2002

MARTHA STEWART LIVING

ANNUAL RECIPES

from the editors of **MARTHA STEWART LIVING**

acknowledgments

It took the collaboration of many talented individuals to create this first volume in a new series of annual cookbooks. Thank you to executive food editor Susan Spungen, deputy food editor Frances Boswell, and Stephana Bottom, for their dedication, expertise, and ability to take on numerous projects simultaneously. Thank you to Shelley Berg and Christine Moller of the books department, for overseeing the creation of this book from start to finish, and to Debra Puchalla and Candice Gianetti, for their keen attention to detail and accuracy. Thanks to Jill Groeber and Scot Schy for developing and directing the design of this book, and to the production team of Duane Stapp, Ted Cannon, and Laura Grady. A very special thank you to the food department, for their tireless creation of wonderful recipes, notably Susan Sugarman, Sara Backhouse, John Barricelli, Tara Bench, Sarah Carey, Samantha Connell, Loren Cunniff, Yolanda Florez, Amy Gropp Forbes, Heidi Johannsen, Wendy Kromer, Judith Lockhart, Samantha Lourie, Amy Marcus, Claire Perez, Gertrude Porter, Joyce Sangirardi, Lucinda Scala Quinn, Mark Ski, Tracey Seaman, Mory Thomas, Laura Trace, and Elizabeth Yeh, and for the support of Najean Lee, Elizabeth Durels, and Suzy Thompson. And many thanks to all who generously contributed their time and energy to the creation of this book, among them Roger Astudillo, Brian Baytosh, Douglas Brenner, Dora Braschi Cardinale, Tara Donne, James Dunlinson, Jamie Fedida, Stephanie Garcia, Amanda Genge, Eric Hutton, Brooke Lyons, Ellen Morrissey, Elizabeth Parson, Eric A. Pike, George D. Planding, Nikki Rooker, Erik Simon, Lauren Podlach Stanich, Gael Towey, Beverly Utt, Alison Vanek, Kathryn Van Steenhuyse, and Bunny Wong, and also to everyone at Oxmoor House, Spectragraphics, and R. R. Donnelley and Sons. Finally, thank you to Martha, for instilling in us a love for creating delicious food from the very best ingredients.

contents

introduction

More than ten years ago, the MARTHA STEWART LIVING test kitchen and magazine were born. During that time, we've grown from infancy to toddler stage, then quickly to adolescence and young adulthood. Now we're all grown up, and have the perspective to look back over our work and reflect. Last year, we published a one-volume collection of recipes from the first ten years. Unfortunately, not every recipe could be included—there just wasn't enough space!

Many of you have kept every issue of our magazine over the years, but now there is an easier and faster way to reference recipes with our first annual book of recipes. Every recipe published in MARTHA STEWART LIVING in 2001, along with some of the best from our BABY, KIDS, and WEDDINGS magazines, appears in these pages. There are color photographs in each chapter to jog your memory and get your mouth watering all over again. The clear, easy-to-read format and clean design make it simple and fun to review the year in recipes and find your favorites. We hope you'll also try recipes that may have escaped your notice when they first appeared.

Every recipe has been tested extensively, but your experience of cooking a particular recipe may stray a bit from the written word. Every kitchen, every pan, every oven, every climate, and even every cook is different from the next. Any of these factors can cause a discrepancy with our account of how we cooked something and achieved a result. Cooking times are especially prone to variation, so always pay close attention to the visual clues for judging doneness that we provide, using the time given as a guide. For instance, if a recipe calls for baking something "until golden brown, about 40 minutes," and after 40 minutes, it's just beginning to brown, by all means extend the baking time, watching carefully, until it matches our description. With that, we sincerely hope that you enjoy using this book as much as we enjoyed putting it together. Give it a prime spot on your cookbook shelf, so we can always be in the kitchen with you.

SUSAN SPUNGEN
Executive Food Editor

january

FAVORITE GOOD THINGS

MINI FRITTATAS

MAKES 4 DOZEN

These frittatas are baked in mini muffin tins and make an easy hors d'oeuvre. Make sure to chop the vegetables extra-fine to suit the size of the hors d'oeuvres.

1 medium zucchini
4 to 6 white mushrooms, wiped clean
1 red bell pepper
1 yellow bell pepper
16 large eggs
2 teaspoons coarse salt
¾ teaspoon freshly ground black pepper
1 tablespoon chopped chives
½ cup finely grated Gruyère or fontina cheese
Vegetable-oil cooking spray

1 Lightly spray two 24-mini-muffin tins with vegetable-oil cooking spray. Slice the zucchini into ⅛-inch rounds. Slice the mushrooms lengthwise into ⅛-inch pieces. Core and seed the red and yellow bell peppers. Chop into ⅛-inch dice, and set aside.

2 Preheat the oven to 400°F. In a large mixing bowl, whisk the eggs, salt, pepper, and chives, and set aside. Arrange the cut zucchini, mushrooms, and peppers in each muffin tin. Ladle the egg mixture into each tin, just even with the rim, and sprinkle with the cheese. Bake until the frittatas are set, 8 to 10 minutes. Serve warm or reheat briefly at 325°F.

FAVORITE BREAKFAST

BEST BUTTERMILK PANCAKES

MAKES 9 SIX-INCH PANCAKES
PHOTOGRAPH ON PAGE 24

If serving these pancakes with bacon, reserve half a teaspoon of bacon drippings to grease the griddle. The batter can be poured onto the griddle in different shapes to appeal to young eaters. For a change of taste, substitute cornmeal, buckwheat flour, or whole-wheat flour for half the all-purpose flour.

2 cups all-purpose flour
2 teaspoons baking powder
1 teaspoon baking soda
½ teaspoon coarse salt
3 tablespoons sugar
2 large eggs, lightly beaten
3 cups nonfat buttermilk
4 tablespoons unsalted butter, melted, plus ½ teaspoon for griddle
1 cup fresh blueberries (optional)

1 Heat an electric griddle to 375°F, or place a griddle pan or cast-iron skillet over medium-high heat. Whisk together the flour, baking powder, baking soda, salt, and sugar in a medium bowl. Add the eggs, buttermilk, and 4 tablespoons melted butter, and whisk to combine. The batter should have small to medium lumps.

2 Preheat the oven to 175°F. Test the griddle by sprinkling a few drops of water on it. If the water bounces and spatters, the griddle is hot enough. Using a pastry brush, brush the remaining ½ teaspoon butter or reserved bacon fat onto the griddle. Wipe off excess with a folded paper towel.

3 Using a 4-ounce (about ½ cup) ladle, pour the batter in pools two inches apart. Scatter with berries, if using. When the pancakes bubble on top and are slightly dry around the edges, about 2½ minutes, flip over. Cook until golden on the bottom, about 1 minute. Repeat with the remaining batter, keeping the finished pancakes on a heat-proof plate in the oven. Serve warm.

FAVORITE SNACKS

AVOCADO FILLED WITH MIXED HERB AND SHALLOT VINAIGRETTE

SERVES 6

3 tablespoons champagne vinegar
1 tablespoon freshly squeezed lemon juice
1½ teaspoons Dijon mustard
¼ cup plus 2 tablespoons canola oil
½ teaspoon coarse salt
⅛ teaspoon freshly ground pepper
1 small shallot, finely chopped
¼ cup loosely packed fresh herbs, such as dill, chervil, parsley, and tarragon, coarsely chopped
3 ripe avocados

1 Combine the vinegar, lemon juice, and mustard in the jar of a blender. Slowly add the oil in a steady stream, blending until all the oil is incorporated. Add the salt and pepper. Stir in the chopped shallot and herbs.

2 Slice the avocados lengthwise, rotating the knife around the pit. Twist the two halves of each avocado in opposite directions to separate. Embed the knife into the pit, and twist to separate the pit from the avocado. Fill each avocado half with a spoonful of vinaigrette, and serve immediately.

APPLESAUCE CAKE

MAKES 1 TEN-INCH CAKE; SERVES
10 TO 12 | **PHOTOGRAPH ON PAGE 25**

*Because of its moistness, this cake keeps
exceptionally well in the refrigerator and
improves with time. Resist eating it fresh
from the oven—the flavor reaches its peak
the next day. You will need a ten-inch
springform pan.*

- 4 ounces pecans
- 1 cup (2 sticks) plus 3 tablespoons unsalted butter, room temperature, plus more for pan
- 2¼ cups superfine sugar
- 2 large eggs
- 2½ cups Applesauce (recipe follows)
- 2¾ cups plus 3 tablespoons all-purpose flour
- 1½ teaspoons ground cinnamon
- ½ teaspoon ground nutmeg
  Pinch of ground cloves
  Pinch of coarse salt
- 1¾ teaspoons baking powder
- 1 teaspoon pure vanilla extract
- 2 tablespoons Calvados or brandy (optional)
- 1 large apple, peeled and very thinly sliced (1 cup)
- ¼ cup packed light-brown sugar
- ¼ teaspoon ground ginger

1 Preheat the oven to 350°F. Place the pecans in a single layer on a rimmed baking sheet; toast until they are golden and aromatic, 8 to 12 minutes. Shake the pan halfway through to make sure the nuts toast evenly. Transfer to a bowl to cool. Reduce the heat to 325°F. Chop the pecans, yielding 1 cup.

2 Brush a 10-inch springform pan with butter. Coat with ¼ cup superfine sugar; tap out any excess. Set the prepared pan aside.

3 In the bowl of an electric mixer fitted with the paddle attachment, combine 1 cup butter and the remaining 2 cups superfine sugar. Beat on medium speed, scraping down the sides with a rubber spatula, until the mixture is light and fluffy, about 5 minutes. Add the eggs, one at a time, beating 1 full minute after each addition. Fold in the applesauce, being careful not to overmix.

4 In a large bowl, sift together 2¾ cups flour, 1 teaspoon cinnamon, ¼ teaspoon nutmeg, the cloves, the salt, and the baking powder.

5 Fold the flour mixture and chopped pecans into the applesauce mixture. Add the vanilla, Calvados, if using, and apple slices, and mix until just combined. Transfer the batter to the prepared pan.

6 Combine the remaining 3 tablespoons butter, 3 tablespoons flour, ½ teaspoon cinnamon, and ¼ teaspoon nutmeg, along with the brown sugar and ginger in a small mixing bowl. Mix with your fingers until just combined; sprinkle lightly over the batter. Place the pan in the oven; bake until a cake tester inserted into the center comes out almost clean, about 1 hour 50 minutes. Transfer to a wire rack to cool completely. Unmold before serving.

APPLESAUCE

MAKES ABOUT 7 CUPS

*All ingredients after the cinnamon are
optional. Homemade applesauce doesn't
need much, if any, sugar, especially when
you use apple cider.*

- 18 McIntosh apples (about 6 pounds), peeled, cored, and quartered
- 1 cup apple cider
- 1 large cinnamon stick
- ½ vanilla bean, split lengthwise
- 1 teaspoon ground ginger, or to taste
- ½ teaspoon ground cardamom, or to taste
- ½ teaspoon ground nutmeg, or to taste
- ½ teaspoon ground mace, or to taste
- ½ cup sugar, or to taste
- 2 tablespoons freshly squeezed lemon juice

1 Combine the apples, apple cider, and cinnamon in a large heavy-bottomed wide saucepan. Scrape the vanilla seeds into the pan, and add the pod. Add ginger, cardamom, nutmeg, mace, sugar, and lemon juice, if using.

2 Place the saucepan over medium heat, and cook, stirring often with a wooden spoon to prevent scorching, until the apples are broken down and saucy, 50 to 60 minutes. Mash any large pieces of apple with the wooden spoon to help them break down. Season with more sugar and spices. Remove the applesauce from the heat, and let stand to cool completely before serving, discarding the cinnamon stick and vanilla pod. Applesauce can be stored in an airtight container for 2 to 3 days in the refrigerator or frozen for up to 2 months.

FAVORITE SANDWICH

MEDITERRANEAN MELT

MAKES 4

- 3 lemons
- 8 baby artichokes
- ½ cup oil-cured black olives, pitted and coarsely chopped
- ¼ cup olive oil
- 1 small garlic clove, minced
  Coarse salt and freshly ground pepper
- 1 cup loosely packed fresh flat-leaf parsley, roughly chopped
- 4 plum tomatoes, sliced ¾ inch thick
- 4 rustic-style rolls
- 8 ounces Taleggio or fontina cheese, sliced ¼ inch thick

1 Slice 2 lemons in half; squeeze the juice into a bowl of cold water. Add the lemon halves to the bowl. Trim the tips and outer leaves from the artichokes. Thinly slice artichokes lengthwise; submerge in the lemon water.

2 Combine the olives with 1 tablespoon oil in a small bowl.

3 Heat 1½ tablespoons oil in a skillet over medium heat; add the garlic. Cook until fragrant, about 30 seconds. Pat the artichoke slices dry; add to the skillet. Cook until golden, about 5 minutes.

4 Squeeze the juice of the remaining lemon over the artichokes; season with salt and pepper. Add ½ cup chopped parsley; toss. Transfer to a small bowl; cover with aluminum foil.

5 Return the skillet to the heat; add the remaining 1½ tablespoons oil. Arrange the tomatoes in the skillet. Sprinkle with the remaining ½ cup chopped parsley, and season with salt and pepper. Cook until the tomatoes are golden around the edges, about 5 minutes. Turn; cook 1 to 2 minutes more.

6 Preheat the broiler to medium-high. Slice the rolls. Scoop out the bottoms, creating a cavity for the filling; spread with the olive mixture. Mound the artichokes over the olive mixture; arrange several tomatoes over the artichokes. Arrange the cheese over the tomatoes. Place the filled rolls and the tops, crumb side up, on a baking sheet; broil until the cheese is melted and the bread is golden, about 2 minutes. Place a top on each filled roll. Serve hot.

FAVORITE QUICK DISHES

MUSSELS IN WHITE WINE AND GARLIC
SERVES 4

Be sure to buy live mussels. Any open mussels that do not close when you press their shells a few times are not alive; discard them.

4 pounds live mussels

2 cups dry white wine

4 large shallots, finely chopped

4 garlic cloves, finely chopped

½ teaspoon coarse salt

⅓ cup mixed fresh herbs, such as flat-leaf parsley, chervil, and basil, chopped

6 tablespoons unsalted butter, cut into pieces

1 Rinse and scrub the mussels under cold running water. Using your fingers or a paring knife, remove the beards (strings that hang from the mussels' shells), and discard.

2 In a large stockpot over medium heat, combine the wine, shallots, garlic, and salt. Simmer 5 minutes. Add the mussels.

3 Cover, and raise the heat to high. Cook until all the mussels are open, about 5 minutes. Stir in the herbs and butter. Remove from the heat. Divide the mussels and broth among four bowls. Serve immediately.

BRAISED COD WITH PLUM TOMATOES
SERVES 4

A cod steak has a row of bones running down its center; to remove the bones, cut around them with a sharp knife, dividing the fish into two pieces.

4 seven-ounce cod steaks, skin and bones removed

1 teaspoon dried oregano

2 teaspoons coarse salt

½ teaspoon freshly ground black pepper

⅛ teaspoon cayenne pepper

4 ripe plum tomatoes, cut into ½-inch-thick slices

1½ teaspoons olive oil

1 cup water

½ teaspoon minced garlic

Fresh flat-leaf parsley, for garnish (optional)

1 Sprinkle both sides of the cod steaks with oregano, ½ teaspoon salt, ¼ teaspoon black pepper, and cayenne pepper. Sprinkle the tomato slices with the remaining 1½ teaspoons salt and ¼ teaspoon black pepper.

2 Heat the olive oil in a large sauté pan over high heat. When hot, add the cod and tomato slices. Cook until the cod steaks are golden on the bottom, about 4½ minutes. Using a metal spatula, flip over the cod steaks and tomatoes. Add the water and the garlic, and bring the liquid to a simmer.

3 Simmer until the cod begins to feel firm when you press it with your finger and it starts to flake, about 4 minutes. Divide the cod, tomatoes, and broth among four shallow soup bowls. Garnish with parsley, if using, and serve.

DINNER-PARTY FAVORITES

SPAGHETTI AND TOMATO SAUCE 101
SERVES 2 TO 4 | **PHOTOGRAPH ON PAGE 29**

This is our simplest, best version of spaghetti with red sauce. Three types of tomatoes can be used with our basic method: sweet, ripe cherry tomatoes; vine-ripened tomatoes; or canned Italian plum tomatoes.

¼ teaspoon coarse salt, plus more for cooking water

1½ pounds cherry tomatoes or vine-ripened tomatoes, or 1 twenty-eight-ounce can Italian plum tomatoes

8 ounces thin spaghetti

¼ cup extra-virgin olive oil

4 garlic cloves, cut into ⅛-inch-thick slices

¼ teaspoon crushed red-pepper flakes

¼ cup loosely packed fresh basil or fresh flat-leaf parsley leaves, torn

Freshly grated Parmigiano-Reggiano cheese (optional)

1 Bring 3 quarts of water to a boil in a large stockpot. Salt the water.

2 If using cherry tomatoes, wash and stem. If using vine-ripened tomatoes, fill a large bowl with ice and water; set aside. Bring a large pot of water to a boil. Using a paring knife, score the nonstem end of each tomato with a shallow "x." Blanch the tomatoes in the boiling water for 30 seconds. With a slotted spoon, transfer the tomatoes to the ice bath. Using a chef's knife, cut the outer flesh into ¼-inch strips; set aside. Press the cores of the tomatoes through a sieve; reserve the pulp, and discard the seeds. If using canned tomatoes, strain, and pass through a food mill fitted with a fine disk.

3 Carefully drop the spaghetti into the boiling water; stir to keep the pasta from sticking together. Cook until al dente, about 11 minutes.

4 Meanwhile, place a 12-inch skillet over medium heat; add the oil. Add the garlic, and cook, stirring occasionally, until the garlic is lightly golden, about 30 seconds. Add the red-pepper flakes and ¼ teaspoon salt. Cook until the garlic is medium golden, about 1 minute more.

5 Raise the heat to high. Tilting the pan at an angle, add the tomato strips and pulp from the sieve, the cherry tomatoes, or the canned tomatoes. Cook, swirling the pan occasionally, until the tomato strips begin to break down, the cherry tomatoes begin to burst, or the canned tomatoes begin to thicken, 5 to 6 minutes. If using cherry tomatoes, mash a few with a spoon; if the mixture starts to get too dry, add a little water from the pasta stockpot.

6 Drain the pasta in a colander, reserving 1 cup of the cooking liquid in case the sauce gets too dry. Add the pasta to the sauce in the skillet; cook until the sauce clings to the pasta, 3 to 4 minutes. Stir in the basil; cook 30 seconds more. Divide among serving bowls, and sprinkle with the cheese, if using. Serve.

CLASSIC CAESAR SALAD

SERVES 4 TO 6

If you prefer not to use the raw yolk in this recipe, substitute one tablespoon prepared mayonnaise. To make a version of the dressing that you can store, simply mince the garlic and anchovies, and place with the salt, pepper, lemon juice, Worcestershire, mustard, egg, and olive oil in a jar. Screw the lid on the jar tightly, and shake to combine. Shake the jar before each use. Store, refrigerated, up to two days. The croutons are best made no more than half an hour before assembling the salad.

FOR THE CROUTONS:

2 tablespoons unsalted butter, melted

2 tablespoons extra-virgin olive oil

1 eight- to ten-ounce loaf rustic Italian bread, crusts removed, cut into ¾-inch cubes

2 teaspoons coarse salt

¾ teaspoon cayenne pepper

½ teaspoon freshly ground black pepper

FOR THE SALAD:

2 garlic cloves

4 anchovy fillets

1 teaspoon coarse salt

1 teaspoon freshly ground black pepper

1 tablespoon freshly squeezed lemon juice

1 teaspoon Worcestershire sauce

½ teaspoon Dijon mustard

1 large egg yolk

⅓ cup extra-virgin olive oil

2 ten-ounce heads romaine lettuce, outer leaves discarded, inner leaves washed and dried

1 cup freshly grated Parmesan or Romano cheese, or 2½ ounces shaved with a vegetable peeler

1 Preheat the oven to 450°F. To make the croutons, combine the butter and olive oil in a large bowl. Add the bread cubes, and toss until coated. Sprinkle with the salt, cayenne pepper, and black pepper; toss until evenly coated. Spread the bread in a single layer in a 12-by-17-inch baking pan. Bake until the croutons are golden, about 10 minutes. Set aside.

2 For the salad, place the garlic, anchovy fillets, and salt in a wooden salad bowl. Using two dinner forks, mash the garlic and anchovies into a paste. Using one fork, whisk in the pepper, lemon juice, Worcestershire sauce, mustard, and egg yolk. Whisk in the olive oil.

3 Chop the romaine leaves into 1- to 1½-inch pieces. Add the croutons, romaine, and cheese to the bowl, and toss well. If you wish, grate extra cheese over the top. Serve immediately.

NOTE: Raw eggs should not be used in food prepared for pregnant women, babies, young children, the elderly, or anyone whose health is compromised.

LEMON CHICKEN

SERVES 4 | **PHOTOGRAPH ON PAGE 27**

Marinate the chicken for at least four hours and up to two days for the best flavor and texture. A salt rub not only seasons the meat but tenderizes it.

⅓ cup coarse salt

3 tablespoons freshly squeezed lemon juice

1 five-pound roasting chicken Gremolata (recipe follows)

6 tablespoons unsalted butter, softened

8 fresh or dried bay leaves

4 lemons, quartered lengthwise

3 lemons, halved (optional)

1 In a small bowl, combine the salt and lemon juice. Loosen the skin of the chicken from the flesh. Rub the mixture under the skin and in the cavity of the chicken. Place the chicken in a large resealable plastic bag; chill at least 4 hours and up to 48 hours, turning occasionally.

2 Preheat the oven to 425°F. Rinse all the salt off the chicken with cold water; pat dry with a paper towel. Set aside.

3 In a small bowl, combine the gremolata and softened butter. Rub two thirds of the gremolata mixture under the chicken's skin; rub the rest on the outside. Stuff the cavity with the bay leaves and the quartered lemons.

4 Place the chicken in a large roasting pan, breast side up. Tuck the tips of the wings under the bottom of the bird. Transfer the pan to the oven. After 40 minutes, baste. If using the lemon halves, place them in the pan, cut side down. Cover the chicken with aluminum foil. Reduce heat to 375°F.

5 Cook, basting occasionally, until the skin is crisp and golden, 40 to 45 minutes more. The juices should run clear when the chicken is pierced; an instant-read thermometer should register 170°F in the deepest part of the thigh when done. Serve alongside the roasted lemon halves, warm or at room temperature.

GREMOLATA

MAKES ⅔ CUP

This mixture, best used as soon as possible, is traditionally made with garlic but here is also flavored with shallots.

Zest of 6 lemons, grated or finely chopped

1 small garlic clove, minced

¼ cup roughly chopped fresh flat-leaf parsley

2 tablespoons (about 2 medium) chopped shallots

On a cutting board, chop all together the lemon zest, garlic, parsley, and shallots until they are well combined.

SPECIAL-OCCASION FAVORITES

CROWN ROAST WITH GRAVY

SERVES 12 TO 18

Ask your butcher to remove the chine, feather bones, and any excess fat from the crown roast.

1 eight- to nine-pound crown roast of pork
  Coarse salt and freshly ground pepper

¼ cup plus 1½ tablespoons olive oil
  Grated zest of 1 orange

4 large garlic cloves, minced

2 tablespoons chopped fresh rosemary
  Wild Rice Dressing (recipe follows)

¾ cup dry white wine

½ cup apple cider

1½ cups Homemade Veal Stock (page 8), Homemade Chicken Stock (page 8), or low-sodium canned chicken broth

1 tablespoon unsalted butter, room temperature

2 tablespoons all-purpose flour

1 Position rack in the lower third of the oven, and preheat to 425°F. Season the roast with salt and pepper, and brush meat with ¼ cup olive oil.

2 In a small bowl, combine the orange zest, garlic, and rosemary and the remaining 1½ tablespoons olive oil.

Spread the mixture evenly over the meat, inside and out. Place the meat in a heavy-duty roasting pan with a rack large enough to hold the roast without crowding the sides. Roast 15 minutes. Reduce the heat to 375°F. Continue roasting, rotating the pan after 45 minutes, until the meat is well browned and an instant-read thermometer registers 150°F, about 1½ hours. (Insert the thermometer into the meaty center of the crown, making sure that it does not touch any ribs. Take several readings to ensure that the temperature is even all around.)

3 While the crown roast is cooking, make the dressing. When the roast is ready, remove it from the oven, transfer to a cutting board with a well, and let stand 20 minutes.

4 Raise the oven temperature to 425°F. Place the dressing in the oven, and bake until heated through, about 20 minutes. Pour the pan juices into a fat separator or glass measuring cup, and let stand 5 to 10 minutes. If using a separator, carefully pour the juices back into the pan; discard the fat. If using a measuring cup, carefully remove the fat with a spoon, and return the juices to the pan.

5 Place the roasting pan on top of the stove over medium-high heat. Add the wine, and bring to a boil. Stir, using a wooden spoon, to loosen any browned bits on the bottom of the pan. Boil until half of the liquid has evaporated, 5 to 7 minutes. Stir in the apple cider and the veal stock; season with salt and pepper, and return the liquid to a boil.

6 In a small bowl, combine the butter and flour. Mix until completely combined. Transfer this mixture to the roasting pan.

Whisk constantly until the gravy has slightly thickened, 4 to 5 minutes. Remove the pan from the heat, and strain the liquid into a gravy boat.

7 Carefully transfer the roast to a serving platter; spoon the dressing into the center of the roast. Carve and serve.

WILD RICE DRESSING

SERVES 12 TO 18

If cooking the dressing on its own, bake in a 425°F oven for twenty minutes.

¼ cup slivered almonds
  Unsalted butter, for casserole

3 tablespoons olive oil

1 medium onion, coarsely chopped

2 celery stalks, strings removed, chopped into ½-inch pieces

3 large garlic cloves, finely minced

1 tablespoon finely chopped fresh rosemary

1 tablespoon finely chopped fresh sage
  Coarse salt and freshly ground pepper

2 tablespoons coarsely chopped fresh flat-leaf parsley

4 ounces sweet fennel sausage, casings removed

1 Granny Smith apple, peeled, cored, and cut into ½-inch dice

¼ cup Calvados or white wine

3 cups cooked wild rice

2 cups cooked white rice

10 dried apricot halves, quartered

6 dried pitted prunes, halved

1 Preheat the oven to 375°F. Place the almonds in a single layer on a rimmed baking sheet; toast until they are golden and aromatic, 5 to 7 minutes. Shake the pan halfway through to make sure the nuts toast evenly. Remove the pan from the oven, and set the almonds aside to cool.

2 Generously butter a 2½-quart casserole, and set aside. Heat 2 tablespoons olive oil in a large sauté pan over medium heat. Add the onion, celery, and garlic. Cook, stirring occasionally, until tender, about 7 minutes.

3 Raise the heat to high, and add the rosemary and sage; season with salt and pepper. Continue cooking until the veg-

etables are golden, 2 to 3 minutes. Remove the pan from the heat; stir in the parsley. Transfer the vegetables to a large bowl, and set aside. Return the pan to the heat.

4 Crumble the sausage, separating the meat. Add 1½ teaspoons olive oil to the sauté pan. Add the sausage, and cook, stirring and breaking up the meat until well browned, 2½ to 3 minutes. Transfer the sausage to the bowl with the reserved vegetables. Return the pan to the heat.

5 Add the remaining 1½ teaspoons olive oil to the pan. Add the apple, and cook, stirring occasionally, until browned, 2 to 3 minutes. Add the Calvados. Stir, using a wooden spoon, to loosen any browned bits on the bottom of the pan. Cook until most of the liquid has evaporated, about 1 minute.

6 Remove the pan from the heat, and transfer the mixture to the bowl with the sausage and vegetables. Add the wild and white rice, the apricots, prunes, and reserved toasted almonds. Season with salt and pepper. Transfer the dressing to the prepared casserole, and cover with aluminum foil.

HOMEMADE VEAL STOCK

MAKES 5 QUARTS

4 sprigs fresh rosemary

8 sprigs fresh flat-leaf parsley

6 sprigs fresh thyme

2 dried bay leaves

1 tablespoon whole black peppercorns

1 pound veal-stew meat, cubed

7 pounds veal bones, such as necks, shanks, and knuckles, sawed or broken into 2-inch pieces

1 pound oxtail (optional)

1 pig's foot (optional)

2 large Spanish onions, unpeeled and quartered

3 large carrots, cut in half

3 celery stalks, strings removed, cut in half

8 ounces mixed mushrooms, wiped clean, stems attached

1 head of garlic, cut in half widthwise

1 six-ounce can tomato paste

1 twenty-eight-ounce can plum tomatoes, drained and quartered

2 cups dry red wine, such as burgundy

8 quarts cold water

1 Preheat the oven to 425°F. Tie the rosemary, parsley, thyme, bay leaves, and peppercorns in a small piece of cheesecloth to make a bouquet garni; set aside.

2 Arrange the veal-stew meat and veal bones (and oxtail and pig's foot, if using) in a single layer in a large heavy roasting pan, and place in the oven. Roast, turning several times, until they turn deep brown, about 1½ hours. Remove from the oven, and place the onions, carrots, celery, mushrooms, garlic, tomato paste, and tomatoes on top of the bones. Reduce heat to 375°F, return the pan to the oven, and roast until the vegetables are brown, about 45 minutes.

3 Transfer the meat, bones, and vegetables to a large stockpot; set aside. Pour off the fat from the roasting pan and discard; set the pan over high heat on the stove. Add the wine, and stir, using a wooden spoon to loosen any browned bits on the bottom of the pan; boil until the wine is reduced by half, about 5 minutes. Pour the mixture into the stockpot.

4 Add the water to the stockpot, just covering the bones; cover, and bring to a boil. Reduce the heat to a simmer, and add the bouquet garni; skim the foam that rises to the surface. Cook 8 to 10 hours, skimming frequently.

5 Fill a large bowl with ice and water; set aside. Strain the stock through a fine sieve or a cheesecloth-lined colander into a large bowl. Discard the solids. Transfer the bowl to the ice bath, and let the stock cool to room temperature.

6 Transfer the stock to airtight containers. They may be labeled at this point and refrigerated for 3 days or frozen for up to 4 months. If using the stock for a recipe, refrigerate for at least 8 hours or overnight so the fat collects on the top and can be removed. If freezing, leave the fat layer intact; it seals the stock.

HOMEMADE CHICKEN STOCK

MAKES 5 QUARTS

If you plan to use the stock for a specific recipe, begin making it at least twelve hours ahead of time, and refrigerate for eight hours so the fat has a chance to collect on top and can be removed.

2 leeks, white and pale-green parts, cut into thirds, well washed

1 teaspoon whole black peppercorns

6 sprigs fresh dill or 2 teaspoons dried

6 sprigs fresh flat-leaf parsley

2 dried bay leaves

2 carrots, cut into thirds

2 celery stalks, cut into thirds

1 four-pound chicken, cut into 6 pieces

1½ pounds chicken wings

1½ pounds chicken backs

2 forty-eight-ounce cans (3 quarts) low-sodium chicken broth, skimmed of fat

6 cups cold water, or more

1 Place the leeks, peppercorns, dill, parsley, bay leaves, carrots, celery, whole chicken, wings, and backs in a large stockpot. Add the chicken broth and water, cover, and bring to a boil. Reduce to a very gentle simmer, and cook, uncovered, about 45 minutes. The liquid should just bubble up to the surface. A skin will form on the surface; skim it off with a slotted spoon, and discard, repeating as needed. After about 45 minutes, remove the whole chicken from the pot, and set it aside until it is cool enough to handle.

2 Remove the meat from the chicken bones, set the meat aside, and return the bones to the pot. Transfer the meat to the refrigerator for another use; if you plan to use it in soup, shred the meat before refrigerating it.

3 Continue to simmer the stock mixture, on the lowest heat possible, for 3 hours, skimming foam from the top as needed. The chicken bones will begin to disintegrate. Add water if at any time the surface level drops below the bones.

4 Fill a large bowl with ice and water; set aside. Strain the stock through a fine sieve or a cheesecloth-lined colander into a very large bowl. Discard the solids. Transfer the bowl to the ice bath; let the stock cool to room temperature.

5 Transfer the stock to airtight containers. Stock may be labeled at this point and refrigerated for 3 days or frozen for up to 4 months. If freezing, leave the fat layer intact; it seals the stock. If refrigerating, chill for at least 8 hours, and remove fat before using.

ROOTS ANNA
SERVES 8 TO 10

We've added slices of rutabaga to pommes Anna, a French dish traditionally made with potatoes alone.

 3 garlic cloves, unpeeled
 ¼ teaspoon olive oil
 1½ pounds Yukon gold or baking potatoes
 1 large (about 2 pounds) rutabaga
 6 tablespoons unsalted butter
 1½ teaspoons coarse salt
 ⅜ teaspoon freshly ground pepper
 1½ teaspoons fresh thyme leaves

1 Preheat the oven to 450°F. Place the garlic in an ovenproof ramekin; drizzle with olive oil. Roast until light brown and very soft, about 20 minutes. Let stand until cool enough to handle. Peel the garlic, cut into slivers, and set aside. Reduce the oven to 425°F.

2 Meanwhile, peel the potatoes and slice them as thinly as possible; place them in a bowl, and put a damp paper towel on top to keep them from turning brown. Peel the rutabaga, and cut in half; slice as thinly as possible, and cover with a damp paper towel.

3 In a 10-inch nonstick ovenproof skillet, melt 2 tablespoons butter, swirling the pan to coat the bottom and sides. Remove from the heat. Starting at the sides of the pan, arrange half of the rutabaga slices in overlapping concentric circles, covering the bottom of the pan; press to compress. Sprinkle the rutabaga with ½ teaspoon salt, ⅛ teaspoon pepper, ½ teaspoon thyme, and a third of the roasted garlic; dot with 1 tablespoon butter.

4 Arrange the potato slices in tight concentric circles over the rutabaga; press down. Season with ½ teaspoon salt, ⅛ teaspoon pepper, ½ teaspoon thyme, and another third of the garlic; dot with 1 tablespoon butter. Arrange the remaining rutabaga on top, and season again with ½ teaspoon salt, ⅛ teaspoon pepper, and the remaining garlic; dot with 1 tablespoon butter.

5 Spread the remaining tablespoon of butter over a large piece of aluminum foil. Cover the skillet with the foil, buttered side down. Place a cast-iron skillet on the foil to weigh it down, and transfer to the oven. Bake until the vegetables are tender when pierced with the tip of a knife, 50 to 60 minutes.

6 Let stand on a wire rack for 15 minutes. Remove the foil, and invert carefully onto a serving dish. Garnish with the remaining ½ teaspoon thyme; serve warm. This can be made a few hours ahead of time and reheated: Cover loosely with foil, and place in a 350°F oven for about 20 minutes or until hot.

PARKER HOUSE ROLLS
MAKES 2 DOZEN

 1 package (about 2½ teaspoons) active dry yeast
 ¼ cup warm water (105°F)
 3 tablespoons plus a pinch of sugar
 13 tablespoons unsalted butter, melted and cooled to room temperature, plus more for plastic wrap, bowl, and baking pan
 1 cup milk, room temperature
 1 tablespoon coarse salt
 3 large eggs, lightly beaten
 4½ to 5 cups all-purpose flour

1 In the detached bowl of an electric mixer, whisk together the yeast, water, and pinch of sugar. Set aside until the mixture is foamy, about 6 minutes.

2 Attach the bowl to the mixer, fitted with the dough-hook attachment. On low speed, add 7 tablespoons butter, the

remaining 3 tablespoons sugar, and the milk, salt, and eggs. Slowly add enough flour to make a sticky dough. Brush the inside of a mixing bowl with butter. Place the dough in the bowl; cover the bowl with buttered plastic wrap. Set aside until dough is doubled in size, about 2½ hours.

3 Generously brush a 9-by-13-inch baking pan with butter. Turn the dough out onto a floured work surface. Roll the dough into a 12-by-16-inch rectangle. Brush it generously with 3 tablespoons butter. Using a pizza wheel or a sharp knife, cut the dough lengthwise into 6 equal strips. Cut the dough crosswise into 4 equal parts. You will have 24 elongated rectangles. Fold each rectangle in half, and place in the prepared baking pan, 4 pieces across and 6 down. Brush the tops with the remaining 3 tablespoons butter. Cover the pan with buttered plastic wrap. Set aside to rise until the dough does not spring back when pressed with a finger, 25 to 30 minutes.

4 Preheat oven to 350°F. Bake until golden, 35 to 40 minutes. Cool for at least 5 minutes before turning out of the pan.

OYSTER BRIOCHE STUFFING
MAKES 6 CUPS

To make this as a dressing and cook it outside a turkey, spread in a buttered nine-by-thirteen-inch baking pan. Bake at 375°F until golden on top, about twenty minutes. Stir, and bake twenty minutes more.

 12 slices Brioche (page 35), ¾ inch thick, crusts removed
 4 tablespoons unsalted butter
 1 onion, cut into ¼-inch dice
 2 celery stalks, strings removed, cut into ¼-inch dice
 1 garlic clove, minced
 1 teaspoon coarse salt
 ½ teaspoon freshly ground black pepper
 ⅛ teaspoon freshly grated nutmeg
 ⅛ teaspoon cayenne pepper
 2 tablespoons cognac (optional)
 2 dozen shucked oysters, ⅓ cup of liquor reserved
 ½ cup heavy cream
 1½ cups fresh flat-leaf parsley, chopped

1 Preheat the oven to 350°F. Cut the brioche into ¾-inch cubes. Spread cubes on a baking sheet; bake until dry and golden, about 10 minutes. Transfer to a wire rack to cool.

2 Melt the butter in a medium skillet over medium heat. When hot, add the onion, celery, garlic, salt, and black pepper. Cook, stirring occasionally, until the onion is softened, about 3 minutes. Add the nutmeg, cayenne, cognac, if using, and oyster liquor; cook until the liquid is absorbed, about 1 minute. Add the oysters and cream; cook 30 seconds more. Remove from the heat.

3 In a large bowl, toss together the brioche cubes, oyster mixture, and parsley. Use immediately.

EGGNOG CUPS

SERVES 8

If you're not sure if your cups are ovenproof, use ordinary six-ounce glass custard dishes to hold these delicious desserts.

7 large egg yolks

⅔ cup granulated sugar

2 tablespoons all-purpose flour, sifted, plus more for work surface

½ vanilla bean, split lengthwise

2 cups milk

1 teaspoon nutmeg, preferably freshly grated

   Pâte Brisée (recipe follows)

1 cup plus 1 tablespoon heavy cream

2 tablespoons confectioners' sugar, sifted

1 tablespoon rum (optional)

1 Combine 6 egg yolks and the granulated sugar in the bowl of an electric mixer fitted with the whisk attachment. Mix on high until thick and pale yellow and a ribbon forms when beaters are lifted, about 5 minutes. Add the flour; mix until fully incorporated.

2 While mixing the egg yolks, in a 2-quart stainless-steel saucepan, scrape the vanilla seeds, and add the pod. Add the milk and nutmeg, and bring to a boil over medium-high heat. With the mixer running, pour about one-quarter of the milk mixture into the egg mixture. Slowly add the egg-milk mixture to the saucepan with the remaining milk mixture. Cook over medium heat, whisking constantly, until the mixture thickens and bubbles in the center, 4 to 5 minutes. Pass through a sieve into a medium bowl. Place plastic wrap directly on the surface of the custard to prevent a skin from forming. Let cool, 30 to 45 minutes. When cool, refrigerate until chilled and set, at least 2 hours.

3 On a lightly floured surface, roll out the pâte brisée ⅛ inch thick. Cut into 8 six-inch squares; discard the extra, or reserve for another use. Place square into an ovenproof ceramic cup; let the excess drape 1 to 1½ inches over the edge. Repeat with the remaining cups.

4 In small bowl, mix the remaining egg yolk and 1 tablespoon cream; brush over the surface of the dough, and refrigerate at least 1 hour.

5 Preheat the oven to 350°F. Transfer the cups to a baking sheet, and gently prick the bottom of the dough inside the cups three to four times with a fork. Bake 20 to 25 minutes, until the crust is deep golden and the inside of the pastry shell is dry. Let cool completely on a wire rack.

6 Meanwhile, chill the bowl and whisk attachment of an electric mixer. Whip the remaining cup of cream on medium high. When the cream starts to thicken, add the confectioners' sugar, and mix until soft peaks form. Add the rum, if using, and continue to whip until soft peaks form.

7 Spoon ¼ cup chilled custard into each cooled pastry shell. Add a dollop of whipped cream, and serve.

PATE BRISEE

MAKES ENOUGH FOR 8 EGGNOG CUPS; 8 TARTLETS; 2 LATTICE TART; 2 EIGHT- TO TEN-INCH SINGLE-CRUST PIES; OR 1 EIGHT- TO TEN-INCH DOUBLE-CRUST PIE

The amount of ice water you need will vary. Add only enough to make the dough come together when you press it between your fingers. If you are using the dough to make Summer Squash Lattice Tart, omit the sugar. The dough may be made one day ahead and refrigerated, well wrapped in plastic, or frozen for up to one month.

2½ cups all-purpose flour

1 teaspoon coarse salt

1 teaspoon sugar

1 cup (2 sticks) chilled unsalted butter, cut into small pieces

¼ to ½ cup ice water

1 Place the flour, salt, and sugar in the bowl of a food processor; pulse to combine, about 30 seconds.

2 Add the butter; pulse until the mixture resembles coarse meal, about 10 seconds. Continue pulsing while adding the ice water in a slow, steady stream through the feed tube; process just until the dough begins to come together. Do not process for more than 30 seconds.

3 Turn the dough out onto a work surface. Divide the dough in half, and place on two separate sheets of plastic wrap. Flatten, and form into two disks or rectangles, depending on the shape of the intended crust. Wrap in plastic, and refrigerate at least 1 hour before using.

FRENCH ONION SOUP

SERVES 6 | **PHOTOGRAPH ON PAGE 26**

Cooking onions for a long time over very low heat mellows their flavor. Avoid the temptation to stir too often, or they won't caramelize. Homemade Beef Stock is best for this soup. Ungarnished soup will keep for up to two days in the refrigerator, or it may be frozen for up to three months.

4 tablespoons unsalted butter

2 pounds yellow onions, sliced into ¼-inch half circles

1 teaspoon sugar

1 tablespoon all-purpose flour

½ cup dry sherry

1½ quarts Homemade Beef Stock (recipe follows), or canned

2 teaspoons chopped fresh thyme leaves, or ¾ teaspoon dried

Coarse salt and freshly ground pepper

1 small baguette, sliced crosswise into ½-inch-thick pieces

8 ounces (about 3 cups) Gruyère cheese, grated on the large holes of a box grater

1 Melt the butter in a large Dutch oven or in a heavy pot set over medium-low heat. Add the onions, and spread out in as thin a layer as possible. Sprinkle with the sugar; cook, stirring just as needed to keep from sticking, until the onions are soft, golden brown, and beginning to caramelize, about 1 hour.

2 Sprinkle the flour over the onions; stir to coat. Add the sherry, beef stock, and thyme, and bring to a simmer. Cook, partly covered, for about 30 minutes, to let the flavors combine. Season with salt and pepper.

3 Preheat the broiler. Lightly toast the bread under the broiler; set aside. Ladle the hot soup into six ovenproof bowls. Arrange the bowls in a baking pan. Place one or two slices of toasted bread over each bowl of soup. Sprinkle ½ cup grated cheese over the bread in each bowl, and place pan under the broiler until the cheese is melted and turning brown around the edges. Serve hot.

HOMEMADE BEEF STOCK

MAKES 6 QUARTS

The butcher can cut veal bones into small pieces for you.

8 sprigs fresh flat-leaf parsley

6 sprigs fresh thyme or ¾ teaspoon dried

4 sprigs fresh rosemary or 2 teaspoons dried

2 dried bay leaves

1 tablespoon whole black peppercorns

1 pound beef-stew meat, cubed

5 pounds veal bones, such as necks, shanks, and knuckles, sawed or broken into 2-inch pieces

1 large onion, unpeeled and quartered

2 large carrots, cut into thirds

2 celery stalks, strings removed, cut into thirds

2 cups dry red wine

6 quarts cold water, or more if needed

1 Preheat the oven to 450°F. Tie the parsley, thyme, rosemary, bay leaves, and peppercorns in a piece of cheesecloth to make a bouquet garni. Set aside.

2 Arrange the beef-stew meat, veal bones, onion, carrots, and celery in an even layer in a heavy roasting pan. Roast, turning every 20 minutes, until the vegetables and the bones are deep brown, about 1½ hours. Transfer the meat, bones, and vegetables to a large stockpot, and set aside. Pour off the fat from the roasting pan, and discard. Place the pan over high heat on the stove. Add the red wine, and stir, using a wooden spoon to loosen any browned bits on the bottom of the pan; boil until the wine is reduced by half, about 5 minutes. Pour the mixture into the stockpot.

3 Add the water to the stockpot, or more if needed, to cover the bones (do not use less water). Cover, and bring to a boil, then reduce to a very gentle simmer so that bubbles occasionally rise to the surface. Add the reserved bouquet garni. Skim the foam from the surface. Continue to simmer the stock over the lowest possible heat for 3 hours. A skin will form on the surface of the liquid; skim off with a slotted spoon. Repeat as needed. Add water if at any time the surface level drops below the bones.

4 Fill a large bowl with ice and water; set aside. Strain the stock through a fine sieve or a cheesecloth-lined colander into a large bowl. Discard the solids. Transfer the bowl to the ice bath, and let the stock cool to room temperature.

5 Transfer the stock to airtight containers. They may be labeled at this point and refrigerated for 3 days or frozen for up to 4 months. If using the stock for a recipe, refrigerate for at least 8 hours or overnight so the fat collects on the top and can be removed. If freezing, leave the fat layer intact; it seals the stock.

FROZEN BLOODY MARYS

SERVES 4 | **PHOTOGRAPH ON PAGE 23**

A Bloody Mary made from puréed frozen cherry tomatoes combines the sweet, spicy taste of the traditional cocktail with the texture of a smoothie. The frozen whole tomatoes won't dilute the drinks the way ice cubes do. For the best results, freeze the cherry tomatoes the night before you plan to make these drinks.

4 cups (1½ pounds) frozen cherry tomatoes, plus more for garnish

6 ounces chilled vodka (optional)

½ cup freshly squeezed lime juice

1 tablespoon freshly grated horseradish

1 teaspoon hot sauce, or to taste

Coarse salt and freshly ground pepper

Celery stalks, for garnish

Place the tomatoes, vodka (if using), lime juice, horseradish, and hot sauce in the jar of a blender; season with salt and pepper. Purée until smooth but still very thick. Divide among chilled glasses, and garnish with celery stalks and frozen cherry tomatoes. Serve immediately.

LETTUCE BUNDLES WITH SPICY PEANUT NOODLES

SERVES 6 TO 8

This is a great dish to serve at an informal lunch or dinner party. Just set out all the ingredients, and let your guests assemble their own lettuce bundles. Store-bought roasted duck or chicken can be used.

½ cup Spanish or other peanuts

2 boneless whole duck or chicken breasts

½ cup plus 3 tablespoons soy sauce
 Canola oil

1 large garlic clove

1 three-quarter-inch piece ginger, peeled and cut in half

2¼ teaspoons chile paste

¼ cup plus 3 tablespoons smooth, good-quality peanut butter

3 tablespoons sugar

¼ cup plus 1½ teaspoons peanut oil
 Juice of 1 lime

4½ tablespoons water, or more if needed
 Coarse salt

6 ounces vermicelli or capellini (angel hair) noodles

2 ounces garlic chives or scallions, cut into 4-inch lengths

1 Japanese or Kirby cucumber, thinly sliced

2 heads Boston or other butterhead lettuce, leaves separated

1 Preheat the oven to 350°F. Place the peanuts in a single layer on a rimmed baking sheet; toast until they are golden and aromatic, 5 to 8 minutes. Shake the pan halfway through to ensure the nuts toast evenly. When cool enough to handle, roughly chop the nuts; set aside.

2 Place the duck or chicken breasts in a resealable plastic bag with ½ cup soy sauce, and let marinate for 1 hour. Heat a lightly oiled grill or cast-iron skillet over medium-high heat until very hot. Grill the duck or chicken breasts until cooked through, 5 to 7 minutes per side for duck and 4 to 6 minutes per side for chicken. Let cool slightly, and shred with your fingers, or cut into ½-inch-wide strips with a knife.

3 In a food processor, pulse the garlic and ginger until finely chopped. Add the remaining 3 tablespoons soy sauce,

the chile paste, peanut butter, sugar, peanut oil, lime juice, and water, and pulse until smooth. If a thinner sauce is desired, add 1 or 2 more teaspoons water, and pulse to combine. Set aside.

4 Bring a large pot of water to a boil. Salt the water, add the noodles, and cook until al dente, about 8 minutes. Drain in a colander, and rinse with cold water to stop the cooking.

5 Dress the noodles with ½ cup of the peanut sauce, and transfer to a medium serving bowl. If desired, set the bowl into a larger bowl filled with ice to keep the noodles chilled at the table. Arrange the reserved peanuts, remaining sauce, chives, cucumber, and lettuce in various serving dishes on the table. Guests can create their own rolls by wrapping noodles, a little sauce, and their choice of meat and fillings in a lettuce leaf.

FAVORITE COOKIE

CHEWY CHOCOLATE GINGERBREAD COOKIES

MAKES 2 DOZEN

7 ounces best-quality semisweet chocolate

1½ cups plus 1 tablespoon all-purpose flour

1¼ teaspoons ground ginger

1 teaspoon ground cinnamon

¼ teaspoon ground cloves

¼ teaspoon ground nutmeg

1 tablespoon unsweetened cocoa powder

8 tablespoons (1 stick) unsalted butter

1 tablespoon freshly grated ginger

½ cup packed dark-brown sugar

¼ cup unsulfured molasses

1 teaspoon baking soda

1½ teaspoons boiling water

¼ cup granulated sugar

1 Chop the chocolate into ¼-inch pieces; set aside. In a medium bowl, sift together the flour, ground ginger, cinnamon, cloves, nutmeg, and cocoa.

2 In the bowl of an electric mixer fitted with the paddle attachment, beat the butter and grated ginger until lightened, about 4 minutes. Add the brown sugar, and beat until combined. Add the molasses; beat until combined.

3 In a small bowl, dissolve the baking soda in the boiling water. Beat half of the flour mixture into the butter mixture. Beat in the baking soda mixture, then the remaining half of the flour mixture. Mix in the chocolate, and turn out onto a piece of plastic wrap. Pat the dough out to about 1 inch thick; seal with plastic wrap, and refrigerate until firm, 2 hours or overnight.

4 Preheat the oven to 325°F, with two racks centered. Line two baking sheets with parchment paper. Roll the dough into 1½-inch balls, and place, 2 inches apart, on the baking sheets. Refrigerate 20 minutes. Place the granulated sugar in a small bowl; roll the cookie balls in the granulated sugar, and return them to the baking sheets. Bake until the surfaces crack slightly, 13 to 15 minutes. Let cool on the baking sheets for 5 minutes, and then transfer to a wire rack to cool completely. Store in an airtight container for up to 1 week.

FAVORITE PIE AND TART

INDIVIDUAL BLUEBERRY PIES A LA MODE

MAKES 4 FIVE-INCH PIES

To serve a crowd, don't double the Large Quantity Pâte Brisée recipe; make as many single batches as needed. This recipe also will make one twelve-inch pie.

6 cups fresh blueberries, preferably wild Maine berries, picked over and cleaned

1 cup sugar, plus more for sprinkling

2 tablespoons all-purpose flour, plus more for work surface
 Pinch of coarse salt
 Large Quantity Pâte Brisée (recipe follows)

2 tablespoons unsalted butter

1 pint vanilla ice cream

1 Preheat the oven to 425°F. Combine the blueberries, sugar, flour, and salt in a large bowl. Gently toss to coat the blueberries. Set aside.

2 On a floured work surface, roll out half the dough to a ⅛-inch-thick square.

Using a sharp knife, quarter the square; carefully drape each quarter over a 5-inch pie plate.

3 Place 1½ cups of the blueberry mixture in each pie plate, mounding the berries in the center. Dot each pie with 1½ teaspoons butter.

4 Again, on a floured work surface, roll the remaining dough into a ⅛-inch-thick square. Using a sharp knife, quarter the square. Using a 1-inch round biscuit cutter, cut a hole in the center of each quarter. Drape each quarter over the berries, centering the steam hole. Seal the edges. Trim the edges around the pie plates to form a ½-inch lip. Chill the dough.

5 Dampen the lip of the dough with water. Using scissors, snip inward from the outside edge at ¾-inch intervals, making each cut about ¾ inch deep. As you cut, carefully fold in alternating tabs to create a bear-tooth crimping design. Chill again, about 30 minutes.

6 Transfer the pies to a baking sheet large enough that the tins do not touch. Brush each lightly with cold water; sprinkle with sugar. Bake until the crust is golden brown, about 20 minutes. Reduce the heat to 375°F; continue baking until the blueberry juice begins to bubble, about 15 minutes more. Remove from the oven; cool slightly. Serve with ice cream.

LARGE QUANTITY PATE BRISEE
MAKES 4 FIVE-INCH PIES

This recipe makes one and a half times the Pâte Brisée recipe on page 10. The amount of water needed will vary, depending on the humidity. Add only enough to make the dough come together when you press it between your fingers. The dough may be made one day ahead and refrigerated, well wrapped in plastic, or frozen for up to one month.

3¾   cups all-purpose flour
1½   teaspoons coarse salt
1½   tablespoons sugar
1½   cups (3 sticks) cold unsalted butter, cut into small pieces
½ to ¾ cup ice water

1 Place the flour, salt, and sugar in the bowl of a food processor; pulse to combine, about 30 seconds.

2 Add the butter; pulse until the mixture resembles coarse meal, about 10 seconds. Continue pulsing while adding the ice water in a slow, steady stream through the feed tube; process just until the dough begins to come together. Do not process for more than 30 seconds.

3 Turn the dough out onto a work surface. Divide the dough in half, and place on two separate sheets of plastic wrap. Flatten, and form into two disks or rectangles, depending on the shape of the intended crust. Wrap in plastic, and refrigerate at least 1 hour before using.

RUSTIC CHERRY TART
MAKES 1 NINE-INCH TART; SERVES 8 TO 10

½   cup blanched-almond flour, plus more for work surface
1   sheet frozen puff pastry, from a 17¼-ounce package, thawed
5   tablespoons unsalted butter, room temperature
⅓   cup plus 4 teaspoons sugar
1   large whole egg
½   teaspoon pure almond extract
1   large egg yolk
1   tablespoon heavy cream
1   pound fresh red cherries, pitted

1 Preheat the oven to 425°F. Line a work surface with parchment paper; sprinkle lightly with blanched-almond flour. Roll out the puff pastry to a ⅛-inch thickness on the paper. Cut a 12-inch circle out of the dough. Roll up the edges, making a 10-inch crust. Transfer the parchment and crust to a baking sheet, and transfer to the refrigerator to chill, about 30 minutes.

2 Place the almond flour, butter, ⅓ cup sugar, egg, and almond extract in a bowl; mix until combined.

3 Remove the crust from the refrigerator, and prick the entire surface with a fork. In a small bowl, combine the egg yolk and cream to make an egg wash; brush the egg wash evenly over the surface and edges of the crust. Using an offset spatula, spread the almond mixture evenly on the crust in a ⅛-inch-thick layer; return to the refrigerator, and chill 15 minutes more.

4 Remove the tart from the refrigerator, and spread the cherries in a single layer over the almond mixture. Bake 15 minutes.

5 Sprinkle the remaining 4 teaspoons sugar over the tart, and continue baking until the edges turn a deep golden brown, 5 to 10 minutes more. Transfer to a wire rack to cool. Serve warm or at room temperature.

FAVORITE CUSTARD AND PUDDING

CARAMEL POTS DE CREME
MAKES 6 | PHOTOGRAPH ON PAGE 30

The name of this delicate dessert comes from the small lidded porcelain pots in which it is traditionally baked. Be careful not to overcook it; doing so would ruin the velvety texture. The cover is not used while the crème is baking; it's added for an elegant presentation. You may also use small white ceramic soufflé ramekins or ovenproof custard cups.

¾   cup sugar
1½   cups heavy cream
1   cup milk
1   whole vanilla bean, split lengthwise
5   large egg yolks
¼   teaspoon coarse salt

1 Preheat the oven to 300°F with a rack in the center. Place 6 four-ounce ovenproof ramekins or pots de crème in a 13-by-9-by-2-inch roasting pan; set aside.

2 Place ½ cup sugar in a medium saucepan set over medium heat. Cook, without stirring, until the sugar has caramelized and is golden brown, about 3 minutes, brushing down the sides of the pan with a pastry brush dipped in water to prevent crystallizing. Swirl the pan, dissolving the unmelted sugar; reduce the heat to low.

3 Slowly whisk in 1 cup cream and the milk. Scrape the vanilla seeds into the pan, and add the pod. Raise the heat to medium high, cover, and bring to a boil; remove the pan from the heat.

4 In a bowl, whisk together the remaining ¼ cup sugar, the egg yolks, and salt; continue whisking until pale yellow. Slowly add the hot cream mixture to the egg mixture, whisking constantly. Pour this new mixture through a fine sieve set over a large liquid measuring cup; discard the vanilla pod.

5 Using a tablespoon or a small ladle, skim the surface to remove any visible air bubbles. Pour about ½ cup of the liquid into each ramekin. Transfer the pan to the oven. Fill the roasting pan with boiling water to within 1 inch of the ramekin tops. Cover the pan with aluminum foil, and poke small holes in two opposite corners for vents.

6 Bake until the custard is just set and is no longer liquid when lightly touched in the center, about 35 minutes. Remove the foil; transfer the ramekins to a wire rack to cool completely. Cover with plastic wrap; refrigerate until chilled.

7 When ready to serve, place the remaining ½ cup cream in a chilled mixing bowl. Using an electric mixer or hand whisk, whip the cream until soft peaks form. Add a dollop of whipped cream to each serving.

CHOCOLATE BREAD PUDDING
SERVES 8 TO 10

A nine-by-thirteen-inch ovenproof baking dish may be used in place of a gratin dish. If you use white bread, trim the crusts.

2 cups heavy cream

2 cups milk

3 cinnamon sticks (optional)

1 whole vanilla bean, split lengthwise

1 one-pound loaf Brioche (page 35), or good-quality white bread

12 ounces Valrhona or other bittersweet chocolate, roughly chopped, plus ½ ounce or ¼ cup shavings, for garnish

8 large egg yolks

¾ cup sugar

8 ounces crème fraîche or heavy cream

1 Preheat the oven to 325°F. Place the cream, milk, and cinnamon sticks, if using, in a medium saucepan; scrape the vanilla seeds into the pan, and add the pod. Bring to a boil. Remove from the heat, cover with plastic wrap, and let sit for 30 minutes to infuse the flavors.

2 Cut the brioche into ¼-inch-thick slices. Cut the slices into quarters, setting aside the rounded top pieces. Fill a 9-by-12-inch gratin dish with the quartered pieces.

3 Return the milk mixture to a boil, remove from the heat, and discard the vanilla pod and cinnamon sticks. Add the chocolate, and whisk until smooth. Combine the egg yolks and sugar in a large bowl, and whisk to combine. Pour the hot chocolate mixture very slowly into the egg-yolk mixture, whisking constantly, until fully combined.

4 Slowly pour half of the chocolate custard over the bread, making sure all the bread is soaked through. Arrange the reserved bread on top in a decorative pattern, and press firmly so the bottom layer of bread absorbs the chocolate mixture.

5 Spoon the remaining custard over the bread until it is completely covered and all cracks are filled. Place a piece of plastic wrap over the dish; press down to soak the bread thoroughly. Remove the plastic, wipe the edges of the dish with a damp towel, and allow to sit for 30 minutes.

6 Place the gratin dish in a roasting pan; transfer the pan to the oven. Fill the roasting pan with boiling water halfway up the sides of the gratin dish. Bake until set, about 35 minutes. Transfer to a wire rack to cool for 15 minutes.

7 Whisk the crème fraîche until soft peaks form. Serve the pudding warm, garnished with crème fraîche and chocolate shavings.

MOST REQUESTED RECIPE

MACARONI AND CHEESE 101
SERVES 12 | **PHOTOGRAPH ON PAGE 28**

For lots of crust, bake this in a broad, shallow casserole dish. You can easily divide this recipe in half; if you do, use a 1½-quart casserole.

8 tablespoons (1 stick) unsalted butter, plus more for casserole dish

6 slices good-quality white bread, crusts removed, torn into ¼- to ½-inch pieces

5½ cups milk

½ cup all-purpose flour

2 teaspoons coarse salt, plus more for water

¼ teaspoon freshly grated nutmeg

¼ teaspoon freshly ground black pepper

¼ teaspoon cayenne pepper

4½ cups (about 18 ounces) grated sharp white cheddar cheese

2 cups (about 8 ounces) grated Gruyère or 1¼ cups (about 5 ounces) grated Pecorino Romano cheese

1 pound elbow macaroni

1 Preheat the oven to 375°F. Butter a 3-quart casserole dish; set aside. Place the bread in a medium bowl. In a small saucepan set over medium heat, melt 2 tablespoons butter. Pour the melted butter into the bowl with the bread, and toss. Set the bread crumbs aside.

2 Warm the milk in a medium saucepan set over medium heat. Melt the remaining 6 tablespoons butter in a high-sided skillet over medium heat. When the butter bubbles, add the flour. Cook, stirring, 1 minute.

3 While whisking, slowly pour in the hot milk a little at a time to keep the mixture smooth. Continue cooking, whisking constantly, until the mixture bubbles and thickens, 8 to 12 minutes.

4 Remove the pan from the heat. Stir in the salt, nutmeg, black pepper, cayenne pepper, 3 cups cheddar cheese, and 1½ cups Gruyère (or 1 cup Pecorino Romano); set the cheese sauce aside.

5 Bring a large pot of water to a boil. Salt the water, and add the macaroni. Cook until the outside of the pasta is cooked and the inside is underdone, 2 to 3 minutes. Transfer the macaroni to a colander, rinse under cold running water, and drain well. Stir the macaroni into the reserved cheese sauce.

6 Pour the mixture into the prepared dish. Sprinkle the remaining 1½ cups cheddar cheese, ½ cup Gruyère (or ¼ cup Pecorino Romano), and the bread crumbs over the top. Bake until golden brown, about 30 minutes. Transfer the dish to a wire rack for 5 minutes; serve.

A DECADE OF DECADENCE

MOIST DEVIL'S FOOD CAKE

MAKES 1 EIGHT-INCH-ROUND THREE-LAYER CAKE; SERVES 8 TO 10

Great swoops of glossy frosting make this a wonderfully exuberant cake with a dark backdrop for birthday candles, but it is just as suitable for afternoon snacks or a Sunday supper. It keeps well for several days stored on the counter: Cover with plastic wrap or a glass dome to keep the cake from drying out. Dutch-process cocoa powder mixed with boiling water gives this cake a rich color and a strong chocolate flavor.

1½ cups (3 sticks) unsalted butter, plus more for pans

¾ cup Dutch-process cocoa powder, plus more for pans

½ cup boiling water

2¼ cups sugar

1 tablespoon pure vanilla extract

4 large eggs, lightly beaten

3 cups sifted cake flour (not self-rising)

1 teaspoon baking soda

½ teaspoon coarse salt

1 cup milk

Mrs. Milman's Chocolate Frosting (recipe follows)

1 Preheat the oven to 350°F; arrange two racks in the center. Butter three 8-by-2-inch round cake pans, and line with parchment paper. Dust the bottoms and sides of the pans with cocoa powder; tap out any excess. Sift ¾ cup cocoa into a medium bowl, and whisk in the boiling water. Set aside to cool.

2 In the bowl of an electric mixer fitted with the paddle attachment, cream the butter on low speed to soften; increase the speed to medium, and beat until light and fluffy. Gradually beat in the sugar until fluffy, 3 to 4 minutes, scraping down the sides twice. Beat in the vanilla. Drizzle in the beaten eggs, a little at a time, beating between each addition until the batter is no longer slick, scraping down the sides twice.

3 In a large bowl, sift together the flour, baking soda, and salt. Whisk the milk into the cooled cocoa mixture. With the mixer on low speed, alternately add the flour and cocoa mixtures to the batter, a little of each at a time, starting and ending with the flour mixture.

4 Divide the batter evenly among the three prepared pans. Bake until a cake tester inserted into the center of each layer comes out clean, rotating the pans for even baking, 35 to 45 minutes. Transfer the pans to wire racks to cool for 15 minutes. Turn out the cakes, and return to the racks, top sides up, until completely cool.

5 Remove the parchment paper from the bottoms of the cakes. Reserve the most attractive layer for the top. Place one cake layer on a serving platter; spread with 1½ cups of the chocolate frosting; repeat with the second layer; top with the reserved third layer. Cover the outside of the cake with the remaining 3 cups of frosting. Serve.

MRS. MILMAN'S CHOCOLATE FROSTING

MAKES 6 CUPS

Lois Milman, the creator of this frosting, always uses Nestlé morsels and makes only one batch at a time; the frosting will not set with more expensive chocolate. Keep the chocolate mixture over the heat until it thickens, or it will not thicken enough in the ice bath; timing will vary, depending on the saucepan used and the heat source. While the frosting is cooling, you'll need to stir it as instructed; otherwise, the frosting around the edge of the bowl will harden and the center will remain liquid. The finished frosting should have a consistent texture. Spread the frosting on our Moist Devil's Food Cake as soon as it is sufficiently chilled; it holds its shape well on the cake.

24 ounces semisweet chocolate morsels

1 quart heavy cream

1 teaspoon light corn syrup

1 Place the chocolate morsels and the cream in a heavy saucepan. Cook over medium-low heat, stirring constantly with a rubber spatula, until combined and thickened, 25 to 35 minutes. Raise the heat to medium; cook, stirring, about 10 minutes more.

2 Remove from the heat, and stir in the corn syrup. Transfer the frosting to a large metal bowl; chill. Stir every 15 to 20 minutes until cool enough to spread, 2 to 3 hours. Use immediately.

MOCHA MAJOLICA CAKE

MAKES 1 SIX-INCH-ROUND THREE-LAYER CAKE; SERVES 10 TO 12

Inspired by a majolica cake stand, this cake is a mocha génoise soaked with coffee syrup and iced lavishly with six shades of Meringue Buttercream.

5 tablespoons unsalted butter, plus more for pans and parchment

⅔ cup sifted cake flour (not self-rising), plus more for pans

⅓ cup unsweetened cocoa powder

1 tablespoon instant-espresso granules

1 teaspoon hot water

1 teaspoon pure vanilla extract

6 large eggs

¾ cup sugar

Coffee Syrup (recipe follows)

Mocha Buttercream (recipe follows)

Meringue Buttercream (recipe follows)

Gel-paste or liquid food coloring

1   Preheat the oven to 350°F. Butter 3 six-inch-round cake pans. Line the bottoms with buttered parchment paper, and dust with flour.

2   Sift the flour and cocoa together twice. Melt the butter. Dissolve the espresso granules in the hot water, and add it, along with the vanilla, to the butter. Keep warm.

3   Break the eggs into a large bowl, and add the sugar. Whisk over a pan of simmering water until warm. Remove from the heat, and beat on high speed until tripled in bulk.

4   In three additions, sift the flour-cocoa mixture over the egg mixture, folding quickly but gently. Scoop a cup of the batter into a small bowl, fold in the hot butter mixture, and then fold back into the rest of the batter. Divide evenly among the pans, and bake 20 to 25 minutes. The cakes will shrink away from the sides of the pan when done. Cool in the pans for 5 minutes, and then turn out onto a rack to cool completely.

5   To assemble the cake, trim off the tops of two layers, and moisten the cut sides with the coffee syrup. Top one trimmed layer with mocha buttercream. Add the second trimmed layer, and cover the top with mocha buttercream. Add the untrimmed layer. Chill until firm.

6   Using a serrated knife, carve the edges of the top layer to make a dome shape. Frost the cake with meringue buttercream. Chill again. Divide the remaining meringue buttercream among five bowls. Tint one each with rose, lavender, blue, and green food coloring; leave the fifth plain. Fill a sixth bowl with the remaining mocha buttercream. Cover the cake with lavender frosting. Chill.

7   With a toothpick, trace six large shell shapes around the cake. Using a #1 plain tip, pipe rows of plain, mocha, blue, and rose frosting inside the shells. Pipe a thick scalloped rose line on top of the outlines. With a pastry brush, brush downward to blend the inside colors. Using a #100 tip, pipe green lines between and over the shells, overlapping on top of the cake. Using a #70 leaf tip, pipe green and rose leaves on top. With the plain tip, pipe green vines around the bottom. Using a #67 tip, pipe on leaves.

COFFEE SYRUP

MAKES ½ CUP

Génoise is always soaked with a sugar syrup to moisten the cake and add flavor.

½ cup water

3 tablespoons sugar

2 tablespoons instant-espresso granules

1 tablespoon Kahlúa (optional)

Combine the water, sugar, espresso granules, and Kahlúa, if using, in a small saucepan over low heat, and bring to a boil. Set aside until ready to use. The syrup can be made up to this point a day ahead and stored, refrigerated, in an airtight container. Before using, return to room temperature, and mix well.

MOCHA BUTTERCREAM

MAKES ABOUT 3½ CUPS

8 ounces semi-sweet or bittersweet chocolate

1 tablespoon instant-espresso granules

1 teaspoon hot water

Meringue Buttercream (recipe follows)

Melt and cool the chocolate. Dissolve the espresso granules in the hot water. Stir the chocolate into the meringue buttercream; add the dissolved espresso granules. Stir to combine.

MERINGUE BUTTERCREAM

MAKES 3 CUPS

This buttercream holds its shape particularly well, making it good for decorating. If the buttercream becomes too soft while piping, stir it over an ice bath until it stiffens. The buttercream can be stored, refrigerated, in an airtight container for up to three days. Return to room temperature and rewhip before using.

1¼ cups sugar

⅓ cup water

5 large egg whites

Pinch of cream of tartar

1 pound (4 sticks) unsalted butter, cut into small pieces

1   In a small saucepan over medium heat, bring the sugar and water to a boil. Clip a candy thermometer onto the saucepan. Continue to boil the syrup, brushing down the sides of the pan with a pastry brush dipped in water to prevent crystallization, until the thermometer registers 238°F (the soft-ball stage).

2   In the bowl of an electric mixer fitted with the whisk attachment, beat the egg whites on low speed until foamy. Add the cream of tartar, and beat on medium high until stiff but not dry peaks form.

3 With the mixer running, pour the sugar syrup, in a steady stream, down the sides of the bowl (to prevent splattering) containing the egg whites. Beat on high speed until steam is no longer visible, about 3 minutes. Beat in the butter piece by piece. After all the butter has been added, beat for 3 to 5 minutes, until the frosting is smooth and spreadable. If it looks curdled at any point during the beating process, continue beating until smooth.

NOTE: Raw eggs should not be used in food prepared for pregnant women, babies, young children, the elderly, or anyone whose health is compromised.

TROMPE L'OEIL EASTER-EGG CAKES

MAKES 6

Spring is the time to serve these little cakes, which resemble hard-boiled eggs sliced in half. Each serving-size pound cake is baked in an easy-to-find egg-cake pan. Then a scoop of cake is removed from the center with a melon baller and replaced with a lemon-curd "yolk" piped from a pastry bag. A "nest" of fruit and mint leaves completes the creation. The cakes can be made up to two weeks in advance and stored in the freezer. Bring to room temperature before glazing.

8 tablespoons (1 stick) unsalted butter, room temperature, plus more for pan
¾ cup plus 3 tablespoons all-purpose flour, plus more for pan
½ cup plus 2 tablespoons granulated sugar
1 teaspoon pure vanilla extract
 Grated zest from ½ lemon
3 large eggs, room temperature
¾ teaspoon baking powder
¼ teaspoon coarse salt
 Colored Butter Glaze (recipe follows)
3 tablespoons confectioners' sugar
½ cup Lemon Curd Filling (recipe follows)
7 cups assorted fruit, such as strawberries, blueberries, blackberries, raspberries, peaches, apricots, and cherries, cut into bite-size pieces
3 tablespoons Grand Marnier (optional)
24 mint leaves, for garnish

1 Preheat the oven to 250°F. Generously butter the wells of an egg-cake pan, and dust the wells with flour; tap out any excess flour. Set the pan aside.
2 In the bowl of an electric mixer fitted with the paddle attachment, combine the butter and granulated sugar. Beat on medium speed until light and fluffy, about 2 minutes. Add the vanilla and the lemon zest; beat to combine. Add the eggs, one at a time, mixing well after each addition and scraping the sides of the bowl.
3 In a medium bowl, whisk together the flour, baking powder, and salt; gradually add to the butter mixture. Beat until just combined. Spoon 3 tablespoons batter into each of six wells in the cake pan, filling to ½ inch below the rim. (If you're using an egg-cake pan with more than six wells, alternate filled and empty ones.)
4 Bake the egg cakes for 10 minutes. Raise the oven temperature to 350°F, and bake until the cakes are golden, about 10 minutes more. Transfer the egg-cake pan to a wire rack, and let cool completely.
5 Invert the pan, and remove the cakes. Using a paring knife, trim the cakes to make a flat surface. (To make trimming easier, place the eggs in resealable plastic bags, and transfer to the freezer for 45 minutes.) Using a melon baller, scoop out a 1-inch-diameter hole in each cake. Set a wire rack over a baking sheet. Place the cakes flat side down on the wire rack. Working quickly, pour the butter glaze over three cakes, completely coating the outsides. Glaze the remaining three cakes. Let the glaze set completely, about 1 hour.
6 Turn the glazed cakes over; trim away any excess glaze with the paring knife so the glaze is flush with the cake's flat side. Wash and dry the wire rack.
7 Place the cakes glazed side down on the wire rack; generously dust the flat side with confectioners' sugar. Fit a pastry bag with a coupler, and fill the bag with lemon curd. Fill each hole with lemon curd until the "yolk" appears slightly rounded.

8 In a large bowl, combine all the fruit. Drizzle with Grand Marnier, if using, and toss to coat. On each dessert plate, make a nest of fruit, and place a filled cake in the center. Garnish each serving with mint leaves.

COLORED BUTTER GLAZE

COATS 6 EGG CAKES

This glaze is spread over the rounded sides of Trompe l'Oeil Easter-Egg Cakes. Experiment with different liquid or paste colors to get the hues you like.

2 tablespoons plus 2 teaspoons milk
 Gel-paste or liquid food coloring
2 cups sifted confectioners' sugar
8 tablespoons (1 stick) unsalted butter

1 Pour the milk into a small bowl, and stir in the food coloring until the desired shade is reached; set aside. Place 1 cup confectioners' sugar in a medium bowl, and set aside.
2 In a small saucepan, melt 4 tablespoons of the butter over medium heat. Remove the pan from the heat, and immediately pour the butter into the bowl with the sugar. Add 1 tablespoon plus 1 teaspoon tinted milk, and whisk until smooth. Immediately glaze three of the cakes; the mixture should be just thin enough so that it runs down the sides of the cake; if not, add a small amount of milk until thinned.
3 Repeat step 2 to glaze the remaining three cakes.

LEMON CURD FILLING

MAKES 1½ CUPS

This lemon curd serves as the "yolk" for Trompe l'Oeil Easter-Egg Cakes. Make it up to two days in advance, and store in the refrigerator; use any extra as a spread for your morning toast.

3 large egg yolks
 Zest of ½ lemon
¼ cup freshly squeezed lemon juice
¼ cup plus 2 tablespoons sugar
4 tablespoons cold unsalted butter, cut into pieces

1   Combine the yolks, lemon zest, lemon juice, and sugar in a small saucepan. Whisk to combine. Set over medium heat, and stir constantly with a wooden spoon, making sure to stir the sides and bottom of the pan. Cook until the mixture is thick enough to coat the back of the spoon, 5 to 7 minutes.

2   Remove the saucepan from the heat. Add the butter, one piece at a time, stirring with the wooden spoon until the consistency is smooth.

3   Transfer the mixture to a medium bowl. Lay a sheet of plastic wrap directly on the surface of the curd to keep a skin from forming; wrap tightly. Let cool; refrigerate until firm and chilled, at least 1 hour. Store, refrigerated, in an airtight container, up to 2 days.

CITRUS POPPY-SEED CAKE

MAKES 1 EIGHT-INCH-ROUND THREE-LAYER CAKE; SERVES 8 TO 10

All the ingredients should be at room temperature to cream properly.

- 1½ cups (3 sticks) unsalted butter, room temperature, plus more for pans
- 3¾ cups all-purpose flour, plus more for pans
- 2½ teaspoons baking powder
- ¾ teaspoon coarse salt
- 2½ cups sugar
- 7 large eggs, lightly beaten
- 1½ teaspoons pure vanilla extract
- 1 cup milk
- ⅓ cup poppy seeds, plus more for sprinkling
- ½ teaspoon each orange, lemon, and lime zest
- Shiny Cream-Cheese Frosting (recipe follows)
- Lemon Glaze (recipe follows)
- 1 navel orange
- 1 lemon

1   Preheat the oven to 350°F with two racks centered. Butter three 8-by-2-inch round cake pans. Line the bottoms of the pans with parchment paper. Dust the bottoms and sides with flour; tap out any excess. Sift together the flour, baking powder, and salt in a medium mixing bowl, and set aside.

2   In the bowl of an electric mixer fitted with the paddle attachment, cream the butter on medium-low speed until lightened, 1 to 2 minutes. Gradually add the sugar, and beat until the color has lightened more, 3 to 4 minutes, scraping down the sides of the bowl once or twice. Gradually drizzle the eggs into the bowl on medium-low speed, beating after each addition until the batter is no longer slick but is smooth and fluffy, about 5 minutes. Stop to scrape down the bowl once or twice. Beat in the vanilla on medium-low speed.

3   Reduce the speed of the mixer to low, and gradually add the flour mixture, alternating with the milk, a little of each at a time, beginning and ending with the flour mixture. Scrape down the bowl once or twice. Beat in the poppy seeds and citrus zest.

4   Divide the batter evenly among the prepared pans, and transfer the pans to the oven. Bake 30 minutes; rotate the pans if needed for even browning. Bake 5 to 10 minutes more, until a cake tester inserted into the center of each comes out clean. Transfer the pans to wire racks; cool about 15 minutes. Remove cakes from pans; cool completely on the wire racks, top sides up.

5   When completely cool, remove the parchment paper from the bottom of each cake. Save the most attractive layer for the top. Place one layer on the serving platter. Spread with 1½ cups frosting. Cover with the second layer, and spread with ½ cup frosting. Place the reserved layer on top. Refrigerate the cake for 1 hour, loosely covered with plastic wrap. To serve, stir the lemon glaze well, then pour onto the center of the top layer of the cake, letting it run down the sides. Cut long strips of zest from the orange and lemon using a single-hole zester. Arrange the zest in loose spirals on the top of the cake, and sprinkle lightly with poppy seeds.

SHINY CREAM-CHEESE FROSTING

MAKES 3 CUPS

This frosting is used to fill the Citrus Poppy-Seed Cake (you will have leftover frosting). Let the frosting chill for three to four hours before spreading on the cake.

- 12 ounces cream cheese, room temperature
- 6 tablespoons unsalted butter, room temperature
- 3 cups confectioners' sugar

In the bowl of an electric mixer fitted with the paddle attachment, beat the cream cheese on medium-low speed until smooth, about 1 minute. Add the butter, and cream for 2 minutes, until smooth. Add the confectioners' sugar on low speed, and mix until completely combined. Beat on medium speed until smooth and fluffy, about 1 minute more. Transfer to an airtight container, and place in the refrigerator until the frosting is chilled and firm, 3 to 4 hours or overnight.

LEMON GLAZE

MAKES ⅔ CUP

- 1½ cups confectioners' sugar
- 3 tablespoons freshly squeezed lemon juice, or more if needed
- 2 teaspoons poppy seeds

Place the sugar in a medium bowl. Gradually add the lemon juice; stir with a fork to combine until smooth, adding more juice if needed; the mixture should be slightly thick. Stir in the poppy seeds. The glaze may be made 3 to 4 hours ahead and kept, tightly covered, in the refrigerator.

RAINBOW SORBET CAKE

MAKES 1 SEVEN-INCH-ROUND
FIVE-LAYER CAKE; SERVES 10

Brightly colored fruit sorbets are layered between delicate, snowy disks of meringue to create a lofty frozen cake. You can use any sorbet flavors in this layer cake; we chose these for the combination of flavors and colors. Make the five meringue disks (steps one through five) up to five days ahead, and store them in an airtight container until you're ready to assemble the cake.

1½ cups sugar

6 large egg whites

⅔ pint mango sorbet

⅔ pint grapefruit sorbet or other pink sorbet

⅔ pint raspberry sorbet

⅔ pint green-apple sorbet or other green sorbet

1 Preheat the oven to 185°F. Cut a 7-inch circle from a 10-inch square of ¼-inch-thick cardboard or Foamcore. Set the circle aside to use for the bottom of the cake, and reserve the cut-out square as a template. Cut three 12-by-17-inch rectangles out of parchment paper, and set the parchment aside.

2 Fill a medium saucepan with 2 inches of water, and bring to a simmer. Place the sugar and egg whites in the bowl of an electric mixer. Hold the bowl over the simmering water, and whisk until the mixture is warm to the touch and the sugar has dissolved, about 3 minutes.

3 Attach the bowl to the mixer, fitted with the whisk attachment, and beat the egg whites on medium speed until stiff and glossy, about 4 minutes; do not overbeat.

4 Place the template over one end of a piece of parchment. Scoop 1 cup of the egg-white mixture into the center. Using an offset spatula, spread the mixture into an even layer. Remove the template. Make another disk on the other end of the parchment. Create three more disks on the remaining two pieces of parchment for a total of five. Slide each piece of parchment onto a 12-by-17-inch baking sheet.

5 Transfer the meringue disks to the oven, and bake 1½ hours, making sure they don't brown. Turn off the heat, and let the disks dry completely in the oven, 6 hours or overnight.

6 Once they are dry, place one meringue disk on the reserved 7-inch cake round. Using a gelato paddle or a large spoon, build up an even layer of the mango sorbet on top of the disk (rough scoops are fine; the layer should not be smooth). Top with a second meringue disk. Continue the layering process, using the remaining grapefruit, raspberry, and green-apple sorbets, and remaining meringue disks, ending with a disk on top.

7 Transfer the cake to the freezer, and freeze until hardened. Using a serrated knife, cut the cake into wedges, and serve. The cake may be assembled up to 4 hours before serving and kept in the freezer.

COCONUT BONBONS

MAKES 1 DOZEN

These delicious frozen bonbons are easy to make; set a rack in a baking pan to catch drips. The chocolate drips can be melted, strained, and reserved for a future use.

12 Nabisco Famous Chocolate Wafers

½ cup shredded sweetened coconut

2 pints coconut sorbet

12 whole almonds

26 ounces semisweet or bittersweet chocolate, chopped

1 tablespoon pure vegetable shortening

1 Set a wire rack over a baking pan. Arrange the wafers, top sides down, on the rack, spaced evenly apart. Place 2 teaspoons shredded coconut in the center of each wafer. Using a 2-inch ice-cream scoop, scoop a ball of coconut sorbet onto each wafer. Place an almond on top of each scoop of sorbet. Transfer the pan to the freezer for 20 minutes.

2 Set a heat-proof bowl or the top of a double boiler over a pan of barely simmering water. Place the chocolate and shortening in the bowl. Melt, stirring occasionally. Remove the bowl from the heat. Let cool slightly.

3 Remove the baking pan from the freezer. Generously ladle the melted

chocolate over the coconut balls, covering them entirely. Return the baking pan to the freezer for 30 minutes more or overnight. Serve frozen.

WATERMELON BOMBE

SERVES 12

Slices of this bombe resemble sweet wedges of watermelon and are just as refreshing. For the mold, choose a deep metal mixing bowl with a nice dome shape. Use one layer of the Vanilla Sponge Cake for the bombe, and freeze the second layer for later use. The bombe may be made up to two days ahead.

1 quart pistachio ice cream

1 pint best-quality vanilla ice cream

1 quart Watermelon Sorbet (page 20), or other red or pink sorbet

4 Nabisco Famous Chocolate Wafers, broken into ¼-inch pieces

1 six-inch-round layer Vanilla Sponge Cake (page 20)

1 Line a 3-quart metal mixing bowl with plastic wrap, and leave the edges overhanging by a few inches. Place the lined bowl in the freezer for 10 minutes; this will be the mold. Chill the bowl of an electric mixer in the freezer as well.

2 Place the pistachio ice cream in the chilled mixer bowl. Attach the bowl to the mixer, fitted with the paddle attachment, and beat on low speed until the ice cream is spreadable, about 30 seconds. Remove the chilled mold from the freezer. Using a rubber spatula, coat the inside of the mold with all the pistachio ice cream, making a ½-inch-thick layer. Return the mold and the empty mixer bowl to the freezer for 30 minutes.

3 Place the vanilla ice cream in the chilled mixer bowl. Beat on low speed until spreadable, about 30 seconds. Remove the mold from the freezer. Using the rubber spatula, coat the pistachio layer with the vanilla ice cream, making a ¼-inch-thick layer. Return the mold and the empty mixer bowl to the freezer for 30 minutes.

4 Place the sorbet in the chilled mixer bowl. Beat on low speed until the sorbet has softened, about 1 minute. Fold in the wafer pieces (these will represent the seeds). Remove the mold from the freezer. Pack the sorbet into the center, making an even layer ⅓ inch below the ice cream. Cover the sorbet portion with the sponge cake; trim the cake if necessary. Return the mold to the freezer until completely hardened.

5 To serve, place a serving plate upside down on top of the mold. Holding the plate against the mold, invert both. Place a hot, wet kitchen towel over the mold. Remove the metal bowl. Immediately, before serving, remove the plastic wrap.

WATERMELON SORBET

MAKES 1 QUART

Choose the ripest watermelon available.

1 cup sugar
¾ cup water
1 tablespoon white crème de menthe or Campari (optional)
3 cups ripe watermelon flesh, seeds removed

1 Fill a large bowl with ice and water; set aside. Place the sugar and water in a small saucepan. Cover, and bring to a boil over medium heat, stirring occasionally. When the sugar has dissolved, remove the pan from the heat, and stir in the crème de menthe, if using. Transfer the syrup to a bowl; set in the ice bath to chill.

2 Place the watermelon flesh in the bowl of a food processor; process until liquefied, about 2 minutes. Add purée to the chilled syrup; stir to combine.

3 Freeze the sorbet in an ice-cream maker according to the manufacturer's instructions. Store in a plastic container in the freezer for up to 1 week.

VANILLA SPONGE CAKE

MAKES 1 NINE-INCH-SQUARE CAKE OR
2 SIX-INCH-ROUND CAKES

1 tablespoon unsalted butter, for pan
½ cup all-purpose flour, plus more for pan
½ cup cornstarch
4 large eggs, separated
1 teaspoon pure vanilla extract
¾ cup sugar
Pinch of coarse salt

1 Preheat the oven to 350°F with a rack in the center. Butter a 9-inch-square baking pan. Line the pan with parchment paper, and butter again. Flour the pan, tapping out the excess flour; set aside. In a small bowl, sift together the flour and cornstarch; set aside.

2 In the bowl of an electric mixer fitted with the whisk attachment, beat the egg yolks, vanilla, and ½ cup sugar on high speed until thick and pale, about 5 minutes. Transfer the egg-yolk mixture to a large bowl. Wash and dry the mixer bowl and the whisk attachment.

3 Combine the egg whites and salt in the mixer bowl, and beat on medium speed until the whites hold soft peaks, about 1½ minutes. With the mixer running, slowly add the remaining ¼ cup sugar. Continue beating until stiff and glossy, about 1 minute.

4 Stir in about one third of the egg-white mixture into the egg-yolk mixture to lighten it, then fold in the remainder. In three additions, fold the reserved flour mixture into this new mixture. Transfer the batter to the prepared pan, and smooth the top with an offset spatula. Bake until a cake tester inserted into the middle comes out clean, 30 to 40 minutes. Transfer the pan to a wire rack to cool; turn out the cake, and wrap it in plastic wrap until ready to use.

FROZEN "TIRAMISU"

MAKES 1 NINE-INCH-SQUARE DESSERT;
SERVES 12

Serve this dessert right from the pan.

1 cup sugar
⅔ cup water
1½ cups strong, freshly brewed espresso
⅓ cup Kahlúa liqueur (optional)
Vanilla Sponge Cake (recipe above)
¼ cup finely ground espresso beans
2 pints espresso ice cream
2 pints coffee ice cream
Chocolate Curls (recipe follows)

1 Place the sugar and water in a small saucepan. Bring to a boil over medium heat, stirring occasionally until the sugar dissolves. Remove from the heat, and stir in the espresso and Kahlúa, if using. Let the syrup cool.

2 Using a long serrated knife, cut the sponge cake in half horizontally, making two layers. Place one layer in the bottom of a 9-by-2-inch baking pan. Using a pastry brush, brush with ¾ cup of the cooled syrup. Sift 2 tablespoons ground espresso over the cake.

3 Place the espresso ice cream in the bowl of an electric mixer fitted with the paddle attachment. Beat on low speed until spreadable. Spread the ice cream over the cake; top with a second layer of the sponge cake. Brush with the remaining syrup. Transfer the cake to the freezer for 20 minutes.

4 Remove the cake from the freezer, and sift the remaining 2 tablespoons ground espresso evenly over the cake. Place the coffee ice cream in the mixer bowl. Beat on low speed until spreadable. Spread the ice cream over the cake, forming large swirls. Return to the freezer, and freeze until completely hardened. To serve, garnish with the chocolate curls.

CHOCOLATE CURLS

MAKES 8 OUNCES

These curls are used to garnish the Frozen "Tiramisu" dessert.

8 ounces semisweet or bittersweet chocolate, chopped into ½-inch pieces

1 teaspoon pure vegetable shortening

1 Set a heat-proof bowl or the top of a double boiler over a pan of barely simmering water. Melt the chocolate and shortening in the bowl, stirring occasionally with a rubber spatula until smooth.

2 Divide the chocolate between two 12-by-17-inch baking pans; spread evenly with an offset spatula. Transfer the pans to the refrigerator, and chill until your finger makes a mark but not a hole when touching the chocolate.

3 Remove the pans from the refrigerator. Holding a sturdy metal pancake turner at a forty-five-degree angle to the pan, scrape away from you, forming curls. If the chocolate is too brittle, quickly wave the pan over the top of a warm stove. If it is too soft, briefly return to the refrigerator to harden. Refrigerate the curls in an airtight container for up to 2 weeks.

SWIRLY CUPCAKES

MAKES 30

Chilling the bowl beforehand helps the cream whip up with the most volume.

Dark Chocolate Cake (recipe follows)

3 pints ice cream, any flavor

5½ cups heavy cream

¼ cup confectioners' sugar

Sprinkles, for decorating

1 Place 30 paper baking cups on two baking sheets. Set aside. Slice each cake layer in half horizontally, making a total of four layers.

2 Using a 2¼-inch-round cookie cutter, cut 30 rounds from the cake layers. Place a round in each baking cup. Using a 2-inch ice-cream scoop, place one scoop of ice cream on each cake round. Transfer baking sheets to freezer for 20 minutes. Chill a medium mixing bowl.

3 Place the heavy cream and the confectioners' sugar in the chilled bowl. Whip until soft peaks form. Fit a 16-inch pastry bag with a coupler. Fill the pastry bag with the whipped cream. Starting at the perimeter of a baking cup, pipe a spiral of whipped cream, covering the ice cream. Repeat with the remaining cupcakes. Return to the freezer, and chill until hard, about 45 minutes. Decorate with sprinkles, and serve.

DARK CHOCOLATE CAKE

MAKES 2 EIGHT-INCH-SQUARE LAYERS

¾ cup (1½ sticks) unsalted butter, melted, plus more for pans

2 cups all-purpose flour, plus more for pans

1½ cups sugar

¾ cup unsweetened cocoa powder

½ teaspoon coarse salt

1½ teaspoons baking powder

¾ teaspoon baking soda

1 large whole egg, room temperature

1 large egg white, room temperature

1 teaspoon pure vanilla extract

1⅓ cups strong, hot coffee

1 Preheat the oven to 325°F. Butter 2 eight-inch-square baking pans. Line the pans with parchment paper, and butter again. Flour the pans, and set aside.

2 In the bowl of an electric mixer fitted with the whisk attachment, mix the butter, flour, sugar, cocoa, salt, baking powder, baking soda, egg, egg white, and vanilla extract. Mix on low speed until combined, about 1 minute. Slowly add the hot coffee. Mix until smooth, about 1 minute. Pour the batter into the prepared pans; smooth the tops with an offset spatula.

3 Bake until a cake tester inserted into the middle comes out clean, 25 to 30 minutes. Transfer the pans to wire racks to cool. Turn out the cakes, and wrap them in plastic wrap until ready to use.

CHOCOLATE CHESTNUT CAKE

SERVES 100 GENEROUSLY

In this extravagant wedding cake, four tiers—three squares atop a round base—are covered in rich ganache and laden with sugar-coated fruit, chestnuts, and laurel leaves. You will need two four-inch-square layers, two six-inch-square layers, two nine-inch-square layers, and three sixteen-inch-round layers. A half-batch of batter makes one four-inch and one six-inch layer; one-and-a-half batches make two nine-inch layers; one batch makes one sixteen-inch layer. For the ganache, you will need three batches for the filling and one for the glaze (the batch for the glaze should be made just before using). The fruits and nuts should be applied with a generous hand, so that every guest gets his or her share when slices of the cake are passed around.

FOR THE CAKE LAYERS:

1 cup (4¼ ounces) whole hazelnuts

8 tablespoons (1 stick) unsalted butter, cut into small pieces, plus more for pans

1 cup all-purpose flour, plus more for pans

4 ounces best-quality semisweet chocolate, chopped into ½-inch pieces

1 cup hot water

1½ cups sugar

2 tablespoons heavy cream

2 tablespoons pure vanilla extract

¼ cup unsweetened cocoa powder

1½ teaspoons baking soda

½ teaspoon baking powder

½ teaspoon coarse salt

9 ounces vacuum-packed chestnuts, ground

2 large eggs

FOR THE GANACHE:

3 pounds best-quality semisweet or bittersweet chocolate chopped into ½-inch pieces

2 cups heavy cream

8 tablespoons (1 stick) unsalted butter

⅔ cup sour cream

4 egg whites or powdered egg whites,
or more if needed

Small pieces of fruit (about 40), such as
lady apples, Seckel pears, and grapes

Superfine sugar

10 to 14 marrons glacés (candied
chestnuts)

Fresh, unsprayed laurel leaves and
sprigs (about 50)

1   To make the cake layers, preheat the
oven to 350°F. Place the hazelnuts in a
single layer on a rimmed baking sheet;
toast until the skins begin to split, about
10 minutes. Rub the warm nuts vigorously with a clean kitchen towel to remove as much skin as possible. When
cool, process in a food processor until
finely ground, about 30 seconds.

2   Reduce the oven heat to 325°F. Brush
the baking pans with butter. Line the
bottom of the pans with parchment paper; brush again with butter. Dust the
pans with flour, tapping out the excess.

3   In a heat-proof bowl or the top of
a double boiler set over a pan of barely
simmering water, combine the butter,
chocolate, and hot water until melted,
about 5 minutes. Transfer the mixture
to the bowl of an electric mixer fitted
with the paddle attachment.

4   Stir the sugar into the chocolate mixture. Let cool to room temperature,
about 10 minutes. Add the cream and
vanilla; stir with a rubber spatula.

5   Sift together the flour, cocoa powder,
baking soda, baking powder, and salt.
Add the ground chestnuts, hazelnuts,
and dry ingredients to the chocolate
mixture. Beat on low speed for 30 seconds to combine. Add the eggs one at a
time, mixing for 30 seconds and scraping
the sides of the bowl after each addition.

6   Pour the batter into the prepared pans
(fill 4-inch and 6-inch pans ½ inch full,
9-inch pans ¾ inch full, and each 16-
inch pan with a full batch). Bake 4-inch,
6-inch, and 16-inch layers for about 35
minutes, 9-inch layers about 45 minutes;
cakes are done when a cake tester inserted
in the center comes out clean.

7   Let cakes cool completely on racks.
Invert onto appropriate-size cardboard
rounds or squares, remove the parchment, and immediately reinvert onto
other rounds or squares so the cakes are
right side up. Wrap with plastic wrap;
store at room temperature.

8   To make the ganache, in a heat-proof
bowl or the top of a double boiler set over
a pan of barely simmering water, melt the
chocolate with the cream. Transfer to
a stainless-steel bowl. Immediately add
butter; stir until the butter is melted.

9   Fold in the sour cream until completely incorporated. If not using within 2
hours, cover the ganache with plastic
wrap, pressing wrap directly on the surface, and refrigerate.

10   To make the sugared fruit and leaves,
beat 4 egg whites (or more as needed;
use powdered whites if concerned about
consuming raw eggs) a few times with a
fork. Brush the apples and pears with the
whites, and roll in the sugar; shake off
excess. Let the fruit dry on parchment-
covered rimmed baking sheets. Store at
room temperature in a nonhumid envi-
ronment for up to 24 hours. Sugar the
grapes, marrons glacés, and laurel (paint
the leaves only halfway; leave the stem
end plain) just before using.

11   To assemble the cake, make 3 batches
of the ganache for icing. Place over a
large bowl of ice and water to cool,
whisking continuously; do not let it solidify. Transfer to the bowl of an electric
mixer fitted with the whisk attachment.
Whip until soft peaks form.

12   Spread ¼ cup ganache on one 4-inch
cake layer (placed on cardboard); place
other 4-inch layer (without cardboard)
on top. Repeat with the other sizes, using 1 cup ganache between the 6-inch
layers, 2 cups between the 9-inch layers,
and 5 cups (total) between the three 16-
inch layers. Use an icing spatula to apply
a thin coating of ganache to each tier.
Refrigerate the tiers until firm, at least
1 hour or overnight.

13   Make one batch of ganache for glazing; it should be warm (125°F on an instant-read thermometer).

14   Place the 16-inch tier on a wire rack
over a rimmed baking sheet (so the excess ganache can be reused). Ladle 16 to
18 ounces ganache on top of the tier;
spread with an offset spatula, pushing
the ganache over the edges. Pour more
ganache over bare spots. Set that tier aside.
Repeat the process for the remaining
tiers, using 4 to 6 ounces for the 4-inch
tier, 8 to 10 ounces for the 6-inch tier,
and 10 to 12 ounces for the 9-inch tier.

15   Place a Masonite board on a cake
turntable. Smear the board with 2 tablespoons ganache; place the 16-inch tier
on top. Insert a ¼-inch-diameter wood-
en dowel into the cake; mark where the
dowel is flush with the glaze; cut 5 pieces
to that length. Insert 4 dowels in a square
pattern on the cake, and 1 in the center.

16   Place the 9-inch tier, on cardboard,
on top, centered over the cake. Repeat
the dowel procedure with the 9-inch tier.
Place the 6-inch tier on top; repeat the
procedure. Place the 4-inch tier on top.

17   Decorate as desired with sugared
fruits, chestnuts, and leaves.

NOTE: Raw eggs should not be used in food
prepared for pregnant women, babies, young
children, the elderly, or anyone whose health is
compromised.

FROZEN BLOODY MARYS | **PAGE 11**

BEST BUTTERMILK PANCAKES

1 Whisk wet ingredients into dry, leaving unmoistened lumps. The interaction of the liquid and pockets of dry ingredients during cooking will result in fluffier pancakes.

2 Flip the pancakes when the surface is covered with little bubbles that have begun to break, but before too many of the bubbles have popped.

3 For blueberry pancakes, place berries on top of the batter right after it's poured onto the griddle. This will distribute the fruit evenly.

BEST BUTTERMILK PANCAKES | **PAGE 3**
with (left to right) cornmeal, blueberries, and whole wheat flour.

APPLESAUCE CAKE | **PAGE 4**

FRENCH ONION SOUP | **PAGE 11**

LEMON CHICKEN | **PAGE 6**

MACARONI AND CHEESE 101

1 To make the white sauce, begin by melting butter in a high-sided skillet over medium heat. When the butter bubbles, add the flour. Cook, stirring one minute.

2 While whisking, slowly pour in hot milk. Continue cooking, whisking constantly, until the sauce becomes thick.

3 The starch from the flour binds the sauce, so when the cheese is stirred in, the result is smooth and creamy. Then, add the cooked macaroni.

INGREDIENTS

elbow macaroni

white cheddar, Gruyère, and Pecorino Romano cheese

bread

milk

freshly ground black pepper

cayenne pepper

butter

salt

nutmeg

flour

SPAGHETTI AND TOMATO SAUCE 101 | **PAGE 5**

CARAMEL POTS DE CREME | PAGE 13

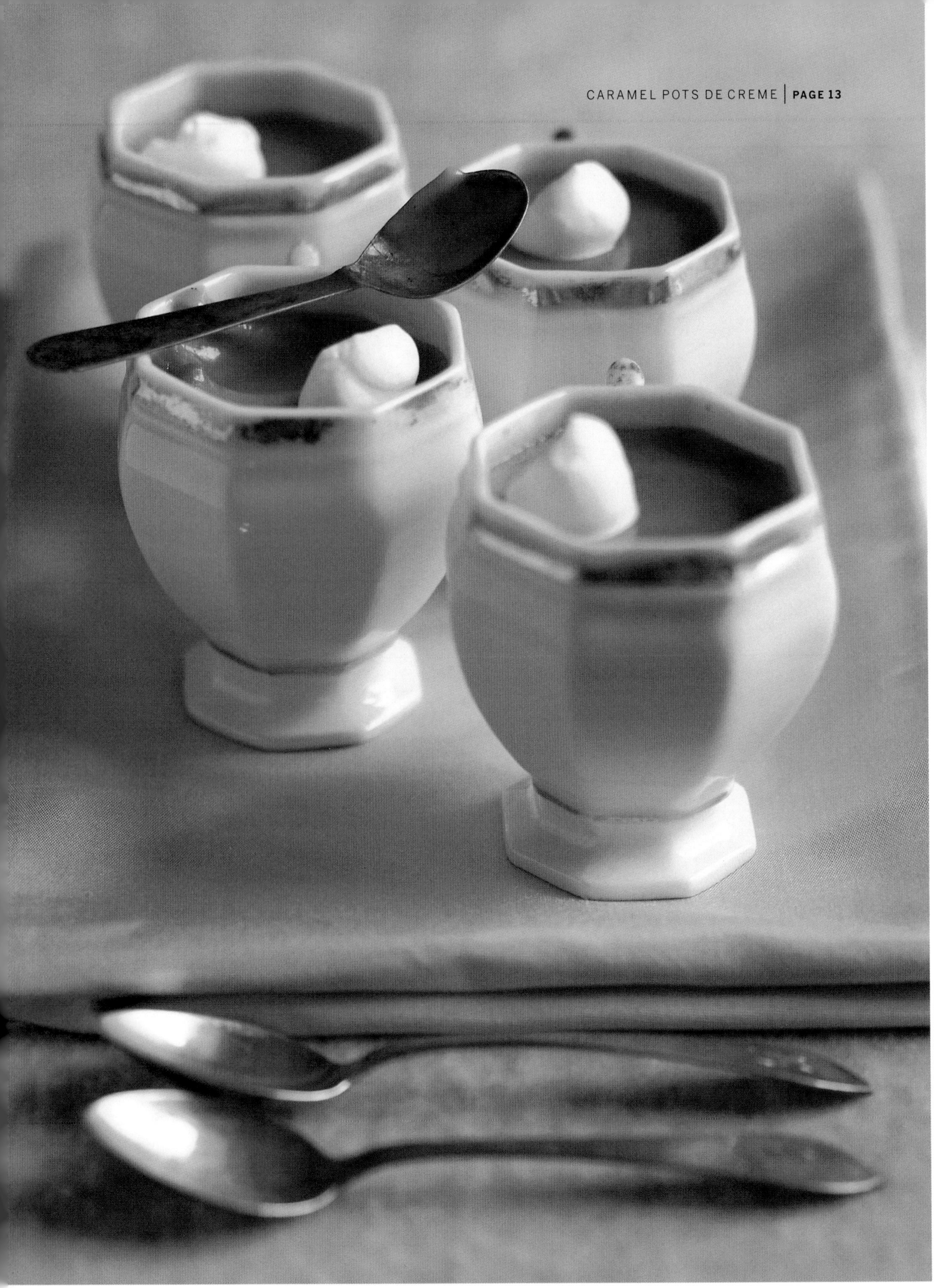

february

Chocolate Soufflé

Chocolate Strawberry Ice Cream
Sandwiches

Classic Brioche Loaves

Individual Paris Brioches

Pastitsio

Macaroni Quattro Formaggi
with Prosciutto

Baked Rigatoni with Sausage
Meatballs and Broccoli Rabe

Baked Mushroom Linguine

Crab-Stuffed Shells with Peas
and Leeks

Butternut Squash Cannelloni
with Sage-Walnut Cream Sauce

Traditional Lasagna Bolognese

Pork Tenderloin with Apricot
Fennel Ragout

Herbed Wild Rice

Roasted Squash Wedges

Chocolate Pistachio Biscotti

Salmon Steamed with Savoy
Cabbage

Blackened Salmon Sandwiches

Poached Salmon, Leek, and
Fennel Soup

Barbecued Salmon Fillets

Slow-Roasted Salmon with
Green Sauce

CHOCOLATE SOUFFLE

MAKES 1 ONE-QUART SOUFFLE; SERVES 2

This soufflé gets its rich flavor from high-quality bittersweet chocolate and cocoa powder; the last-minute addition of whisked egg whites keeps the batter supremely fluffy. A parchment collar ensures maximum height. If desired, serve the soufflé with whipped cream, crème anglaise, or fruit sauces such as orange, raspberry, or strawberry.

Unsalted butter, room temperature, for dish and collar

½ cup plus 2 tablespoons granulated sugar, plus more for dish

¾ cup milk

3 tablespoons all-purpose flour

4 large eggs, separated

2 ounces (about ½ cup) Valrhona or best-quality bittersweet chocolate, finely chopped

¼ cup Valrhona or unsweetened cocoa powder, sifted

¼ teaspoon cream of tartar

Confectioners' sugar, for dusting (optional)

1 Preheat the oven to 400°F with rack in center. Cut a parchment collar about 20 inches long by 6 inches high. Brush the top half of one side with butter. Butter the sides only of a 1-quart soufflé dish; coat with an even layer of granulated sugar, and set aside.

2 In a small heavy-bottomed saucepan, whisk together ¼ cup sugar and the milk. Bring to a boil; remove from heat.

3 In a medium bowl, whisk together ¼ cup sugar, the flour, and the egg yolks. Slowly pour the hot-milk mixture into the egg-yolk mixture, whisking constantly.

4 Transfer the milk-and-yolk mixture to the saucepan. Whisk over medium-high heat until mixture thickens, about 40 seconds. Make sure to whisk along the sides of the pan to prevent scorching.

5 Remove the pan from the heat, add the chopped chocolate, and whisk until melted. Add the cocoa powder; whisk until combined. Transfer chocolate pastry cream to a large mixing bowl, and set aside.

6 In the bowl of an electric mixer fitted with the whisk attachment, combine the egg whites and cream of tartar on low speed until frothy. Increase to medium speed until soft peaks form. Gradually add the remaining 2 tablespoons sugar. Increase mixer speed to high, and whisk until stiff but not dry peaks form.

7 Whisk the chocolate pastry cream to loosen and release steam; add one third of the egg-white mixture, and whisk vigorously until the mixture is combined and lightened.

8 Using a rubber spatula, lightly stir the remaining egg-white mixture to loosen (this will keep you from overmixing the soufflé), then fold the remaining egg-white mixture into the lightened chocolate pastry cream.

9 Transfer the soufflé batter to the prepared dish, and smooth the top with a spatula. Secure the parchment collar around the dish with kitchen twine so that the collar extends 3 inches above the dish. Place in the oven, and bake for 10 minutes; reduce oven temperature to 350°F, and bake 20 minutes more for a creamy center or 25 minutes more for a slightly drier center.

10 If desired, dust the soufflé with confectioners' sugar; serve immediately.

SOUFFLE TIPS

All equipment that comes into contact with egg whites must be perfectly clean and dry: Any grease or water will prevent the whites from reaching full volume. A copper bowl produces the most stable beaten egg whites. It also makes them hard to overbeat. A second choice is stainless steel, and third is glass. Never use plastic. Omit the cream of tartar if using a copper bowl. Use eggs that are at least three days old—older eggs beat up fluffier and are more stable than fresh eggs. Make sure the oven is fully heated before baking. An oven thermometer is helpful; precise temperature is important when baking soufflés. Position a rack in the lower third of the oven, and remove the other racks. A soufflé should be served straight from the oven, but you can keep it at its peak for up to five minutes by turning off the oven and leaving the door ajar. Avoid drafts.

CHOCOLATE STRAWBERRY ICE CREAM SANDWICHES

MAKES 2 DOZEN | PHOTOGRAPH ON PAGE 47

Bottled pure vanilla extract can be substituted for homemade. These dessert sandwiches may be made with cookie cutters of any shape, but heart shapes are ideal for creating a Valentine's Day treat.

- 2¾ cups all-purpose flour, plus more for work surface
- ½ cup unsweetened cocoa powder
- 2½ teaspoons baking powder
- ¼ teaspoon coarse salt
- 12 tablespoons (1½ sticks) unsalted butter, softened
- 1½ teaspoons Vanilla Extract (recipe follows)
- 1½ cups sugar
- 2 large eggs
- 1 tablespoon milk
- 2 to 2½ pints strawberry ice cream

1 In a medium bowl, sift together the flour, cocoa powder, baking powder, and salt, and set aside. In the bowl of an electric mixer fitted with the paddle attachment, cream the butter, vanilla, and sugar. Add the eggs and milk, and mix until combined. Add the reserved flour mixture, and mix on low speed until incorporated, scraping the sides of the bowl at least once. Divide the dough in half, and shape each half into a flat disk. Wrap each disk in plastic wrap, and chill until firm, about 1 hour.

2 Preheat the oven to 350°F. Roll out one disk on a floured work surface, releasing the dough with an offset spatula every few turns of the rolling pin. Roll the dough to ⅛ inch thick. Cut the dough using a variety of heart-shape cookie cutters 2½ to 3 inches in diameter, making sure each cookie has a match to make a sandwich. Place the hearts on a parchment-lined baking sheet; chill until firm, about 30 minutes.

3 Remove cookies from the refrigerator, and use a fork to prick them with holes. Bake until just firm, 12 to 15 minutes. Let cool on the baking sheet; transfer to a wire rack.

4 Turn half the cookies upside down, and spoon onto them the softened ice cream; spread ice cream about ½ inch thick. Place the matching cookie on top of ice cream, top side facing out. Transfer immediately to the freezer to harden. Repeat the process with the remaining ingredients. Serve sandwiches directly from the freezer. Sandwiches can be kept stored in an airtight container, frozen, for 3 to 4 days.

VANILLA EXTRACT

MAKES 1 CUP

This extract is best used after resting for two months or longer.

- 2 whole vanilla beans, split lengthwise
- 8 ounces vodka

Place the vanilla beans in a clean jar with a lid. Pour the vodka over the beans, and place the lid on the jar. Allow to sit in a cool, dark place for 2 to 5 months, shaking the jar occasionally.

BRIOCHE

BRIOCHE DOUGH

MAKES ENOUGH FOR 2 MEDIUM LOAVES, OR 1 LARGE LOAF AND 4 INDIVIDUAL BRIOCHES, OR 1 RECTANGULAR LOAF AND 8 INDIVIDUAL BRIOCHES, OR 22 INDIVIDUAL BRIOCHES

Because there is so much butter in brioche, it is important to use the best-quality butter you can find. Rather than measure by volume, weigh your ingredients using an accurate scale, as professional bakers do. And remember: The butter and eggs must be cold, or you may produce something that looks more like cake batter than bread dough. If this happens, chill the dough until it becomes workable. Never add more flour, which will toughen the dough. Preheat the oven to 375°F when you think the dough is about a half-hour from doubling.

- ⅓ cup warm water
- 1 tablespoon active dry yeast or ½ ounce fresh yeast
- 9 ounces bread flour or all-purpose flour
- 5 ounces pastry flour or all-purpose flour
- 10 ounces unsalted butter
- 4 large eggs
- 3 tablespoons (1 ounce) sugar
- ½ ounce milk powder
- 1 teaspoon coarse salt

1 For the sponge, pour the warm water into a medium bowl; sprinkle the yeast over the surface. Stir with a fork until dissolved. Let stand until creamy looking, about 5 minutes.

2 Add 2 ounces bread flour; stir until well combined. Cover with a dry towel; let rise in a warm spot until doubled in bulk and bubbles appear on the surface, about 1 hour.

3 Place the remaining 7 ounces bread flour, and the pastry flour, butter, 4 eggs, sugar, and milk powder in the bowl of an electric mixer fitted with the dough-hook attachment. Beat on low speed until well combined, about 5 minutes. Add the sponge; beat on low speed for

5 minutes more. Increase the speed to medium; beat 5 minutes more. Sprinkle in the salt; beat on medium speed for 5 minutes more, until the dough is smooth, shiny, and elastic.

4 Cover the bowl with plastic wrap; immediately place in the freezer for 30 minutes. Remove from the freezer; punch down the dough in the bowl. Turn out onto the plastic wrap. Working quickly, use your fingers to press the dough out into a ½-inch-thick disk. Wrap well, place on a tray, and chill 10 hours or overnight.

CLASSIC BRIOCHE LOAVES
PHOTOGRAPHS ON PAGES 48-49

The dough balls for brioche loaves will vary in weight according to the pan size: An eight-inch-round fluted pan takes five balls at five-and-a-half ounces each; a seven-inch-round pan takes five balls at three ounces each. A rectangular loaf pan takes four balls at five-and-a-half ounces each, or the same amount of dough can be split into eight balls. Adjust the ball size for slightly larger or smaller pans.

Unsalted butter, for pan
Brioche Dough (recipe above)
All-purpose flour, for shaping and work surface
1 egg, beaten, for glaze

1 Butter a round fluted pan or rectangular loaf pan; set aside. Remove the disk of dough from the refrigerator. Weigh out enough pieces of dough for one loaf. Return the unused dough to the refrigerator. On a lightly floured wooden surface, roll each piece of dough into a ball with the floured palm of your cupped hand, using slight pressure. Roll the ball quickly in a circular motion until it is smooth. Add as little extra flour as possible. If using a rectangular loaf pan, roll four balls into log shapes, or make eight balls; skip to step 6. For a round loaf, shape each ball into a teardrop shape.

2 Arrange four teardrop shapes around the sides of the prepared pan, leaving a hole in the center. Use your forefingers to press and smear the dough together a bit on the bottom of the pan, leaving only a little pan showing. This will help the balls bake cohesively so the baked loaf won't fall apart.

3 Using your thumbs, press lightly on the middle part of the dough balls while turning the pan, nudging the teardrops together and creating a slight bulge.

4 Lightly brush the inside of the partially formed loaf with the beaten egg.

5 Drop in the last teardrop shape, letting it rest higher than the others.

6 Cover the loaves with a bowl or other container large enough to give the dough ample room to double. The bowl should not touch the rising loaves. Set aside in a warm, nondrafty place until more than fully doubled in bulk, this could take anywhere from 1 to 3 hours. Be patient. Repeat with the remaining dough. Just before baking, brush the loaves gently but generously with the beaten egg. Bake medium loaves 40 to 45 minutes and large loaves for 45 minutes or until they sound hollow when the bottom is tapped. Immediately tip the loaves in their tins to cool, or transfer to wire racks.

BRIOCHE DOUGH

Making an admirable brioche is not so difficult, but it requires the finest ingredients, patience, and a basic understanding of the dough's properties. It helps if you have very fresh eggs, unsalted creamery butter, and fine high-gluten bread flour. Brioche dough is unusually dense from the weight of all its butter and eggs, so it takes longer than ordinary bread to rise to double in bulk, as required, before baking. To make a dough that can be handled, the butter and the eggs must be cold going in, and the dough itself must be kept cold while you're working with it. Shaping the dough well will present the biggest challenge—the dough is sticky (and meant to be that way); just use lightly floured hands and an easy, quick touch. It will take practice to form handsome loaves, but if you follow all the other steps properly and precisely, even less than beautiful brioches will taste wonderful.

INDIVIDUAL PARIS BRIOCHES

MAKES 22 | **PHOTOGRAPHS ON PAGES 48–49**

Unsalted butter, for pan

Brioche Dough (page 34)

All-purpose flour, for shaping and work surface

1 egg, beaten, for glaze

1 Butter a few 3-inch fluted pans; set aside. Remove the disk of dough from the refrigerator, and weigh out 1½-ounce pieces. Return all but the pieces you are immediately using to the refrigerator. On a lightly floured wooden surface, roll each piece of dough into a ball with the palm of your cupped hand, exerting only slight pressure. You may need to flour your hand or the surface during the shaping process, but use as little extra flour as possible.

2 Using the edge of your hand, roll the dough back and forth to create a "neck" for the classic "head" *(tête)* of the brioche. Do not separate this ball of dough. It should be about one sixth of the total ball of dough (marble size).

3 Pick up the dough by the head, and lower it into the prepared pan.

4 Using your lightly floured forefinger, nudge the dough up to create a slight bulge while rotating the tin. You are deepening the space in which the head will sit.

5 Press the head gently into the space created in step 4 without flattening it too much.

6 The head should be level with the rest of the dough. Cover each loaf with a bowl or container large enough to give the dough ample room to double. The bowl should not touch the loaves as they rise. Set aside in a warm, nondrafty place until more than fully doubled in bulk.

This could take anywhere from 1 to 3 hours. Be patient. Repeat with the remaining dough, making a few loaves at a time. Just before baking, brush gently but generously with the beaten egg. Bake for 8 to 12 minutes or until they sound hollow when tapped on the bottom. Timing will vary, depending on your oven. Do not overbake. Immediately remove from the pans, and cool on a wire rack.

BAKED PASTA

PASTITSIO

SERVES 10 TO 12

FOR THE MEAT SAUCE:

2 tablespoons extra-virgin olive oil

2 white onions, cut into ¼-inch dice

2 pounds ground lamb

2 teaspoons coarse salt

2 teaspoons ground cinnamon

½ teaspoon freshly ground black pepper

¼ teaspoon ground nutmeg

½ cup red wine

1 six-ounce can tomato paste

2 bay leaves

2 cups water

FOR THE BECHAMEL:

6 tablespoons unsalted butter

½ cup plus 1 tablespoon all-purpose flour

2 teaspoons baking powder

3 cups milk

1 cup (about 3 ounces) freshly grated Parmesan cheese

2 teaspoons coarse salt, plus more for cooking water

¼ teaspoon freshly ground black pepper

¼ teaspoon ground nutmeg

Pinch of cayenne pepper

FOR THE ASSEMBLY:

Unsalted butter, for baking dish

1 pound curly elbow macaroni

1 To make the sauce, heat the olive oil in a large skillet with high sides over medium heat. Add the onions, and cook until they begin to soften, about 3 minutes. Add the lamb, salt, cinnamon, pepper, and nutmeg. Cook, breaking into pieces, until the lamb is no longer pink. Add the wine, and cook until the liquid is almost evaporated. Stir in the tomato paste, bay leaves, and water. Cover, and let simmer 30 minutes, skimming the fat occasionally. Remove from the heat, and set aside, covered.

2 For the béchamel, melt the butter in a large saucepan over medium heat. When the butter is bubbling, add the flour and baking powder. Cook, stirring constantly with a wire whisk, for 1 minute. While whisking, slowly pour in the milk. Continue cooking, whisking constantly, until the mixture bubbles and becomes thick. Remove the pan from the heat, and stir in the Parmesan, salt, black pepper, nutmeg, and cayenne pepper. Set aside, covered, until ready to assemble.

3 Preheat the oven to 375°F. Butter a 9-by-13-inch glass or other ovenproof baking dish; set aside. Bring a large saucepan of water to a boil. Salt the water, and add the pasta; cook 2 to 3 minutes less than the manufacturer's instructions, until very al dente. Transfer to a colander, and rinse with cold water to stop the cooking; drain well. Stir the noodles into the meat mixture. Pour the meat-and-pasta mixture into the prepared pan. Spread the béchamel over the mixture, and bake until the top is set and golden brown, 30 to 40 minutes. Let sit 10 minutes before serving.

MACARONI QUATTRO FORMAGGI WITH PROSCIUTTO

SERVES 10 TO 12 | **PHOTOGRAPH ON PAGE 51**

6 tablespoons unsalted butter, plus more for baking dish

1 medium onion, diced

½ cup all-purpose flour

5½ cups milk

2 teaspoons coarse salt, plus more for cooking water

¼ teaspoon freshly ground black pepper

Pinch of cayenne pepper, or to taste

1½ cups (about 4½ ounces) freshly grated Parmesan cheese

1½ cups (about 6 ounces) grated Gruyère cheese

1½ cups (about 6 ounces) grated fontina cheese

1½ cups (about 6 ounces) Gorgonzola cheese, broken into small pieces

1 pound ziti or mostaccioli pasta

8 ounces thinly sliced prosciutto

1 Preheat the oven to 375°F. Butter a 3-quart casserole dish; set aside. Melt the butter in a large saucepan over medium heat. Add the onion, and cook until softened but not browned, about 5 minutes. While the butter is bubbling, add the flour. Cook, stirring constantly with a wire whisk to coat the onions, for 1 minute. While whisking, slowly pour in the milk. Continue cooking, whisking constantly, until the mixture bubbles and becomes thick. Remove the pan from the heat; stir in the salt, black pepper, cayenne pepper, and all the cheese. Set the cheese sauce aside.

2 Bring a large saucepan of water to a boil. Salt the water, add the pasta, and cook 2 to 3 minutes less than the manufacturer's instructions, until the outside of the pasta is cooked and the inside is underdone. Transfer the pasta to a colander, and rinse under cold running water to stop the cooking; drain well. Stir the pasta into the reserved cheese sauce.

3 Shred about three slices of the prosciutto to yield ¼ cup; set aside. Place half of the remaining prosciutto in the bottom of the prepared baking dish. Layer with half of the pasta mixture. Place the remaining prosciutto in a layer over the pasta, and top with the remaining pasta mixture. Sprinkle the shredded prosciutto on top. Bake until browned on top, about 30 minutes. Transfer the dish to a wire rack, and cool 5 minutes before serving.

BAKED RIGATONI WITH SAUSAGE MEATBALLS AND BROCCOLI RABE

SERVES 10 TO 12

FOR THE TOMATO CREAM SAUCE:

2 tablespoons extra-virgin olive oil

1 onion, diced

2 ounces vodka

1 sixteen-ounce can tomato sauce

1 twenty-eight-ounce can plum tomatoes, cut into pieces, with juice

1½ cups heavy cream

4 sprigs fresh oregano

4 sprigs fresh thyme

FOR THE MEATBALLS:

2 pounds sweet Italian sausage, casings removed

FOR THE ASSEMBLY:

1 pound rigatoni

Unsalted butter, for baking dish

Coarse salt, for cooking water

1 bunch broccoli rabe

4 ounces fontina cheese, cut in ½-inch cubes

1 To make the sauce, heat the olive oil in a large saucepan over medium heat. Add the onion, and cook until softened, about 5 minutes. Add the vodka, and cook until the liquid has almost evaporated, about 3 minutes. Stir in the tomato sauce, canned tomatoes, cream, oregano, and thyme. Cook at a gentle simmer about 30 minutes to let the sauce thicken and the flavors infuse.

2 While the sauce is cooking, make the meatballs. Using your hands, roll the sausage into balls about 1 inch in diameter. Heat a medium skillet over medium-high heat, and sauté the meatballs in

PERFECT PASTA

The pasta should not be crowded in the cooking water; always use five to six quarts of water for every pound of pasta. Long, wide noodles, such as lasagna and pappardelle, require even more water. Use more than one pot, if necessary. Add the pasta all at once; if the pasta is too long to fit into the pot, don't break it. Push the tops down gently with a wooden spoon as the bottoms soften in the hot water. Stir the pasta to separate the strands or shapes and stir occasionally while it cooks. The only way you'll know when the pasta is al dente (which means "to the tooth" in Italian) is by tasting it. When it's ready it should be tender but still a bit chewy, offering some resistance but not a "crunch" when you bite into it. Start testing sooner rather than later (and well before the time given on the package).

batches until well browned and cooked through, about 6 minutes. Add to the tomato sauce.

3 Bring a large saucepan of water to a boil. Salt the water, and add the pasta; cover and cook 2 to 3 minutes less than the manufacturer's instructions, until very al dente. Transfer the pasta to a colander, and rinse with cold running water to stop the cooking; drain well. Stir the pasta into the sauce mixture.

4 Preheat the oven to 375°F. Butter a 3-quart casserole dish; set aside. Bring a large saucepan of water to a boil; salt the water. Trim and discard the tough ends of the broccoli rabe; cut the broccoli rabe into 1-inch lengths. Blanch in boiling water until bright green and just tender, about 1 minute. Drain in a colander, and rinse under cold water to stop the cooking. Add to the pasta mixture, and stir to combine. Pour into the prepared baking dish, and top with cheese. Bake until the mixture is bubbling and the top is slightly browned, about 30 minutes.

BAKED MUSHROOM LINGUINE
SERVES 10 TO 12 | PHOTOGRAPH ON PAGE 50

4 ounces dried mushrooms (such as porcini or chanterelle), wiped clean

1 quart boiling water

2 sprigs fresh rosemary

2 sprigs fresh thyme, plus 2 teaspoons finely chopped

7 tablespoons unsalted butter, plus more for pan

¼ cup plus 1 tablespoon all-purpose flour

1½ cups heavy cream

1 onion, diced

1 pound button mushrooms, wiped clean, stems removed and quartered

1 pound shiitake mushrooms, wiped clean, stems removed and sliced

2½ teaspoons coarse salt, plus more for cooking water

½ teaspoon freshly ground pepper

1 pound linguine

½ cup grated Romano cheese

1 Place the dried mushrooms in a bowl, and pour the boiling water over them. Let sit 30 minutes to allow the flavors to infuse. Wrap the rosemary and thyme sprigs in cheesecloth, and tie with kitchen twine; set aside. Lift out the mushrooms with a slotted spoon, and place in another bowl. Press the mushrooms to release any retained liquid, and pour the liquid back into the first bowl; set the mushrooms aside. Strain the mushroom liquid through a fine-mesh sieve lined with a paper towel. You should have about 4 cups of mushroom stock; set aside.

2 Melt 5 tablespoons butter in a large saucepan over medium heat. When bubbling, add the flour. Cook, stirring, until the mixture begins to brown, about 3 minutes. While whisking, slowly pour in the mushroom stock. Continue cooking, whisking constantly, until the mixture bubbles and becomes thick. Stir in the cream and reserved herb bundle. Reduce to a gentle simmer, and cook 30 minutes, stirring occasionally, to allow flavors to infuse.

3 Meanwhile, heat the remaining 2 tablespoons butter in a large skillet over medium heat. Add the onion, and cook until it begins to soften, about 3 minutes. Add the button mushrooms, and cook until they release their juices and make room in the pan. Add the shiitake mushrooms and chopped thyme, and cook until all the mushrooms are tender, about 5 minutes. Add the dried-mushroom sauce to the skillet, and stir to combine. Season with salt and pepper, and set aside.

4 Preheat the oven to 375°F. Butter a 9-by-13-inch baking dish; set aside. Bring a large pot of water to a boil. Salt the water, and add the pasta. Cover, and cook

2 to 3 minutes less than the manufacturer's instructions, until very al dente. Transfer the pasta to a colander, and rinse with cold water to stop the cooking; drain well. Stir the pasta into the mushroom mixture. Transfer the mixture to the prepared pan. Sprinkle with grated cheese, and bake until browned on top and the mixture is bubbling, about 30 minutes. Transfer the dish to a wire rack to cool 5 minute before serving.

CRAB-STUFFED SHELLS WITH PEAS AND LEEKS
SERVES 10 TO 12

2 leeks, white and light-green parts only

9 tablespoons (1 stick plus 1 tablespoon) unsalted butter

1 cup fresh or defrosted frozen peas

2½ teaspoons coarse salt, plus more for cooking water

½ teaspoon freshly ground pepper

8 ounces lump crabmeat, picked over

¼ cup plus 2 tablespoons all-purpose flour

2 cups milk

1 cup heavy cream

Juice of 1 lemon

1 pound jumbo shells

½ cup bread crumbs

6 garlic cloves, very finely minced

¼ cup fresh flat-leaf parsley leaves

1 tablespoon extra-virgin olive oil

1 Preheat the oven to 375°F. Cut the leeks in half lengthwise, then crosswise into ¼-inch half moons. Place them in a large bowl of cold water, and stir to release sand. Transfer the leeks to a colander, and drain.

2 Melt 3 tablespoons butter in a medium skillet over medium heat. Add leeks, and cook until tender, about 5 minutes. Add peas, and cook until bright green, about 3 minutes more. Transfer to a bowl, and season with ½ teaspoon salt and ¼ teaspoon pepper. Stir in crabmeat, and set aside in the refrigerator until ready to assemble the shells.

3 Melt the remaining 6 tablespoons butter in a large saucepan over medium heat. While the butter is bubbling, add the flour. Cook, stirring constantly with a wire whisk, for 1 minute. While whisking, slowly pour in the milk. Continue cooking, whisking constantly, until the mixture bubbles and becomes thick. Remove from the heat, and stir in the cream, lemon juice, and remaining 2 teaspoons salt and ¼ teaspoon pepper.

4 Bring a large saucepan of water to a boil. Salt the water, and add the pasta; cook 2 to 3 minutes less than the manufacturer's instructions, until very al dente. Transfer the pasta to a colander, and rinse with cold water to stop the cooking; drain well. Meanwhile, in a small bowl, combine bread crumbs, garlic, parsley, and olive oil; set aside. Stir 1 cup of the cream sauce into the crab-and-pea mixture. Pour another cup of cream sauce into the bottom of a 9-by-13-inch baking dish.

5 Fill each shell with a heaping tablespoon of the crab mixture; place in the baking dish. Spoon the remaining cream sauce over the shells, and sprinkle with the bread-crumb mixture. Bake until the mixture is bubbling and the top is golden brown, about 30 minutes. Serve.

BUTTERNUT SQUASH CANNELLONI WITH SAGE-WALNUT CREAM SAUCE

SERVES 8 TO 10 | PHOTOGRAPH ON PAGE 50

3 tablespoons unsalted butter

1 onion, diced

1 butternut squash (2½ to 3 pounds), peeled, seeded, and roughly chopped (about 1-inch pieces)

1 teaspoon ground cinnamon

¼ teaspoon ground nutmeg

¼ teaspoon cayenne pepper

1 teaspoon ground cumin

1 tablespoon plus 2½ teaspoons coarse salt

½ teaspoon freshly ground black pepper

1 cup water

1 cup (about 3 ounces) freshly grated Parmesan cheese

1 cup ricotta cheese

1 pound spinach, Swiss chard, or other greens

2 tablespoons extra-virgin olive oil

8 ounces dried pasta sheets (about twelve 5-by-7-inch rectangles), or Fresh Pasta, (page 40)

Sage-Walnut Cream Sauce (page 40)

Fresh sage leaves, for garnish

1 To make the filling, heat 2 tablespoons butter in a large skillet with high sides over medium heat. Add the onion; cook until it begins to soften, about 3 minutes. Add the squash; cook, stirring occasionally, until it begins to soften, about 5 minutes. Add the cinnamon, nutmeg, cayenne pepper, cumin, 1½ teaspoons salt, ¼ teaspoon black pepper, and water. Reduce the heat, cover, and cook, stirring occasionally, until very tender, about 20 minutes.

2 Mash the mixture with a potato masher or wooden spoon. Transfer to a medium bowl; cool. Stir in Parmesan and ricotta. Transfer to the refrigerator until ready to assemble.

3 Wash the spinach or greens well. Remove and discard the stems. Roughly chop the spinach into smaller pieces. Heat the remaining tablespoon butter in

BAKED PASTA

A delicious meat sauce starts with onions, carrots, and celery, which are cooked until soft and sweet. Meat sauce should simmer slowly until it is rich and flavorful. This takes time, but the results are well worth it. Use the best ingredients you can find to create the filling. Sample the mixture while you cook it, and add more herbs and spices as needed. If your pasta lacks creaminess, the solution is probably béchamel. Not all baked pasta dishes call for béchamel, but those that do, cannot succeed without it. Béchamel is easy to make. Start with a roux (a mixture of butter and flour), slowly add milk and cream, and then let the sauce simmer until it bubbles and thickens. Fight the temptation to delve immediately into a piping hot dish. Wait a few minutes to allow the pasta to set before serving.

a large skillet over medium heat. Add the spinach a little at a time; cook, tossing, until wilted and any liquid has evaporated. Season with 1 teaspoon salt and ¼ teaspoon black pepper. Refrigerate until ready to assemble.

4 Preheat the oven to 375°F. Bring a large pot of water to a boil. Add the olive oil and the remaining tablespoon salt. One at a time, add the pasta sheets to the boiling water, and cook until very al dente, 2 to 3 minutes less than the manufacturer's instructions for dried pasta, and 2 to 3 minutes total cooking time for fresh pasta. Remove the pasta sheets with tongs, and drain them in a colander.

5 To assemble the cannelloni, lay out the pasta sheets on a work surface. Spoon about ½ cup filling down the center of a sheet, and top with a heaping tablespoon of spinach. Brush one long side of pasta with water; roll up, starting with the other long side, and seal. Repeat with the remaining pasta and filling. Spread half of the sage-walnut cream sauce in the bottom of a 13-by-9-by-2-inch baking dish. Place the cannelloni in the bottom of the dish, and cover with the remaining sauce. Garnish with a few sage leaves. Bake until the top starts to brown and the filling is bubbling, about 30 minutes. Serve.

SAGE-WALNUT CREAM SAUCE
MAKES ABOUT 3 CUPS

4 tablespoons unsalted butter
¼ cup all-purpose flour
2 cups milk
1 cup heavy cream
2 sprigs fresh sage, chopped
¼ cup chopped walnuts
1 teaspoon coarse salt
¼ teaspoon freshly ground pepper
Pinch of ground nutmeg

1 Heat the butter in a large saucepan over medium heat. When bubbling, add the flour. Cook, stirring constantly with a wire whisk, for 1 minute. While whisking, slowly pour in the milk. Continue cooking, whisking constantly, until the mixture bubbles and becomes thick.

2 Remove the pan from the heat; stir in the cream, sage, walnuts, salt, pepper, and nutmeg. Cover; set aside to infuse for 30 minutes.

FRESH PASTA
MAKES 1 POUND

This pasta can be used for any recipe that calls for ribbon or filled pasta. The recipe can easily be halved; work in smaller quantities until you are comfortable with the technique. Rolling pasta by hand is undeniably a challenge. The dough must be rolled and stretched rapidly before it dries out, and rare is the novice who produces a flawless sheet on the first try. No matter. Perfectly good pasta can be cut from less-than-perfect sheets. Fresh pasta must be dried for several hours, until no moisture remains, before it is stored.

2 cups all-purpose flour, plus more for work surface
4 large eggs
Coarse salt
2 tablespoons oil

1 Mound the flour in the center of a work surface, and make a well in the middle. Crack the eggs into the well.

2 Beat the eggs with a fork until smooth, then begin to work the flour into the eggs with the fork.

3 Use a bench scraper to work in the rest of the flour, a bit at a time.

4 Once all the flour has been incorporated, start working the dough with your hands to form a rounded mass for kneading. Be sure your work surface is clean of all loose bits of dough; lightly dust with flour. Knead the dough about 10 minutes, or until smooth and elastic.

5 Cover the dough with an inverted bowl or plastic wrap, and allow to rest 1½ hours at room temperature, or refrigerate overnight.

6 Roll out the dough. If rolling by hand, proceed to step 8. To roll using a pasta machine, divide the dough into four pieces. Quickly knead and flatten a portion of the dough into a disk shape somewhat narrower than the machine opening; very lightly dust the dough with flour. Feed the dough through at the machine's widest setting. (If the pasta pulls or tears when passing through the machine, simply sprinkle a little more flour over the dough, just before it's fed, to keep it from sticking. When finished, remove the excess flour with a dry brush.) As the pasta sheet emerges, gently support it with your palm, and guide it onto the work surface. Fold the sheet lengthwise into thirds. Repeat the sequence twice with the same setting to smooth the dough and increase its elasticity.

7 Thin the dough by passing it through ever finer settings, one pass on each setting from the widest to the narrowest (machine settings differ; some have as many as ten, others only six). Roll the remaining three portions of the dough as soon as the first is finished. (For filled pasta, it's best to roll and cut a single portion at a time, otherwise the dough will dry out.) If your pasta machine comes with cutting rollers (most are equipped to make capellini, linguine, or fettuccine pasta), cut the sheets in the desired width. Alternatively, cut the sheets by hand as in step 9.

8 To roll by hand, lightly flour a clean work surface. Divide the dough into four pieces. Vigorously roll each piece into a very thin circle; apply even pressure. As the dough stretches, roll constantly. Do not bear down too hard or it will tear. Roll for several minutes, until the dough is as thin as possible, almost translucent. If it shrinks back as you roll, cover with a towel, and let rest 10 minutes before you resume rolling. Repeat with the remaining pieces of dough.

9 To cut the sheets, lightly fold the sheets one at a time into thirds. Cut crosswise with a sharp knife to desired width.

10 Bring a large pot of water to a boil. Salt the water, and add the oil. Place pasta in the water. Cook until al dente, 2 to 3 minutes. Drain in a colander.

TRADITIONAL LASAGNA BOLOGNESE
SERVES 10 TO 12

This lasagna was designed for a deep-dish baking pan. You can use a standard nine-by-thirteen-inch baking pan, but you will have excess sauce; the sauce can be frozen and used over pasta another time. Bake the lasagna on a rimmed baking sheet to avoid oven spills. The lasagna can be assembled and refrigerated up to a day ahead: Cool completely, cover, and refrigerate or freeze, unbaked, up to three weeks. Defrost overnight in the refrigerator; bake as directed below.

Bolognese Sauce (page 42)

3 pounds ricotta cheese

3 large egg yolks

1 cup (about 3 ounces) freshly grated Parmesan cheese

1 tablespoon plus 1½ teaspoons coarse salt

¼ teaspoon freshly ground black pepper

¼ teaspoon ground nutmeg

  Pinch of cayenne pepper

  Unsalted butter, for pan

2 tablespoons extra-virgin olive oil

1 pound dried lasagna noodles, or Fresh Pasta (recipe above)

1 pound fresh mozzarella, sliced into ¼-inch rounds

1 Bring the sauce to room temperature. In a large bowl, whisk together the ricotta, egg yolks, Parmesan, 1½ teaspoons salt, black pepper, nutmeg, and cayenne pepper. Refrigerate until ready to assemble the lasagna.

2 Preheat the oven to 400°F. Butter a 14-by-11-by-3-inch lasagna baking pan. Bring a large pot of water to a boil. Add the olive oil and the remaining tablespoon of salt. One at a time, add the lasagna noodles; cook until very al dente, 2 to 3 minutes less than the manufacturer's instructions for dried pasta, and 2 to 3 minutes total cooking time for fresh pasta. Remove the noodles with tongs; drain in a colander.

3 Spread about 3 cups of sauce on the bottom of the baking pan. Place a single layer of lasagna noodles over the sauce, overlapping the noodles slightly. Spread about 2 cups of sauce over the noodles and about half of the ricotta mixture over the sauce.

4 Top with a layer of lasagna noodles, again slightly overlapping the noodles. Repeat with more sauce and the remaining ricotta mixture. Top with a final layer of lasagna noodles. Spread a layer of sauce over the noodles, and finish with a layer of sliced mozzarella rounds.

5 Bake until the sauce is bubbling and the cheese is melted, at least 1 hour. Cover with aluminum foil if the cheese starts to brown too early. Let the lasagna stand 10 to 15 minutes before serving.

FRESH OR DRIED?

With all the good-quality dried pastas available, there is little reason to make fresh—unless you really want to. Making fresh pasta by hand is appealing for the pure sensual pleasure of it—kneading the dough into a silky ball, then rolling it out into gold sheets can be very satisfying. Handmade pasta doesn't necessarily require special skill, only time and space. Clear enough tabletops and chair backs for draping the dough after rolling and cutting; cover chairs with clean dishcloths, and dust flat surfaces with flour. Pasta dough must be thoroughly worked to develop the flour's gluten, which gives the dough the elasticity necessary to produce a pasta both chewy and tender. If kneading and cutting by hand isn't an option, a food processor and hand-cranked roller can do the job.

BOLOGNESE SAUCE

MAKES ABOUT 3 QUARTS

- 3 tablespoons unsalted butter
- 3 tablespoons extra-virgin olive oil
- 2 onions, cut into ¼-inch dice
- 3 celery stalks, strings removed, cut into ¼-inch dice
- 3 carrots, cut into ¼-inch dice
- 2 pounds ground sirloin
- 2 pounds ground veal
- 1 quart whole milk
- 2 cups red wine
- 2 fourteen-and-a-half-ounce cans beef stock, or about 3½ cups Homemade Beef Stock (page 11)
- 1 cup tomato paste
- 1½ teaspoons coarse salt
- ¾ teaspoon freshly ground pepper

1 Heat the butter and olive oil in a large cast-iron or enamel pot over medium heat.

2 Add the onions, and cook until they begin to soften, about 5 minutes. Add the celery and carrots, and cook until the vegetables are tender, 8 to 10 minutes. Add the ground sirloin and veal, and cook, stirring occasionally, until the meat is no longer pink. Add the milk, and cook at a gentle simmer, skimming fat from the surface, until the liquid has reduced by half, about 50 minutes.

3 Add the wine, and simmer until the liquid is reduced by half again, about 40 minutes.

4 Add the beef stock, tomato paste, salt, and pepper; simmer gently until the sauce thickens, 40 to 45 minutes. If using for lasagna, set aside to cool slightly before assembling.

WHAT TO HAVE FOR DINNER

menu

PORK TENDERLOIN WITH APRICOT FENNEL RAGOUT

HERBED WILD RICE

ROASTED SQUASH WEDGES

CHOCOLATE PISTACHIO BISCOTTI

PORK TENDERLOIN WITH APRICOT FENNEL RAGOUT

SERVES 4

- 3 tablespoons grainy mustard
- 2 tablespoons Dijon mustard
- 2 twelve-ounce pork tenderloins, tied with kitchen twine
  Coarse salt and freshly ground pepper
- ½ cup bread crumbs
- 3 tablespoons vegetable oil
- 1 tablespoon unsalted butter
- 4 large (or 8 medium) shallots, ends trimmed, peeled and quartered
- 1 small fennel bulb, fronds trimmed, cut into thin slices
- 1½ cups Homemade Chicken Stock (page 8) or low-sodium canned
- 12 dried apricots
- ¼ cup cognac
- 1 teaspoon fresh thyme, plus more for garnish

1 Preheat the oven to 400°F. Combine the mustards. Season the pork with salt and pepper. Rub with the mustards; sprinkle with the bread crumbs. Pat the coating. Set aside.

2 Heat a large, heavy skillet over medium-high heat. Add 2 tablespoons oil. Sear the pork, turning until brown on all sides, about 5 minutes. Remove from the pan; set aside. Add the remaining tablespoon oil and the butter to the pan. Add the shallots and fennel. Cook until tender, about 5 minutes. Add ½ cup stock; cook, stirring, until the liquid evaporates, 1 to 2 minutes.

3 Return the pork to the pan; add the apricots, ½ cup stock, and cognac. Roast in the oven, stirring the vegetables occasionally, until the pork registers 160°F on an instant-read thermometer, about 20 minutes. Transfer the pork to a cutting board; place the pan over medium-low heat. Add the remaining ½ cup stock and

the thyme; stir, using a wooden spoon, to loosen any browned bits on the bottom of the pan. Simmer 5 minutes. Season with salt and pepper; slice the pork. Serve with vegetables and sauce. Garnish with thyme.

HERBED WILD RICE

SERVES 4

Wild rice is actually a long-grain marsh grass that has a chewy texture and a nutty flavor. The rice is cooked, uncovered, in a large amount of water and then drained.

- 2 cups wild rice
- 3 tablespoons extra-virgin olive oil
- ¼ cup chopped fresh flat-leaf parsley
- ¼ cup chopped fresh marjoram
  Coarse salt and freshly ground pepper

1 Rinse the wild rice well under cold running water. Drain well, and set aside.

2 Bring a large saucepan of water to a boil. Stir in the rice, reduce to a simmer, and cook until the rice is tender, about 40 minutes.

3 Drain the rice, transfer to a bowl, and stir in the olive oil, parsley, and marjoram. Season with salt and pepper, and serve at room temperature or chilled.

ROASTED SQUASH WEDGES

SERVES 4

We used acorn squash for this recipe, but pumpkins or other squash such as butternut work just as well.

- 2 acorn squash
- 2 tablespoons unsalted butter, melted
- 2 tablespoons honey
- 1 teaspoon ground cinnamon
  Pinch of ground nutmeg
- ½ teaspoon coarse salt
- ¼ teaspoon freshly ground pepper

1 Preheat the oven to 400°F. Cut the squash in half through the stem end, and remove the seeds. Cut each half into three wedges, 1½ to 2 inches thick. Place the wedges in a large roasting pan.

2 Toss with the butter, honey, cinnamon, nutmeg, salt, and pepper. Roast the squash, tossing occasionally, until tender and golden brown, 35 to 45 minutes.

CHOCOLATE PISTACHIO BISCOTTI

SERVES 4 | PHOTOGRAPH ON PAGE 54

Softer than traditional biscotti, these are baked for a shorter time.

6 tablespoons unsalted butter, softened, plus more for baking sheet
2 cups all-purpose flour, plus more for baking sheet
½ cup unsweetened cocoa powder
1 teaspoon baking soda
¼ teaspoon coarse salt
1 cup sugar
2 large eggs
1 cup shelled green pistachio nuts
½ cup chocolate chips
  Pistachio ice cream or Pistachio Gelato (recipe follows)

1 Preheat the oven to 350°F. Butter and flour a baking sheet; set aside.
2 In a medium bowl, whisk together the flour, cocoa powder, baking soda, and salt. In the bowl of an electric mixer fitted with the paddle attachment, cream the butter and sugar until light and fluffy. Add the eggs; beat until well combined, scraping down the sides of the bowl if necessary. Add the flour mixture, and stir to form a stiff dough. Stir in the pistachios and chocolate chips.
3 Transfer the dough to the prepared baking sheet; form into a slightly flattened log, 12 by 4 inches. Bake until slightly firm, about 25 minutes. Cool 5 minutes. Reduce oven to 300°F.
4 On a cutting board, use a sharp serrated knife to cut the biscotti diagonally into 1-inch-thick slices. Arrange the biscotti, cut sides down, on the baking sheet, and bake until crisp but still slightly soft in the center, about 8 minutes. Serve with pistachio ice cream or gelato.

PISTACHIO GELATO

MAKES ABOUT 1 QUART

2 cups (8 ounces) shelled pistachios
3 cups milk
5 large egg yolks
⅔ cup sugar
1 cup heavy cream

1 Preheat the oven to 350°F. Bring a saucepan of water to a boil. Add the pistachios, and cook for 30 seconds. Remove from the heat, and drain in a sieve. When the pistachios are cool enough to handle, remove the outer skins; discard the skins. Place the pistachios in a single layer on a rimmed baking sheet; toast until they are aromatic, about 5 minutes. Transfer to a bowl to cool completely; grind the nuts coarsely.
2 Combine the milk and ground pistachios in a medium saucepan. Bring to a gentle boil. Cover, and remove from the heat. Steep for 2 hours at room temperature. Strain the mixture through a fine sieve, or a cheesecloth-lined colander, into a large bowl, pressing hard on the nuts; set the nut milk aside, and discard the solids.
3 In the bowl of an electric mixer fitted with the whisk attachment, combine the egg yolks and sugar. Beat on medium-high until the mixture is very thick and pale yellow, about 5 minutes.
4 Pour the nut milk back into the medium saucepan. Bring to a simmer. Fill a large bowl with ice and water; set aside. Whisking constantly, add half the nut milk to the egg-yolk mixture. Slowly whisk the egg-yolk-and-milk mixture into the remaining nut milk in the saucepan. Cook over low heat, stirring constantly with a wooden spoon, until the mixture is thick enough to coat the back of the spoon.
5 Remove from the heat, and immediately stir in the cream. Pass the mixture through a fine sieve into a medium bowl set over the ice bath to chill. Freeze in an ice-cream maker according to the manufacturer's instructions. Store, frozen, in an airtight container for up to 1 week.

FIT TO EAT: SALMON DISHES

SALMON STEAMED WITH SAVOY CABBAGE

SERVES 6 | PHOTOGRAPH ON PAGE 52

You will need a two-level bamboo steamer for this recipe.

2 heads (2 pounds each) savoy cabbage
½ cup Homemade Chicken Stock (page 8) or low-sodium canned, skimmed of fat
¼ cup honey
¼ cup rice-wine vinegar
1 teaspoon grated fresh ginger, with juice
2 garlic cloves, very thinly sliced
2 tablespoons low-sodium soy sauce
2 teaspoons sesame oil
8 ounces rice noodles
6 three-ounce salmon fillets, about 1½-by-3-inches each, skin removed
½ teaspoon coarse salt
¼ teaspoon freshly ground pepper
2 scallions, white and light-green parts only, thinly sliced

1 Bring a large saucepan of water to a boil. Peel off 6 of the big outer leaves, without holes, from each cabbage; set aside. Core and thinly slice the cabbages. Fill a medium bowl with ice and water; set aside. Blanch the cabbage leaves in boiling water until bright green and flexible, about 1 minute; plunge into the ice bath. Drain on paper towels. Blanch the remaining sliced cabbage until just tender, about 1 minute. Drain the cabbage; immerse in the ice bath. When cool, drain in a colander; set aside.
2 In a small bowl, combine the chicken stock, honey, vinegar, ginger, garlic, soy sauce, and sesame oil; set aside. Bring a saucepan of water to a boil. Cook the rice noodles until tender, about 3 minutes. Transfer the noodles to a colander; rinse under cold water to stop the cooking. Drain well; transfer to a bowl. Toss with ⅓ cup of the soy mixture; set aside.
3 Bring a wok or large skillet of water to a simmer. Season each salmon fillet with salt and pepper. Carefully cut out

the stiff stems of the reserved cabbage leaves. Place 2 leaves on a work surface, slightly overlapping. Place a fillet on each leaf. Top with about ½ cup sliced cabbage, and roll leaves "burrito" style. Divide the remaining sliced cabbage among the bottom of each level of the bamboo steamer. Place the salmon packages seam side down on the cabbage. Cover the steamer; place in the wok or skillet. Steam until the salmon is just cooked through, 15 to 18 minutes. For the sauce, add the scallions to the remaining soy mixture. Serve the salmon packages and steamed cabbage over the noodles with the sauce.

PER SERVING: 364 CALORIES, 7 G FAT, 47 MG CHOLESTEROL, 47 G CARBOHYDRATE, 476 MG SODIUM, 22 G PROTEIN, 2 G FIBER

BLACKENED SALMON SANDWICHES

MAKES 4 | PHOTOGRAPH ON PAGE 53

The spice rub can be stored in an airtight container for up to one month.

1 teaspoon whole cumin seed
1 teaspoon whole fennel seed
1 teaspoon dried oregano
1 teaspoon dried thyme
2 teaspoons paprika
½ teaspoon cayenne pepper
2 teaspoons coarse salt
½ teaspoon freshly ground black pepper
2 tablespoons prepared horseradish
¼ cup plain low-fat yogurt
1 tablespoon honey
4 four-ounce salmon fillets, skin removed
4 slices crusty bread
1 bunch arugula, stems trimmed
½ small red onion, thinly sliced crosswise

1   Place the cumin seed, fennel seed, oregano, and thyme in a spice grinder. Pulse until finely chopped but not powdery. Transfer to a small bowl; stir in the paprika, cayenne pepper, 1½ teaspoons salt, and ¼ teaspoon black pepper; set aside. In another small bowl, whisk together the horseradish, yogurt, honey, remaining ½ teaspoon salt, and ¼ teaspoon black pepper; set aside.

2   Heat a heavy skillet over medium-high heat. Coat each fillet with 2 teaspoons of the spice blend; pat with your fingers. Place the fillets in the hot skillet. Cook until well browned, about 5 minutes. Turn the fillets; cook through, about 5 minutes more. Transfer to a plate; set aside.

3   To assemble, spread the bread with the horseradish mixture. Top with the arugula and onion. Flake the salmon into chunks; place on the sandwiches. Drizzle with the remaining horseradish mixture, and serve.

PER SERVING: 261 CALORIES, 8 G FAT, 63 MG CHOLESTEROL, 21 G CARBOHYDRATE, 772 MG SODIUM, 26 G PROTEIN, 1 G FIBER

POACHED SALMON, LEEK, AND FENNEL SOUP

SERVES 6

3 leeks, white and light-green parts only
1 tablespoon extra-virgin olive oil
3 carrots, cut into ¼-inch-thick slices
1 small fennel bulb, trimmed and cut into wedges, fronds reserved for garnish
2 celery stalks, strings removed, cut crosswise into ¼-inch-thick slices
4 sprigs fresh flat-leaf parsley
4 sprigs fresh thyme
1 fourteen-and-a-half-ounce can fat-free vegetable stock or about 1¾ cups Homemade Vegetable Stock (recipe follows)
2 teaspoons coarse salt
½ teaspoon freshly ground pepper
5 cups water
1 one-pound salmon fillet, skin removed, cut into 1-inch cubes
3 ounces spinach, washed and cut into 1½-inch-wide strips

1   Slice the leeks crosswise into ¼-inch coins. Place in a bowl of cold water; move the leeks around so the sand falls to the bottom. Lift the leeks from the water with your fingers or a slotted spoon, and drain; set aside.

2   Heat the oil in a saucepan over medium heat. Add the leeks, carrots, fennel, and celery. Cook until softened, about 5 minutes. Add the parsley, thyme, stock,

salt, pepper, and water. Bring to a boil; reduce to a simmer. Cook, uncovered, 30 minutes. Turn off the heat; add the salmon and spinach. Poach until just cooked through, about 3 minutes. Garnish with fennel fronds; serve.

PER SERVING: 177 CALORIES, 8 G FAT, 42 MG CHOLESTEROL, 10 G CARBOHYDRATE, 202 MG SODIUM, 17 G PROTEIN, 3 G FIBER

HOMEMADE VEGETABLE STOCK

MAKES 3 QUARTS

1 tablespoon unsalted butter
1 tablespoon olive oil
1 large onion, coarsely chopped
2 large carrots, coarsely chopped
2 parsnips, coarsely chopped
1 celery stalk, coarsely chopped
1½ pounds red or green Swiss chard, cut into 1-inch pieces
   Several sprigs fresh thyme
   Several sprigs fresh flat-leaf parsley
1 dried bay leaf
3½ quarts cold water

1   In a medium stockpot, melt the butter and oil, stirring occasionally, over medium-low heat. Add the onion; cook until caramelized, 15 to 25 minutes. Add the carrots, parsnips, and celery, and cook until tender, about 20 minutes.

2   Add the Swiss chard to the vegetable mixture. Add the thyme, parsley, bay leaf, and water. Bring to a boil; reduce heat, and let simmer, uncovered, for about 1 hour.

3   Remove from the heat. Strain the stock through a fine sieve, or a cheesecloth-lined colander, into a large bowl, pressing on the vegetables to extract the juices. Discard the vegetables. The stock can be refrigerated in an airtight container for up to 4 days or frozen for up to 3 months.

BARBECUED SALMON FILLETS

SERVES 6

2 teaspoons canola oil
1 onion, coarsely chopped
2 garlic cloves, smashed
1 carrot, coarsely chopped
1 celery stalk, strings removed, coarsely chopped
2 tomatoes, seeded and coarsely chopped
2 tablespoons tomato paste
2 tablespoons unsulfured molasses
2 tablespoons honey
2 tablespoons packed brown sugar
2 teaspoons dry mustard
1 teaspoon ground cumin
1½ teaspoons coarse salt
½ teaspoon freshly ground black pepper
    Pinch of cayenne pepper, or to taste
2 cups water
6 five-ounce salmon steaks or fillets
    Spiced Pilaf (recipe follows)

1 Heat the oil in a saucepan over medium heat. Add the onion, garlic, carrot, and celery. Cook the vegetables until softened, 5 to 7 minutes. Add the tomatoes; cook the vegetables until very tender, about 10 minutes more. Add the tomato paste, molasses, honey, sugar, mustard, cumin, 1 teaspoon salt, ¼ teaspoon black pepper, cayenne pepper, and water; stir to combine. Simmer gently until thickened, about 30 minutes. Transfer to a food processor or blender; purée until smooth. Refrigerate until ready to serve.

2 Heat a grill or grill pan over high heat. Season the salmon with the remaining ½ teaspoon salt and ¼ teaspoon pepper. Brush generously with the sauce. Grill until the fish is cooked through, 2 to 3 minutes per side. When the fish is done, remove and discard the skin. Serve over pilaf drizzled with sauce.

PER SERVING: 300 CALORIES, 11 G FAT, 78 MG CHOLESTEROL, 21 G CARBOHYDRATE, 363 MG SODIUM, 29 G PROTEIN, 2 G FIBER·

SPICED PILAF

SERVES 6

2 teaspoons canola oil
1 red onion, cut into ¼-inch dice
2 small carrots, cut into ¼-inch dice
1 celery stalk, strings removed, cut into ¼-inch-thick slices
¼ cup dry white wine
1½ cups brown rice
1 teaspoon coarse salt
¼ teaspoon freshly ground pepper
½ teaspoon paprika
¼ teaspoon ground turmeric
½ teaspoon ground cumin

1 Heat the oil in a medium skillet over medium heat. Add the onion, carrots, and celery. Cook until tender, 3 to 4 minutes. Add the wine, and cook until most of the liquid has evaporated, about 2 minutes. Transfer to a medium bowl, and set aside to cool.

2 Meanwhile, cover and bring to a boil a medium saucepan of water. Stir in the rice, and cook until tender, 25 to 30 minutes. Drain, and add to the bowl of vegetables. Season with salt, pepper, paprika, turmeric, and cumin. Serve with barbecued salmon fillets.

PER SERVING: 213 CALORIES, 3 G FAT, 0 MG CHOLESTEROL, 40 G CARBOHYDRATE, 203 MG SODIUM, 6 G PROTEIN, 3 G FIBER

SALMON

The bright orange-pink of salmon stands out at the fish market. But its color isn't salmon's only attractive quality: It is remarkably healthful. Salmon is full of protein, vitamin A, and Omega fatty acids, which are essential to the proper functioning of the heart and brain. Salmon is flavorful, too. Whether you choose to steam, roast, or grill it, you'll find the fish softer and richer than other seafood and buttery in flavor—almost sweet.

SLOW-ROASTED SALMON WITH GREEN SAUCE

SERVES 6

Save any remaining green sauce to use as salad dressing or as a sandwich spread.

1 small white onion, chopped

2 garlic cloves, minced

1 cup fresh flat-leaf parsley

4 ounces watercress leaves, plus 2 bunches for serving

8 ounces spinach leaves

½ cup nonfat buttermilk

½ cup low-fat sour cream

Juice of 1 lemon

2 teaspoons coarse salt

½ teaspoon freshly ground pepper

1½ teaspoons extra-virgin olive oil

4 five-ounce salmon fillets, skin removed, each about 1½ by 4 inches

¼ cup water

1 Place the onion, garlic, parsley, watercress, spinach, buttermilk, sour cream, lemon juice, 1 teaspoon salt, and ¼ teaspoon pepper in a food processor. Purée until smooth, and transfer to the refrigerator.

2 Preheat the oven to 300°F. Rub the bottom of a 9-by-13-inch glass baking dish with ½ teaspoon oil. Arrange the salmon fillets in the dish, and rub the tops with the remaining teaspoon oil. Sprinkle with the remaining teaspoon salt and ¼ teaspoon pepper. Pour the water in the dish to cover bottom in a thin layer. Cook the fish until just cooked through, 20 to 25 minutes. Serve immediately over a bed of watercress drizzled with cold green sauce. Extra sauce can be refrigerated up to 4 days.

PER SERVING: 199 CALORIES, 9 G FAT, 53 MG CHOLESTEROL, 7 G CARBOHYDRATE, 839 MG SODIUM, 23 G PROTEIN, 2 G FIBER

CHOCOLATE STRAWBERRY ICE CREAM SANDWICHES | **PAGE 34**

INDIVIDUAL PARIS BRIOCHES

1 Roll pieces of dough into balls. Use only slight pressure and as little extra flour as possible on your hands and work surface.

2 Using the edge of your hand, roll dough back and forth to create a "neck" for the classic "head" (or *tête*) of the brioche.

3 Pick up the dough by the head, and lower it into a buttered three-inch pan.

4 Using your forefinger, nudge the dough up while rotating the pan to create a slight bulge, deepening the space in which the head will sit.

5 Press the head gently into the space created in step 4. You should be able to do this without flattening it too much.

6 The head should be level with the rest of the dough. Let the loaves fully double in size, one to three hours, before baking.

CLASSIC BRIOCHE LOAVES

1 Roll five pieces of dough into balls, using slight pressure. Roll each quickly in a circular motion until smooth. Shape balls into teardrop shapes.

2 Arrange four teardrops around sides of pan. Press and smear dough together on bottom. Press lightly on middle part of balls while turning pan, creating a slight bulge.

3 Using a pastry brush, lightly brush the inside of the partially formed loaf with beaten egg.

4 Drop in the last teardrop, letting it rest higher than the others. Alternatively, make rectangular loaves by placing four logs or eight balls of dough in a loaf pan.

CLASSIC BRIOCHE LOAF | **PAGE 35**

INDIVIDUAL PARIS BRIOCHE | **PAGE 36**

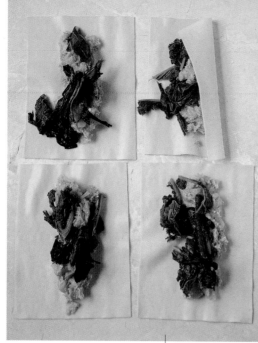

To fill cannelloni, place filling and greens in the center of a pasta sheet. Brush edge with water, and roll into a tubular shape, sealing the filling.

BUTTERNUT SQUASH CANNELLONI WITH
SAGE-WALNUT CREAM SAUCE | **PAGE 39**

BAKED MUSHROOM LINGUINE | **PAGE 38**

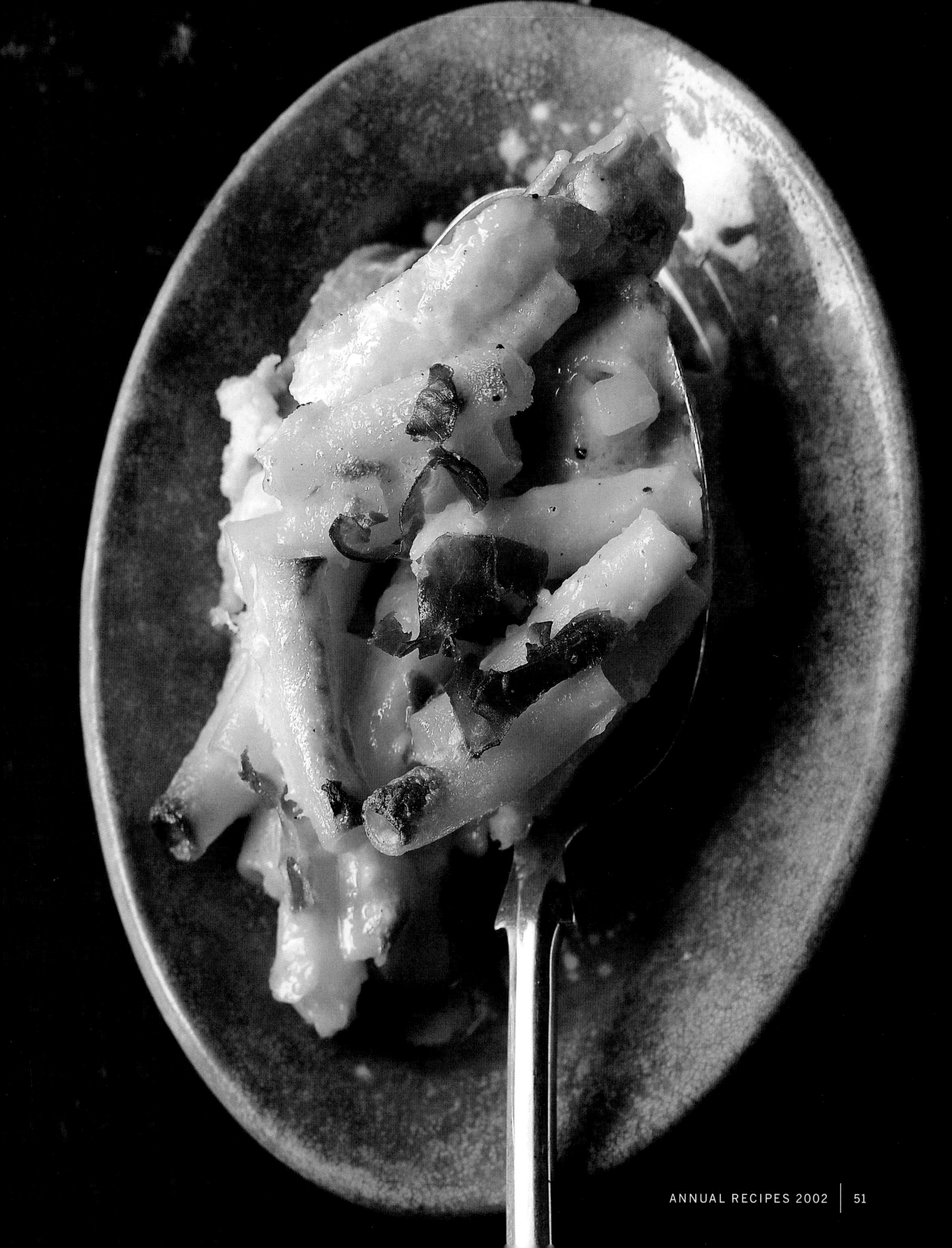

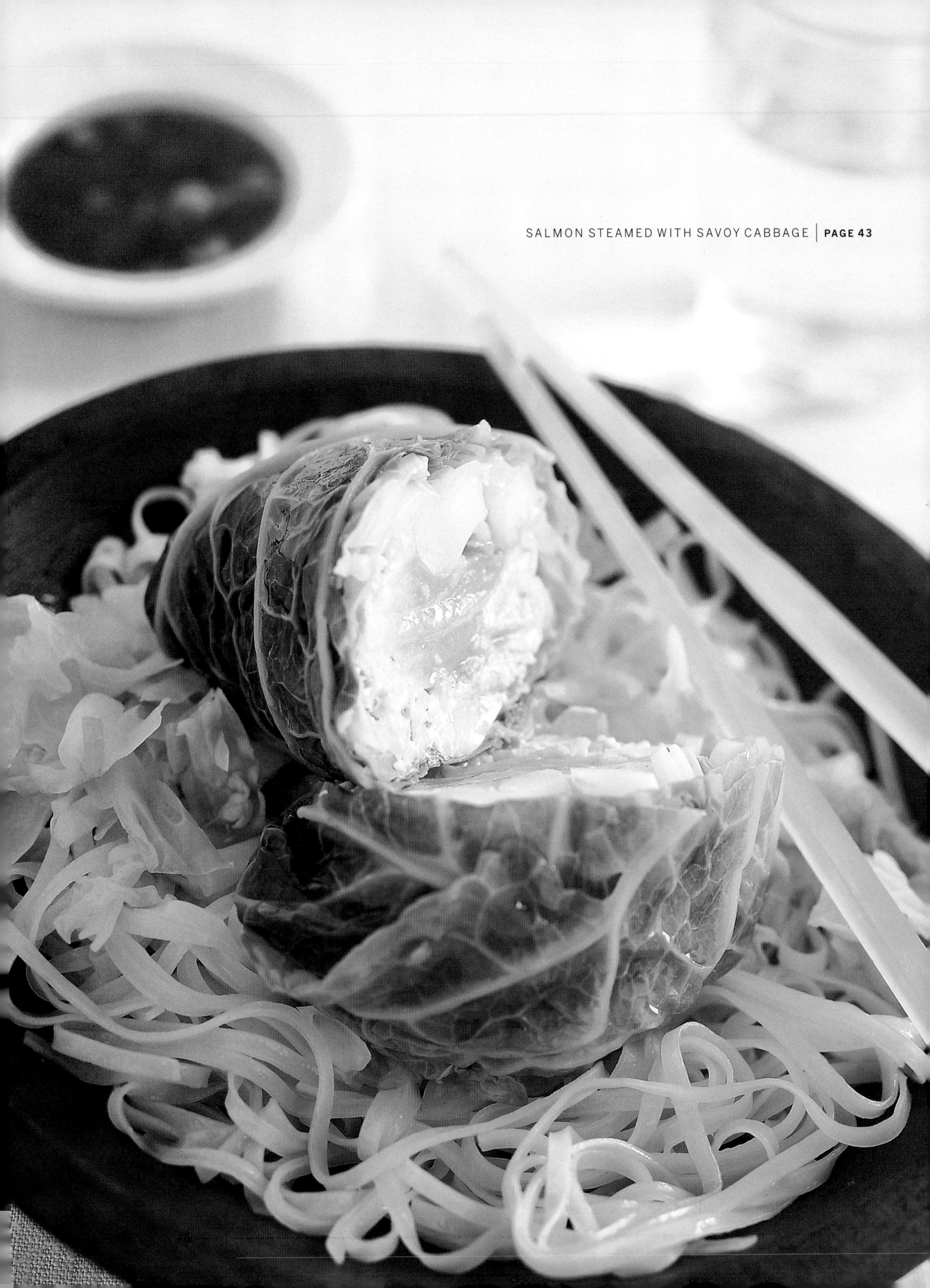

SALMON STEAMED WITH SAVOY CABBAGE PAGE 43

BLACKENED SALMON SANDWICHES | PAGE 44

CHOCOLATE PISTACHIO BISCOTTI | **PAGE 43**

march

Pastel de Tres Leches

Violet-Mint Jelly

Hibiscus Sorbet

Hibiscus Punch

Jasmine Rice Pudding

Navettes

Rose-Water Madeleines

Lavender Galaktoboureko
  (Custard-Filled Phyllo)

Eggplant Caviar

Grilled Eggplant

Warm Eggplant Salad

Summer Squash Lattice Tart

Squash Blossom Risotto

Stuffed Squash Two Ways

Summer Vegetable Pot au Feu

Roasted Squash

Sliced Zucchini and Yellow
  Squash Salad

Zucchini Bruschetta

Three Variety Squash Tian

Batter Fried Stuffed Squash
  Blossoms

Two-Colored Squash Loaf Cake

Celery Sticks with Horseradish
  Cream Cheese

Baked Flounder with Onion
  and Lemon

Saffron Rice with Tomatoes and
  Fresh Oregano

Bread-and-Butter Pudding with
  Strawberries

Steak "Frites"

Salade Niçoise

Poached Chicken and Vegetables
  (Poule au Pot)

Celery Root Rémoulade
  (Céleri Rémoulade)

Warm Leeks Vinaigrette
  (Poireaux Tiedes en Vinaigrette)

Apple Galette

PASTEL DE TRES LECHES

SERVES 12

The most time-consuming step is making the coconut curls; in a pinch you can use store-bought shaved coconut. The cake must be made in a metal nine-by-thirteen-inch baking pan.

8 tablespoons (1 stick) unsalted butter, melted and cooled, plus more for pan

6 large eggs, separated

¼ teaspoon baking soda

¼ teaspoon coarse salt

1 cup sugar

1 cup all-purpose flour

2½ cups milk, room temperature

1 twelve-ounce can evaporated milk

1 fourteen-ounce can sweetened condensed milk

1 fresh coconut

2 cups heavy cream

Assorted tropical fruits, such as pineapple, star fruit, mango, and pepino, for garnish

1 Preheat the oven to 350°F. Generously butter a 9-by-13-inch metal baking pan. In the bowl of an electric mixer fitted with the whisk attachment, combine the egg whites, baking soda, and salt, and beat on medium speed until soft peaks form, 2 to 3 minutes.

2 Add the yolks to the egg-white mixture, and beat until completely combined. With the mixer running, slowly add the sugar until combined. Remove the bowl from the mixer. Using a rubber spatula, fold in the butter.

3 Sift ¼ cup flour on top of the mixture, and fold in to combine. Repeat with the remaining flour, folding in ¼ cup at a time. Pour the batter into the prepared pan, and bake until golden and a cake tester inserted into the middle comes out clean, 20 to 25 minutes. Remove from the oven, and transfer to a wire rack.

4 About 5 minutes before the cake is done, whisk together the three milks, and set aside. As soon as the cake is removed from the oven, slowly pour the milk mixture over the entire cake. The cake should absorb all the liquid within 3 to 5 minutes. Set the cake aside, and let stand until cool. Cover the cake well, and transfer to the refrigerator to chill, at least 5 hours or overnight.

5 Before serving, preheat the oven to 450°F. Place the whole coconut in the oven, and bake for 20 minutes. Remove from the oven, and using an awl or a screwdriver, pierce the three "eyes" of the coconut. Turn over, and drain the liquid. Using a hammer, break open the coconut. Insert a small spatula or a grapefruit knife between the flesh and the shell to pry the meat out in large pieces. Using a vegetable peeler, shave off thin curls of coconut. Transfer the curls to a rimmed baking sheet, and let stand uncovered for 30 minutes. Place in the oven, and bake until the edges are golden, about 10 minutes. Remove from the oven, and set aside until cool. These curls can be stored in an airtight container for up to 5 days or frozen for future use.

6 When ready to serve the cake, whip the cream to soft peaks. Slice the cake into twelve servings, top with whipped cream, and serve with the fruits and toasted coconut curls.

FLOWER ESSENCES

VIOLET-MINT JELLY

MAKES ABOUT 1 QUART

This jelly is a variation on rose-petal jelly, a delicacy popular in the Balkans, Turkey, and Iran. Mint adds depth to the subtle flavor of violets. Try it with scones or as a pastry glaze. Be sure to use only unsprayed violets.

½ cup (about 1 ounce) violets

1 cup packed mint leaves, chopped

2 cups water

2 tablespoons white-wine vinegar

4 cups sugar

1 three-ounce pouch liquid pectin

FLOWER ESSENCES

If you cook with flower essences, you'll soon appreciate their different strengths: Essential oils are stronger than floral waters; fresh petals impart subtler flavors than dried. Too much extract will ruin a dish, so floral essences must be used judiciously. Part of the pleasure in using an essence comes from its delicate nature. Showcase it in a simple dish with few other seasonings to avoid overpowering the taste in a clamor of competing flavors. A dish or drink graced by flowers should be a celebration of a distinctive and lovely scent.

1 Place the flowers and mint in a small saucepan with the water. Bring to a boil. Cover, remove from the heat, and let steep for 20 minutes. Strain through a fine sieve or a cheesecloth-lined colander, and reserve the liquid.

2 Pour the liquid into a large heavy saucepan, and stir in the vinegar and sugar. Bring to a boil over medium-high heat, and cook, stirring constantly, until the sugar is dissolved, about 10 minutes. Add the pectin, and bring to a boil. Boil for 1 minute, and remove from the heat. Skim off any foam that collects on the top.

3 Ladle the jelly into hot sterilized jars; seal. Let cool, and refrigerate for up to 2 months, or freeze in a plastic airtight container for up to 1 year.

HIBISCUS SORBET

MAKES ABOUT 1 QUART

Hibiscus sorbet has a brilliant color and a tangy flavor.

1 quart Hibiscus Syrup (recipe follows)

Freeze the hibiscus syrup in an ice-cream maker according to the manufacturer's instructions.

HIBISCUS PUNCH

SERVES 8

2 cups Hibiscus Syrup (recipe follows)
2 quarts chilled ginger ale
Lemon zest, for garnish

Combine the syrup and ginger ale in a large pitcher or bowl. Serve in a pitcher, or pour over ice into glasses. Garnish with lemon zest.

HIBISCUS SYRUP

MAKES 1 QUART

5 cups water
1½ cups sugar
4 ounces dried hibiscus flowers
Zest and juice of 1 lemon

1 Combine the water and sugar in a medium saucepan. Bring to a boil. Stir until the sugar is dissolved. Remove from the heat; stir in the flowers and lemon zest. Cover, and let steep for 1 hour.

2 Fill a large bowl with ice and water; set aside. Strain the syrup through a sieve into a medium bowl, and discard the solids. Chill in the ice bath. When cool, stir in the lemon juice. Keep refrigerated up to 1 week.

JASMINE RICE PUDDING

SERVES 6 TO 8

Jasmine extract is a Thai staple that adds a floral note to this creamy rice pudding.

1 quart whole milk
¼ cup jasmine tea leaves or a few drops jasmine essence
3 cups water
1⅓ cups jasmine rice
1 teaspoon coarse salt
1 tablespoon unsalted butter
1½ cups sugar

1 Heat the milk in a medium saucepan until hot but not boiling. Add the tea leaves or essence. Remove from heat. If using tea leaves, cover the saucepan, and let steep 20 minutes; strain milk, and set aside. If using essence, proceed to step 2.

2 In a medium saucepan, bring the water to a boil. Stir in the rice and salt. Reduce heat to low; cover, and cook until rice is tender and liquid has evaporated, 15 to 20 minutes. Stir the flavored milk, butter, and ½ cup sugar into rice. Cover, and cook over medium-low heat, stirring occasionally, until sugar is dissolved and pudding is thick, about 30 minutes.

3 Spoon the pudding into dessert dishes. Lay a piece of plastic wrap directly on the surface of each pudding to prevent

a skin from forming; transfer dishes to the refrigerator. Place the remaining cup sugar in a medium skillet over medium-low heat. Cook, without stirring, until dark amber in color, about 15 minutes. Pour caramel over top of each pudding. Serve immediately or bring to room temperature.

NAVETTES

MAKES ABOUT 2 DOZEN | **PHOTOGRAPH ON PAGE 71**

These boat-shaped cakes from Provence are unassertive pastries that benefit from additional flavoring. Orange-flower water is traditional for navettes.

1 teaspoon active dry yeast
2 tablespoons lukewarm water
4 cups all-purpose flour, plus more for work surface
Pinch of coarse salt
4 tablespoons unsalted butter, room temperature
1 cup granulated sugar
2 large whole eggs
3 tablespoons orange-flower water
Grated zest of 1 lemon
Grated zest of 1 orange
Olive oil, for bowl and baking sheet
1 large egg yolk, beaten with 1 tablespoon water, for glaze
Crystal sugar, for sprinkling (optional)

1 In a small bowl, dissolve the yeast in the lukewarm water. Let stand until creamy, about 10 minutes.

2 Meanwhile, in another bowl, whisk together the flour and salt. Place the butter and granulated sugar in the bowl of an electric mixer fitted with the paddle attachment. Beat until soft and crumbly. Add the dissolved yeast, whole eggs, orange-flower water, and both zests. Add the flour a cup at a time, and beat on low speed until just combined.

3 Transfer the dough to a floured work surface, and knead with your hands until it's smooth and no longer sticky. Form into a ball, and place in an oiled bowl. Cover, and leave to rest in a warm place for 30 minutes.

4 Rub a large baking sheet with olive oil. Turn the dough out onto a lightly floured work surface, and cut it into three equal portions. Using your hands, roll each portion into a log about 1 inch thick. Cut each log crosswise into pieces about 2½ inches long. Shape the pieces into tapered boat shapes by rounding and somewhat raising the middle portions and pinching the ends into points.

5 Transfer the shapes to the baking sheet. Cover the baking sheet with a kitchen towel, and leave in a warm place for 2 hours. Navettes will rise somewhat but will not double.

6 Preheat the oven to 375°F. Using a razor blade or very sharp knife, make a lengthwise slash down each navette, to about one-third of its depth. Using a pastry brush, coat the surface of each navette with the egg-yolk glaze. Sprinkle with the crystal sugar, if using. Bake until golden, 25 to 30 minutes. Transfer to a wire rack to cool.

ROSE-WATER MADELEINES
MAKES ABOUT 2 DOZEN

Madeleines are the sophisticated cousins of navettes. Rose water, popular in British tea cakes, works well with rich madeleines.

¾ cup plus 1 tablespoon all-purpose flour
1 teaspoon baking powder
½ teaspoon coarse salt
3 large eggs
½ cup sugar
1 teaspoon pure vanilla extract
2 tablespoons plus 2 teaspoons rose water
8 tablespoons (1 stick) unsalted butter, melted and cooled to room temperature
Butter-flavored cooking spray

1 In a medium bowl, sift together the flour, baking powder, and salt; set aside.
2 In the bowl of an electric mixer fitted with the whisk attachment, beat the eggs and sugar on medium speed until pale and foamy, 3 to 4 minutes. Beat in the vanilla

and 2 teaspoons rose water. Fold in the flour mixture. Fold in the butter. Cover with plastic; chill for 30 minutes.
3 Meanwhile, preheat the oven to 400°F with a rack in the center. Coat two madeleine or scallop-shell pans with cooking spray. Use a spoon to fill the molds three-quarters full. Bake 5 minutes. Reduce the heat to 375°F. Bake 5 to 8 minutes more, until lightly golden. Immediately tap out madeleines onto a cooling rack. Drizzle with the remaining 2 tablespoons rose water. Let the madeleines cool scallop side up to avoid any creases or lines from rack. Repeat with the remaining batter.

LAVENDER GALAKTOBOUREKO (CUSTARD-FILLED PHYLLO)
SERVES 8 TO 10

This classic Greek pastry is typically made with orange-flower water. We have infused it with lavender and honey for a different, yet delicate, flavor.

8 tablespoons (1 stick) unsalted butter, plus more for pan
1 cup sugar
½ cup water
¼ cup honey
2 teaspoons brandy
1 tablespoon freshly squeezed lemon juice
1 tablespoon freshly squeezed orange juice
Zest of 1 orange
3 cups milk
2 tablespoons dried or fresh lavender flowers
½ cup semolina flour
2 large eggs
1 pound phyllo pastry

1 To clarify the butter, place it in a small saucepan, and melt over medium heat until bubbling. Remove the pan from the heat, and cool 2 to 3 minutes. Using a spoon, carefully skim the milky foam from the top of the butter, and discard. Carefully pour the skimmed golden butter into another bowl, leaving behind

MAKING SORBET WITHOUT AN ICE-CREAM MAKER

If an ice-cream maker is unavailable, place the mixture in an 11-by-6-by-2¾-inch plastic container (this size container works best) in the freezer for 1 hour. After 1 hour, stir with a fork to break up the ice. Continue to freeze, stirring every 30 minutes, until the sorbet has set and is completely frozen, about 4 hours. This process will make an icier sorbet than those made in ice-cream makers.

RICE PUDDINGS

Choosing the rice for your pudding is important: Different varieties of rice yield different textures. Arborio rice yields a creamier, thicker pudding with grains of rice that are slightly al dente, or toothsome (the same quality that this rice gives to risotto). Basmati, jasmine, or other long-grain white rices have soft and tender grains and yield a lighter pudding that can be enhanced with delicate flavors like rose water and citrus zests.

the milk solids; set clarified butter aside, and discard milk solids.

2 Combine ½ cup sugar and the water in a small saucepan. Stir in the honey. Bring to a boil, and stir until the sugar is dissolved. Remove from the heat, and stir in the brandy, lemon juice, orange juice, and zest; set syrup aside to cool.

3 Preheat the oven to 350°F. Lightly butter an 8-inch-square ovenproof baking dish or metal pan. Heat the milk in a medium saucepan until hot but not boiling. Add the lavender flowers, cover, and let steep about 20 minutes. Strain, and return the milk to the saucepan.

4 Whisk the remaining ½ cup sugar and the semolina into the milk. Place over medium-low heat. Cook, stirring constantly with a wooden spoon, until thick and creamy, 8 to 10 minutes. Remove from the heat, and cool slightly.

5 Beat the eggs by hand or with an electric mixer until pale and creamy 2 to 3 minutes. Quickly pour the eggs into the semolina mixture, stirring constantly. Let the mixture cool before assembling the pastry.

6 Layer 8 sheets of phyllo pastry in the baking dish, brushing with clarified butter between each layer and overhanging the edge of the baking dish. Spread the semolina mixture over the phyllo, and top with 6 more sheets of phyllo, brushing with butter between each sheet. Fold over the edges of phyllo, and brush the top with butter.

7 Cut 2 sheets of phyllo into shreds, and toss in a bowl with some of the butter until coated. Sprinkle over the top of the pastry. Bake until the phyllo is golden brown and the filling is set, 50 minutes to 1 hour. Remove from the oven, and immediately pour ¼ cup of cooled syrup over the top, making sure it is evenly distributed. Let cool, and serve, if desired, with remaining syrup.

EGGPLANT

EGGPLANT CAVIAR

MAKES 3½ CUPS | **PHOTOGRAPH ON PAGE 72**

An old favorite in Russia, this dish calls for purple-globe eggplants. Instead of cooking them over an open flame (as described on page 72), you can use the oven: Place the eggplants in a shallow baking pan, and place under the broiler. Broil, turning eggplants every five minutes, until the skin is blackened all over and the flesh is falling-apart tender, twenty to thirty minutes.

2 purple-globe eggplants (1½ pounds each)
¼ cup minced onion
2 plum tomatoes, seeded and finely chopped
¼ cup coarsely chopped fresh flat-leaf parsley
½ cup extra-virgin olive oil
1½ teaspoons freshly squeezed lemon juice
Coarse salt and freshly ground pepper
Pita or rye bread

1 Roast the eggplants; peel away the blackened skin.

2 Place the eggplants in a food processor; pulse until puréed. Transfer to a large bowl; stir in the onion, tomatoes, parsley, olive oil, and lemon juice. Season with salt and pepper. Serve warm or at room temperature with pita or rye bread.

GRILLED EGGPLANT

SERVES 6

3 pounds eggplant, cut into ½-inch-thick slices
3 tablespoons coarse salt, plus more for serving
⅓ cup extra-virgin olive oil
Freshly ground pepper

1 Sprinkle the eggplant slices with salt on both sides. Place in a colander set over a bowl, and let stand 1 hour to drain. Discard the liquid, and rinse the slices under cold running water. Place the slices on several layers of paper towels; press out the water.

2 Heat a grill or grill pan over medium-high heat. Generously brush both sides of the eggplant slices with oil; sprinkle with pepper. Place on the grill; cook until browned on one side, 5 to 6 minutes. Turn the eggplant slices over; cook until browned on the other side. Serve drizzled with olive oil and sprinkled with salt and pepper.

WARM EGGPLANT SALAD

SERVES 4 | **PHOTOGRAPHS ON PAGES 72-73**

12 ounces small, round white eggplants, sliced ¼ inch thick
Coarse salt
Extra-virgin olive oil
Freshly ground pepper
1 small red onion, thinly sliced
2 ounces feta cheese, crumbled
⅓ cup oil-cured black olives, pitted and quartered lengthwise
2 teaspoons fresh oregano leaves

1 Sprinkle the eggplant slices with salt on both sides. Place in a colander set over a bowl, and let stand 1 hour to drain. Discard the liquid, and rinse the slices under cold running water. Place the eggplant slices on several layers of paper towels; press out the water.

2 Transfer the eggplant to a nonreactive surface. Generously brush both sides of the eggplant slices with oil; sprinkle with pepper. Heat 2 tablespoons oil in a large skillet over medium-high heat. Add slices of eggplant (without crowding); cook until golden brown on both sides, about 6 minutes total. Drain on paper towels. Repeat the process with remaining slices.

3 Place the eggplant, onion, feta, olives, and oregano in a large bowl. Drizzle with olive oil, and season with salt and pepper, if desired. Gently toss mixture to combine, and serve warm or at room temperature.

SUMMER SQUASH

SUMMER SQUASH LATTICE TART

SERVES 6 | **PHOTOGRAPHS ON PAGE 74**

All-purpose flour, for work surface

½ recipe Pâte Brisée, sugar omitted (page 10)

2 medium (about 10 ounces) zucchini

2 medium (about 10 ounces) yellow squash

Coarse salt

2 tablespoons unsalted butter

2 large (about 12 ounces) leeks, white part only, cut into ⅓-inch dice, well washed

Freshly ground pepper

½ cup (1 ounce) grated Gruyère cheese

1 large whole egg

1 large egg yolk

¼ cup heavy cream

Olive oil, for brushing

1 Preheat the oven to 375°F. Have ready a 4½-by-14-inch bottomless rectangular tart form or one with a removable bottom on a parchment-lined baking sheet. On a lightly floured surface, roll the dough into a 7-by-16-inch rectangle. Fit the dough into the mold, and trim the sides flush with the top of the mold. Transfer the shell to the freezer to chill for 20 minutes.

2 Remove the shell from the freezer, prick the bottom with a fork, and line with parchment paper cut to fit. Fill with dried beans or metal pie weights. Bake until the crust is just beginning to brown, about 15 minutes. Remove from the oven, and remove the beans or weights. Return the crust to the oven, and bake until golden brown, about 10 minutes more. Remove from the oven, and set aside on a wire rack.

3 Using a mandoline or vegetable peeler, very thinly slice 1 green zucchini and 1 yellow squash lengthwise. Place the slices in a colander in a single layer, and sprinkle lightly with salt. Place the colander in a bowl, and set aside to drain for 30 minutes.

4 Cut the remaining zucchini and squash into ⅓-inch dice. Melt the butter in a large skillet over high heat. Add the leeks,

WORKING WITH PHYLLO

Phyllo, also spelled "filo," can be found frozen in supermarkets and fresh in Greek markets. Packages labeled as strudel leaves may also be used. Frozen phyllo must be thawed in the refrigerator overnight before using. Do not refreeze. Phyllo can be defrosted at room temperature in about an hour, but it may be more difficult to work with. Cover the sheets you're not using with a damp kitchen towel so they do not dry out: Phyllo dries out easily and cannot be salvaged. Mend rips by brushing with melted butter or oil and patching them with another piece of phyllo. If all the sheets are torn in the same place throughout all the layers, alternate the way you arrange the sheets on top of one another.

EGGPLANT VARIETIES

The differences among the varieties of eggplants are more than skin deep. White eggplants are firmer, drier, less bitter, and closer-grained than their purple cousins. They hold their shape better when baked, steamed, or fried. Slim, pale-violet eggplants, popular in Chinese cooking, have earned a reputation for being sweeter and more tender, with fewer seeds. Long, slender eggplants have the thinnest skins, making them ideal for slicing to top pizza. Round or pear-shape eggplants are terrific stuffed with rice, ground meat, or other fillings.

zucchini, and squash, and season with salt and pepper. Cook until golden brown but still firm, about 8 minutes. Evenly distribute the cooked vegetables in the crust. Sprinkle the Gruyère cheese on top.

5 Place the salted zucchini and squash slices in between double layers of paper towels. Gently press down to remove as much liquid as possible. Alternating squash colors, weave a lattice pattern over the top of the cheese and vegetables, covering the entire surface. Trim or tuck in the ends to fit.

6 In a medium bowl, whisk together the egg, egg yolk, and cream, and season with salt and pepper. Lift the edges of the lattice in several places, and pour in the egg mixture. Using a pastry brush, coat the lattice with olive oil. Bake, loosely covered with aluminum foil, until the custard is set, 30 to 35 minutes. Remove the tart from the oven, and place on a wire rack to cool slightly before serving.

SQUASH BLOSSOM RISOTTO
SERVES 4

Squash blossoms are generally available only in the late spring and early summer, before the squash are fully grown on their vines. Traditionally filled and sautéed, these delicate blossoms infuse risotto with their flavors. Squash blossoms should be used as soon as possible after they are picked.

2½ cups Homemade Chicken Stock (page 8) or low-sodium canned

2½ cups water

11 squash blossoms (about 2 ounces)

2 tablespoons extra-virgin olive oil

3 shallots, coarsely chopped (about ¼ cup)

Coarse salt and freshly ground pepper

1½ cups Arborio rice

¼ cup dry white wine

¾ cup (about 4 ounces) sliced yellow baby squash

1 tablespoon unsalted butter

⅓ cup freshly grated Parmesan cheese

6 fresh basil leaves, chopped, plus sprigs for garnish

1 Combine the chicken stock and water in a medium saucepan, place over medium-low heat, and bring to a simmer. Quarter each blossom lengthwise, and cut in half crosswise; set aside.

2 Heat the olive oil in another medium saucepan over medium heat. Add the shallots, season with salt and pepper, and cook until translucent, about 2 minutes. Add the rice, and cook, stirring, until slightly opaque, about 2 minutes. Add the wine, and cook, stirring constantly, until almost all the wine is absorbed, about 30 seconds.

3 Add about ½ cup of the simmering stock to the rice. Raise the heat to medium-high, and cook, stirring constantly, until nearly all the stock is absorbed. Continue adding stock, about ½ cup at a time, stirring constantly and letting each addition be nearly absorbed before adding the next.

4 After about 10 minutes, add the sliced squash; continue cooking, adding stock until the rice is creamy looking and each grain is tender but slightly firm in the center. This process will take 15 to 20 minutes more.

5 Stir in the blossoms, butter, and Parmesan, and cook, stirring, for 1 minute. Remove from the heat, and stir in the basil leaves. Adjust the seasoning with salt and pepper. Serve immediately, garnished with basil sprigs.

STUFFED SQUASH TWO WAYS
MAKES 6 OF EACH FILLING

You can make this recipe using only one or both fillings. If making both fillings, you will need twice the amount of tomato sauce.

FOR SQUASH AND LAMB FILLING:

6 medium (about 2¾ pounds) round squash, such as 'Roly Poly,' 'Ronde de Nice,' or 'Sundrop'

2 tablespoons olive oil

¼ cup finely chopped onions

2 garlic cloves, minced

Coarse salt and freshly ground pepper

8 ounces twice-ground lamb

⅓ cup dry red wine

½ cup fresh bread crumbs

3 tablespoons pine nuts, coarsely chopped

2 tablespoons currants

¼ cup (about 1 ounce) crumbled feta cheese

1 teaspoon ground cumin

1 teaspoon ground coriander

1 teaspoon ground cinnamon

3 tablespoons finely chopped fresh mint

Fresh Tomato Sauce (recipe follows)

1 Preheat the oven to 350°F. Have ready a 1½-quart baking dish. Slice off 1 inch crosswise from the stem end of each squash; set aside. Use a melon baller to remove the flesh from the squash, hollowing out the squash bottoms and leaving a ⅛-inch-thick shell. Remove any flesh from the reserved squash top. Coarsely chop the flesh; set aside. Place the squash tops and bottoms in a steamer, and steam until just tender, about 15 minutes. Remove from the steamer; set on a wire rack, cut side down.

2 Heat the olive oil in a large skillet over high heat. Add the onions, garlic, and reserved chopped squash. Season with salt and pepper, and cook until tender, about 6 minutes.

3 Transfer the mixture to a medium bowl. Return the skillet to the heat. Add the lamb, and cook, breaking up the meat with the back of a wooden spoon, until crumbly and lightly browned, about 5 minutes. Stir in the wine, and cook until all the liquid is absorbed, about 1 minute. Add the meat to the onion mixture, and add the bread crumbs, pine nuts, currants, feta, cumin, coriander, cinnamon, mint, and 3 tablespoons tomato sauce. Stir well to combine.

4 Stuff each squash with the meat mixture, brimming the tops. Place squash tops on top. Pour the remaining tomato sauce into the baking dish, and place the stuffed squash in the sauce. Bake until squash is tender, about 30 minutes. Divide the sauce among plates, place the squash on top, and serve.

FOR SQUASH AND BREAD-CRUMB FILLING:

6 medium (about 2¾ pounds) round squash, such as 'Roly Poly,' 'Ronde de Nice,' or 'Sundrop'

4 slices white bread

2 tablespoons olive oil

1 small onion, cut into ¼-inch dice

2 garlic cloves, minced

½ cup fresh corn kernels

2 yellow squash (about 10 ounces), cut into ¼-inch dice

Coarse salt and freshly ground pepper

2 tablespoons chopped fresh flat-leaf parsley

3 tablespoons Homemade Chicken Stock (page 8) or low-sodium canned

Fresh Tomato Sauce (recipe follows)

1 Prepare the squash as in step 1 of the squash-and-lamb-filling recipe above. Place the bread in a food processor, and pulse to form crumbs. Transfer to a medium skillet, and place over medium-high heat. Toast the bread crumbs, stirring constantly, until light golden, about 2 minutes. Remove from the heat, and transfer to a medium bowl.

2 Return the skillet to the heat, and add the olive oil. Add the onion, garlic, corn, and yellow squash, and season with salt and pepper. Cook until the vegetables are just tender, 5 to 6 minutes. Remove from the heat, add to the bread crumbs along with the parsley and chicken stock, and toss to combine.

3 Stuff each squash with the bread-crumb mixture, brimming the tops. Place squash tops on top. Pour the remaining tomato sauce into the baking dish, and place the stuffed squash in the sauce. Bake until squash is tender, about 30 minutes. Divide the sauce among plates, place the squash on top, and serve.

FRESH TOMATO SAUCE

MAKES 1½ CUPS

It's easy to blanch tomatoes for too long, causing the flesh to become mushy. To determine the proper cooking time, remove a tomato from the water, beginning after ten seconds, and gently pinch with two fingers. The skin should have just a slight give and feel a bit less taut than when raw.

15 plum tomatoes (about 2 pounds)

3 tablespoons olive oil

2 garlic cloves, peeled

Coarse salt and freshly ground pepper

1 Fill a large bowl with ice and water; set aside. Bring a large pot of water to a boil. Place the tomatoes in the boiling water until the skins just begin to loosen, 10 to 20 seconds. Remove the tomatoes, and transfer them to the ice bath. Remove them from the ice bath, core, and peel. Slice the tomatoes in half; remove and discard the seeds and liquid. Cut the flesh into ¼-inch dice.

2 Heat the olive oil in a large skillet over medium-low heat. Add the garlic; cook until well browned all over, about 10 minutes. Add the tomatoes; season with salt and pepper. Raise heat to medium. Simmer the sauce until the tomatoes break down somewhat to a saucy consistency, about 5 minutes. Remove the pan from the heat, and discard the garlic.

MAKING BREAD CRUMBS

Bread crumbs have two very appealing characteristics: They are simple to make, and they are an economical use of leftover unsweetened breads. Bread crumbs can be either fresh or dried. For fresh, simply remove the crusts from the bread, place the bread in the bowl of a food processor, and process until fine. For dried bread crumbs, toast the bread in a 250°F oven until fully dried out, 12 to 15 minutes. Let the bread cool, and process until fine. Store in an airtight container in the refrigerator for up to 1 week or in the freezer for up to 6 months. Never use stale bread to make bread crumbs: They will taste that way—stale. Bread crumbs can also be made from darker breads. These somewhat earthier crumbs add interesting flavor to gratins and breaded meats.

SUMMER VEGETABLE POT AU FEU

SERVES 4

Summer is the time to look for produce that is flavorful and delicate. This dish highlights this produce. Look for baby carrots and squash at your green market.

2 teaspoons extra-virgin olive oil

2 ounces pearl onions, peeled

3 garlic cloves, peeled

¼ cup dry white wine

4 ounces round baby orange and yellow carrots, thinly sliced

1 small bay leaf

2 sprigs fresh thyme

2 sprigs fresh flat-leaf parsley

¾ cup Homemade Chicken Stock (page 8) or low-sodium canned

¾ cup water

4 ounces baby new potatoes

9 ounces assorted baby summer squash, cut in half

1 ounce young sugar snap peas, stem ends trimmed

1 ounce fresh lima beans, shelled, or defrosted frozen

1 Heat the oil in a large skillet over medium-high heat. Add the onions and garlic; cook until golden. Add the white wine; cook until most of it has evaporated, about 3 minutes. Add the carrots, bay leaf, thyme, parsley, stock, and water; simmer 5 minutes. Add the potatoes; simmer 7 minutes. Add the squash; cook until just tender, about 5 minutes. Add the peas and lima beans, and cook 2 minutes more.

2 Remove the skillet from the heat; remove and discard the herb sprigs. Divide the vegetables and broth among four shallow bowls, and serve.

ROASTED SQUASH

SERVES 4 | **PHOTOGRAPH ON PAGE 75**

The baking pan must be removed from the oven just before placing the squash slices on it. It is best to use small, long, thin squash—try 'Costata Romanesco'—for this recipe.

1½ pounds zucchini and yellow squash, sliced ⅜ inch thick

2 tablespoons extra-virgin olive oil

2 tablespoons coarsely chopped summer savory, plus sprigs for garnish

Coarse salt and freshly ground pepper

1 Preheat the oven to 500°F. Place a shallow baking pan large enough for the squash, without crowding, in the oven for 30 minutes.

2 Place the squash in a bowl. Add the oil and savory; season with salt and pepper. Toss well.

3 Remove the pan from the oven; quickly arrange the squash in a single layer. Roast, turning halfway through, until golden brown on both sides, 15 to 20 minutes. Serve garnished with savory sprigs.

SLICED ZUCCHINI AND YELLOW SQUASH SALAD

SERVES 6

Use young squash for this recipe; larger ones have too many seeds and are more fibrous.

10 ounces (about 3) small, tender yellow squash

10 ounces (about 3) small, tender zucchini

Coarse salt and freshly ground pepper

2 tablespoons extra-virgin olive oil

2 lemons

½ ounce Parmesan cheese

Using a mandoline or vegetable peeler, very thinly slice the yellow squash into rounds and the zucchini lengthwise. Arrange the squash rounds and zucchini slices on six salad plates. Sprinkle the rounds and slices with salt and pepper, drizzle with olive oil, and squeeze the juice of 1 lemon over them. Very thinly shave the Parmesan cheese directly on top, and serve with the other lemon cut into wedges.

ZUCCHINI BRUSCHETTA

SERVES 8

4 ciabatta or rustic rolls, sliced in half crosswise

3 garlic cloves, peeled

3 tablespoons extra-virgin olive oil

4 zucchini, cut into ¼-inch dice

Coarse salt and freshly ground pepper

1 tablespoon coarsely chopped fresh tarragon, plus sprigs for garnish

1 tablespoon chopped fresh flat-leaf parsley

2 tablespoons nonpareil capers

2 teaspoons freshly squeezed lemon juice

1 Grill or toast the roll halves until golden. Rub each side with garlic, and set aside.

2 Heat the olive oil in a large skillet over high heat. Add the zucchini, and cook, stirring occasionally, until slightly golden, crunchy, but still bright green, about 8 minutes. Season with salt and pepper. Add the tarragon, parsley, capers, and lemon juice, and toss to combine. Divide the mixture over the toasted bread, and serve garnished with tarragon sprigs.

THREE VARIETY SQUASH TIAN

SERVES 6

For the best flavor, use freshly made bread crumbs for this dish, because they have a much fluffier texture. Place as many slices of white bread as will comfortably fit in the bowl of your food processor, and pulse the bread until crumbly. Any leftover crumbs can be placed in a resealable plastic bag and frozen for future use.

1¼ pounds assorted squash, such as 'Costata Romanesco,' pattypan, yellow, green, and black, sliced ⅛ inch thick

2 medium (1 pound) ripe tomatoes, sliced ⅛ inch thick

3 tablespoons olive oil

¼ cup plus 1 tablespoon Homemade Chicken Stock (page 8) or low-sodium canned

Coarse salt and freshly ground pepper

2 tablespoons fresh thyme leaves, plus sprigs for garnish

1 cup fresh bread crumbs

2 tablespoons unsalted butter, melted

1 Preheat the oven to 350°F. In a 10-inch-round gratin dish, arrange the squash slices and tomatoes in an overlapping pattern to fill the dish. Brush the vegetables with olive oil; drizzle the remaining oil on top. Drizzle the chicken stock on top. Sprinkle with salt and pepper and 1 tablespoon thyme leaves.
2 In a medium bowl, combine the bread crumbs, butter, and remaining tablespoon thyme; season with salt and pepper. Arrange the bread-crumb mixture on top of the vegetables. Bake until the vegetables are tender and the bread crumbs are golden, about 50 minutes. Remove from the oven, garnish with thyme sprigs, and serve.

BATTER FRIED STUFFED SQUASH BLOSSOMS

SERVES 4 TO 6 | PHOTOGRAPHS ON PAGE 74

To stuff the squash blossoms easily, spoon the filling into a pastry bag fitted with a coupler; pipe it directly into each blossom.

 1 cup ricotta cheese
 1 cup all-purpose flour
   Coarse salt and freshly ground pepper
 1 cup plus 2 tablespoons milk
 3 ounces (about 1 cup) mozzarella cheese, cut into ¼-inch cubes, room temperature
 1 tablespoon coarsely chopped fresh marjoram
 2 tablespoons coarsely chopped fresh flat-leaf parsley
16 large (about 4 ounces) squash blossoms
 1 quart light olive oil

1 Place the ricotta cheese in a double layer of cheesecloth. Tie up the ends, and hang over a bowl to drain. Place in the refrigerator for 2 to 3 hours, or overnight.
2 In a medium bowl, whisk together the flour with salt and pepper to taste. Slowly whisk the milk into the flour to make a paste. Continue to add milk slowly, whisking constantly, until the batter is slightly thickened and has a very smooth consistency; set aside.
3 Remove the ricotta from the cheesecloth, and discard the liquid. In another medium bowl, stir together the drained ricotta, mozzarella, marjoram, and parsley, and season with salt and pepper. Gently open the squash-blossom petals, and, using a small spoon or pastry bag, fill a blossom about two-thirds full with the ricotta mixture. Wrap the petals around the mixture to seal. Using your fingers, gently press the blossom to evenly distribute the filling. Repeat, filling all the blossoms.
4 In a small saucepan fitted with a deep-frying thermometer, heat the olive oil over medium-high heat to 375°F. Place the stuffed blossoms in the reserved batter until completely coated. Lift out, and gently drag the blossom against the edge of the bowl to remove excess batter. Carefully slip as many blossoms into the hot oil as will comfortably fit without crowding. Fry the blossoms until golden brown, 2 to 3 minutes. Remove from the oil with a slotted spoon, and transfer to several layers of paper towels to drain. Sprinkle with salt, and serve immediately.

TWO-COLORED SQUASH LOAF CAKE

SERVES 12

Purchase high-quality pistachios, and pick through the nuts for the greenest ones.

 1 cup shelled, unsalted green pistachio nuts, coarsely chopped
10 tablespoons (1¼ sticks) unsalted butter, room temperature, plus more for pan
 2 cups all-purpose flour, plus more for pan
 2 medium yellow squash
 2 medium zucchini
 1 teaspoon coarse salt
1½ teaspoons baking powder
1¼ cups sugar
 4 large eggs
 1 teaspoon pure vanilla extract
 2 teaspoons whole fennel seeds

WHAT IS A SQUASH?

The squash grown by American gardeners fall into four species or a cross among the species. The earliest gardeners discovered that the members of the squash family love to cross-pollinate. Thousands of years ago Native Americans began the process when they started cultivating squash for larger seeds and less bitter flesh. In the nineteenth century, Europeans and Americans continued the selection process with the development of the zucchini in Europe and the straightneck squash in America. Today, so much cross-pollination has occurred that trying to figure out what's what only leads to confusion. It is easiest to rely on one question: Can I eat it? If you can't eat it, call it a gourd and grow it for ornamental use. The rest call squash, except for pumpkins, which are just squash by another name.

1 Preheat the oven to 425°F. Place the pistachios in a single layer on a rimmed baking sheet; toast for 5 minutes. Remove from oven; rub the warm nuts between your palms to eliminate as much brown skin as possible. Set aside to cool.

2 Meanwhile, generously butter a 5-by-9-inch loaf pan. Sprinkle the pan with flour; tap out excess flour, and set the pan aside. Using a box grater, coarsely grate the squash and zucchini. Place the grated squash in a piece of cheesecloth, and squeeze out as much liquid as possible; set the squash aside.

3 In a medium bowl, sift together the flour, salt, and baking powder; set aside.

4 In the bowl of an electric mixer fitted with the paddle attachment, combine the butter and sugar; beat on medium-high speed until light and fluffy. Add the eggs one at a time, and mix until combined. Beat in the vanilla. Add the flour mixture, and beat until just combined.

5 Remove the bowl from the mixer stand; fold in the squash, pistachios, and fennel seeds. Spoon the batter into the prepared loaf pan; bake 10 minutes.

6 Reduce the oven temperature to 350°F, and bake the cake until golden brown and a cake tester inserted into the center comes out clean, about 1 hour. Remove the cake from the oven, and transfer to a wire rack until cool.

menu

CELERY STICKS WITH HORSERADISH CREAM CHEESE

BAKED FLOUNDER WITH ONION AND LEMON

SAFFRON RICE WITH TOMATOES AND FRESH OREGANO

BREAD-AND-BUTTER PUDDING WITH STRAWBERRIES

CELERY STICKS WITH HORSERADISH CREAM CHEESE
SERVES 4

1 bunch (2½ pounds) celery

8 ounces cream cheese, room temperature

2 tablespoons prepared horseradish, or more to taste

5 drops hot sauce, or more to taste

½ teaspoon coarse salt

¼ teaspoon freshly ground pepper

1 Separate the celery stalks. Rinse them free of grit, and use a vegetable peeler to remove strings if desired. Cut the stalks into 3- to 4-inch pieces, leaving the tender inner stalks whole. Wrap the celery sticks in a damp cloth, and chill for 1 hour before serving.

2 In a small bowl, combine the cream cheese, horseradish, and hot sauce. Season with salt and pepper. Serve the cream-cheese mixture with the celery.

BAKED FLOUNDER WITH ONION AND LEMON
SERVES 4

Be careful when transferring the fish from the baking dish to the plate—flounder is a fragile fish that falls apart easily.

2 lemons, sliced into ¼-inch-thick rounds

2 medium onions, sliced into very thin rounds

4 tablespoons unsalted butter

1 cup dry white wine

¼ cup cold water

1 teaspoon chopped fresh thyme, plus several sprigs, for garnish

Coarse salt and freshly ground pepper

4 six-ounce flounder fillets

1 Preheat the oven to 400°F. Arrange the lemons and onions in a 9-by-13-inch ovenproof baking dish. Dot with butter; add the wine and cold water. Sprinkle with the chopped thyme; season with salt and pepper. Bake until the onions are soft and translucent, about 40 minutes.

2 Remove the baking dish from the oven. Arrange the fish fillets over the lemons and onions. Season the fillets with salt and pepper. Scatter the thyme sprigs over the fish, and baste with a little cooking liquid. Bake until the fish is just opaque and cooked through, 16 to 18 minutes. Do not overcook. Serve the fish with the cooked onions and lemons.

SAFFRON RICE WITH TOMATOES AND FRESH OREGANO
SERVES 4

In this recipe, the rice is cooked in boiling water just like pasta. Toss the cooked rice very gently, or it will become gummy.

Pinch of saffron

2 tablespoons coarse salt, plus more for seasoning

1½ cups jasmine or long-grain white rice

3 tablespoons unsalted butter, softened

2 ripe beefsteak tomatoes, seeded and cut into ¼-inch dice (about 1 cup)

Freshly ground pepper

6 sprigs fresh oregano, leaves picked from stem

1 Fill a medium saucepan with cold water. Add the saffron. Bring the water to a boil; add the salt. Stir in the rice, and cook, uncovered, until the rice is tender, 12 to 14 minutes. Remove from the heat, and drain well.

2 Place the rice in a serving bowl. Add the butter and tomatoes, and toss very gently. Season with salt, pepper, and oregano leaves.

BREAD-AND-BUTTER PUDDING WITH STRAWBERRIES

SERVES 4 TO 6 | **PHOTOGRAPH ON PAGE 78**

Allowing the bread to soak in the custard batter for a full hour is the secret to a good bread-and-butter pudding.

4 large eggs
¾ cup milk
¾ cup heavy cream
¼ cup plus 3 tablespoons sugar
2 tablespoons dark rum (optional)
8 slices white bread
4 tablespoons unsalted butter, very soft
1 pint fresh strawberries, hulled and cut in half

1 Whisk together the eggs, milk, heavy cream, 3 tablespoons sugar, and rum, if using. Set aside.
2 Spread the top of each slice of bread with a generous amount of butter. Cut the slices in half diagonally. In a 9-inch-round baking dish or cake pan, fan overlapping slices in one layer. It is also fine for bread to overlap randomly. Pour the egg mixture over the bread, and let stand 1 hour.
3 Preheat the oven to 400°F. Sprinkle the pudding with 2 tablespoons sugar. Bake until puffed and golden brown and pudding has set, about 20 minutes.
4 Meanwhile, combine the strawberries with the remaining 2 tablespoons sugar. Let stand while pudding bakes. Serve strawberries with the baked pudding.

FIT TO EAT: HEALTHY FRENCH BISTRO DISHES

STEAK "FRITES"

SERVES 4 | **PHOTOGRAPH ON PAGE 76**

4 baking potatoes (about 2½ pounds)
2 teaspoons extra-virgin olive oil
2 teaspoons coarse salt
½ teaspoon freshly ground pepper
4 four-ounce slices of filet mignon (beef tenderloin)
 Dijon mustard, for serving
 Cooking spray

1 Preheat the oven to 450°F with two baking sheets inside. Peel the potatoes; cut into ¼-inch sticks. Place in a bowl; toss with the olive oil, 1½ teaspoons salt, and ¼ teaspoon pepper. Carefully remove the baking sheets from the oven; coat with cooking spray. Divide the potatoes between the hot baking sheets in a single layer. Bake, tossing occasionally, until golden brown, 20 to 30 minutes.
2 While the potatoes are cooking, heat a cast-iron or heavy skillet over medium heat until very hot. Place the filet slices in a layer of plastic wrap; lightly pound with the flat side of a meat tenderizer until ½ inch thick. Season the steaks on both sides with the remaining ½ teaspoon salt and ¼ teaspoon pepper. Sear in the hot skillet until browned on both sides and medium rare in the center, about 2 minutes per side. Serve immediately with fries and Dijon mustard.

PER SERVING: 378 CALORIES, 12 G FAT, 70 MG CHOLESTEROL, 38 G CARBOHYDRATE, 625 MG SODIUM, 28 G PROTEIN, 3 G FIBER

BISTRO FARE

Savoring the flavors of traditional French bistro foods does not require overindulgence. Steak Frites is a quick, hearty meal, here kept lean by baking the potatoes and using a lean cut of beef. Another essential French dish, Poule au Pot—made with poached skinless chicken breasts and plenty of vegetables—adds a simple meal to any cook's repertoire. And healthful variations on Warm Leeks Vinaigrette, Salade Niçoise, and Celery Root Rémoulade add important vitamins and minerals to any menu. Then try a rustic, unpretentious Apple Galette. After all, any bistro meal would be incomplete without dessert.

SALADE NIÇOISE

SERVES 8

1 large shallot, minced

1 tablespoon capers

2 tablespoons Dijon mustard

2 tablespoons white-wine vinegar

1 teaspoon coarse salt

¼ teaspoon freshly ground pepper

¼ cup plus 2 tablespoons extra-virgin olive oil

8 ounces green beans

1 pound small red potatoes

2 large eggs

1 small head Romaine lettuce, cut into bite-size pieces

1 celery stalk, strings removed, cut into ¼-inch slices

2 tomatoes, cut into wedges

4 radishes, thinly sliced

1 six-ounce can water-packed solid white tuna, drained

3 ounces (about 24) Niçoise or other olives

8 anchovies (optional)

1 Whisk together the shallot, capers, mustard, vinegar, salt, and pepper. Slowly whisk in the oil; set dressing aside.

2 Fill a large bowl with ice and water; set aside. Bring a saucepan of water to a boil. Add the green beans, and cook until bright green, about 1 minute. Drain; plunge into the ice bath to stop the cooking. Drain again, cut into 1½-inch pieces, and set aside.

3 Refill the saucepan with cold water, and add the potatoes. Bring to a boil. Reduce to a simmer; cook, uncovered, until the potatoes are tender, about 15 minutes. Drain the potatoes, and let cool slightly. When cool enough to handle, cut the potatoes into 1-inch pieces. Place in a bowl. Toss with ¼ cup dressing; set aside.

4 Place the eggs in a small saucepan of cold water. Bring to a boil; cover. Remove from the heat. Let sit for 11 minutes. Rinse in cold water. Peel the eggs, and cut into wedges. Set aside.

5 To assemble, arrange the lettuce on individual plates. Arrange the green beans, potato mixture, egg wedges, celery, tomatoes, radishes, tuna, olives, and anchovies, if using. Drizzle with the remaining dressing, and serve.

PER SERVING: 210 CALORIES, 13 G FAT, 62 MG CHOLESTEROL, 14 G CARBOHYDRATE, 491 MG SODIUM, 11 G PROTEIN, 2 G FIBER

POACHED CHICKEN AND VEGETABLES (POULE AU POT)

SERVES 6

This is a low-fat version of the classic French dish in which chicken and vegetables are served in bowls with their flavorful stock.

FOR THE STOCK:

4 sprigs fresh flat-leaf parsley

4 sprigs fresh thyme

1 teaspoon whole black peppercorns

2 bay leaves

4 whole cloves

2 teaspoons extra-virgin olive oil

1 carrot, cut into 4 pieces

1 celery stalk, strings removed, cut into 4 pieces

1 onion, quartered

¼ cup dry white wine

2 fifteen-ounce cans low-sodium chicken broth, or Homemade Chicken Stock (page 8), skimmed of fat

1 quart water

FOR THE SOUP:

3 whole (16 ounce) chicken breasts on the bone, split, skin removed

4 ounces button mushrooms, wiped clean, cut in half

8 ounces small red potatoes, cut into 1-inch pieces

4 ounces white or green asparagus, stems peeled, cut into 1-inch pieces

1 carrot, cut into ¼-inch slices

1 celery stalk, strings removed, cut into ¼-inch slices

4 ounces pearl onions, peeled

8 ounces baby turnips, peeled, or medium turnips, peeled and cut into wedges

1½ teaspoons coarse salt

½ teaspoon freshly ground pepper

1 Wrap the parsley, thyme, peppercorns, bay leaves, and cloves in a piece of cheesecloth; tie with kitchen twine. Heat the oil in a stockpot over medium-low heat. Add the carrot, celery, and onion; cook, stirring occasionally, until softened and just starting to brown, 4 to 5 minutes. Add the wine; cook until the liquid has evaporated, 5 to 6 minutes. Add the stock, herb bundle, and water. Bring to a boil; reduce to a gentle simmer. Cover, and simmer 30 minutes.

2 Strain the stock through a fine sieve or cheesecloth-lined colander; discard the vegetables. Return the stock to the stockpot. Bring to a simmer. Add the chicken, mushrooms, potatoes, asparagus, carrot, celery, onions, and turnips. Simmer gently over medium heat with the cover ajar, skimming occasionally, until the chicken is cooked through, 30 to 40 minutes. Season with salt and pepper, and serve immediately.

PER SERVING: 255 CALORIES, 5 G FAT, 88 MG CHOLESTEROL, 13 G CARBOHYDRATE, 687 MG SODIUM, 35 G PROTEIN, 3 G FIBER

CELERY ROOT REMOULADE
(CELERI REMOULADE)

SERVES 6

Traditional rémoulade is made with mayonnaise. We have lightened this traditional side dish with a lemony yogurt dressing.

1 medium (about 12 ounces) celery root
1 Granny Smith apple
   Juice of 1 lemon (about 2 tablespoons)
½ cup nonfat plain yogurt
2 tablespoons heavy cream
1 tablespoon plus 1 teaspoon
   Dijon mustard
1 teaspoon coarse salt
¼ teaspoon freshly ground pepper

1 Peel the celery root, and core the apple. Grate both on the large holes of a box grater. Place in a medium bowl, and toss with the lemon juice.
2 In another bowl, whisk together the yogurt, cream, mustard, salt, and pepper. Add to the grated celery root and apple, and toss to combine. Refrigerate until ready to serve.

PER SERVING: 61 CALORIES, 2 G FAT, 7 MG CHOLESTEROL, 9 G CARBOHYDRATE, 454 MG SODIUM, 2 G PROTEIN, 3 G FIBER

WARM LEEKS VINAIGRETTE
(POIREAUX TIEDES EN
VINAIGRETTE)

SERVES 6

1 tablespoon plus 1 teaspoon sherry
   vinegar
1 tablespoon plus 1 teaspoon
   Dijon mustard
1 tablespoon honey
1 teaspoon coarse salt
¼ teaspoon freshly ground pepper
1 tablespoon plus 1 teaspoon
   extra-virgin olive oil
3 bunches (about 15) leeks

1 Whisk together the vinegar, mustard, honey, salt, and pepper in a large bowl. Slowly drizzle in the olive oil, whisking constantly, until well combined; set aside.
2 Trim the leek greens to about 6 inches, leaving only the white and light-green parts. Trim the roots, and cut the leeks in half lengthwise. Wash well under

STORING OILS AND VINAIGRETTES

Store olive oil away from light and heat. Both will cause the oil to turn more quickly and develop a bitter, rancid taste. The oil should be stored in a closed cabinet or, if you want to keep it out in the open, in a dark bottle. Never store it near the stove. Keep all nut oils in the refrigerator because they can go rancid with prolonged exposure to heat. Most other oils should be kept in a dark, cool place to extend their shelf life. Most vinaigrettes can keep for at least a week in a jar in the refrigerator. Those with fresh herbs should be used within a day or two of making them. Bring to room temperature before serving.

CLEANING LEEKS

A member of the allium family, the leek is the restrained, shy relative of onions and garlic. Leeks vary enormously in size; the smaller the leek, the more tender the stalk. Before using, trim the tiny roots that hang off the root end, and trim the thick leaf end. Leeks grow into the soil, so they retain lots of dirt in their layers and leaves. Always wash them thoroughly before proceeding with a recipe. The best way to ensure that every bit of dirt is washed from leeks is to cut them first into the size that is called for in the recipe. Generally they are halved lengthwise, then sliced crosswise into pieces. Transfer the pieces to a large bowl of cold water, stir, and let stand for five minutes to let the dirt and sand settle to the bottom. Lift pieces out of the water with a slotted spoon, and drain on paper towels.

cold running water to remove any dirt; set aside.

3 Place a steamer basket in a large saucepan filled with water to the bottom of the basket. Bring the water to a boil. Add the leeks. Cover, and steam until tender, about 10 minutes. Remove the leeks, and drain on paper towels to remove any water. Place the leeks in the bowl with the vinaigrette, and toss to combine. Serve hot or at room temperature.

PER SERVING: 121 CALORIES, 4 G FAT, 0 MG CHOLESTEROL, 22 G CARBOHYDRATE, 255 MG SODIUM, 2 G PROTEIN, 3 G FIBER

APPLE GALETTE

SERVES 8 TO 10 | PHOTOGRAPH ON PAGE 77

1½ cups all-purpose flour, plus more for work surface

3 tablespoons granulated sugar

¼ teaspoon coarse salt

6 tablespoons unsalted butter, chilled and cut into pieces

3 to 4 tablespoons ice water

5 McIntosh or other red apples

1 teaspoon ground cinnamon

¼ cup freshly squeezed lemon juice

¼ cup confectioners' sugar

1 Preheat the oven to 400°F. Place the flour, 1 tablespoon granulated sugar, and salt in the bowl of a food processor, and pulse to combine. Add the butter, and pulse until the mixture resembles coarse meal. With the food processor running, add the ice water in a thin stream, processing until just combined, forming clumps. Gently press the dough into a disk, and wrap the disk in plastic wrap. Refrigerate the dough until firm, about 30 minutes.

2 Peel, core, and coarsely chop 2 apples. Heat a medium skillet over medium heat. Add the chopped apples, 1 tablespoon granulated sugar, and ½ teaspoon cinnamon. Cook, stirring occasionally, until the apples are very tender and the mixture is the consistency of chunky applesauce, about 15 minutes. If the pan gets too dry while the apple mixture is cooking, add water, ¼ cup at a time. Transfer the apple mixture to a bowl to cool. When cool, stir in 3 tablespoons lemon juice, and set aside.

3 On a lightly floured surface, roll the reserved dough into a 12-inch circle, about ⅛ inch thick. Sprinkle the dough with the remaining tablespoon granulated sugar, and prick the dough with a fork several times to prevent puffing. Bake on a baking sheet until just starting to set, 8 to 10 minutes. Place the baking sheet with crust on a wire rack to cool.

4 Peel and core the remaining 3 apples. Cut into ⅛-inch wedges, and place in a bowl. Toss with the remaining tablespoon lemon juice and remaining ½ teaspoon cinnamon. Spread the crust with the cooked apple mixture, leaving a ½-inch border. Arrange the apple slices over the mixture in a spiral pattern, slightly overlapping each piece. Sift confectioners' sugar over the galette, and bake until the crust is golden brown and cooked through, about 30 minutes.

PER SERVING: 217 CALORIES, 8 G FAT, 20 MG CHOLESTEROL, 34 G CARBOHYDRATE, 126 MG SODIUM, 2 G PROTEIN, 4 G FIBER

NAVETTES | **PAGE 58**

ROASTING EGGPLANT

1 Pierce eggplants all over with a wooden skewer. Turn two gas burners or gas grill to high flame; place eggplants over flames. Cook, turning, until skins are completely black and flesh is falling-apart tender.

2 Remove from the flame; transfer to a nonreactive baking dish. Place the dish on a slant so that the juices can run from the eggplants.

3 When cool enough to handle, peel away all blackened skin, dipping fingertips in cold water frequently to rinse off any charred residue. Discard the juices.

EGGPLANT CAVIAR | **PAGE 60**

To make Warm Eggplant Salad, first salt eggplant slices on both sides to remove any bitter flavor. Drain in a colander for one hour.

WARM EGGPLANT SALAD | **PAGE 60**

To assemble the squash lattice tart, weave a lattice pattern over the filling, alternating slices of green zucchini and yellow squash. Trim or tuck in ends to fit.

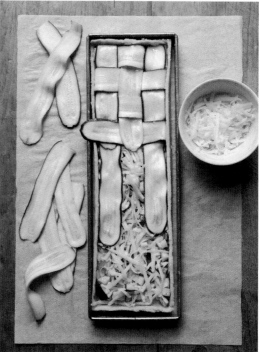

To stuff squash blossoms, use a small spoon to fill each blossom about two-thirds full with ricotta filling. Wrap petals around mixture to seal. Gently place stuffed blossoms in batter, dragging against bowl to remove excess.

BATTER FRIED STUFFED SQUASH BLOSSOMS | PAGE 65

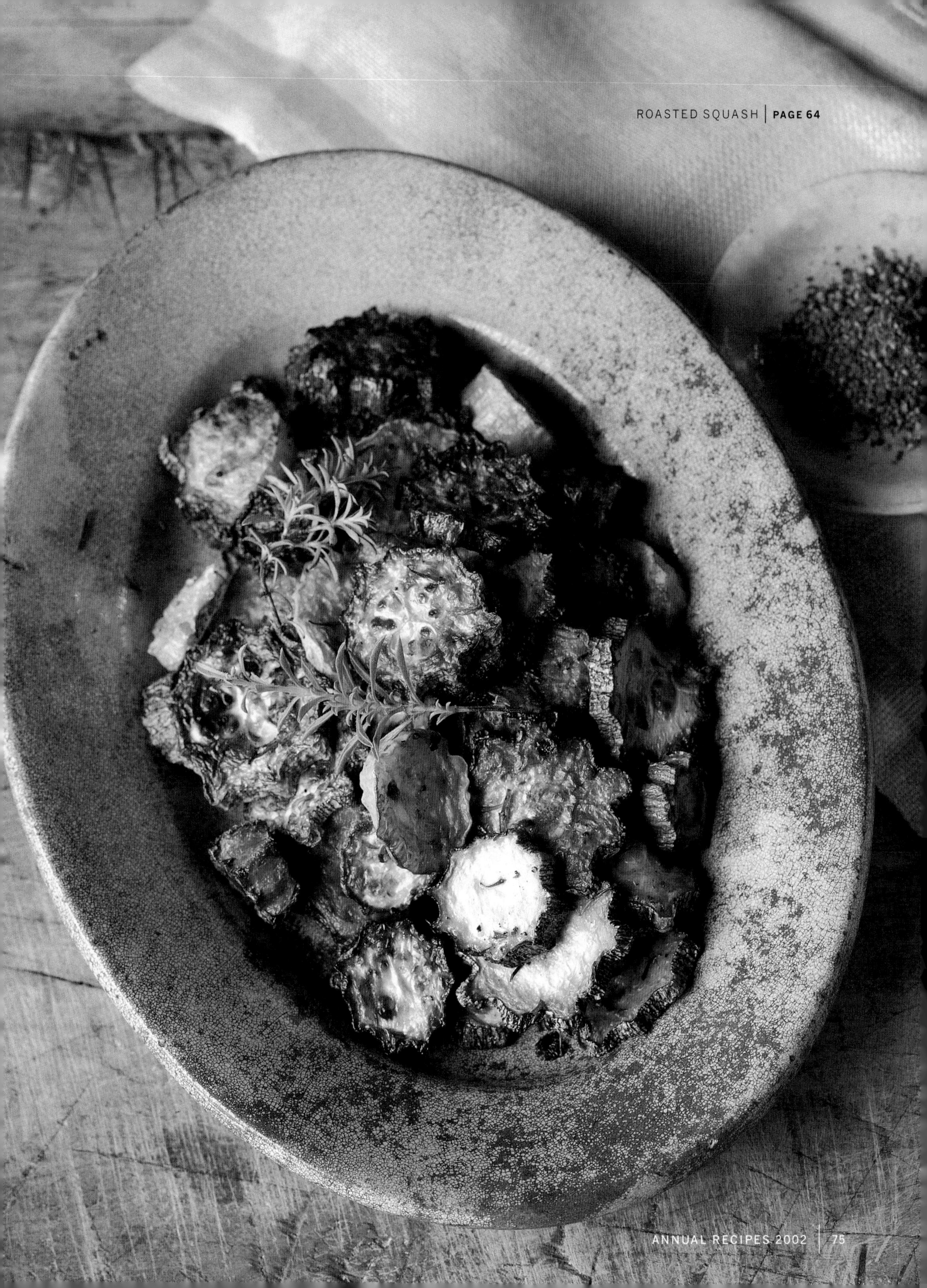

STEAK "FRITES" | **PAGE 67**

APPLE GALETTE | PAGE 70

BREAD-AND-BUTTER PUDDING WITH STRAWBERRIES | **PAGE 67**

april

Apricot Torte

Herb Fritters

Classic French Toast

Cinnamon-Raisin French Toast

Savory French Toast Sticks

Banana-Nut French Toast

Orange Croissant French Toast

Sugar-Coated Bunnies and Chicks

Chocolate-Coated Marshmallow
Chicks

Coconut-Coated Marshmallow
Shapes

Flat Marshmallow Shapes

Grilled Ramps with Asparagus

Charoset

Caviar and Chopped Eggs
on Biscuits

Watercress and Ramp Soup

Leg of Lamb with Spicy Mustard
Marinade

Glazed Baby Carrots with Chives

Crab-Apple Jelly

Fresh Mint Jelly

Blackberry Tartlets

Brandy Snaps

Tuna with Mustard Seed Crust

Warm Mustard and Olive Oil Sauce

Perfect Mustard Vinaigrette

Grilled Cheese with Grainy Mustard

Poached Chicken with Hot English
Mustard

Cold Poached Mussels with Creamy
Mustard Sauce

Potato Gratin with Mustard

Steamed Artichokes with Grainy
Mustard and Bacon Dressing

Hot Mustard Biscuits

Romaine Salad with Prosciutto
Crisps

Almond Crusted Chicken

Orzo with Peas and Mint

Marsala Cheese Tart with Oranges

Spinach Dill Pie

Spinach Salad

"Creamed" Spinach

Spinach Soufflé

Spinach Egg Broth

APRICOT TORTE

MAKES 1 TEN-INCH CAKE; SERVES 8

Centuries of working with the Jewish holidays' dietary restrictions have produced treats worth indulging in anytime. In this luscious Passover torte, whisked egg whites give height and finely chopped apricots impart moisture and texture. The torte is brushed with an apricot glaze, sliced almonds, and Passover Powdered Sugar, made with potato starch instead of cornstarch. You will need a ten-inch springform pan.

8 ounces blanched, whole almonds
¼ cup blanched, sliced almonds, for garnish
　Margarine, for pan
1 cup granulated sugar, plus more for pan
8 ounces dried apricots
　Zest and juice of 1 lemon
2 teaspoons ground cinnamon
½ teaspoon ground nutmeg
¼ teaspoon ground cloves
8 large eggs, separated
½ teaspoon coarse salt
¼ cup apricot jam
　Passover Powdered Sugar (recipe follows)

1　Preheat the oven to 325°F. Place the whole almonds in a single layer on a rimmed baking sheet and the sliced almonds in a single layer on another sheet. Toast until golden and aromatic, 8 to 10 minutes. Shake the pans halfway through to make sure the nuts brown evenly. Set aside to cool.

2　Grease the springform pan with margarine, sprinkle with sugar, and tap out excess; set aside. Place ¼ cup sugar, the whole almonds, and the apricots in the bowl of a food processor; process until finely chopped, 1 to 2 minutes. Transfer to a medium bowl, add the lemon zest, cinnamon, nutmeg, and cloves, and stir to combine; set aside. In the bowl of an electric mixer fitted with the whisk attachment, whisk the egg yolks and ½ cup sugar on high speed until light and fluffy, 3 to 4 minutes. Transfer the mixture to a large bowl; set aside.

3　Clean and dry the mixer bowl and whisk; use to beat the egg whites with the salt and lemon juice until frothy. Slowly add the remaining ¼ cup sugar, and continue whisking on medium until the peaks are stiff but not dry. Fold the beaten whites into the beaten egg yolks. Add the apricot-and-almond mixture, and fold in until just combined. Pour the batter into the prepared pan, and bake until the torte is golden brown and a cake tester inserted into the middle comes out clean, 50 to 60 minutes. It may be necessary to cover the torte lightly with foil to keep the top from burning. Transfer to a wire rack to cool for 10 minutes. Run a knife around the edge of the torte, and release from the pan. Allow to cool.

4　Place the apricot jam in a small saucepan over medium heat, and bring to a boil. Remove from the heat, and strain. Brush the glaze onto the cooled torte. Sprinkle with the sliced almonds and Passover powdered sugar.

PASSOVER POWDERED SUGAR

MAKES 1 CUP

1 tablespoon potato starch
1 cup granulated sugar

In the bowl of a food processor, combine the potato starch and sugar. Process until it is very powdery and resembles confectioners' sugar, about 2 minutes. Let the sugar settle for about 1 minute before removing the processor cover.

FRENCH TOAST

The secret to perfect French toast—lightly crisp on the outside and tender on the inside—is using day-old bread. Soak it for several minutes in a mixture of cream and eggs, and fry it in a hot skillet.

A SELECTION OF BREADS

baguette

brioche

challah

cinnamon-raisin

country French

croissant

pugliese

pullman

sesame

sourdough boule

whole grain

GOOD THINGS

HERB FRITTERS

SERVES 4

Crisp herb fritters are an unusual way to savor the individual pleasures of a full range of fresh herbs. Dipped in beer batter, fried lightly in oil, and served with lemon wedges, they make a delightful accompaniment to a glass of wine. If the batter is too thick, thin with a little water; if it is too thin, add a little flour.

- 2 large eggs, separated
- 1½ tablespoons vegetable oil, plus more for frying
- ½ cup beer
- ¾ cup all-purpose flour
- 3 ounces assorted herbs, such as basil, mint, sage, parsley, oregano, tarragon, and chives
- 1 teaspoon coarse salt, plus more for seasoning
- ¼ teaspoon freshly ground pepper
- 1 lemon, cut into wedges

1 Whisk together the yolks, oil, and beer in a bowl. Slowly add the flour, whisking until just combined. Set aside for 20 minutes. Wash and dry the herbs. Whisk the egg whites to soft peaks; fold into the beer batter. Add the salt and pepper.
2 In a heavy-bottomed saucepan, heat 1 inch of oil over medium heat until hot but not smoking, about 375°F on a frying thermometer. Dip each herb into the batter, shaking off excess, until lightly coated. Place the herbs in the oil, turning until golden, about 1 minute. Drain on paper towels; season with salt. Serve with lemon wedges.

FRENCH TOAST

CLASSIC FRENCH TOAST

SERVES 6 | **PHOTOGRAPH ON PAGE 95**

We used challah for this recipe, but any dense bread, such as brioche or sourdough, will make rich French toast. Pure maple syrup and a pat of butter are the only condiments needed. Serve with crisp bacon, café au lait, and fresh fruit juice for the perfect breakfast.

- 6 large eggs
- 1½ cups heavy cream, half-and-half, or milk
- 2 tablespoons pure vanilla extract
- ½ teaspoon ground cinnamon
- Pinch of ground nutmeg
- Pinch of coarse salt
- 6 one-inch-thick slices bread, preferably a day old
- 4 tablespoons unsalted butter
- ¼ cup vegetable oil
- Pure maple syrup (optional)

1 Whisk together the eggs, cream, vanilla, cinnamon, nutmeg, and salt in a medium bowl; set aside.
2 Place the bread slices in a shallow baking dish large enough to hold them in a single layer. Pour the egg mixture over the bread; let sit 10 minutes. Turn the slices over; let sit 10 minutes more or until soaked through.
3 Preheat the oven to 250°F. Place a wire rack on a baking sheet, and set aside. Heat 2 tablespoons butter and 2 tablespoons oil in a large skillet over medium heat. Fry half the bread slices until golden brown, 2 to 3 minutes per side. Transfer to the wire rack, and place in the oven while cooking the remaining bread. Wipe out the skillet, and repeat with the remaining 2 tablespoons butter, 2 tablespoons oil, and 3 slices of bread. Serve hot with maple syrup, if using.

CINNAMON-RAISIN FRENCH TOAST

SERVES 6

Any bread is lovely in this buttermilk batter, which has a tang that balances the sweetness of the bread and syrup.

- 6 large eggs
- 1½ cups nonfat buttermilk
- 2 tablespoons pure vanilla extract
- ½ teaspoon ground cinnamon
- Pinch of ground nutmeg
- Pinch of coarse salt
- 6 one-inch-thick slices cinnamon-raisin bread, preferably a day old
- 2 tablespoons unsalted butter
- 2 tablespoons vegetable oil
- Pure maple syrup (optional)

1 Whisk together the eggs, buttermilk, vanilla, cinnamon, nutmeg, and salt in a medium bowl; set aside.
2 Place the bread slices in a shallow baking dish large enough to hold them in a single layer. Pour the egg mixture over the bread; let sit 10 minutes. Turn the slices over; let sit 10 minutes more or until soaked through.
3 Preheat the oven to 250°F. Place a wire rack on a baking sheet, and set aside. Heat 1 tablespoon butter and 1 tablespoon oil in a large skillet over medium heat. Fry half the bread slices until golden brown, 2 to 3 minutes per side. Transfer to the wire rack, and place in the oven while cooking the remaining bread. Wipe out the skillet, and repeat with the remaining tablespoon butter, tablespoon oil, and 3 slices of bread. Serve hot with maple syrup, if using.

SAVORY FRENCH TOAST STICKS

SERVES 6

French toast becomes a cozy dinner with the addition of a few unexpected toppings, such as bacon, onions, mushrooms, and grated Parmesan cheese. Serve these sticks with a simple green salad for a perfectly balanced meal.

5 ounces (about 6 slices) bacon

2 onions, cut into ¼-inch dice

12 ounces button mushrooms, wiped clean, stemmed and quartered

6 large eggs

1½ cups heavy cream, half-and-half, or milk

½ cup (about 1½ ounces) freshly grated Parmesan cheese, plus more for serving

1 teaspoon coarse salt

6 one-inch-thick slices bread, such as sourdough, preferably a day old, each cut into 3 strips

2 tablespoons unsalted butter

2 tablespoons vegetable oil

1 Heat a skillet over medium heat. Add the bacon; cook until browned, 3 to 4 minutes. Remove the bacon with tongs; drain on paper towels, crumble, and set aside. Add the onions to the skillet with the bacon drippings; cook, stirring constantly, until the onions begin to soften, about 3 minutes. Add the mushrooms; cook until tender and most of the liquid released has evaporated, 5 to 6 minutes. Transfer the mixture to a bowl to cool. When cool, set aside half the mixture; finely chop the other half.

2 Whisk together the eggs, cream, Parmesan, and salt in a medium bowl. Stir in the finely chopped vegetables, and set aside.

3 Place the bread strips in a shallow baking dish large enough to hold them in a single layer. Pour the egg mixture over the bread; let sit 10 minutes. Turn the strips over, and let sit 10 minutes more or until the bread is soaked through.

4 Preheat the oven to 250°F. Place a wire rack on a baking sheet; set aside. Heat 1 tablespoon butter and 1 tablespoon oil in a large skillet over medium heat. Fry half the bread strips until golden brown, 2 to 3 minutes per side. Transfer to the wire rack, and place in the oven while cooking the remaining bread. Wipe out the skillet, and repeat with the remaining tablespoon butter, tablespoon oil, and strips of bread. Keep in the oven until ready to serve.

5 Heat the remaining onion mixture in a small skillet until warm. Serve the French toast hot, topped with the onion mixture, crumbled bacon, and Parmesan.

BANANA-NUT FRENCH TOAST

SERVES 6

1½ cups walnuts

6 large eggs

1½ cups heavy cream, half-and-half, or milk

2 tablespoons pure vanilla extract

½ teaspoon ground cinnamon

Pinch of ground nutmeg

Pinch of coarse salt

6 ripe but firm bananas, peeled and cut into ¼-inch rounds

1½ cups packed dark-brown sugar

12 one-half-inch-thick slices bread, such as brioche or challah, preferably a day old

8 tablespoons (1 stick) unsalted butter

¼ cup vegetable oil

Pure maple syrup (optional)

1 Preheat the oven to 350°F. Place the walnuts in a single layer on a rimmed baking sheet, and toast until lightly golden and aromatic, 8 to 12 minutes. When cool, chop the walnuts coarsely. Set aside.

2 Whisk together the eggs, cream, vanilla, cinnamon, nutmeg, and salt in a medium bowl, and set aside.

3 Combine the bananas, sugar, and walnuts in another bowl. Lay out 6 slices of bread on a work surface. Spoon ⅓ cup of the banana mixture onto each slice. Set aside the remaining mixture. Top with the remaining bread slices; press gently to seal the sandwiches.

4 Place the sandwiches in a shallow baking dish (or two dishes) large enough to hold them in a single layer. Pour the egg mixture over the bread, and let sit 10 minutes. Carefully turn the sandwiches over, and let sit 10 minutes more or until the bread is soaked through.

5 Reduce the oven temperature to 250°F. Place a wire rack on a baking sheet, and set aside. Heat the remaining banana mixture in a small skillet over medium-low heat until the sugar is melted and the bananas are soft and slightly translucent, about 3 minutes. Add 4 tablespoons butter, and stir to combine; keep warm.

6 Heat 2 tablespoons butter and 2 tablespoons vegetable oil in a large skillet over medium heat. Fry half of the sandwiches until golden brown, 2 to 3 minutes per side. Transfer to the wire rack, and place in the oven while cooking the remaining sandwiches. Wipe out the skillet, and repeat with the remaining 2 tablespoons butter, 2 tablespoons oil, and 3 sandwiches. Cut into triangles, and serve hot with the warm banana mixture and maple syrup, if using.

ORANGE CROISSANT FRENCH TOAST

SERVES 6

In this version of French toast, flaky croissants are filled with sweetened cream cheese and thick orange marmalade, then soaked in a cream-based batter that has been laced with Grand Marnier and orange zest.

6 large eggs

1½ cups heavy cream, half-and-half, or milk

2 tablespoons Grand Marnier (optional)

1 teaspoon pure vanilla extract

½ teaspoon ground cinnamon

Pinch of ground nutmeg

Pinch of coarse salt

Grated zest of 1 orange

4 ounces cream cheese, softened

2 tablespoons confectioners' sugar

6 croissants, preferably a day old

½ cup orange marmalade, plus more for serving if desired

2 tablespoons unsalted butter, plus more for serving if desired

2 tablespoons vegetable oil

Orange Syrup (page 84)

2 oranges, segmented (optional)

1 Whisk together the eggs, cream, Grand Marnier, if using, vanilla, cinnamon, nutmeg, salt, and orange zest in a medium bowl, and set aside. Stir together the cream cheese and confectioners' sugar in a small bowl.

2 Halve the croissants crosswise. Spread the bottoms with the cream-cheese mixture, then with the marmalade. Place the tops back on to seal. Place the stuffed croissants in a shallow baking dish large enough to hold them in a single layer. Pour the egg mixture over the croissants; let sit 5 minutes. Turn the croissants over; let sit 5 minutes more or until they are soaked through.

3 Preheat oven to 250°F. Place a wire rack on a baking sheet, and set aside. Heat 1 tablespoon butter and 1 tablespoon oil in a large skillet over medium heat. Fry half the croissants until golden brown, about 3 minutes per side. Transfer to the wire rack, and place in the oven while cooking the remaining croissants. Wipe out the skillet, and repeat with the remaining tablespoon butter, tablespoon oil, and 3 croissants. Serve hot with orange syrup, butter, marmalade, and orange segments, if desired.

ORANGE SYRUP

MAKES 1¼ CUPS

This syrup can be poured over French toast or pancakes as a delicious alternative to maple syrup.

1 cup sugar
½ cup water
¾ cup freshly squeezed orange juice
1 tablespoon cornstarch
2 tablespoons unsalted butter

Combine the sugar and water in a small saucepan. Bring to a boil; stir until the sugar has dissolved. Combine the juice and cornstarch in a bowl; pour into the sugar syrup. Simmer gently until thick, 6 to 8 minutes. Add the butter; stir until it melts. Serve warm.

MARSHMALLOW TREATS

SUGAR-COATED BUNNIES AND CHICKS

MAKES ABOUT 2 DOZEN

Line a baking sheet with colored sugar or other coating so you can pipe in assembly-line fashion, and the process goes quickly. You can use luster dust or sparkle dust to custom-color white crystal sugar.

1½ cups fine crystal colored sugar, or turbinado sugar
Luster dust or sparkle dust (optional)
Marshmallow for Piping (recipe follows)
Single-Batch Royal Icing (recipe follows)

1 Fill a rimmed baking sheet or several shallow bowls with sugar. If desired, color white crystal sugar by stirring in luster dust or sparkle dust a little at a time, using a toothpick.

2 For bunnies, use a ½-inch (#11 Ateco) tip to pipe a 1¼-inch mound of marshmallow about ½ inch tall directly onto the sugar. Pipe a small mound on one side for the tail; pipe a larger mound for the head on the opposite side. With a damp finger, pat down the spikes formed from piping the body, tail, and head. Pipe the ears, starting from the top of the head, and pipe onto the body, pulling forward and off to finish. Pat down the spikes on the ears. For chicks, pipe an oval shape about 1 inch wide, tapering the end and pulling upward to finish with the tail. On the opposite end, for the neck and face, pipe a mound about the width of the body, pushing toward the tail and up. Pull away from the face to form the beak. Make large and small chicks by changing the dimensions.

3 Working quickly so the marshmallow surface does not dry, use a spoon to sprinkle sugar over the entire surface. Allow the shape to sit a few minutes to set, and lift out of the sugar with a spoon or small offset spatula. Transfer the icing to a small pastry bag fitted with a ¹⁄₃₂-inch (#1 Ateco) tip. Pipe eyes on both sides of coated chicks and two eyes and a nose on bunnies. Place in a parchment-lined airtight container until ready to serve, up to 2 weeks.

MARSHMALLOW FOR PIPING

MAKES ABOUT 1½ CUPS

2½ teaspoons (1 envelope) unflavored gelatin
⅓ cup plus ¼ cup cold water
1 cup sugar

1 In the bowl of an electric mixer, sprinkle the gelatin over ⅓ cup cold water. Allow the gelatin to soften, about 5 minutes.

2 In a small saucepan, combine ¼ cup water and the sugar, and stir over medium-high heat until dissolved. Stop stirring, and place a candy thermometer into the sugar; wipe sides of the pan with a wet brush if the sugar crystals have splattered up. Boil the sugar until the temperature reaches the soft-ball stage (238°F). Remove the syrup from the heat, and add to the softened gelatin. Using the mixer's whisk attachment, hand stir the mixture a few minutes to cool; place the bowl on the mixer stand, and attach the whisk. Beat on medium-high until soft peaks form and the marshmallow mixture holds its shape, 8 to 10 minutes.

3 Transfer the mixture to a 14-inch pastry bag fitted with a ½-inch (#11 Ateco) tip, and pipe immediately.

SINGLE-BATCH ROYAL ICING

MAKES 1 CUP

While not in use, the tip of the icing bag should be wrapped in a damp paper towel—the icing hardens quickly when exposed to air.

8 ounces (2 cups) confectioners' sugar
2½ tablespoons meringue powder
¼ cup water
Black or dark-brown gel-paste food coloring

1 In the bowl of an electric mixer fitted with the paddle attachment, combine the confectioners' sugar, meringue powder, and water on low speed. Mix until fluffy yet dense, 10 to 15 minutes.

2 Color the icing as needed, starting with a small amount of food coloring. Transfer to a small pastry bag fitted with a ¹⁄₃₂-inch pastry tip (#1 Ateco).

3 Store the royal icing in an airtight container up to a week, and stir before using.

CHOCOLATE-COATED MARSHMALLOW CHICKS

MAKES ABOUT 2 DOZEN

When dipping chicks in chocolate, work quickly so the chocolate does not go out of temper. If out of temper, it will set with gray streaks.

Cornstarch

Marshmallow for Piping (recipe above)

Tempered Chocolate (recipe follows)

Single-Batch Royal Icing (page 84)

1 Sift a thin layer of cornstarch onto the bottom of a rimmed baking sheet to cover the surface completely. Pipe the chicks directly onto the cornstarch (see step 2 of Sugar-Coated Bunnies and Chicks recipe, above), and allow to set uncovered for 30 to 45 minutes. Meanwhile, temper the chocolate.

2 Line a second baking sheet with parchment paper or a Silpat baking mat. Set aside. Dust fingers with cornstarch, and gently pick up a chick, dusting off any excess cornstarch from its bottom; place in the bowl of tempered chocolate. Using a free hand or chocolate-dipping fork, cover the chick with chocolate; lift out, and let the excess drip back into the bowl. Gently place the chick on the lined baking sheet; touch up any bare spots with a chocolate-coated finger. Allow to set at least 3 hours. Pipe on royal-icing eyes with a 1/32-inch (#1 Ateco) tip. Store in an airtight container until ready to serve, up to 2 weeks.

TEMPERED CHOCOLATE

MAKES ENOUGH FOR 2 DOZEN CHICKS

We used Valrhona chocolate; temperatures vary with different chocolates. Call the manufacturer or check the package for exact tempering temperatures for the chocolate you choose. Do not use a wooden spoon to stir. Be careful not to let any water droplets get in the bowl of chocolate, and be sure the thermometer tip is not touching the bottom of the bowl, or the temperature reading will be inaccurate.

1½ pounds good-quality dark or milk chocolate

1 Finely chop 1 pound of chocolate with a serrated knife, and place it in a metal bowl.

2 Bring a medium saucepan with about 2 inches of water to a simmer, and turn off the heat. Set the bowl of chopped chocolate over the saucepan, and melt the chocolate. Stir gently with a rubber spatula until the chocolate reaches 118°F on a chocolate thermometer.

3 Remove the bowl from the saucepan, and add the remaining ½ pound chocolate in one piece to the melted chocolate. Stir with a rubber spatula until the melted chocolate cools to 84°F. If necessary, remove the unmelted piece of chocolate, and reserve for future baking. Once the temperature reaches 84°F, place the bowl back over the saucepan.

4 For dark chocolate, stir until the thermometer reaches 88°F to 90°F. For milk chocolate, stir until the thermometer reaches 85°F to 88°F. Use immediately.

COCONUT-COATED MARSHMALLOW SHAPES

MAKES 10 NESTS OR 2 DOZEN BUNNIES

Use toasted angel flake coconut for an authentic-looking nest; fill with jelly beans. For fluffy bunnies, use untoasted macaroon coconut (also known as desiccated or unsweetened coconut).

2½ cups (7 ounces) angel flake coconut or 2 cups macaroon coconut

Marshmallow for Piping (page 84)

1 To make nests, preheat the oven to 350°F; toast the angel flake coconut on a rimmed baking sheet, stirring occasionally, until light brown, 7 to 10 minutes. Place the cooled coconut on a rimmed baking sheet or in shallow bowls.

2 Using a ½-inch (#11 Ateco) tip, pipe marshmallow onto the coconut, making a flat spiral about 3 inches in diameter. Build up the sides by spiraling up the edge of the disk, about ¾ inch. Completely cover the nest with coconut, filling the inside; allow to set a few minutes. Remove the excess coconut from the center of the nest. Repeat to make 10 nests.

3 To make bunnies, pipe marshmallow shapes directly onto untoasted macaroon coconut (see step 2 of Sugar-Coated Bunnies and Chicks recipe, page 84). Completely cover the bunnies with coconut, and allow to set a few minutes.

4 Transfer nests and bunnies to a parchment-lined airtight container until ready to serve, up to 2 weeks.

FLAT MARSHMALLOW SHAPES

MAKES 2 TO 3 DOZEN

1½ cups fine crystal colored sugar

Luster dust or sparkle dust (optional)

Marshmallow for Piping (page 84)

Single-Batch Royal Icing (page 84)

1 Fill a rimmed baking sheet or several shallow bowls with sugar. If desired, color white crystal sugar by stirring in luster dust or sparkle dust a little at a time, using a toothpick.

2 For flat bunnies, use a ½-inch (#11 Ateco) tip; start with the tail, and pipe an outline directly onto the sugar. In a continuous motion, fill in the center of the shape. Using a damp finger, pat down any spikes left from piping. Working quickly, use a spoon to cover the shape with sugar, and allow it to set a few minutes. Pipe on royal-icing eyes using a 1/32-inch (#1 Ateco) tip. Place in

a parchment-lined airtight container until ready to serve, up to 2 weeks.

3 For flat chicks, use a ½-inch tip; start piping directly onto the sugar at the tail end. In a continuous motion, adding more pressure, form the body and head, pulling away from the head to create the beak. Working quickly, spoon sugar around and over the shape; allow to set a few minutes. Pipe on royal-icing eyes with a ¹/₃₂-inch tip, and store as above.

4 For large flowers, use a ½-inch tip, and pipe directly onto the sugar in a continuous motion, forming five petals 1 to 2 inches long, all connected in the center. Or form each petal individually, then connect them in the center. Using a damp finger, pat down any spikes left from piping; spoon the sugar around and over the shape. When the flower is set, pipe a mound in the center of the petals, and carefully cover the freshly piped center with a different color of sugar. Gently shake off excess. Place in a parchment-lined airtight container until ready to serve, up to 2 weeks.

5 For small flowers, use a ³/₁₆-inch (#4 Ateco) tip. Pipe directly onto the sugar in a continuous motion, forming the outline of a flower, finishing in the center. Pat down any spikes with a damp finger, cover with sugar, and store as above.

RAMPS

GRILLED RAMPS WITH ASPARAGUS

SERVES 4 TO 6 AS A SIDE DISH | **PHOTO-GRAPH ON PAGE 96**

Ramps mostly grow wild, so their season is short. Look for them in your market from late March to mid-May. They grow along the eastern seaboard and into Canada but are perhaps best loved in Appalachia, where festivals mark their season. Grill ramps quickly to make the most of their flavor.

1 bunch (about 20) ramps, well washed

1 bunch thin asparagus

3 tablespoons extra-virgin olive oil

Coarse salt and freshly ground pepper

1 Heat a grill or grill pan to medium-high heat. Trim and discard the root hairs from the ramps. Trim the tough ends from the asparagus.

2 Place the ramps and asparagus on a rimmed baking sheet or in a shallow baking dish. Drizzle with olive oil, and toss to coat evenly. Season with salt and pepper, and toss to combine.

3 Arrange the ramps and asparagus on the hot grill in a single layer. Grill until hot and grill marks appear, about 1 minute per side. Transfer to a platter, and serve hot or at room temperature.

THE SEDER RITUAL

CHAROSET

MAKES ABOUT 3 CUPS

Kosher wine is generally sweeter than other red wines and is essential to this recipe.

¾ cup walnuts

2 Granny Smith apples

¼ cup kosher red wine

2 tablespoons sugar

1 Preheat oven to 350°F. Place the walnuts in a single layer on a rimmed baking sheet; toast until they are lightly browned and aromatic, about 10 minutes. Set aside. When cool, chop coarsely.

2 Peel, core, and finely chop the apples. Add the wine, sugar, and chopped walnuts, and stir to combine. Serve.

EASTER AT THE BLUE BARN

CAVIAR AND CHOPPED EGGS ON BISCUITS

SERVES 8

3 large eggs

2 teaspoons Dijon mustard

1 tablespoon mayonnaise

Coarse salt and freshly ground pepper

16 whole-wheat digestive biscuits

2 fifty-gram tins black caviar

Freshly chopped chives, for garnish

1 Place the eggs in a saucepan with enough cold water to cover by two inches. Bring to a boil over medium-high heat. Cook for 1 minute, cover, and remove from the heat. Let stand for 10 minutes. Drain the eggs, cover with ice, and place under cold running water to stop the cooking.

2 Peel the eggs, and finely chop them. Place them in a bowl with the mustard and mayonnaise; stir to combine. Season with salt and pepper.

3 To serve, place a rounded teaspoon of egg mixture on a digestive biscuit, top with caviar, and garnish with chives.

WATERCRESS AND RAMP SOUP

SERVES 8

If ramps are unavailable in your area, using more leeks makes an equally delicious soup.

5 tablespoons unsalted butter

5 cups (7 to 8 medium) thinly sliced leeks, white and pale-green parts only, well washed

2 cups thinly sliced ramps, well washed

1 quart water

2 cups milk

2 medium (about 1 pound) russet potatoes, peeled and cut into ½-inch cubes

1 tablespoon plus ½ teaspoon coarse salt

¼ teaspoon freshly ground pepper

2 bunches (about 8 ounces) watercress, washed, tough ends trimmed

1 Melt 3 tablespoons butter in a 5-quart saucepan over medium heat. Add 3 cups leeks and 1 cup ramps; reduce the heat to medium-low. Sauté until tender, about 10 minutes. Add the water, 1 cup milk, potatoes, 1 tablespoon salt, and pepper; bring to a boil over high heat. Reduce the heat to medium-low, and simmer until the potatoes are tender, about 7 minutes. Add the watercress; raise the heat to medium. Cook about 3 minutes, until the watercress is tender and bright green. Cool slightly. Purée in 1-cup batches in the jar of a blender. Return all of the soup to the pot over low heat; add the remaining cup milk.

2 In a medium sauté pan, melt the remaining 2 tablespoons butter over medium-low heat. Add the remaining 2 cups leeks, remaining cup ramps, and ½ teaspoon salt. Sauté, stirring frequently, until the leeks are tender but still green, 5 to 10 minutes. Do not let them brown. Ladle the soup into bowls, and garnish with the leek mixture. Serve.

LEG OF LAMB WITH SPICY MUSTARD MARINADE

SERVES 8 TO 10

For the most flavorful results, the lamb should marinate overnight. Serve with Glazed Baby Carrots and Crab-Apple and Fresh Mint Jellies (recipes follow).

½ cup Dijon mustard
3 tablespoons freshly chopped rosemary
3 tablespoons soy sauce
2 garlic cloves, minced (2 teaspoons)
¼ teaspoon ground ginger
2 tablespoons olive oil
1 seven- to eight-pound leg of lamb (leg bone in, hip bone removed)

1 Whisk together the mustard, rosemary, soy sauce, garlic, ginger, and olive oil in a glass bowl.

2 Trim the lamb of excess fat; coat with the marinade using a pastry brush. Place on a rack in a roasting pan, and cover with plastic wrap. Marinate, refrigerated, 6 hours or overnight.

3 Remove the lamb from the refrigerator, and let sit at room temperature for 1 hour.

4 Preheat the oven to 450°F. Place the lamb in the oven; immediately reduce the temperature to 350°F. Roast for 15 to 20 minutes per pound. To check doneness, insert an instant-read thermometer into the thickest part of the meat, without touching the bone. The temperature should register 135°F to 140°F for medium rare (2 hours 15 minutes for a 7½-pound leg of lamb). Let rest at least 15 minutes before carving.

5 Carve the meat with the tip end of the lamb bone toward you. Slice away from you and toward 2 o'clock, holding the knife parallel to the bone. Slice thin or thick pieces according to your preference, turning the lamb as you carve.

GLAZED BABY CARROTS WITH CHIVES

SERVES 8

2 pounds baby carrots
1 tablespoon unsalted butter
1 tablespoon sugar
1 teaspoon coarse salt
1 tablespoon snipped chives

In a 12-inch sauté pan over high heat, place the carrots, butter, sugar, salt, and enough water to cover. Bring to a simmer. Cook at a gentle boil until tender and slightly caramelized, about 15 minutes. Serve garnished with chives.

CRAB-APPLE JELLY

MAKES ABOUT 4 CUPS

Make this jelly in the fall, when crab apples are plentiful. Can it and enjoy throughout the year.

4 pounds crab apples
1½ quarts water
3 cups sugar

1 Wash and quarter the apples; place in a 6-quart saucepan. Add the water, place over medium-high heat, and bring to a boil. Reduce to a simmer. Cook until very soft, 45 to 60 minutes, and remove from the heat. Pour the apples into a bowl through a fine sieve lined with two layers of damp cheesecloth. Gather the cheesecloth, and tie into a bundle. Suspend from a wooden-spoon handle set over the bowl; drain, without pressing solids, for 1 hour, to yield about 4 cups juice.

2 Place the juice in a saucepan over medium-high heat; bring to a simmer. Cook for 10 minutes, and skim the foam. Add the sugar; stir to dissolve. Clip on a candy thermometer. Cook until the temperature reaches 220°F, skimming the foam. Pour into sterilized jars, let cool, and keep refrigerated for up to 6 months.

FRESH MINT JELLY

MAKES 1 EIGHT-INCH-SQUARE PAN

You can substitute three tablespoons powdered pectin for liquid pectin. Dissolve it in a half cup of warm water before adding to the mint mixture.

2 cups firmly packed mint leaves and stems (3 to 4 bunches)
2 cups water
3 tablespoons freshly squeezed, strained lemon juice
3½ cups sugar
3 ounces liquid pectin
2 drops green gel-paste or liquid food coloring

1 Place the mint and water in the jar of a blender; blend for 10 seconds until the mint is finely chopped. Pour into a medium saucepan, and bring to a boil. Cover, and remove from the heat. Let steep for 45 minutes to infuse the flavors. Strain mint into a bowl through a fine sieve lined with damp cheesecloth, squeezing out all the liquid to yield 1¾ to 2 cups liquid.

2 Place the mint and water in a clean saucepan; add the lemon juice and sugar. Bring to a boil; cook for 1 minute, skimming the foam. Add the pectin, and return to a full boil. Cook 1 minute more. Remove from the heat; stir in the food coloring. Skim the surface. Pour into an 8-inch-square baking pan; let cool on a rack. Cover with plastic wrap, and chill overnight.

3 Run a paring knife around the edges of the pan. Slice the jelly into ½-inch cubes. Use an offset spatula to lift them from the pan; transfer to a serving dish.

BLACKBERRY TARTLETS

MAKES 8 | **PHOTOGRAPH ON PAGE 102**

If you have enough tartlet pans, place a second one inside each dough-lined pan during baking. This will keep the crust from shrinking down the sides. You can also line tartlet shells with parchment paper and dried beans; the shells will take a few minutes longer to bake.

Pâte Brisée (page 10)
All-purpose flour, for work surface
1 pint (2½ cups) blackberries
¼ cup sugar
1 teaspoon grated lemon zest
1 cup heavy cream
Elderflower Ice Cream (recipe follows)
8 fresh pansies, for garnish (optional)

1 Divide the dough evenly into 8 pieces. On a lightly floured surface, roll out each piece into a rough circle ⅛ inch thick; fit into eight fluted tartlet pans (3½ inches in diameter, 1½ inches deep). Chill for at least 30 minutes.

2 Preheat the oven to 375°F. Line each tartlet shell with a second pan or parchment paper and dry beans. Transfer pans to a rimmed baking sheet, and place in the oven; bake until golden brown, 20 to 25 minutes. Remove the top pans or parchment lining; return the baking sheet to the oven if the bottoms of the shells are not fully browned. Set on a wire rack until completely cool.

3 Fill a bowl with ice and water; set aside. Place the blackberries, 2 tablespoons sugar, and lemon zest in a medium saucepan over medium heat. Cook until the berries release their juices, the sugar dissolves, and the mixture begins to bubble, about 5 minutes. Remove from the heat, and set the pan in the ice bath to cool.

4 Chill a bowl and a large whisk. Place the cream and the remaining 2 tablespoons sugar in the bowl; whip until soft peaks form. Fold ½ cup berry mixture into the whipped cream. Fill the tartlet shells with the mixture; top with the remaining mixture. Serve with elderflower ice cream, and garnish with fresh pansies, if using.

ELDERFLOWER ICE CREAM

MAKES ABOUT 1 QUART

Elderflower cordial makes this ice cream an unusual accompaniment to blackberry tartlets; you may also omit the cordial to make delicious vanilla ice cream.

1 whole vanilla bean
2 cups milk
6 large egg yolks
¾ cup sugar
2 cups very cold heavy cream
1 cup elderflower cordial

1 Split the vanilla bean lengthwise with a sharp paring knife. Place in a medium saucepan with the milk. Bring to a gentle boil, and remove from the heat.

2 Combine the egg yolks and sugar in the bowl of an electric mixer fitted with the whisk attachment. Beat on medium-high speed until pale yellow, 3 to 5 minutes. Fill a large bowl with ice and water, and set aside.

3 Using a measuring cup or ladle, slowly pour about ½ cup of the hot milk into the egg-yolk mixture, whisking constantly on low speed until blended. Keep adding milk, about ½ cup at a time, until all has been added. Whisk until combined.

4 Pour the mixture back into the saucepan; cook over medium heat, stirring constantly with a wooden spoon, 3 to 5 minutes, until the mixture is thick enough to retain a line drawn across the back of the spoon with your finger.

5 Remove the pan from the heat; immediately stir in the cold cream to stop the cooking. Pour the custard through a fine sieve into a medium bowl set in the ice bath to chill; stir occasionally until cooled. Stir the elderflower cordial into the cooled custard. Cover the bowl; transfer to the refrigerator to chill, at least 30 minutes or overnight.

6 Pour the custard into a chilled ice-cream maker; prepare according to the manufacturer's instructions (ice cream will be just set when done). Transfer the soft ice cream to an airtight container; freeze at least 4 hours or up to 1 week.

BRANDY SNAPS

MAKES 1½ DOZEN

You may substitute dark corn syrup for the golden syrup, but the flavor will differ slightly. If the cookies get difficult to shape, return them to the oven for a few seconds until they soften.

½ cup all-purpose flour
½ teaspoon ground ginger
5 tablespoons unsalted butter
⅓ cup sugar
¼ cup golden syrup

1 Preheat the oven to 350°F. Combine the flour and ginger with a whisk. Melt the butter in a small saucepan over medium heat. Add the sugar and golden syrup; cook, stirring with a wooden spoon, until the sugar has dissolved. Remove from the heat, and stir in the flour-ginger mixture.

2 Line a rimmed baking sheet with a Silpat baking mat or parchment paper. Drop 6 even tablespoons of batter about 2 inches apart onto the Silpat; place in the oven. Bake until flat and golden brown, about 10 minutes.

3 Let the cookies cool 2 minutes, until slightly firm; immediately wrap them, one at a time, around a wide round wooden spoon handle, and let set for 30 seconds. Transfer from the spoon handle to a wire rack. Repeat with the remaining batter.

MUSTARD

TUNA WITH MUSTARD SEED CRUST

SERVES 4 | **PHOTOGRAPH ON PAGE 98**

You can also coat whole tuna steaks or salmon fillets with the crust mixture.

2 one-pound sushi-quality tuna steaks, 1½ inches thick
½ cup mustard seeds
1 teaspoon coarse salt
½ teaspoon freshly ground pepper
3 tablespoons extra-virgin olive oil, or more to taste
1 small bunch arugula
2 lemons, halved

1 Using a sharp knife, slice each tuna steak into pieces that are about 1½ inches square. Grind the mustard seeds to a coarse powder in a spice grinder. Combine the ground seeds with salt and pepper; spread the mixture on a plate.
2 Dredge each piece of tuna in the mustard mixture, gently pressing the ground seeds against the tuna so that they adhere.
3 Place a large skillet over medium heat; let stand about 1 minute so the skillet feels hot when you place your palm just above it. Add 1½ tablespoons olive oil to the skillet. Heat the oil until it is hot but not smoking, about 1 minute more.
4 Carefully arrange the pieces of tuna in the skillet about 1 inch apart (it is easiest to cook 2 pieces at a time; if you do so, add 1½ tablespoons oil for the second batch). Sear the tuna about 1 minute, until it releases easily from the skillet and the crust is a deep golden brown. Continue the process until all sides are seared. (The tuna will be very rare in the center; if you want it more well done, increase the cooking time and reduce the heat, if necessary.)
5 Arrange the tuna on four plates, each with a handful of arugula and half a lemon. Drizzle the arugula with the remaining 1½ tablespoons olive oil.

WARM MUSTARD AND OLIVE OIL SAUCE

MAKES ¾ CUP | **PHOTOGRAPH ON PAGE 98**

This sauce is a good alternative to hollandaise. Serve with asparagus, poached eggs, and smoked salmon for a delicious brunch dish.

1 cup dry white wine
½ cup champagne vinegar, or other mild-flavored vinegar, such as rice-wine vinegar
2 large egg yolks
½ cup extra-virgin olive oil
1 tablespoon Dijon mustard
Coarse salt and freshly ground pepper

1 Combine the wine and vinegar in a small saucepan. Bring to a simmer over medium-high heat. Reduce the heat to medium, and simmer until the liquid is reduced by three-quarters, about 12 minutes.
2 Set a heat-proof bowl or the top of a double boiler over a pan of barely simmering water. Transfer the reduced liquid to the bowl. Lightly beat the egg yolks, and whisk them into the wine reduction, whisking constantly until the mixture is thick enough to form ribbons, about 3 minutes.
3 Remove from the heat, and slowly add the olive oil, pouring in a steady stream and whisking constantly until all the oil is incorporated. Whisk in the mustard, and season with salt and pepper. Serve immediately.

PERFECT MUSTARD VINAIGRETTE

MAKES 1⅓ CUPS | **PHOTOGRAPH ON PAGE 101**

Extra-virgin olive oil yields a flavorful, rich vinaigrette. If you prefer a lighter taste, try using vegetable or canola oil.

2 tablespoons Dijon mustard
⅓ cup champagne vinegar, or other mild-flavored vinegar, such as rice-wine vinegar
1 cup extra-virgin olive oil
½ teaspoon coarse salt, or more to taste
¼ teaspoon freshly ground pepper, or more to taste

Whisk the mustard and vinegar together in a small bowl. Slowly add the oil in a steady stream, whisking constantly until all the oil is added and the dressing is creamy and emulsified. Add the salt and pepper; season with additional salt and pepper if desired.

GRILLED CHEESE WITH GRAINY MUSTARD

SERVES 4

We used cheddar cheese in these sandwiches, but any type of cheese that oozes when it melts, such as Swiss, will produce sandwiches just as delicious.

2 tablespoons unsalted butter, room temperature
8 slices hearty whole-grain or other bread, about ⅓ inch thick
3 tablespoons grainy mustard, or more to taste
6 ounces sharp cheddar cheese, thinly sliced

1 Preheat oven to 300°F. Spread the butter over one side of each slice of bread.
2 Arrange the bread, butter side down, on a piece of plastic wrap or wax paper. Spread each slice with mustard. Arrange the cheese over 4 slices of bread, and sandwich together with the remaining bread, butter side out.
3 Set a large cast-iron skillet or sauté pan over medium heat. Working in batches, use a spatula to press down firmly on the sandwiches. Cook until the bread is golden brown, 2 to 3 minutes. Reduce the heat to medium-low. Turn the sandwiches over, press down with the spatula, and cook until the bread is golden and the cheese is starting to melt, about 2 minutes more.
4 Transfer the sandwiches to a baking sheet, and place in the oven. Bake until the cheese is completely melted.

POACHED CHICKEN WITH HOT ENGLISH MUSTARD

SERVES 4 | PHOTOGRAPH ON PAGE 98

This recipe yields excess chicken stock.
The excess can be kept in plastic containers
and frozen for up to four months.

2 carrots, cut in half
1 celery stalk, cut in half
2 onions, cut in half
3 stems fresh flat-leaf parsley
10 whole black peppercorns
1 four-pound whole chicken
  Coarse salt
4 slices French bread, about ⅓ inch thick
1 tablespoon extra-virgin olive oil
1 small bunch watercress
¼ cup hot English mustard, or to taste

1 Place the carrots, celery, onions, parsley, and peppercorns in a stockpot. Rinse the chicken with cold water, and pat dry. Add the chicken to the pot, and fill with enough cold water to cover the chicken by 1 inch.
2 Set the stockpot over medium-high heat, and bring the water to a boil. Reduce the heat, and allow to simmer, covered, for 1 hour, skimming off any foam that rises to the surface.
3 Fill a large bowl with ice and water; set aside. Remove the chicken from the pot; set aside. Strain the stock through a very fine sieve or chinois; discard the solids. Transfer the stock to a metal bowl, and set the bowl in the ice bath. Let stand until the stock is completely chilled and the fat can be skimmed off the surface, replacing ice if necessary.
4 Meanwhile, when the chicken is cool enough to handle, remove the skin and discard. Carefully pull the meat off the bones; it should fall away easily. Keep the meat in large chunks when possible.
5 Return 5 cups of stock to the stockpot or a large saucepan. Bring to a boil; adjust seasoning with salt. Reduce the heat to a simmer; simmer uncovered until the stock has become very flavorful and reduced by 1 cup, about 15 minutes. Add the pieces of chicken; cook just until the chicken is heated through, about 5 minutes.

6 Toast the bread until golden, and brush with olive oil. Serve the chicken in a wide bowl with a ladleful of hot broth. Add a handful of watercress to each bowl. Place a spoonful of mustard on the toast, sprinkle with salt, and serve on the side.

COLD POACHED MUSSELS WITH CREAMY MUSTARD SAUCE

SERVES 4 AS AN APPETIZER | PHOTO-GRAPH ON PAGE 99

Poach the mussels in advance so they have
time to chill, and assemble just before
serving. Sour cream makes a fine substitute
for crème fraîche.

2 tablespoons unsalted butter
3 shallots, finely chopped
1 garlic clove, minced
½ teaspoon coarse salt, plus more for seasoning
¼ teaspoon freshly ground pepper, plus more for seasoning
2 pounds mussels, rinsed, debearded, and scrubbed
1 cup dry white wine
¾ cup crème fraîche
1 tablespoon Dijon mustard, or more to taste
2 teaspoons champagne vinegar, or other mild-flavored vinegar, such as rice-wine vinegar
  Zest of ½ lemon
¼ cup loosely packed fresh chervil leaves, snipped

1 Melt the butter in a high-sided medium saucepan over medium heat. Add the shallots and garlic. Cook, stirring, until the shallots are translucent and the garlic is very fragrant but not brown, about 2 minutes. Add the salt and pepper. Add the mussels and wine. Cover the saucepan, and cook until the mussels open and are cooked through, about 8 minutes. Discard any mussels that have not opened.

2 Remove the mussels from the saucepan with a slotted spoon. Transfer the cooking liquid to a small bowl, and set aside to cool; when cool, transfer to the refrigerator to chill.
3 Remove the mussels from the shells, reserving the shells for serving, if desired. Place the mussels in a small bowl, cover with plastic wrap, and transfer to the refrigerator.
4 Whisk together the crème fraîche, mustard, and vinegar. Stir the reserved cooking liquid, and add about 4 tablespoons of it to the crème-fraîche mixture to make a nice thin sauce with just enough body to cling to the mussels. Adjust the seasoning with salt and pepper and more mustard, if desired. Stir in half the lemon zest and half the chervil.
5 Gently toss the cold mussels in the mustard sauce. Spoon a mussel and a large puddle of sauce into each reserved mussel shell. Sprinkle the mussels with the remaining lemon zest and chervil, and serve with any remaining sauce on the side.

POTATO GRATIN WITH MUSTARD

SERVES 6 TO 8

The size of the baking dish will affect the
gratin's cooking time. If your dish is slightly
smaller than the one suggested, increase
the cooking time; if slightly larger, reduce
the cooking time.

1 tablespoon unsalted butter, room temperature
6 Yukon gold potatoes (about 2 pounds), sliced ¼ inch thick
1 garlic clove, cut in half
3 cups milk
1 cup heavy cream
¼ cup Dijon mustard
  Coarse salt and freshly ground pepper
1 tablespoon all-purpose flour
4 ounces Gruyère cheese, grated on the large holes of a box grater
2 teaspoons yellow or brown mustard seeds

1 Preheat oven to 325°F. Brush a shallow, oval baking dish (about 12-by-7 inches) with butter.

2 In a high-sided medium saucepan, combine the sliced potatoes, garlic, and milk, and set over high heat. Bring to a boil, then reduce heat, and let simmer until the potatoes just begin to get tender, about 8 minutes.

3 Drain the potatoes, reserving 1 cup milk. Combine the reserved cup of milk with the heavy cream. Whisk in the mustard. Season well with salt and pepper.

4 Layer the potatoes in the baking dish, sprinkling the flour and scattering cheese between each layer but reserving half the cheese for the top. Pour the cream mixture over the potatoes; the liquid should come just to the top of the potatoes.

5 Scatter the remaining cheese over the top of the gratin; sprinkle with the mustard seeds. Bake until the potatoes are completely soft when pricked with a fork and the cream has thickened and is just starting to bubble up but is not boiling, about 25 minutes. Turn the oven to broil. Position the oven rack in the top slot. Transfer the gratin to the rack, and broil until the top is golden brown, about 3 minutes. Serve hot.

STEAMED ARTICHOKES WITH GRAINY MUSTARD AND BACON DRESSING

SERVES 4 | PHOTOGRAPH ON PAGE 98

The dressing is best when made and served immediately. The artichokes, however, can be prepared in advance.

4 large artichokes
  Juice of 4 lemons, halves reserved
1 teaspoon coarse salt, plus more
  for seasoning
1 teaspoon whole black peppercorns
  Large sprig fresh thyme
2 garlic cloves
2 tablespoons extra-virgin olive oil, plus
  more for vegetable-cooking liquid
6 strips thick bacon, cut into
  ¼-inch pieces
2 shallots, finely chopped
2 carrots, finely diced
1 celery stalk, strings removed,
  finely diced
2½ tablespoons grainy mustard,
  or more to taste
  Freshly ground black pepper

1 Fill a bowl with ice and water; set aside. Snap off the tough outer leaves of each artichoke. Cut each artichoke in half lengthwise, and cut off and discard the top quarter. Snip the remaining leaf tips with scissors. Trim the bottom of the stem; using a vegetable peeler, peel off the tough outer skin. Spread the leaves to gain easier access to the choke, scoop it out with a melon baller, then rub some lemon juice onto the heart. Pour the remaining lemon juice into the ice bath; add the reserved lemon halves and artichokes to the ice bath.

2 Fill a saucepan large enough to accommodate all of the artichokes and 2 inches of water. Add the salt, peppercorns, thyme, garlic, and olive oil; bring to a simmer. Add the artichokes, stem end up; cover the saucepan. Steam until tender, about 25 minutes. The leaves should pull off easily; the heart should feel tender when pierced. Drain well. Cool to room temperature.

3 Meanwhile, cook the bacon in a large sauté pan over medium-low heat until it is brown and crisp and the fat is rendered. Using a slotted spoon, remove the bacon from the pan, and set aside.

4 Depending on the amount of bacon fat in the pan, add enough olive oil to make a total of ⅓ cup fat and oil. Add the shallots, carrots, and celery, and cook until the vegetables are soft and fragrant, about 4 minutes. Stir in the grainy mustard, and season with salt and pepper. Return the reserved bacon to the pan. Arrange the artichokes on a serving platter. Spoon the hot mixture into the cavity of each artichoke. Serve.

HOT MUSTARD BISCUITS

MAKES ABOUT 1½ DOZEN

These biscuits go well with ham. When preparing them, dip the biscuit cutter in a little flour before cutting the dough to keep it from sticking. Be economical when cutting the biscuits to get as many of them from the dough as possible. The dough can be reformed and patted out again, though this may toughen the biscuits.

8 tablespoons (1 stick) plus 1
  tablespoon cold unsalted butter,
  cut into small pieces
2 small shallots, minced
1½ tablespoons fresh rosemary, chopped
3½ cups all-purpose flour, plus
  more for surface
2½ teaspoons baking powder
¼ cup plus 1 tablespoon ground mustard
½ teaspoon coarse salt
¼ cup pure vegetable shortening, cold
1 cup milk
¼ cup grainy mustard
3 tablespoons honey

1 Preheat oven to 425°F. Melt 1 tablespoon butter in a sauté pan over medium heat. Stir in the shallots and rosemary; cook until the shallots are soft, about 2 minutes. Set aside.

2 In a large bowl, whisk together the flour, baking powder, ¼ cup ground mustard, and salt. Using two knives or a pastry cutter, cut the remaining 8 tablespoons butter into the dry ingredients until the mixture is coarse and crumbly. Cut in the shortening.

3 Line a baking sheet with parchment paper, and set aside. Combine the milk, mustard, and reserved shallot-and-rosemary mixture. Make a well in the center of the dry ingredients, and pour in the milk mixture. Slowly mix in the dry ingredients until they are completely incorporated. Make sure the dough is mixed well but not overworked. Turn the dough out onto a lightly floured work surface. Pat into a rectangular shape about 1 inch thick. Using a 2-inch biscuit cutter, cut out biscuits, and transfer to the parchment-lined baking sheet.

4 Transfer biscuits to the oven to bake. Combine the remaining tablespoon ground mustard with the honey, stirring until smooth. When the biscuits are puffed up and golden brown, about 25 minutes, remove them from the oven, and brush with the mustard glaze. Return them to the oven, and bake 5 minutes more. Serve hot.

WHAT TO HAVE FOR DINNER

menu

ROMAINE SALAD WITH PROSCIUTTO CRISPS

ALMOND CRUSTED CHICKEN

ORZO WITH PEAS AND MINT

MARSALA CHEESE TART WITH ORANGES

ROMAINE SALAD WITH PROSCIUTTO CRISPS

SERVES 4 | **PHOTOGRAPH ON PAGE 100**

The small inner leaves of romaine lettuce are tender and crisp, perfect for this salad. Use a vegetable peeler to shave the Pecorino Romano.

2 tablespoons extra-virgin olive oil, plus more for pan

4 slices (about 2 ounces) prosciutto

1 tablespoon balsamic vinegar

1 teaspoon fresh thyme leaves, coarsely chopped

Coarse salt and freshly ground pepper

6 ounces romaine hearts, leaves torn in half

1 ounce Pecorino Romano cheese, shaved

1 Preheat the oven to 400°F. Lightly brush a rimmed baking sheet with olive oil, and arrange the prosciutto in a single layer. Place in the oven, and bake until crisp, 5 to 10 minutes. Remove from the oven, and let cool on a wire rack.
2 Combine the olive oil, balsamic vinegar, and thyme in a bowl; season with salt and pepper, and whisk to combine. Add the romaine and shaved Pecorino Romano; toss to combine. Arrange on 4 plates; serve topped with the prosciutto crisps.

ALMOND CRUSTED CHICKEN

SERVES 4 | **PHOTOGRAPH ON PAGE 100**

¾ cup dry bread crumbs

Coarse salt and freshly ground pepper

2 large eggs

2 teaspoons water

2 whole boneless, skinless chicken breasts (1½ to 2 pounds), split

1½ cups sliced almonds, broken into pieces

2 tablespoons unsalted butter

2 tablespoons canola oil

1 Preheat the oven to 400°F. In a medium bowl, season the bread crumbs with salt and pepper. Place the eggs in a small bowl with the water, and beat lightly. Dip the chicken in the egg, wiping away the excess with your fingers, then dredge in the bread-crumb mixture until lightly coated. Dip the chicken in the egg again, and coat thoroughly with the almonds.
2 Heat the butter and oil in a 12-inch ovenproof skillet over medium heat. Sauté the chicken until nicely browned, about 3 minutes, and turn over. Cook 1 minute more. Transfer the pan to the oven, and bake until the chicken is cooked through, about 10 minutes.

ORZO WITH PEAS AND MINT

SERVES 4 | **PHOTOGRAPH ON PAGE 100**

1 cup orzo (Greek pasta)

2 tablespoons unsalted butter

1 shallot, minced (about 2 tablespoons)

Zest of 1 lemon

1 pound fresh peas, shelled, or 2 cups defrosted frozen peas

Coarse salt and freshly ground pepper

2 tablespoons freshly chopped mint

1 Cook the orzo according to the package directions. Melt the butter in a medium saucepan over medium heat. Add the shallot and lemon zest, and sauté until translucent.
2 Add the peas, and cook until bright green and tender, adding a little water if the shallots brown before the peas are tender.
3 Add the cooked orzo, season with salt and pepper, and toss to combine. Remove from the heat, and stir in the mint. Serve immediately.

MARSALA CHEESE TART WITH ORANGES

MAKES 1 EIGHT-INCH TART

5 ounces gingersnaps, broken into pieces

4 tablespoons unsalted butter, melted

8 ounces cream cheese, room temperature

½ cup sugar

2 tablespoons Marsala wine

1 teaspoon pure vanilla extract

½ cup heavy cream

3 navel oranges

1 Place the gingersnaps in the bowl of a food processor, and process until finely ground. Transfer to a bowl, add the melted butter, and stir until well combined. Transfer to an 8-inch fluted tart pan with a removable bottom, and press into bottom and up sides to form an even crust. Place in the freezer.
2 Place the cream cheese and sugar in the bowl of an electric mixer fitted with the paddle attachment; beat until fluffy. Add the Marsala and vanilla extract, and beat until combined. Whip the heavy cream to stiff peaks, and fold into the cream-cheese mixture. Spoon the mixture into the prepared crust; return to the freezer for at least 1 hour 15 minutes or until firm.
3 Cut the ends off the oranges, and remove the peel, pith, and outer membranes, following the curve of the fruit with a paring knife. Lift the sections away from the inner membranes. Serve the tart garnished with the orange sections.

FIT TO EAT: SPINACH DISHES

SPINACH DILL PIE

SERVES 6 TO 8

Serve this pie warm or at room temperature. For brunch, couple it with a green salad.

10 ounces fresh spinach, well washed, tough stems removed
1 tablespoon unsalted butter
1 onion, cut into ¼-inch pieces
2 garlic cloves, minced
1 cup low-fat ricotta cheese
2 large whole eggs
2 large egg whites
2 tablespoons finely chopped fresh flat-leaf parsley
¼ cup chopped fresh dill
1 cup (about 2 ounces) freshly grated Parmesan cheese
¼ teaspoon ground cumin
½ teaspoon coarse salt
¼ teaspoon freshly ground pepper
8 sheets phyllo dough, thawed
   Vegetable-oil cooking spray

1 Preheat the oven to 375°F. Coarsely chop the spinach leaves; set aside. Heat the butter in a nonstick skillet over medium heat. Add the onion and garlic, and cook until tender, about 3 minutes. Add the spinach; cook until wilted and bright green, about 2 minutes. Transfer the mixture to a colander to cool and drain. When the mixture is cool enough to handle, press lightly with paper towels to remove excess moisture; set aside to cool completely.
2 In a medium bowl, combine the ricotta, eggs, egg whites, parsley, dill, Parmesan, cumin, salt, and pepper. Stir in the cooled spinach mixture; set aside.
3 Dampen a large kitchen towel with water, and squeeze dry. Unroll the phyllo; place on a work surface. Cover with plastic wrap and then the kitchen towel. Lightly coat a 9-inch ovenproof pie plate with cooking spray. Remove 1 sheet of phyllo, keeping the remaining phyllo covered; place in the prepared baking dish. Coat lightly with cooking spray. Repeat with

the remaining 7 sheets of phyllo, spraying between each layer. Trim the edges with scissors, leaving a slight overhang.
4 Spoon the filling into the dish, spreading it evenly. Bake until the phyllo is golden brown and the filling is set, about 1 hour. Cool for at least 15 minutes before cutting into wedges.

PER SERVING: 217 CALORIES, 9 G FAT, 81 MG CHOLESTEROL, 21 G CARBOHYDRATE, 463 MG SODIUM, 13 G PROTEIN, 2 G FIBER

SPINACH SALAD

SERVES 6

It is much healthier, and just as flavorful, to wilt the spinach in a salad with a warm beet dressing instead of hot bacon dressing.

1 red onion, sliced into ¼-inch rings
2 to 3 slices whole-grain bread, cubed
8 ounces (about 2 small) beets
¼ cup extra-virgin olive oil
1 small shallot, minced
1 tablespoon honey mustard
¼ cup red-wine vinegar
2 tablespoons sugar
½ teaspoon coarse salt
¼ teaspoon freshly ground pepper
12 ounces spinach, well washed, stems removed
4 ounces button mushrooms, wiped clean, stems trimmed, sliced

1 Preheat the oven to 350°F. Fill a bowl with ice and water; add the onion. Let sit for 30 minutes. Drain, and set aside. Meanwhile, place the bread on a baking tray; toast, tossing occasionally, until golden and crisp, 10 to 15 minutes; set the croutons aside to cool.
2 Place the beets in a small saucepan, and cover with cold water. Bring to a boil, and cook until tender, about 30 minutes. Drain; when cool enough to be handled, peel and cut into ½-inch cubes. Set aside.

3 While the beets are cooking, make the dressing: Heat 1 tablespoon olive oil in a medium skillet over medium heat. Add the shallot, and cook until tender, about 3 minutes. Whisk in the honey mustard, vinegar, sugar, salt, and pepper. Cook, whisking constantly, until the sugar has dissolved, about 1 minute. Slowly whisk in the remaining 3 tablespoons olive oil. Reduce the heat to low; keep the dressing warm. Add the cooked beet cubes to the dressing, and stir to coat.
4 Place the onions, spinach, and mushrooms in a bowl. Drizzle with the warm dressing; toss to coat evenly. Garnish with croutons. Serve warm or at room temperature.

PER SERVING: 193 CALORIES, 10 G FAT, 0 MG CHOLESTEROL, 25 G CARBOHYDRATE, 361 MG SODIUM, 5 G PROTEIN, 4 G FIBER

"CREAMED" SPINACH

SERVES 4 | PHOTOGRAPH ON PAGE 100

1¼ pounds (2 bunches) spinach, well washed, tough stems removed
1 cup skim milk
1 teaspoon whole black peppercorns
2 dried bay leaves
4 whole cloves
2 tablespoons unsalted butter
2 tablespoons all-purpose flour
½ teaspoon coarse salt
¼ teaspoon white pepper
¼ teaspoon freshly grated nutmeg
2 tablespoons half-and-half
1 medium onion, cut into ¼-inch pieces

1 Roughly chop the spinach leaves; set aside. Combine the milk, peppercorns, bay leaves, and cloves in a small saucepan. Warm over medium heat until hot but not boiling. Remove from the heat, cover, and let steep for 30 minutes. Strain into a bowl or measuring cup, discarding solids; set aside.
2 Melt 1 tablespoon butter in a saucepan over medium heat. Whisk in the flour;

cook, whisking constantly, for 1 minute. Gradually whisk in the milk mixture. Cook, whisking constantly, until the mixture thickens, about 3 minutes. Stir in the salt, white pepper, nutmeg, and half-and-half. Cover, and keep warm over low heat.

3 Heat the remaining tablespoon butter in a large nonstick skillet over medium-low heat. Add the onion; cook until tender, about 5 minutes. Add the spinach a little at a time; turn with tongs until all the spinach is added and just wilted. Pour the sauce over the spinach, and stir to combine. Serve immediately.

PER SERVING: 146 CALORIES, 7 G FAT, 19 MG CHOLESTEROL, 17 G CARBOHYDRATE, 465 MG SODIUM, 8 G PROTEIN, 4 G FIBER

SPINACH SOUFFLE

SERVES 6

Serve this soufflé immediately in the dish, or let cool and unmold for a denser version.

3 tablespoons bread crumbs

10 ounces spinach, well washed, tough stems removed

1 tablespoon plus 1 teaspoon unsalted butter

3 tablespoons all-purpose flour

1½ cups skim milk

½ teaspoon coarse salt

¼ teaspoon freshly ground pepper

2 whole large eggs, separated

1 cup (2 ounces) freshly grated Parmesan cheese

2 large egg whites
Pinch of cream of tartar
Vegetable-oil cooking spray

1 Preheat the oven to 400°F. Position the rack in the center of the oven. Coat a 2-quart soufflé dish or six individual (8-ounce) dishes with cooking spray. Coat with the bread crumbs. Tap out excess; set aside.

2 Fill a bowl with ice and water; set aside. Place a steamer basket in a medium saucepan filled with 1 inch of water. Bring to a boil, and add the spinach. Steam until wilted, about 3 minutes. Drain, and plunge into the ice bath to stop the cooking. Let cool, and squeeze out excess water. Place the spinach in the bowl of a

food processor; pulse until finely chopped; set aside. You should have about 1 cup.

3 Melt the butter in a small saucepan over medium heat. Whisk in the flour, and cook, stirring constantly, for 3 minutes. Gradually whisk in the milk, and bring just to a simmer. Cook, stirring constantly, until slightly thickened, about 3 minutes. Stir in the salt and pepper. Remove from the heat, and set the white sauce aside.

4 In a large bowl, whisk together the 2 egg yolks until blended. Whisk in a little white sauce to temper the eggs, then add the remaining sauce, whisking until combined. Add the cooked spinach and grated cheese.

5 Place the 4 egg whites and cream of tartar in the bowl of an electric mixer fitted with the whisk attachment. Beat on low until soft peaks begin to form. Increase the speed to high; beat until stiff peaks form and the egg whites are smooth.

6 Using a rubber spatula, transfer one third of the egg whites to the spinach mixture; gently fold in until blended. Add the spinach mixture to the remaining egg whites; gently fold in until just combined. Pour into the prepared dish or dishes.

7 Place the soufflé in the oven, and reduce the heat to 375°F. Bake until puffed and golden, 20 to 30 minutes. Serve.

PER SERVING: 149 CALORIES, 7 G FAT, 85 MG CHOLESTEROL, 11 G CARBOHYDRATE, 488 MG SODIUM, 11 G PROTEIN, 2 G FIBER

SPINACH EGG BROTH

SERVES 4 | **PHOTOGRAPH ON PAGE 97**

This recipe can easily be doubled.

5 ounces spinach, well washed, tough stems removed

1 onion, coarsely chopped

2 carrots, coarsely chopped

2 celery stalks, strings removed, coarsely chopped

¼ cup dry white wine

2 fourteen-and-a-half-ounce cans low-sodium chicken broth, or Homemade Chicken Stock (page 8), skimmed of fat

2 cups water

1 teaspoon whole black peppercorns

2 dried bay leaves

3 large eggs, lightly beaten

1 teaspoon coarse salt

¼ teaspoon freshly ground black pepper

1 Cut the spinach leaves into ½-inch strips; set aside. Add the onion, carrots, and celery to a saucepan set over medium heat. Cook, stirring occasionally, until the vegetables are golden and tender, about 10 minutes.

2 Add the wine, and cook until evaporated, about 3 minutes, stirring with a wooden spoon to loosen any browned bits on the bottom of the pan.

3 Add the stock, water, peppercorns, and bay leaves; bring to a boil. Reduce to a gentle simmer, and cook 30 minutes to allow the flavors to infuse.

4 Strain the stock through a fine sieve, discarding the solids. Place the strained stock in a clean saucepan, and bring to a simmer. Add the beaten eggs, stirring gently so they form long threads. Stir in the spinach, and cook until just wilted, about 1 minute. Season with salt and pepper, and serve immediately.

PER SERVING: 85 CALORIES, 4 G FAT, 160 MG CHOLESTEROL, 2 G CARBOHYDRATE, 719 MG SODIUM, 6 G PROTEIN, 1 G FIBER

CLASSIC FRENCH TOAST | **PAGE 82**

GRILLED RAMPS WITH
ASPARAGUS | PAGE 86

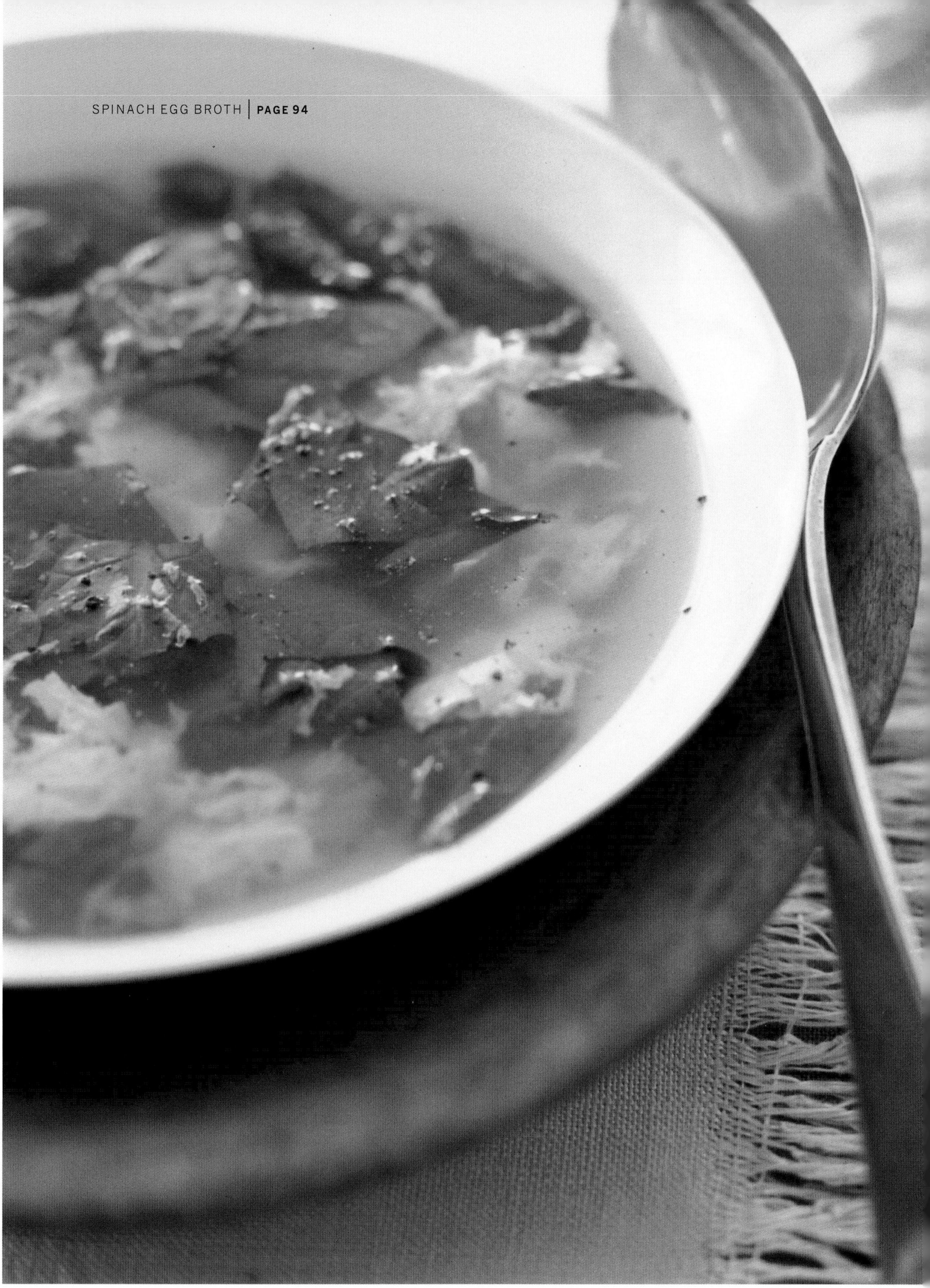
SPINACH EGG BROTH | PAGE 94

POACHED CHICKEN WITH HOT
ENGLISH MUSTARD | **PAGE 90**

WARM MUSTARD AND OLIVE OIL SAUCE | **PAGE 89**

STEAMED ARTICHOKES WITH
GRAINY MUSTARD AND
BACON DRESSING | **PAGE 91**

TUNA WITH MUSTARD SEED CRUST | **PAGE 89**

COLD POACHED MUSSELS WITH
CREAMY MUSTARD SAUCE | **PAGE 90**

ALMOND CRUSTED CHICKEN | **PAGE 92**

ROMAINE SALAD WITH PROSCIUTTO CRISPS | **PAGE 92**

"CREAMED" SPINACH | **PAGE 93**

ORZO WITH PEAS AND MINT | **PAGE 92**

PERFECT MUSTARD VINAIGRETTE | PAGE 89

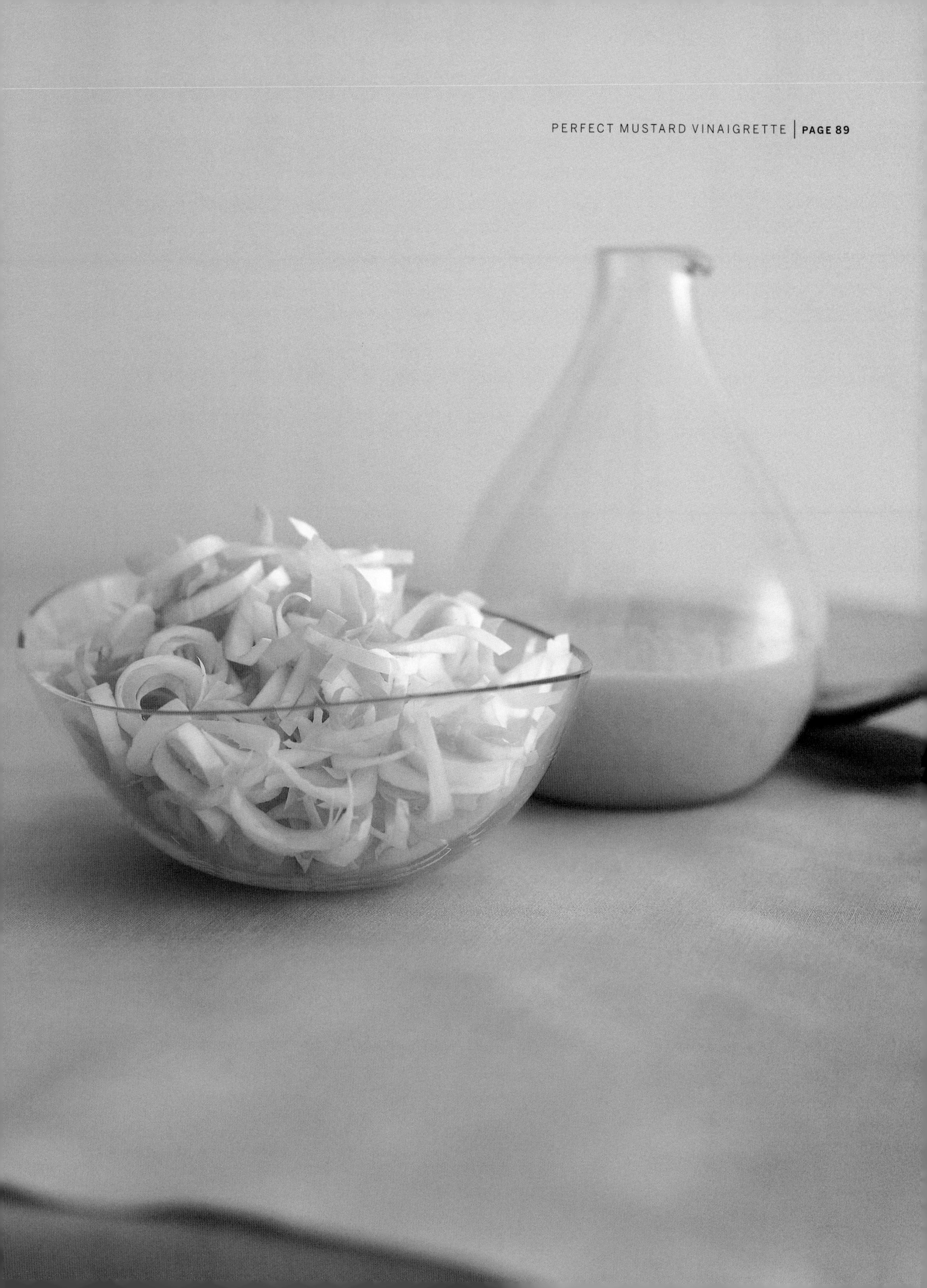

BLACKBERRY TARTLETS | **PAGE 88**

may

Maypole Cake

Hollandaise Sauce

Hollandaise Sauce, Blender Method

Béarnaise Sauce

Classic Crumb Cake

Yeasted Coffee Cake with
  Poppy-Seed Filling

Ultimate Streusel Cake

Whole-Wheat Apple Cake

Rhubarb and Strawberry Ice Cream

Whole Rhubarb Chutney

Meringue Cupcakes with
  Stewed Rhubarb and Raspberries

Cream Cheese and Mascarpone
  Cheesecake

Rhubarb and Blackberry Snack Cake

Breakfast Blintzes with Caramelized
  Rhubarb and Sour Cream

Individual Rhubarb and Raspberry
  Tartlets

Balsamic Marinated Skirt Steak

Cucumber, String Bean, and
  Olive Salad

Grated Potato Pancake

Sunken Chocolate Cakes with
  Coffee Ice Cream

Breakfast Smoothies

Edamame

Sautéed Tofu with Bitter Greens

White Bean Chili with Herbed
  Yogurt Cheese

Broccoli Cheese Frittata

Salmon Cakes

MAYPOLE CAKE

SERVES 10 TO 12 | **PHOTOGRAPH ON PAGE 125**

This edible version of May Day's traditional maypole uses a central layer cake to anchor a gumdrop-topped pole strung with ribbons and ringed by cupcake "dancers." To make the maypole, you will need a wooden dowel, painted white, and six pieces of one-eighth-inch satin ribbon, each three times the length of the dowel.

1½ cups (3 sticks) unsalted butter, room temperature, plus more for pans

4½ cups sifted cake flour (not self-rising), plus more for pans

1½ tablespoons baking powder

¾ teaspoon table salt

3 cups superfine sugar

2 teaspoons pure vanilla extract

6 large eggs, lightly beaten

1½ cups milk

Seven-Minute Frosting (page 106)

6 ounces cream-colored sprinkles

1 pound assorted jellied citrus slices

14 assorted small gumdrops (about 1½ ounces)

Maypole Cupcakes (page 106)

1 Preheat the oven to 375°F with a rack in the lower third of the oven. Butter two 9-by-2-inch-round cake pans; line with parchment paper, and butter again. Dust the bottoms and sides with flour, and tap out excess. Set aside. In a medium bowl, sift together the flour, baking powder, and salt three times. Set aside.

2 In the bowl of an electric mixer fitted with the paddle attachment, cream the butter on low speed to soften. Increase the speed to medium, and beat until fluffy and light in color. Keep beating while gradually adding the sugar; beat until fluffy, about 3 minutes. Beat in the vanilla.

3 Gradually drizzle in the eggs, beating between additions and scraping down the sides of the bowl twice, until the batter is no longer slick. With the mixer on low, add the reserved flour mixture alternately with the milk, beginning and ending with the flour. Beat mixture until just incorporated after each addition. Scrape down the sides of the bowl; mix 10 seconds more.

4 Divide the batter evenly between the pans. Bake until a cake tester inserted into the center of each comes out clean, 45 to 50 minutes. Transfer the pans to a wire rack to cool for 10 minutes. Remove the cakes from the pans, remove the parchment, and return the cakes to the rack to cool, top sides up.

5 To assemble, turn the cakes upside down. Using a long serrated knife, slice each cake in half horizontally. Place a layer on a cake stand large enough to hold a circle of cupcakes around the cake. Spread the top of the layer with 1½ cups frosting. Stack the second layer over the frosted layer; spread another 1½ cups of frosting over the top of this layer; repeat with the third layer and more frosting; cover with the top layer. Using a dry pastry brush, gently brush any loose crumbs away from the cake. Frost the cake thinly to seal in the crumbs. Use 3 cups frosting for the final coating. You will have leftover frosting to use on the cupcakes.

6 To decorate, evenly distribute sprinkles over the top of the cake. Using a ⅛-inch petal-shape cutter, cut petals from jellied citrus slices. You will need 84 petals. Gently press the gumdrops, evenly spaced, around the perimeter of the cake. Arrange six jellied petals around each gumdrop to form flowers. Place the maypole cupcakes around the cake on the cake stand. Gather the ribbons together, and pin them through their centers to one end of the dowel. Gently press a Lifesaver over the pinned ribbons, and top with a small gumdrop. Insert the maypole into the center of the cake, and fan the ribbons out around the cake stand, taping in place and letting the ends trail over the table.

WHAT IS A MAYPOLE?

The Maypole tradition we recognize today evolved in medieval England. On the first day of May, a pole made from a birch tree and decorated with flowers was erected on the village green. At the end of the day, young women performed ritual dances around the Maypole while young men with bells strapped to their arms and legs provided the rhythm. In more recent times, ribbons were affixed to the Maypole, and the dancers, holding the ribbons, plaited the pole in colorful patterns.

MAYPOLE CUPCAKES

MAKES 1 DOZEN | PHOTOGRAPHS ON
PAGE 124

4½ cups cake flour (not self-rising), sifted

1½ teaspoons baking powder

¾ teaspoon table salt

1 pound plus 4 tablespoons (4½ sticks)
 unsalted butter, room temperature

3 cups sugar

6 large eggs

1 tablespoon pure vanilla extract

1½ cups nonfat buttermilk

6 ounces green sprinkles

6 ounces cream-colored sprinkles

2 pounds assorted jellied citrus slices

12 ounces jellied grapefruit slices

12 assorted large gumdrops
 (about 5 ounces)

1 Preheat the oven to 350°F. Line two 6-cup jumbo cupcake tins (1¾-inch-deep, 4-inch-diameter) with paper liners, and set aside. In a medium bowl, sift together the flour, baking powder, and salt; set aside.

2 In the bowl of an electric mixer fitted with the paddle attachment, cream the butter and sugar on medium speed until light and fluffy, about 3 minutes. With the mixer on medium, add the eggs, one at a time; add the vanilla.

3 With the mixer on low speed, add one-third of the reserved flour mixture, and mix until combined. Add 1 cup buttermilk, and mix until combined. Add another third of the flour mixture, then the remaining ½ cup buttermilk. Add the last third of the flour, and mix until smooth.

4 Divide the batter among the cups, and bake until golden, about 30 minutes. Transfer the cupcake tins to a wire rack to cool. When cool, remove the cupcakes from the tins.

5 To decorate, frost the cupcakes with the remaining frosting. Fill a small, shallow bowl with green sprinkles and another with cream-colored sprinkles. Gently press each frosted cupcake into the sprinkles, rolling the cupcake so the entire surface is coated. Alternate colors so that you have 6 green and 6 cream-colored cupcakes.

6 Using a 2-inch petal-shape cutter, cut petals from the jellied citrus and grapefruit slices. You will need 72 petals. Using scissors or a knife, cut off the bottom third of the gumdrops, and discard. Gently press a gumdrop top into the center of each cupcake, and arrange six jellied petals around each gumdrop to form flowers.

SEVEN-MINUTE FROSTING

MAKES ABOUT 13 CUPS

This cake frosting is named for the length of time it must be beaten in the final stage. Because this is a large batch, it requires more time to beat. Have the cake you are going to frost already prepared before making this frosting; it must be spread on while the beaten egg whites and sugar are still pliable. Once frosted, the cake may sit out for several hours before serving.

2½ cups plus 2 tablespoons sugar

3 tablespoons light corn syrup

¼ cup plus 2 tablespoons water

9 large egg whites

1 In a medium heavy saucepan, combine 2¼ cups sugar, the corn syrup, and water. Cook over medium heat, stirring occasionally, until the sugar has dissolved. Rub a bit between your fingers to make sure there is no graininess. Raise heat, and bring to a boil. Do not stir anymore. Boil, washing down the sides of the pan with a pastry brush dipped in cold water from time to time to prevent the sugar from crystallizing, until a candy thermometer registers 230°F, about 5 minutes. (Depending on the humidity, this can take anywhere from 4 to 10 minutes.)

2 Meanwhile, in the bowl of an electric mixer fitted with the whisk attachment, whisk the egg whites on medium speed until soft peaks form, about 2½ minutes. Gradually add the remaining ¼ cup plus 2 tablespoons sugar. Remove the syrup from the heat when the temperature reaches 230°F (it will keep rising as the

pan is removed from the heat). To avoid splattering, pour the syrup in a steady stream down the side of the bowl containing the egg-white mixture, with the mixer on medium-low speed.

3 Beat the frosting on medium speed until it is cool, about 15 minutes. The frosting should be thick and shiny. Use immediately.

HOLLANDAISE SAUCE 101

HOLLANDAISE SAUCE

MAKES ABOUT 1½ CUPS | PHOTOGRAPH
ON PAGE 122

12 tablespoons (1½ sticks) unsalted butter

3 large egg yolks

2 tablespoons freshly squeezed
 lemon juice, or more to taste

½ teaspoon coarse salt

¼ cup boiling water

 Pinch of cayenne pepper

1 Melt the butter in a small saucepan over medium-low heat. Keep warm until ready to use.

2 Place the egg yolks in a copper or stainless-steel bowl or the top of a double boiler. Fill a medium saucepan or the bottom of a double boiler with 2 inches of water, and bring to a boil. Off the heat, whisk the yolks until they become pale. Add 1 tablespoon lemon juice and the salt, and whisk until well combined. Gradually add the boiling water, whisking constantly. Place the bowl over the saucepan or double boiler, and reduce the heat to the lowest setting. Whisking constantly, cook until the whisk leaves a trail in the mixture and the sauce begins to hold its shape. Remove from the heat.

3 Pour the warm melted butter into a glass measuring cup. Add to the yolk mixture one drop at a time, whisking constantly. After you have added about a tablespoon of butter, you can start adding it slightly faster, still whisking constantly. If the butter is added too quickly, the emulsion will be too thin or will "break" (separate).

4 Once all the butter is incorporated, adjust the seasoning with the remaining

tablespoon lemon juice and the cayenne pepper. If the sauce is too thick, you may thin it with a little additional lemon juice or water. If not serving immediately, place the sauce over a pot of simmering water that has been removed from the heat, or in a warm spot on the stove, for up to 1 hour. Alternatively, store it in a clean thermos that has been warmed with hot but not boiling water for up to 3 hours.

HOLLANDAISE SAUCE, BLENDER METHOD
MAKES 1 CUP

This nearly foolproof way to make hollandaise yields a slightly thicker sauce.

3   large egg yolks
2   tablespoons freshly squeezed lemon juice, or more to taste
½   teaspoon coarse salt
    Pinch of cayenne pepper
12 tablespoons (1½ sticks) unsalted butter, melted

Place the egg yolks, lemon juice, salt, and cayenne pepper in the jar of a blender. With the motor running, add the melted butter very slowly. Transfer the sauce to a bowl. If the sauce is too thick, thin by whisking in a tablespoon of water at a time.

BEARNAISE SAUCE
MAKES ABOUT 1½ CUPS

½   cup white wine
2   tablespoons white-wine vinegar
2   tablespoons finely chopped shallots
2   tablespoons plus 1 teaspoon freshly chopped tarragon
3   whole black peppercorns
12 tablespoons (1½ sticks) unsalted butter
3   large egg yolks
½   teaspoon coarse salt
¼   cup boiling water
1   tablespoon freshly squeezed lemon juice, or more to taste

1   Place the wine, vinegar, shallots, 2 tablespoons tarragon, and the peppercorns in a small saucepan set over medium-high heat. Bring the mixture to a boil, and cook until it is reduced to about 2 tablespoons.

2   Melt the butter in a small saucepan over medium-low heat. Keep warm until ready to use.
3   Place the egg yolks in a copper or stainless-steel bowl or the top of a double boiler. Fill a medium saucepan or the bottom of a double boiler with 2 inches of water, and bring to a boil. Off the heat, whisk the yolks until they become pale. Add the wine mixture and salt, and whisk until well combined. Gradually add the boiling water, whisking constantly. Place the bowl over the saucepan or double boiler; reduce the heat to the lowest setting. Whisking constantly, cook until the whisk leaves a trail in the mixture and the sauce begins to hold its shape. Remove from the heat.
4   Pour the warm melted butter into a glass measuring cup. Add to the yolk constantly. After you have added about a tablespoon of butter, you can start adding it slightly faster, still whisking constantly. If the butter is added too quickly, the emulsion will be too thin or will "break" (separate).
5   Once all the butter is incorporated, adjust the seasoning with the lemon juice, and stir in the remaining teaspoon tarragon. If the béarnaise becomes too thick, you may thin it with a little additional lemon juice or water. If not serving immediately, place the sauce over a pot of simmering water that has been removed from the heat, or in a warm spot on the stove, for up to 1 hour. Alternatively, store it in a clean thermos that has been warmed with hot but not boiling water for up to 3 hours.

HOLLANDAISE SAUCE

The rich yet airy sauces of the hollandaise family are made with lemon juice or another liquid that is thickened with egg yolks and butter or oil. By altering the ingredients, you can produce a variety of sauces. Béarnaise sauce is flavored with a reduction of white wine, vinegar, shallots, and tarragon. Add tomato purée to a béarnaise, and you have Choron sauce. A hollandaise in which orange juice, simmered with the zest, replaces the lemon juice is a Maltaise sauce. A mikado sauce is a hollandaise made with cooked tangerine juice and zest. A half cup of whipped cream folded into a hollandaise sauce produces the lighter mousseline.

COFFEE CAKE

CLASSIC CRUMB CAKE

MAKES 1 NINE-INCH CAKE

For variation, stir blueberries into the batter and the crumb topping.

2½ cups all-purpose flour
1 teaspoon baking soda
1 teaspoon baking powder
¼ teaspoon coarse salt
10 tablespoons (1¼ sticks) unsalted butter, room temperature, plus more for pan
1 cup granulated sugar
3 large eggs
1 teaspoon pure vanilla extract
1¼ cups sour cream
3 cups blueberries (optional)
Crumb Topping (recipe follows)
Confectioners' sugar for dusting (optional)

1 Preheat the oven to 350°F. Sift the flour, baking soda, baking powder, and salt into a bowl; set aside. Butter a 9-inch-square baking pan; set aside.
2 In the bowl of an electric mixer fitted with the paddle attachment, cream the butter and granulated sugar until light and fluffy, about 4 minutes. Add the eggs one at a time, until well combined. Add the vanilla, and stir until combined. Add the reserved flour mixture and sour cream, and stir just until combined. Fold in 2 cups blueberries, if using.
3 Spoon the batter into the prepared pan. Toss remaining cup blueberries, if using, with the crumb topping. Sprinkle topping over the cake. Bake until golden brown and a cake tester comes out clean, 50 to 60 minutes. Transfer to a wire rack to cool for 20 minutes. Remove from the pan. Dust with confectioners' sugar, if using. Serve warm or at room temperature.

CRUMB TOPPING

MAKES ENOUGH FOR 1 NINE-INCH CAKE

1½ teaspoons ground cinnamon
½ teaspoon coarse salt
½ cup packed light-brown sugar (or ¾ cup confectioners' sugar)
1½ cups all-purpose flour
12 tablespoons (1½ sticks) unsalted butter, room temperature

In a medium bowl, combine the cinnamon, salt, sugar, and flour; cut in the butter using your hands, two knives, or a pastry cutter until well combined and crumbly. (Alternatively, use an electric mixer.) Store the topping in an airtight container in the refrigerator for up to 1 week, or freeze for up to 2 months.

YEASTED COFFEE CAKE WITH POPPY-SEED FILLING

MAKES 2 NINE-INCH CAKES | **PHOTO-GRAPHS ON PAGES 120–21**

This coffee cake may take longer to make than others, but the results are worth it. Freeze a cake for later.

1½ cups warm water
1½ cups warm milk
8 tablespoons (1 stick) unsalted butter, melted, plus more for bowl and pans
1 tablespoon coarse salt
½ cup granulated sugar
1 teaspoon ground cardamom
2 large eggs
2 packages (about 5 teaspoons) active dry yeast
10 cups all-purpose flour, plus more for work surface
½ cup packed dark-brown sugar
Poppy-Seed Filling (recipe follows)

1 In the bowl of an electric mixer fitted with the paddle attachment, combine the warm water, milk, 4 tablespoons butter, salt, granulated sugar, cardamom, and eggs. Sprinkle the yeast over the top; let stand until foamy, 10 to 15 minutes.
2 With the mixer running, gradually add the flour. Mix until well combined; the dough will be sticky. Turn the dough out onto a floured work surface, and gently knead until the dough forms a ball. Place in a large buttered bowl to rise, covered loosely with a kitchen towel or plastic wrap, until doubled, about 1½ hours.
3 Preheat the oven to 375°F. Butter two 9-inch tube pans; sprinkle the bottom of each with ¼ cup brown sugar. Punch down the dough; turn out onto the lightly floured surface. With a rolling pin, roll into a rectangle that is about 14 by 17

inches and about ½ inch thick. Brush a third of the remaining butter over the middle third of the dough, and sprinkle with 1 cup of the filling. Fold the bottom third of the dough over the filling and overlap the top third, forming an envelope. Rotate the dough 90 degrees. Roll the dough again into a rectangle roughly the same size, and repeat with half of the remaining butter and filling. Repeat one more time, three rollings in all, using the remaining butter and filling. Rotate the dough 90 degrees, and let rest, covered with a damp cloth or plastic wrap, for 15 minutes. Roll the dough one final time into a long rectangle, 11 by 17 inches and about 1 inch thick. With a sharp knife, cut a 1-inch slice from the end of the dough. Pick it up, twisting it gently into a spiral so that the filling spirals through the dough. Place the twist in the bottom of the pan, forming a circle. Repeat, using the remaining dough, filling each tube pan with 2 layers of twisted dough. Cover each cake with plastic wrap, and let rise until doubled, about 45 minutes.
4 Bake the cakes until golden brown, 40 to 50 minutes. Transfer to a wire rack to cool for about 20 minutes before inverting. Flip cakes over so attractive side is up. Serve cakes warm or at room temperature. After cooling completely, cakes can be frozen, wrapped in two layers of plastic wrap, for up to a month.

POPPY-SEED FILLING

MAKES ENOUGH FOR 2 YEASTED COFFEE CAKES

1 cup packed dark-brown sugar
½ cup all-purpose flour
½ cup finely chopped walnuts
¼ teaspoon ground cinnamon
¼ teaspoon ground nutmeg
⅓ cup poppy seeds
8 tablespoons (1 stick) unsalted butter, room temperature

Combine the sugar, flour, walnuts, cinnamon, nutmeg, and poppy seeds in a medium bowl. Using your hands or a pastry cutter, mix in the butter until well combined and crumbly; chill until ready to use.

ULTIMATE STREUSEL CAKE

MAKES 1 TEN-INCH CAKE

2½ cups all-purpose flour
1 teaspoon baking soda
1 teaspoon baking powder
¼ teaspoon coarse salt
10 tablespoons (1¼ sticks) unsalted butter, room temperature, plus more for pan
1 cup granulated sugar
3 large eggs
1 teaspoon pure vanilla extract
1¼ cups sour cream (or 1 cup nonfat buttermilk)
Pecan-Streusel Filling (recipe follows)
2½ cups sifted confectioners' sugar
¼ cup milk

1 Preheat the oven to 350°F. Sift together the flour, baking soda, baking powder, and salt into a bowl; set aside. Butter a 10-inch Bundt pan (or other tube pan with 3-quart capacity); set aside.
2 In the bowl of an electric mixer fitted with the paddle attachment, cream the butter and granulated sugar until light and fluffy, about 4 minutes. Add the eggs one at a time, until well combined. Add the vanilla; stir until combined. Add the reserved flour mixture and sour cream, and stir just until combined.
3 Spoon half the batter into the prepared pan. Make a well in the batter, and crumble two thirds of the filling into the well. Top with the remaining batter, smoothing the top. Sprinkle the remaining filling evenly over the top. Bake until golden brown and a cake tester comes out clean, about 1 hour. Transfer the cake to a wire rack to cool for about 20 minutes.
4 In a medium bowl, whisk together the confectioners' sugar and milk until well combined; set the icing aside, covered with plastic wrap, until ready to use. Remove the cake from the pan, drizzle with icing, and serve warm.

PECAN-STREUSEL FILLING

MAKES ENOUGH FOR 1 TEN-INCH CAKE

1½ cups lightly packed light-brown sugar
½ cup granulated sugar
1½ cups chopped pecans
½ cup all-purpose flour
1 tablespoon ground cinnamon
Pinch of ground cloves
8 tablespoons (1 stick) unsalted butter, room temperature

Combine the sugars, pecans, flour, cinnamon, and cloves in a medium bowl. Using your hands or a pastry cutter, mix in the butter until well combined and crumbly; set aside in the refrigerator until ready to use.

WHOLE-WHEAT APPLE CAKE

MAKES 1 NINE-INCH CAKE

Using whole-milk yogurt yields the best results for this cake. You will need a nine-inch springform pan.

3 Granny Smith apples, peeled, cored, and cut into ½-inch pieces
¾ cup packed light-brown sugar
2 teaspoons ground cinnamon
Pinch of ground cloves
1¼ cups all-purpose flour
1¼ cups whole-wheat flour
1 teaspoon baking soda
1 teaspoon baking powder
¼ teaspoon coarse salt
10 tablespoons (1¼ sticks) unsalted butter, room temperature, plus more for pan
1 cup granulated sugar
3 large eggs
1 teaspoon pure vanilla extract
1¼ cups plain whole-milk yogurt

1 Preheat the oven to 350°F. In a medium bowl, combine the apples, ½ cup brown sugar, cinnamon, and cloves, and set aside. Sift together both flours, the baking soda, baking powder, and salt into a medium bowl, and set aside. Butter the springform pan, and set aside.
2 In the bowl of an electric mixer fitted with the paddle attachment, cream the

YEAST

Yeast is key in making airy loaves of bread. Most recipes require proofing the yeast by combining it with warm water (110°F) and sugar. If the yeast is alive, it will bubble and foam. Cake yeast, also known as compressed fresh yeast, is dry, crumbly, and white and comes in six-ounce squares. It is equivalent in potency to a one-quarter-ounce package of active dry yeast. Cake yeast is moist and must be used within a week or two of being made (or by the date indicated on the package.) If frozen, defrost before using. Professional bakers prefer cake yeast, as it is fresher, but home bakers can also keep active dry yeast fresh in the freezer for years. Less common is quick-rise yeast, which causes bread to rise twice as fast and is packaged as pellets in an airtight can.

butter and granulated sugar until light and fluffy, about 4 minutes. Add the eggs one at a time, until well combined. Add the vanilla, and stir until combined. Add the reserved flour mixture and yogurt, and stir just until combined. Fold in two-thirds of the reserved apple mixture.

3   Spoon half the batter into the prepared pan. Sprinkle the remaining apple mixture evenly over the batter. Top with the remaining batter, and smooth with a spatula. Sprinkle the top with the remaining ¼ cup brown sugar. Bake until golden brown and a cake tester comes out clean, 1 hour 10 minutes to 1 hour 20 minutes. Cover with foil after 45 minutes of baking. Transfer to a wire rack to cool for about 20 minutes. Remove the cake from the pan, and serve warm or at room temperature.

RHUBARB

RHUBARB AND STRAWBERRY ICE CREAM

MAKES 1 QUART | PHOTOGRAPH ON PAGE 124

Unlike most ice-cream recipes, this one contains no eggs.

1   pound trimmed rhubarb, cut into ½-inch pieces (about 3½ cups)
¾   cup plus 2 tablespoons sugar
2   tablespoons water
8   ounces ripe strawberries
1   cup heavy cream
½   cup milk
2   tablespoons kirsch (optional)

1   Place the rhubarb, ½ cup sugar, and the water in a saucepan over medium heat. Bring to a boil. Reduce the heat to medium-low; let simmer, stirring frequently, until the rhubarb is very tender and beginning to fall apart, about 12 minutes. Remove from the heat; transfer to a bowl, and set aside.

2   Place the strawberries in the bowl of a food processor, and purée. Strain through a fine sieve or chinois into a bowl, and set aside.

3   Scald the cream and milk in a saucepan over medium heat. Do not let boil. Remove from the heat, add the remaining 6 tablespoons sugar, and stir until the sugar is dissolved. Allow the mixture to cool to room temperature.

4   In a medium bowl, combine cooked rhubarb, strawberry purée, cream mixture, and kirsch, if using. Cover with plastic wrap, and chill at least 2 hours or overnight. Freeze in an ice-cream maker according to manufacturer's instructions.

WHOLE RHUBARB CHUTNEY

MAKES 2½ CUPS

Serve as a condiment with pâtés or roast meats, such as pork.

½   red onion, cut into ¼-inch-thick rounds
¼   cup golden raisins
1   teaspoon freshly grated ginger
    Zest of 1 orange
½   cup white wine
¼   cup white-wine vinegar
1   cup packed light-brown sugar
1   pound trimmed rhubarb, cut into 6-inch lengths
2   celery stalks, strings removed, cut into 6-inch lengths

1   Combine the onion, raisins, ginger, zest, wine, vinegar, and sugar in a saucepan; bring to a simmer over medium heat.

2   Add the rhubarb and celery; cover, and reduce the heat. Simmer gently until the rhubarb is tender but not falling apart, about 5 minutes.

3   Remove the rhubarb with a slotted spoon, and set aside. Continue to simmer the liquid until it has thickened and reduced and the celery is tender, about 10 minutes more. Transfer the celery and liquid to a bowl, and add the cooked rhubarb. Let cool, and chill until ready to use. Chutney will last several days refrigerated in an airtight container.

MERINGUE CUPCAKES WITH STEWED RHUBARB AND RASPBERRIES

MAKES 1 DOZEN

Take extra care when filling cupcake liners with meringue. If any of the meringue spills over onto the muffin tin, it will make removing the baked cupcakes difficult.

6   large egg whites, room temperature
½   teaspoon table salt
1   teaspoon vinegar
1   teaspoon pure vanilla extract
1¾   cups sugar
    Stewed Rhubarb, chilled (recipe follows)
½   pint raspberries
1   cup crème fraîche
½   cup heavy cream

1   Preheat the oven to 225°F. Line every other cup of two nonstick 12-cup muffin tins with cupcake liners, and set aside. Combine the egg whites, salt, vinegar, and vanilla in the bowl of an electric mixer fitted with the whisk attachment. Beat on medium-high speed until frothy. Add the sugar 1 tablespoon at a time, beating a full 2 minutes after each addition and making sure the sugar has completely dissolved. Use a rubber spatula to scrape down the sides of the bowl after each addition so that undissolved sugar does not build up. The egg whites should form glossy, firm peaks.

2   Using a rubber spatula, spoon the meringue equally into the 12 paper cups so it mounds about 2 inches above the rims. Clean up the edges so no meringue is touching the muffin tins. Do not smooth meringue or worry about peaks and odd shapes. Place in the oven, and bake until very light brown and completely dry on the outside but still soft in the middle, about 2½ hours. Rotate the tins after 1½ hours. Remove from the oven, remove the cupcakes from the tins, and peel off the liners. Let cool.

3   Combine the stewed rhubarb and raspberries. Combine the crème fraîche and heavy cream; whip to soft peaks. Using a serrated knife, gently slice the tops off the cupcakes; do not worry if they crack. Spoon the whipped crème-fraîche mixture into the center of each cupcake, and cover with the fruit. Cover with top of cupcake.

STEWED RHUBARB

MAKES 1 CUP

It is important that the rhubarb is cooked at a gentle simmer, or it will quickly turn to mush. Do not recombine the rhubarb and cooking liquid until the liquid is cool, or the rhubarb will overcook.

- 10 ounces trimmed rhubarb, cut into ¼-inch pieces (about 2¾ cups)
- ⅔ cup sugar, plus more to taste
- 2 tablespoons water

1 Place the rhubarb, sugar, and water in a medium saucepan set over medium-low heat. Simmer gently, stirring occasionally, until the sugar is dissolved and the rhubarb is almost tender, about 8 minutes. Using a slotted spoon, remove the rhubarb, and transfer it to a medium bowl; set aside.

2 Raise the heat to medium, and continue simmering the liquid until thickened and reduced to ½ cup, about 10 minutes. Remove from heat. Transfer the reduced liquid to a small bowl to cool. Add the cooled, thickened liquid to the reserved cooked rhubarb, and stir to combine.

MERINGUES

Eggs are easier to separate when cold, but egg whites create more volume when beaten at room temperature. If egg whites do not beat up, it may be due to the tiniest bit of egg yolk or fat, which can cling to plastic bowls even after washing. This is why bakers use copper, metal, or glass bowls. Acid, usually a small amount of cream of tartar, also stabilizes beaten egg whites. Fail to beat whites long enough, and the bubbles won't stiffen; they will lack volume. Overbeat the whites and they will turn liquidy or curdle. Begin to whip whites on low speed. The clear liquid will turn white and smooth as you increase the speed to medium-high. Stop when the whites are stiff enough to stand in peaks. If the whites turn lumpy, you have beaten too long and must start over.

ICE-CREAM MAKING TIPS

Make sure that the custard mixture is cold before putting it in the machine. In order to give the ice cream an opportunity to aerate in the machine, do not fill the ice-cream maker more than three-quarters full. Vanilla extract and other extracts lose their flavor if added while the custard is hot; wait until the custard has cooled. Not only does the flavor of ice cream fade over time, but it has a tendency to absorb the odors of the food around it. Seal it tightly and eat it within a week. Storing ice cream in a shallow container makes it easier to form scoops for a cone or sundae.

CREAM CHEESE AND MASCARPONE CHEESECAKE

MAKES 1 TEN-BY-THREE-INCH CAKE;
SERVES 10 | PHOTOGRAPH ON PAGE 124

This rich cheesecake is baked in a cornmeal rather than a graham-cracker crust. Spoon stewed rhubarb and raspberries over every slice. Do not worry if the cheesecake sinks and cracks while it cools: The fruit will conceal any imperfections. You will need a ten-by-three-inch springform pan.

12 tablespoons (1½ sticks) unsalted butter, room temperature

1¾ cups plus 2 tablespoons sugar

1¼ cups all-purpose flour

1¼ cups yellow cornmeal

½ teaspoon table salt

1½ pounds cream cheese, room temperature

8 ounces mascarpone cheese, room temperature

5 large whole eggs

1 large egg yolk

¼ cup heavy cream

1 tablespoon pure vanilla extract

Zest of 1 orange and 1 lemon

Stewed Rhubarb, chilled (page 111)

½ pint raspberries

1 Preheat the oven to 350°F. In the bowl of an electric mixer fitted with the paddle attachment, cream the butter and ½ cup plus 2 tablespoons sugar until light and fluffy. Add the flour, cornmeal, and salt, and mix until well combined. Press the mixture onto the bottom and three-quarters of the way up the sides of the springform pan to form a neat crust. Place in the oven, and bake until lightly golden, 20 to 25 minutes. Remove from the oven, and place on a wire rack. Gently press the sides of the crust back into place, if necessary. Let cool to room temperature.

2 Reduce the oven temperature to 325°F. In the bowl of an electric mixer fitted with the paddle attachment, beat the cream cheese, mascarpone, and remaining 1¼ cups sugar on low speed until smooth and well combined. Add the eggs and egg yolk one at a time, beating on low speed after each addition until combined, scraping down the sides of the bowl with a rubber spatula as needed.

3 Add the cream, extract, and orange and lemon zests. Beat just until combined; do not overbeat. Pour the mixture into the cooled shell. Place in the oven; bake until set but still wobbly in the center, 65 to 70 minutes. Turn the oven off, and allow the cheesecake to sit in the oven 1 hour longer. Remove the cheesecake from the oven, and place on a wire rack to cool. When completely cool, chill at least 2 hours or overnight. Remove the outside ring of the springform pan.

4 Combine the stewed rhubarb with the raspberries. Spoon the fruit over the cheesecake immediately before serving.

RHUBARB AND BLACKBERRY SNACK CAKE

MAKES ONE 13¾-BY-4¼-INCH CAKE

Draining the rhubarb will keep the cake from becoming soggy.

4 tablespoons unsalted butter, softened, plus more for pan

½ cup all-purpose flour, plus more for pan

5 ounces rhubarb, cut into ¼-inch-thick slices (scant 1½ cups)

1 cup plus 1 tablespoon sugar

½ teaspoon baking powder

Pinch of coarse salt

2 large eggs

1 whole vanilla bean, split lengthwise

1 large handful blackberries (about ⅓ cup)

1 Preheat the oven to 350°F. Butter and flour a 13¾-by-4¼-inch fluted tart pan with a removable bottom, and set aside. Combine the rhubarb and ⅓ cup sugar in a medium bowl, and allow to sit, stirring occasionally, until the rhubarb has released its juice and the sugar has dissolved, about 45 minutes.

2 Sift together the flour, baking powder, and salt into a small bowl; set aside. In the bowl of an electric mixer fitted with the paddle attachment, cream the butter with ⅔ cup sugar. Add the eggs one at a time, beating well after each addition. Scrape the seeds from the vanilla pod, and add the seeds to the mixture. Beat to combine. Add the reserved flour mixture, and beat to combine. Using a rubber spatula, spoon the batter into the prepared pan, and spread flat.

3 Strain the rhubarb, discarding the juice; add the blackberries, and toss to combine. Spoon the fruit on top of the batter in the pan. Sprinkle with the remaining tablespoon sugar, place in the oven, and bake until the cake is golden and the center is set, about 1 hour. Remove from the oven, and place on a wire rack to cool slightly before removing the tart from the pan.

BREAKFAST BLINTZES WITH CARAMELIZED RHUBARB AND SOUR CREAM

MAKES 1 DOZEN

Cooking blintzes takes a bit of practice. A nonstick skillet is a great help. The first blintz is almost never perfect; just discard it and start again. The blintzes can be made to step five up to two hours ahead. The extra quarter tablespoon of sugar in the batter is important — it is a generous pinch.

11 tablespoons (1⅜ sticks) unsalted butter, plus more for pan
1 cup all-purpose flour
¼ teaspoon table salt
1 cup plus 2¼ tablespoons sugar
4 large eggs
1 cup milk
1½ pounds trimmed rhubarb, cut into ½-inch lengths (about 5 cups)
¼ cup plus 2 tablespoons brandy
½ pint sour cream, or more if desired

1 Melt 2 tablespoons butter; let cool. Combine the flour, salt, ¼ tablespoon sugar, eggs, milk, and the 2 tablespoons reserved melted, cooled butter in the bowl of a food processor, and process until smooth. Transfer to a medium bowl, cover with plastic wrap, and place in the refrigerator at least 1 hour or overnight.
2 Fill a large bowl with ice and water; set aside. Melt the remaining 9 tablespoons butter in a large sauté pan over medium heat. Sprinkle the remaining 1 cup plus 2 tablespoons sugar over the butter; cook until the sugar has dissolved and starts to turn golden brown, about 5 minutes. Add the rhubarb; cook, shaking the pan vigorously to coat in the caramelized sugar, until the rhubarb is tender and just starting to fall apart, about 5 minutes. Add the brandy, shake the pan, and cook just until the liquid comes to a boil, about 30 seconds. Remove from the heat. Transfer the rhubarb to a small bowl; set the bowl in the ice bath to stop the cooking.

3 Heat a 10-inch nonstick sauté pan over medium heat. Melt about ½ tablespoon butter in the sauté pan; swirl to coat. If the butter pools, gently wipe with a paper towel. Pour a scant ¼ cup chilled batter into the hot pan. Swirl to form a thin, even layer; cook the blintz until the bottom is very lightly browned, about 2 minutes. Do not turn. Loosen the edge of the blintz with a spatula; slide it out of the pan onto a piece of waxed paper. Continue making blintzes until all the batter is used (you may not need to add butter to the pan each time); place a piece of waxed paper between each one.
4 Transfer a blintz, cooked side up, onto a plate. Spoon a generous ¼ cup of rhubarb filling (getting a nice proportion of fruit to liquid) into the center of the blintz. Carefully fold up the blintz, creating an envelope for the filling; set aside, seam up, on a baking sheet. Continue filling and folding until all the blintzes and filling have been used.
5 Set a large sauté pan (use the same pan or a slightly larger one, if you wish) over medium-low heat. Melt just enough butter to lightly coat the bottom of the pan, and place on it two or three filled blintzes, depending on the size of the pan. Cook until the blintzes are golden and crisp on both sides, about 4 minutes per side. Repeat with the remaining blintzes. Serve immediately with sour cream.

RHUBARB

Rhubarb is commonly used in pies and jams, but it is actually a vegetable. It is also delicious stewed until almost falling apart and paired with something rich—a thick pudding or vanilla ice cream—or served as a complement to savory foods such as pork or lamb. Rhubarb needs to be sweetened, but not by too much. Sugar should be added a little at a time until the right level of sweetness is reached. The same rule applies when adding fruits or berries. Rhubarb absorbs the flavors of fruits and makes them taste even better, but be cautious. It is easy to overwhelm the subtle flavor of rhubarb by adding too much fruit.

INDIVIDUAL RHUBARB AND RASPBERRY TARTLETS

MAKES 8

The extra tablespoon of flour, sprinkled into the center of each pastry circle, helps thicken the rhubarb juices as the tartlets cook.

1½ pounds trimmed rhubarb, cut into ¼-inch pieces (about 5½ cups)

8 ounces (about 1 pint) raspberries

1 cup all-purpose flour, plus more for work surface

2 cups sugar, plus more for sprinkling Pâte Brisée (page 10), chilled

1 Combine the rhubarb, berries, ½ cup flour, and sugar in a medium bowl; set aside.

2 Divide the dough evenly into 8 pieces. On a lightly floured surface, roll out each piece of dough into a rough circle about 7 inches in diameter and ⅛ inch thick. Chill the dough until just cold and easy to work with, about 30 minutes.

3 Spoon 1 tablespoon flour in the center of each unbaked shell. Cover with about ½ cup rhubarb mixture, spreading the mixture out to about 1 inch from the edge of the shell. Fold the edges of the shells over the rhubarb filling, leaving the tarts open in the center. Gently brush between the folds with water, and press gently on the folds so that the dough adheres. Place the tarts on two parchment-lined baking sheets, arranging them so that they are several inches apart. Transfer to the refrigerator to chill at least 30 minutes.

4 Preheat the oven to 400°F. Remove the tarts from the refrigerator, brush them with water, and sprinkle with sugar. Place in the oven to bake until the crusts are golden brown, about 30 minutes; rotate the pans halfway through. Reduce the

heat to 350°F, and continue to bake until the juices are bubbly and just starting to run out from the center of each tartlet, 10 to 12 minutes more, rotating the pans as needed. Transfer immediately to a wire rack, and let cool before serving.

WHAT TO HAVE FOR DINNER

menu

BALSAMIC MARINATED SKIRT STEAK

CUCUMBER, STRING BEAN, AND OLIVE SALAD

GRATED POTATO PANCAKE

SUNKEN CHOCOLATE CAKES WITH COFFEE ICE CREAM

BALSAMIC MARINATED SKIRT STEAK

SERVES 4 | **PHOTOGRAPH ON PAGE 123**

½ cup balsamic vinegar

¼ cup olive oil

3 fresh rosemary sprigs

3 garlic cloves, thinly sliced

1½ pounds skirt steak

Coarse salt and freshly ground pepper

1 Combine the vinegar, oil, rosemary, and garlic in a glass or plastic dish, and stir to combine. Add the skirt steak, and coat well with the marinade. Cover; refrigerate for at least 30 minutes, or up to 2 hours.

2 Preheat the broiler or grill. Remove the steak from the marinade, and transfer to a rimmed baking sheet. Season the meat generously with salt and pepper on both sides. Place under the broiler or on the grill, and cook about 3 minutes; turn over, and cook for 3 minutes more for medium rare.

3 Transfer to a cutting board to rest for 5 to 10 minutes. Slice thinly across the grain, and serve.

CUCUMBER, STRING BEAN, AND OLIVE SALAD

SERVES 4 | **PHOTOGRAPH ON PAGE 123**

To pit the olives, place them on a cutting board, and press firmly with your thumb. The olives will split, and the pits can be easily removed.

Coarse salt

8 ounces string beans, ends snapped off

2 cucumbers (1¼ pounds)

4 ounces oil-cured black olives, pitted and torn in half

¼ cup fresh flat-leaf parsley leaves

1 teaspoon Dijon mustard

1 tablespoon red-wine vinegar

Freshly ground pepper

2 tablespoons extra-virgin olive oil

1 Fill a large bowl with ice and water; set aside. Bring a pot of water to a boil. Salt the water; add the string beans, and cook until bright green and just tender, 3 to 4 minutes. Drain, and transfer to the ice bath until cool. Drain, and cut in half lengthwise; set aside.

2 Peel the cucumbers, and split lengthwise. Remove the seeds using a melon baller or a spoon. Cut into ½-inch-thick slices on the diagonal. Combine with the string beans, olives, and parsley leaves in a medium serving bowl.

3 Place the mustard and vinegar in a small bowl; season with salt and pepper. Whisk to combine. Slowly add the olive oil, whisking constantly until well combined. Toss with salad just before serving.

GRATED POTATO PANCAKE

SERVES 4 | PHOTOGRAPH ON PAGE 123

It is important to wring all excess moisture from the potatoes to ensure a crisp pancake. If you are uncomfortable flipping the pancake, you may invert it onto a plate and slide it back into the pan after adding the remaining oil.

2 baking potatoes (about 1¼ pounds)

2 teaspoons canola oil

Coarse salt and freshly ground pepper

1 Peel the potatoes, and grate on the large holes of a box grater. Place the grated potatoes in a clean kitchen towel, and squeeze tightly to remove all excess moisture.

2 Heat a 10-inch nonstick skillet over medium-high heat, and add 1 teaspoon oil. When very hot, add the potatoes, and season with salt and pepper. Use a spatula to press the potatoes into a flat, round shape. Reduce the heat to medium. Cook, shaking the pan periodically, until the pancake is nicely browned, 5 to 7 minutes. Flip the pancake, and add the remaining teaspoon of oil, drizzling it around the edges of the pancake. Gently swirl the pan to distribute the oil. Season again with salt and pepper. Continue cooking until the pancake is golden brown and crisp on both sides, 5 to 7 minutes more.

3 Transfer to a cutting board, and cut into wedges. Serve immediately.

SUNKEN CHOCOLATE CAKES WITH COFFEE ICE CREAM

SERVES 4 | PHOTOGRAPH ON PAGE 126

The center of each cake makes a bowl for a scoop or two of coffee ice cream. Coating the muffin tin with butter and sugar gives the cakes sparkle and a bit of crunch.

8 tablespoons (1 stick) unsalted butter, cut into pieces, plus more for pan

¼ cup sugar, plus more for pan

5 ounces best-quality bittersweet chocolate, coarsely chopped

2 large egg yolks

2 large whole eggs, separated

1 pint coffee ice cream

1 Preheat the oven to 350°F. Lightly butter four cups in a jumbo nonstick muffin pan, leaving the two center cups empty. Coat lightly with sugar, and set aside. Place the butter and chocolate in a heat-proof bowl or the top of a double boiler set over a pan of barely simmering water. Stir occasionally until melted and thoroughly combined. Remove from the heat; set aside.

2 Combine the egg yolks with 2 tablespoons sugar, and whisk until the mixture is pale yellow and thick. Stir in the chocolate-and-butter mixture.

3 Whisk the egg whites until soft peaks form, add the remaining 2 tablespoons sugar, and whisk until stiff and shiny but not dry. Fold into the chocolate mixture. Divide the batter among the prepared muffin cups, and bake until set and slightly springy to the touch, about 25 minutes. Remove from the oven, and transfer to a wire rack. Allow to cool for 15 minutes in the pan; carefully run a knife around the edges of the cakes, and unmold. The cakes will sink in the middle as they cool. Serve each with a scoop or two of coffee ice cream.

FIT TO EAT: CALCIUM-RICH FOODS

BREAKFAST SMOOTHIES

SERVES 4 | PHOTOGRAPH ON PAGE 119

A quick, satisfying breakfast, these smoothies are high in calcium, vitamin C, and flavor. Any other ripe fruit, such as peaches or raspberries, can be substituted for the strawberries.

1½ cups (12 ounces) plain fat-free yogurt

3 to 4 bananas, peeled and cut into chunks

14 ounces strawberries, stems removed and coarsely chopped (about 3 cups)

¼ cup skim milk or soy milk

2 tablespoons honey

1 cup ice

Gradually add the yogurt, bananas, strawberries, milk, honey, and ice to the jar of a blender; purée until smooth. Serve.

PER SERVING: 207 CALORIES, 209 MG CALCIUM, 1 G FAT, 2 MG CHOLESTEROL, 76 MG SODIUM, 7 G PROTEIN, 3 G DIETARY FIBER

CALCIUM

Calcium is critical to strong bones and teeth. But ensuring you get the proper amount of the mineral doesn't require drinking massive quantities of milk. A variety of foods are packed with calcium. Edamame or soybeans—delicious simply boiled—are rich with calcium and other nutrients. Salmon cakes, white bean chili, and frittatas also contain plenty of calcium. And for a double shot of this essential mineral, try sautéed tofu with bitter greens.

EDAMAME

SERVES 4

Edamame (soybeans) are often served in Japanese restaurants preceding sushi. They are found in the freezer section of the grocery store. Discard the pods after stripping the beans.

1 pound frozen edamame

1 teaspoon coarse or sea salt

Bring a saucepan of water to a boil. Cook the edamame until just tender, 4 to 5 minutes. Drain well; sprinkle with salt. Serve.

PER SERVING: 180 CALORIES, 222 MG CALCIUM, 8 G FAT, 0 MG CHOLESTEROL, 295 MG SODIUM, 15 G PROTEIN, 8 G DIETARY FIBER

SAUTEED TOFU WITH BITTER GREENS

SERVES 4 TO 6 | PHOTOGRAPH ON PAGE 122

1 one-pound block extra-firm tofu

3 tablespoons low-sodium soy sauce

2 tablespoons toasted sesame oil

½ teaspoon chili paste or hot sauce (optional)

3 tablespoons freshly squeezed lime juice

1 tablespoon freshly grated ginger

6 garlic cloves, thinly sliced

2 pounds bitter greens, such as collard, mustard, baby bok choy, or dandelion, washed, trimmed, and torn into pieces

1 teaspoon sesame seeds, lightly toasted

¼ teaspoon crushed red-pepper flakes

1 Cut the tofu in half lengthwise, then cut each piece across into six slices. Place the tofu on a paper-towel-lined plate. Cover with more paper towels; place another plate on top. Weight with a few soup cans. Chill 30 minutes so the towels absorb excess water.

2 In a medium bowl, combine the soy sauce, sesame oil, chili paste or hot sauce (if using), lime juice, ginger, and garlic.

Set aside. Transfer the tofu to a medium bowl; toss with half the marinade, and let sit for 30 minutes.

3 Heat a nonstick skillet over medium heat. Working in batches, arrange the tofu in a single layer in the pan. Cook until golden brown, about 2 minutes per side; transfer to a platter. Repeat with the remaining tofu. Gradually add the greens to the skillet with the remaining marinade. Cook, tossing occasionally, until the greens are wilted and most of the liquid has evaporated, 5 to 8 minutes. Transfer to the platter with the tofu. Sprinkle with sesame seeds and pepper flakes; serve.

PER SERVING: 223 CALORIES, 271 MG CALCIUM, 11 G FAT, 0 MG CHOLESTEROL, 412 MG SODIUM, 15 G PROTEIN, 1 G DIETARY FIBER

WHITE BEAN CHILI WITH HERBED YOGURT CHEESE

SERVES 6

3 cups dried navy or other white beans

2 small poblano chile peppers

1 tablespoon unsalted butter

4 garlic cloves, minced

1 onion, cut into ¼-inch pieces

1 large carrot, cut into ¼-inch pieces

2 celery stalks, strings removed, cut into ¼-inch dice

1 teaspoon ground cumin

1 teaspoon ground coriander

½ teaspoon paprika

¼ teaspoon cayenne pepper (optional)

30 ounces Homemade Chicken Stock (page 8) or low-sodium canned, skimmed of fat

2 quarts water

1½ teaspoons coarse salt

¼ teaspoon freshly ground black pepper

4 radishes, grated

Cilantro sprigs, for garnish

Herbed Yogurt Cheese (recipe follows)

1 Pick over the dried beans, discarding any stones or broken beans; rinse. Place in a large saucepan, cover with cold water by 2 inches, and bring to a strong boil over high heat. Remove from the heat; let stand 1 hour. Drain the beans; set aside.

2 Meanwhile, place the peppers directly on the trivet of a gas-stove burner over high heat or on a grill. As they turn black, turn them with tongs. (Alternatively, place the peppers in a baking pan; broil in the oven, turning as peppers become charred.) Transfer the charred peppers to a medium bowl; cover with plastic wrap. Let peppers rest 15 minutes. Transfer to a work surface (do not rinse). Peel off and discard the blackened skin. Halve the peppers; remove the seeds and ribs, and discard. Cut the peppers into ¼-inch pieces; set aside.

3 Heat the butter in a large saucepan over medium heat. Add the garlic, onion, carrot, and celery. Cover; cook, stirring occasionally, until softened and slightly browned, about 15 minutes. Add the cumin, coriander, paprika, and cayenne, if using; stir to combine. Stir in the stock, water, beans, and half the roasted peppers. Cover; cook until the beans are soft, about 1½ hours. Uncover; simmer gently until the beans begin to fall apart, about 30 minutes more. Season with salt and pepper. Serve the chili garnished with the remaining peppers, and the radish, cilantro, and yogurt cheese.

PER CHILI SERVING: 369 CALORIES, 169 MG CALCIUM, 4 G FAT, 6 MG CHOLESTEROL, 572 MG SODIUM, 22 G PROTEIN, 11 G DIETARY FIBER

HERBED YOGURT CHEESE

MAKES ABOUT 1 CUP

8   ounces plain fat-free yogurt
2   teaspoons freshly squeezed lime juice
¼   cup chopped fresh cilantro
¼   cup chopped fresh flat-leaf parsley
¼   teaspoon coarse salt
    Pinch of freshly ground pepper

Line a colander or sieve with several thicknesses of cheesecloth; set over a bowl. Add the yogurt; drain for 1 hour. Transfer the yogurt to the bowl of a food processor; add the lime juice, cilantro, parsley, salt, and pepper. Purée until well combined. Chill until ready to use, up to 1 week.

PER SERVING: 8 CALORIES, 29 MG CALCIUM, 0 G FAT, 0 MG CHOLESTEROL, 29 MG SODIUM, 1 G PROTEIN, 0 G DIETARY FIBER

BROCCOLI CHEESE FRITTATA

SERVES 8 | PHOTOGRAPH ON PAGE 122

Grated Parmesan cheese and broccoli florets and stems are added to a frittata to make it a good source of calcium.

2   heads (about 2 pounds) broccoli
2   teaspoons unsalted butter
2   small onions, cut into ½-inch pieces
1   cup water
1½   teaspoons coarse salt
¼   teaspoon freshly ground pepper
3   large whole eggs
9   large egg whites
½   ounce (¼ cup) freshly grated
     Parmesan cheese
2   ounces (⅓ cup) goat cheese
     Vegetable-oil cooking spray

1   Preheat the oven to 375°F. Cut the broccoli stems into ½-inch pieces, and cut the florets into 1-inch pieces; set aside. Melt the butter in a 12-inch sauté pan over medium heat. Add the onions; cook until translucent, about 5 minutes. Add the broccoli stems, and cook until they begin to soften, about 5 minutes. Add the florets and water, and cook until the broccoli is tender and the liquid has evaporated, about 5 minutes more. Add the salt and pepper. Transfer to a bowl to cool completely.

2   Wipe out the pan; coat with cooking spray. In the bowl of an electric mixer fitted with the whisk attachment, combine the eggs and egg whites. Beat until extremely light and foamy, 8 to 10 minutes. Heat the pan over medium-high heat. Fold the Parmesan and the broccoli mixture into the eggs. Transfer the mixture to the pan; dot the top with goat cheese. Cook, without stirring, for 2 minutes. Transfer the pan to the oven; bake until the top is golden brown and the frittata is set, about 30 minutes. Let cool 1 minute before removing from the pan. Serve hot or at room temperature.

PER SERVING: 128 CALORIES, 103 MG CALCIUM, 5 G FAT, 87 MG CHOLESTEROL, 381 MG SODIUM, 12 G PROTEIN, 4 G DIETARY FIBER

WHAT IS A FRITTATA?

A frittata is an Italian omelet with the ingredients mixed into the eggs rather than sprinkled over them in a hot skillet, as in a French omelet. A frittata is firmer than a traditional omelet because it's cooked very slowly over low heat (an omelet is usually cooked quickly over moderately high heat). The result is a soft, fluffy egg pie, delicious hot or at room temperature.

SALMON CAKES

MAKES 1 DOZEN; SERVES 4
PHOTOGRAPH ON PAGE 122

Flaked salmon and black beans are both good sources of calcium.

1 fifteen-ounce can salmon, drained and flaked (about 2 cups)

1 cup canned black beans, rinsed and drained

1 small red bell pepper (or ½ large pepper), seeds and ribs removed, finely chopped

3 scallions, white and light-green parts only, finely chopped

1 large whole egg

3 large egg whites

1 teaspoon mustard powder

½ teaspoon paprika

¼ teaspoon coarse salt

¼ teaspoon freshly ground black pepper

Few dashes of hot sauce (optional)

1 cup bread crumbs

Mixed greens, for serving

Vegetable-oil cooking spray

1 Preheat the oven to 450°F. Coat a baking sheet with cooking spray. In a bowl, combine the salmon, beans, bell pepper, scallions, egg, egg whites, mustard, paprika, salt, pepper, hot sauce (if using), and ½ cup bread crumbs. Using hands, combine well.

2 Pour the remaining ½ cup bread crumbs into a shallow bowl. Form the salmon mixture into twelve 2½-inch patties. Coat the patties in bread crumbs; place on the prepared baking sheet. Cook until golden brown and crisp, about 30 minutes, flipping the cakes over halfway through cooking. Serve warm over greens.

PER SERVING: 353 CALORIES, 351 MG CALCIUM, 9 G FAT, 95 MG CHOLESTEROL, 1,080 MG SODIUM, 35 G PROTEIN, 5 G DIETARY FIBER

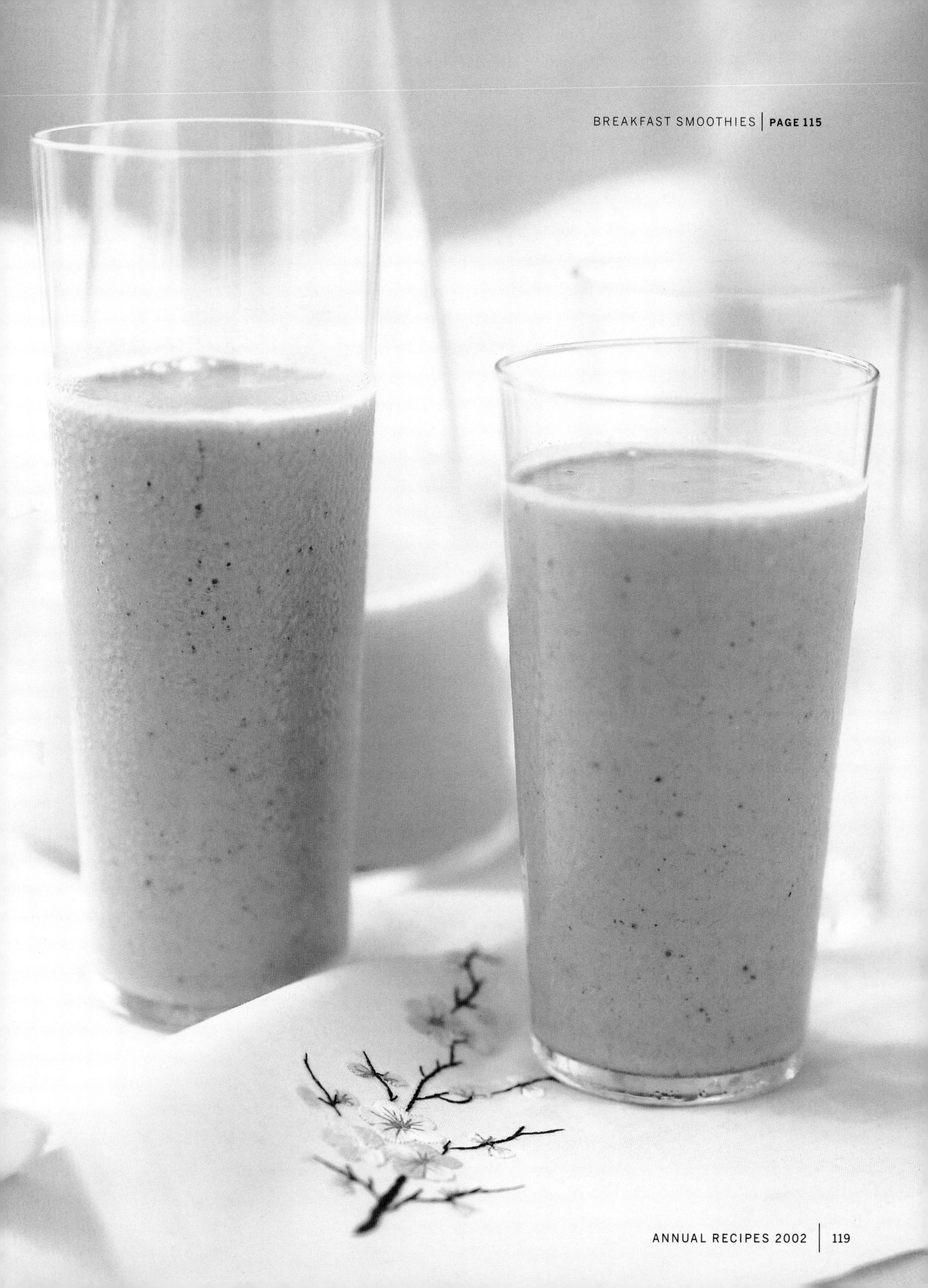

BREAKFAST SMOOTHIES | PAGE 115

1 After the dough has risen, roll it out on a lightly floured surface into a large rectangle; brush melted butter over the middle third of the dough.

2 Sprinkle one-third of the poppy-seed filling across the middle of the rectangle. Then fold the dough over the center to make an envelope, and rotate the dough 90 degrees.

3 Repeat the process in steps 1 and 2: Roll the dough into another rectangle, brush the middle third with butter, and sprinkle half the remaining filling across the center.

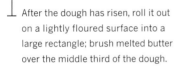

4 Repeat the process a third and final time. Let the dough rest, then roll one final time into a long rectangle.

5 Using a sharp knife, cut the dough crosswise into one-inch-wide strips, and gently pull and twist each of the strips into a spiral.

6 Place the twists in two layers in the bottom of two tube pans, forming circles around the bottom. Set the cakes aside to rise until doubled, then bake at 375° F.

YEASTED COFFEE CAKE WITH POPPY-SEED FILLING | **PAGE 108**

BROCCOLI CHEESE FRITTATA | **PAGE 117**

HOLLANDAISE SAUCE | **PAGE 106**

SAUTEED TOFU WITH BITTER GREENS | **PAGE 116**

SALMON CAKES | **PAGE 118**

BALSAMIC MARINATED SKIRT STEAK | **PAGE 114**

CUCUMBER, STRING BEAN, AND OLIVE SALAD | **PAGE 114**

GRATED POTATO PANCAKE | **PAGE 114**

MAYPOLE CUPCAKES | **PAGE 106**

To make flowers for maypole cake and cupcakes, use a gum-paste petal cutter to cut petals from jellied citrus slices. For cupcakes, use the tops of large gumdrops as flower centers. For maypole cake, use small gumdrops as centers. A Life Saver and small gumdrop top the maypole.

CREAM CHEESE AND MASCARPONE CHEESECAKE | **PAGE 112**

RHUBARB AND STRAWBERRY ICE CREAM | **PAGE 110**

MAYPOLE CAKE | **PAGE 105**

SUNKEN CHOCOLATE CAKES WITH COFFEE ICE CREAM | **PAGE 115**

june

Frozen Lemon Mousse

Gougères

Beef Paillards with Arugula and
Capers

Grilled Chicken Paillards with Endive
and Radicchio

Pork Paillards with Grilled Pineapple

Grilled Turkey Sandwich

Spicy Asian Slaw

French Crudités

Southwestern Cobb Salad

Green Gazpacho Salad

Grilled Vegetable Salad

Pan-fried Soft-Shell Crabs

Creamed Cornbread

Chopped Coleslaw

Outer Banks Clam Chowder

Alma Etheridge Wilson's
Roanoke Sixteen-Layer
Chocolate Fudge Cake

Coffee Praline Checkerboard Bombe

Spumoni Bombe

Orange Sherbet Bombe

Malt Ball Bombes

Tropical Bombe

Banana Split Bombe

Raspberry Pavlova Bombe

Grilled Lamb Chops with
Lemon Yogurt Sauce

Grilled Mixed Peppers and Onions

Eggplant Fritters

Plum, Raspberry, and Tarragon Soup

Dolmades

Zucchini Pie

Pink Potato Salad

Moussaka

Stewed Baby Artichokes with
Fava Beans

DESSERT OF THE MONTH

FROZEN LEMON MOUSSE

SERVES 8 | PHOTOGRAPHS ON PAGE 148

This mousse can be made up to three days before serving. Ring molds can be purchased at specialty cookware stores; you can also use an eight-inch springform pan.

8 to 10 lemons
2 cups sugar
8 large egg yolks
2 large whole eggs
1 cup (2 sticks) unsalted butter, cut into pieces
1½ cups plus 2 tablespoons heavy cream, chilled
   Candied Lemon Zest (recipe follows)
8 ounces crème fraîche

1 Fill a large bowl with ice and water; set aside. Juice 1 lemon; reserve the juice. Juice the additional lemons to yield 1 cup. To make the lemon curd, place 1 cup lemon juice, sugar, egg yolks, whole eggs, and butter in a saucepan; whisk to combine. Cook over medium heat, whisking constantly, until the mixture begins to boil, about 10 minutes.

2 Strain the curd through a fine sieve into a bowl set in the ice bath. Stir periodically until cool; remove from the ice bath. Lay a sheet of plastic wrap directly on the surface of the curd to keep a skin from forming; refrigerate at least 1 hour and up to 3 days.

3 Place 1½ cups chilled heavy cream in a large mixing bowl; whisk until soft peaks form. Reserve ½ cup of the lemon curd for the sauce; add the remaining lemon curd to the whipped cream. Fold gently until well combined.

4 Place eight ring molds, 3 inches in diameter and 2¼ inches high, on a baking sheet lined with parchment. Divide the mousse among the molds, filling each mold with about ¾ cup of mousse. Place in the freezer, on the baking sheet, until firm, at least 4 hours.

5 Drain the candied lemon zest; reserve the syrup. Whisk ⅓ cup syrup and the reserved ½ cup lemon curd and juice of 1 lemon in a small bowl. Place the frozen mousse on plates; let rest 4 to 5 minutes before removing the molds.

6 Meanwhile, whisk the crème fraîche and the remaining 2 tablespoons cream in a medium bowl until soft peaks form. Remove the molds. Spoon the lemon sauce around the mousse, and top with the crème fraîche mixture. Garnish with the candied zest; serve.

CANDIED LEMON ZEST

GARNISHES 8 SERVINGS

Use the juice of these lemons for the Frozen Lemon Mousse, and use some of the syrup for the lemon sauce. Make this recipe a day before the mousse.

4 lemons, well scrubbed
2 cups sugar
1 cup cool water

1 Remove the zest from the lemons with a vegetable peeler, keeping the pieces long. Remove any white pith with a paring knife. Using a very sharp knife, cut zest into a fine julienne; place it in a small bowl, and cover with boiling water. Let stand 30 minutes; drain.

2 Place the sugar and water in a small saucepan, cover, and bring to a boil over medium-high heat. When the sugar is completely dissolved, add the julienned zest. Reduce the heat to medium-low, and cook, uncovered, for 10 minutes more. Remove from the heat, cover, and let stand overnight. Store the zest in the syrup in an airtight container in the refrigerator for up to 2 weeks.

GOOD THINGS

GOUGERES

MAKES ABOUT 6 DOZEN

Gougères, savory bites made with a steam-leavened dough called pâte à choux, are one of the simplest and most versatile of the French pastry doughs, and the basis for cream puffs, éclairs, and Paris-Brest. Adding grated cheese and herbs to the dough—here, Parmesan and chives, with a pinch of cayenne pepper—produces a savory puff that is an exceptional partner to wine or champagne.

1 cup plus 1 tablespoon water
8 tablespoons (1 stick) unsalted butter
1 teaspoon table salt
   Pinch of cayenne pepper
1 cup all-purpose flour
5 large eggs
¾ cup finely grated Parmesan cheese
1 tablespoon snipped fresh chives

1 Preheat the oven to 375°F. Combine 1 cup water, butter, salt, and cayenne in a saucepan. Bring to a boil. When the butter melts, add the flour; reduce the heat to medium-low. Stir constantly with a wooden spoon until the dough pulls away from the edges; it should not stick to your fingers and will appear shiny and smooth. Transfer to a medium bowl; let cool 5 minutes.

2 One at a time, add 4 eggs; mix well between each addition. Add the Parmesan and chives; mix until combined. Transfer the mixture to a pastry bag fitted with a plain ½-inch round tip (Wilton #1A). To form each gougère, pipe 1 teaspoon of dough onto a parchment-lined baking sheet. Allow 2 inches between each gougère. Pat down the peaks of the dough with a finger dipped in water.

3 Combine the remaining egg with the remaining tablespoon water; brush on the gougères with a pastry brush. Bake 20 to 25 minutes, rotating the pan after 12 minutes, until golden. Serve. Can be frozen in an airtight container for up to 1 month; reheat in a 350°F oven for 15 minutes or until heated through before serving.

PAILLARDS

BEEF PAILLARDS WITH ARUGULA AND CAPERS

SERVES 6

2¼ pounds beef tenderloin, cut into 12 three-ounce steaks
Basic Marinade (recipe follows)
1 small red onion, cut in paper-thin rounds
3 tablespoons red-wine vinegar
Coarse salt
6 ounces baby arugula (or chopped arugula)
2 celery stalks, strings removed, very thinly sliced on the bias
1 tablespoon freshly squeezed lemon juice
1 tablespoon extra-virgin olive oil
Freshly ground pepper
¼ cup capers, drained

1 Cut open the two sides of a resealable plastic bag. Place 1 steak in the bag; pound to ¼-inch thickness using a meat pounder. Transfer to a nonmetal container. Repeat with the remaining steaks. Add the marinade. Chill for 2 hours.
2 Place the onion in a bowl with the vinegar and salt to taste; toss to combine.
3 Heat a grill or grill pan to medium-high heat. Place the arugula, celery, lemon juice, and olive oil in a medium bowl; toss to combine. Season with salt and pepper. Remove the meat from the marinade; season with salt and pepper. Grill for 1 minute on each side, until browned. Place two pieces of beef on each plate; sprinkle with capers. Top with the arugula salad and pickled onions. Serve.

BASIC MARINADE

MAKES ABOUT ½ CUP

If you marinate the meat overnight, omit the lemon juice and add it two hours before cooking.

⅓ cup extra-virgin olive oil
2 sprigs fresh rosemary, crushed
3 sprigs fresh thyme
3 large garlic cloves, peeled and smashed
Juice of 1 lemon
Pinch of freshly ground pepper

Combine the oil, rosemary, thyme, garlic, lemon juice, and pepper, and stir to combine.

GRILLED CHICKEN PAILLARDS WITH ENDIVE AND RADICCHIO

SERVES 6

3 whole boneless, skinless chicken-breast halves (about 2 pounds)
Basic Marinade (recipe above)
3 heads Belgian endive, halved lengthwise
2 large heads radicchio, each cut into 6 wedges
3 lemons, cut in half crosswise
2 tablespoons extra-virgin olive oil
Coarse salt and freshly ground pepper
Rosemary sprigs, for garnish
Thyme sprigs, for garnish

1 Cut open the two sides of a resealable plastic bag. Place 1 chicken-breast half in the bag; pound to ¼-inch thickness using a meat pounder. Transfer to a nonmetal container. Repeat with the remaining chicken. Add the marinade. Chill for 2 hours.
2 Brush the endive, radicchio, and cut sides of the lemons with the olive oil; sprinkle the endive and radicchio with salt and pepper; set aside.
3 Heat a grill or grill pan to medium-high heat. Remove the chicken from the marinade; season with salt and pepper. Grill until browned and cooked through, 2 to 3 minutes on each side. Transfer to a serving platter. Grill the endive, radicchio, and lemons until nicely browned, about 3 minutes; turn as needed. Serve on a platter with the chicken paillards, garnished with the rosemary and thyme.

PORK PAILLARDS WITH GRILLED PINEAPPLE

SERVES 6 | PHOTOGRAPH ON PAGE 146

6 seven-ounce boneless pork loin chops
Basic Marinade (recipe above)
½ pineapple, peeled, cored, and cut into ½-inch-thick rings
3 tablespoons extra-virgin olive oil
Coarse salt and freshly ground pepper
2 heads butter lettuce, torn into bite-size pieces
1 bunch fresh cilantro, leaves only
2 tablespoons freshly squeezed lime juice, plus 3 limes for garnish

1 Cut open the two sides of a resealable plastic bag. Place 1 chop in the bag; pound to ¼-inch thickness using a meat pounder. Transfer to a nonmetal container. Repeat with the remaining chops. Add the marinade. Chill 2 hours.
2 Heat a grill or grill pan to medium-high heat. Brush the pineapple with 1 tablespoon olive oil; sprinkle with salt and pepper. Grill until browned, about 4 minutes, turning as needed. Transfer to a cutting board; cut into ½-inch cubes. Set aside.
3 Remove the pork from the marinade; season with salt and pepper. Grill until cooked through and browned on both sides, 1½ to 2 minutes per side. Combine the lettuce, cilantro, lime juice, remaining 2 tablespoons olive oil, and salt and pepper to taste in a bowl; toss to combine. Serve on a platter with the pork paillards, chopped pineapple, and halved limes.

GRILLED TURKEY SANDWICH

SERVES 6

Cook the tomatoes on only one side to prevent them from getting too soft.

½ boneless turkey breast (1¾ pounds)
Basic Marinade (recipe above)
1 sweet onion, cut into ¼-inch-thick rounds
5 plum tomatoes, cut into ¼-inch rounds
2 twenty-five-inch baguettes, halved lengthwise
¼ cup extra-virgin olive oil
Coarse salt and freshly ground pepper
2 ounces Parmesan cheese, sliced paper thin
1 cup fresh basil leaves
1 bunch watercress, tough stems discarded

1 Remove the tenderloin from the turkey; cut the tenderloin in half lengthwise. Cut the breast into ½-inch-thick medallions. Cut open the two sides of a resealable plastic bag. Place 1 medallion in the bag; pound to ¼-inch thickness using a meat pounder. Transfer to a nonmetal container. Repeat with the remaining turkey. Add the marinade. Chill for 2 hours.
2 Heat a grill or grill pan to medium-high heat. Brush the onion, tomatoes, and bread with the oil. Season the onion and tomatoes with salt and pepper. Grill the onion until browned and soft, about 2

minutes per side. Set aside on a plate. Grill the tomatoes without turning until lightly browned, about 2 minutes. Grill the bread until just toasted, 1 to 2 minutes.

3 Remove the turkey from the marinade; season with salt and pepper. Grill until browned and cooked through, 1 to 2 minutes per side. Layer the bread with the onion, turkey, Parmesan, basil, tomatoes, and watercress; top with the remaining bread. Serve.

SHREDDED AND CHOPPED SALADS

SPICY ASIAN SLAW
SERVES 6 TO 8 AS A SIDE DISH

If you don't want to chop all of the vegetables by hand, use the grater attachment on your food processor.

FOR THE DRESSING:

1 cup mayonnaise

2 tablespoons toasted sesame oil

2 tablespoons mirin or rice-wine vinegar

¼ cup chili sauce

3 tablespoons freshly squeezed lime juice

1 tablespoon grated ginger

1 teaspoon coarse salt

¼ teaspoon freshly ground pepper

2 teaspoons sesame seeds

FOR THE SLAW:

½ small head (about 1 pound) red cabbage

½ head (about 1 pound) napa cabbage

1 turnip (about 9 ounces), peeled

1 small daikon (about 8 ounces), peeled

1 large carrot

4 scallions, thinly sliced on the diagonal

1 red bell pepper, seeds and ribs removed, thinly sliced

¼ cup finely chopped fresh mint leaves

¼ cup finely chopped fresh cilantro

1 To make the dressing, in a medium bowl, whisk together the mayonnaise, sesame oil, vinegar, chili sauce, lime juice, ginger, salt, pepper, and sesame seeds; set dressing aside.

2 To make the slaw, core, quarter, and very thinly slice the red and napa cabbages. Transfer to a large bowl, and fill it with cold water to cover the cabbage. Swish the cabbage around with your hands so any dirt settles to the bottom of the bowl. Lift the cabbage from the bowl, and transfer to a colander to drain. Place in a large bowl; set aside.

3 Using the large holes of a box grater, grate the turnip, daikon, and carrot. Add to the bowl of cabbage, along with the scallions, red bell pepper, mint, and cilantro. Add the reserved dressing, and toss to combine. Cover with plastic wrap, and let refrigerate at least 2 hours, preferably overnight, and up to 4 days. Serve chilled.

FRENCH CRUDITES
SERVES 6

Serve this assortment of grated salads as a first course with French bread and butter.

½ cup walnuts

4 large (about 2 pounds) beets, scrubbed

2 pounds (about 2) seedless cucumbers

1 teaspoon coarse salt, plus more for seasoning

1 bunch red radishes, tops removed, grated on large holes of box grater

5 large (about 2 pounds) carrots, grated on large holes of box grater

½ cup golden raisins

3 tablespoons finely chopped fresh flat-leaf parsley

2 medium (2 pounds) celery root

¼ cup minced cornichons or gherkins

¼ cup capers, drained and coarsely chopped

¼ cup snipped chives, or more for garnish

½ cup mayonnaise

1 tablespoon Dijon mustard

¾ cup red-wine vinegar

1 cup extra-virgin olive oil
Freshly ground pepper

1 Preheat the oven to 350°F. Place the walnuts in a single layer on a rimmed baking sheet. Toast until aromatic, 8 to 12 minutes, shaking the pan halfway through to make sure the nuts toast evenly. Set aside to cool, and chop coarsely.

2 Place the beets in a saucepan; cover with cold water. Bring to a boil, and reduce to a simmer. Cook until the beets are tender when pierced with the tip of

HOW TO MAKE PAILLARDS

Beef, pork, and chicken and turkey breasts can all be prepared as paillards. Cut turkey breasts into cross sections before pounding; otherwise they are too large and thick.

1 Cut open the two sides of a thick-ply plastic bag, such as a resealable bag or freezer bag, so you can easily move the pieces of meat in and out of it.

2 Place the meat inside the bag, and pound, using a heavy tool and a slightly outward motion, working to yield a uniform one-quarter-inch thickness. The heavier the tool, the more concentrated the weight, and the fewer times you will have to hit each piece. If you use a meat pounder, use the smooth side, not the textured one; the goal is to flatten the meat as evenly as possible.

3 Place the paillards in a nonmetallic container; marinate at least two hours.

a paring knife, about 30 minutes, depending on their size. Drain, and rinse well with cold water. Let sit until cool enough to handle. Peel, and grate the beets into a bowl using the large holes of a box grater. Add the chopped nuts. Toss to combine; set aside.

3 Peel the cucumbers. Grate on the large holes of a box grater, and place in a colander set over a bowl. Sprinkle with 1 teaspoon salt, and set aside for 20 minutes to let the juices drain. Discard the accumulated juices, transfer the cucumbers to a clean kitchen towel, and wring out any additional moisture. Transfer to a bowl, and add the radishes; set aside.

4 In another bowl, combine the carrots, raisins, and parsley; set aside. Peel the celery root; grate on the large holes of a box grater. Place in a bowl; add the cornichons, capers, chives, and mayonnaise; stir to combine.

5 In another bowl, whisk together the mustard and vinegar until well combined. Drizzle in the olive oil, and whisk until the dressing is smooth and emulsified. Season with salt and pepper; set aside.

6 Drizzle half the dressing over each salad, tossing to combine. Season each with salt and pepper. Garnish the beets and celery root with additional chives, if desired. Serve at room temperature.

SOUTHWESTERN COBB SALAD

SERVES 6 TO 8 AS A MAIN DISH | **PHOTO-GRAPH ON PAGE 146**

¼ cup freshly squeezed lime juice, plus juice of 2 limes

¼ cup plus 2 tablespoons extra-virgin olive oil

¼ cup soy sauce

1 teaspoon ground cumin

1 teaspoon crushed red-pepper flakes

4 boneless, skinless chicken-breast halves

4 large eggs

8 ounces thickly sliced bacon

1 yellow bell pepper

1 poblano chile

1 tomato, seeded and cut into ½-inch pieces

½ cup (2½ ounces) coarsely chopped pitted black olives

1 sweet onion, cut into ¼-inch pieces

Coarse salt and freshly ground black pepper

2 ripe but firm Hass avocados, peeled and cut into ½-inch pieces

½ cup chopped fresh cilantro

⅛ teaspoon ground cayenne pepper (optional)

1 fifteen-ounce can black beans, rinsed and drained

1 small head romaine, torn in 1-inch pieces

Green Goddess Dressing (recipe follows)

1 Combine ¼ cup lime juice, ¼ cup oil, the soy sauce, ½ teaspoon cumin, and the red-pepper flakes in a small bowl. Place the chicken breasts in a large resealable plastic bag. Pour the marinade into the bag, and refrigerate at least 1 hour or overnight.

2 Heat a grill or grill pan to medium-high heat. Lift the chicken from the bag, allowing the excess marinade to drain off. Place on the grill, and cook until grill marks appear and the chicken is cooked through, about 5 minutes per side. Cool the chicken completely, and cut into ½-inch pieces; set aside.

3 Place the eggs in a saucepan with cold water to cover. Cover the pan, and bring to a boil. Remove from the heat. Let sit 11 minutes. Drain; rinse under cold running water until cooled. Peel and coarsely chop the eggs; set aside.

4 Heat a skillet over medium heat. Cook the bacon until crisp, and drain on paper towels. Crumble when cool; set aside.

5 Place the yellow and poblano peppers directly on the trivet of a gas burner over high heat or on the grill or grill pan used for the chicken. Turn the peppers with tongs as they char. (Alternatively, place the peppers on a rimmed baking sheet, and broil in the oven, turning as each side becomes charred.) Transfer to a large bowl; cover immediately with plastic wrap. Let the peppers sweat until cool enough to handle. Peel off and discard the blackened skin. Remove the seeds; chop the yellow pepper into ½-inch pieces and the poblano into ¼-inch pieces; set them aside separately.

6 In a bowl, combine the yellow pepper, tomato, olives, and half the onion. Season with salt and pepper, and set aside.

7 In another bowl, combine the poblano with the avocados, ¼ cup cilantro, remaining juice of 2 limes, cayenne pepper (if using), and remaining ½ teaspoon cumin. Season with salt and pepper; set aside.

8 Combine the black beans with the remaining ¼ cup cilantro and onion. Drizzle with the remaining 2 tablespoons olive oil, and season with salt and pepper; set aside.

9 Arrange the romaine on a platter. Arrange the chicken, eggs, and bacon and the yellow pepper, poblano, and bean mixtures in sections across the romaine. Drizzle with the dressing; serve.

GREEN GODDESS DRESSING

MAKES 1½ CUPS

Let the dressing sit overnight to meld the flavors.

½ cup mayonnaise

½ cup sour cream

2 tablespoons nonfat buttermilk

1 tablespoon white-wine vinegar

1 teaspoon Worcestershire sauce

1 bunch chives, coarsely chopped (⅓ cup)

2 scallions, white and green parts, coarsely chopped

2 tablespoons chopped fresh cilantro

2 tablespoons chopped fresh flat-leaf parsley

1 teaspoon sugar

1 teaspoon coarse salt

½ teaspoon freshly ground black pepper
    Pinch of cayenne pepper (optional)

Combine all ingredients in a blender or food processor; process until smooth. Refrigerate in an airtight container up to 3 days.

GREEN GAZPACHO SALAD

SERVES 6 | PHOTOGRAPH ON PAGE 146

½ cup slivered almonds

4 ounces baguette or other French bread, cut into ½-inch cubes (1½ cups)

1 yellow tomato, seeded and cut into ½-inch dice

1 green bell pepper, seeds and ribs removed, cut into ½-inch dice

1 cucumber, peeled and seeded, cut into ½-inch dice

2 celery stalks, strings removed, cut into ½-inch dice

1 small red onion, cut into ½-inch dice

2 scallions, thinly sliced

1 cup (about 6 ounces) green seedless grapes, cut in half

¼ cup finely chopped fresh flat-leaf parsley

2 tablespoons finely chopped fresh tarragon

¼ cup extra-virgin olive oil

2 tablespoons sherry or white-wine vinegar

1 teaspoon coarse salt

¼ teaspoon freshly ground pepper

1 head butter lettuce, torn into bite-size pieces

1 Preheat the oven to 350°F. Place the almonds in a single layer on a rimmed baking sheet and the bread cubes on a baking sheet. Toast until the nuts are golden and aromatic and the bread is dried and barely golden, 8 to 10 minutes; set aside.

2 In a large bowl, combine the tomato, bell pepper, cucumber, celery, red onion, scallions, grapes, parsley, tarragon, ¼ cup almonds, and the bread cubes. Drizzle with the olive oil and vinegar. Add the salt and pepper. Toss well to combine. Let sit for 30 minutes for the flavors to blend. Serve over the lettuce garnished with the remaining ¼ cup almonds.

GRILLED VEGETABLE SALAD

SERVES 6 TO 8

Substitute vegetables according to what you have on hand.

1 tablespoon plus 1 teaspoon coarse salt

1 teaspoon freshly ground black pepper

2 teaspoons dried oregano

1 eggplant (1 pound), sliced ½ inch thick

1 red bell pepper, seeds and ribs removed, cut in half

1 yellow bell pepper, seeds and ribs removed, cut in half

1 green bell pepper, seeds and ribs removed, cut in half

1 medium zucchini, cut lengthwise into ½-inch-thick slices

1 yellow summer squash, cut lengthwise into ½-inch-thick slices

1 head radicchio, quartered lengthwise

2 heads Belgian endive, halved lengthwise

1 large onion, cut into ½-inch-thick slices

¾ cup extra-virgin olive oil

¼ cup finely chopped fresh flat-leaf parsley

1 tablespoon chopped fresh thyme

1 In a small bowl, combine 2 teaspoons coarse salt, the black pepper, and oregano; set aside.

2 Place the sliced eggplant in a colander, and sprinkle both sides with the remaining 2 teaspoons salt. Let sit 1 hour. Rinse quickly, and pat dry with paper towels; set aside.

3 Heat a grill or grill pan to medium-high heat. Arrange the eggplant, bell peppers, zucchini, summer squash, radicchio, endive, and onion on a large rimmed baking sheet. Brush with the olive oil; sprinkle with the salt-oregano mixture. Toss gently until evenly coated. Grill in batches until tender and grill marks appear (times will vary with each vegetable). Return to the baking sheet; let sit until cool enough to handle. Cut into 1-inch pieces, and transfer to a bowl. Add the parsley and thyme, and toss to combine. Season with any remaining salt-oregano mixture if desired. Serve warm or at room temperature.

SOFT-SHELL CRABBING

PAN-FRIED SOFT-SHELL CRABS

SERVES 6 | PHOTOGRAPH ON PAGE 145

Ask your fishmonger to clean the soft-shell crabs for you. They should be cooked no more than six hours after they are cleaned.

1½ cups all-purpose flour

2 teaspoons coarse salt

1 teaspoon freshly ground pepper

12 soft-shell crabs, cleaned

¾ cup vegetable oil

6 tablespoons unsalted butter

¼ cup loosely packed fresh flat-leaf parsley leaves, chopped

3 lemons, cut in half

1 Whisk together the flour, salt, and pepper; place on a dinner plate. Dredge 2 crabs in the flour mixture, shaking off the excess (make sure they are completely coated).

2 Heat 2 tablespoons oil in a medium sauté pan over medium-high heat. The oil should be very hot but not smoking. Place the flour-coated crabs, back side down, in the sauté pan; reduce the heat to medium if the pan starts to smoke. Sauté the crabs until golden and crisp, about 3 minutes (do not stand too close

to the pan; the crabs tend to spatter during cooking). Turn the crabs over, and cook 2 minutes more.

3 Add 1 tablespoon butter and a pinch of parsley to the skillet. Squeeze the juice of half a lemon over the crabs. Keep warm in a low oven. Repeat the process until all the crabs are cooked.

CREAMED CORNBREAD

MAKES 1 EIGHT-INCH-SQUARE
LOAF | **PHOTOGRAPH ON PAGE 144**

2 tablespoons unsalted butter, melted, plus more for pan
1 cup all-purpose flour
¾ cup yellow cornmeal
1 tablespoon baking powder
½ teaspoon coarse salt
½ cup milk
½ cup sour cream
1 large egg
⅓ cup sugar
1 fourteen-and-three-quarter-ounce can creamed corn

1 Preheat the oven to 425°F. Brush an 8-inch-square baking pan with butter. Set aside.
2 Combine the flour, cornmeal, baking powder, and salt in a medium mixing bowl; set aside.
3 Whisk together the milk, sour cream, egg, sugar, and butter in a small bowl. Stir in the creamed corn. Fold the wet ingredients into the dry ingredients until well combined.
4 Pour the batter into the prepared pan, and bake until set and golden brown on top, about 30 minutes. Cool slightly on a wire rack before cutting into squares.

CHOPPED COLESLAW

SERVES 6 TO 8 | **PHOTOGRAPH ON PAGE 145**

1 large head (3½ pounds) green cabbage
3 tablespoons coarse salt
½ cup sugar
2 tablespoons cider vinegar
¾ cup mayonnaise
3 large carrots

1 Grate the cabbage on the large holes of a box grater or in a food processor. Fill a large bowl three quarters full with cold water. Add the salt and grated cabbage. Cover, and refrigerate overnight.
2 Drain the cabbage, squeezing out the excess moisture with your hands, and pat dry.
3 Whisk together the sugar, vinegar, and mayonnaise. Peel and grate the carrots on the large holes of the box grater.
4 Combine the cabbage and the carrots in a large bowl. Add the dressing, and toss well to mix. Chill at least 1 hour before serving.

OUTER BANKS CLAM CHOWDER

SERVES 6 TO 8 | **PHOTOGRAPH ON PAGE 144**

1 quart cold water
3 dozen cherrystone clams, scrubbed
6 ounces good-quality bacon, cut into 1-inch pieces
2 medium yellow onions, cut into ¼-inch dice
2 garlic cloves, minced
3 medium russet potatoes, cut into ½-inch pieces
¼ cup white wine
Coarse salt and freshly ground pepper

1 Fill a large high-sided saucepan with the water. Set over high heat; bring to a boil. Add the clams, cover with the lid slightly askew, and cook 5 minutes. Remove any of the clams that have opened, and transfer to a bowl. Continue cooking the clams, removing them as they open, for 5 to 10 minutes more. Discard any clams that have failed to open by this time. Strain the cooking liquid through a cheesecloth-lined sieve. Set aside.
2 Wipe out the saucepan; set over medium heat. Add the bacon; cook until golden and crisp, about 7 minutes. Using a slotted spoon, remove the bacon, and transfer to a paper towel-lined plate to drain, leaving the fat in the pan.
3 Add the onions and garlic to the saucepan, and cook in the bacon fat until soft and translucent, stirring often so they do not brown, about 5 minutes. Add

3½ cups of reserved clam broth and the potatoes. Bring to a simmer, and cook until the potatoes are very tender, about 20 minutes.
4 Coarsely chop the clams. Add the clams, wine, the reserved bacon, and an additional ½ cup broth to the saucepan. Season with salt and pepper. Heat through, and serve. Keep the chowder, covered, in the refrigerator 1 to 2 days.

ALMA ETHERIDGE WILSON'S ROANOKE SIXTEEN-LAYER CHOCOLATE FUDGE CAKE

MAKES 1 EIGHT-INCH CAKE | **PHOTO-GRAPH ON PAGE 143**

Do not overbake the layers, or the cake will be dry. Make the frosting after all the layers are baked. The cake is best eaten shortly after it is assembled and should not be refrigerated. It will keep at room temperature for one to two days.

3 cups all-purpose flour, plus more for dusting
1 pound (4 sticks) unsalted butter, room temperature
⅓ cup pure vegetable shortening
3 cups sugar
6 large eggs, room temperature
½ teaspoon baking powder
Pinch of coarse salt
1 cup evaporated milk
1 tablespoon pure vanilla extract
Chocolate Glaze (recipe follows)
Vegetable-oil cooking spray

1 Preheat the oven to 325°F. Coat two 8-inch cake pans, preferably nonstick, with cooking spray. Line each with a parchment circle slightly smaller than the pan. Coat the parchment with cooking spray, and dust with flour, shaking out the excess. Set the pans aside.
2 In the bowl of an electric mixer fitted with the paddle attachment, cream the butter and shortening on medium-high, about 1 minute.
3 Add the sugar, and beat until fluffy, about 3 minutes. Use a rubber spatula to scrape down the sides as needed.
4 Add the eggs one at a time, mixing after each addition. Scrape down the sides of the bowl after adding the last egg; beat 1 minute more.

5 Sift together the flour, baking powder, and salt. Combine the milk and vanilla. Reduce the speed of the mixer to low, and add the flour mixture alternately with the milk, beginning and ending with the flour mixture. Beat until incorporated after each addition.

6 Spoon exactly ½ cup of the batter into each of the prepared pans. Using a small offset spatula, spread the batter evenly. Place the pans on the center rack in the oven; bake until the cakes are set and barely golden along the edges, 8 to 10 minutes. Rotate the pans halfway through baking.

7 Remove the cakes from the oven, and let them cool on a wire rack about 3 minutes. Use an offset spatula to loosen the edges of the cakes, and invert onto the wire rack. Peel off the parchment. The baked layers should be approximately ¼ inch thick. Repeat the process, in freshly prepared pans, until 16 layers are baked. Keep the batter in a bowl at room temperature while you work. Stack the slightly warm cake layers with a piece of parchment between each. Wrap the stack with plastic wrap to keep the layers fresh as you work.

8 Prepare the chocolate glaze only after all the cake layers are baked. To glaze the cake, place one layer on a cardboard cake round, slightly smaller than the layer. Place on a wire rack with a baking sheet underneath the rack. Ladle a scant 2 tablespoons of glaze over the layer. Use a small offset spatula to spread the glaze over the entire surface of the layer. The glaze should just coat the layer. Scrape off any excess glaze. Place the second cake layer on top of the first, pressing down gently to secure and create a level cake. Repeat the process until all 16 layers are stacked on top of one another. Make sure that the cake remains level as you stack the layers; pressing down on the cake should help with this.

9 Pour the remaining glaze over the top of the cake, and let it drip down the sides. Using a small offset spatula, smooth the sides so they are completely covered. Let stand 30 minutes before serving.

CHOCOLATE GLAZE
MAKES 3¾ CUPS

Make this glaze just before you plan to use it.

7½ ounces unsweetened chocolate, chopped into small chunks
3 cups sugar
1¼ cups evaporated milk
¼ cup plus 1 tablespoon light corn syrup

1 Place the chocolate in a heat-proof bowl or the top of a double boiler. Set aside.

2 Combine the sugar, milk, and corn syrup in a small saucepan. Set over medium-high heat; bring to a boil. Stirring often, boil for 1 minute. Immediately pour the hot mixture over the chocolate; stir until the chocolate melts.

3 Fill a large pan or the bottom of the double boiler with water, and bring to a boil. Remove from the heat. Set the bowl of glaze over the double boiler to keep it warm while glazing the cake.

ICE CREAM BOMBES

COFFEE PRALINE CHECKERBOARD BOMBE
SERVES 12 | PHOTOGRAPH ON PAGE 149

3 pints coffee ice cream
3 pints praline or hazelnut ice cream
1 tablespoon sliced almonds (optional)
   Cooking spray

1 Coat two 9-by-5-inch straight-sided loaf pans with cooking spray. Line each with two strips of overlapping parchment paper, one placed along the width and the other placed along the length of the pan (make them long enough to generously hang over the edges of the pans).

2 Beat the coffee ice cream in the bowl of an electric mixer fitted with the paddle attachment until soft but still holding its shape, 1 to 2 minutes; work in batches if necessary. Spread the ice cream into one of the prepared pans to about 2 inches thick; smooth the top with a small offset spatula. Transfer the pan to the freezer, and let the ice cream solidify, about 2 hours. Repeat the process with the praline ice cream, filling the second pan. Freeze the ice cream until it hardens, about 2 hours.

3 Place a large sheet of plastic wrap over a baking sheet. When the ice cream has hardened, remove the pans from the freezer. To unmold, dip the pans into very hot water for a few seconds; invert onto a cutting board. Remove the parchment. Working quickly, cut each block lengthwise into two long equal-size logs. Using a long spatula, transfer one coffee log and one praline log, long sides touching, to the plastic wrap. Stack the remaining coffee log on top of the praline log, and the remaining praline log on top of the coffee log to form the checkerboard. Wrap quickly in plastic; return to the freezer. Once the checkerboard is hardened, about 2 hours, remove from the freezer. Unwrap on a clean cutting board sprinkled with sliced almonds, if using, to keep the ice cream from slipping. Slice crosswise into 12 pieces, and transfer to a serving tray or plates.

SPUMONI BOMBE
SERVES 10 TO 12 | PHOTOGRAPH ON PAGE 149

1 pint green pistachio ice cream
½ cup shelled pistachios, coarsely chopped
1 cup dried cherries
⅔ cup light rum
¼ cup water
⅓ cup heavy cream
1 cup vanilla ice cream
1 pint chocolate ice cream
1 tablespoon sliced almonds (optional)
   Cooking spray

1 Coat the inside of an 8½-by-4½-inch loaf pan with cooking spray. Line with two strips of overlapping parchment paper, one placed along the width and the other placed along the length of the pan (make them long enough to generously hang over the edges of the pan). Place in the freezer to chill for 15 minutes. Beat the pistachio ice cream in the bowl of an electric mixer fitted with the paddle attachment until soft but still holding its shape, 1 to 2 minutes. Add the pistachios; remove the pan from the freezer. Transfer the pistachio ice cream to the pan, forming a 1-inch layer; smooth with a small offset spatula. Return the pan to the freezer until the ice cream hardens, about 40 minutes.

2 In a small saucepan, combine the cherries, rum, and water. Bring to a boil over medium-high heat (be careful not to ignite). Reduce the heat; cover the pan. Let the cherries simmer until all the liquid is absorbed, 10 to 12 minutes. Remove from the heat; let cool.

3 In a medium bowl, whip the cream until soft peaks form; set aside. Soften the vanilla ice cream as above; fold the whipped cream into it. Remove the pan from the freezer; add a layer of the vanilla mixture, smoothing the top with a small offset spatula. Return the pan to the freezer.

4 When the vanilla layer is firm to the touch, about 45 minutes, soften the chocolate ice cream as above. Add the cooled cherries; mix until just combined. Remove the pan from the freezer; fill to the top with the chocolate-cherry mixture. Smooth the top with an offset spatula; cover with plastic wrap. Return to the freezer until completely hardened, about 4 hours or overnight. To unmold, remove from the freezer; dip the pan in very hot water for a few seconds. Sprinkle sliced almonds, if using, over the chocolate ice cream to keep the ice cream from sliding when turned out. Using the overhanging parchment, gently lift the ice cream out of the pan. Invert onto a cutting board. Use a sharp knife to slice into servings; transfer to a platter. Serve.

ORANGE SHERBET BOMBE

SERVES 10 TO 12

This is made in a six-cup kugelhopf mold.

1½ pints orange sherbet
1½ pints vanilla ice cream
1 tablespoon sliced almonds (optional)

1 Chill the mold in the freezer for about 30 minutes. Beat the orange sherbet in the bowl of an electric mixer fitted with the paddle attachment until soft but still holding its shape, 1 to 2 minutes. Remove the mold from the freezer. Using a small spoon, spread the sherbet on the bottom and up the sides of the mold, creating a well for the vanilla ice cream. If the sherbet slips down the sides of the mold, return mold to the freezer to chill, about 10 minutes, and then finish lining. Transfer the finished mold to the freezer; let the sherbet harden.

2 Soften the vanilla ice cream as above. Remove the mold from the freezer; using a spoon, fill the sherbet-lined mold with the vanilla ice cream, pressing down on the ice cream so there are no air pockets. Cover with plastic wrap; return to the freezer. Chill until firm, 4 hours or overnight. To unmold, sprinkle the top with sliced almonds, if using, to prevent slipping when the bombe is turned out. Dip the mold in hot water for 6 seconds; invert onto a serving platter. Use a sharp knife to slice into servings.

MALT BALL BOMBES

MAKES 5 TO 6 | **PHOTOGRAPHS ON PAGE 148**

Each ball, made in two half-moon metal molds can easily serve two people.

3 pints chocolate ice cream
1¼ cups vanilla ice cream
3½ tablespoons malted milk powder
1 pound semisweet chocolate, chopped

1 Chill the molds in the freezer. Beat the chocolate ice cream in the bowl of an electric mixer fitted with the paddle attachment until soft but still holding its shape, 1 to 2 minutes; work in batches if necessary. Wearing rubber gloves, remove the molds one at a time from the freezer; fill them with the chocolate ice cream, pushing down on the ice cream to prevent air pockets. Make the top even and smooth with an offset spatula; return the filled molds immediately to the freezer. Let the chocolate ice cream become firm but not too hard to spoon out, about 1 hour.

2 Remove the molds from the freezer one at a time; use a 1-ounce ice-cream scoop or round tablespoon to scoop out ice cream from the center, leaving a ½-inch border around the edges. Return the molds immediately to the freezer.

3 Soften the vanilla ice cream as above. Add the malted-milk powder, and stir just to combine. Remove the molds from the freezer, and fill each center with the malted vanilla ice cream, smoothing the top with an offset spatula. Return to the freezer, and chill until firm, 1 hour more.

4 Working with two molds at a time, remove from the freezer; dip in warm water for a few seconds. Use your finger to gently slide the ice cream out of the molds. Match two halves, flat sides together, and wrap in plastic wrap. Gently press the halves together; return to the freezer. Repeat with the remaining molds. Let the balls harden, about 1 hour.

5 Melt the chocolate in a heat-proof bowl or the top of a double boiler, set over a pan of barely simmering water. When melted, remove from the heat; stir the chocolate occasionally to let it cool, 8 to 10 minutes. Place a wire rack over a rimmed baking sheet; set aside.

6 Line a rimmed baking sheet with waxed paper; set aside. Remove 1 malt ball at a time from the freezer; dip in the melted chocolate. Using a spoon or a small offset spatula, very quickly turn the ball to coat, and lift it out of the chocolate. Place ball on the wire rack, and let excess chocolate drip off (chocolate will adhere to the wire rack if allowed to sit too long). Gently transfer the malt ball bombe to the prepared sheet; return to the freezer before the chocolate is completely set. Repeat the process with the remaining balls. If not serving immediately, wrap each ball in plastic wrap after it is completely frozen. Serve.

TROPICAL BOMBE

SERVES 24 TO 32 | PHOTOGRAPH ON
PAGE 150

To determine the volume of your mold, fill it with water, and pour the water into a liquid measuring cup. The amount of water will show how much ice cream you need for that mold. If the mold is cylindrical, divide the total amount of the mold by four flavors; plan according to your needs. Alternatively, for a triangular or dome-shaped mold, use less sorbet on the first layer, as we did. Remember to press down as you fill the mold to prevent air pockets from forming.

2 pints mango sorbet, or more depending on mold
3 pints coconut sorbet
3 pints strawberry sorbet
4 pints pineapple-coconut ice cream
2 tablespoons sliced almonds (optional)

1 Beat the mango sorbet in the bowl of an electric mixer fitted with the paddle attachment until soft but still holding its shape, 1 to 2 minutes. Using a spoon, place the sorbet in the bottom of the mold, spreading it into any details of the mold. A rubber spatula or offset spatula will help. Smooth the top; place the mold in the freezer to let the sorbet harden, about 1 hour.

2 Soften the coconut sorbet as above, working in batches if necessary. Remove the mold from the freezer; spoon the coconut sorbet in a layer over the mango sorbet. Smooth the top; return to the freezer.

3 When the coconut sorbet has hardened, soften the strawberry sorbet as above. Remove the mold from the freezer; add a layer of strawberry sorbet. Freeze until hardened. Repeat the process with the pineapple-coconut ice cream, finishing the top of the mold by smoothing the surface and covering with plastic wrap. Freeze until hardened, a few hours or overnight.

4 Remove the mold from the freezer; dip into very hot water, 7 to 8 seconds. Sprinkle the almonds, if using, over the ice cream to keep it from slipping. Using some force, invert the bombe onto a cutting board; return the bombe to the freezer for 15 minutes so the outside refreezes. Use a very sharp knife to cut the bombe into servings.

BANANA SPLIT BOMBE

SERVES 10 TO 12

Each of this bombe's layers must freeze solid before the next is added. Don't rush the freezing time, or the layers will run together. You will need an eight-by-three-inch springform pan.

1 cup walnuts, coarsely chopped
2 pints chocolate ice cream
3 medium (about 1¼ pounds) bananas
2 teaspoons milk
½ cup sugar
½ teaspoon pure vanilla extract
  Hot Fudge Sauce, room temperature (page 138)
1 pint vanilla ice cream
2 tablespoons cold water
  Cooking spray

1 Preheat the oven to 350°F. Place the walnuts in a single layer on a rimmed baking sheet. Toast until golden and aromatic, about 7 minutes, shaking the pan halfway through to toast evenly. Remove from the oven, and let cool. Set aside.
2 Place a circle of parchment in the bottom of the springform pan. Lightly coat the bottom of the pan with cooking spray to adhere the parchment. Chill the pan in the freezer for 30 minutes.
3 Beat 1½ pints chocolate ice cream in the bowl of an electric mixer fitted with the paddle attachment until soft but still holding its shape, 1 to 2 minutes. Using a small offset spatula or a spoon, spread the ice cream evenly on the bottom and up the sides of the pan. Work quickly, or the ice cream will not stay on the sides very long; if it starts to fall, return the pan to the freezer for 10 minutes, and then finish lining. Transfer the ice cream-lined pan to the freezer until hardened, about 45 minutes.
4 In the bowl of a food processor, combine 2 bananas, the milk, ¼ cup sugar, and the vanilla. Process 30 seconds or until smooth, and add the remaining banana. Pulse until there are only small pieces of banana, about the size of peas. Transfer the mixture to a bowl.
5 Remove the pan from the freezer, and spread half the banana mixture, about ¾ cup, into the bottom of the chocolate ice

ICE CREAM BOMBES

To make ice cream easier to work with while making bombes, it is beaten in an electric mixer for 1 to 2 minutes, until soft but still holding its shape. Very hard ice cream can take up to 4 minutes. A small offset spatula helps to smooth the ice cream; a rubber spatula also works. Wear rubber gloves when unmolding the ice cream to protect your hands from the cold. Scattering a few sliced almonds on the surface of the ice cream before unmolding it will help keep the bombe from sliding around the cutting board or serving plate. Shredded coconut and cake or cookie crumbs work, too. Before you begin, clear out enough space in the freezer to hold the mold, and be careful not to open the door unnecessarily. Home freezers vary in temperature; adjust freezing time accordingly. To unmold, fill the sink with very hot water, and dip the mold in the water for several seconds. Bombes can be made several days in advance.

cream-lined pan. Return to the freezer until hardened, about 2 hours. Cover the remaining banana mixture with plastic wrap, and refrigerate. When the banana layer has hardened, remove the pan from the freezer; ladle 1 cup hot fudge sauce over the banana layer. Return to the freezer until hardened, about 15 minutes. Set aside the remaining fudge sauce to serve with the finished bombe.

6 Soften the vanilla ice cream as above. Remove the pan from the freezer, and add 1 cup softened vanilla ice cream, using a small offset spatula or spoon to spread it evenly. Return the pan to the freezer, and let the ice cream harden, about 1 hour. Return the remaining soft vanilla ice cream to its container and store in the freezer; it will soften quickly when you need it again.

7 In a medium nonstick sauté pan, combine the remaining ¼ cup sugar and the water. Stir over medium-high heat until the sugar is dissolved; stop stirring, and let boil. The sugar will begin to caramelize in the pan; pick up the pan and slightly swirl the sugar for even caramelizing. Let the caramel turn to a dark golden brown, about 5 minutes, and immediately add the nuts to the pan. Turn off the heat. Using a wooden spoon, stir the nuts in the caramel to coat them evenly. Transfer the nuts directly onto a Silpat baking mat or parchment paper, and spread them into an even layer. Let cool; break into small pieces.

8 Remove the ice cream mold from the freezer, and sprinkle an even layer of nuts over the vanilla layer. Remove the banana mixture from the refrigerator, and spread the remaining ¾ cup over the nuts. Quickly return the mold to the freezer, and let solidify. When the banana layer has hardened, about 2 hours, resoften the remaining cup of vanilla ice cream, and spread evenly over the banana mixture with a small offset spatula or spoon.

9 When the vanilla ice cream has hardened, soften the remaining ½ pint of chocolate ice cream; remove the mold from the freezer. Add the final layer of chocolate ice cream, spreading it all the way to the edges and smoothing the top. If chocolate ice cream extends above the inside rim of the mold, run your finger around the top of the inside of the rim to give a clean edge. Cover with plastic wrap, and place in the freezer to harden completely, about 4 hours, or overnight. When ready to serve, remove mold from freezer, and dip in very hot water for a few seconds. Unlatch the ring, and gently pull away from the bombe. Slide the bombe and parchment off the pan base. Transfer the bombe to a serving platter. Using a sharp knife, slice the bombe into wedges, and serve with remaining fudge sauce, if desired.

HOT FUDGE SAUCE
MAKES 2⅓ CUPS

10 ounces bittersweet chocolate, chopped
8 tablespoons (1 stick) unsalted butter
½ cup plus 2 tablespoons sugar
½ cup water
   Pinch of coarse salt
½ cup light corn syrup

1 In a medium saucepan over medium-high heat, combine the chocolate, butter, sugar, water, and salt. Stir continuously until melted and combined. Add the corn syrup, and bring the mixture to a boil.

2 Reduce the heat, and simmer on low, stirring occasionally, until thickened, about 10 minutes. Remove from the heat, and cool to room temperature. Store refrigerated, in an airtight plastic container, for up to a week.

RASPBERRY PAVLOVA BOMBE
SERVES 10 TO 12

This bombe calls for lining the entire mold with raspberries, which is best done when berries are in season, but this step can be skipped and berries used only on the inside of the bombe.

2 large egg whites
½ cup sugar
   Pinch of cream of tartar
11 cups (about 9 pints) raspberries
1 pint plus 1 cup raspberry sorbet
2 pints vanilla ice cream
2 tablespoons sliced almonds (optional)

1 Preheat the oven to 200°F. Line a baking sheet with parchment; set aside. In the bowl of an electric mixer, whisk together the egg whites, sugar, and cream of tartar. Set the bowl over a pan of simmering water; continue to whisk until the sugar is dissolved and the mixture is warm to the touch. Transfer the bowl to the mixer fitted with the whisk attachment; mix on medium-high until stiff peaks form, about 10 minutes.

2 Transfer the meringue to the parchment-lined baking sheet; spread into a 5-inch-diameter disk that is ½ inch thick. Transfer to the oven. Let dry but don't let it brown; this will take about 4 hours. Remove from the oven; let cool. Remove from the parchment, break into 2- to 4-inch shards, and set aside.

3 Meanwhile, line a 9-inch-diameter, 4-inch-deep metal bowl with raspberries. With open sides of berries facing the wall of the bowl, place the raspberries neatly in the bottom and up the sides as far as you can; if the berries start to fall, add them later. Transfer the bowl to the freezer, and let berries completely freeze to the bowl, about 2 hours.

4 Beat 1 cup raspberry sorbet in the bowl of an electric mixer fitted with the paddle attachment until soft but still holding its shape, 1 to 2 minutes. Remove the mold from the freezer, and gently layer the sorbet in the bottom of the bowl, smoothing it toward the edges with an offset spatula. Return the mold to the freezer until the sorbet has hardened. Remove the mold from the freezer; cover the sorbet with a single layer of raspberries, about 1½ cups. Return to the freezer until the berries are solid, about 20 minutes. Soften 1 pint vanilla ice cream as above. Remove the mold from the freezer; spread a layer of vanilla ice cream over the frozen berries, making sure the ice cream

is spread all the way to the sides of the bowl. Return the mold to the freezer, and let the vanilla ice cream become firm, about 15 minutes.

5   Soften the remaining pint raspberry sorbet as above; set aside. Remove the mold from the freezer; layer the meringue on top of the vanilla ice cream in a single layer. It is fine if some pieces overlap. On top of the meringue, spread the raspberry sorbet, making sure it touches the berry-lined edges of the bowl. Return the mold to the freezer. Continue the process with one more single layer of raspberries, about 2 cups. Soften remaining pint vanilla ice cream as above, and add to bombe in an even layer. Add the berries as needed to the bowl's lining so they completely encase the ice cream to the top of the bowl. Cover with plastic wrap; let the bombe completely freeze overnight. Scatter the sliced almonds, if using, over the vanilla ice cream to keep it from slipping when turned out. To unmold, dip the bowl into very hot water for 7 seconds. Using some force, invert onto a cutting board. Transfer to a serving platter. Working quickly, using a sharp knife, slice the bombe into wedges; serve.

WHAT TO HAVE FOR DINNER

menu

GRILLED LAMB CHOPS WITH LEMON YOGURT SAUCE

GRILLED MIXED PEPPERS AND ONIONS

EGGPLANT FRITTERS

PLUM, RASPBERRY, AND TARRAGON SOUP

GRILLED LAMB CHOPS WITH LEMON YOGURT SAUCE

SERVES 4 | PHOTOGRAPH ON PAGE 147

Low-fat plain yogurt can also be used.

1   cup whole-milk plain yogurt
1   tablespoon freshly squeezed lemon juice
⅛   teaspoon paprika
⅛   teaspoon ground cumin
8   rib lamb chops
1½ teaspoons coarse salt
½   teaspoon freshly ground pepper
    Mint sprigs, for garnish (optional)

1   To make the yogurt sauce, combine the yogurt, lemon juice, paprika, and cumin in a small bowl, and refrigerate.
2   To make the chops, heat a grill to medium heat. Sprinkle the chops with salt and pepper, and grill until cooked through, 5 to 6 minutes per side. Serve with the reserved yogurt sauce and mint sprigs, if using.

GRILLED MIXED PEPPERS AND ONIONS

SERVES 4

Skewering the onion slices through all the layers keeps the pieces of onion from falling through the grill.

1   white onion, cut into ¼-inch-thick rounds
1   red onion, cut into ¼-inch-thick rounds
1   green bell pepper, seeds and ribs removed, cut into quarters
1   red bell pepper, seeds and ribs removed, cut into quarters
1   orange bell pepper, seeds and ribs removed, cut into quarters
1   yellow bell pepper, seeds and ribs removed, cut into quarters
3   tablespoons olive oil
½   teaspoon coarse salt
½   teaspoon freshly ground black pepper

1   Soak four wooden skewers in warm water for 20 to 30 minutes. Heat a grill to medium heat. Skewer the white and red onion slices, passing the skewer through each layer; skewer the green, red, orange, and yellow peppers. Place the skewered vegetables, olive oil, salt, and pepper in a shallow bowl, and turn the vegetables until they are coated.

2   Place the vegetables on the grill, and cook until lightly charred, 6 to 8 minutes per side. Remove the vegetables from the skewers; cut the peppers into ½-inch-thick slices. Transfer the vegetables to a serving platter.

EGGPLANT FRITTERS

SERVES 4

1   large eggplant (about 2½ pounds)
¼   cup olive oil
1   small garlic clove, minced
2   tablespoons coarsely chopped fresh flat-leaf parsley
½   cup fresh or dry bread crumbs
1   tablespoon grated Parmesan cheese
1   large egg, lightly beaten
¼   teaspoon ground cumin
¼   teaspoon ground coriander
¾   teaspoon coarse salt
¼   teaspoon freshly ground pepper
2   tablespoons canola oil
1   head frisée lettuce, washed and dried
1   tablespoon balsamic vinegar

1   Preheat the oven to 425°F. Cut the eggplant in half, and place on a rimmed baking sheet. Drizzle with 2 tablespoons olive oil. Place in the oven; cook until tender, about 40 minutes. Remove from the oven; when cool enough to handle, scoop the flesh into a colander to drain. Transfer the drained eggplant to a bowl; add the garlic, parsley, bread crumbs, Parmesan, egg, cumin, coriander, salt, and pepper. Stir to combine. Form the mixture into 2-inch patties.
2   Heat the canola oil in a large skillet over medium heat. Add the patties, and cook until golden brown, about 2 minutes per side. Drain on paper towels. Place the frisée on a serving platter; drizzle with the remaining 2 tablespoons olive oil and the balsamic vinegar. Top with the fritters.

PLUM, RASPBERRY, AND TARRAGON SOUP

SERVES 4

1½ pounds (about 6) ripe red plums; plus 1 plum, skin on and cut into ¼-inch dice, for garnish

6 ounces raspberries, plus more for garnish

1 cup white wine

¼ cup plus 2 tablespoons sugar

3 sprigs tarragon, plus more for garnish

2 tablespoons triple sec, Cointreau, or Grand Marnier (optional)

¼ cup water

1 Fill a large bowl with ice and water; set aside. Bring a medium pot of water to a boil. Add the plums; blanch until the skins begin to peel, 2 to 3 minutes. Remove the plums from the water; place in the ice bath until cool. Remove the plums, reserving the ice bath.

2 Peel the plums, remove the pits, cut flesh into chunks, and place in a medium saucepan. Add the raspberries, wine, sugar, tarragon, triple sec (if using), and water to the saucepan; cover, and bring to a simmer over medium heat. Reduce the heat to medium-low, and allow to simmer until the plums are falling apart, 15 to 20 minutes. Remove from the heat, transfer mixture to a clean bowl, and place in the reserved ice bath, stirring occasionally, until cold.

3 Remove the tarragon sprigs, and transfer the mixture to a blender. Purée, working in batches if necessary. Serve garnished with the diced plum, raspberries, and tarragon. Serve cold.

FIT TO EAT: GREEK DISHES

DOLMADES

MAKES 3 DOZEN

Simple changes to traditional Greek dishes make them healthier. Stuffed grape leaves, called dolmades, are filled with nutrient-rich brown rice instead of white. Brown rice, with its nutty flavor and chewy texture, is a better source of iron, magnesium phosphate, and potassium. Dolmades can be made a day in advance and refrigerated.

1 red bell pepper

1 tablespoon plus 1 teaspoon olive oil

1 medium yellow onion, finely diced

1 teaspoon ground oregano

1 teaspoon coarse salt

2 cups cooked brown rice

½ cup currants

½ cup chopped fresh flat-leaf parsley

Grated zest and juice of 2 lemons

1 one-pound jar grape leaves, rinsed

1 Place the pepper directly on the trivet of a gas-stove burner over high heat. As each section turns puffy and black, turn the pepper with tongs. (If you don't have a gas stove, place the pepper in a baking pan, and broil, turning pepper as each side chars.) Transfer the pepper to a small bowl, and cover with plastic wrap. Let sweat until it is cool enough to handle, about 15 minutes. Transfer to a work surface. Peel off and discard the blackened skin. Cut the pepper into ¼-inch dice, discarding the seeds and the ribs. Transfer to a bowl; set aside.

2 Heat 1 teaspoon olive oil in a skillet set over medium heat. Add the onion, oregano, and salt; cook until the onion is beginning to brown, about 4 minutes. Transfer to the bowl with the red pepper. Add the rice, currants, parsley, zest, and all but 1 tablespoon of the lemon juice; stir to combine.

3 Remove the stem from a rinsed grape leaf, and lay the leaf on a work surface. Place 1 tablespoon filling at the stem end; roll the leaf tightly, tucking in the ends. Repeat with additional leaves until all the filling is used.

4 Line an 8-inch saucepan with the remaining leaves; arrange the stuffed leaves, seam side down, in the pan. They may be stacked in 2 layers. Drizzle with the remaining tablespoon olive oil and the remaining tablespoon lemon juice. Add enough water to the pan to just cover the stuffed leaves; weight the leaves for cooking with a kitchen plate or a lid smaller than the diameter of the pan.

5 Place the saucepan over high heat, cover, and bring to a boil. Reduce the heat to medium-low; allow to simmer gently with lid ajar until the leaves are tender, about 45 minutes. Transfer the stuffed leaves to a serving platter, and allow to cool. Serve at room temperature or chilled.

PER DOLMA: 30 CALORIES, 1 G FAT, 0 MG CHOLESTEROL, 4 G CARBOHYDRATE, 32 MG SODIUM, 0 G PROTEIN, 0 G FIBER

ZUCCHINI PIE

SERVES 6

If yellow squash are unavailable, use all green zucchini.

2 teaspoons olive oil

1 pound (about 2 or 3) green zucchini, cut into ½-inch pieces

4 scallions, thinly sliced

4 garlic cloves, minced

1 teaspoon dried marjoram

1 teaspoon coarse salt

½ teaspoon freshly ground pepper

1 pound (about 2 or 3) yellow squash, cut into ½-inch pieces

½ cup freshly chopped dill

¼ cup freshly chopped flat-leaf parsley

5 large whole eggs

5 large egg whites, lightly beaten

1 tomato, thinly sliced

2 ounces low-fat feta cheese, crumbled

1 Preheat the oven to 325°F. Heat 1 teaspoon olive oil in a large skillet set over medium heat. Add the zucchini, half the scallions, half the garlic, ½ teaspoon marjoram, ½ teaspoon salt, and ¼ teaspoon pepper. Cook, stirring frequently, until the zucchini has softened and is beginning to brown, about 5 minutes. Remove from the heat; transfer to a large bowl, and set aside.

2 Rinse the skillet. Repeat the process with the yellow squash and the remaining teaspoon olive oil, scallions, garlic, ½ teaspoon marjoram, ½ teaspoon salt, and ¼ teaspoon pepper. Transfer to the bowl with the cooked zucchini; let sit until cooled. Drain, and discard any liquid.

3 Add the dill, parsley, eggs, and egg whites to the zucchini; stir to combine. Pour into a 9½-inch-round deep baking dish. Cover with the tomato slices; sprinkle with the feta. Bake until set, about 1 hour. Serve hot or at room temperature.

PER SERVING: 146 CALORIES, 8 G FAT, 186 MG CHOLESTEROL, 8 G CARBOHYDRATE, 336 MG SODIUM, 12 G PROTEIN, 1 G FIBER

PINK POTATO SALAD

SERVES 6

Use red or white small potatoes if fingerlings are unavailable.

2 cups plain nonfat yogurt
1½ pounds fingerling potatoes
1 seedless cucumber, cut into ¼-inch-thick half moons
4 ounces (about 1 cup) kalamata olives, pitted and cut in half
1 small red onion, sliced into thin half moons
¼ cup fresh chervil leaves
3 tablespoons red-wine vinegar
½ teaspoon ground cinnamon
½ teaspoon ground nutmeg
½ teaspoon coarse salt
¼ teaspoon paprika

1 Drain the yogurt in a cheesecloth-lined sieve placed over a bowl for 30 minutes.
2 Place the potatoes in a medium pot, and cover with cold water; cover, and bring to a boil over high heat. Boil until tender, about 20 minutes. Remove from

the heat. Drain; run under cold water to stop the cooking. Set aside until completely cool.

3 Cut the potatoes into 1-inch pieces; place in a bowl. Add the cucumber, olives, onion, and chervil; set aside.

4 Place the drained yogurt (about 1½ cups) in a bowl. Add the vinegar, cinnamon, nutmeg, salt, and paprika; stir until well combined. Pour over the potato mixture; stir until the potatoes are well coated. Transfer to a serving bowl; serve immediately.

PER SERVING: 192 CALORIES, 7 G FAT, 1 MG CHOLESTEROL, 27 G CARBOHYDRATE, 158 MG SODIUM, 7 G PROTEIN, 2 G FIBER

MOUSSAKA

SERVES 6

Moussaka may be assembled a day in advance and refrigerated unbaked, wrapped in plastic wrap. To serve, bake for an additional fifteen to twenty minutes or until the center is hot, for a total cooking time of forty-five to fifty minutes.

2 cups plain nonfat yogurt
1 pound ground turkey
1 yellow onion, cut into ¼-inch dice
1 garlic clove, minced
1 teaspoon ground cinnamon
1 teaspoon coarse salt, plus more for eggplant
¼ teaspoon ground nutmeg
¼ teaspoon freshly ground pepper
1 twenty-eight-ounce can whole peeled tomatoes, coarsely chopped
¼ cup tomato paste
¼ cup chopped fresh oregano
½ cup chopped fresh flat-leaf parsley
2 medium (about 2 pounds) eggplants
¼ cup (1 ounce) grated Parmesan cheese
1 large whole egg
1 large egg white
Olive-oil cooking spray

1 Drain the yogurt in a cheesecloth-lined sieve placed over a bowl until thickened, 2 hours or overnight.
2 Place the turkey in a medium saucepan over medium heat; cook until browned, about 6 minutes. Using a slotted spoon, transfer to a medium bowl. Add the onion, garlic, cinnamon, salt, nutmeg,

and pepper to the saucepan; cook until the onion is translucent, about 10 minutes. Return the turkey to the saucepan, and add the tomatoes, tomato paste, and oregano. Bring to a boil; reduce the heat to medium-low, and simmer until the sauce has thickened, about 1 hour. Remove from the heat. Stir in the chopped parsley, and set aside.

3 Meanwhile, preheat the broiler. Cut the eggplants crosswise into ¼-inch-thick slices. Sprinkle with salt on both sides. Place in a colander set over a bowl; let stand 1 hour to drain. Discard the liquid; rinse each slice under cold running water to remove all salt and juice. Place the slices on several layers of paper towels; press out the water. Arrange a single layer of dry slices on a clean baking sheet; coat with olive-oil spray. Broil until browned, about 2 minutes. Turn; coat with olive-oil spray, and broil until browned, about 2 minutes more. Repeat until all the eggplant slices have been broiled; set the cooked eggplant aside.

4 Place the drained yogurt in a small bowl. Add the Parmesan, egg, and egg white. Whisk together briskly with a fork; set aside.

5 Preheat the oven to 400°F. To assemble the moussaka, place a layer of eggplant on the bottom of an 8-inch-square baking pan. Cover with half the turkey sauce. Place another eggplant layer, then the remaining turkey mixture. Add a final eggplant layer; cover with the yogurt mixture. Bake until the mixture is bubbling and the top starts to brown, about 30 minutes. Transfer to a heat-proof surface; let sit until the moussaka cools slightly and firms, about 10 minutes. Cut into 6 pieces; serve.

PER SERVING: 266 CALORIES, 9 G FAT, 102 MG CHOLESTEROL, 23 G CARBOHYDRATE, 510 MG SODIUM, 25 G PROTEIN, 3 G FIBER

STEWED BABY ARTICHOKES WITH FAVA BEANS

SERVES 6 | **PHOTOGRAPH ON PAGE 146**

Defrosted frozen lima beans may be substituted for the fava beans. If you choose to do so, start with the second step.

1½ pounds fava beans, shelled

1 quart water

3 tablespoons freshly squeezed lemon juice, plus 1 lemon half for artichokes

2¼ pounds (about 24) baby artichokes

2 teaspoons olive oil

1 shallot, peeled and finely chopped

3 garlic cloves, peeled and lightly crushed

1 teaspoon coarse salt

¼ teaspoon freshly ground black pepper

¼ teaspoon crushed red-pepper flakes

4 sprigs fresh thyme

4 sprigs fresh flat-leaf parsley

1 Fill a large bowl with ice and water; set aside. Bring a medium pot of water to a boil. Add the fava beans; blanch 30 seconds. Remove from the water; transfer to the ice bath until cool. Peel the outer skin from the beans; set aside.

2 Place the water in a large bowl; add the lemon juice. Set aside. Remove the tough outer leaves from the artichokes; cut 1 inch from the tip of each artichoke. Trim and peel the stem of each; rub all over with the lemon half. Place in the reserved lemon water.

3 Heat the olive oil in a saucepan over medium heat. Add the shallot, garlic, salt, black pepper, and red-pepper flakes; cook, stirring frequently, until the shallot is lightly browned, about 2 minutes. Add the artichokes, 1 cup lemon water, thyme, and parsley; bring to a simmer. Reduce the heat to medium-low, and cover; simmer until the artichokes are tender, about 14 minutes.

4 Add the fava beans. Cook until the beans are tender, about 3 minutes more. Serve hot or at room temperature.

PER SERVING: 197 CALORIES, 3 G FAT, 0 MG CHOLESTEROL, 39 G CARBOHYDRATE, 544 MG SODIUM, 15 G PROTEIN, 9 G FIBER

CREAMED CORNBREAD | **PAGE 134**

OUTER BANKS CLAM CHOWDER | **PAGE 134**

CHOPPED COLESLAW | **PAGE 134**

PAN-FRIED SOFT-SHELL CRABS | **PAGE 133**

GREEN GAZPACHO SALAD | **PAGE 133**

SOUTHWESTERN COBB SALAD | **PAGE 132**

STEWED BABY ARTICHOKES
WITH FAVA BEANS | **PAGE 142**

PORK PAILLARDS WITH GRILLED
PINEAPPLE | **PAGE 130**

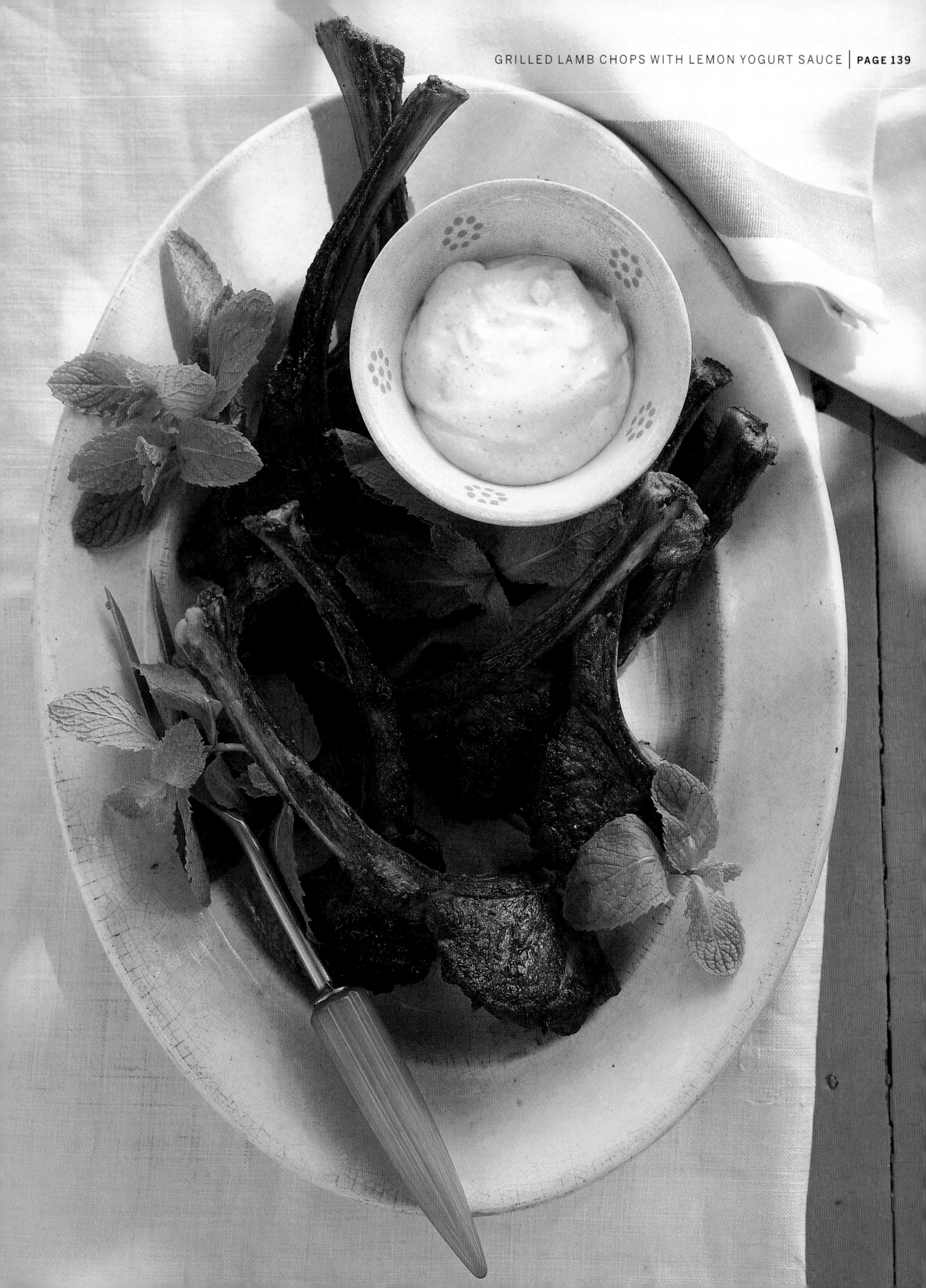

To make Frozen Lemon Mousse, fold chilled lemon curd into whipped cream. Pour the mousse into ring molds that have been placed on parchment-lined baking sheets, and freeze.

To form Malt Ball Bombes, fill half-moon metal molds with chocolate ice cream; freeze. Scoop out ice cream from the centers using a small ice-cream scoop. Return to freezer. Fill centers with malted vanilla ice cream, smoothing tops.

MALT BALL BOMBES | **PAGE 136**

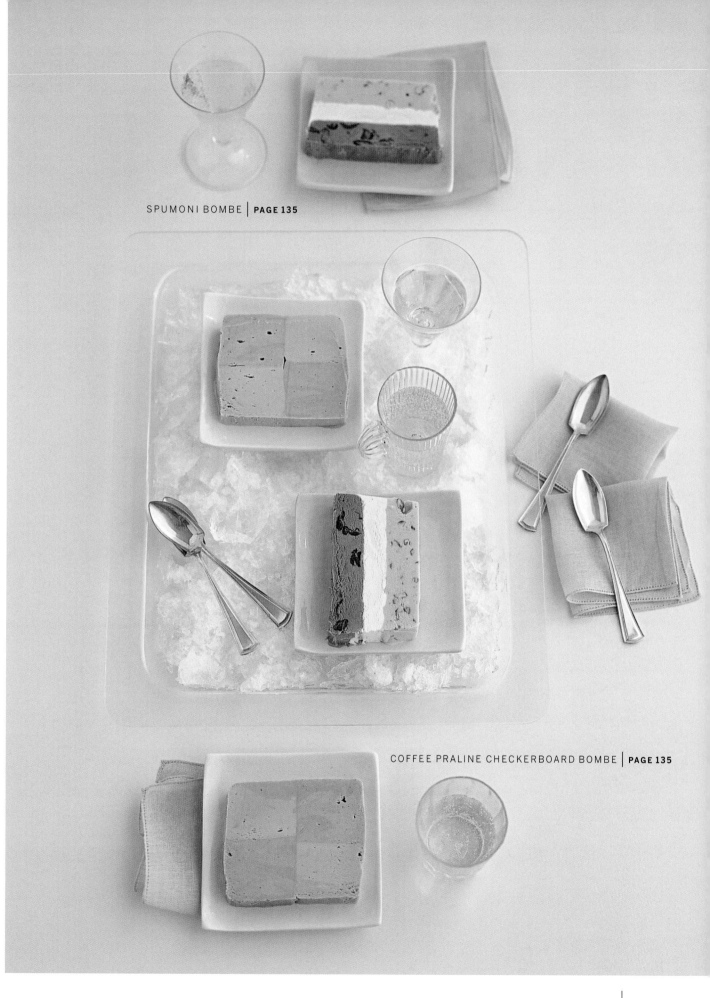

SPUMONI BOMBE | **PAGE 135**

COFFEE PRALINE CHECKERBOARD BOMBE | **PAGE 135**

TROPICAL BOMBE | **PAGE 137**

july

Star-Spangled Shortcake

Crisp Topping

Chocolate Chunk Cookies

Orange-Sable Cookies

Raspberry Sauce

Chocolate Fudge Sauce

Caramel Bourbon Vanilla Sauce

Margaritas

Guacamole

Grilled Cheese and
    Tomato Quesadillas

Basic Vinaigrette

Red-Wine Vinaigrette

Sherry-Walnut Vinaigrette

Buttermilk Herb Vinaigrette

Summer Sun Cocktails

Lemonade

Deviled Eggs with Crème Fraîche

Fennel Crab Salad on
    Beefsteak Tomatoes

Farm-Stand Salad

Marinated Baby Artichokes

Steamed White Corn

Sweet Corn Ice Cream

Orange Cornmeal Shortbread

White Sangria

Chicken and Vegetable Skewers

Barbecued Clams and Oysters

Grilled Quesadillas

Pan Tomate con Jamón

Cilantro Gazpacho

Paella

Lemon Pound Cake

Key Lime Ice Cream

Poached Fruits

Lemon Curd

Spicy Grilled Shrimp
    with Plum Salad

Honeydew Cucumber Soup

Tomato, Cantaloupe, and Basil Salad
    with Tomato Water

Lobster Salad with Grapefruit,
    Avocado, and Hearts of Palm

Lamb Koftas with Cucumber Raita

Chopped Lemongrass Chicken Salad

Escabèche

(continued on next page)

(continued from previous page)

Marinated Tofu with
    Cold Peanut Noodles

Watermelon Ice

Hearts of Lettuce with
    Russian Dressing

Monogram Cupcakes

Herb Marinated Cheese

Grilled Sausage with Arugula Pesto

Minestrone Salad

Macerated Berry and
    Crème Fraîche Parfait

Cucumber Cups

Pita Pizzas

Spicy Seared Scallops

Black Bean Salsa with
    Tortilla Chips

Tea Sandwiches with Horseradish-
    Salmon Spread and Asparagus

STAR-SPANGLED SHORTCAKE

MAKES 1 RING PLUS 4 STARS; SERVES
10 TO 12 | PHOTOGRAPHS ON PAGE 172

 4   cups all-purpose flour
 1   cup plus 2 tablespoons sugar
 2   tablespoons baking powder
 1   teaspoon table salt
12   tablespoons (1½ sticks) cold
     unsalted butter, cut into pieces
 3½ cups plus 2 to 3 tablespoons
     heavy cream
 1   large egg
 1   pint raspberries
 1   pint blueberries
 2   pints strawberries, cut in half or
     quarters, depending on size
 ½   pint red currants (optional)
     Confectioners' sugar (optional)

1   Combine flour, ¾ cup sugar, baking powder, and salt in a large bowl. Add the butter; use a pastry cutter or two knives to incorporate the butter until the mixture resembles coarse meal.
2   Blend 2 cups heavy cream into the flour mixture using a fork. Turn dough out onto a clean work surface; press away from you with the heel of your hand just to incorporate ingredients. Add 1 tablespoon cream if the dough is too dry to combine.
3   Prepare an egg wash: Place the egg and 2 tablespoons cream in a small bowl, and whisk to combine. Set aside.
4   Press the dough into a 7-by-10-inch rectangle, 1 inch thick. Use a 3½-inch star cutter to cut out six biscuits. Press down three of the stars to flatten slightly. Form the stars into a ring on a parchment-lined baking sheet, alternating flattened stars with unflattened stars. Brush with egg wash to join them along common edges. Gather the remaining dough; cut out four more stars for additional servings, if desired. Refrigerate the dough and remaining egg wash for 1 hour.
5   Preheat the oven to 400°F. Remove the dough from the refrigerator. Brush the top of the star ring and individual stars with egg wash, and sprinkle with 2 tablespoons sugar. Bake for 5 minutes, then reduce heat to 350°F; continue baking until golden brown, about 25 minutes more. Transfer the ring and stars to a wire rack to cool.
6   Combine the raspberries, blueberries, strawberries, red currants, if using, and the remaining ¼ cup sugar in a large bowl; toss to combine. Allow the berries to macerate for at least 30 minutes, until very juicy. Whip the remaining 1½ cups cream to soft peaks.
7   Use a serrated knife to cut the star ring in half crosswise. Cut the four extra stars in half as well. Using two large offset spatulas, carefully lift the top half of the ring, and set aside, leaving the spatulas in place. Set aside the tops of the individual stars as well. Transfer the bottom half of the ring to a serving platter. Transfer the bottoms of the stars to plates, if desired. Spoon macerated berries, with juice, and whipped cream over the bottom halves of the star ring and individual stars. Using the spatulas, place the tops of the ring and individual stars over the whipped cream; dust with confectioners' sugar, if using. Serve immediately.

CRISP TOPPING

MAKES 2 QUARTS

For a delicious, easy dessert, sprinkle this topping over a baking dish filled with chopped peaches and berries to make a fruit crisp. Bake in a 375°F oven until the topping is brown and the juices are bubbling, thirty-five to forty-five minutes. This makes enough for two large crisps.

 ½   cup whole almonds
 2¼ cups all-purpose flour
 ¾   cup packed light-brown sugar
 ⅓   cup granulated sugar
 ½   teaspoon ground cinnamon
 ½   teaspoon coarse salt
 1   cup (2 sticks) chilled unsalted
     butter, cut into small pieces

1   Preheat the oven to 350°F. Place the almonds in a single layer on a rimmed baking sheet; toast until aromatic, about 8 minutes. Shake the pan halfway through to ensure that the nuts toast evenly. Remove from the oven; let cool.
2   Place the toasted almonds in the bowl of a food processor; process until coarsely ground. Transfer to the bowl of an electric mixer fitted with the paddle attachment. Add the flour, brown sugar, granulated sugar, cinnamon, and salt, and mix until just combined. Add the butter; mix on low speed until pea-size clumps form, 4 to 5 minutes. Chill before using. Crisp topping can be frozen in an airtight bag or container for up to two months.

CHOCOLATE CHUNK COOKIES

MAKES ABOUT 4 DOZEN

The dough for cookies can be prepared, rolled into logs, and frozen until ready to bake.

 2½ cups all-purpose flour
 1   teaspoon baking soda
 ½   teaspoon baking powder
 1   teaspoon table salt
 1   cup (2 sticks) unsalted butter,
     room temperature
 ⅔   cup granulated sugar
 ⅔   cup packed light-brown sugar
 2   large eggs
 1   teaspoon pure vanilla extract
 8   ounces bittersweet chocolate,
     chopped into small chunks

1   In a small bowl, combine the flour, baking soda, baking powder, and salt; set aside.
2   Cream the butter and sugars in the bowl of an electric mixer fitted with the paddle attachment until light and fluffy. Add the eggs and vanilla; beat until combined. Add the flour mixture; beat until combined. Stir in the chocolate chunks.
3   Divide the dough in half, and place on sheets of plastic wrap or parchment paper. Roll each half into a log about 1½ inches in diameter. Refrigerate until firm, 2 hours or overnight, or freeze for up to 3 months.
4   Preheat the oven to 350°F. Place Silpat baking mats or parchment paper on baking sheets; set aside. Unwrap the logs; cut into ¼-inch-thick slices. Place on baking sheets, leaving 1½ inches between cookies. Bake until golden, 10 to 12 minutes. Transfer to a wire rack to cool. Serve, or store in an airtight container for up to 2 weeks.

ORANGE-SABLE COOKIES

MAKES ABOUT 4 DOZEN

1¼ cups whole blanched almonds

1 cup confectioners' sugar

¾ cup (1½ sticks) unsalted butter, room temperature

3 tablespoons finely grated orange zest

1 large egg

1 tablespoon freshly squeezed lemon juice

1½ cups all-purpose flour

1 Place the almonds and sugar in the bowl of a food processor. Process until the mixture resembles coarse cornmeal; set aside.

2 Place the butter and zest in the bowl of an electric mixer fitted with the paddle attachment. Beat on medium until pale and fluffy, 2 to 3 minutes. On low, add the almond mixture; beat until combined, 10 to 15 seconds. Add the egg and lemon juice; combine. Add the flour; beat until combined.

3 Divide the dough in half; place on sheets of plastic wrap or parchment paper. Roll each half into a log 1½ inches in diameter. Refrigerate until firm, 2 hours or overnight, or freeze for up to 3 months.

4 Preheat the oven to 350°F. Place Silpat baking mats or parchment paper on baking sheets; set aside. Unwrap logs; cut into ¼-inch-thick slices. Place on baking sheets, leaving 2 inches between cookies. Transfer to the oven, and bake until the edges are golden, about 15 minutes. Transfer to a wire rack to cool. Serve, or store in an airtight container for up to 2 weeks.

RASPBERRY SAUCE

MAKES 1¼ CUPS

This quick sauce makes a delicious and simple topping for ice cream.

2 cups raspberries

¼ cup sugar

2 tablespoons water

1 tablespoon freshly squeezed lemon juice

Combine the raspberries, sugar, water, and lemon juice in a small pan over medium-low heat. Cook until the berries release juice but stay whole, about 5 minutes. Serve warm or at room temperature.

CHOCOLATE FUDGE SAUCE

MAKES ABOUT 1 QUART

1 pound bittersweet chocolate

2½ cups heavy cream

1 Chop the chocolate finely using a serrated knife, and place in a heat-proof bowl.

2 Bring the cream to a boil over medium-high heat; pour directly over the chopped chocolate. Let sit 10 minutes; use a rubber spatula to stir the chocolate and cream gently until smooth and combined. Store in an airtight container, refrigerated, for up to a week. Before using, warm gently in a heat-proof bowl or the top of a double boiler. Set over a pan of barely simmering water.

CARAMEL BOURBON VANILLA SAUCE

MAKES ABOUT 2 CUPS

2 cups sugar

½ cup water

1 cup heavy cream

1 whole vanilla bean, split lengthwise

2 teaspoons freshly squeezed lemon juice

2 tablespoons unsalted butter

1 tablespoon bourbon

Combine the sugar and water in a 2-quart saucepan over medium heat. Stir until the sugar is dissolved; stop stirring, and let boil. Cook until dark amber in color, swirling the pan carefully while cooking, about 20 minutes. Reduce the heat to low. Slowly add the cream, stirring with a wooden spoon. Scrape the vanilla seeds into the pan; add the pod. Add the lemon juice, butter, and bourbon. Stir to combine. Remove the vanilla pod. Store in an airtight container, refrigerated, for up to a week. Bring the sauce to room temperature, or warm over low heat, before using.

MARGARITAS

SERVES 6

1 fresh lime wedge

Coarse salt for glasses

1 cup freshly squeezed lime juice

¾ cup tequila

3 tablespoons Grand Marnier

3 tablespoons Simple Syrup I (recipe follows)

Rub the rims of six glasses with lime. Spread the salt out on a plate; dip the rims of the glasses in the salt to coat. Place ice in each glass. In a pitcher, combine the lime juice, tequila, Grand Marnier, and simple syrup; divide the mixture among the glasses. Serve.

SIMPLE SYRUP I

MAKES 6 CUPS

Use this to sweeten iced tea and lemonade, or to cut the acidity of margaritas.

2½ cups sugar

4¾ cups water

Fill a bowl with ice and water; set aside. In a saucepan, combine the sugar and water; boil over medium-high heat. Cook until the sugar dissolves, about 10 minutes. Transfer syrup to a bowl; set over the ice bath. Let stand, stirring occasionally, until chilled. Store refrigerated in an airtight container for up to 2 months.

GUACAMOLE

MAKES ABOUT 2 CUPS

2 ripe avocados

½ garlic clove

1 jalapeño pepper, seeds and ribs removed, minced

2 tablespoons freshly squeezed lime juice

1 teaspoon coarse salt

½ teaspoon freshly ground black pepper

½ cup loosely packed fresh cilantro, chopped

1 To pit the avocados, slice them lengthwise, rotating the knife around the pit. Twist the two halves of each avocado in opposite directions to separate. Embed the knife in the pit, and twist to separate the pit from the avocado. Peel the avocados.

2 Combine the avocado flesh, garlic, jalapeño, lime juice, salt, and pepper in a large bowl. Mash with a large metal spoon until combined but avocados are still chunky. Stir in the cilantro, and serve.

GRILLED CHEESE AND TOMATO QUESADILLAS

MAKES 4

8 eight-inch flour tortillas

2 cups grated white cheddar cheese

2 tomatoes, thinly sliced

1 Heat a grill or skillet to high heat. Sprinkle each of 4 tortillas with ¼ cup cheese; cover with tomatoes; sprinkle with ¼ cup more cheese; and top with the remaining 4 tortillas. Grill each until the bottom tortilla is golden brown and the cheese starts to melt.

2 Flip. Cook until the tortilla is golden brown, the cheese is completely melted, and the tomato is hot. Transfer to a cutting surface; cut into wedges.

VINAIGRETTE 101

BASIC VINAIGRETTE

MAKES ⅔ CUP | **PHOTOGRAPH ON PAGE 170**

This is a good vinaigrette for a simple green salad. Use extra-virgin olive oil if you prefer a fruitier flavor.

2 tablespoons good-quality white-wine vinegar

1 teaspoon Dijon mustard

1 small shallot, finely chopped

1 teaspoon coarse salt, or more for seasoning

¼ teaspoon freshly ground pepper, or more for seasoning

6 tablespoons good-quality olive oil

1 Combine the vinegar, mustard, shallot, salt, and pepper in a bowl. Let the ingredients macerate for 10 minutes to allow the flavors to infuse.

2 While whisking, slowly add the olive oil, drop by drop at first, until the vinaigrette begins to emulsify. Still whisking, continue to add the oil in a slow, steady stream until combined. Adjust the seasoning with salt and pepper, if desired.

RED-WINE VINAIGRETTE

MAKES ABOUT ½ CUP

2 tablespoons red-wine vinegar

1 garlic clove, smashed

1 teaspoon coarse salt, or more for seasoning

¼ teaspoon freshly ground pepper, or more for seasoning

3 tablespoons extra-virgin olive oil

3 tablespoons canola oil

1 Place the vinegar, garlic, salt, and pepper in the jar of a blender. Let the ingredients macerate for 10 minutes to allow the flavors to infuse. Remove the garlic; discard.

2 With the blender running, add the olive oil and canola oil in a slow, steady stream until the mixture is well combined. Adjust the seasoning with salt and pepper, if desired.

SHERRY-WALNUT VINAIGRETTE

MAKES ⅓ CUP

Make sure your oil is fresh. Some oils, such as walnut, tend to turn rancid quickly. Store them in the refrigerator.

2 tablespoons sherry-wine vinegar

2 teaspoons freshly squeezed lemon juice

1 teaspoon Dijon mustard

1 teaspoon coarse salt, or more for seasoning

¼ teaspoon freshly ground pepper, or more for seasoning

¼ cup walnut oil

2 tablespoons fresh flat-leaf parsley, finely chopped

1 Combine the vinegar, lemon juice, mustard, salt, and pepper in a bowl. Let the ingredients macerate for 10 minutes to allow the flavors to infuse.

2 While whisking, slowly add the oil, drop by drop at first, until the vinaigrette begins to emulsify. Still whisking, continue to add the oil in a slow, steady stream until combined. Stir in the parsley. Adjust the seasoning with salt and pepper, if desired.

BUTTERMILK HERB VINAIGRETTE

MAKES ABOUT ½ CUP

¼ cup buttermilk

2 tablespoons white-wine vinegar

½ garlic clove, minced

½ teaspoon coarse salt, or more for seasoning

¼ teaspoon freshly ground pepper, or more for seasoning

2 tablespoons extra-virgin olive oil

¼ cup fresh herbs, such as chives, parsley, thyme, tarragon, and dill, chopped

1 Combine the buttermilk, vinegar, garlic, salt, and pepper in a bowl. Let the ingredients macerate for 10 minutes to allow the flavors to infuse.

2 While whisking, slowly add the olive oil, drop by drop at first, until the vinaigrette begins to emulsify. Still whisking, continue to add the oil in a slow, steady stream until combined. Stir in the herbs. Adjust the seasoning with salt and pepper, if desired.

NASTURTIUMS

SUMMER SUN COCKTAILS

SERVES 2

2 red, ripe tomatoes (1 pound), quartered

4 medium carrots

2 ounces tequila

Table salt and freshly ground pepper

Nasturtium flowers and leaves, for garnish

1 Using a juice extractor, process the tomatoes and carrots. Transfer juice to a small pitcher.

2 Stir in the tequila, and season with salt and pepper.

3 Pour the mixture into two ice-filled tumblers. Garnish with nasturtium flowers and leaves, and serve.

LUNCH UNDER A TREE

LEMONADE

MAKES 3 QUARTS

2½ cups sugar

6½ cups filtered water

3 cups freshly squeezed lemon juice (15 to 20 lemons), plus 1 lemon for garnish

4 cups ice

1   In a small saucepan, combine the sugar and 2½ cups water. Bring to a boil over medium-high heat, stirring until the sugar is dissolved. Remove from the heat; let cool.

2   In a punch bowl or large container, combine the lemon juice, sugar syrup, remaining 4 cups water, and ice. Stir well to combine. Thinly slice the remaining lemon, and add to the lemonade. Serve.

DEVILED EGGS WITH CREME FRAICHE

SERVES 6 TO 8

6   large eggs
2   tablespoons mayonnaise
2   tablespoons crème fraîche
1   teaspoon Dijon mustard
    Coarse salt and freshly ground pepper
2   chives, finely chopped
½   tablespoon fresh flat-leaf parsley, finely chopped
½   tablespoon fresh tarragon, finely chopped
1   small bunch bronze fennel or dill

1   Place the eggs in a saucepan, completely cover with cold water, and bring to boil over medium-high heat. Boil 2 minutes; remove from the heat, and cover. Let the eggs stand for 12 minutes. Rinse with cold water to stop the cooking. Let cool completely. Peel. Slice in half crosswise, and separate the yolks from the whites. Trim the bottom of the whites so they don't wobble. Set aside.

2   Place the yolks in a sieve over a medium bowl; press through with a spoon. Mix in mayonnaise, crème fraîche, and mustard; season with salt and pepper. Transfer to a pastry bag fitted with a medium star tip (Ateco #35). Pipe into egg-white cups; set aside.

3   In a small bowl, combine the chives, parsley, and tarragon. Snip some fennel or dill over the eggs. Arrange the remaining fennel or dill on a serving plate, and place the eggs on top. Garnish the eggs with the chopped-herb mixture, and serve.

FENNEL CRAB SALAD ON BEEFSTEAK TOMATOES

SERVES 6 TO 8

1½ pounds (about 2) beefsteak tomatoes, preferably orange or yellow
10 ounces (about 3 or 4) baby fennel bulbs
1   tablespoon freshly squeezed lemon juice
½   pound jumbo lump crabmeat
5   ounces purslane or watercress
2   tablespoons olive oil
    Coarse salt and freshly ground pepper

1   Cut the tomatoes into ½-inch slices; set aside. Remove the outer peel from the fennel, if necessary. Using a mandoline, thinly shave the fennel; toss with the lemon juice, and set aside. Remove any shells from the crabmeat, and set aside.

2   Arrange the purslane or watercress on a serving dish, and top with the tomatoes, shaved fennel, and crabmeat. Lightly drizzle the tomato slices with olive oil, and sprinkle with salt and pepper. Serve immediately.

FARM-STAND SALAD

SERVES 6 TO 8

3   pounds small mixed beets, trimmed
1¼ pounds small red potatoes
2½ teaspoons coarse salt
8   ounces haricots verts or small green beans, trimmed
8   ounces Romano beans, trimmed
8   ounces sugar snap peas, trimmed, tough strings removed
3   small zebra green tomatoes or cherry tomatoes
    Lemon Vinaigrette (recipe follows)

1   Bring a large saucepan of water to a boil; cook the beets for 15 minutes. Turn off the heat; cover the pan. Let sit until tender, about 45 minutes. When cool, drain. Rub off skins, trim ends, and cut into ¼-inch rounds.

2   In a saucepan, cover the potatoes with cold water; add ½ teaspoon salt. Bring to a boil over medium-high heat. Reduce the heat to medium; simmer until tender. Set aside.

3   Fill a large bowl with ice and water; set aside. Fill a small stockpot halfway with water. Bring to a boil; add 1 teaspoon salt. Blanch the haricots verts 2 to 3 min-

utes, or until bright green and still crisp. Transfer to the ice bath to stop the cooking. Remove from the ice bath when cool. Repeat blanching and cooling with the Romano beans and snap peas.

4   Slice the cooled potatoes into quarters; arrange on a platter with the blanched vegetables. Slice the tomatoes into eighths, and use to garnish platter. Season with the remaining teaspoon salt. Serve with lemon vinaigrette.

LEMON VINAIGRETTE

MAKES ABOUT 1 CUP

This makes enough to dress the Farm-Stand Salad and Marinated Baby Artichokes.

1   shallot, finely chopped
2   tablespoons Dijon mustard
4   tablespoons white-wine vinegar
3   tablespoons freshly squeezed lemon juice
    Coarse salt and freshly ground pepper
¾   cup plus 2 tablespoons olive oil
1   tablespoon tarragon, finely chopped

1   Combine the shallot, mustard, vinegar, lemon juice, salt, and pepper in a bowl. Let the ingredients macerate for 10 minutes to allow the flavors to infuse.

2   While whisking, slowly add the oil, drop by drop at first, until the vinaigrette begins to emulsify. Still whisking, continue to add the oil in a slow, steady stream until combined. Stir in the tarragon.

MARINATED BABY ARTICHOKES

SERVES 6 TO 8

1   lemon
2   pounds baby artichokes, tough outer leaves removed
    Lemon Vinaigrette (recipe above)
4   sprigs thyme

1   Fill a bowl with cold water, and juice the lemon into the water; set aside. Trim the artichoke tops, trim the tough stems, and halve lengthwise. Trim any pink choke from the centers, leaving half intact. Transfer the artichokes to the lemon water.

2 Bring a medium saucepan of water to a boil over high heat. Drain the artichokes; add them to the boiling water. Reduce the heat to medium; gently simmer the artichokes until just tender, 5 to 7 minutes. Drain, and set aside.

3 Toss the artichokes with ½ cup vinaigrette; transfer to a serving dish. Strip the leaves from 1 thyme sprig, and sprinkle them on the artichokes. Garnish the platter with the remaining 3 sprigs. Serve with extra vinaigrette on the side.

STEAMED WHITE CORN
SERVES 6

6 ears white corn, shucked and cleaned
Coarse salt

Fill a large stockpot with 1 to 2 inches of water, and bring to a boil. Stand the ears of corn on end, and cover. Steam 4 to 5 minutes or until tender, and remove the corn from the pot. Drain, and arrange on a serving platter. Sprinkle with salt, and serve.

SWEET CORN ICE CREAM
MAKES 1½ QUARTS

4 ears fresh sweet corn, shucked
2 cups milk
2 cups heavy cream
¾ cup sugar
9 large egg yolks
Blackberries, for garnish

1 Using a large knife, slice the kernels from the cobs; place kernels in a large saucepan. Cut or break the cobs into thirds; add to the pot with the milk, cream, and ½ cup sugar. Bring the mixture to a boil, stirring occasionally; turn off the heat. Remove and discard the cobs. Using an immersion blender or regular blender, purée the mixture. Allow flavors to infuse for 1 hour by covering the pan with a tight-fitting lid.

2 Uncover, bring to a simmer, and turn off the heat. In a small bowl, whisk together the egg yolks and the remaining ¼ cup sugar. Add a cup of hot cream to the yolk mixture, stirring constantly so the yolks do not curdle. Add the yolk mixture to the saucepan, stirring. Cook

over medium-low heat, stirring constantly, until the mixture is thick enough to coat the spoon, about 10 minutes.

3 Pass the custard through a coarse sieve, then through a fine sieve or chinois, pressing down on solids; discard the solids. Let the custard cool. Cover; chill at least 4 hours. Freeze in an ice-cream maker according to the manufacturer's directions. Serve garnished with blackberries.

ORANGE CORNMEAL SHORTBREAD
MAKES 2 DOZEN

1 cup (2 sticks) unsalted butter, softened
¾ cup confectioners' sugar, plus more for dusting
2 teaspoons pure vanilla extract
1½ teaspoons orange zest
2 cups all-purpose flour
¼ cup plus 2 tablespoons yellow cornmeal
1 teaspoon table salt

1 Using an electric mixer fitted with the paddle attachment, beat butter and sugar until creamy and smooth, about 2 minutes. Add the vanilla and zest. Beat well, scraping down the sides of the bowl as necessary. With the mixer on low speed, add the flour, 2 tablespoons cornmeal, and salt until well combined, about 3 minutes. Form the dough into two logs about 1½ inches in diameter; wrap in plastic wrap, and chill at least 1 hour.

2 Preheat the oven to 300°F. Place the remaining ¼ cup cornmeal on a sheet of parchment or waxed paper. Remove the plastic from the chilled dough; roll the logs in the cornmeal to coat. Slice the logs into ¼-inch rounds. Place on a parchment-lined baking sheet about 1 inch apart. Bake until pale golden all over, 25 to 30 minutes. Cool on a wire rack. Before serving, dust with sugar.

SKYLANDS DINNER PARTY

WHITE SANGRIA
MAKES ABOUT 1 QUART

½ cantaloupe, seeds removed
1 peach, sliced into ½-inch wedges
1 apricot, sliced into ½-inch wedges
¼ cup sugar
2 tablespoons freshly squeezed lime juice
750 ml white Rioja, chilled
¼ cup Grand Marnier

Scoop out the melon using a melon baller; place balls in a large pitcher. Add the peach and apricot wedges, sugar, and lime juice to the pitcher. Toss to combine, and allow to macerate for 1 hour. Add the wine and Grand Marnier. Keep in the refrigerator until ready to serve. Serve over ice.

CHICKEN AND VEGETABLE SKEWERS
MAKES 2 DOZEN; SERVES 12
PHOTOGRAPH ON PAGE 169

¼ cup whole almonds
¾ cup extra-virgin olive oil
12 garlic cloves, finely chopped
1 cup sherry-wine vinegar
¾ cup fresh flat-leaf parsley, finely chopped
Coarse salt and freshly ground pepper
1 twelve-ounce boneless skinless chicken breast, cut into ¾-inch pieces
1 yellow bell pepper, seeds and ribs removed, cut into 1-inch pieces
2 small zucchini, stems trimmed, cut into ¾-inch pieces
24 cherry tomatoes
24 red and white pearl onions, peeled

1 Soak 24 bamboo skewers in warm water for at least 1 hour. Process the almonds in a food processor until smooth, about 2 minutes; set aside.

2 Place a large skillet over medium heat. Add the olive oil and garlic; sauté until golden, about 3 minutes. Add the vinegar; cook 5 minutes. Add the reserved almonds, and cook 3 minutes more. Remove from the heat, and stir in the parsley. Season with salt and pepper. Set aside.

3 Heat a grill to medium-high heat. Thread the chicken and vegetables onto the skewers. Season with salt and pepper. Brush with the reserved sauce; grill until cooked through. Serve hot or at room temperature.

BARBECUED CLAMS AND OYSTERS

SERVES 12 | PHOTOGRAPH ON PAGE 168

2 dozen littleneck clams
2 dozen oysters
Romesco Sauce (recipe follows)
Hogwash (recipe follows)

Heat a grill to medium heat. Shuck the clams and oysters. Place on the grill; top each with a teaspoon of either sauce. Cook until the edges begin to curl, about 5 minutes. Serve.

ROMESCO SAUCE

MAKES ABOUT 2 CUPS

5 plum tomatoes (about 1 pound)
1 pasilla chile, soaked for 1 hour, seeded and minced
½ teaspoon cayenne pepper, or to taste
3 garlic cloves, minced
1 tablespoon fresh flat-leaf parsley, finely chopped
¼ cup olive oil
1 half-inch-thick slice country bread, crusts removed
1½ cups coarsely chopped onion
¼ cup red-wine vinegar
1¼ cups Homemade Chicken Stock (page 8) or low-sodium canned
1½ teaspoons coarse salt, or to taste
¼ teaspoon freshly ground black pepper, or to taste

1 Preheat broiler. Slice the tomatoes in half, and remove the seeds. Line a baking sheet with parchment paper. Place the tomatoes on the sheet, skin side up; broil until the skins are charred, 10 to 12 minutes. Transfer to a wire rack to cool. Peel off the charred skin, and discard.
2 In a bowl, combine the pasilla chile, cayenne pepper, garlic, parsley, and 1 tablespoon olive oil. Set aside.
3 Heat 2 tablespoons olive oil in a medium skillet over medium-high heat; fry the bread until golden brown. Drain the bread on a paper towel-lined plate. Reduce the heat to medium low; add the remaining tablespoon oil and the chopped onion to the pan; sauté until softened and translucent. Add the chile mixture to the onion. Stir in the vinegar. Cook 3 minutes. Add the tomatoes, fried bread, and stock. Bring to a boil. Lower the heat; simmer, covered, for 30 minutes.
4 Purée mixture in the bowl of a food processor. Season with salt and black pepper. Serve at room temperature.

HOGWASH

MAKES 1⅓ CUPS

Martha loves this recipe from the Hog Island Oyster Company. Drizzle it over grilled fish or shrimp.

½ cup rice-wine vinegar
½ cup seasoned rice vinegar
2 shallots, finely chopped
3 tablespoons freshly squeezed lime juice
1 small jalapeño pepper, seeds and ribs removed, finely chopped
1 small bunch cilantro, coarsely chopped

Combine the rice-wine vinegar, rice vinegar, shallots, lime juice, jalapeño, and cilantro in a medium bowl. Refrigerate at least 1 hour before using.

GRILLED QUESADILLAS

SERVES 12 | PHOTOGRAPH ON PAGE 168

These quesadillas, filled with mango chutney and cheese, can be assembled ahead of time and wrapped in plastic until you're ready to grill.

¾ cup Major Grey's chutney
12 six-inch flour tortillas
1½ cups grated sharp cheddar cheese
¾ cup sour cream, for garnish
Tomatillo Salsa (recipe follows)

Heat a grill or grill pan to medium-low heat. Using a spatula, spread 2 tablespoons chutney evenly over each of 6 tortillas; sprinkle ¼ cup cheese over the chutney. Top with the remaining tortillas. Grill until the cheese is melted and the tortilla is slightly golden, about 2 minutes on each side. Using a sharp knife or scissors, cut into 6 wedges. Serve with sour cream and salsa.

TOMATILLO SALSA

MAKES 3 CUPS

1½ pounds tomatillos, husks removed
1 jalapeño pepper
1 small yellow onion, finely chopped
2 tablespoons red-wine vinegar
¼ cup chopped fresh cilantro
Coarse salt and freshly ground pepper

Heat a grill or grill pan to medium heat. Roast the tomatillos and jalapeño until soft and slightly charred, about 10 minutes. Set aside to cool. Remove the charred skin from the jalapeño, and discard. Halve the jalapeño lengthwise; remove seeds and ribs, and discard. Chop finely, and set aside. Chop the tomatillos; place in a bowl, and add the jalapeño, onion, vinegar, and cilantro. Season with salt and pepper.

PAN TOMATE CON JAMON

MAKES 2 DOZEN; SERVES 12

1 baguette, cut diagonally into ¼-inch-thick slices
2 garlic cloves, crushed
¼ cup extra-virgin olive oil
2 ripe plum tomatoes, halved and seeded
6 ounces Serrano ham, thinly sliced
24 Oven-Dried Tomatoes (recipe follows)
2 tablespoons fresh marjoram leaves

Heat a grill or grill pan to medium-low heat. Rub the bread with the garlic cloves. Brush lightly with olive oil. Grill until crisp, about 1 minute on each side. Rub with the plum tomatoes. Drape the ham over the bread. Garnish with the dried tomatoes and marjoram. Serve.

OVEN-DRIED TOMATOES

MAKES ABOUT 2 DOZEN

6 small ripe plum tomatoes, cored
2 tablespoons extra-virgin olive oil
2 teaspoons marjoram, chopped
1 teaspoon thyme leaves
Coarse salt and freshly ground pepper

1 Preheat the oven to 250°F. Line a baking sheet with a Silpat baking mat or parchment paper, and set aside. Slice the tomatoes lengthwise into four ¼-inch-thick slices; toss with the olive oil, marjoram, thyme, and salt and pepper.

2 Arrange the tomato slices in a single layer on the Silpat. Bake 1 hour. Reduce the temperature to 200°F; continue baking 2 hours more, until the tomatoes are shriveled. Oven-dried tomatoes can be kept refrigerated in an airtight container for up to 4 days.

CILANTRO GAZPACHO

SERVES 12

This gazpacho can be served over tomato aspic in a glass as a portable first course, or on its own.

5 pounds ripe tomatoes, seeds removed
2½ pounds cucumbers, peeled, seeds removed
2 red bell peppers, seeds and ribs removed
1 jalapeño pepper, seeds and ribs removed
4 scallions, white and light-green parts only
1 large garlic clove, peeled
½ cup extra-virgin olive oil
¾ cup fresh cilantro, coarsely chopped
5 tablespoons freshly squeezed lime juice
    Coarse salt and freshly ground pepper
    Hot-pepper sauce
    Tomato Aspic (recipe follows)
    Big Croutons (recipe follows)

1 Coarsely chop the tomatoes, cucumber, red and jalapeño peppers, scallions, and garlic. Place in a large bowl; toss with ¼ cup olive oil, ½ cup cilantro, and the lime juice. In a food processor or blender, purée half the vegetables until smooth. With the motor running, slowly add the remaining ¼ cup olive oil to the purée in a steady stream until emulsified. Pass the purée through a fine sieve into a medium bowl, and set aside. Discard the pulp in the sieve.
2 In a food processor or blender, pulse the remaining vegetables in batches, letting them remain chunky. Alternatively, chop the vegetables by hand. Combine the vegetables with the reserved purée; mix well. Stir in the remaining ¼ cup cilantro. Season with salt, pepper, and hot-pepper sauce to taste.
3 Pour ¼ cup aspic into each of 12 six-ounce glasses; chill until set, at least 1 hour. Ladle about ½ cup gazpacho into each glass, and serve garnished with a big crouton.

TOMATO ASPIC

MAKES 3 CUPS

4 pounds ripe tomatoes, seeds removed
1 jalapeño pepper, seeds and ribs removed
1½ teaspoons coarse salt
½ cup cold water
¼ cup plus 2 teaspoons (6 envelopes) unflavored gelatin

1 In a food processor or blender, purée the tomatoes and jalapeño until smooth. Line a large bowl with a double layer of cheesecloth. Transfer the purée to the prepared bowl. With kitchen twine, tie the cheesecloth to enclose the tomato purée; tie the bundle to a large wooden spoon. Rest the spoon across the top of a stockpot or deep jar, letting the juices drip into the pot for about 3 hours. Pour the tomato juice through a fine chinois or sieve into a bowl; discard purée in cheesecloth. Add the salt; stir to combine.
2 Place the cold water in a small heat-proof bowl. Sprinkle the gelatin evenly over it; set aside for 5 minutes to soften. Bring a small saucepan of water to a simmer; place the bowl of gelatin over it. Stir until the gelatin is dissolved; remove the bowl from the heat. Stir in some of the tomato juice to reduce the temperature, then stir all of the gelatin mixture into the remaining tomato juice.

BIG CROUTONS

MAKES 1 DOZEN

These can be made a day ahead and stored in an airtight container after cooling.

¼ cup extra-virgin olive oil
4 tablespoons unsalted butter
¼ cup chopped fresh flat-leaf parsley
1 baguette, cut into twelve ¼-inch-thick slices

Combine the olive oil and butter in a small saucepan; place over medium heat until the butter is melted. Stir in the parsley. Spread over one side of each slice of bread; grill until crisp, 1 to 2 minutes on each side. Alternatively, toast the croutons in a 350°F oven until golden brown, 10 to 15 minutes.

PAELLA

SERVES 10 TO 12 | **PHOTOGRAPHS ON PAGE 170**

Unless you have a large paella pan, you will need to divide this recipe between two shallow twelve-inch pans that have a large surface area, such as skillets. For twenty to twenty-five servings, the recipe can be doubled.

2 whole chicken legs, cut off the bone and chopped into pieces
¼ cup plus 2 tablespoons extra-virgin olive oil
2 tablespoons paprika
1½ tablespoons coarse salt, plus more for seasoning
1 one-and-a-quarter-pound lobster
½ pound boneless pork loin, cut into 1-inch cubes
    Freshly ground black pepper
½ pound chorizo, cut into 1-inch pieces
⅓ cup onion, diced
⅓ cup minced garlic
12 ounces squid, cleaned and cut into 1-inch rings and tentacle sections
½ pound medium shrimp, peeled and deveined
12 ounces scallops, muscles trimmed
1 green bell pepper, seeds and ribs removed, cut into strips
¼ pound asparagus, trimmed, cut into 1-inch pieces
1 cup fresh or defrosted frozen peas
1 cup tomatoes, peeled, seeded, and chopped
12 small mussels, scrubbed and debearded
6 to 8 cups Homemade Chicken Stock (page 8) or low-sodium canned
4 cups long-grain white rice
½ cup brandy
1½ teaspoons Spanish saffron threads
1 lemon

1 Coat the chicken pieces with 2 tablespoons oil, paprika, and 1½ teaspoons salt; let sit 2 hours.
2 Bring a large pot of water to a boil; cook the lobster, covered, for 4 minutes, and drain. When cool enough to handle, remove the tail from the shell; cut the meat into bite-size pieces. Cut the claws in half, leaving the meat in the shells. Discard the bodies, or save to make stock.
3 Heat the remaining ¼ cup olive oil in a paella pan or two 12-inch skillets over a

gas grill set on medium heat, a burner set on medium, or a hardwood fire (place grid 3 inches from fire). Cook the chicken pieces in the oil, turning occasionally until browned, about 4 minutes per side.

4 Add the pork, sprinkle with salt and pepper, and cook until browned, about 2 minutes, stirring occasionally. Add the chorizo, and cook for 2 minutes. Add the onion and garlic, and cook for 3 minutes more. Add the squid, stir to combine, and cook 1 minute.

5 Add the lobster, shrimp, scallops, bell pepper, and asparagus, and cook for 3 to 4 minutes. Add the peas, tomatoes, mussels, and 1 cup broth; cook for 2 minutes. Sprinkle the rice evenly over the top, and stir until combined. Add 4 cups broth and the brandy. With a mortar and pestle or spice grinder, combine the saffron with the remaining tablespoon salt. Add to 1 cup stock, and pour over the rice. Season with black pepper.

6 Reduce the heat to medium-low, and cook until most of the liquid is absorbed and the rice is al dente, 15 to 20 minutes. Cooking times will vary; add more stock 1 cup at a time as needed. Just before serving, squeeze the lemon over the paella.

LEMON POUND CAKE

MAKES 1 NINE-INCH CAKE |
PHOTOGRAPH ON PAGE 174

Serve with Key Lime Ice Cream, Poached Fruits, and Lemon Curd (recipes follow).

1 cup (2 sticks) unsalted butter, room temperature, plus more for pan

3 cups sifted all-purpose flour, plus more for pan

2 teaspoons baking powder

½ teaspoon table salt

½ cup dried currants

2 tablespoons freshly squeezed lemon juice

2 cups sugar

5 large eggs

¾ cup buttermilk

2 tablespoons lemon zest

1 Preheat the oven to 325°F. Butter a 9-by-4½-inch Bundt pan; dust with flour. Sift together the flour, baking powder, and salt; set aside. Place the currants in a small bowl, cover with the lemon juice, and set aside.

2 Place butter in the bowl of an electric mixer fitted with the paddle attachment; beat on medium until soft, 2 to 3 minutes. Add the sugar; beat until fluffy, 1 to 2 minutes. Add the eggs, one at a time, beating until incorporated and scraping down the sides of the bowl as necessary. Reduce the speed to low. Add the flour mixture alternately with the buttermilk, beginning and ending with the flour mixture; beat until incorporated after each addition. Stir in the zest and currants and juice.

3 Pour the batter into the prepared pan; bake until a cake tester inserted in the center comes out clean, 50 to 60 minutes. Unmold by inverting onto a wire rack; allow to cool.

KEY LIME ICE CREAM

MAKES ABOUT 1½ QUARTS |
PHOTOGRAPH ON PAGE 174

8 Key limes or 5 regular limes

2 cups milk

6 large egg yolks

¾ cup plus 2 tablespoons sugar

2 cups very cold heavy cream

1 Grate the zest from all the limes; reserve. Squeeze the limes over a bowl to yield ½ cup juice; set aside. Place the zest in a saucepan with the milk. Scald the milk; cover. Remove from the heat. Steep for 30 minutes.

2 Combine the egg yolks and sugar in a bowl; whisk until pale yellow and thick.

3 Fill a large bowl with ice and water; set aside. Return the milk to the stove, and bring to a simmer. Slowly pour it into the egg-yolk mixture, whisking constantly.

4 Return the mixture to the saucepan; cook over low heat, stirring constantly with a wooden spoon, until the mixture is thick enough to coat the back of the spoon, about 5 minutes.

5 Remove the pan from the heat; stir in the chilled cream to stop the cooking. Pour through a fine sieve into a bowl set in the ice bath; stir occasionally until cooled. Stir the reserved lime juice into the custard. Cover; chill at least 30 minutes or overnight.

6 Pour the custard into an ice-cream maker, following the manufacturer's directions. Churn until the ice cream is just set, but not hard. Transfer to an airtight container; freeze at least 4 hours and up to a week. Serve with Lemon Pound Cake, Poached Fruits, and Lemon Curd, if desired.

POACHED FRUITS

SERVES 12 | **PHOTOGRAPH ON PAGE 174**

Cook the fruit until tender but not soft. Use a heat-proof plate to keep the fruit submerged as it poaches.

2 cups red wine

8½ cups sugar

3 star anise

11 cups water

6 plums (about 3 pounds)

3 cinnamon sticks

6 peaches

1 vanilla bean, split lengthwise

1 pineapple, peeled, cored, and cut into ½-inch-thick rounds

1 Place the wine, 2 cups sugar, star anise, and 2 cups water in a saucepan over high heat; bring to a boil. Reduce to a simmer, and add the plums. Poach until tender, about 5 minutes. Remove from the liquid; let cool. Reserve the liquid.

2 Fill a large bowl with ice and water; set aside. In a second saucepan, combine 4½ cups sugar, 6 cups water, and the cinnamon sticks. Set the saucepan over high heat; bring to a boil. Reduce to a simmer, and add the peaches. Cook until tender, about 5 minutes. Transfer the peaches and enough liquid to cover them to a bowl set over the ice bath; cool.

3 In a third saucepan, combine the remaining 2 cups sugar and 3 cups water.

Scrape the vanilla seeds into the pan, and add the pod. Set the saucepan over high heat; bring to a boil. Reduce to a simmer, and add the pineapple. Cook until tender, about 5 minutes. Remove from the liquid; let cool.

4 Return the plum poaching liquid to a boil; reduce to a syrup that coats the back of a spoon, about 20 minutes. Remove from the heat; cool.

5 Halve the plums, and remove the pits and skin. Halve the peaches, and remove the pits. Quarter the pineapple rings. Arrange the fruit in bowls. Serve with reserved syrup, Lemon Pound Cake, Key Lime Ice Cream, and Lemon Curd, if desired.

LEMON CURD

MAKES 1¼ CUPS | **PHOTOGRAPH ON PAGE 174**

4 large egg yolks

1 large whole egg

1 cup sugar

½ cup freshly squeezed lemon juice, strained

8 tablespoons (1 stick) unsalted butter, cut into pieces

1 tablespoon grated lemon zest

1 Strain the yolks and whole egg through a sieve into a heavy nonreactive saucepan. Add the sugar and juice; whisk to combine.

2 Cook over low heat, stirring constantly with a wooden spoon until the mixture thickens and coats the back of the spoon, 10 to 12 minutes. Transfer to a heat-proof bowl. Stir in the butter, one piece at a time, until fully incorporated. Stir in the zest. If not using immediately, cover the surface with plastic wrap to prevent a skin from forming. Chill in an airtight container up to 3 days. Serve with Lemon Pound Cake, Key Lime Ice Cream, and Poached Fruits, if desired.

COOL FLAVORS

SPICY GRILLED SHRIMP WITH PLUM SALAD

SERVES 8 AS AN APPETIZER

⅓ cup olive oil

1 jalapeño pepper, seeds and ribs removed, cut in half lengthwise

1 garlic clove, smashed

6 plums, pitted and cut into ½-inch dice

1 tablespoon sugar

3 tablespoons sake

4 shiso leaves, finely chopped, plus more for garnish

Zest of 1 lime

2 pounds (28 to 30) large shrimp, peeled with tails intact, deveined

Coarse salt and freshly ground black pepper

1 Combine the oil, jalapeño, and garlic in a saucepan; bring to a simmer. Remove from the heat; set aside until completely cool.

2 Place the plums in a bowl; sprinkle with the sugar. Toss to combine. Add the sake, shiso leaves, and zest; stir to combine. Set aside for at least 15 minutes to allow flavors to meld.

3 Heat a grill or broiler. Toss the shrimp with the oil mixture; season with salt and pepper. Grill until cooked through, about 4 minutes per side. Serve with plum salad.

HONEYDEW CUCUMBER SOUP

SERVES 16 AS AN APPETIZER

We like to serve this soup in demitasse cups and fill the saucers with ice to keep it chilled.

1 ripe honeydew melon, rind and seeds removed, cut into chunks

4 cucumbers, peeled, seeded, and cut into chunks

¼ cup crème fraîche, plus more for garnish

1 teaspoon minced, seeded jalapeño pepper, or more to taste

¼ cup loosely packed fresh cilantro leaves, plus more for garnish

¼ cup freshly squeezed lime juice

1 teaspoon coarse salt

1 Place the honeydew in the bowl of a food processor; purée until smooth. Line a bowl with a double thickness of cheesecloth; transfer the purée to the bowl.

Gather the cheesecloth; tie into a bundle. Suspend the bundle from a spoon over a bowl for 1 hour, to yield 4 cups liquid. Discard any solids in cheesecloth.

2 Place the cucumbers in the food processor; purée until smooth. Add ¼ cup crème fraîche, the jalapeño, cilantro, lime juice, and salt; purée until smooth. Add the honeydew liquid; purée until combined. Chill well. Serve with a dollop of crème fraîche and a cilantro leaf.

TOMATO, CANTALOUPE, AND BASIL SALAD WITH TOMATO WATER

SERVES 8

Take the time to find perfectly ripe tomatoes for this salad. Besides being sweet, ripe tomatoes yield a large amount of flavorful water to ladle around each serving.

4 pounds ripe beefsteak tomatoes, cored

3 tablespoons coarse salt, plus more for seasoning

1 ripe cantaloupe, cut in half and seeded

2 pounds small ripe heirloom and cherry tomatoes

½ cup loosely packed basil leaves

1 tablespoon olive oil

Freshly ground pepper

1 Place the beefsteak tomatoes and 3 tablespoons salt in the bowl of a food processor; blend until smooth. Line a bowl with a double thickness of cheesecloth; transfer the purée to the bowl, and set aside.

2 Using a melon baller, scoop out the cantaloupe; set balls aside. Scoop out any cantaloupe remaining in the skins, and purée in the food processor; add to the tomato purée. Gather the cheesecloth; tie into a bundle. Suspend the bundle from a spoon over a bowl for 2 hours, to yield 4 cups liquid. Discard purée in cheesecloth.

3 Core the heirloom tomatoes; slice into wedges and rounds for a variety of shapes. Place in a bowl; add the reserved melon balls, the basil, and the olive oil. Season with salt and pepper; toss to combine. Divide the salad among eight shallow bowls, heaping it in the center. Ladle tomato-melon water around the salad, and serve.

LOBSTER SALAD WITH GRAPEFRUIT, AVOCADO, AND HEARTS OF PALM

SERVES 8 AS AN APPETIZER

- 4 one-and-a-quarter-pound lobsters
- 2 ruby-red or pink grapefruits
- 1 tablespoon finely minced shallots
- 1¼ teaspoons Dijon mustard
- 2 tablespoons white-wine vinegar
- 1 tablespoon freshly chopped lemon basil or regular basil, plus leaves for garnish
  Coarse salt and freshly ground pepper
- ¼ cup extra-virgin olive oil
- 2 avocados, peeled and pitted
- 4 hearts of palm, cut into ½-inch-thick rounds
- 1 large head (8 ounces) Boston lettuce

1 Fill a large bowl with ice and water; set aside. Bring a stockpot of water to a boil. Boil the lobsters, covered, for 10 minutes; transfer to the ice bath until cool. Break off the claws and tails; use the bodies to make stock, or discard. Split the tails lengthwise with a sharp knife; remove the meat, and slice it into bite-size pieces. Remove the claw meat from the shells, keeping it whole if possible. Chill the lobster meat.
2 Cut the ends off the grapefruits; remove the peel, pith, and outer membranes. Lift the sections away from the membranes, and reserve. Squeeze juice from the membranes into a bowl, and reserve.
3 Place the shallots, mustard, vinegar, basil, and ½ cup grapefruit juice in a bowl. Season with salt and pepper. Whisk to combine. Gradually whisk in the olive oil; adjust the seasoning.
4 Cut the avocados into ½-inch-thick wedges. Coat with a little grapefruit juice to prevent discoloration, and place in a bowl. Add the lobster, grapefruit sections, and hearts of palm. Line each of 8 bowls with a lettuce leaf. Tear the remaining lettuce into bite-size pieces; add to the lobster mixture. Drizzle with the dressing; toss. Fill the bowls with the salad; garnish with basil leaves.

LAMB KOFTAS WITH CUCUMBER RAITA

MAKES 3 DOZEN | PHOTOGRAPH ON PAGE 168

- ½ cup coarsely chopped onion
- ½-inch piece ginger, peeled
- 1 garlic clove
- ½ cup mint leaves, plus sprigs for garnish
- ¼ cup fresh cilantro leaves
- 1 teaspoon garam masala
- 1 teaspoon coarse salt
- ¼ teaspoon freshly ground pepper
- 1 large egg
- 1 pound ground lamb
- 3 tablespoons canola oil
  Cucumber Raita (recipe follows)

1 Place the onion, ginger, and garlic in the bowl of a food processor; pulse until finely chopped. Add the mint, cilantro, garam masala, salt, and pepper; pulse until finely chopped, scraping down the sides of the bowl as needed. Add the egg and lamb; process until fully combined, scraping down the sides as needed. Shape the mixture into 1-inch balls; flatten into patties.
2 Heat a sauté pan over medium-high heat; add the oil. When hot, add the patties in batches; cook until cooked through, about 2 minutes per side. Transfer to a paper towel-lined baking sheet to drain.
3 Insert a toothpick or skewer into each patty; place on a platter. Serve with raita, and garnish with fresh mint sprigs.

CUCUMBER RAITA

MAKES 1¾ CUPS

- 1 ten-ounce cucumber, peeled
- 1 cup plain yogurt
- ¼ cup freshly chopped mint leaves
  Juice of 1 lime (2 tablespoons)
- 1 teaspoon coarse salt
- 1 tablespoon canola oil
- 1 tablespoon black mustard seeds

Slice the cucumber in half lengthwise; scoop out the seeds with a spoon. Cut the cucumber into ¼-inch dice. Transfer to a bowl; add the yogurt, mint, lime juice, and salt. Stir to combine. Heat a skillet over medium heat; add the oil. When very hot, add the mustard seeds; cook until they pop. Add the seeds to the yogurt mixture; stir to combine.

CHOPPED LEMONGRASS CHICKEN SALAD

SERVES 8 | PHOTOGRAPH ON PAGE 167

- 4 whole boneless skinless chicken breasts (4 pounds)
  Lemongrass Marinade (recipe follows)
- 2 teaspoons coarse salt, plus more for seasoning and cooking water
- ½ teaspoon freshly ground black pepper, plus more for seasoning
- 1 pound sugar snap peas, strings removed
- 2 shallots, coarsely chopped
- 1 inch piece ginger, coarsely chopped
- ½ cup freshly squeezed lime juice
- ¾ cup fresh mint
- ¾ cup fresh cilantro
- 6 tablespoons canola oil
- 1 head romaine lettuce, chopped into pieces
- 2 mangoes, peeled, pitted, and cut into ½-inch dice
- 3 red bell peppers, seeds and ribs removed, cut into 1-inch-long matchsticks
- 1 fennel bulb, trimmed, cored, and cut into ¼-inch dice
- 6 scallions, thinly sliced, white and pale-green parts only

1 Place the chicken between sheets of plastic wrap; pound to ½-inch thickness. Place in a plastic or glass dish; coat with the marinade. Cover; chill 4 hours or overnight.
2 Heat a grill or broiler. Season the chicken with salt and black pepper; grill until golden brown and cooked through, 4 to 5 minutes per side. Set aside to cool.
3 Fill a large bowl with ice and water; set aside. Bring a large saucepan of water to a boil; salt the water. Add the snap peas; cook until bright green and still crisp, about 2 minutes. Transfer to the ice bath to cool. Drain; cut into ¾-inch pieces.
4 Place the shallots and ginger in the bowl of a food processor; process until very finely chopped. Add the lime juice, ½ cup mint, ½ cup cilantro, the remaining 2 teaspoons salt, and remaining ½ teaspoon black pepper. Process until the herbs are finely chopped. Slowly add the oil through the feed tube with the motor running.

5 Layer the romaine, mangoes, chicken, bell peppers, fennel, snap peas, and scallions in a large bowl. Top with the remaining ¼ cup mint and ¼ cup cilantro. Serve with the dressing on the side, or add the dressing to the bowl.

LEMONGRASS MARINADE
MAKES 1⅔ CUPS

This marinade may be made in advance and kept in the refrigerator for two days.

4 stalks lemongrass, tough outer leaves removed, cut into pieces

1 inch piece ginger, peeled and coarsely chopped

4 garlic cloves

2 shallots, peeled and coarsely chopped

2 tablespoons light-brown sugar

½ cup mirin (Japanese cooking wine)

2 tablespoons fish sauce

6 tablespoons canola oil

Add the lemongrass, ginger, garlic, and shallots through the feed tube of a food processor with the motor running. Process until very finely chopped. Add the sugar, mirin, and fish sauce; process until puréed, scraping down the sides as needed. With the motor running, slowly add the oil; process until incorporated.

ESCABECHE
SERVES 8 AS AN APPETIZER

2 pounds lemon sole or red snapper (6 fillets)

Coarse salt and freshly ground pepper

6 tablespoons olive oil

1 red bell pepper, seeds and ribs removed, cut into ¼-inch-thick rings

1 navel orange, sliced ¼ inch thick

1 red onion, very thinly sliced

4 mild chile peppers

8 garlic cloves, smashed

6 fresh bay leaves

1 tablespoon whole black peppercorns

2 cups white-wine vinegar, or more if needed

2 cups water, or more if needed

¼ cup freshly squeezed lime juice (about 3 limes), plus lime wedges for garnish

24 cracked green olives

¼ cup chopped fresh flat-leaf parsley

1 Cut each fillet into 3 pieces; season with salt and pepper. Heat 2 tablespoons oil in a skillet over medium heat. Working in batches, sauté the fish until golden brown and cooked through, about 2 minutes on each side, adding the remaining 4 tablespoons oil to the pan as needed. Transfer the fish to a plate to cool completely.
2 Layer the fish with the bell pepper, orange, onion, chiles, garlic, bay leaves, and peppercorns in a large wide-mouthed jar. Combine the vinegar, water, and lime juice, and pour over the fish and vegetables in the jar; if the liquid doesn't cover completely, continue adding equal parts vinegar and water. Cover with plastic wrap or a lid; refrigerate 3 hours or overnight. Serve garnished with lime wedges, olives, and parsley.

MARINATED TOFU WITH COLD PEANUT NOODLES
SERVES 8

1 tablespoon coarse salt

8 ounces soba or other thin wheat noodles

Coconut Peanut Sauce (recipe follows)

¼ cup soy sauce

¼ cup mirin (Japanese cooking wine)

2 tablespoons freshly grated ginger

2 12.3-ounce packages firm silken tofu

12 radishes, sliced paper thin

8 ounces jícama, peeled and cut into 1-inch-long matchsticks

1 3.5-ounce package pea shoots or pea sprouts

1 Bring a large pot of water to a boil; add the salt. Add the noodles; cook until al dente, 4 to 5 minutes. Drain in a large colander; rinse with cold water until completely cool. Drain well. Transfer the noodles to a large bowl; add the peanut sauce to coat.
2 Combine the soy sauce, mirin, and ginger in a bowl. Cut the tofu into 8 pieces; place one piece on each plate. Drizzle with the soy sauce mixture. Divide the noodles among the plates; top with the radishes, jícama, and pea shoots.

COCONUT PEANUT SAUCE
MAKES ABOUT ½ CUP

¼ cup coconut milk, well shaken

2 tablespoons peanut butter

1 tablespoon soy sauce

1 tablespoon mirin

½ inch piece ginger, peeled and coarsely chopped

1½ teaspoons light-brown sugar

Place the coconut milk, peanut butter, soy sauce, mirin, ginger, and brown sugar in a small food processor or blender; blend until smooth. Can be stored in an airtight container in the refrigerator for up to 5 days.

WATERMELON ICE
MAKES 5 CUPS

4 pound wedge of watermelon

½ cup superfine sugar

¼ cup freshly squeezed lime juice

2 tablespoons Campari

1 Remove the rind from the watermelon, cut the fruit into 2-inch chunks, and remove the seeds. Arrange chunks in a single layer on a parchment-lined baking sheet or in a resealable plastic bag; place in the freezer until frozen, about 1½ hours. Transfer to airtight freezer bags if not using immediately.
2 Place the frozen chunks in the bowl of a food processor; process until smooth. Add the sugar, lime juice, and Campari; process until fully incorporated, about 5 minutes, scraping down the sides of the bowl as needed. Freeze in an airtight container, at least 2 hours, until firm. Stir if the juice starts to separate from the ice.

HEARTS OF LETTUCE WITH RUSSIAN DRESSING

SERVES 8 TO 10

3 small heads lettuce
1½ cups mayonnaise
½ cup ketchup or chili sauce
½ cup sour cream
½ cup finely chopped cornichons or sweet pickle relish
2 tablespoons chopped fresh dill
4 teaspoons chopped, drained capers
2 shallots, finely chopped

Cut the lettuce in wedges; arrange in a bowl. Whisk together the mayonnaise, ketchup, sour cream, cornichons, dill, capers, and shallots. Pour the dressing over the lettuce; serve. The dressing can be stored, refrigerated, for up to 1 week.

MONOGRAM CUPCAKES

MAKES 1 DOZEN

Pipe guests' initials onto the tops of these cupcakes, or create a message that is spelled out when the cupcakes are lined up.

6 ounces semisweet chocolate, chopped
4 tablespoons heavy cream
2 tablespoons unsalted butter
Vanilla Cupcakes (recipe follows)
2 large egg whites
8 ounces confectioners' sugar
Gel-paste food coloring, optional

1   Place the chocolate, cream, and butter in a heat-proof bowl or the top of a double boiler over a pan of barely simmering water. Stir occasionally until melted. Remove from the heat; let cool slightly. Transfer the mixture to a bowl; dip the top of each cupcake into the glaze, letting the excess drip off. Chill until just set, about 10 minutes.
2   In the bowl of an electric mixer fitted with the paddle attachment, combine egg whites and sugar on low speed until

spreadable. Add the food coloring, if using. Transfer icing to a pastry bag fitted with the desired tip, and pipe letters or initials immediately (or store in an airtight container, refrigerated, 1 to 2 days; beat with a rubber spatula before using).

NOTE: Raw eggs should not be used in food prepared for pregnant women, babies, young children, the elderly, or anyone whose health is compromised.

VANILLA CUPCAKES

MAKES 1 DOZEN

For chocolate cupcakes, substitute one-half cup cocoa powder for one-half cup all-purpose flour.

8 tablespoons (1 stick) unsalted butter, room temperature
1 cup sugar
3 large eggs
1½ teaspoons pure vanilla extract
1½ cups all-purpose flour
1 teaspoon baking powder
½ teaspoon table salt
¾ cup milk

1   Preheat the oven to 350°F. Place paper liners in 12 cupcake tin wells; set aside. In the bowl of an electric mixer fitted with the paddle attachment, cream the butter and sugar until light and fluffy. Add the eggs one at a time, scraping down the sides of the bowl as needed; beat in the vanilla.
2   Sift together the flour, baking powder, and salt. Add the flour mixture to the mixer bowl alternately with the milk, beginning and ending with the flour mixture. Mix until incorporated after each addition.
3   Divide the batter evenly among the liners; use about ⅓ cup each. Bake, rotating the pan once, until just golden and tops spring back to the touch, about 20 minutes. Transfer to a wire rack until completely cooled.

menu

HERB MARINATED CHEESE

GRILLED SAUSAGE WITH ARUGULA PESTO

MINESTRONE SALAD

MACERATED BERRY AND CREME FRAICHE PARFAIT

HERB MARINATED CHEESE

SERVES 4

Serve this quick appetizer with a hearty whole-grain bread.

8 ounces Bûcheron or other ripened goat's-milk cheese
½ small red onion, thinly sliced into half-moons
1 teaspoon fresh thyme
1 teaspoon fresh oregano
Pinch of crushed red-pepper flakes
¼ cup extra-virgin olive oil
1 tablespoon red-wine vinegar
Coarse salt and freshly ground black pepper
Sliced whole-grain bread

1   Cut the cheese crosswise into ½-inch slices, and arrange on a serving platter.
2   Sprinkle the cheese with the onion, thyme, oregano, and red-pepper flakes. Drizzle with the olive oil and vinegar. Season with salt and pepper.
3   Let sit at room temperature for about 30 minutes. Serve with sliced bread.

GRILLED SAUSAGE WITH ARUGULA PESTO

SERVES 4 │ **PHOTOGRAPH ON PAGE 171**

Save any extra pesto to use on other grilled meats or fish. It will last for up to a week in the refrigerator.

1 bunch (about 4 ounces) arugula, washed, stems trimmed
4 garlic cloves, peeled and smashed
1 cup freshly grated Parmesan cheese
1½ teaspoons coarse salt
½ teaspoon freshly ground pepper
½ cup extra-virgin olive oil
8 assorted Italian pork sausages, both hot and sweet varieties (about 1 pound)

1 To make the pesto, place the arugula and garlic in the bowl of a food processor. Pulse until finely chopped, scraping down the sides of the bowl as needed. Add the cheese, salt, pepper, and olive oil, and purée until smooth and well combined.

2 Heat a grill to medium-high heat. Prick the sausages with a fork to allow excess fat to drip. Grill until cooked through, about 4 minutes per side. Serve the pesto over the grilled sausages.

MINESTRONE SALAD

SERVES 4 | PHOTOGRAPH ON PAGE 171

1 teaspoon coarse salt, plus more for seasoning

8 ounces gemelli or other pasta, such as penne or rotini

¼ cup extra-virgin olive oil

1 small onion, cut into ¼-inch dice

2 garlic cloves, minced

1 carrot, cut into ½-inch dice

1 zucchini (about 6 ounces), cut into ½-inch dice

4 ounces green beans, cut into 1-inch pieces

1¼ cups corn kernels, cut from 1 ear, or defrosted frozen

Freshly ground pepper

2 tablespoons balsamic vinegar

1 fifteen-ounce can cannellini beans, rinsed and drained

1 pound assorted tomatoes, coarsely chopped

1 Bring a medium saucepan of water to a boil; add 1 teaspoon salt. Add the pasta, and cook until al dente, 8 to 10 minutes. Drain, and rinse under cold water; set aside.

2 Heat 2 tablespoons olive oil in a large skillet over medium heat. Add the onion and garlic, and cook until they begin to soften, about 2 minutes. Add the carrot, and cook until it softens, about 4 minutes. Add the zucchini, green beans, and corn. Cook until the vegetables are tender, stirring occasionally, 10 to 15 minutes more. Season with salt and pepper. Transfer to a medium bowl to cool. Stir in the remaining 2 tablespoons olive oil, vinegar, cannellini beans, tomatoes, and reserved pasta. Season to taste with more salt and pepper, if desired. Serve chilled or at room temperature.

MACERATED BERRY AND CREME FRAICHE PARFAIT

SERVES 4 | PHOTOGRAPH ON PAGE 173

The rich, tangy crème fraîche and a bit of vinegar cut the sweetness of the berries. You can use vanilla ice cream in place of the crème fraîche.

12 ounces assorted berries, such as strawberries, blueberries, raspberries, and blackberries

2 tablespoons superfine sugar

2 tablespoons balsamic vinegar

8 ounces crème fraîche
Amaretti biscuits, crumbled

1 Combine the berries in a medium bowl. Sprinkle with the sugar and vinegar. Let sit, stirring occasionally, until the berries soften and start to release juices, about 30 minutes.

2 Layer the berries with the crème fraîche in parfait glasses. Serve immediately or refrigerate up to 3 hours. Just before serving, sprinkle with crumbled amaretti biscuits.

FIT TO EAT: HORS D'OEUVRES

CUCUMBER CUPS

MAKES 4 DOZEN | PHOTOGRAPH ON PAGE 168

2 seedless cucumbers (each 9½ inches long), washed

½ cup low-fat cottage cheese
Clover sprouts, for garnish

Slice the cucumbers in half lengthwise; trim ends. Cut each half into ¾-inch pieces. Scoop out the center of each piece with a melon baller, and fill with about ½ teaspoon cottage cheese. Garnish with clover sprouts, and serve.

PER PIECE: 4 CALORIES, 0 G FAT, 0 MG CHOLESTEROL, 0 G CARBOHYDRATE, 9 MG SODIUM, 0 G PROTEIN, 0 G FIBER

PITA PIZZAS

MAKES 4 DOZEN WEDGES

¼ teaspoon olive oil

1 small yellow onion, chopped into ¼-inch dice

2 garlic cloves, minced

½ teaspoon dried oregano

½ teaspoon dried basil

¼ teaspoon crushed red-pepper flakes

1 bay leaf

14 ounces whole peeled tomatoes, coarsely chopped

¼ cup tomato paste

4 whole-wheat pita breads (each 7½ inches)

1 yellow bell pepper, seeds and ribs removed, cut into ⅛-inch-thick strips

3 ounces mozzarella cheese, grated
Fresh basil, thinly sliced for garnish

1 To make the tomato sauce, heat the olive oil in a medium saucepan set over medium heat. Add the onion and garlic, and cook, stirring frequently, until browned, about 4 minutes. Add the oregano, basil, red-pepper flakes, bay leaf, chopped tomatoes, and tomato paste. Bring the mixture to a boil. Reduce the heat to medium-low, and let simmer, stirring occasionally, until the liquid has evaporated and the sauce is thick, about 35 minutes.

2 Preheat the oven to 350°F. To assemble the pizzas, arrange the pita breads on two baking sheets. Spread about 6 tablespoons tomato sauce on each. Scatter the strips of bell pepper on top, and then sprinkle with the cheese. Transfer the baking sheets to the oven, and bake the pizzas until the peppers begin to wilt and the cheese has melted, about 20 minutes. Remove the pizzas from the oven, and transfer to a cutting board. Sprinkle with the basil, and cut each pita pizza into 12 wedges. Serve warm or at room temperature.

PER WEDGE: 24 CALORIES, 1 G FAT, 1 MG CHOLESTEROL, 4 G CARBOHYDRATE, 44 MG SODIUM, 1 G PROTEIN, 1 G FIBER

SPICY SEARED SCALLOPS

MAKES 4 DOZEN | PHOTOGRAPH ON
PAGE 168

- 6 tablespoons all-purpose flour
- 1½ teaspoons cayenne pepper, or more to taste
- 3 teaspoons ground cumin
- 3 teaspoons ground coriander
- 1½ teaspoons coarse salt
- ¾ teaspoon ground cardamom
- 24 sea scallops (about 1½ pounds), halved
- 1 twelve-inch-long daikon radish, peeled and cut into forty-eight ¼-inch-thick rounds
- 5 romaine lettuce leaves, very thinly sliced
  Olive-oil cooking spray

1 Combine the flour, cayenne pepper, cumin, coriander, salt, and cardamom in a small bowl. Dip each scallop half into the mixture to coat; set aside.

2 Place the daikon rounds on a serving platter. Top each with shredded lettuce; set aside.

3 Heat a medium nonstick skillet over medium heat. Coat with olive-oil spray, and add the scallops. Sear until light golden brown and cooked through, about 1 minute per side. Transfer each seared scallop half to a daikon round. Serve warm or at room temperature.

PER SCALLOP HALF: 20 CALORIES, 0 G FAT,
5 MG CHOLESTEROL, 2 G CARBOHYDRATE,
59 MG SODIUM, 3 G PROTEIN, 0 G FIBER

BLACK BEAN SALSA WITH TORTILLA CHIPS

MAKES 2 CUPS SALSA AND
4 DOZEN CHIPS

- 1 nineteen-ounce can black beans
- 1 small tomato, seeded and cut into ½-inch dice
- 2 scallions, finely chopped
- 1 jalapeño pepper, seeds and ribs removed, minced
- ½ cup chopped fresh cilantro
- 2 tablespoons freshly squeezed lime juice
- ½ teaspoon coarse salt
- 6 flour tortillas (each 7½ inches)
  Olive-oil cooking spray

1 Preheat the broiler. Rinse the beans under cold running water. To make the salsa, place ¼ cup black beans in the bowl of a food processor. Pulse until coarsely chopped; transfer to a bowl. Add the remaining beans, tomato, scallions, jalapeño, cilantro, lime juice, and salt. Stir to combine; set aside.

2 To make the chips, cut each tortilla into eight wedges. Arrange on a baking sheet; coat with cooking spray. Place under the broiler, and broil until crisp and golden brown, 1 to 2 minutes per side. Transfer the chips to a wire rack to cool. Serve the chips with salsa.

PER CHIP PLUS SALSA: 23 CALORIES, 0 G
FAT, 0 MG CHOLESTEROL, 4 G CARBOHYDRATE,
62 MG SODIUM, 1 G PROTEIN, 1 G FIBER

TEA SANDWICHES WITH HORSERADISH-SALMON SPREAD AND ASPARAGUS

MAKES 4 DOZEN

The spread can be made an hour or two ahead and chilled; assemble the sandwiches just before serving.

- 4 cups water
- 1 onion, cut in half
- 5 sprigs fresh flat-leaf parsley
- 5 sprigs fresh thyme
- 1 bay leaf
- 20 whole black peppercorns
- 3 salmon steaks (about 2¼ pounds total), deboned
- ¼ cup finely grated fresh horseradish
- 1½ cups nonfat sour cream
- 1 teaspoon coarse salt
- 36 spears asparagus (about 3 pounds), ends trimmed
- 1½ loaves whole-grain bread, cut into 24 thin slices

1 Place the water, onion, parsley, thyme, bay leaf, and peppercorns in a medium pan set over high heat; bring to a boil. Reduce the heat to medium-low. Add the salmon, cover, and allow to simmer until the salmon is cooked through, about 8 minutes. Remove the salmon from the water; when cool enough to handle, flake it into small pieces, and transfer to a medium bowl. Add the horseradish, sour cream, and salt; stir to combine. Set mixture aside.

2 Fill a large bowl with ice and water; set aside. Bring a wide, shallow pan of water to a simmer over medium heat. Add the asparagus; let simmer until tender, about 3 minutes. Transfer to the ice bath; let cool. Drain well. Transfer to a cutting board, and slice the asparagus in half lengthwise; set aside.

3 To assemble the sandwiches, spread the reserved horseradish-salmon mixture onto each slice of bread. Top half the slices with six asparagus-spear halves each, then cover with the remaining slices of bread. Trim the crusts, cut each sandwich into four triangles, and serve immediately.

PER SANDWICH: 71 CALORIES, 2 G FAT,
12 MG CHOLESTEROL, 9 G CARBOHYDRATE,
102 MG SODIUM, 6 G PROTEIN, 1 G FIBER

CHOPPED LEMONGRASS CHICKEN SALAD | **PAGE 162**

CHICKEN AND VEGETABLE SKEWERS | PAGE 157

To toss a salad, place dried greens in a bowl. Season with coarse salt. Pour vinaigrette over the greens, being careful not to overdress. Toss with tongs or hands until the leaves are coated. Serve immediately.

BASIC VINAIGRETTE | PAGE 155

Paella is a traditional Spanish dish named for the wide, shallow pan in which it is cooked and served. Be sure to assemble and measure all ingredients before you start cooking.

PAELLA | PAGE 159

GRILLED SAUSAGE WITH ARUGULA PESTO | **PAGE 164**

MINESTRONE SALAD | **PAGE 165**

STAR-SPANGLED SHORTCAKE

1 After the baked ring has cooled, cut it in half crosswise with a serrated knife: Place it on a turntable, and rotate as you cut to achieve an even thickness.

2 Remove the top of the ring, using two offset spatulas. Transfer the bottom layer to a serving platter; cover with berries, juices, and whipped cream.

3 Place the top layer of the ring over the fruit and cream using the offset spatulas. Dust with confectioners' sugar, if desired.

STAR-SPANGLED SHORTCAKE | **PAGE 153**

MACERATED BERRY AND CREME FRAICHE PARFAIT | PAGE 165

POACHED FRUITS | PAGE 160
KEY LIME ICE CREAM | PAGE 160
LEMON POUND CAKE | PAGE 160
LEMON CURD | PAGE 161

august

Melon with Orange-Ginger Syrup

Chocolate Seashells

Vegetarian Summer Rolls

Shrimp and Chive Summer Rolls

Pork and Mango Summer Rolls

Shrimp Kabobs with Lemon Wedges
    and Cilantro

Barbecued Chicken Kabobs with
    Potatoes and Summer Squash

Tuna Kabobs with Marinated
    Baby Artichokes

Scallop Kabobs with Beets and
    Prosciutto

Curried Lamb Kabobs with Cherry
    Tomatoes and Red Onions

Brine-Cured Pork Kabobs
    with Jalapeños and Pineapple

Grilled Bread with Olive Oil,
    Garlic, and Salt

Tomato and Corn Tabbouleh Salad

Lemon Relish

Herbed Aïoli

Salsa Verde

Grilled Plum Kabobs

Frozen Tequila Sunrises

Latin Lovers

Arctic Mint Juleps

Raspberry Surfs

Frozen White Sangria

Mango Coolers

Frozen Banana Daiquiris

Frozen Margaritas

Piña Coladas

Orange Clouds

Frozen Marys

Grilled Cheese with Tomato
    and Basil

Corn on the Cob with Lime
    and Melted Butter

Quick Pickled Cucumber and
    Red-Onion Salad

Peach and Blueberry Cobbler

Stuffed Peppers

Golden Pepper Soup

Peperonata Sandwiches

Spicy Red-Pepper Sauce

Healthy Pepper Hash

MELON WITH ORANGE-GINGER SYRUP

SERVES 8

The exact size of the melon balls is unimportant; it's nice to have a variety of sizes.

1 cup freshly squeezed and strained orange juice (about 4 oranges), plus zest of 2 oranges

1 cup sugar

½ ounce ginger, thinly sliced

2 tablespoons Cointreau (optional)

1 small honeydew melon, cut in half and seeded

1 small canary or crenshaw melon, cut in half and seeded

1 cantaloupe, rind and seeds removed, cut into 1-inch wedges

Mint sprigs, for garnish

Orange Lace Cookies (recipe follows)

1 Fill a large bowl with ice and water; set aside. Place the orange juice, sugar, and ginger in a small saucepan set over medium heat; bring to a boil. Let simmer, stirring occasionally, until the sugar has dissolved and the syrup has thickened, about 15 minutes. Remove from the heat; strain the syrup into a clean bowl. Add the Cointreau, if using, and stir to combine. Set the bowl in the ice bath, or chill in the refrigerator, until the syrup is cold.

2 Using different sizes of melon ballers, cut balls from the honeydew and canary melons. Place the balls in a medium bowl; add ½ cup cold syrup and the orange zest. Toss to combine.

3 To serve, arrange the cantaloupe on a platter. Spoon the melon balls on top. Serve extra melon balls on the side. Drizzle the melons with syrup; garnish with mint. Serve with orange lace cookies and the remaining syrup on the side.

ORANGE LACE COOKIES

MAKES ABOUT 3 DOZEN

¼ cup light corn syrup

¼ cup packed light-brown sugar

4 tablespoons unsalted butter

1 tablespoon Cointreau (optional)

½ cup plus 2 tablespoons all-purpose flour

1 tablespoon orange zest (about 1 orange), finely chopped

⅛ teaspoon table salt

1 Preheat the oven to 350°F. Place a Silpat baking mat or parchment paper, on a baking sheet; set aside. Combine the corn syrup, sugar, butter, and Cointreau, if using, in a small saucepan set over low heat; stir until the butter melts. Remove from the heat. Add the flour, orange zest, and salt; stir until combined.

2 Drop heaping teaspoons of the batter, about 2½ inches apart, onto the prepared baking sheet. Place the sheet in the oven; bake until the cookies spread out, bubble, and turn golden brown, about 14 minutes. Remove from the oven, and let stand until the cookies firm slightly, about 4 minutes. Using a spatula, remove the cookies from the sheet; place on a wire rack, and let cool until crisp. Repeat until all the batter has been used, stirring the batter in between batches. Cool the cookies completely. Cookies can be stored in an airtight container for up to 2 days.

CHOCOLATE SEASHELLS

MAKES ABOUT 14

These chocolate shells make edible serving dishes for ice cream. Choose large, unbroken scallop shells; the shells we used measured three inches by four inches.

8 ounces white chocolate, broken into pieces

¾ teaspoon vegetable shortening

2 ounces semisweet chocolate, broken into pieces

1 To prepare the scallop shells, wrap each shell tightly in plastic wrap, making certain that the wrap is tight and smooth over the exterior (convex side) of the shell, securing excess wrap on the interior. Set aside.

2 Combine the white chocolate and ½ teaspoon shortening in a heat-proof bowl or the top of a double boiler set over a pan of barely simmering water; melt the mixture gently. Remove from the heat; set aside.

3 Combine the semisweet chocolate and the remaining ¼ teaspoon shortening in the cleaned heat-proof bowl or top of the double boiler; melt as above.

4 Drizzle 2 tablespoons melted semisweet chocolate into the melted white chocolate. Swirl the bowl to slightly combine the chocolates and create a marbled effect. Holding the very edges of a scallop shell, dip the exterior side into the swirled chocolate. Lift the shell out, and turn over, tilting it to evenly distribute the chocolate over the surface. Place the shell, chocolate side up, on a rimmed baking sheet; transfer to the freezer. Repeat with the remaining shells and chocolate. Freeze for at least 2 hours.

5 When the shells are frozen, remove from the freezer. Carefully loosen the plastic wrap from the edges of the shell. Gently separate the shell from the chocolate. Slowly peel the plastic wrap away from the chocolate. Return the chocolate shells to the freezer, and store in an airtight container until ready to use, up to 1 day ahead.

SUMMER ROLLS

VEGETARIAN SUMMER ROLLS
MAKES 1 DOZEN

12 eight-and-a-half-inch rice-paper wrappers

1 medium head frisée lettuce

4 medium carrots, cut into matchsticks

1 daikon radish, peeled and cut into matchsticks

1 red bell pepper, seeds and ribs removed and cut into matchsticks

4 scallions, peeled, ends trimmed, washed, and cut into matchsticks

1 bunch fresh mint

1 bunch fresh cilantro

Red Chile Dipping Sauce (recipe follows)

1 Dip a rice-paper wrapper into a bowl of warm water for 5 seconds; transfer to a clean work surface (the wrapper will still feel hard but will soften as it sits).
2 Lay a piece of frisée on the bottom third of the rice paper; top with some carrots, daikon, pepper, scallions, mint, and cilantro.
3 Roll, tucking in one end as you go and leaving the other end open. Place the roll on a plate; cover with a damp paper towel. Continue filling and rolling the rice-paper wrappers until all the ingredients are used. Do not refrigerate. Serve within 30 minutes with red chile dipping sauce.

RED CHILE DIPPING SAUCE
MAKES ABOUT 1½ CUPS

For a milder sauce, remove the seeds and ribs from the chile peppers before chopping.

8 fresh red chile peppers, stems removed

1 cup rice-wine vinegar

¼ cup sugar

In the bowl of a food processor, process the peppers until finely chopped. Transfer to a bowl, and add the vinegar and sugar. Stir to combine, and transfer to a serving bowl.

SHRIMP AND CHIVE SUMMER ROLLS
MAKES 1 DOZEN | **PHOTOGRAPHS ON PAGE 194**

2 pounds (about 60) small shrimp, peeled and deveined

4 ounces rice vermicelli

¼ cup freshly squeezed lime juice (2 limes)

2 tablespoons sesame oil

¼ teaspoon coarse salt

12 eight-and-a-half-inch rice-paper wrappers

½ seedless cucumber, cut into matchsticks

½ pound (about 2 cups) bean sprouts

1 bunch fresh chives, ends trimmed

1 head Boston lettuce, washed

1 bunch fresh mint

1 bunch fresh cilantro

Nuoc Cham (recipe follows)

1 Bring a large pot of water to a boil. Reduce to a simmer. Add the shrimp; poach until pink and cooked through, about 2 minutes. Slice 12 cooked shrimp in half lengthwise. Set all shrimp aside.
2 Bring a medium pot of water to a boil. Add the vermicelli; cook until softened, about 2 minutes. Remove from the heat; drain. Transfer to a bowl. Add the lime juice, sesame oil, and salt; toss to combine. Set aside.
3 Dip a rice-paper wrapper into a bowl of warm water for 5 seconds; transfer to a clean work surface (the wrapper will still feel hard but will soften as it sits).
4 Lay ¼ cup vermicelli on the bottom third of the rice paper; top with about 4 uncut shrimp and some cucumber and bean sprouts. Roll halfway, tucking in the ends. Place some chives and 2 shrimp halves on top of the roll; continue to roll so the chives and shrimp halves are enclosed but are still showing through the rice paper. Place the finished roll on a plate; cover with a damp paper towel. Continue filling and rolling the rice-paper wrappers until all ingredients are used. Serve with lettuce, mint, and cilantro, which are held around the rolls as they are eaten, and nuoc cham for dipping.

NUOC CHAM (VIETNAMESE DIPPING SAUCE)
MAKES ABOUT 1 CUP

½ cup freshly squeezed lime juice (4 to 5 limes)

¼ cup fish sauce

¼ cup rice-wine vinegar

2 teaspoons sugar

1 green chile pepper, very thinly sliced

In a small bowl, combine the lime juice, fish sauce, vinegar, sugar, and chile. Transfer to a serving bowl. Nuoc cham can be made several hours ahead, and refrigerated in an airtight container.

PORK AND MANGO SUMMER ROLLS
MAKES 2 DOZEN HORS D'OEUVRES | **PHOTOGRAPH ON PAGE 195**

½ cup fish sauce

¼ cup canola oil

¼ cup rice-wine vinegar

1 stalk lemongrass, crushed

2 garlic cloves, finely sliced

½ inch piece ginger, finely sliced

1 green chile pepper, finely sliced

2 teaspoons freshly ground black pepper

1 pork tenderloin (about 1 pound), silver skin trimmed

6 eight-and-a-half-inch rice-paper wrappers

1 bunch watercress, washed

½ mango, peeled and cut into matchsticks

½ small jícama, peeled and cut into matchsticks

1 cup fresh basil leaves, washed and dried

Peanut Dipping Sauce (recipe follows)

1 To make the marinade, combine the fish sauce, oil, vinegar, lemongrass, garlic, ginger, chile pepper, and black pepper in a medium bowl. Transfer to a resealable plastic bag; add the pork, coat with the marinade, and refrigerate 3 hours or overnight.
2 Heat a grill or grill pan to medium heat. Remove the pork from the marinade. Place on the grill; cook, turning as necessary, until a meat thermometer registers 160°F. Remove from the grill;

let cool. When cool enough to handle, slice the meat ⅛ inch thick; set aside.

3 Dip a rice-paper wrapper into a bowl of warm water for 5 seconds; transfer to a clean work surface (the wrapper will still feel hard but will soften as it sits).

4 Lay some watercress on the bottom third of the rice-paper wrapper. Top with some pork, mango, jícama, and basil. Roll; you needn't tuck in the ends. Place on a plate; cover with a damp paper towel. Continue filling and rolling the rice-paper wrappers until all the ingredients are used. Trim the ends; halve. Halve each half again on the diagonal to make hors d'oeuvres. Serve with peanut dipping sauce.

PEANUT DIPPING SAUCE

MAKES ABOUT 1½ CUPS

If the sauce thickens on standing, thin with water.

1 cup blanched unsalted peanuts
2 tablespoons sesame oil
1 shallot, peeled and finely chopped
1 garlic clove, minced
½ green chile pepper, seeds and ribs removed, minced, or more to taste
2 tablespoons tomato paste
1 cup Homemade Chicken Stock (page 8) or low-sodium canned
2 tablespoons fish sauce
1 teaspoon sugar
1 tablespoon freshly squeezed lime juice (about 1 lime)

1 Heat a skillet over medium heat. Add the peanuts; roast, stirring, until browned, about 3 minutes. Remove from heat; let cool. Transfer to the bowl of a food processor; process until finely ground, and set aside.

2 Warm the oil in a small saucepan over medium heat. Add the shallot, garlic, and chile pepper; cook until they begin to brown, about 4 minutes. Add the tomato paste; cook, stirring, about 1 minute more. Add the reserved nuts, stock, fish sauce, and sugar; stir. Simmer 5 minutes. Stir in the lime juice. Transfer to a serving bowl. Serve warm or at room temperature. Sauce can be made several hours ahead and refrigerated in an airtight container. Return to room temperature before serving.

KABOB PARTY

SHRIMP KABOBS WITH LEMON WEDGES AND CILANTRO

MAKES 8 | **PHOTOGRAPH ON PAGE 193**

½ cup loosely packed cilantro leaves, chopped
½ cup extra-virgin olive oil
32 large shrimp (about 2 pounds)
4 lemons, each cut into 8 wedges
1 teaspoon coarse salt
¼ teaspoon freshly ground pepper

1 Combine the cilantro and olive oil in a large bowl. Set aside. Peel the shrimp to the first knuckle, and devein. Rinse; pat dry. Place in the bowl with the cilantro-oil mixture, and coat.

2 Thread 4 shrimp, alternating with the lemon wedges, onto each of 8 skewers. Gently brush with a little of the olive oil mixture remaining in the bowl. Season with salt and pepper.

3 Heat a grill to medium heat. Arrange the skewers on the grill off direct heat. Grill, rotating the skewers and brushing with the olive oil mixture as necessary to prevent sticking, until cooked through, about 6 minutes, depending on the heat of the grill. The lemons should be soft and lightly charred. Serve with your choice of condiments.

BARBECUED CHICKEN KABOBS WITH POTATOES AND SUMMER SQUASH

MAKES 8 | **PHOTOGRAPH ON PAGE 193**

The potatoes need to be parboiled so they will be done grilling at the same time as the chicken.

1½ chicken breasts (3 halves), cut into 1-inch cubes
Spicy Barbecue Sauce (page 180), or 2 cups good-quality store-bought barbecue sauce
1 cup water
1½ tablespoons coarse salt
1¼ pounds new or fingerling potatoes
12 ounces (about 2) green or yellow summer squash cut into 1-inch pieces
2 tablespoons olive oil
1 teaspoon freshly ground pepper

BUYING RICE-PAPER WRAPPERS

The tissue-thin dough of rice-paper wrappers is made by sun-drying rice-flour paste on woven bamboo mats, which leave an attractive basket-weave imprint. Make sure to purchase Vietnamese rice-paper wrappers (bánh tráng) rather than the thicker Chinese wrappers, which may tear more easily. In Asian grocery stores, you'll usually find the Vietnamese wrappers in cellophane packets in the dry-noodle section. Rice-paper wrappers come in various sizes and shapes; we used 8½-inch rounds, but any size will work as long as you adjust the amount of filling to the size of the wrapper.

1   Place the chicken in a large bowl. Add the barbecue sauce; toss. Cover, and refrigerate for at least 30 minutes or overnight.
2   Place the water in a large saucepan. Add 1 tablespoon salt and the potatoes. Bring to a boil over high heat. Reduce the heat; simmer until the potatoes are almost tender when pierced with a knife, about 10 minutes. Do not overcook. Drain; halve. Set aside.
3   Thread 4 cubes of chicken, alternating with the potatoes and squash, onto each of 8 skewers. Gently brush the vegetables with a little olive oil. Season with the remaining ½ tablespoon salt and the pepper.
4   Heat a grill to medium heat. Arrange the skewers on the grill off direct heat. Grill, rotating the skewers and brushing with olive oil as necessary to prevent sticking, until cooked through, about 12 minutes, depending on the heat of the grill. The vegetables should be soft and lightly charred. Serve with your choice of condiments.

SPICY BARBECUE SAUCE
MAKES 2 CUPS

3   tablespoons extra-virgin olive oil
1   small onion, finely chopped
2   garlic cloves, minced
½   teaspoon cayenne pepper
1   teaspoon ground ginger
1   teaspoon dry mustard
1   teaspoon coarse salt
¼   teaspoon allspice
1   fifteen-ounce can tomato purée
1   teaspoon Worcestershire sauce
2   tablespoons dark molasses
¼   cup cider vinegar
¼   teaspoon freshly ground black pepper

1   Heat the oil in a saucepan over medium heat. Add the onion and garlic; cook, stirring, until translucent, about 3 minutes. Add the cayenne, ginger, mustard, salt, and allspice; cook just until the spices become very fragrant, about 2 minutes more.

2   Add the tomato purée, Worcestershire, molasses, and vinegar. Bring to a boil. Reduce the heat to low. Simmer, stirring often, until slightly thickened, about 15 minutes. Season with pepper. Use immediately, or cool and refrigerate in an airtight container until needed, up to 1 week.

TUNA KABOBS WITH MARINATED BABY ARTICHOKES
MAKES 8 | PHOTOGRAPH ON PAGE 192

The baby artichokes are cooked in advance so they only need to be grilled for a short time.

3   tablespoons Dijon mustard
1   tablespoon freshly squeezed lemon juice
½   teaspoon crushed red-pepper flakes
8   tablespoons extra-virgin olive oil
1   garlic clove, minced
1½   pounds tuna loin, cut into 1½-inch cubes
     Marinated Baby Artichokes (recipe follows)
1   tablespoon coarse salt
½   teaspoon freshly ground black pepper

1   Whisk together the mustard, lemon juice, red-pepper flakes, 6 tablespoons olive oil, and garlic in a large bowl. Add the tuna, and toss to coat.
2   Thread 4 cubes of tuna, alternating with the artichokes, onto each of 8 skewers. Gently brush with some of the remaining 2 tablespoons olive oil. Season with salt and pepper.
3   Heat a grill to medium heat. Arrange the skewers on the grill off direct heat. Grill, rotating the skewers and brushing with olive oil as necessary to prevent sticking, until the tuna is brown and charred on the outside and warm but still rare in the middle, about 5 minutes, depending on the heat of the grill. The artichokes should be tender and lightly charred. Serve with your choice of condiments.

MARINATED BABY ARTICHOKES
MAKES 2 CUPS

In addition to using these artichokes to make Tuna Kabobs, they are a wonderful addition to any summer salad or antipasto. They can also be served as a side dish for roasted or grilled lamb.

2   lemons
1½   pounds baby artichokes
1   head garlic, cut in half
2   tablespoons whole black peppercorns
2   tablespoons coarse salt
¼   cup extra-virgin olive oil
1   small bunch fresh thyme
     Pinch of freshly ground black pepper

1   Fill a large bowl with cold water; juice the lemons into the water. Set aside. Trim the spiky tops, tough stems, and outer leaves from the artichokes; halve lengthwise. Scrape any pink choke out from the centers, leaving the artichoke halves intact. Immediately transfer each artichoke to half the lemon water.
2   Drain the artichokes. Fill a large saucepan with water. Add the artichokes, garlic, peppercorns, 1½ tablespoons salt, 2 tablespoons olive oil, and thyme to the saucepan. Set over high heat; bring to a boil. Reduce the heat. Simmer, using a few layers of cheesecloth or a plate to keep the artichokes submerged, until tender when pierced with a sharp knife, about 5 minutes.
3   Remove from the heat, and drain. Reserve the artichoke halves, some of the garlic, and a few sprigs of thyme. Place in a bowl, and drizzle with the remaining 2 tablespoons olive oil. Season with the remaining 1½ teaspoons salt and ground pepper. Keep refrigerated in an airtight container up to 5 days, until needed.

SCALLOP KABOBS WITH BEETS AND PROSCIUTTO

MAKES 8 | PHOTOGRAPH ON PAGE 192

If baby beets are not available, use large beets cut into one-inch chunks.

1½ pounds baby beets, scrubbed, tops trimmed

2 pounds sea scallops, muscle removed

¼ pound prosciutto, thinly sliced

4 sprigs fresh mint

2 lemons

2 tablespoons extra-virgin olive oil

1 tablespoon coarse salt

1 teaspoon freshly ground pepper

1 Fill a large saucepan with cold water. Add the beets; bring to a boil. Reduce the heat to a simmer; cook until the beets are fork tender, about 15 minutes. Remove from the heat. Let cool slightly; rub away skins with a paper towel. Cut the beets in half, and set aside.

2 Rinse the scallops; pat dry. Wrap each scallop in a piece of prosciutto, tucking a leaf or two of mint between the scallop and prosciutto. Thread 4 scallops, alternating with the beets, onto each of 8 skewers. Squeeze the juice of 1 lemon over the skewers. Brush gently with some olive oil, and season with salt and pepper.

3 Heat a grill to medium heat. Arrange the skewers on the grill off direct heat. Grill, rotating the skewers and brushing with olive oil as needed to prevent sticking, until cooked through, about 5 minutes, depending on the heat of the grill. The beets should be soft and slightly charred. Remove from the grill; squeeze the remaining lemon over the skewers. Serve with your choice of condiments.

CURRIED LAMB KABOBS WITH CHERRY TOMATOES AND RED ONIONS

MAKES 8 | PHOTOGRAPH ON PAGE 193

1 garlic clove, minced

1 teaspoon ground coriander

1 teaspoon ground cumin

½ teaspoon ground turmeric

½ teaspoon dried oregano

6 tablespoons extra-virgin olive oil

1 tablespoon freshly squeezed lemon juice

¼ cup loosely packed mint leaves, chopped

2 pounds lamb shoulder, cut into 1-inch cubes

1 pound cherry tomatoes, mixed colors

4 small red onions, each cut into 8 wedges

1½ tablespoons coarse salt

2 teaspoons freshly ground pepper

1 Whisk together the garlic, coriander, cumin, turmeric, oregano, 4 tablespoons olive oil, lemon juice, and mint in a small bowl. Add the lamb. Toss to coat; refrigerate, covered, for at least 2 hours or overnight.

2 Thread 4 cubes of lamb, alternating with the tomatoes and onion wedges, onto each of 8 skewers. Brush with some of the remaining 2 tablespoons olive oil. Sprinkle with the salt and pepper.

3 Heat a grill to medium heat. Arrange the skewers on the grill off direct heat. Grill, rotating the skewers and brushing with olive oil as necessary to prevent sticking, until the lamb is cooked through but still pink inside, about 8 minutes, depending on the heat of the grill. The vegetables should be soft and lightly charred. Serve with your choice of condiments.

SKEWERS

To keep bamboo skewers from burning, soak them in warm water for at least thirty minutes before using. Cooking times may be a bit shorter if you use metal skewers, which conduct heat.

BRINE-CURED PORK KABOBS WITH JALAPEÑOS AND PINEAPPLE

MAKES 8 | **PHOTOGRAPH ON PAGE 192**

Brine-curing the pork makes it soft, tender, and juicy. The pork is cut into small pieces, so it needs to be cured for only four hours.

6 cups cold water

¼ cup sugar

3 tablespoons coarse salt, plus more for seasoning

2 bay leaves

1 tablespoon whole black peppercorns

1 tablespoon allspice berries

3 garlic cloves, chopped

1¾ pounds pork loin, cut into 1½-inch cubes

½ pineapple, peeled, cored, and cut into 1-inch chunks

16 medium jalapeño or other hot peppers, cut in half lengthwise

Spicy Molasses Glaze (recipe follows)

Freshly ground black pepper

2 tablespoons extra-virgin olive oil

1 Combine the water, sugar, salt, bay leaves, peppercorns, allspice, and garlic in a nonreactive bowl. Add the pork, cover, and refrigerate for at least 4 hours or overnight. Drain.

2 Thread 4 cubes of pork, alternating with the pineapple and pepper halves, onto each of 8 skewers. Brush with glaze, and season with salt and pepper.

3 Heat a grill to high heat. Arrange the skewers on the grill off direct heat. Grill, rotating the skewers and brushing with the remaining glaze and the olive oil to prevent sticking as necessary, until the pork is cooked through but juicy in the center, about 12 minutes, depending on the heat of the grill. The pineapples and peppers should be soft and lightly charred. Serve with your choice of condiments.

SPICY MOLASSES GLAZE

MAKES ABOUT 1 CUP

Brush on fish, chicken, and burgers.

2 tablespoons dark molasses

3 garlic cloves, minced

2 serrano chiles or jalapeño peppers, minced

1 inch piece fresh ginger, peeled and grated

½ teaspoon crushed red-pepper flakes

¾ cup extra-virgin olive oil

½ tablespoon coarse salt

Pinch of freshly ground black pepper

Whisk the molasses, garlic, chiles, ginger, pepper flakes, and oil in a small bowl. Add the salt and pepper. Keep the glaze in an airtight container at room temperature for up to 1 week.

GRILLED BREAD WITH OLIVE OIL, GARLIC, AND SALT

SERVES 8

1 loaf rustic bread, sliced

1 large garlic clove

¼ cup extra-virgin olive oil

Coarse salt

Heat a grill to high heat. Arrange the bread on the grill off direct heat, working in batches if necessary. Grill until golden brown. Turn the slices over; grill the other sides. Remove from the grill. Rub one side of each piece of grilled bread with the garlic clove. Brush with olive oil, and sprinkle with salt. Serve immediately.

TOMATO AND CORN TABBOULEH SALAD

SERVES 8

1 cup bulghur wheat

3 cups boiling water

6 ears corn, husked

½ cup extra-virgin olive oil

2 teaspoons coarse salt, or to taste

¼ teaspoon freshly ground pepper, or to taste

2 garlic cloves, minced, or to taste

Juice of 4 limes

4 large ripe tomatoes, diced

½ cup loosely packed fresh mint, finely chopped

½ cup loosely packed fresh flat-leaf parsley, finely chopped

¼ cup fresh chives, cut into small pieces

1 In a bowl, cover the bulghur with the boiling water. Let stand 45 minutes. Drain well; return bulghur to the bowl. Set aside.

2 Stand the corn on end on a cutting board, and, using a sharp knife, carefully cut the kernels from the cob. Heat 2 tablespoons olive oil in a large sauté pan over medium heat. Add one-third of the corn, season with salt and pepper, and cook, stirring, until the corn is caramelized and golden, about 7 minutes. One minute before the corn is done, add one-third of the minced garlic, and mix with the corn. Transfer the corn to a baking pan to cool. Deglaze the sauté pan with a little lime juice: Stir, using a wooden spoon, to loosen any browned bits on the bottom of the pan. Add the juice and bits to the corn, and set aside to cool. Repeat twice with the remaining corn.

3 Combine the bulghur with the remaining 2 tablespoons oil, tomatoes, remaining lime juice, mint, parsley, and chives. Add the corn; mix well. Chill 30 minutes before serving. Adjust the seasoning with salt and pepper.

LEMON RELISH

MAKES 2 CUPS

Try replacing some of the lemon with lime or orange segments for a mixed-citrus relish. Serve as a condiment for any of the kabobs.

8 lemons
  Lemon Oil (recipe follows)
1 medium red onion, diced
6 tablespoons sugar
4 ounces niçoise or Gaeta olives, pitted and chopped
½ teaspoon coarse salt
½ teaspoon freshly ground pepper
½ cup loosely packed fresh cilantro, coarsely chopped

1 Trim away the peel and white pith from the lemons. Working over a bowl to catch the juices, slice between the sections and membranes of the lemons; remove the segments whole. Place each segment in a bowl as completed. Cut the segments in half. Set aside.
2 Combine the lemon oil and red onion in a medium sauté pan. Set over medium-low heat, and cook, stirring, until the onion is translucent, about 4 minutes. Add the sugar, and cook until it melts, about 30 seconds. Remove from the heat, and let cool 5 minutes.
3 Transfer the onion mixture to a medium bowl. Add the lemon segments, olives, salt, pepper, and cilantro. Mix carefully, trying not to break up the lemon sections too much. Let stand at least 30 minutes before serving. Serve chilled or at room temperature.

LEMON OIL

MAKES ½ CUP

Keep lemon oil on hand to make salad dressings or to use when cooking fish.

½ cup extra-virgin olive oil
  Zest of 2 lemons

Combine the oil and zest in a small saucepan. Set over low heat, and cook very gently to infuse the oil with the lemon, about 10 minutes. Remove from the heat; let cool. The oil can be kept at room temperature in an airtight container for up to 1 month.

HERBED AIOLI

MAKES 2 CUPS

This condiment can be made up to a day in advance and refrigerated until serving. Serve as a condiment with the kabobs.

1 tablespoon freshly squeezed lemon juice
1 tablespoon champagne vinegar or sherry vinegar
2 garlic cloves
½ teaspoon paprika
1 large whole egg
1 large egg yolk
1 cup vegetable oil
¼ cup loosely packed tarragon, coarsely chopped
1½ teaspoons coarse salt
  Pinch of freshly ground pepper
½ cup extra-virgin olive oil

1 Combine the lemon juice, vinegar, garlic, paprika, whole egg, and egg yolk in the bowl of a food processor. Process just until the ingredients are blended.
2 With the processor running, slowly drizzle the vegetable oil into the mixture (it should begin to come together like mayonnaise). Add the tarragon, salt, and pepper. Slowly drizzle the olive oil into the processor. Chill for 30 minutes, and serve.

NOTE: Raw eggs should not be used in food prepared for pregnant women, babies, young children, the elderly, or anyone whose health is compromised.

SALSA VERDE

MAKES 2 CUPS

This is a very versatile condiment. Besides serving it with kabobs, try it with poached fish or grilled meats or drizzled over sliced ripe tomatoes. The sauce can also be prepared in a food processor but will have a more pastelike consistency.

2 cups loosely packed basil leaves
2 cups loosely packed marjoram leaves
2 cups loosely packed fresh flat-leaf parsley leaves
2 cups loosely packed mint leaves
3 anchovy fillets
3 garlic cloves
2 tablespoons capers
1¼ cups extra-virgin olive oil
½ teaspoon coarse salt, or more to taste
¼ teaspoon freshly ground pepper, or more to taste

1 Finely chop the basil, marjoram, parsley, and mint. Transfer to a bowl.
2 Chop the anchovies, garlic, and capers; combine to form a paste, and add to the herbs. Add the oil, salt, and pepper; stir to combine. Refrigerate in an airtight container until needed, up to 5 days. Bring to room temperature before serving.

GRILLED PLUM KABOBS

MAKES 8

Any ripe stone fruits, such as peaches and apricots, can be substituted for or mixed and matched with the plums.

8 ripe plums, quartered and pitted
2 tablespoons grapeseed oil or vegetable oil
2 pints vanilla ice cream
  Caramel Sauce (page 184)

1 Arrange 4 plum quarters on each of 8 skewers so that the cut sides of the fruit all face in the same direction. Heat a grill to medium heat. Brush the cut side of the fruit with some of the oil, and place, cut side down, on the grill off direct heat.
2 Grill just until the fruit begins to turn golden brown, about 2 minutes. Brush the bottoms of the fruit with oil, and turn over. Grill until the pit cavity fills with

juices and the fruit is soft, about 5 minutes, depending on the ripeness of the fruit and the heat of the grill.

3 Serve with bowls of vanilla ice cream, and drizzle with caramel sauce.

CARAMEL SAUCE

MAKES 2 CUPS

2 cups sugar

½ cup water

1 cup heavy cream

1 vanilla bean, split lengthwise

2 teaspoons freshly squeezed lemon juice

2 tablespoons unsalted butter

1 tablespoon bourbon (optional)

1 Combine the sugar and water in a 2-quart saucepan over medium heat. Stir until the sugar is dissolved; stop stirring, and let boil. Cook until dark amber, swirling the pan carefully while cooking, about 12 minutes.

2 Reduce the heat to low. Slowly add the cream, stirring with a wooden spoon. Scrape the vanilla seeds into the pan; add the pod. Add the lemon juice, butter, and bourbon, if using. Stir to combine. Remove the pod. Sauce can be stored in an airtight container in the refrigerator for up to 1 week. Bring to room temperature, or warm over low heat, before using.

BLENDER DRINKS

FROZEN TEQUILA SUNRISES

SERVES 2 | **PHOTOGRAPH ON PAGE 198**

The grenadine will sink to the bottom of the glass to create the sunrise effect. In addition to drizzling each drink, you can also pour some of the grenadine on the bottom of the glasses.

1½ ounces gold tequila

5 tablespoons frozen orange juice concentrate

1½ cups small ice cubes

2 tablespoons grenadine syrup

1 orange, sliced and cut into fans, for garnish (optional)

Combine the tequila, orange juice, and ice in the jar of a blender; process until smooth. Pour the mixture into two glasses. Carefully drizzle 1 tablespoon grenadine around the inside rim of each glass. Garnish with orange fans, if using, and serve.

LATIN LOVERS

SERVES 2 | **PHOTOGRAPH ON PAGE 198**

Fresh sugarcane can be found in some Latin markets. Have it cut into sections and then quartered lengthwise.

4 tablespoons frozen pineapple juice concentrate

2 tablespoons frozen orange juice concentrate

2 tablespoons frozen cranberry juice concentrate

1 tablespoon freshly squeezed lime juice

2 ounces Malibu rum

1½ cups small ice cubes

Fresh sugarcane skewers, for garnish (optional)

Combine the juices, rum, and ice in the jar of a blender; process until smooth. Pour the mixture into two glasses. Garnish with sugarcane skewers, if using, and serve.

ARCTIC MINT JULEPS

SERVES 2

6 teaspoons Mint Syrup (recipe follows)

2 ounces bourbon

1⅔ cups small ice cubes

Mint sprigs, for garnish

Pour 2 teaspoons mint syrup into each of two glasses. Combine the bourbon and ice in the jar of a blender; process until smooth. Spoon the bourbon mixture into each glass. Drizzle another teaspoon of mint syrup on top of each drink, garnish with a mint sprig, and serve.

MINT SYRUP

MAKES ABOUT ¾ CUP

1 bunch (2 cups packed) fresh mint, leaves only

¾ cup Simple Syrup II (recipe follows)

1 Fill a large bowl with ice and water; set aside. Bring a saucepan of water to a boil. Add the mint; cook just until bright and wilted, 3 to 5 seconds. Using a slotted spoon, transfer to the ice bath briefly. Drain.

2 Combine the syrup and mint leaves in the jar of a blender, and process until puréed. Let stand for 10 minutes. Pass through a fine sieve, pressing down firmly to extract as much syrup as possible; discard the solids. Store in an airtight container in the refrigerator until ready to use or up to 10 days.

SIMPLE SYRUP II

MAKES ABOUT 3 CUPS

3 cups sugar

1½ cups water

Fill a large bowl with ice and water; set aside. Combine the sugar and water in a small saucepan; place over medium-high heat. Cook, stirring frequently, until the sugar is completely dissolved, about 4 minutes. Transfer the syrup to a medium bowl, and place the bowl in the ice bath until chilled. Store in an airtight container, refrigerated, for up to 2 months.

RASPBERRY SURFS

SERVES 2

Chambord is a raspberry-flavored liqueur that can be found in liquor stores.

1 ounce Chambord

1 ounce raspberry-flavored vodka

3 tablespoons Fresh Raspberry Sauce (recipe follows)

1½ cups small ice cubes

Raspberries on a skewer, for garnish (optional)

Combine the Chambord, vodka, raspberry sauce, and ice in the jar of a blender; process until smooth. Pour the mixture into two glasses. Garnish with a raspberry skewer, if using, and serve.

FRESH RASPBERRY SAUCE

MAKES ABOUT 1¼ CUPS

In addition to being used to make Raspberry Surfs, the sauce can also be served over ice cream and with other desserts.

⅔ cup sugar

1 pint raspberries

Combine the sugar and raspberries in a small saucepan, and place over medium heat. Cook, stirring occasionally, until the raspberries break down and liquefy, about 10 minutes. Remove from the heat, and pass through a fine sieve to remove the seeds (if sieve is not fine enough, you may need to repeat this). Let stand until cool. Refrigerate in an airtight container until ready to use or up to 1 week.

FROZEN WHITE SANGRIA

SERVES 2

Superfine sugar, also called castor sugar, dissolves almost instantly.

½ peach, cut up and frozen

½ plum, cut up and frozen

3 strawberries, cut up and frozen

1 tablespoon frozen orange juice concentrate

3 tablespoons superfine sugar

½ cup dry white wine

1 ounce brandy or cognac

1½ cups small ice cubes

Combine the peach, plum, strawberries, orange juice, sugar, wine, brandy, and ice cubes in the jar of a blender, process until smooth. Pour the mixture into two glasses, and serve.

MANGO COOLERS

SERVES 2

Look for fragrant mangoes with unblemished skin.

1 cup ripe mango, cut into 1-inch cubes and frozen, plus more for garnish

1½ ounces dark rum

2 tablespoons freshly squeezed lemon juice

1 tablespoon Simple Syrup II (recipe above)

1½ cups small ice cubes

Cut a 1-inch square of mango flesh into tiny cubes, and set aside, covered. Combine 1 cup mango, rum, lemon juice, syrup, and ice in the jar of a blender; process until smooth. Pour the mixture into two glasses. Garnish with the reserved mango cubes and serve.

TIPS FOR BLENDER DRINKS

Perfecting these chilly drinks comes easily if you prepare ahead. First, you'll need a blender that is powerful enough to process ice to the desired smoothness. The quality of the liquor is essential: No amount of flavorful fruit will mask second-rate rum or tequila. Freeze fresh fruit for a smoother, less watery drink. Cut fruit into chunks, then lay the pieces flat in the freezer in a plastic bag. Depending on the variety of fruit, the slices will be ready in 30 minutes to an hour. Where juice is required, follow the recipe to the letter. If the recipe calls for concentrated juice, use it; substituting fresh will make a watery drink. Take ice out of the freezer right before blending to ensure that it is dry. To start, ice pieces should be in about ¾-inch cubes. Place larger cubes in a cloth towel and break them up with a meat tenderizer or hammer before blending. Start the blender on low until the ice begins to incorporate and crush, then switch to high speed.

FROZEN BANANA DAIQUIRIS

SERVES 2

Sweetened or unsweetened banana chips are available at most health-food stores and specialty-food shops.

1 tablespoon freshly squeezed lemon juice
3 tablespoons superfine sugar
2 ounces white rum
2 ripe bananas, cut into pieces
1½ cups small ice cubes
    Banana chips, for garnish (optional)

Combine the lemon juice, sugar, rum, bananas, and ice in the jar of a blender; process until fully blended and smooth. Pour the mixture into two glasses. Garnish with banana chips, if using, and serve.

FROZEN MARGARITAS

SERVES 2

For a strawberry margarita, add 1 cup frozen sliced, fresh strawberries, and do not salt the rim.

    Lime wedges, for garnish (optional)
    Coarse salt, for the glasses
3 tablespoons superfine sugar
¼ cup freshly squeezed lime juice (about 2 limes)
1½ ounces gold tequila
1¼ ounces Cointreau
2 cups small ice cubes

Run a wedge of lime, if using, around the rims of two glasses. Invert each glass, and dip the rim into the salt. Set aside. Combine the sugar and lime juice in a bowl; stir until the sugar is dissolved. Pour into the jar of a blender. Add the tequila, Cointreau, and ice; process until smooth. Pour the mixture into the two glasses. Garnish with lime wedges, if using, and serve.

PIÑA COLADAS

SERVES 2

You can buy shaved coconut in health-food stores. Toast the coconut curls in a 375°F oven until slightly golden on the edges. Shredded coconut can also be used.

2 ounces white rum
2 tablespoons coconut cream
1½ cups ripe golden pineapple chunks, frozen
1½ heaping cups small ice cubes
    Toasted fresh coconut curls, for garnish (optional)

Combine the rum, coconut cream, pineapple, and ice in the jar of a blender; process until smooth. Pour the mixture into two glasses. Garnish with coconut curls, if using, and serve.

ORANGE CLOUDS

SERVES 2

This drink is reminiscent of Creamsicles.

1 lemon wedge
    Orange Powder (recipe follows), or sugar, for glasses
¼ cup frozen orange juice concentrate
1 tablespoon heavy cream
1 ounce Cointreau
1 ounce Galliano
1½ cups small ice cubes

Run a lemon wedge around the rims of two glasses. Invert each glass, and dip the rim into the orange powder. Set aside. Combine the orange juice, cream, Cointreau, Galliano, and ice in the jar of a blender; process until smooth. Pour the mixture into the glasses, and serve.

ORANGE POWDER

MAKES ABOUT 3 TABLESPOONS

2 juice oranges
1 cup water
½ cup sugar
    Vegetable-oil cooking spray

1 Preheat the oven to 200°F. Using a vegetable peeler, peel the zest from the oranges, leaving behind the white pith.
2 In a saucepan, combine the zest, water, and sugar; bring to a boil over medium heat. Reduce the heat to low, and simmer 30 minutes.

3 Coat a parchment-lined rimmed baking sheet with cooking spray. Remove the orange zest from the heat, and strain. Spread the zest in a single layer on the prepared baking sheet. Bake until dry, 45 to 60 minutes. Remove from the oven, and set aside until completely cool.
4 Place the dried zest in a clean spice grinder, and process until powdery. Store at room temperature in an airtight container for up to 6 weeks.

FROZEN MARYS

SERVES 2

To make yellow and orange Marys, use only one teaspoon Worcestershire sauce, and instead of bottled juice, use a juice extractor to get juice from orange and yellow tomatoes.

½ cup bottled red tomato juice
1 tablespoon freshly squeezed lemon juice
1 cup fresh tomato chunks, frozen
1 tablespoon plus 1 teaspoon Worcestershire sauce
3 dashes hot-pepper sauce
2 ounces vodka
¼ teaspoon table salt
1½ cups small ice cubes
    Freshly ground black pepper
    Skewers of grape or cherry tomatoes, fresh basil, and cubed mozzarella, for garnish (optional)

Combine the tomato juice, lemon juice, frozen tomatoes, Worcestershire sauce, hot-pepper sauce, vodka, salt, and ice in the jar of a blender; season with pepper. Process until smooth. Pour the mixture into two glasses. Garnish with the skewers of tomatoes, basil, and mozzarella, if using, and serve.

menu

GRILLED CHEESE WITH TOMATO AND BASIL

SERVES 4 | PHOTOGRAPH ON PAGE 196

We cooked these sandwiches on a grill, but a skillet works just as well. Choose your favorite kind of cheese. We prefer a variety that melts easily, such as Gouda or Swiss, but cheddar is also good.

2 tablespoons unsalted butter, room temperature
8 slices white bread
12 ounces Gouda or Swiss cheese, sliced
1 large ripe tomato, thinly sliced
   Handful fresh basil leaves

1 Butter one side of each slice of bread. Arrange 4 slices, buttered side down, on a clean work surface. Divide the cheese evenly among the slices. Arrange the tomato slices over the cheese, cutting the slices to fit, if necessary. Scatter basil leaves over the tomatoes. Top with the remaining slices of bread, buttered side up.
2 Place the sandwiches on a medium-hot grill off direct heat. Cook until the bread is golden and the cheese is beginning to melt, about 4 minutes, depending on the heat of the grill.
3 Turn the sandwiches over, and continue grilling until the bread is golden and the cheese is completely melted. Move to a slightly cooler part of the grill to melt the cheese if the bread is darkening too much.

CORN ON THE COB WITH LIME AND MELTED BUTTER

SERVES 4

Ears of corn, cut into small pieces, make a perfect summer side dish. Plan on one whole ear per person.

4 ears corn, husked
4 tablespoons unsalted butter, melted
   Coarse salt and freshly ground pepper
2 limes, cut into wedges

1 Bring a large pot of water to a boil. Using a sharp knife, cut each ear of corn into 3 or 4 pieces about 1½ inches long. Add the corn to the boiling water, and cook just until tender, 3 to 4 minutes; this should not take much longer than the time required for the water to return to a boil.
2 Drain the corn. Toss with the melted butter, and season with salt and pepper. Serve with lime wedges to squeeze directly onto the corn.

QUICK PICKLED CUCUMBER AND RED-ONION SALAD

SERVES 4 | PHOTOGRAPH ON PAGE 196

This salad is best when served very cold.

1 large red onion, peeled and very thinly sliced
2 large cucumbers, peeled if waxed and cut into ¼-inch-thick slices
   Coarse salt and freshly ground pepper
3 tablespoons rice-wine vinegar
¼ cup loosely packed fresh dill leaves, or more to taste

1 Place the onion and cucumbers in a serving bowl. Season with salt and pepper, and sprinkle with the rice-wine vinegar. Toss to combine, and transfer to the refrigerator to chill, about 30 minutes.
2 Just before serving, scatter the dill over the salad, and toss well.

PEACH AND BLUEBERRY COBBLER

SERVES 4 | PHOTOGRAPH ON PAGE 197

3 to 4 ripe peaches (1¼ pounds), each cut into eighths
1 cup blueberries
¼ cup plus 1 tablespoon sugar
½ teaspoon ground cinnamon
2 teaspoons cornstarch
1 large egg
3 tablespoons unsalted butter, melted and cooled to room temperature
¼ cup heavy cream
½ cup plus 2 tablespoons all-purpose flour
   Pinch of table salt
1 teaspoon baking powder
   Vanilla ice cream (optional)

1 Preheat the oven to 350°F. Combine the peaches and blueberries in a bowl. Whisk together ¼ cup sugar, cinnamon, and cornstarch. Add to the fruit; toss to combine. Set aside.
2 Combine the egg, 2 tablespoons melted butter, and the cream in a bowl; whisk with a fork. Set aside.
3 Sift together the flour, salt, baking powder, and remaining tablespoon sugar. Make a well in the center of the dry ingredients, and pour the egg mixture into the well. Using your hands, slowly draw the dry ingredients into the wet ingredients, and work the dough until just mixed together.
4 Divide the fruit mixture among four 8-ounce ramekins. Gently pat the dough into 4 disks just big enough to fit on top of the ramekins. Place the dough on top, and brush the dough with the remaining tablespoon melted butter. Place the ramekins on a baking sheet. Bake until the juices bubble up and the crust is golden brown, 15 to 17 minutes. Serve hot, with ice cream, if using.

STUFFED PEPPERS

SERVES 6 | **PHOTOGRAPH ON PAGE 191**

- 6 medium (3 pounds) assorted bell peppers
- 1 large leek, white and light-green parts only
- 1 tablespoon extra-virgin olive oil
- 3 cloves garlic, minced
- 1 carrot, cut into ¼-inch dice
- 1 medium poblano pepper, seeds and ribs removed, cut into ¼-inch dice
- 4 ounces button mushrooms, wiped clean, stemmed and cut into ¼-inch dice
- ¾ cup uncooked long-grain white rice
- 1 fourteen-and-a-half-ounce can low-sodium chicken broth, or Homemade Chicken Stock (page 8), skimmed of fat
- 1½ cups water
- 1½ teaspoons coarse salt
- ¼ teaspoon freshly ground black pepper
- ½ teaspoon ground cumin
- ½ teaspoon ground turmeric
- ½ teaspoon paprika
- 1 cup corn kernels, fresh or defrosted frozen
- 1 cup canned black beans, rinsed and drained
- ¾ cup (3 ounces) grated Monterey Jack cheese

1 Slice off the tops of the bell peppers about ½ inch from the stems, reserving the tops for another use if desired. Remove and discard the seeds and ribs. If any pepper doesn't stand upright, shave a little off the bottom, making sure not to cut into the cavity; set aside.

2 Cut the leek into quarters lengthwise; slice ¼ inch thick. Place in a bowl of cold water, and soak 5 to 10 minutes to remove the dirt and sand. Lift the leek slices out of the water; discard sandy water. Drain in a colander; set aside.

3 Preheat the oven to 350°F. Heat the oil in a large nonstick skillet over medium heat. Add the leek and garlic. Cook, stirring occasionally, until they begin to soften, about 5 minutes. Add the carrot and poblano pepper; cook until just soft, about 5 minutes. Add the mushrooms; cook until the vegetables are just tender, about 4 minutes.

4 Stir in the rice; cook the mixture, tossing to coat, for 1 minute. Stir in the stock, water, salt, black pepper, cumin, turmeric, and paprika. Bring to a boil, and then reduce to a simmer; cook, uncovered, until the rice is just tender and most of the liquid has evaporated, 15 to 20 minutes. Stir in the corn, black beans, and ½ cup grated cheese. Divide the mixture among the bell-pepper shells, mounding it. The peppers can be made a day ahead up to this point.

5 Place the peppers in a glass baking dish, and fill the dish with ¼ inch of water. Bake until the peppers are tender and the filling is hot, about 1 hour. Sprinkle with the remaining ¼ cup cheese, and cook until the cheese is melted, about 1 minute more.

PER PEPPER: 277 CALORIES, 7 G FAT, 0 MG CHOLESTEROL, 44 G CARBOHYDRATE, 386 MG SODIUM, 11 G PROTEIN, 6 G DIETARY FIBER

GOLDEN PEPPER SOUP

SERVES 6 | **PHOTOGRAPH ON PAGE 196**

This puréed soup is good served either hot from the saucepan or chilled.

- 3 cups Homemade Chicken Stock (page 8), or low-sodium canned, skimmed of fat
- Generous pinch of saffron threads
- 1 tablespoon unsalted butter
- 1 large onion, diced
- 3 garlic cloves, minced
- 2 celery stalks, diced
- 4 large (about 2 pounds) yellow bell peppers, seeds and ribs removed, diced
- ¼ cup dry white wine
- 1 teaspoon coarse salt
- ½ teaspoon ground cumin
- 2 tablespoons half-and-half or milk
- Freshly ground black pepper
- Pinch of cayenne pepper
- Low-fat sour cream, for garnish

1 Bring the stock to a boil in a small saucepan. Add the saffron, and stir to dissolve. Turn off the heat, and let infuse. Set aside.

2 Heat the butter in a large saucepan over medium-low heat. Add the onion and garlic; cook until they begin to soften, about 4 minutes. Add the celery and bell peppers; cook, covered, stirring occasionally, until softened, 18 to 20 minutes.

3 Add the wine, and cook, stirring occasionally, until the liquid has evaporated. Add the infused chicken stock, salt, and cumin. Bring to a simmer, and cook until the vegetables are very tender, about 10 minutes.

4 Let the soup cool slightly. Purée, in batches if necessary, in a food processor or blender (do not fill more than halfway). Return to the cleaned saucepan; stir in the half-and-half or milk, and then reheat gently (do not boil; the mixture will curdle). Season with black pepper to taste and cayenne. Serve hot or chilled, garnished with sour cream.

PER SERVING: 84 CALORIES, 3 G FAT, 8 MG CHOLESTEROL, 11 G CARBOHYDRATE, 226 MG SODIUM, 3 G PROTEIN, 2 G DIETARY FIBER

PEPERONATA SANDWICHES

SERVES 6

The peperonata topping in this recipe can also be tossed with cooked pasta for a light summer dinner.

- 2 teaspoons extra-virgin olive oil
- 1 large onion, cut into ½-inch strips
- 6 large (about 3 pounds) assorted bell peppers, seeds and ribs removed, cut into ½-inch strips
- 1 teaspoon sugar
- 1 sprig fresh thyme
- 1 sprig fresh rosemary
- 1 teaspoon coarse salt
- ¼ teaspoon freshly ground black pepper
- 2 baguettes
- 1 tablespoon balsamic vinegar
- Herbed Goat-Cheese Spread (recipe follows)

1 Heat the olive oil in a large nonstick skillet over medium heat. Add the onion, and cook until it begins to soften, 3 to 4 minutes. Add the bell peppers, sugar, thyme, rosemary, salt, and black pepper. Toss until well combined. Cover the pan, and reduce the heat to low. Cook, stirring occasionally, until the peppers are very soft, about 30 minutes.

2 Slice the baguettes lengthwise, stopping before reaching the bottom of roll. Scoop out some of the top halves so they will sit nicely on top of the peppers; set the loaves aside, and reserve the scooped-out bread for another use. Uncover the skillet; raise the heat to medium. Cook, stirring often, until most of the liquid evaporates and the peppers are nicely glazed, about 3 minutes. Stir in the balsamic vinegar. Add a little water, if necessary, to avoid scorching. Transfer the peperonata to a bowl to cool. When cool, the peperonata can be stored, refrigerated in an airtight container, for up to 4 days.

3 Spread the herbed goat cheese on the bread, and top with the cooled peperonata. Slice each baguette into 3 sandwiches, and serve.

PER SANDWICH: 294 CALORIES, 9 G FAT, 13 MG CHOLESTEROL, 43 G CARBOHYDRATE, 743 MG SODIUM, 12 G PROTEIN, 4 G DIETARY FIBER

HERBED GOAT-CHEESE SPREAD
MAKES ABOUT 1 CUP

6 ounces fresh goat cheese
2 tablespoons chopped fresh flat-leaf parsley
2 tablespoons chopped chives
2 tablespoons freshly squeezed lemon juice
½ teaspoon coarse salt
¼ teaspoon freshly ground pepper

Combine the goat cheese, parsley, chives, lemon juice, salt, and pepper in the bowl of a food processor. Purée until smooth and well combined. Transfer to an airtight container, and refrigerate until needed, up to 4 days.

PER SERVING: 78 CALORIES, 6 G FAT, 13 MG CHOLESTEROL, 1 G CARBOHYDRATE, 198 MG SODIUM, 5 G PROTEIN, 0 G DIETARY FIBER

HOW TO BLANCH VEGETABLES

Blanching is a simple way to capture the fresh flavor of summer vegetables. Very briefly cooking vegetables in boiling water to just a step or two beyond raw prevents discoloration and retains vitamins. In minutes, vibrant blanched produce, full of flavor, becomes a crisp-cool side dish, part of a salad, or a meal in itself.

PREPARE Choose the freshest-possible produce from a farmers' market or your garden. Clean it, then cut to uniform size to ensure even cooking. Each variety should be blanched on its own.

BOIL The faster, the better. Bring a large pot of water to a vigorous boil, so it boils again quickly when the produce is dropped in. Add salt for flavor; this also hastens the cooking. Cook produce in batches from light-colored produce to dark. Cook until brightened, 45 to 60 seconds. Use a slotted spoon to remove from the water.

SHOCK Shocking, also called refreshing, stops the cooking and starts the crisping. Have ready a large bowl of water and ice. Immediately transfer the blanched vegetables to the ice bath. Remove when they're cool to the touch. Work quickly. If the water is not icy or the vegetables soak after shocking, they will wilt and discolor.

STRAIN Remove the vegetables from the ice bath, and transfer them to a colander. Shake gently over the sink to remove as much excess water as possible.

PAT DRY To keep blanched vegetables at their best, spread them on a clean kitchen towel, and gently pat away any remaining moisture. Loosely wrap vegetables in the towel, and chill up to two hours. Serve on a platter with lemon wedges, coarse salt, and vinaigrette.

SPICY RED-PEPPER SAUCE

MAKES ABOUT 2 QUARTS

Serve tossed with hearty fettuccine noodles and freshly grated Parmesan cheese.

2 tablespoons extra-virgin olive oil

1 large onion, cut into ½-inch dice

4 garlic cloves, minced

4 red bell peppers (about 2 pounds), seeds and ribs removed, cut into ½-inch dice

⅓ cup dry white wine

1 twenty-eight-ounce can crushed tomatoes, with juice

1 fourteen-and-a-half-ounce can low-sodium chicken stock, or Homemade Chicken Stock (page 8), skimmed of fat

1 fifteen-ounce can tomato sauce

2 cups water

½ teaspoon crushed red-pepper flakes, or more to taste

½ teaspoon coarse salt

½ teaspoon freshly ground black pepper

Few dashes hot-pepper sauce (optional)

1 Heat the oil in a large skillet over medium heat. Add the onion and garlic. Cook until softened, about 5 minutes.

2 Add the bell peppers; cook until tender, about 8 minutes. Raise the heat to medium-high; add the wine. Cook, stirring with a wooden spoon to loosen any browned bits on the bottom of the pan, until the liquid evaporates.

3 Stir in the crushed tomatoes with juice, stock, tomato sauce, water, red-pepper flakes, salt, black pepper, and hot-pepper sauce, if using. Bring to a boil, and then reduce to a gentle simmer. Cook, stirring occasionally, until the sauce is slightly thickened, about 1 hour.

PER SERVING: 135 CALORIES, 5 G FAT, 0 MG CHOLESTEROL, 15 G CARBOHYDRATE, 562 MG SODIUM, 3 G PROTEIN, 4 G DIETARY FIBER

HEALTHY PEPPER HASH

SERVES 6 | **PHOTOGRAPH ON PAGE 196**

Hash is often served at breakfast or brunch, but this dish also makes an easy dinner. Serve topped with poached eggs or eggs "fried" in a nonstick skillet with cooking spray.

1 tablespoon unsalted butter

1 red onion, cut into ½-inch dice

2 garlic cloves, minced

1 carrot, cut into ½-inch dice

1 medium (about 9 ounces) Idaho potato, peeled and cut into ½-inch dice

3 assorted bell peppers, seeds and ribs removed, cut into ½-inch dice

6 ounces button mushrooms, wiped clean, stems trimmed and cut into ½-inch pieces

8 ounces ground turkey

2 tablespoons all-purpose flour

¼ cup dry sherry

2 cups Homemade Chicken Stock (page 8) or low-sodium canned, skimmed of fat

1 teaspoon coarse salt

¼ teaspoon freshly ground black pepper

¼ teaspoon chile powder

¼ teaspoon paprika

2 tablespoons finely chopped fresh flat-leaf parsley

1 Heat the butter in a large nonstick sauté pan over medium-high heat. Add the onion, garlic, carrot, and potato. Cook until the vegetables soften and begin to brown, 6 to 7 minutes.

2 Reduce the heat to medium; add the bell peppers and mushrooms, and cook until the vegetables are just tender, 8 to 10 minutes.

3 Add the turkey; sauté until cooked through. Sprinkle with the flour; stir to combine.

4 Add the sherry; stir, scraping any browned bits from the bottom of the pan. Cook until most of the liquid has evaporated. Add the stock, salt, black pepper, chile powder, and paprika; bring to a boil. Reduce to a simmer; cook until the liquid thickens and reduces by half. Stir in the parsley. Serve hot.

PER SERVING: 243 CALORIES, 11 G FAT, 249 MG CHOLESTEROL, 18 G CARBOHYDRATE, 309 MG SODIUM, 16 G PROTEIN, 3 G DIETARY FIBER

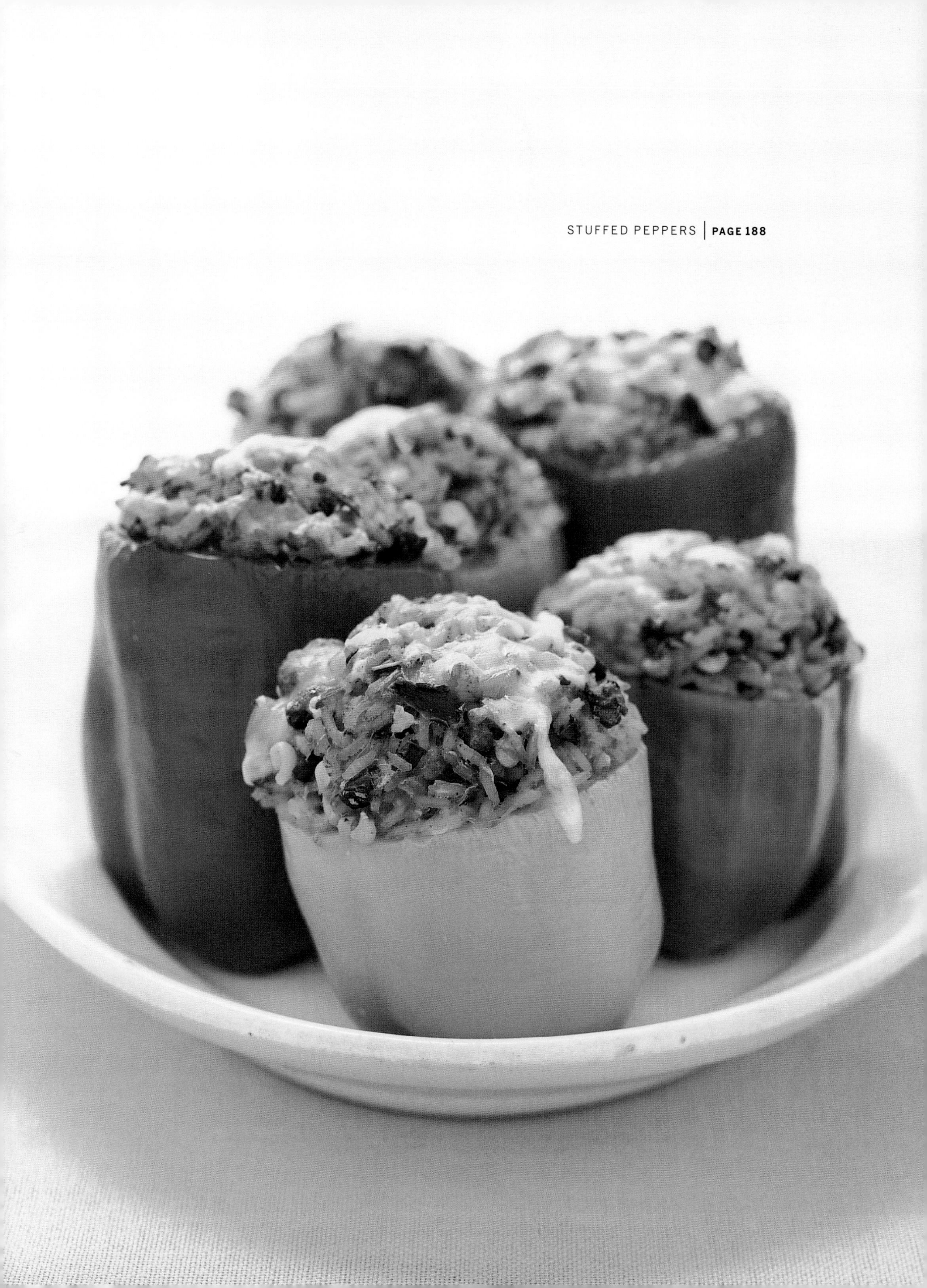

STUFFED PEPPERS | PAGE 188

BRINE-CURED PORK KABOB WITH JALAPEÑOS AND PINEAPPLE | **PAGE 182**

SCALLOP KABOB WITH BEETS AND PROSCIUTTO | **PAGE 181**

TUNA KABOB WITH MARINATED BABY ARTICHOKES | **PAGE 180**

CURRIED LAMB KABOB WITH CHERRY TOMATOES AND RED ONIONS | **PAGE 181**

BARBECUED CHICKEN KABOB WITH POTATOES AND SUMMER SQUASH | **PAGE 179**

SHRIMP KABOB WITH LEMON WEDGES AND CILANTRO | **PAGE 179**

SHRIMP AND CHIVE SUMMER ROLLS

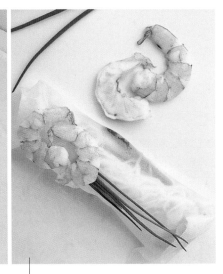

1 Dip the wrapper in warm water for five seconds to soften—no longer or it will get soggy and tear. The wrapper will still feel hard but will soften as it sits.

2 To get a tight roll, arrange the filling into a firm cylinder near one end of the rice-paper wrapper.

3 Fold in the top and bottom of the wrapper. Keeping the ends folded in, wrap the short edge over the filling; tuck it underneath to secure. Roll once. Arrange shrimp and chives on top, and finish rolling.

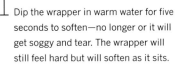

SHRIMP AND CHIVE SUMMER ROLLS | **PAGE 178**

Serve Shrimp and Chive Summer Rolls with lettuce, cilantro, and mint, which are held around the rolls as they are eaten. Dip the rolls in Nuoc Cham, a traditional sauce made with lime juice, fish sauce, rice-wine vinegar, sugar, and thinly sliced chile peppers.

HEALTHY PEPPER HASH | **PAGE 190**

QUICK PICKLED CUCUMBER AND
RED-ONION SALAD | **PAGE 187**

GOLDEN PEPPER SOUP | **PAGE 188**

GRILLED CHEESE WITH TOMATO AND BASIL | **PAGE 187**

PEACH AND BLUEBERRY COBBLER | **PAGE 187**

FROZEN TEQUILA SUNRISE | **PAGE 184**

LATIN LOVER | **PAGE 184**

september

Plum and Raspberry
Upside-Down Cake

Wild Mushroom Crackers

Classic Panzanella

New Classic Panzanella

Fried Okra

Sautéed Okra

Baby-Spinach Salad

Potato "Sushi" Rolls

Salmon Ceviche

Miso-Glazed Eggplant

Barbecued Oysters with
Cucumber Sauce

Barbecued Oysters with Del's
Homemade Ketchup

Barbecued Oysters with
Lemon Olive Sauce

Chilled Oysters on the Halfshell

Clam Custard (Chawon Mushi)

Wok-Smoked Mussels

Tuna Tartare with Asian Pears

Shiso-Wrapped Crab

Creamy Tomato Soup

Basil Croutons with Cherry Tomatoes

Salmon Salad with Horseradish
Vinaigrette

Cornmeal Cake with
Cream and Berries

Lemon-Saffron Millet Pilaf

Polenta Wedges

Wheat Berries with Vegetables

Wild- and Brown-Rice Salad

Quinoa Spinach Bake

Tomato, Cucumber, and Barley Salad

Whole-Wheat Couscous Salad

DESSERT OF THE MONTH

PLUM AND RASPBERRY UPSIDE-DOWN CAKE

MAKES 1 EIGHT-AND-A-HALF-INCH CAKE
PHOTOGRAPH ON PAGE 222

We used black plums, but red or Italian plums are just as delicious. Use more or fewer plums depending on their size. You will need an eight-and-a-half-by-two-and-a-half-inch round springform pan.

10 tablespoons (1¼ sticks) unsalted butter, room temperature, plus more for pan
⅓ cup packed light-brown sugar
6 medium plums, halved and pitted
½ pint raspberries
1½ cups all-purpose flour
1 teaspoon ground cinnamon
¾ teaspoon baking powder
¼ teaspoon baking soda
¼ teaspoon table salt
¼ teaspoon grated nutmeg
¾ cup granulated sugar
1 teaspoon pure vanilla extract
3 large egg yolks
½ cup sour cream

1   Preheat the oven to 375°F. Butter an 8½-by-2½-inch round springform pan; line with parchment paper. Melt 2 tablespoons butter; pour into the pan. Using a sieve, sprinkle the brown sugar evenly over the melted butter. Arrange the plum halves cut side down on top of the brown sugar, squeezing in as many plums as possible to allow for shrinkage during baking. Fill in the gaps with the raspberries; set aside.
2   In a medium bowl, sift together the flour, cinnamon, baking powder, baking soda, salt, and nutmeg; set aside. In the bowl of an electric mixer fitted with the paddle attachment, cream the remaining 8 tablespoons butter and the granulated sugar until light. Beat in the vanilla extract. Add the egg yolks one at a time, beating well after each addition. Add half the flour mixture, and beat until combined. Beat in the sour cream, and then beat in the remaining flour mixture.
3   Spoon the cake batter on top of the plums and raspberries, spreading evenly with a small spatula. Place the pan on a rimmed baking sheet to catch any juices; transfer to the oven, and bake until a cake tester inserted into the middle comes out clean, 60 to 70 minutes. Transfer to a wire rack to cool, about 1 hour. Run a knife around the edge of the pan to loosen the cake. Remove the ring; invert onto a serving plate. Serve slightly warm or at room temperature.

GOOD THINGS

WILD MUSHROOM CRACKERS

MAKES ABOUT 7 DOZEN
2-INCH CRACKERS

These crackers use mushroom powder, made from dried mushrooms ground with a mortar and pestle or in a spice grinder.

8 tablespoons (1 stick) unsalted butter, room temperature
½ pound (8 ounces) goat cheese
2 cups all-purpose flour, plus more for work surface
⅓ cup mushroom powder, from ¾ ounce dried mushrooms
¼ teaspoon freshly ground pepper
¼ cup milk
   Coarse salt

1   Preheat the oven to 350°F. In the bowl of an electric mixer fitted with the paddle attachment, mix the butter and goat cheese on medium until well combined. Add the flour, mushroom powder, and pepper; mix until just combined and crumbly. Scrape down the sides of the bowl, and add the milk. Mix on low speed until the dough comes together; it should be quite stiff.
2   Divide the dough into thirds. Wrap two pieces in plastic wrap; set aside. On a lightly floured work surface, roll out the third piece to ⅛ inch thick. Cut out rounds with a 2-inch cookie or biscuit cutter, arrange on a baking sheet, and prick each with a fork once or twice. Sprinkle with salt, and bake for 15 to 20 minutes or until the crackers start to brown.
3   Remove from the oven; let cool on a wire rack. Repeat with the remaining dough, rerolling scraps once. Serve when cool, or store in an airtight container for up to a week.

GROUND MUSHROOMS

Finely ground dried mushrooms add a savory, earthy flavor to bread crumbs and biscuit-and-cracker mixes. You can also try them as a meat rub or as a condiment sprinkled over baked vegetables. Pulverize several types of dried wild mushrooms in a mortar and pestle or a spice grinder. Keep the reserves in a jar on the spice shelf.

PANZANELLA TWO WAYS

CLASSIC PANZANELLA

SERVES 6 | PHOTOGRAPHS ON PAGE 218

For this recipe we soaked the onions in cold water to lessen their bite. If you prefer a stronger onion flavor, eliminate this step.

1 medium red onion, peeled and thinly sliced

5 one-inch-thick slices 1- to 4-day-old stale Tuscan-style bread

1 teaspoon coarse salt, plus more for seasoning

2 pounds ripe beefsteak tomatoes, cored and cut into large chunks

4 Kirby cucumbers (about 12 ounces), peeled and sliced

5 tablespoons extra-virgin olive oil

3 tablespoons red-wine vinegar
Freshly ground pepper

1 cup packed fresh basil leaves

1 Fill a bowl with enough cold water to cover the onion slices. Let them soak about 30 minutes, changing the water three or four times. Drain, and transfer to a large bowl or dish. Cover the bread with cold water, and let stand until the bread is softened and heavy with water, about 10 minutes.

2 Squeeze the bread between your palms to remove as much water as possible. Arrange the bread on a double layer of paper towels. Cover with another double layer of paper towels, and press down to extract any remaining water. Remove the top layer of towels, and sprinkle the bread with the salt. Set aside for 5 minutes. Using fingers, pluck bread into bite-size pieces, and transfer to the dish containing the onions.

3 Add the tomatoes and cucumbers. Drizzle the oil and vinegar over the salad; season with salt and pepper.

4 Tear the basil leaves in half; add to the bowl. Gently toss to combine. Set aside in a cool place, 30 to 45 minutes. Toss, and serve.

NEW CLASSIC PANZANELLA

SERVES 6 | PHOTOGRAPHS ON PAGES 218–19

You can intensify the garlic flavor by rubbing an additional clove on one side of the toasted bread before tearing it into chunks.

1 garlic clove

2 pounds ripe beefsteak tomatoes, cored and cut into large chunks

1 medium red onion, peeled and thinly sliced

5 tablespoons extra-virgin olive oil

3 tablespoons red-wine vinegar
Coarse salt and freshly ground pepper

5 one-inch-thick slices day-old Tuscan-style bread

4 Kirby cucumbers (about 12 ounces), peeled and sliced

1 cup packed fresh basil leaves, torn in half

1 Place the garlic on a cutting board; hit it with the side of a large knife to break it open a bit. Place the garlic, tomatoes, and onion in a large nonreactive bowl. Drizzle the oil and vinegar over the vegetable mixture; season with salt and pepper. Toss; let stand, covered, in a cool place, about 1 hour or more.

2 Place the bread on a hot grill or under a heated broiler; toast until both sides are slightly charred, 2 to 3 minutes. Remove from the heat, and rub lightly with garlic if desired; tear the bread into bite-size chunks.

3 When ready to serve, add the cucumbers, basil, and bread to the tomato mixture. Toss to coat the bread thoroughly with the marinating liquid. Adjust the seasoning with salt and pepper, and remove the garlic clove. Serve.

VARIATIONS: To either salad, try adding cubed fresh mozzarella or bocconcini, roasted bell peppers, sliced fresh fennel, or capers. Experiment using other in-season vegetables.

OKRA

FRIED OKRA

MAKES 2 POUNDS | PHOTOGRAPH ON PAGE 220

1 quart vegetable oil

2 pounds okra

2 large eggs

¼ cup milk

2 cups yellow cornmeal

1 cup all-purpose flour

1 tablespoon coarse salt, plus more for seasoning

1 teaspoon freshly ground black pepper

½ teaspoon cayenne pepper
Hot-pepper sauce (optional), for serving

1 Heat the oil in a cast-iron or other heavy skillet until a deep-frying thermometer registers 375°F.

2 Meanwhile, wash the okra under cold water, and pat dry with paper towels. Trim the stem ends; cut each pod crosswise into ¾-inch pieces.

3 Whisk together the eggs and milk in a medium bowl; set aside. Place the cornmeal, flour, salt, black pepper, and cayenne in another bowl; whisk to combine.

4 Add the okra to the egg mixture; stir until evenly coated. Add the cornmeal mixture; toss with your hands or a spatula until evenly coated.

5 Fry the okra in batches until golden brown, turning as necessary, 1 to 2 minutes per batch. Drain on paper towels, and season with salt. Serve warm with hot-pepper sauce, if using.

PANZANELLA

This salad originated in Tuscany as a tasty way to use the last scraps of stale bread. In the classic recipe, slices of bread are briefly soaked in cold water, squeezed dry, and added to roughly chopped tomatoes, other vegetables, olive oil, and vinegar. Soaking softens the bread and gives it a fluffy texture. Some cooks prefer to forgo the water bath and break the bread directly into the salad, arguing that dry bread more readily soaks up the flavorful juices. Other cooks hasten the staling process by toasting fresh bread. We provide two recipes: one with presoaked bread and one with toasted bread.

OKRA

Fresh okra is available from the garden in late summer. Okra pods become tough when they grow longer than about four inches; two to three inches is best. Choose bright-green ones with few, if any, black age spots. To test for firmness, snap off a tip: It should break crisply and readily without flexing or splintering. Fresh okra keeps best if stored in the refrigerator in a breathable container, such as a brown-paper bag. It will keep in the refrigerator for several days. For longer-term storage, chop the pods into half-inch rounds, immerse in water, and freeze as a block. Before cooking, use a sharp knife to trim, but not remove, the pods. The feathery spines are soft and will disappear when cooked. One reason okra hasn't become a popular ingredient in more North American households may be its misplaced reputation for having a slimy, unappealing consistency. Blame the cooks, not the vegetable. When heated slowly, okra releases complex sugars and moisture. They give the vegetable a slippery, ropy consistency that's useful to thicken lusty stews and Creole gumbos but that is undesirable when okra is served on its own. However, there are plenty of tricks for avoiding gummy okra. The simplest is to cook it quickly over high heat; try sautéing it in a hot, bacon-greased skillet for a few minutes or grilling it over glowing barbecue coals, which adds an alluring smokiness to the flesh. Another excellent way to lose the ooze is to cook the pods whole instead of slicing them. Okra's flavor is a natural partner for the sweetness of corn and onions, and stewing all three vegetables with fresh tomatoes is a wonderful way to chase off fall's first blustery days.

SAUTEED OKRA

SERVES 4 TO 6 AS A SIDE DISH
PHOTOGRAPH ON PAGE 220

For the best flavor and texture, cook okra quickly over high heat.

2 pounds okra

4 slices (about 4 ounces) bacon

Coarse salt and freshly ground black pepper

Crushed red-pepper flakes, for garnish (optional)

1 Wash the okra under cold water, and pat dry with paper towels. Trim the stem ends.

2 Heat a cast-iron or other heavy skillet over medium-high heat until hot. Add the bacon, and cook, turning occasionally, until golden. Drain the bacon on paper towels, and crumble into pieces.

3 Discard all but 3 tablespoons of bacon fat; return the pan to heat. When the fat is hot but not smoking, add the okra. Cook, turning occasionally, until the okra is bright green and slightly browned, 8 to 10 minutes. Season with salt and pepper; transfer to a platter. Sprinkle with crumbled bacon and pepper flakes, if using. Serve immediately.

ENTERTAINING AT YAKE-DONO

BABY-SPINACH SALAD

SERVES 6

1 log (6 ounces) soft goat cheese

½ cup cracker crumbs (Saltines)

1 tablespoon red-wine vinegar

1 teaspoon sugar

1 teaspoon coarse salt

6 tablespoons olive oil

9 ounces baby spinach, washed and dried

1 pink grapefruit, peeled, sectioned, and chopped into 1-inch pieces

½ cup pine nuts, toasted

½ cup dried currants

1 Divide the goat cheese into six equal portions. Gently dredge each in the cracker crumbs, pressing lightly to adhere. Set aside in the refrigerator.

2 In a bowl, combine the vinegar, sugar, and salt. Whisk in ¼ cup olive oil. Set aside.

3 Combine the spinach with most of the vinaigrette; arrange in a bowl. Top with the grapefruit, pine nuts, and currants. Drizzle with the remaining vinaigrette.

4 Heat the remaining 2 tablespoons oil in a large nonstick skillet over medium heat. Sauté the goat cheese until golden, about 30 seconds on each side. Transfer to the salad bowl. Serve.

POTATO "SUSHI" ROLLS

MAKES 3 ROLLS; SERVES 6 TO 8
PHOTOGRAPH ON PAGE 217

For best results, use small, creamy Yukon gold potatoes.

2 pounds Yukon gold potatoes, peeled and halved

2 tablespoons sugar

½ teaspoon coarse salt

1 tablespoon powdered wasabi (Japanese horseradish)

2 teaspoons water

3 nori sheets, 8-by-7½ inches

Pickled ginger, for garnish

Daikon sprouts, for garnish

Tamari or soy sauce, for serving

1 Place the potatoes in a medium saucepan, cover with cold water, and bring to a boil. Cook for 10 to 12 minutes or until tender. Drain well; return to the saucepan. Heat the potatoes over low heat, stirring until dry, 3 to 4 minutes. Remove from the heat. Using a potato ricer or a food mill fitted with the medium-holed blade, press the potatoes into a medium bowl. Add the sugar and salt. Stir to combine.

2 On a clean work surface, "knead" the potato mixture gently until it becomes smooth and dry, about 2 minutes. Set the mixture aside.

3 Combine the wasabi powder and the water in a small bowl to make a paste. Set aside.

4 Toast the nori sheets: Working one sheet at a time, fan each side of the nori over a gas burner on low heat until it stiffens and is paperlike, 1 to 1½ minutes. Set the toasted nori aside.

5 To prepare the sushi rolls, place 1 nori sheet shiny side down, horizontally, on a sushi roller or clean kitchen towel. Using an offset spatula, spread 1 cup potato mixture evenly over the nori, leaving a 1¼-inch border at the top of the sheet and a ⅛-inch border at the bottom. Spread ½ teaspoon wasabi paste, or more to taste, in a narrow line ½ inch from the bottom of the potato mixture. Starting at the bottom, roll up the nori evenly and tightly. Remove the roll from the sushi roller. Moisten the edge of the nori with water, and press gently to seal; set aside. Repeat with the remaining nori, potato, and wasabi.

6 Using a very sharp knife, cut each sushi roll into eight pieces, trimming the ends. Serve the sushi pieces at room temperature, cut side up. Garnish with pickled ginger and daikon sprouts, and serve with a small dish of tamari or soy sauce for dipping.

SALMON CEVICHE

MAKES 35 TO 40

½ cup white wine

½ cup freshly squeezed lemon juice

1 tablespoon coarse salt

1¼ pounds salmon fillet, skin removed, cut into ¼-inch dice

2 bay leaves

1 baguette or ficelle, cut into ¼-inch slices

3 tablespoons extra-virgin olive oil

1½ tablespoons whole green peppercorns in brine, finely chopped, for garnish

1 Combine the wine, lemon juice, and salt in a nonreactive bowl. Add the salmon and bay leaves. Toss gently to combine. Refrigerate for 2 hours, stirring occasionally.

2 Drain the salmon, and discard the bay leaves.

3 To serve, place 1 rounded tablespoon of salmon on each baguette slice. Drizzle with olive oil, and garnish with chopped peppercorns.

MISO-GLAZED EGGPLANT

SERVES 6 AS AN HORS D'OEUVRE

PHOTOGRAPH ON PAGE 216

5 tablespoons white miso
3 tablespoons sake
2 tablespoons sugar
2 tablespoons peanut or grapeseed oil
6 Japanese eggplants (1½ pounds),
  sliced in half lengthwise
  Zest of 1 lemon, finely grated

1 To prepare the miso paste, combine the miso, sake, and sugar in a small saucepan. Warm over low heat, stirring until the sugar has dissolved. Set aside.
2 Line a baking sheet with a paper towel; set aside. Heat the oil in a large skillet over high heat until almost smoking. Place the eggplant halves cut side up in the skillet. Cook for 5 minutes, turn over, and continue cooking for 1 to 2 minutes more or until golden brown and very soft. Remove the eggplant halves from the skillet, and transfer to the prepared baking sheet.
3 Using an offset spatula, spread 2 teaspoons of the reserved miso paste evenly over each eggplant half. Garnish with lemon zest. Cut the eggplant halves into pieces. Serve warm.

BARBECUED OYSTERS WITH CUCUMBER SAUCE

MAKES 1 DOZEN

8 ounces seedless cucumber, peeled
  and chopped into 1-inch pieces
¼ cup rice-wine vinegar
½ teaspoon coarse salt
4 tablespoons sesame oil
12 fresh oysters, scrubbed

1 Place the cucumber, vinegar, and salt in the bowl of a food processor. Purée until the mixture is smooth, about 10 seconds. With the motor running, slowly add the sesame oil until blended. Transfer the mixture to a small bowl, and set aside.
2 Heat a grill until very hot. Place the oysters on the grill. When the shells open, after 5 to 7 minutes, use an oyster knife to detach the oysters from the top (flat) shells. Discard the top shells. Place the oysters in the bottom (rounded) shells. Serve with cucumber sauce.

BARBECUED OYSTERS WITH DEL'S HOMEMADE KETCHUP

MAKES 1 DOZEN

12 fresh oysters, scrubbed
1 cup Del's Homemade Ketchup
  (page 206)
2 ounces soft goat cheese, crumbled
  (optional)
  Fresh chives, chopped, for garnish

1 Heat a grill until very hot. Place the oysters on the grill. When the shells open, after 5 to 7 minutes, use an oyster knife to detach the oysters from the top (flat) shells. Discard the top shells.
2 Place the oysters in the bottom (rounded) shells, add 1 heaping tablespoon ketchup and a little goat cheese, if using, to each, and return the shells to the grill. Heat 1 minute more, until hot. Garnish with chopped chives.

SHUCKING OYSTERS

Wearing work gloves, scrub the shells with a firm vegetable brush to remove any grit. Hold the oyster flat side up. Wedge a knife between the halves, at the joint. Twist the knife, and pry apart the shells. Hold the lid open with your thumb, and slide the knife across the roof until the muscle releases.

DEL'S HOMEMADE KETCHUP

MAKES 10 CUPS

10 pounds ripe tomatoes, chopped

3 cups water

8 onions, cut into ½-inch dice

6 Anaheim chiles, seeds removed, cut into ½-inch pieces

2 red bell peppers, seeds and ribs removed, cut into ½-inch pieces

6 garlic cloves

2 bay leaves

1 stick cinnamon

1 teaspoon whole allspice

1 teaspoon whole black peppercorns

1 teaspoon whole cloves

2 cups cider vinegar

1 cup sugar

1 tablespoon coarse salt

1 tablespoon dry mustard

1 teaspoon celery seed

1 teaspoon mace

1 Place a 12- to 20-quart stainless-steel pasta cooker in a large stockpot. Place 5 pounds tomatoes in the pot. Add 1 cup water, cover, and cook over medium-high heat until the tomatoes are very soft, about 10 minutes. Drain the tomatoes; reserve the cooking liquid. Pass the soft tomatoes through a food mill, fitted with a medium-holed blade, into a clean stockpot. Add the reserved cooking liquid to the puréed tomatoes. Repeat the cooking process with the remaining 5 pounds tomatoes and 1 cup water. Set aside.

2 Place the onions, chiles, bell peppers, and garlic in the pasta cooker. Add the remaining cup water, cover, and cook over medium-high heat until soft, about 20 minutes. Working in batches, transfer the vegetables with a slotted spoon to the bowl of a food processor; reserve the cooking liquid. Process the vegetables until smooth, about 10 seconds. Pass the puréed vegetables through the food mill, and add to the stockpot along with the reserved cooking liquid. Set aside.

3 Make a bouquet garni: Gather the bay leaves, cinnamon, allspice, peppercorns, and cloves in a tea ball or small piece of cheesecloth. Add the bouquet garni, vinegar, sugar, salt, mustard, celery seed, and mace to the stockpot; stir to combine.

4 Bring the ketchup to a boil over medium-high heat, and then reduce to a simmer; cook, stirring occasionally, until thickened, 2 to 2½ hours. Can immediately, or let cool. When cool, the ketchup may be frozen for up to 6 months.

BARBECUED OYSTERS WITH LEMON OLIVE SAUCE

MAKES 1 DOZEN

⅔ cup Meyer Lemon Oil (recipe follows)

2 ounces Kalamata olives, pits removed, halved and sliced

1 shallot, minced

12 fresh oysters, scrubbed

1 ounce manchego cheese, shaved (optional)

1 Combine the lemon oil, olives, and shallot in a small bowl. Whisk to combine, and set aside.

2 Heat a grill until very hot. Place the oysters on the grill. When the shells open, after 5 to 7 minutes, use an oyster knife to detach the oysters from the top (flat) shells. Discard the top shells. Place the oysters in the bottom (rounded) shells; add 1 to 2 teaspoons of sauce and a shaving or two of cheese, if using, to each. Return to the grill. Heat 1 minute more, until hot.

MEYER LEMON OIL

MAKES ⅔ CUP

⅓ cup freshly squeezed lemon juice, preferably Meyer

½ cup extra-virgin olive oil

1 Heat the lemon juice in a small saucepan over high heat until reduced by half, about 3 minutes.

2 Combine the lemon juice and oil in a glass jar. Store in the refrigerator for up to 2 weeks.

CHILLED OYSTERS ON THE HALFSHELL

MAKES 4 DOZEN

Plan to serve between three and six oysters per person for a first-course serving, and between eight and twelve for a main-course serving.

Crushed ice

4 dozen fresh oysters

Lemon wedges

Black-Pepper Ponzu Mignonette (recipe follows)

Red Oyster Sauce (recipe follows)

Arrange the crushed ice on a large platter. Open the oysters, and place on the ice. Serve with lemon wedges and sauces.

BLACK-PEPPER PONZU MIGNONETTE

MAKES ½ CUP

This is an Asian version of the classic mignonette sauce of red-wine vinegar, shallots, fresh lemon juice, and black pepper.

¼ cup rice-wine vinegar

1 teaspoon sugar

1 tablespoon freshly squeezed lemon juice

2 tablespoons soy sauce

¼ teaspoon freshly ground pepper

In a small bowl, whisk together the rice-wine vinegar, sugar, lemon juice, soy sauce, and pepper.

RED OYSTER SAUCE

MAKES 1 CUP

Thai red-curry paste usually comes in a fourteen-ounce bucket and can be bought at most Asian markets.

 4 tablespoons unsalted butter
 ½ cup extra-virgin olive oil
 1 large garlic clove, minced
 ¼ cup sun-dried-tomato paste
 ¼ teaspoon Thai red-curry paste
 10 fresh basil leaves

Melt the butter in a medium saucepan over medium-low heat. Add the olive oil, garlic, tomato paste, and red-curry paste, and simmer until the butter is brown, about 15 minutes. Coarsely chop the basil, and add it to the sauce. Serve warm.

CLAM CUSTARD (CHAWON MUSHI)

SERVES 6

To prepare this savory custard, you will need either a bamboo steamer or a water bath.

 12 Manila or littleneck clams
 1 cup water
 6 fresh morel or shiitake mushrooms, wiped clean and quartered
 6 snow peas, cut diagonally into ⅛-inch slices
 ¼ cup pine nuts
 2 scallions, white and light-green parts only, thinly sliced
 5 large eggs, lightly beaten

 1 If using a water bath, preheat the oven to 300°F with a rack in the center. Place 6 six-ounce ramekins in a 13-by-9-by-2-inch roasting pan; set aside. If using a bamboo steamer, place the ramekins on a work surface.
 2 Combine the clams with the water in a medium saucepan; cover, and place over medium-high heat. Simmer the clams until they open, 4 to 5 minutes. Remove the clams with a slotted spoon, and transfer to a small bowl. Set the clams aside to cool. Discard any unopened shells. Detach the clams from their shells; discard the shells. Reserve 1 cup cooking liquid; cool, and strain.

 3 Divide the clams, mushrooms, snow peas, pine nuts, and scallions among the six ramekins. Whisk together the reserved cup cooking liquid and eggs in a bowl. Ladle about 2½ ounces egg mixture into each ramekin.
 4 If using a bamboo steamer, place it over a wok filled with simmering water. Place the ramekins in the steamer, and steam, covered, over medium-low heat, for 15 minutes, until the custard has set. If using a water bath, bring a kettle filled with water to a boil. Transfer the roasting pan with the ramekins to the oven. Fill the pan with the boiling water halfway up the sides of the ramekins. Bake until the custard is set, 30 to 40 minutes. Remove the ramekins from the water bath. Serve warm.

WOK-SMOKED MUSSELS

SERVES 6

This recipe is adapted from one served at Bacar, a popular restaurant in San Francisco. Preheating the wok for seven minutes creates the smoky flavor.

 2 tablespoons peanut or grapeseed oil
 12 garlic cloves
 3 bay leaves
 1 jalapeño pepper, seeds and ribs removed, julienned
 1 teaspoon sea salt
 ½ teaspoon freshly ground black pepper
 2 pounds mussels, scrubbed and debearded
 ½ cup dry white wine
 Crusty bread, for serving

Heat a dry wok over high heat for 7 minutes. Add the oil, garlic, bay leaves, jalapeño pepper, salt, and black pepper, stirring constantly until the garlic becomes golden. Add the mussels, and stir occasionally until the shells open, 2 to 3 minutes. Add the wine, and cook until the liquid is reduced by half, 5 to 10 minutes; discard any unopened shells. Serve in deep bowls with crusty bread.

A HINT OF GARLIC

A sauté of greens and fresh garlic is a fast and nourishing meal or side dish when you find yourself in a hurry. Sliced garlic, though, will often char when cooked too quickly over high heat, and its strong flavor may prove overwhelming. To lend a milder garlic flavor to a dish, spear a large peeled clove with a fork and use the fork to stir as you cook. Discard the clove when you're finished.

TUNA TARTARE WITH ASIAN PEARS

MAKES 2 DOZEN; SERVES 6 TO 8

Set out chopsticks to use with this dish.

- 2 Asian pears (1¼ pounds)
- 1½ teaspoons soy sauce
- 1 tablespoon freshly squeezed lemon juice
- ½ teaspoon coarse salt
- ½ teaspoon freshly ground pepper
- 2 tablespoons olive oil
- ½ pound fresh tuna, cut into ¼-inch dice
- 1 large shallot, minced
- 1½ teaspoons fresh ginger, grated
- 2 tablespoons chives, finely chopped, plus more for garnish
- 24 shiso leaves
   Daikon sprouts, for garnish

1 Cut 1 pear in half crosswise. Peel one half, and cut into ¼-inch dice. Set aside. Cut the remaining 1½ pears into about 24 eighth-inch rounds. Set aside.
2 To prepare the marinade, place the soy sauce, lemon juice, salt, and pepper in a small bowl. Add oil, and whisk to combine. Set aside.
3 Combine the diced pear, tuna, shallot, ginger, and chives in a nonreactive bowl. Add the marinade, and toss gently.
4 Place a shiso leaf on each pear round. Top with a tablespoon of tuna tartare. Garnish with chives and daikon sprouts.

SHISO-WRAPPED CRAB

SERVES 8 | **PHOTOGRAPH ON PAGE 215**

Shiso leaves can vary in size. This recipe makes enough filling for thirty large or sixty small shiso leaves. Basil leaves can be used as well.

- ½ pound Dungeness or jumbo lump crabmeat
- ½ cup cracker crumbs (Saltines)
- 1 large shallot, minced
- 2 tablespoons store-bought or Homemade Mayonnaise (recipe follows)
- 1 tablespoon Dijon mustard
- 1 large egg, beaten
- 1 teaspoon Worcestershire sauce
- 1 teaspoon coarse salt
   Zest of 1 lemon
   Pinch of cayenne pepper
- 30 large or 60 small shiso leaves
- 4½ tablespoons all-purpose flour
- 6 tablespoons water
- 1½ cups canola oil
   Tamari or soy sauce, for serving

1 In a medium bowl, combine the crabmeat, cracker crumbs, shallot, mayonnaise, mustard, egg, Worcestershire, salt, lemon zest, and cayenne. Mix well to combine.
2 Line a baking sheet with a paper towel, and set aside. Place between 1 and 2 generous teaspoons of the crab mixture on each shiso leaf, depending on the size of the leaf. Fold each leaf in half. Set the leaves aside on the prepared baking sheet (this can be done up to 2 hours ahead).
3 To prepare the batter, combine the flour and water in a small bowl. Stir until just combined (be sure not to overmix), and set aside.
4 Heat the oil in a large skillet or a wok set over medium-high heat. Working with a few at a time, dip the leaf packets halfway into the batter, leaving the tips of the leaves uncoated. Gently shake off the excess batter. Carefully place the packets in the hot oil, and fry until golden and crisp, about 20 seconds. Remove, and drain the leaf packets on a paper towel. Repeat with the remaining leaf packets. Serve warm with tamari or soy sauce for dipping.

HOMEMADE MAYONNAISE

MAKES 2½ CUPS

A food processor helps make homemade mayonnaise quickly, but a whisk works just as well. Martha prefers to use entire eggs, not just the yolks, for a lighter texture. Add the oil very slowly, literally drop by drop. This prevents the oil from overwhelming the egg yolks and produces a smooth, creamy spread. By varying the ingredients, you can create endless combinations. Substitute a flavored vinegar such as tarragon or sherry for the lemon juice, or alter the flavor by trying different olive oils. Seasonings or chopped fresh herbs may be added to the mayonnaise after it is made.

- 1 cup light olive oil
- 1 cup canola oil
- 2 large eggs
- ¼ teaspoon dry mustard
- ¼ teaspoon coarse salt
- 2 tablespoons freshly squeezed lemon juice

1 Combine the oils in a large glass measuring cup. Place the eggs, mustard, and salt in the bowl of a food processor. Process until the mixture is foamy and pale, about 1½ minutes.
2 With the machine running, add the oil, drop by drop, through the feed tube, until the mixture starts to thicken (about ½ cup oil); do not stop the machine at this point or the mayonnaise may not come together. Add the remaining oil in a slow, steady stream. When all the oil has been incorporated, slowly add the lemon juice. The fresh mayonnaise can be kept, refrigerated in an airtight container, for up to 5 days.

NOTE: Raw eggs should not be used in food prepared for pregnant women, babies, young children, the elderly, or anyone whose health is compromised.

WHAT TO HAVE FOR DINNER

menu

CREAMY TOMATO SOUP

BASIL CROUTONS WITH CHERRY
TOMATOES

SALMON SALAD WITH HORSERADISH
VINAIGRETTE

CORNMEAL CAKE WITH CREAM
AND BERRIES

CREAMY TOMATO SOUP

SERVES 4

6 tablespoons unsalted butter

2 small onions, finely chopped

4 garlic cloves, minced

½ cup dry white wine

3 pounds chopped ripe summer tomatoes
(4 cups chopped)

1 teaspoon coarse salt, plus more for
seasoning

¼ teaspoon freshly ground pepper,
plus more for seasoning

1 cup fresh basil leaves, loosely packed

½ cup heavy cream

1   Melt the butter in a medium saucepan over medium heat. Add the onions
and garlic, and cook, stirring, until the
onions are translucent, about 3 minutes.
Add the wine, tomatoes, salt, and pepper. Cook just until the tomatoes are
falling apart, about 5 minutes. Stir in the
basil, and remove from the heat.
2   Let cool slightly. Transfer the tomato
mixture to the jar of a blender, filling
it no more than halfway; work in batches
if necessary. Cover the lid with a clean
dish towel, and press the lid securely in
place; blend the soup until smooth.
3   Return the soup to the saucepan. Add
the cream, and adjust the consistency
with water if necessary. Season with salt
and pepper.

BASIL CROUTONS WITH
CHERRY TOMATOES

MAKES 1 DOZEN

*Serve these large croutons as hors d'oeuvres
or as a soup garnish.*

½ loaf French bread

2 cups fresh basil leaves, loosely packed,
finely chopped

2 garlic cloves, or to taste, minced

2 ounces Parmesan cheese, grated

2 tablespoons extra-virgin olive oil

½ teaspoon coarse salt, plus more
for seasoning

¼ teaspoon freshly ground pepper,
plus more for seasoning

12 to 15 cherry tomatoes

1   Preheat the oven to 400°F. Slice the
bread on a slight diagonal into 12 slices,
about ¼ inch thick. Arrange the slices
on a baking sheet, and toast until golden,
about 3 minutes per side. Remove from
the oven, and set aside.
2   Mix together the basil, garlic, and
Parmesan in a small bowl. Slowly add
the oil, and mix to combine. Add the salt
and pepper; mix to combine.
3   Spoon a small amount of the basil
mixture onto each crouton, using the
back of the spoon to spread slightly. Slice
the cherry tomatoes in half, and place
the halves, face down, on the croutons.
Season with salt and pepper.

KEEPING TOMATOES

The area surrounding the stem of a
tomato is firm enough for the fruit to
hang securely on the vine through
wind and rain. Use nature's design to
extend the shelf life of fresh tomatoes
by placing them upside down on
a windowsill or countertop to ripen.
The tomatoes will keep longer without going flat and becoming spongy
on the bottom.

SALMON SALAD WITH HORSERADISH VINAIGRETTE

SERVES 4

The salmon can be poached a day ahead if desired and refrigerated until needed.

4 cups cold water

1 cup dry white wine

1 onion, thickly sliced

2 carrots, cut in half

1 bay leaf

1½ pounds salmon fillet, skin on

1½ pounds (about 10) new potatoes

1½ tablespoons coarse salt, plus more for seasoning

10 ounces haricots verts, stem ends trimmed

¼ cup red-wine vinegar or sherry vinegar

¼ cup grated fresh horseradish or prepared horseradish

½ cup extra-virgin olive oil
Freshly ground pepper

½ cup finely diced red onion

¼ cup finely diced fresh chives

6 ounces greens (optional)

1 Fill a large straight-sided skillet with the water and wine. Add the onion, carrots, and bay leaf. Set over high heat, and bring to a boil. Reduce the heat, and let simmer about 20 minutes. Add the salmon. If the liquid does not cover the salmon, adjust the level by adding more water to the skillet. Poach the salmon, skimming off any foam that rises to the surface, until the flesh is opaque and the fish is cooked through, 8 to 10 minutes. Remove from the liquid, and let cool completely.

2 Place the potatoes in a large saucepan, and fill to cover with cold water. Add 1 tablespoon salt, and bring to a boil. Reduce to a simmer, and cook until fork tender, 30 to 35 minutes. Remove from the heat, and drain. Set the potatoes aside.

3 Fill a large bowl with ice and water, and set aside. Rinse out the saucepan, and fill with cold water. Bring to a rolling boil. Add ½ tablespoon salt and the haricots verts, and cook until the beans are bright green and tender, about 5 minutes. Remove from the heat. Drain, and plunge into the ice bath. Drain, and pat dry.

4 Combine the vinegar and horseradish in a small bowl. Slowly whisk in the oil; season with salt and pepper.

5 Slice the potatoes and haricots verts in half, and place in a medium bowl. Add the red onion, chives, and half the dressing; toss gently to combine. Divide the vegetables among four plates. Remove the skin from the salmon, and slice the fillet into fork-size pieces. Place the salmon on top of the vegetables, and drizzle with the remaining dressing. Serve with greens if using.

CORNMEAL CAKE WITH CREAM AND BERRIES

MAKES 1 NINE-INCH SQUARE CAKE

1 cup (2 sticks) plus 2 tablespoons unsalted butter, room temperature, plus more for pan

2 cups all-purpose flour, plus more for pan

1 cup sugar

3 tablespoons honey

3 large eggs, room temperature

½ cup sour cream

1¼ cups yellow cornmeal

2 teaspoons baking powder
Pinch of table salt

1 tablespoon water

½ pint heavy whipping cream

2 cups blackberries

1 Preheat the oven to 375°F. Brush a 9-inch square baking pan with butter. Sprinkle with flour, and shake to coat. Tap out any excess; set aside.

2 In the bowl of an electric mixer fitted with the paddle attachment, cream the butter, ¾ cup sugar, and honey until fluffy, about 3 minutes. Add the eggs one at a time, beating until incorporated after each addition; do not overbeat. Add the sour cream; mix to combine. In a bowl, whisk together the flour, cornmeal, baking powder, and salt. Add the dry ingredients to the batter; mix to combine. Scrape the sides of the bowl with a spatula, and mix again.

3 Spread the batter in the prepared pan. Brush with the water, and sprinkle with the remaining ¼ cup sugar. Bake until the cake springs back when gently pressed in the center, about 30 minutes. Cool slightly on a wire rack. Whip the cream. Cut the cake into 4 squares; slice each square in half horizontally. Spoon whipped cream and berries over the bottom half of each cake, and cover with the top half.

FIT TO EAT: GRAINS

LEMON-SAFFRON MILLET PILAF

SERVES 8 TO 10 AS A SIDE DISH
PHOTOGRAPH ON PAGE 220

We served this pilaf with grilled shrimp. It would be just as good with any roasted or grilled fish.

2 teaspoons olive oil

2 shallots, peeled and finely diced

2 garlic cloves, minced

3 carrots, finely chopped

2 celery stalks, strings removed, finely chopped

¾ teaspoon coarse salt

¼ teaspoon freshly ground pepper

¼ teaspoon saffron threads, crumbled

1½ cups millet

3 cups water

3 tablespoons freshly squeezed lemon juice plus 1 tablespoon finely chopped lemon zest, plus more zest for garnish

¾ cup chopped fresh flat-leaf parsley

1 Heat the oil in a medium saucepan over medium heat. Add the shallots, garlic, carrots, celery, salt, and pepper, and cook until the vegetables begin to brown, about 5 minutes. Add the saffron and millet, and cook, stirring, 1 minute more. Add the water, lemon juice, and lemon zest. Bring to a simmer; cover, reduce the heat to low, and let cook until all the water has been absorbed, about 25 minutes. Turn off the heat, and let sit, covered, until tender, 10 minutes more.

2   Add the parsley, and stir with a fork to combine the parsley and fluff the pilaf. Serve garnished with lemon zest.

PER SERVING: 150 CALORIES, 2 G FAT, 0 MG CHOLESTEROL, 16 G CARBOHYDRATE, 112 MG SODIUM, 4 G PROTEIN, 2 G DIETARY FIBER

POLENTA WEDGES

SERVES 8 AS A SIDE DISH

You will need an eight-and-a-half-inch springform pan.

3   cups skim milk
3   tablespoons finely chopped fresh chives
2   garlic cloves, minced
½   teaspoon coarse salt
¼   teaspoon paprika
¾   cup quick-cooking polenta
2   ounces Parmesan cheese, grated
1   tablespoon unsalted butter
    Olive-oil cooking spray

1   Combine the milk, chives, garlic, salt, and paprika in a medium saucepan, and bring to a boil over high heat. While whisking, slowly sprinkle in the polenta. Reduce the heat to medium-low; cook, stirring occasionally with a wooden spoon, until the polenta has thickened, 5 to 8 minutes. Add the Parmesan and butter, and stir until combined. Pour the polenta into an 8½-inch springform pan; let rest until completely set, about 45 minutes at room temperature.

2   Preheat the broiler. Remove the outer ring from the springform pan. Cut the polenta into eight wedges. Coat with olive-oil spray, and place on a rack in the oven several inches below the broiler. Broil the polenta until golden brown on top and heated through, about 8 minutes. Serve.

PER SERVING: 127 CALORIES, 4 G FAT, 13 MG CHOLESTEROL, 15 G CARBOHYDRATE, 225 MG SODIUM, 7 G PROTEIN, 0 G DIETARY FIBER

PREPARING FRUIT ZEST

The zest, or outer layer of the peel, of lemons and oranges contains aromatic and highly flavorful citrus oils, making it a wonderful addition to many dishes, both sweet and savory. It is important to use just the colored part of the peel, since the white pith beneath it is bitter. To remove the zest, use a vegetable peeler or a zester, a tool with tiny holes that is dragged across the surface of the fruit, creating very thin strips. Since the peel of citrus fruits is not normally consumed, most people don't think about washing them, but it is necessary when using the zest. Washing with warm water and a scrub brush (a brush should be reserved just for washing produce) will remove the thin, waxy coating that's used to help some fruits and vegetables last longer and look more attractive in the supermarket; apples, cucumbers, and citrus fruits commonly bear this coating. Fruits and vegetables without a waxy coating should also be given more than a douse of water before being eaten. Wash them thoroughly—use the brush if necessary—since even those that look clean may have been handled quite a bit before reaching you.

WHEAT BERRIES WITH VEGETABLES

SERVES 8 TO 10 AS A SIDE DISH

This is an excellent accompaniment to meat or fish; it can also be served as an entrée.

1 cup wheat berries

1 quart water

1 small head broccoli (about 15 ounces), trimmed and cut into florets

2 teaspoons olive oil

1 medium yellow onion, peeled and diced

2 garlic cloves, minced

1 twenty-eight-ounce can tomatoes, chopped

¼ cup chopped fresh oregano

1 large yellow squash, quartered length-wise and cut into ¼-inch slices

½ small eggplant, cut into ½-inch pieces

½ teaspoon coarse salt

¼ teaspoon freshly ground pepper

1 Place the wheat berries in a small stockpot over high heat. Add the water. Cover, and bring to a boil. Reduce the heat to low. Simmer until tender, at least 40 minutes. Drain; set aside.

2 Fill a large bowl with ice and water; set aside. Bring a medium pot of water to a boil. Add the broccoli, and blanch until bright green, 1 to 2 minutes. Transfer to the ice bath, and set aside.

3 Heat the oil in a large skillet over medium-low heat. Add the onion and garlic, and cook, stirring frequently, until the onion is translucent, about 10 minutes. Raise the heat to medium, and add the tomatoes, oregano, squash, eggplant, salt, and pepper. Cook, stirring occasionally, until the vegetables have softened, about 15 minutes. Add the broccoli and wheat berries, and continue to cook until they are heated through, about 3 minutes more. Serve.

PER SERVING: 64 CALORIES, 2 G FAT, 0 MG CHOLESTEROL, 39 G CARBOHYDRATE, 260 MG SODIUM, 8 G PROTEIN, 9 G DIETARY FIBER

WILD- AND BROWN-RICE SALAD

SERVES 8 TO 10 AS A SIDE DISH |
PHOTOGRAPH ON PAGE 221

Any combination of rice or commercial blend of rice works well in this recipe.

1 tablespoon olive oil

1½ tablespoons balsamic vinegar

1 teaspoon coarse salt

¼ teaspoon freshly ground black pepper

¼ teaspoon Dijon mustard

1½ cups cooked wild rice

3 cups cooked brown and/or brown basmati rice (about 1⅓ cups uncooked)

1 yellow bell pepper, seeds and ribs removed, cut into ½-inch pieces

½ red onion, finely chopped

2 celery stalks, strings removed, cut into ½-inch pieces

½ seedless cucumber, quartered lengthwise and cut into ¼-inch slices

6 ounces cherry tomatoes, quartered

¼ cup chopped fresh cilantro

1 In a small bowl, whisk together the oil, vinegar, salt, pepper, and mustard; set aside.

2 Place the wild rice, brown rice, bell pepper, onion, celery, cucumber, cherry tomatoes, and cilantro in a medium bowl. Add the dressing, and toss well to combine. Transfer to a serving bowl.

PER SERVING: 152 CALORIES, 2 G FAT, 0 MG CHOLESTEROL, 29 G CARBOHYDRATE, 136 MG SODIUM, 4 G PROTEIN, 2 G DIETARY FIBER

QUINOA SPINACH BAKE

SERVES 8 AS A SIDE DISH | PHOTOGRAPH ON PAGE 220

In place of fresh spinach, you can use ¾ cup frozen, chopped spinach that has been thawed.

Bread crumbs, for baking dish

1 pound spinach, leaves picked and washed

2 teaspoons olive oil

1 medium yellow onion, peeled and diced

2 garlic cloves, minced

1 tablespoon picked fresh thyme leaves

1 teaspoon finely chopped fresh rosemary

¼ teaspoon crushed red-pepper flakes

2 cups cooked quinoa (about 1 cup uncooked)

1 cup nonfat cottage cheese

¼ teaspoon freshly ground black pepper

2 large eggs, lightly beaten

Olive-oil cooking spray

1 Preheat the oven to 350°F. Coat an 8-inch square glass or ceramic baking dish with cooking spray. Coat with bread crumbs; set aside.

2 Fill a large bowl with ice and water; set aside. Bring a medium pot of water to a boil. Add the spinach; blanch until bright green, about 10 seconds. Transfer to the ice bath. When the spinach is cold, remove it from the ice bath, squeeze out all the water, and finely chop; set aside. If using frozen spinach, defrost it and squeeze out excess water.

3 Heat the oil in a medium sauté pan. Add the onion, garlic, thyme, rosemary, and red-pepper flakes, and sauté until the onion is translucent, about 8 minutes. Remove from the heat, and transfer to a medium bowl.

4 Add the spinach, quinoa, cottage cheese, pepper, and eggs to the onion mixture, and stir until well combined. Pour the mixture into the prepared baking dish, and place in the oven. Bake until set and edges are brown, 60 to 70 minutes. Slice, and serve warm or at room temperature.

PER SERVING: 218 CALORIES, 5 G FAT, 55 MG CHOLESTEROL, 33 G CARBOHYDRATE, 174 MG SODIUM, 12 G PROTEIN, 4 G DIETARY FIBER

TOMATO, CUCUMBER, AND BARLEY SALAD

SERVES 12

Inspired by the classic Middle Eastern bulghur dish, this salad is every bit as refreshing and healthy.

5 cups water
¾ cup barley
2 teaspoons coarse salt
3 large (about 2 pounds) tomatoes, seeded and cut into ¾-inch dice
1½ cucumbers (about 1 pound), peeled, seeded, and cut into ½-inch dice
2 celery stalks, strings removed, finely chopped
2 scallions, white parts only, thinly sliced crosswise
½ cup finely chopped fresh flat-leaf parsley
1 cup finely chopped fresh mint
⅛ teaspoon cayenne pepper
3 tablespoons freshly squeezed lime juice
1 tablespoon plus 1 teaspoon extra-virgin olive oil
¼ teaspoon freshly ground black pepper

1 Bring the water to a boil in a saucepan. Stir in the barley and 1 teaspoon salt. Reduce the heat to medium, and cook until tender, about 35 minutes. Drain; rinse with cool water. Set aside.
2 Combine the tomatoes and cucumbers in a large bowl. Add the barley, celery, scallions, parsley, mint, and cayenne. Toss to combine, and set aside.
3 In a small bowl, whisk together the lime juice, olive oil, remaining teaspoon salt, and the pepper; add to the barley mixture. Toss to combine. Serve immediately, or refrigerate, covered, for up to 8 hours.

PER HALF-CUP SERVING: 78 CALORIES, 2 G FAT, 0 MG CHOLESTEROL, 14 G CARBOHYDRATE, 371 MG SODIUM, 2 G PROTEIN, 2 G DIETARY FIBER

WHOLE-WHEAT COUSCOUS SALAD

SERVES 6

2 beets, trimmed and scrubbed
2 tablespoons olive oil
½ cup finely chopped onion
¾ teaspoon ground cumin
1½ cups whole-wheat couscous
1½ cups boiling water
¾ teaspoon coarse salt
⅛ teaspoon freshly ground pepper
3 tablespoons freshly squeezed lemon juice
1 cucumber (8 ounces), cut into ½-inch dice
½ cup chopped fresh mint
½ cup chopped fresh flat-leaf parsley
1 bunch watercress (3 ounces), leaves only
4 wedges Moroccan Preserved Lemons, rinsed and thinly sliced (optional; page 214)

1 Preheat the oven to 425°F. Wrap the beets in aluminum foil, and bake until tender when pierced with the tip of a knife, 30 to 60 minutes, depending on the size of the beets. Unwrap, let cool enough to handle, and rub off the beet skins. Cut the beets into ½-inch pieces, and set aside.
2 Heat 1 tablespoon oil in a large skillet over medium heat. Add the onion and cumin, and cook, stirring, until translucent, about 8 minutes. Add the couscous, boiling water, salt, and pepper; stir. Turn off the heat, cover, and let sit 10 minutes, until all the water has been absorbed. Fluff with a fork. Transfer to a large serving bowl. Add the reserved beets, lemon juice, cucumber, mint, parsley, watercress, remaining tablespoon oil, and the preserved lemons, if using. Toss to combine. Serve.

PER SERVING: 259 CALORIES, 3 G FAT, 0 MG CHOLESTEROL, 64 G CARBOHYDRATE, 852 MG SODIUM, 8 G PROTEIN, 6 G DIETARY FIBER

GRAINS

Grains are a delicious source of carbohydrates and protein, and there are many wonderful choices besides the typical wheat, corn, and white rice. Though less familiar, basmati rice, quinoa, and millet offer a wide range of flavors. In a hearty salad, try nutty brown rice, which provides plenty of fiber and iron. For a side dish, prepare quinoa, a mild, light grain containing all eight essential amino acids. Or, as the foundation of a richly flavored pilaf, use delicate millet, complemented by aromatic saffron.

MOROCCAN PRESERVED LEMONS

MAKES 2 QUARTS

Lemons pickled in salt and lemon juice will keep for up to 6 months. Dice or cut the rind into matchsticks, and add to salads, pastas, and condiments.

8 lemons, scrubbed

½ cup coarse salt

2 one-inch cinnamon sticks

½ teaspoon whole black peppercorns

6 dried bay leaves

1 quart freshly squeezed lemon juice (about 24 lemons), or more if needed

1 Cut each lemon lengthwise into quarters, but only two-thirds of the way through, so one end remains intact. Rub the insides with 1 to 2 teaspoons salt. In 2 one-quart jars or 1 two-quart jar, layer the lemons, remaining salt, cinnamon sticks, peppercorns, and bay leaves. Pack the lemons as tightly as possible. Pour the lemon juice over the lemons until they are submerged. The lemons must be completely covered with the juice.

2 Close the jars tightly. Place in a warm spot to ripen for at least 1 week before using. Gently shake the jars daily to redistribute the salt. Transfer the jars to the refrigerator. To use the preserved lemons: Remove the amount needed from the jar, remove the flesh and discard, and rinse the rind under cold water to remove excess salt.

PER ¼ LEMON WEDGE: 6 CALORIES, 0 G FAT, 0 MG CHOLESTEROL, 3 G CARBOHYDRATE, 108 MG SODIUM, 0 G PROTEIN, 0 G DIETARY FIBER

SHISO-WRAPPED CRAB | **PAGE 208**

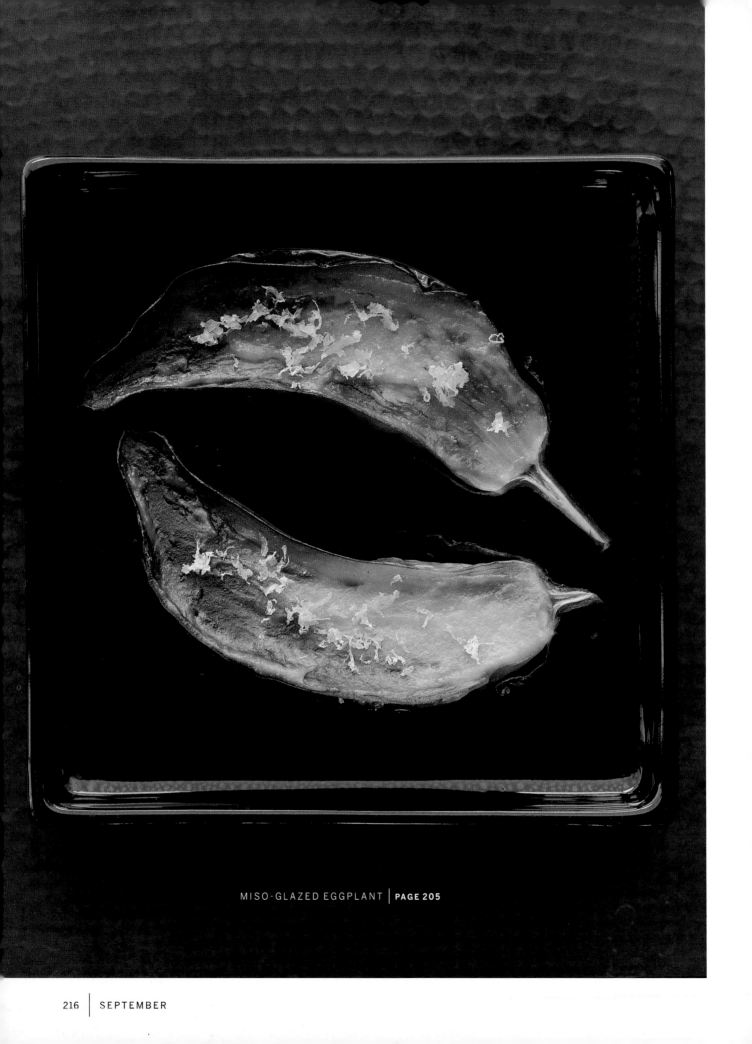

MISO-GLAZED EGGPLANT | **PAGE 205**

POTATO "SUSHI" ROLLS | PAGE 204

CLASSIC PANZANELLA

1 Soak onion slices in a bowl to lessen their bite. Cover slices of bread with cold water; let stand until the bread is softened and heavy with water.

2 Squeeze the bread between your palms to remove as much of the water as possible.

3 Add tomatoes, cucumber, oil, vinegar, salt, pepper, and torn basil leaves to the onion and bread.

CLASSIC PANZANELLA | **PAGE 202**

NEW CLASSIC PANZANELLA | **PAGE 202**

Once the ingredients for Classic Panzanella are combined, set aside the bowl in a cool place for 30 to 45 minutes. Toss before serving.

FRIED OKRA | **PAGE 202**

LEMON-SAFFRON MILLET PILAF | **PAGE 210**

QUINOA SPINACH BAKE | **PAGE 212**

SAUTEED OKRA | **PAGE 204**

WILD- AND BROWN-RICE SALAD | **PAGE 212**

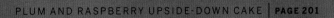
PLUM AND RASPBERRY UPSIDE-DOWN CAKE | **PAGE 201**

october

Peanut Butter Tart

Pumpkin Seed Pesto

Chicken Enchiladas

Orange Rice with Mushrooms

Buttermilk Ranch Dressing

Caramel Pecan Brownies

Endive and Treviso Radicchio Salad
     with Anchovy Dressing

Endive and Ham Gratin

Grilled Radicchio and Endive

Hearty Bacon and Lemon
     Chicory Salad

Sautéed Escarole with Garlic

Beef Stew

Caramelized Pineapple with
     Vanilla Ice Cream

Rigatoni with Pumpkin and Bacon

Pumpkin Soup with
     Wild Rice and Apples

Pumpkin Ice Cream

Pumpkin Cornmeal Doughnuts

Sweet Pumpkin Maple Custard

Pumpkin Molasses Tea Bread

Potatoes, Beans, and Peas in Cream

Florence's Potato Salad

Potato Focaccia

Best Baked Potatoes

Potato Gratin

Home Fries

Potato Seafood Chowder

Shepherd's Pie

Rachel Good's Glazed
     Potato Doughnuts

Julia Dunlinson's Potato
     Griddle Scones

Boneless Pork Chops with
     Apple Chutney

Herb Roasted Sweet Potatoes

Mustard Greens and Onions

Ice Cream with Caramel
     Brioche Croutons

Indian-Spiced Halibut with Yogurt

Red Lentil and Squash Curry Soup

Yellow Curry Chicken

Beef Rendang with Broccoli

Chickpea Apple Curry

Thai Green Shrimp Curry

PEANUT BUTTER TART

MAKES ONE 13¾-BY-4¼-INCH TART

- 10 graham crackers, 4¾-by-2½ inches broken into pieces
- 6 tablespoons unsalted butter, melted
- 3 ounces best-quality milk chocolate, plus more for curls
- 1¾ cups heavy cream
- ¾ cup creamy peanut butter
- 4 ounces cream cheese
- ⅓ cup sweetened condensed milk

1 Place the graham crackers in the bowl of a food processor, and pulse until fine crumbs are formed. Transfer to a medium bowl, and add the butter. Stir with a fork until thoroughly combined. Place the crumbs in a 13¾-by-4¼-inch rectangular tart pan with a removable bottom. Press the crumbs up the sides of the pan to form the edge of the tart, and then spread evenly over the bottom of the pan. Transfer to the refrigerator while making the filling.
2 Fill a large bowl with ice and water. Finely chop the chocolate, and place in a medium bowl. Place ½ cup cream in a small saucepan over medium heat, and bring to a boil. Pour the cream over the chopped chocolate, and set aside for 5 minutes. Whisk to combine. Set the bowl of ganache in the ice bath until cool, whisking constantly. Once cool, remove from the ice bath; whisk until the ganache is just thick enough to hold its shape. Do not overbeat. Spread the ganache in bottom of prepared crust, and return to the refrigerator until set.
3 Combine the peanut butter, cream cheese, and condensed milk in the bowl of a food processor; process until smooth. Transfer to a mixing bowl.
4 Whip ¾ cup heavy cream to soft peaks. Add the whipped cream to the peanut butter mixture, and whisk to combine.
5 Spoon the mixture into the prepared crust, and return to the refrigerator for 2 hours or overnight. Remove the tart from the refrigerator, and transfer to a serving platter 10 minutes before serving. Whip the remaining ½ cup cream, and top the tart with dollops of it. Use a vegetable peeler to make chocolate curls for garnish.

PUMPKIN SEED PESTO

MAKES 2½ CUPS

Pumpkin seeds, also known as pepitas, are an essential element of Southwestern cuisine, but their culinary possibilities are truly international. An example is this fragrant pesto, which features toasted pumpkin seeds and parsley in place of the usual pine nuts and basil for a seasonal variation on the Italian classic. Serve tossed with cooked pasta and topped with freshly grated Parmesan cheese.

- 3 cups hulled pumpkin seeds (pepitas)
- 1 cup fresh flat-leaf parsley, cleaned and stemmed
- 2 garlic cloves
- 1 small dried chile pepper
- ¼ teaspoon ground cinnamon
- 1½ cups extra-virgin olive oil
  Coarse salt and freshly ground black pepper

1 Preheat the oven to 350°F. Spread the seeds in a single layer on a rimmed baking sheet. Toast until fragrant, about 10 minutes. Transfer to a bowl to cool.
2 In the bowl of a food processor, combine the seeds, parsley, garlic, chile, and cinnamon. Pulse to combine. With the processor running, slowly add the oil in a steady stream until combined. Season with salt and pepper. Pesto can be stored, refrigerated, in an airtight container, for up to 3 days.

CHICKEN ENCHILADAS

SERVES 6 TO 8

- 1 chicken (3 to 4 pounds)
- 2 quarts Homemade Chicken Stock (page 8) or low-sodium canned
- 2 tablespoons extra-virgin olive oil
- 1 onion, halved, cut into ¼-inch slices
- 2 green or red bell peppers, seeds and ribs removed, cut into ¼-inch strips
  Enchilada Sauce (page 226)
- 12 corn tortillas (6 inch)
- 2 cups (about 6 ounces) grated Monterey Jack cheese
- 2 cups (about 6 ounces) grated sharp cheddar cheese
  Pepper and Tomato Salsa (optional, page 226)
  Sour cream (optional)

1 Place the chicken in a large pot, and pour the stock over it. If necessary, add water to cover the chicken. Bring to a boil, reduce to a simmer, and cook until the chicken is cooked through and very tender, about 1 hour. Transfer the chicken to a bowl to cool, and reserve the stock to use for enchilada sauce, if desired. When the chicken is cool enough to handle, remove the meat from the bones, and shred; set aside.
2 Heat the olive oil in a large skillet over medium heat. Add the onion, and cook until the slices start to soften, about 5 minutes. Add the peppers, and cook until tender, about 7 minutes. Transfer to a bowl, and set aside.
3 When ready to assemble, preheat the oven to 350°F. Place the enchilada sauce in a medium saucepan over medium heat. When hot, dip the tortillas into the sauce one at a time to soften, and place them side by side on two baking sheets. Divide the shredded chicken and the pepper mixture among the tortillas. Place the cheeses in a bowl, and toss to combine. Top each tortilla with 2 tablespoons grated cheese. Roll up the tortillas, and place snugly seam side down in a 9-by-13-inch ovenproof baking dish. Top them with the remaining enchilada sauce and grated cheese. Bake until the enchiladas are heated through and the cheese is melted, about 30 minutes. Serve with salsa, sour cream, or both, if using.

ENCHILADA SAUCE

MAKES 4 CUPS

To tone down the sauce for a milder flavor, omit some of the chiles.

5 long fresh red chiles
1 cup Homemade Chicken Stock (page 8) or low-sodium canned
2 cups water
4 large tomatoes
1 small poblano pepper
¼ cup extra-virgin olive oil
1 white onion, cut into ½-inch pieces
2 scallions, chopped
3 garlic cloves, minced
½ cup tomato paste
1 teaspoon ground cumin
1 teaspoon fresh oregano, chopped
½ teaspoon coarse salt

1   Cut the red chiles in half lengthwise; remove and discard the seeds and any ribs. Set aside. In a small saucepan, bring the chicken stock and the water to a simmer. Add the chiles, and simmer until tender, about 15 minutes. Set the saucepan aside. Fill a medium saucepan with water, and bring to a boil. Fill a large bowl with ice and water, and set aside. Cut an X in the bottom of each tomato, and add to the boiling water one at a time. Simmer until the skins begin to peel. Transfer the tomatoes to the ice bath immediately to cool. When cool, peel and discard the skins; chop, and set aside.

2   Place the poblano pepper directly on the burner of a gas stove over high heat or on a grill. Turn the pepper with tongs just as each side blackens. (You may also place the pepper on a rimmed baking sheet and broil in the oven, turning as each side becomes charred.) Transfer the poblano to a bowl, cover with plastic wrap, and let steam until cool enough to handle, about 15 minutes. Transfer the pepper to a work surface. Peel off and discard the blackened skin. Cut the pepper in half, and discard the seeds. Roughly chop the pepper, and set aside, along with any juices that have collected in the bowl.

3   Heat the olive oil in a large high-sided skillet over medium heat. Add the onion, scallions, and garlic; sauté until translucent, about 10 minutes. Add the chopped tomatoes, tomato paste, red chiles and liquid, poblano and liquid, cumin, oregano, and salt. Stir to combine. Simmer gently for 15 minutes. Transfer to the jar of a blender or the bowl of a food processor, filling no more than halfway; purée until smooth. Return to the pan; keep hot if assembling enchiladas, or refrigerate for up to 4 days.

PEPPER AND TOMATO SALSA

MAKES 1½ CUPS

2 cups Homemade Chicken Stock (page 8) or low-sodium canned
2 poblano peppers
3 large tomatoes
6 ounces tomatillos, husks removed
¼ cup olive oil
6 scallions, chopped
3 garlic cloves, minced
1 teaspoon chopped fresh oregano
1 teaspoon ground cumin
1 teaspoon coarse salt

1   Place the chicken stock in a small saucepan, and bring to a boil. Reduce to a simmer, and cook until reduced to 1 cup; set aside. Place the poblanos directly on the burner of a gas stove over high heat or on a grill. Turn the peppers with tongs just as each side blackens. (You may also place the peppers on a rimmed baking sheet and broil in the oven, turning just as each side becomes charred.) Transfer the poblanos to a large bowl, cover with plastic wrap, and let steam until cool enough to handle, about 15 minutes. Transfer the peppers to a work surface. Peel off and discard the blackened skin. Halve the peppers, and discard the seeds. Coarsely chop, and set aside.

2   Coarsely chop the tomatoes, and set aside in a bowl. Coarsely chop the tomatillos, and add to the tomatoes, tossing to combine. Place half of the tomato mixture in the bowl of a food processor, and pulse until finely chopped. Set aside the remaining tomato mixture.

3   Heat the olive oil in a large skillet, and add the scallions and garlic. Sauté until translucent, about 5 minutes. Add the processed tomato mixture and reduced stock. Bring to a simmer, and add the roasted poblanos, oregano, cumin, and salt. Simmer until the sauce has thickened slightly, about 15 minutes. Stir in the remaining tomato mixture, and cook until just softened, about 2 minutes. Serve immediately, or refrigerate for up to 3 days.

ORANGE RICE WITH MUSHROOMS

SERVES 6 TO 8

1 cup uncooked long-grain white rice
2 tablespoons extra-virgin olive oil
1 red onion, cut into ½-inch dice
2 celery stalks, strings removed, cut into ½-inch slices
8 ounces button mushrooms, wiped clean and stems removed, cut into ½-inch pieces
½ cup sliced scallions
Zest and juice of 1 orange
1 teaspoon coarse salt
¼ teaspoon freshly ground pepper

1   Bring a medium saucepan of water to a boil. Add the rice, and simmer until tender, 20 to 25 minutes. Drain, and set aside.

2   Heat the oil in a large saucepan over medium heat. Add the onion and celery, and cook until softened, about 10 minutes. Add the mushrooms, and cook until softened, about 5 minutes. Stir in the cooked rice, scallions, zest, and juice. Season with salt and pepper. Serve warm or at room temperature.

BUTTERMILK RANCH DRESSING

MAKES ABOUT 1½ CUPS

Drizzle this creamy dressing over Romaine lettuce, sliced carrots, and black olives.

1 cup mayonnaise

½ cup nonfat buttermilk

2 tablespoons freshly squeezed lemon juice

1 teaspoon coarse salt

1 teaspoon celery seed

1 tablespoon finely chopped fresh oregano (or 1 teaspoon dried)

½ teaspoon onion powder

¼ teaspoon freshly ground black pepper

Pinch of cayenne pepper

Whisk together the mayonnaise, buttermilk, lemon juice, salt, celery seed, oregano, onion powder, black pepper, and cayenne in a medium bowl. Store, refrigerated in an airtight container, for up to a week.

CARAMEL PECAN BROWNIES

MAKES 1 DOZEN | PHOTOGRAPH ON PAGE 246

1 cup (2 sticks) unsalted butter, plus more for dish

12 ounces bittersweet chocolate, finely chopped

2 cups all-purpose flour

¼ teaspoon cayenne pepper, or to taste

½ teaspoon coarse salt

1¾ cups sugar

4 large eggs

1 tablespoon pure vanilla extract

6 ounces semisweet chocolate chunks

3 ounces (about 1 cup) chopped pecans

Caramel Topping (optional, recipe follows)

1 Preheat the oven to 350°F. Butter a 9-by-13-inch glass baking dish. Line the bottom of the pan with parchment paper. Butter the paper, and set aside. Place the butter and the bittersweet chocolate in the top of a double boiler or a heat-proof bowl; set the bowl over a pan of barely simmering water. Stir occasionally until melted. Remove the pan from the heat, and set aside.

2 Sift together the flour, cayenne, and salt, and set aside. Place the sugar and eggs in the bowl of an electric mixer fitted with the paddle attachment, and beat until fluffy and well combined, 3 to 5 minutes. Add the vanilla and chocolate mixture, and stir to combine. Add the flour mixture, and stir to combine. Stir in the semisweet chocolate. Pour into the prepared dish, and sprinkle with the chopped pecans. Bake until set, 35 to 40 minutes. Transfer the pan to a wire rack to cool. When cool, drizzle with caramel sauce, if using.

CARAMEL TOPPING

MAKES 2 CUPS

We like this sauce over cooled brownies, but it also makes a rich topping for ice cream.

1 cup sugar

¼ cup water

½ cup heavy cream

1 small vanilla bean, split lengthwise

1 teaspoon freshly squeezed lemon juice

1 tablespoon unsalted butter

1 Stir together the sugar and water in a 2-quart saucepan over medium heat. Cook, without stirring, until the mixture is dark amber in color, occasionally swirling the pan carefully while cooking, about 20 minutes.

2 Reduce the heat to low. Slowly and carefully add the cream, stirring with a wooden spoon when the bubbling dies down. Scrape the vanilla seeds into the pan, and add the pod. Add the lemon juice and butter. Stir to combine. Remove the pod.

3 Cover, and store, refrigerated, for up to a week. Bring the sauce to room temperature, or warm over low heat, before using.

CHICORIES

ENDIVE AND TREVISO RADICCHIO SALAD WITH ANCHOVY DRESSING

SERVES 4

Soaking anchovies in red-wine vinegar gives them a wonderful pickled flavor.

6 anchovy fillets

¼ cup plus 1 tablespoon red-wine vinegar

1 garlic clove, smashed and peeled

½ teaspoon coarse salt

3 tablespoons extra-virgin olive oil

¼ teaspoon freshly ground pepper

4 endives, cut lengthwise into ¼-inch slices

1 head Treviso radicchio, leaves separated

1 In a small bowl, submerge the anchovies in ¼ cup red-wine vinegar. Let them soak for 30 minutes; drain, and discard the liquid.

2 Place the anchovies and garlic on a cutting board. Sprinkle with the salt, and mince into a paste. Transfer the mixture to a medium bowl. Whisk in the remaining tablespoon vinegar, the olive oil, and pepper. Set aside.

3 Arrange the endives and radicchio on four salad plates. Drizzle the anchovy mixture over each. Serve immediately.

ENDIVE AND HAM GRATIN

SERVES 6 AS A SIDE DISH | PHOTOGRAPH ON PAGE 240

4 tablespoons unsalted butter, plus more for dish

6 endives

¾ teaspoon coarse salt

1 cup milk

2 tablespoons all-purpose flour

¼ teaspoon freshly grated nutmeg

3 ounces Black Forest or Virginia ham, sliced ⅛ inch thick and cut lengthwise into 2½-inch-wide strips

1 ounce Gruyère cheese, grated

1 Preheat the oven to 400°F. Melt 2 tablespoons butter in a Dutch oven over medium heat. Add the endives and ¼ teaspoon salt. Cook, turning occasionally, until golden brown, about 6 minutes.

Reduce the heat to low, and cover. Cook until soft and tender, about 30 minutes more. Remove from the heat, and set aside, covered.

2 Butter a 6-by-10-inch baking dish, and set aside. Place the milk in a small saucepan over low heat. In another small pan, melt the remaining 2 tablespoons butter over medium heat. Whisk in the flour. Cook, whisking constantly, for 1 minute. Slowly pour the heated milk into the mixture. Whisk constantly, preventing lumps. Add the remaining ½ teaspoon salt and the nutmeg. Cook the mixture, whisking slowly but constantly, until thick and bubbling, about 1 minute. Remove from the heat, and set aside.

3 Wrap a piece of ham around each endive, and place in the prepared baking dish. Spoon the sauce over the endives. Sprinkle the cheese over the sauce. Bake until golden brown on top, 20 to 25 minutes. Serve immediately.

GRILLED RADICCHIO AND ENDIVE

SERVES 6 AS A SIDE DISH

For flavorful and moist radicchio and endives, place them close together on the grill.

1 head radicchio
6 heads Belgian endive
¼ cup plus 2 tablespoons extra-virgin olive oil
1½ teaspoons coarse salt
½ teaspoon freshly ground pepper

Heat a grill to medium heat. Slice the radicchio lengthwise into six wedges. Slice each head of Belgian endive lengthwise into four wedges. Using a pastry brush, brush the olive oil over all sides of the radicchio and endive wedges. Sprinkle the wedges with salt and pepper. Place the wedges on the grill, away from direct flame. Cook, turning occasionally, until golden and tender, 6 to 8 minutes, depending on the heat of the grill. Serve immediately.

HEARTY BACON AND LEMON CHICORY SALAD

SERVES 4 | **PHOTOGRAPH ON PAGE 241**

8 slices bacon
1 medium red onion, thinly sliced lengthwise
1 small head chicory, coarsely chopped
1 small head frisée, coarsely chopped
   Juice of 1 lemon
3 tablespoons extra-virgin olive oil
1 teaspoon coarse salt
½ teaspoon freshly ground pepper

1 Place the bacon in a large skillet over medium heat. Cook until it is golden and crisp. Drain on paper towels. Break into 1- to 1½-inch pieces, and set aside. Drain all but 1½ tablespoons bacon fat from the pan. Add the onion to the pan. Cook over medium heat until soft and golden, about 5 minutes. Remove from the heat.

2 Place the bacon, onion, chicory, and frisée in a serving bowl. In another bowl, whisk together the lemon juice, olive oil, salt, and pepper. Drizzle the dressing over the salad, and toss. Serve immediately.

SAUTEED ESCAROLE WITH GARLIC

SERVES 4 AS A SIDE DISH

¼ cup extra-virgin olive oil
3 garlic cloves, sliced ⅛ inch thick lengthwise
1 large head escarole, leaves separated
¾ teaspoon coarse salt, plus more for seasoning
¼ teaspoon freshly ground pepper

Heat the oil in a large high-sided skillet over medium-low heat. Add the garlic, and cook, stirring occasionally, until pale golden, about 2 minutes. Add the escarole, salt, and pepper. Raise the heat to high, and cook, stirring occasionally, until the escarole is soft and the white parts are tender, 6 to 8 minutes. Season with salt, if desired. Serve immediately.

BROWNING AND DEGLAZING

BEEF STEW

SERVES 6

Browning the beef before adding the other ingredients adds a rich flavor to the stew. Avoid crowding the pan or the meat will steam, not sear; cook in batches if necessary.

2½ pounds beef-stew meat, cut into 1½- to 2-inch cubes
    Coarse salt and freshly ground pepper
4 tablespoons all-purpose flour
3 to 4 tablespoons olive oil
⅔ to 1 cup dry red wine
8 ounces pearl onions, peeled
2¼ cups Homemade Beef Stock (page 11) or low-sodium canned
1 cup canned whole plum tomatoes, strained, seeded, and crushed
5 carrots, cut into 1-inch pieces
12 ounces small button mushrooms, wiped clean, quartered if large

1 Since moisture impedes browning, pat the cubed meat dry with paper towels; season with salt and pepper. Toss the meat in the flour; this helps the browning process and provides a thickening agent for the stew.

2 Heat a large Dutch oven over medium-high heat. Add 1 tablespoon oil. Add meat in a single layer without crowding, and brown on all sides, 5 to 6 minutes. Remove the meat from the pot, and transfer to a bowl. Add ⅓ cup wine to the pot, and stir with a wooden spoon, scraping loose any browned bits on the bottom of the pan. Transfer the cooking liquid to the bowl with the meat. Wipe the pot clean, and repeat the cooking procedure if necessary with the remaining meat, 1 tablespoon oil, and ⅓ cup wine.

3 Add the remaining 2 tablespoons olive oil to the pot. Add the onions, and cook, stirring occasionally, until golden all over, about 3 minutes.

4 Deglaze the pan with the remaining ⅓ cup wine, and return the reserved beef and cooking liquid to the pot. Add the stock and the tomatoes, and season with salt and pepper. Bring to a boil, reduce the heat to low, and cook, covered, for 1 hour 20 minutes. Add the carrots and the mushrooms, and cook, covered, until the meat and vegetables are tender, 45 to 50 minutes more.

CARAMELIZED PINEAPPLE WITH VANILLA ICE CREAM

SERVES 6

This dessert relies on the same browning and deglazing techniques used for savory dishes. Many fruits benefit from a quick sauté, and their natural sugars—brought to the surface as juices evaporate—aid in the caramelization process. You can substitute more pineapple juice for the rum.

½ cup dark rum

½ cup pineapple juice

4 tablespoons unsalted butter

1 ripe pineapple, peeled, cored, and sliced into ½-inch-thick rounds

½ cup sugar

Vanilla ice cream

1 Combine the rum and juice in a glass measuring cup. Set aside. Heat 2 tablespoons butter in a large skillet over medium-high heat until foaming. Add half of the pineapple slices, and cook until well browned on both sides, 5 to 8 minutes. Transfer to a baking pan.

2 Sprinkle the skillet with ¼ cup sugar, and cook until the sugar caramelizes to a golden brown, 1 to 2 minutes.

3 Turn off the heat or hold the skillet away from the heat, and carefully add ½ cup rum mixture.

4 Turn the heat on or return the skillet to heat, and stir with a wooden spoon, scraping loose any caramelized bits on the bottom of the skillet. Simmer the sauce until it is reduced and slightly thickened, about 3 minutes. Pour the sauce through a fine sieve into a bowl, and set aside. Wash out the skillet, and repeat the cooking procedure with the remaining 2 tablespoons butter, pineapple slices, ¼ cup sugar, and ½ cup rum mixture. Cut the pineapple slices, and serve over the ice cream, drizzled with the warm sauce.

PUMPKIN FOODS

RIGATONI WITH PUMPKIN AND BACON

SERVES 4 TO 6

Hulled pumpkin seeds can be found in most health-food stores.

8 slices bacon, cut into 1-inch pieces

1 onion, cut into ½-inch dice

1½ teaspoons coarse salt, plus more for cooking water

¼ teaspoon freshly ground pepper

1 two-pound pumpkin, such as 'Cheese' or 'Small Sugar Pie,' peeled, and cut into ¾-inch cubes

1 tablespoon chopped fresh sage

¼ teaspoon ground allspice

1½ cups Homemade Chicken Stock (page 8) or low-sodium canned

3 tablespoons heavy cream

1 pound rigatoni

1 cup freshly grated Parmesan cheese

2 tablespoons hulled pumpkin seeds (pepitas)

1 Cook the bacon in a large, deep skillet over medium heat until the fat is rendered and the bacon is almost crisp, about 5 minutes. Remove from the skillet with a slotted spoon, and drain on paper towels; set aside.

2 Add the onion, salt, and pepper to the skillet, and cook, stirring occasionally, until the onion is soft, about 5 minutes. Add the pumpkin, sage, and allspice, and cook, stirring frequently, until the pumpkin is coated with bacon fat, about 5 minutes.

3 Add the stock, and bring to a simmer. Reduce the heat to medium-low, and stir in the cream. Gently simmer until the pumpkin is soft and the sauce has slightly thickened, about 20 minutes.

4 Meanwhile, bring a large pot of water to a boil. Salt the water, and add the rigatoni. Cook until tender. Drain the pasta.

5 Add the cooked pasta and bacon to the skillet, and stir gently to combine. Divide the pasta among serving bowls. Serve topped with grated Parmesan cheese and pumpkin seeds.

BROWNING AND DEGLAZING CHICKEN

Roasted chicken creates mouthwatering pan drippings, which can be used to make a quick sauce. First, skim away any excess fat from the pan, leaving behind only the juices and browned bits. Pour enough wine or stock into the pan to make a shallow layer, and then use a wooden spoon to loosen any cooked-on bits, stirring to incorporate them into the sauce.

PUMPKIN SOUP WITH WILD RICE AND APPLES

SERVES 4 TO 6 | **PHOTOGRAPH ON PAGE 239**

We served this soup in pumpkin shells, but it is just as delicious served in a regular soup bowl. 'Small Sugar Pie' pumpkins are ideal for converting into bowls. To do so, remove all the seeds and string with a sharp-edged spoon. Fill the pumpkin with boiling water moments before serving the soup in it to temper the flesh and keep the soup hot.

- 2 tablespoons slivered almonds
- 3 tablespoons unsalted butter
- 1 onion, cut into ½-inch dice
- 1 leek, white part only, well washed and thinly sliced
- 1 pumpkin (1½ pounds), such as 'Cheese' or 'Small Sugar Pie,' peeled, seeded, cut into 1-inch wedges, and thinly sliced (to yield about 4 cups)
- 1 large turnip, peeled, cut into 4 to 6 pieces, and thinly sliced
- 2 carrots, thinly sliced
- 1 large parsnip, peeled and thinly sliced
- 2¾ teaspoons coarse salt
- ¼ teaspoon freshly ground black pepper
- 3½ to 4 cups Homemade Chicken Stock (page 8) or low-sodium canned
- 2 sprigs fresh thyme
- ⅓ cup wild rice
- 1 apple, cored and cut into ½-inch dice
- 2 scallions, thinly sliced on the bias
- Pinch of cayenne pepper

1 Preheat the oven to 350°F. Place the almond slivers on a rimmed baking sheet, and toast until golden brown, about 10 minutes, shaking the pan halfway through. Transfer to a cutting board and chop; set aside.

2 Heat 2 tablespoons butter in a large saucepan over medium-low heat. Add the onion, and cook, stirring occasionally, until soft, about 10 minutes. Add the leek, and cook, stirring occasionally, until soft, about 5 minutes more. Add the pumpkin, turnip, carrots, parsnip, 2 teaspoons salt, and pepper. Cook, stirring, until vegetables are well mixed and coated with butter.

3 Add 3½ cups stock and the thyme, and bring to a boil over medium heat. Reduce the heat to medium-low, and gently simmer until the vegetables are very tender, about 30 minutes.

4 Meanwhile, fill a saucepan with cold water. Add ½ teaspoon salt and the rice. Bring to a boil over high heat, and then reduce to a simmer. Cook until the rice is tender, about 45 minutes, or according to the package instructions. Drain, and set aside.

5 Remove the soup from the heat, and let cool slightly. Purée the soup in batches using an immersion blender, food processor, or blender (fill the blender only halfway—hot liquids expand). Add stock to thin if necessary. Reheat the soup over medium-low heat.

6 Heat the remaining tablespoon butter in a sauté pan over medium heat. Add the apple, and cook until brown and soft, about 3 minutes. Add the scallions, the remaining ¼ teaspoon salt, and the cayenne; cook until the scallions soften, about 1 minute. Add the rice and the reserved almonds, and cook until heated through, 1 to 2 minutes more.

7 Ladle soup into pumpkin shells, and garnish with the wild-rice mixture. Serve.

PUMPKIN ICE CREAM

MAKES 1 QUART

This is best served soon after it is made.

- 1 cup milk
- ½ cup heavy cream
- ½ cup Milk Caramel, or more for serving (recipe follows)
- 6 large egg yolks
- ¼ cup sugar
- ½ teaspoon pure vanilla extract
- 2 tablespoons freshly squeezed lemon juice
- ½ cup cooked Pumpkin Purée (recipe follows) or canned
- Candied Pumpkin Slices (optional, recipe follows)

1 Combine the milk, cream, and caramel in a saucepan over medium heat. Bring to a simmer, stirring frequently as the caramel melts.

2 Fill a large bowl with ice and water, and set aside. Whisk together the egg yolks and sugar in a bowl until thick and pale, about 4 minutes. While whisking, very slowly add a little hot milk mixture. Slowly add the remaining milk mixture, whisking until combined. Add the vanilla, lemon juice, and pumpkin purée; combine. Strain into a clean bowl, and transfer to the ice bath to cool.

3 Freeze in an ice-cream maker according to the manufacturer's instructions. After churning, transfer to the freezer until firm. Serve with more milk caramel and candied pumpkin, if using.

MILK CARAMEL

MAKES ABOUT 1 CUP

Cook caramel very slowly or it will scorch.

- 1 can (14 ounces) sweetened condensed milk
- 1 small cinnamon stick

1 Combine the milk and cinnamon stick in the top of a double boiler or a heatproof bowl set over a pan of simmering water. Cook, stirring every 10 to 15 minutes, until the milk has reduced by almost half and is thick and amber in color, 1½ to 2 hours.

2 Remove the pan from the heat, and discard the cinnamon stick. Beat with a wooden spoon. Transfer the mixture to a clean bowl, cover, and refrigerate for up to several weeks, until ready to use.

PUMPKIN PUREE

MAKES 3 CUPS

- 1 pumpkin (3½ pounds), such as 'Small Sugar Pie,' cut in half

Preheat the oven to 425°F. Place the pumpkin halves cut side down on a baking pan, and roast until tender, 50 to 60 minutes. Remove from the oven, and let cool. Using a large spoon, scrape out and discard the seeds. Remove the flesh, and transfer to the bowl of a food processor. Purée until completely smooth without any solid pieces, about 1 minute. Transfer to a bowl. Refrigerate for up to several days, or freeze for up to 1 month.

CANDIED PUMPKIN SLICES

MAKES ABOUT 5 DOZEN

This recipe works best with firm, orange-skinned pumpkins, such as 'Cheese' or 'Small Sugar Pie.'

1 pumpkin (1½ pounds), peeled and seeded
3 cups sugar
½ cup freshly squeezed lemon juice
Zest of 2 limes, cut into very thin strips

1 Cut the pumpkin into wedges about 3 to 4 inches wide. Cut across the wedges to form slices about ¼ inch thick; set aside.
2 Combine 2 cups sugar, the lemon juice, and the zest in a medium bowl. Add the pumpkin pieces, and stir until well coated. Cover with plastic wrap, and refrigerate overnight.
3 Transfer the mixture to a medium heavy-bottomed saucepan, and bring to a simmer over medium heat. Reduce the heat to medium-low. Cook, stirring occasionally, until the pumpkin is translucent and the sugar has formed a light-amber-colored caramel, 1 hour 10 minutes to 1 hour 15 minutes.
4 Remove the pumpkin from the caramel with a slotted spoon, and dry on a rack set over a baking sheet for at least 12 hours, turning the pumpkin pieces once or twice.
5 Place the remaining cup sugar in a medium bowl. Add several pieces of candied pumpkin to the bowl at a time, and coat in the sugar. Transfer to a bowl to serve, or store in an airtight container for several days.

PUMPKIN CORNMEAL DOUGHNUTS

MAKES ABOUT 14 THREE-INCH DOUGHNUTS AND 14 DOUGHNUT HOLES

If you do not have a doughnut cutter, use a three-inch cookie cutter to cut out the doughnuts and a one-inch cookie cutter to cut out the centers.

2¾ cups all-purpose flour, plus more for work surface
4 teaspoons baking powder
¼ teaspoon table salt
1 teaspoon ground cinnamon
¾ teaspoon ground allspice
1 tablespoon minced orange zest
1 cup fine cornmeal
3 large eggs, lightly beaten
½ cup granulated sugar
½ cup sweetened condensed milk
1 cup Pumpkin Purée (recipe above), or canned
4 tablespoons unsalted butter, melted
8 cups vegetable oil, for frying
¼ cup confectioners' sugar

1 Sift together the flour, baking powder, salt, ½ teaspoon cinnamon, and the allspice into a large bowl. Add the orange zest and cornmeal; mix until combined. Set aside.
2 In the bowl of an electric mixer fitted with the paddle attachment, beat the eggs and ¼ cup granulated sugar until the mixture is pale yellow, about 5 minutes. Add the condensed milk, and beat well. Add the pumpkin purée and melted butter, and beat until combined. Add the reserved flour mixture, and mix until the dough holds together. Cover the dough with plastic wrap, and refrigerate overnight.
3 Heat the vegetable oil in a large deep pan over medium heat until a deep-frying thermometer reads 365°F.
4 While the oil is heating, roll out the dough on a lightly floured surface to about ⅓ inch thick. Using a 3-inch doughnut cutter, cut out doughnuts, and set aside. Reroll the scraps of dough, and continue to cut out more doughnuts. Mix together the remaining ½ teaspoon cinnamon and ¼ cup granulated sugar in a small bowl, and set aside.

5 Add 4 doughnuts to the hot oil, and fry until golden brown, about 1½ minutes. Turn the doughnuts over, and fry until golden brown on the other side, about 1 minute more. Transfer the doughnuts to several layers of paper towels to drain. Repeat until all the doughnuts have been fried.
6 Roll half the warm doughnuts, one at a time, in cinnamon sugar to coat. Transfer to a serving platter. Dust the remaining doughnuts with confectioners' sugar. Transfer to the serving platter. Serve warm.

SWEET PUMPKIN MAPLE CUSTARD

SERVES 6

This custard can be baked in two small pumpkins or in individual ramekins. The baking time for custards baked in pumpkin shells is slightly longer, because the pumpkins insulate the custard as it bakes.

1 tablespoon vegetable oil, for baking dish
2 pumpkins (1½ pounds each), such as 'Small Sugar Pie' (optional)
1 cup Pumpkin Purée (recipe above), or canned
½ cup pure maple syrup, plus more for serving
¼ cup sugar
4 large eggs, lightly beaten
2 cups heavy cream
Pinch of table salt
½ teaspoon ground cinnamon
1 teaspoon ground ginger
Pinch of freshly ground nutmeg

1 Preheat the oven to 325°F. Oil a 9-by-13-inch metal baking pan, and set aside. If baking in pumpkin shells, place a steamer basket in a medium saucepan filled with several inches of water; cover, and bring the water to a boil. Add the

pumpkins, and steam until just tender, 10 to 20 minutes. Remove from the steamer, and set aside to cool.

2 Cut off the tops of the pumpkins, and remove the seeds and stringy pulp. Transfer to the baking pan, and set aside.

3 Place the purée, ½ cup maple syrup, sugar, eggs, 1 cup cream, salt, cinnamon, ginger, and nutmeg in a medium bowl; whisk until well combined. Pour the custard into the prepared pumpkins, up to the lower edge of the opening. Bake until the custard puffs and sets and a knife inserted into the center comes out clean, 40 to 90 minutes, depending on the shape and thickness of the pumpkin. Alternatively, pour ¾ cup mixture each into 6 six-ounce ovenproof ramekins or custard cups. Set the ramekins in a water bath, and bake until the edges of the custard are firm and the center is still slightly wobbly, 25 to 30 minutes.

4 Remove from the oven, and transfer to a wire rack to cool completely. Whip the remaining cup cream. Cut the pumpkin into wedges, and serve the wedges or ramekins with whipped cream and maple syrup.

PUMPKIN MOLASSES TEA BREAD

MAKES 1 NINE-INCH LOAF

We used apple juice to sweeten the bread, but this recipe is equally tasty made with orange or cranberry juice.

Soft butter, for pan

2 cups all-purpose flour, plus more for pan

½ teaspoon baking powder

1 teaspoon baking soda

1 teaspoon table salt

½ cup molasses

½ cup sugar

½ cup vegetable oil

2 large eggs, lightly beaten

1 cup cooked Pumpkin Purée (page 230), or canned

2 tablespoons apple juice

½ cup coarsely chopped dried cranberries

½ cup coarsely chopped walnuts

8 ounces cream cheese, room temperature

¼ cup honey

1 Preheat the oven to 350°F. Butter and flour a 5-by-9-inch loaf pan; set aside. In a medium bowl, combine the flour, baking powder, baking soda, and salt; set aside.

2 In the bowl of an electric mixer fitted with the paddle attachment, beat the molasses, sugar, oil, eggs, pumpkin, and apple juice. Add the flour mixture, and mix until combined. Fold in the cranberries and walnuts. Spoon the mixture into the prepared pan, and bake until a cake tester inserted into the center comes out clean, about 1 hour. Let the bread sit for about 10 minutes, and then turn it out of the pan onto a wire rack to cool completely.

3 While the bread cools, make the frosting. Combine the cream cheese and honey in the bowl of an electric mixer fitted with the paddle attachment. Beat until smooth and well combined. Once the bread is completely cool, spread the top with frosting. Serve.

POTATO HARVEST

POTATOES, BEANS, AND PEAS IN CREAM

SERVES 6 TO 8

Any small round white or red potato, or any of the fingerling varieties, works well for this dish. If you use large potatoes, cut them into bite-size pieces.

2 pounds small potatoes

Coarse salt

12 ounces yellow beans, green beans, or both, trimmed and cut into 2-inch-long pieces

12 ounces fresh peas in the pod (about 1 cup shelled)

1½ cups heavy cream

2 tablespoons unsalted butter

Freshly ground pepper

1 Place the potatoes in a medium saucepan, and cover with water. Bring to a boil over high heat, and salt the water. Reduce the heat slightly, and simmer until tender, 10 to 12 minutes. Drain in a colander. Transfer to a medium bowl, and cover loosely.

2 Place a steamer basket in a medium pot with about 2 inches of water. Steam the beans and peas until tender, 5 to 6 minutes. Remove, and add to the bowl with the cooked potatoes.

3 Combine the cream and butter in a small saucepan, and bring to a boil over medium-high heat. Reduce the heat to medium, and gently boil until slightly thickened, 5 to 6 minutes. Pour the cream over the vegetables, and season with salt and pepper. Toss to combine.

FLORENCE'S POTATO SALAD

SERVES 8

If making this salad in advance, wait to add the cucumber until just before serving.

2 pounds russet potatoes, scrubbed
  Coarse salt

3 large hard-boiled eggs, peeled and cut into ½-inch dice

1 celery stalk, strings removed, finely chopped

1 red onion, finely chopped

1 cucumber, peeled, seeded, and cut into ¼-inch dice

¼ cup coarsely chopped fresh flat-leaf parsley

3 tablespoons cider vinegar

6 tablespoons mayonnaise
  Freshly ground pepper

1 Place the potatoes in a medium saucepan, and cover with water. Bring to a boil over high heat; salt the water. Reduce the heat to medium, and simmer until tender, about 20 minutes. Drain in a colander. When cool enough to handle, peel and cut into ½-inch pieces. Transfer to a medium bowl. Add the eggs, celery, onion, cucumber, and parsley.

2 In a small bowl, whisk together the vinegar and mayonnaise; season with salt and pepper. Pour the dressing over the vegetables, and stir gently to combine. Serve at room temperature.

POTATO FOCACCIA

MAKES 1 TWELVE-BY-18-INCH LOAF

Fingerlings are grown in yellow, pink, and blue varieties. For a special touch, use an assortment of them for the slices that top the bread. Any small potatoes will work just as well as fingerlings.

7 tablespoons olive oil, plus more for bowl and plastic wrap

1 pound assorted fingerling potatoes

4½ teaspoons coarse salt, plus more for seasoning

1 package (about 2½ teaspoons) active dry yeast

6 cups all-purpose flour

1½ tablespoons fresh rosemary, coarsely chopped
  Freshly ground pepper

1 Place half the potatoes in a small saucepan. Cover with cold water, and bring to a boil over high heat. Add 3 teaspoons salt. Reduce the heat to medium-high, and cook until the potatoes are tender, 10 to 12 minutes. Drain in a colander, reserving the liquid. Pass through a potato ricer or a food mill into a bowl; set aside.

2 Place ¼ cup reserved warm cooking liquid into the bowl of an electric mixer fitted with the paddle attachment. Sprinkle in the yeast, and stir well. Let stand until creamy, 5 to 10 minutes. Add 2¼ cups more reserved cooking liquid, 2 tablespoons olive oil, and the reserved mashed potatoes; beat until combined. In a large bowl, whisk together the flour and 1½ teaspoons salt; add to the potato mixture. Mix on low speed until the flour is incorporated, about 3 minutes. Change to the dough hook, and knead on medium high until the dough is smooth and elastic and is slightly tacky when squeezed but does not stick to your fingers, 4 to 5 minutes.

3 Turn the dough out onto a clean surface, and knead into a ball. Place in a lightly oiled large bowl, cover with plastic wrap, and let stand at room temperature until doubled in size, 1 to 1½ hours.

4 Preheat the oven to 425°F. Pour 2 tablespoons olive oil into a 12-by-18-inch rimmed baking sheet, and spread all over using your fingertips. Spread the dough evenly on the baking sheet. Cover with oiled plastic wrap, and let stand in a warm place until the dough has filled the entire pan and has increased in size by about one third, about 30 minutes.

5 Using a mandoline or a knife, slice the remaining ½ pound of potatoes into very thin rounds. Transfer to a bowl. Add ¾ tablespoon rosemary and 1 tablespoon olive oil, and season with salt and pepper. Toss to coat the potatoes well.

6 Remove the plastic wrap, and dimple the dough with your fingertips, leaving deep indentations. Drizzle with the remaining 2 tablespoons oil. Gently press the reserved sliced potatoes into the dough. Sprinkle with the remaining ¾ tablespoon rosemary. Bake until golden brown, 30 to 35 minutes. Remove from the oven, and transfer to a wire rack. Serve warm.

BEST BAKED POTATOES

SERVES 6

Hitting the potatoes with your hand before slicing them open creates a fluffy interior.

6 russet potatoes (about 3 pounds), scrubbed and dried

Preheat the oven to 450°F. Using a fork, pierce the potatoes all over. Place in the oven directly on the rack, and bake until fork-tender, 50 to 60 minutes. Remove from the oven. Put on an oven mitt, or hold a folded kitchen towel. Place the potatoes on a clean surface, and hit them with your hand. Slice the potatoes open, and serve.

POTATO GRATIN

SERVES 6 | **PHOTOGRAPH ON PAGE 244**

Reblochon is a French cow's-milk cheese. It has a smooth yellow-to-pink rind and a rich, creamy interior. Ripe Camembert can be used in its place.

3 tablespoons unsalted butter, plus more for dish

1 tablespoon olive oil

2 yellow onions, sliced into ¼-inch-thick half circles

1 teaspoon sugar

2½ pounds all-purpose Maine potatoes, peeled
  Coarse salt and freshly ground pepper

9 ounces Reblochon cheese, coarsely chopped

1 tablespoon fresh thyme leaves

1 Generously butter a 5-cup gratin dish. Melt 1 tablespoon butter and the olive oil in a large skillet over low heat. Add the onions, sprinkle with the sugar, and cook, stirring occasionally, until the onions are very soft and golden, 15 to 20 minutes; set aside.

2 Preheat the oven to 400°F. Using a mandoline or a knife, slice the potatoes ⅛ inch thick. Arrange one-third of the potatoes in the gratin dish so they overlap. Sprinkle with salt and pepper. Cover the potatoes with half of the reserved onions, half the cheese, and 1 teaspoon thyme. Arrange another third of the potatoes so that they overlap; sprinkle with salt and pepper. Repeat layering with the remaining onions, 4½ ounces cheese, and 1 teaspoon thyme. Arrange the remaining potatoes on top so they overlap. Melt the remaining

2 tablespoons butter, and brush it over the top layer of potatoes. Sprinkle with the remaining teaspoon thyme, and season with salt and pepper.

3 Cover the dish tightly with aluminum foil, and place in the oven. Bake for 40 minutes; remove the foil, and continue baking until golden brown, 20 to 30 minutes more. Remove from the oven, let stand 5 minutes, and serve.

HOME FRIES

SERVES 6

We used small potatoes for this recipe. Adjust the cooking time for larger potatoes.

2½ pounds small Yukon gold potatoes
Coarse salt
¾ pound thick-sliced bacon, cut into ½-inch pieces
1 small red bell pepper, seeds and ribs removed, cut into ½-inch dice
1 small yellow bell pepper, seeds and ribs removed, cut into ½-inch dice
1 red onion (about 10 ounces), cut into ½-inch dice
1 tablespoon fresh thyme leaves
2 tablespoons coarsely chopped fresh flat-leaf parsley
Freshly ground black pepper

1 Place the potatoes in a medium saucepan. Cover with water, and bring to a boil over high heat. Salt the water. Reduce the heat to medium-high, and cook until the potatoes have softened but are still slightly firm, 12 to 15 minutes. Drain in a colander. When cool enough to handle, peel the potatoes, and cut into 1-inch pieces. Set aside.

2 Cook the bacon in a large skillet over medium heat until all the fat has been rendered and the bacon is crisp and brown, about 15 minutes. Remove the bacon with a slotted spoon, and set aside on paper towels to drain. Pour off all but 2 tablespoons of the bacon fat. Add the reserved potatoes to the skillet, and cook over medium heat, stirring occasionally, until golden on all sides, about 10 minutes. Add the reserved bacon, peppers, onion, and thyme, and cook until the vegetables have softened, 5 to 7 minutes. Stir in the parsley, and season with salt and pepper. Remove from the heat, and serve.

POTATO SEAFOOD CHOWDER

SERVES 6

The clams will not all open at the same time. To prevent overcooking, check them frequently while they cook, and remove them as they open.

2 cups water
2 pounds littleneck clams, well scrubbed
2 tablespoons unsalted butter
1 medium yellow onion, cut into ½-inch dice
2 celery stalks, strings removed, sliced ⅛ inch thick
1 tablespoon all-purpose flour
1½ pounds small Yukon gold potatoes, peeled and cut into ¾-inch dice
1 bay leaf
4 sprigs fresh thyme
1 pound firm white fish, such as cod or red snapper, cut into bite-size pieces
½ pound medium shrimp, peeled, deveined, and cut in half crosswise
1½ cups half-and-half
Coarse salt and freshly ground pepper

1 Bring the water to a boil in a medium saucepan over high heat. Reduce the heat to medium-high, and add the clams. Cover the pan, and cook, stirring occasionally, until the clams have opened, 5 to 8 minutes. Remove the clams, discard the shells, and pass the broth through a cheesecloth-lined colander, reserving the broth and clams separately. Set both aside.

2 Melt the butter in a stockpot over medium heat. Add the onion and celery, and cook, stirring frequently, until the onion is translucent, 8 to 10 minutes. Add the flour, and cook, stirring, 1 minute. Add the reserved clam broth and the potatoes, bay leaf, and thyme. Cover, and simmer until the potatoes are tender, 10 to 12 minutes. Uncover, and add the fish and shrimp. Simmer until cooked through, about 3 minutes. Add the half-and-half and the reserved clams; season with salt and pepper. Cook until heated through, about 3 minutes; serve.

SHEPHERD'S PIE

SERVES 6

If you do not have leftover cooked lamb on hand, you may use one-and-a-quarter pounds uncooked lamb stew meat cut into one-inch pieces. To cook, sprinkle the lamb with salt and pepper. Heat two tablespoons olive oil in a large skillet. Add the lamb, and cook until deeply browned on all sides, five to seven minutes. Remove from the pan, finely dice the meat, and use in step two.

2 pounds russet potatoes, peeled and cut into large chunks
Coarse salt
3 tablespoons olive oil
1 medium yellow onion, peeled and finely chopped
1 garlic clove, minced
1 celery stalk, strings removed, finely chopped
2 medium carrots, cut into ¼-inch dice
½ pound button mushrooms, wiped clean, trimmed, and cut into ½-inch pieces
1 pound cooked lamb, finely diced
1 six-ounce can (8 tablespoons) tomato paste
1⅔ cups Homemade Beef Stock (page 11) or low-sodium canned
1 teaspoon dried oregano
Freshly ground pepper
1 cup milk
6 tablespoons unsalted butter

1 Preheat the oven to 400°F. Have ready six 1½-cup (12-ounce) ramekins or a 2½-quart casserole. Place the potatoes in a large saucepan, and cover with cold water. Bring to a boil over high heat, and salt the water. Reduce the heat to medium-high. Cook until tender, about 25 minutes. Drain in a colander. Pass through a potato ricer or a food mill into a large bowl. Cover and keep warm.

2 While the potatoes cook, pour the oil into a large skillet, and place over medium heat. Add the onion, garlic, celery, and carrots. Cook, stirring frequently, until the onions are translucent, about 10 minutes. Add the mushrooms, and cook until softened, about 7 minutes. Stir in the lamb, tomato paste, beef stock, and oregano; season with salt and pepper. Cook until the mixture bubbles and thickens, 12 to 15 minutes. Remove from the heat. Divide the mixture among the ramekins, or pour into the casserole. Set aside.

3 Warm the milk and butter in a small saucepan over low heat. Pour into the bowl with the potatoes, season with salt and pepper, and stir until combined and smooth. Spread and swirl about 1 cup of the potatoes in each ramekin, or spread the potatoes over the casserole, on top of the lamb mixture, covering the entire surface. Place the ramekins in a baking pan, and bake until the potatoes are golden, 40 to 45 minutes. Remove from the oven, and let stand about 5 minutes. Serve.

RACHEL GOOD'S GLAZED POTATO DOUGHNUTS

MAKES ABOUT 3 DOZEN |
PHOTOGRAPH ON PAGE 245

If you do not have a doughnut cutter, use a two-and-a-half-inch cookie cutter to cut out the doughnuts and a three-quarter-inch cookie cutter to cut out the centers. These doughnuts are best eaten slightly warm.

8 ounces russet potatoes, peeled and sliced ¼ inch thick

¼ cup warm water, plus 6 tablespoons water

1 package (about 2½ teaspoons) active dry yeast

1 cup milk, scalded

¼ cup solid pure vegetable shortening

¾ cup granulated sugar

1 teaspoon table salt

2 large eggs, lightly beaten

5 cups all-purpose flour, plus more if needed for dough and for work surface

2 quarts vegetable oil, plus more for bowl

4 cups confectioners' sugar

1 teaspoon pure vanilla extract

½ teaspoon ground cinnamon

1 Have ready two parchment-lined baking pans. Place the potatoes in a small saucepan, cover with cold water, and bring to a boil over high heat. Cook until tender, about 15 minutes. Drain in a colander. Pass the potatoes through a potato ricer or food mill into a medium bowl; set aside.

2 Place the warm water in a small bowl. Sprinkle with the yeast, stir gently, and let stand until creamy, 5 to 10 minutes. In the bowl of an electric mixer fitted with the paddle attachment, combine the milk, shortening, ¼ cup granulated sugar, and the salt. Let stand until cooled to just warm. Add the yeast mixture, reserved potatoes, and the eggs. Beat until combined. Fit the mixer with the dough-hook attachment. Add 5 cups flour, and mix on medium-low speed until combined, adding more flour if necessary, until a smooth and elastic dough is formed, about 5 minutes. Transfer the dough to a large, lightly oiled bowl, and cover. Let stand in a warm place until the dough is doubled in size, about 55 minutes.

3 Transfer the dough to a lightly floured surface. Roll out to ½ inch thick. Using a 2½-inch-diameter doughnut cutter, cut out shapes and place on the prepared baking sheets. Loosely cover with plastic wrap, and let stand in a warm place until the dough has risen by about a third, about 30 minutes.

4 Combine the confectioners' sugar, vanilla, and remaining 6 tablespoons water in a medium bowl, stirring until smooth; set the glaze aside. In a medium bowl, whisk together the remaining ½ cup granulated sugar and the cinnamon until well combined; set aside.

5 In a large, low-sided saucepan over medium heat, heat the oil until a deep-frying thermometer registers 375°F. Drop the doughnuts into the oil; fry in batches until golden, 1 to 2 minutes per side. Transfer to several layers of paper towels to drain. Place the drained doughnuts on a wire rack set over a baking pan. Dip half the doughnuts in the glaze, and return to the wire rack. Roll the remaining doughnuts in the cinnamon-sugar mixture until well coated.

JULIA DUNLINSON'S POTATO GRIDDLE SCONES

MAKES 16

These British scones, created by Martha Stewart Living deputy art director James Dunlinson's mother, resemble small, thick pancakes.

1½ pounds russet potatoes, peeled and sliced

1 tablespoon unsalted butter, melted, plus more for griddle and serving

½ cup all-purpose flour, plus more for work surface

1 teaspoon table salt

Jam, for serving (optional)

1 Place the potatoes in a small saucepan, cover with cold water, and bring to a boil over high heat. Cook until very tender, about 12 minutes. Drain, and transfer to a medium bowl. Pass the potatoes through a potato ricer or a food mill into a medium bowl (you should have 5 cups mashed). Add the melted butter, flour, and salt. Stir, using a wooden spoon, until the dough comes together. Transfer to a clean work surface, and knead until smooth, being careful not to overwork the dough.

2 Heat a griddle over medium heat. Roll out the dough to ¾-inch thickness on a lightly floured surface. Using a 2½-inch cookie cutter, cut out rounds, and prick with a fork. Lightly butter the griddle. Cook the scones in batches until golden brown, about 5 minutes per side. Transfer to a clean kitchen towel, keeping the scones covered while cooking the remaining scones. Serve warm with butter and jam, if desired.

menu

BONELESS PORK CHOPS WITH
APPLE CHUTNEY

HERB ROASTED SWEET POTATOES

MUSTARD GREENS AND ONIONS

ICE CREAM WITH
CARAMEL BRIOCHE CROUTONS

BONELESS PORK CHOPS
WITH APPLE CHUTNEY

SERVES 4 | PHOTOGRAPH ON PAGE 243

4 tablespoons olive oil

2 teaspoons coarse salt,
plus more for seasoning

1 teaspoon freshly ground black pepper,
plus more for seasoning

4 boneless center-cut pork chops
(1¼ pounds), cut ¾ inch thick

1 large onion, cut into ½-inch dice

4 green apples (such as Granny Smith),
peeled, cored, and cut into ½-inch dice

½ cup cider vinegar

½ cup golden raisins

1 teaspoon ground ginger

¼ teaspoon dry mustard

Pinch of cayenne pepper

1   Preheat the oven to 400°F. Heat 2 tablespoons olive oil in an ovenproof skillet
over medium heat. Sprinkle the salt and
pepper on both sides of the pork chops,
and add to the skillet. Sauté until golden
brown, about 2 minutes; flip over. Cook
2 minutes more, and transfer the skillet
to the oven. Roast until the meat is cooked
through and registers 155°F on an instant-
read thermometer, about 5 minutes.
Transfer to a platter.
2   Meanwhile, in a large saucepan, heat
the remaining 2 tablespoons olive oil over
medium heat, and add the onion. Sauté
until translucent and beginning to brown,
about 6 minutes. Add the apples, and
sauté 4 minutes more. Add the vinegar,
raisins, ginger, mustard, and cayenne. Stir
well to combine, and cover. Continue
cooking, stirring occasionally, until the
apples are very tender but hold their
shape, about 3 minutes. Season with salt
and pepper, and serve over the pork chops.

HERB ROASTED
SWEET POTATOES

SERVES 4 | PHOTOGRAPH ON PAGE 243

4 medium sweet potatoes, peeled
and cut into 1½-inch rounds

3 tablespoons olive oil

1 tablespoon fresh thyme leaves,
plus a few sprigs for garnish

2 small garlic cloves, minced

¼ teaspoon crushed red-pepper flakes

1 teaspoon coarse salt

1   Preheat the oven to 400°F. In a medium bowl, toss the sweet-potato rounds
with the olive oil, thyme, garlic, pepper
flakes, and salt.
2   Transfer to a rimmed baking sheet,
garnish with thyme sprigs, and place
in the oven. Roast until tender and starting
to brown, 40 to 45 minutes. Transfer
to a platter, and serve.

MUSTARD GREENS AND
ONIONS

SERVES 4 | PHOTOGRAPH ON PAGE 243

3 tablespoons unsalted butter

1 medium onion, cut into ¼-inch dice

2 pounds mustard greens, washed
and cut into 3-inch pieces

1 teaspoon coarse salt

¼ teaspoon freshly ground pepper

1 teaspoon freshly squeezed lemon juice

1   In a large high-sided skillet, heat
the butter over medium-high heat. Add
the onion, and sauté until translucent
and beginning to brown, about 6 minutes.
Add as many mustard greens as will fit,
and sprinkle with salt and pepper.
2   Toss until the greens are just wilted,
adding more greens as they will fit into
the pan. Toss with lemon juice just before serving.

ICE CREAM WITH CARAMEL
BRIOCHE CROUTONS

SERVES 4

6 tablespoons unsalted butter

1 cup sugar

¼ cup water

1 small loaf (4 to 5 ounces) Brioche
(page 35), cut into ¾-inch cubes

1½ pints vanilla ice cream

1   Line a baking sheet with parchment
paper, and set aside. In a medium saucepan over medium-high heat, combine
the butter, sugar, and water. Stir until
the sugar is dissolved, about 2 minutes.
2   Without stirring, allow the mixture
to boil. The sugar will begin to caramelize
in the pan; pick up the pan and slightly
swirl the sugar for even caramelizing. Let
the caramel turn a medium amber color,
about 4 minutes. Remove from the heat.
Add the cubes of brioche a handful at
a time, and stir to coat. When all croutons
are coated, transfer them to the prepared
baking sheet. Quickly spread the croutons
so they are not touching. Let cool. To serve,
fill four serving dishes with ice cream,
and garnish with the caramel croutons.

FIT TO EAT: CURRIES —

INDIAN-SPICED HALIBUT
WITH YOGURT

SERVES 6 | PHOTOGRAPH ON PAGE 242

*If you cannot find fenugreek seed, you can
substitute ground fenugreek; add with the
other ground spices.*

2 tomatoes

2 tablespoons Curry Powder
(recipe follows)

1 teaspoon whole fenugreek seed

2 teaspoons coarse salt

2 teaspoons ground mustard

¼ teaspoon ground cardamom

Pinch of ground cloves

4 garlic cloves, minced

1 tablespoon freshly grated ginger

1 tablespoon dark-brown sugar

1 tablespoon water

4 teaspoons unsalted butter

1 large onion, thinly sliced

1 can (14½ ounces) low-sodium
vegetable stock or Homemade
Vegetable Stock (page 44)

1 green chile, finely chopped

1½ pounds halibut fillets (or other firm-
fleshed white-fish fillets, such as cod),
cut into 6 pieces

1 cup plain nonfat yogurt

1 Bring a saucepan of water to a boil. Fill a bowl with ice and water. Cut an X in the bottom of each tomato, and plunge into the boiling water. Cook until the skin starts to peel back, about 30 seconds. Plunge into the ice bath to stop the cooking. When cool, peel off and discard the skin. Cut the tomatoes in half, and squeeze out the seeds. Chop, and set aside.

2 In the bowl of a food processor, combine the curry powder, fenugreek, salt, mustard, cardamom, and cloves. Pulse to combine. Add the garlic, ginger, brown sugar, and water. Purée until a smooth paste forms. Set the curry paste aside.

3 Heat the butter in a large saucepan over medium heat. Stir in the curry paste, and cook until fragrant, about 1 minute. Add the onion and half the stock; cook until the onion starts to soften, about 3 minutes. Add the chile and the remaining stock. Bring to a boil. Reduce to a gentle simmer, add the fish and reserved tomatoes, and cook until the fish is opaque in the center, 6 to 8 minutes. Remove from the heat, and stir in the yogurt just before serving.

PER SERVING: 234 CALORIES, 6 G FAT, 44 MG CHOLESTEROL, 16 G CARBOHYDRATE, 595 MG SODIUM, 27 G PROTEIN, 2 G DIETARY FIBER

CURRY POWDER

MAKES ABOUT 2 TABLESPOONS

2 teaspoons coriander seed

2 teaspoons cumin seed

½ teaspoon ground cayenne pepper

¾ teaspoon ground turmeric

¼ teaspoon cinnamon

Heat a skillet over medium-high heat. Add the coriander and cumin. Toast the seeds, tossing constantly, until fragrant. Transfer to a spice grinder. Add the cayenne, turmeric, and cinnamon. Pulse to combine. Use immediately.

PER RECIPE: 36 CALORIES, 2 G FAT, 0 MG CHOLESTEROL, 6 G CARBOHYDRATE, 11 MG SODIUM, 1 G PROTEIN, 0 G DIETARY FIBER

RED LENTIL AND SQUASH CURRY SOUP

SERVES 6 TO 8

2 teaspoons coarse salt

2 tablespoons Curry Powder (recipe above)

12 ounces red lentils

2 tablespoons unsalted butter

1 onion, cut into ½-inch dice

4 garlic cloves, minced

1 tablespoon freshly grated ginger

1 butternut squash (about 1½ pounds), peeled, seeded, and cut into ½-inch pieces

2 cans (14½ ounces each) low-sodium canned, or Homemade Chicken Stock (page 8), skimmed of fat

2 cups water

In a small bowl, combine the salt and curry powder, and set aside. Rinse the lentils, and set aside. Heat the butter in a large saucepan over medium heat. Add the curry mixture, and stir until fragrant, about 1 minute. Add the onion, garlic, and ginger, and cook until the onion is translucent, about 4 minutes. Add the squash, and cook until just beginning to soften, about 5 minutes. Add the stock and water. Bring to a boil, and reduce to a simmer. Cook until the squash is tender, about 10 minutes. Stir in the lentils, and cook until soft, 10 to 15 minutes. Serve hot.

PER SERVING: 264 CALORIES, 5 G FAT, 9 MG CHOLESTEROL, 43 G CARBOHYDRATE, 545 MG SODIUM, 15 G PROTEIN, 7 G DIETARY FIBER

YELLOW CURRY CHICKEN

SERVES 6

Serve with jasmine rice tossed with scallions, chopped cilantro, salt, and pepper.

6 dried red Thai chiles

1 cup boiling water, plus ½ cup water

2 tablespoons Curry Powder (recipe above)
  Lemongrass Paste (recipe follows)

1 teaspoon coarse salt
  Pinch of ground cloves

1 Idaho potato (about 8 ounces)

1 pound boneless, skinless chicken breasts (about 4 breasts)

1 tablespoon cornstarch

1 tablespoon extra-virgin olive oil

1 onion, cut into ½-inch slices

3 garlic cloves, sliced

2 carrots, cut into ¼-inch-thick rounds

¼ cup low-fat canned coconut milk

2 cups Homemade Chicken Stock (page 8) or low-sodium canned, skimmed of fat

2 tablespoons chopped fresh cilantro
  Chopped peanuts (optional)
  Crushed red-pepper flakes (optional)

1 Place the chiles in a small bowl, and pour the boiling water over them. Let soak until softened, about 10 minutes. Drain. In the bowl of a food processor, combine the chiles, curry powder, lemongrass paste, salt, and cloves. Purée until smooth, adding water if necessary.

2 Peel the potato, and cut it into ¾-inch pieces. Place in a bowl of cold water to prevent discoloring. Cut the chicken into 1-inch cubes, and place in a bowl. Sprinkle with the cornstarch, and toss to combine. Set aside.

3 Heat the olive oil in a large nonstick skillet over medium heat. Add the curry paste, and cook until fragrant, about 1 minute. Add the onion and garlic, and cook until they start to soften, about 4 minutes. Add the potato, chicken, carrots, coconut milk, remaining ½ cup water, stock, and cilantro. Cover, and simmer until the chicken is cooked through, about 10 minutes. Uncover; simmer until slightly thickened and the vegetables are tender, about 10 minutes more. Serve garnished with chopped peanuts and pepper flakes, if using.

PER SERVING: 248 CALORIES, 7 G FAT, 61 MG CHOLESTEROL, 19 G CARBOHYDRATE, 398 MG SODIUM, 25 G PROTEIN, 2 G DIETARY FIBER

LEMONGRASS PASTE

MAKES 1 CUP

Look for fresh lemongrass in Asian markets and some supermarkets.

2 teaspoons extra-virgin olive oil

6 shallots, finely chopped

1 tablespoon freshly grated ginger

3 garlic cloves, minced

1 stalk lemongrass, pounded, cut into ½-inch pieces (or 1 tablespoon dried)

¼ cup water

Heat the oil in a medium saucepan over medium-low heat. Add the shallots, ginger, garlic, lemongrass, and water. Cover, and cook until very tender, 8 to 10 minutes. Uncover, and cook until the liquid has evaporated, about 1 minute more. Transfer to the bowl of a food processor, and purée to form a smooth paste. Keep, refrigerated, for up to 2 days.

PER RECIPE: 137 CALORIES, 9 G FAT, 0 MG CHOLESTEROL, 13 G CARBOHYDRATE, 11 MG SODIUM, 2 G PROTEIN, 0 G DIETARY FIBER

BEEF RENDANG WITH BROCCOLI

SERVES 6 | **PHOTOGRAPH ON PAGE 242**

This goes well with mashed sweet potatoes.

1 cup Lemongrass Paste (page 237)
1½ teaspoons coarse salt
2 tablespoons Curry Powder (page 237)
2 medium leeks (about 8 ounces), white and light-green parts only
16 ounces lean flank steak, cut into thin strips
3 tablespoons all-purpose flour
1 teaspoon extra-virgin olive oil
¼ cup low-fat coconut milk
½ cup water
1 can (14½ ounces) low-sodium fat-free beef broth
1 head broccoli (1 pound), cut into florets

1 In a small bowl, combine the lemongrass paste with the salt and curry powder. Set the curry paste aside.
2 Halve the leeks lengthwise, and cut across into ½-inch-wide half circles. Place in a large bowl of cold water, and swish around to release the dirt. Place in a colander to drain. Place the steak in a bowl, and sprinkle with the flour. Toss to coat, and set aside.
3 Heat the oil in a large nonstick skillet over medium heat. Add the curry paste, and cook until fragrant, about 1 minute. Add the leeks, and cook, stirring occasionally, until tender, about 3 minutes. Add the beef, and sauté until browned. Add the coconut milk, water, beef stock, and broccoli. Cover; cook, stirring occasionally, until the broccoli is just tender, about 5 minutes more. Uncover, and cook until slightly thickened, about 4 minutes more. Serve.

PER SERVING: 236 CALORIES, 12 G FAT, 39 MG CHOLESTEROL, 14 G CARBOHYDRATE, 490 MG SODIUM, 18 G PROTEIN, 3 G DIETARY FIBER

CHICKPEA APPLE CURRY

SERVES 6 | **PHOTOGRAPH ON PAGE 242**

Serve with cucumber-yogurt salad.

1 tablespoon extra-virgin olive oil
2 tablespoons Curry Powder (page 237)
1 large onion, cut into ¼-inch-wide slivers
2 tablespoons freshly grated ginger
4 garlic cloves, minced
½ cup chopped fresh cilantro, plus more for garnish
1 can (28 ounces) whole tomatoes
2 Granny Smith apples, peeled, cored, and cut into ½-inch pieces
2 cans (15½ ounces each) chickpeas, rinsed and drained
1 tablespoon freshly squeezed lemon juice
1 cup plain nonfat yogurt

Heat the olive oil in a large saucepan over medium-low heat. Add the curry powder, and cook until fragrant, about 1 minute. Add the onion, ginger, and garlic, and cook until the onion starts to soften and is well coated with the curry mixture, 2 to 3 minutes. Add the cilantro, tomatoes, apples, and chickpeas. Cover, and simmer until the apples are tender, 30 to 40 minutes. Uncover, and simmer until slightly thickened, about 5 minutes. Remove from the heat, and stir in the lemon juice. Just before serving, stir in the yogurt.

PER SERVING: 259 CALORIES, 5 G FAT, 1 MG CHOLESTEROL, 43 G CARBOHYDRATE, 314 MG SODIUM, 12 G PROTEIN, 10 G DIETARY FIBER

THAI GREEN SHRIMP CURRY

SERVES 6 | **PHOTOGRAPH ON PAGE 242**

3 large fresh green chiles, seeds and ribs removed, coarsely chopped, plus a few thinly sliced, for garnish (optional)
2 tablespoons Lemongrass Paste (page 237)
3 tablespoons chopped fresh cilantro
1 tablespoon coriander seed
1 teaspoon cumin seed
1 teaspoon coarse salt
1 lime
8 ounces dried rice noodles
4 teaspoons vegetable oil
1 red onion, cut into 1-inch pieces
1 red bell pepper, ribs and seeds removed, cut into 1-inch pieces
2 tablespoons cornstarch
2¾ cups cold water
1 small (or ½ large) pineapple, peeled, cored, and cut into 1-inch pieces
1 package (3½ ounces) Enoki mushrooms
¼ cup low-fat canned coconut milk
12 jumbo shrimp, peeled and deveined, tails intact

1 Place the chopped chiles, lemongrass paste, cilantro, coriander and cumin seed, and salt in the bowl of a food processor. Zest the lime, and add the zest. Purée until smooth, adding water a tablespoon at a time if necessary, and set aside. Bring a pan of water to a boil. Add the noodles, and cook until just tender, about 5 minutes. Drain, and set aside in a bowl of cold water.
2 Heat the oil in a large nonstick skillet over medium heat. Add the lemongrass mixture, and cook until fragrant, about 1 minute. Add the onion, and cook until just softened, 6 to 8 minutes. Add the bell pepper, and cook until just tender, about 3 minutes. In a small bowl, combine the cornstarch with the water; add to the pan. Add the pineapple, mushrooms, and coconut milk, and bring to a simmer. Add the shrimp, and cook until pink and opaque. Squeeze the juice from the lime into the skillet, and stir to combine. Serve garnished with sliced chiles, if using.

PER SERVING: 277 CALORIES, 6 G FAT, 43 MG CHOLESTEROL, 50 G CARBOHYDRATE, 239 MG SODIUM, 7 G PROTEIN, 2 G DIETARY FIBER

PUMPKIN SOUP WITH WILD RICE AND APPLES | PAGE 230

BEEF RENDANG WITH BROCCOLI | **PAGE 238**

CHICKPEA APPLE CURRY | **PAGE 238**

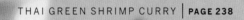
THAI GREEN SHRIMP CURRY | **PAGE 238**

INDIAN-SPICED HALIBUT WITH YOGURT | **PAGE 236**

MUSTARD GREENS AND ONIONS | **PAGE 236**
HERB ROASTED SWEET POTATOES | **PAGE 236**
BONELESS PORK CHOPS WITH APPLE CHUTNEY | **PAGE 236**

POTATO GRATIN | **PAGE 233**

RACHEL GOOD'S GLAZED POTATO DOUGHNUTS | **PAGE 235**

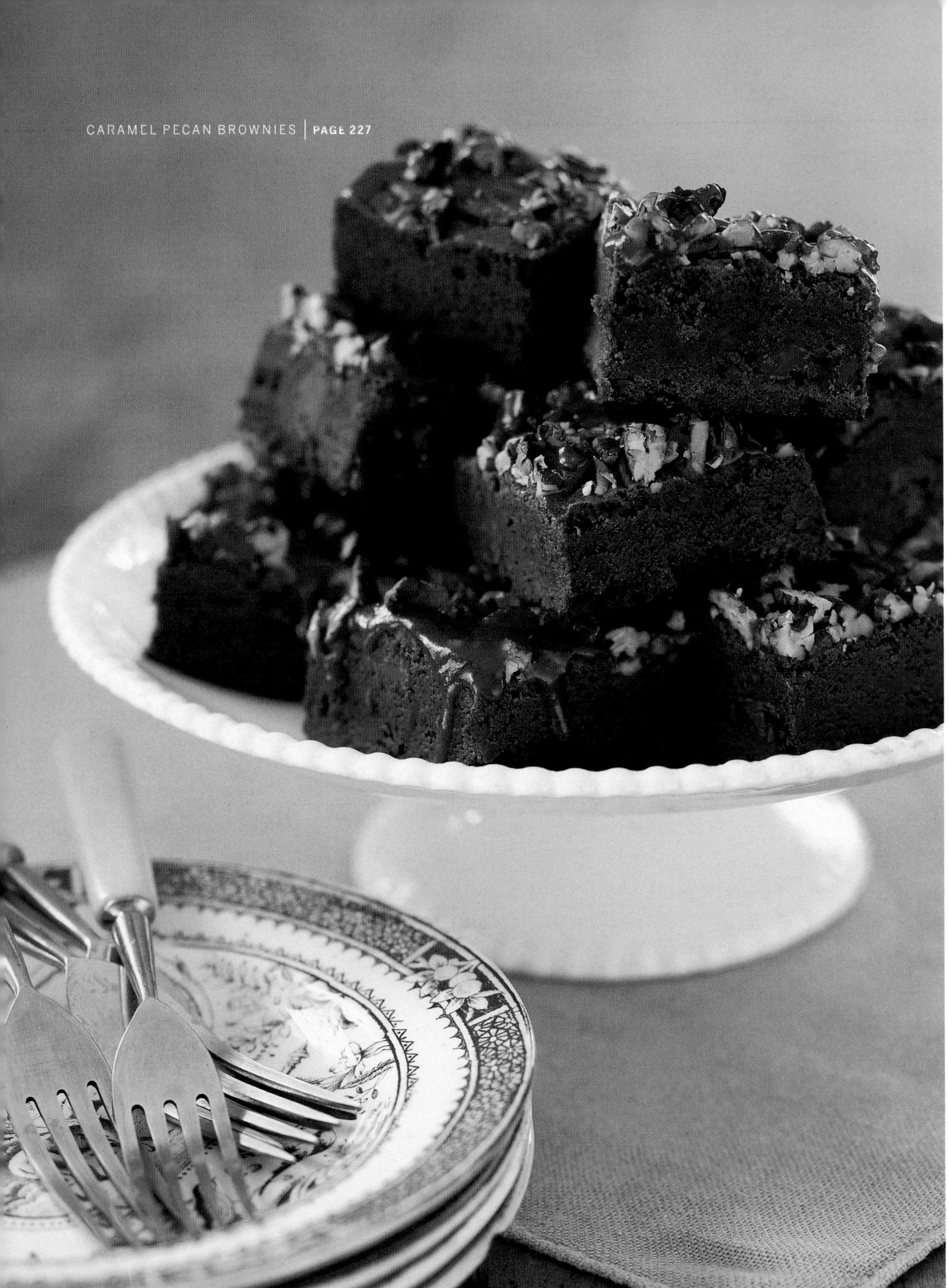

CARAMEL PECAN BROWNIES | **PAGE 227**

november

Apple Praline Tart

Buttermilk Biscuits

Angel Biscuits

Cornmeal Drop Biscuits

Baking Powder Biscuits

Layered Biscuits

Steamed Brussels Sprouts with
    Lemon-Dill Butter

Wilted Brussels Sprouts Salad with
    Warm Apple-Cider Dressing

Fettuccine with Brussels
    Sprouts Leaves, Brown Butter,
    and Toasted Walnuts

Shrimp Cocktail

Cocktail Sauce

Lemon Aïoli

Pumpkin Dip

Vegetarian Pâté

Flame-Grilled Eggplant Dip

Spice-Cured Turkey

Cauliflower with Hazelnut
    Brown Butter

Braised Onions

Mashed Potatoes and Celery Root

Vegetarian Mushroom Gravy

Chopped Beet Salad with
    Feta and Pecans

Honey-Roasted Squash

Cranberry Sauce with Dried Cherries

Escarole with Persimmons,
    Pomegranate Seeds, and
    Lemon-Shallot Vinaigrette

Apple-Chestnut Stuffing

Homemade Ginger Beer

Sorrel Punch

Coconut Patties

Pear-Cranberry Upside-Down Cake

Sweet Potato Flan

Chestnut Mushroom Soup

Frisée, Chestnut, and Pear Salad

Lamb and Chestnut Stew

Perciatelli with Roasted Chestnuts,
    Butternut Squash, and Goat Cheese

Chestnut Espresso Caramel-Swirl
    Ice Cream

Chestnut Flour Crêpes

Pan-Fried Fennel

Sea Scallops with Sherry and
    Saffron Couscous

Sausage-and-Pepper Stew

(continued on next page)

(continued from page 247)

Grapes with Sour Cream and
    Brown Sugar

Baked Sweet Potatoes with
    Caramelized Onions and
    Shaved Parmesan

Spinach Roulade

Whole-Wheat Penne with
    Butternut Squash and Beet Greens

Carrot Soup

Braised Escarole with Currants

DESSERT OF THE MONTH

APPLE PRALINE TART

MAKES 1 EIGHT-INCH TART
PHOTOGRAPH ON PAGE 263

This tart may also be made in an eight-inch spring form pan. Fit the pâte brisée into the pan, and press it up the sides. Trim so the pastry is one and three-quarter inches high.

½ recipe Pâte Brisée (page 10)

½ cup all-purpose flour, plus more for work surface

½ cup dried apricots, quartered

½ cup dried figs, preferably Calimyrna, cut into ½-inch pieces

2 tablespoons cognac

¼ cup water

3 Granny Smith apples, cored (about 1¼ pounds)

Juice of 1 lemon

½ cup roughly chopped Almond Praline (recipe follows), plus more for garnish

3 large eggs

¾ cup sugar

12 tablespoons unsalted butter

1 vanilla bean, split lengthwise

Vanilla ice cream, for serving

1 Place an 8-by-1¾-inch cake ring on a parchment-lined baking sheet. Roll pâte brisée on lightly floured surface to ⅛-inch thick. Fit gently into ring, easing dough into corners and up sides; remove excess dough so tart shell is flush with top of cake ring. Pierce bottom of tart shell with fork; transfer to freezer for 30 minutes.

2 Preheat oven to 350°F. Place apricots, figs, cognac, and water in a medium saucepan over medium heat; bring to a simmer. Cook, stirring occasionally, until all liquid has been absorbed and fruit is softened, about 4 minutes. Set aside.

3 Peel apples; cut into ¾-inch cubes. Place in bowl. Combine with lemon juice, tossing to coat. Add dried fruit mixture and chopped praline; stir to combine.

4 Combine eggs, sugar, and flour in a medium bowl; whisk until smooth. Place butter in a sauté pan; scrape the vanilla seeds into the pan, and add the pod. Cook over medium-high heat until butter begins to brown. Add to egg mixture. Whisk until fully incorporated. Remove the pod, and discard.

5 Remove baking sheet with tart shell from the freezer; fill with apple mixture, making sure dried fruits are evenly distributed. Slowly pour egg mixture over fruit, letting it seep into all gaps, until it is ⅛ inch from the top of tart shell.

6 Place tart in the oven; bake until cake tester inserted into center comes out clean and top is nicely browned, about 1 hour 30 minutes. Transfer to wire rack to cool for 30 minutes; remove ring.

7 Serve warm or at room temperature, topped with vanilla ice cream and garnished with almond praline.

ALMOND PRALINE

MAKES 1 TEN-BY-FIFTEEN INCH SHEET

1½ cups sliced almonds

1 tablespoon unsalted butter, room temperature

2 cups sugar

½ cup water

Juice of half a lemon (1 tablespoon)

1 Preheat oven to 350°F. Place almonds on a rimmed baking sheet; toast until golden brown and fragrant, about 10 minutes. Remove from oven; set aside to cool.

2 Butter a 10-by-15-inch rimmed baking sheet. Spread the toasted almonds in an even layer on the sheet.

3 Place sugar and water in a medium saucepan; stir to combine. Place over medium-high heat; bring to a boil, brushing down sides of pan with a pastry brush dipped in water to prevent crystals from forming. Once sugar has dissolved, cook without stirring until liquid is deep amber. Add lemon juice, and immediately pour caramel over the almonds, coating with a thin layer. If caramel doesn't cover all almonds, tilt pan slightly to distribute, or stir in almonds with a wooden spoon, being careful not to touch caramel or hot pan. Set aside to cool completely.

4 Gently twist the pan to release the praline. Break into pieces. Store in an airtight container for up to 1 week.

BISCUITS

BUTTERMILK BISCUITS

MAKES 15   PHOTOGRAPH ON PAGE 265

Buttermilk makes biscuits airy and tangy.

4 cups all-purpose flour, plus more for work surface

4 teaspoons baking powder

1 teaspoon baking soda

1½ teaspoons coarse salt

1 teaspoon sugar

1 cup (2 sticks) cold unsalted butter, cut into pieces

2 cups buttermilk

1 Preheat oven to 375°F. In a bowl, whisk together the flour, baking powder, baking soda, salt, and sugar. Cut in butter, using a pastry blender or two knives, until mixture resembles coarse crumbs.

2 Add the buttermilk; stir just until the dough comes together; it will be sticky. Transfer the dough to a lightly floured work surface. With floured fingers, pat the dough to a 1-inch thickness. Use a 2½-inch round biscuit or cookie cutter to cut out biscuits, cutting as close together as possible to minimize scraps.

3 Transfer to a baking sheet; bake for 18 to 20 minutes or until lightly browned. Remove from the oven, and cool on a wire rack. Serve warm.

CHEDDAR MIX-IN: Add 3 cups (9 ounces) grated cheddar cheese to the flour mixture after the butter has been cut in. Proceed with the remainder of the recipe.

ANGEL BISCUITS

MAKES 24   PHOTOGRAPH ON PAGE 265

Yeast is used as part of the leavening to give these biscuits the light, airy texture for which they are named.

6 cups all-purpose flour, plus more for work surface

2 teaspoons sugar

1 teaspoon baking soda

1 tablespoon baking powder

1½ teaspoons coarse salt

1 package active dry yeast (2½ teaspoons)

¼ cup warm water

1 cup (2 sticks) butter, melted and cooled to 115°F

2 cups buttermilk, room temperature

1 In a medium bowl, sift or whisk together flour, sugar, baking soda, baking powder, and salt; set aside. In a bowl, sprinkle yeast over water; allow to stand until creamy looking, about 5 minutes.

2 In a medium bowl, place 1 cup flour mixture, the yeast mixture, melted butter, and 1 cup buttermilk. Stir to combine. Add remaining flour and buttermilk mixtures alternately, stirring between additions. When a sticky dough forms, cover it with plastic wrap; transfer to refrigerator for 2 hours.

3 Preheat oven to 450°F. Remove dough from refrigerator; turn out onto a lightly floured work surface. Knead a few times; roll to a ½-inch thickness. Cut out shapes using a 2¼-inch round biscuit or cookie cutter; place on a baking sheet, about 1 inch apart. Bake 12 to 15 minutes, until golden on top and cooked in middle. Remove from oven; cool on a wire rack. Serve warm.

CORNMEAL DROP BISCUITS

MAKES 10 | PHOTOGRAPH ON PAGE 265

1½ cups all-purpose flour

1 cup yellow cornmeal, preferably stone-ground

2½ teaspoons baking powder

½ teaspoon coarse salt

2 teaspoons sugar

8 tablespoons (1 stick) cold unsalted butter, cut into pieces

1 cup plus 1 tablespoon milk

1 Preheat oven to 375°F. In a medium bowl, combine flour, cornmeal, baking powder, salt, and sugar. Whisk to combine. Cut in butter, using a pastry blender or two knives, until mixture resembles coarse crumbs. Add milk; stir until just combined.

2 Spoon 10 mounds, about ½ cup each, onto a baking sheet spaced 1 inch apart; bake until biscuits start to brown, about 20 minutes. Remove from the oven; cool on a wire rack. Serve warm.

BACON-AND-ONION MIX-IN: Cut 6 ounces bacon into ½-inch pieces. Cook over medium heat, stirring occasionally, until crisp, about 4 minutes. Transfer to a paper towel–lined bowl. Add 1 small onion, cut into ¼-inch dice, to hot fat in skillet; cook until translucent, about 3 minutes. Drain on paper towels. Add bacon and onion to flour mixture after butter has been cut in. Proceed with remainder of recipe.

BAKING POWDER BISCUITS

MAKES 1 DOZEN |
PHOTOGRAPH ON PAGE 265

These are flaky and rich. Add more sugar to taste for a breakfast or dessert biscuit.

4 cups all-purpose flour, plus more for work surface

2 tablespoons baking powder

1 teaspoon coarse salt

2 teaspoons sugar

1 cup (2 sticks) cold unsalted butter, cut into pieces

2 cups heavy cream

1 Preheat the oven to 400°F. In a medium mixing bowl, whisk together the flour, baking powder, salt, and sugar; whisk well. Cut in the butter, using a pastry blender or two knives, until the mixture resembles coarse crumbs.

2 Add the heavy cream; stir just until dough comes together; it will be sticky.

3 Transfer to lightly floured work surface. With floured fingers, pat dough to a 1-inch thickness. Using a 2½-inch round biscuit or cookie cutter, cut out biscuits; cut as close as possible so there are few scraps.

4 Transfer to baking sheet. Bake until lightly browned, about 20 minutes. Remove from oven; cool on wire rack. Serve warm.

HERB MIX-IN: Finely chop and then mix together a variety of fresh herbs—such as rosemary, oregano, thyme, parsley, and chives—to yield 4 tablespoons. Add herbs to flour mixture after the butter has been cut in. Proceed with remainder of recipe.

LAYERED BISCUITS

MAKES 15 | PHOTOGRAPH ON PAGE 265

For a more savory version of these layered biscuits, omit the cinnamon and sugar.

1 tablespoon cinnamon

3 tablespoons sugar

3½ cups all-purpose flour, plus more for work surface

1 teaspoon coarse salt

2 teaspoons baking powder

¼ teaspoon baking soda

1 cup (2 sticks) cold unsalted butter, cut into pieces

1½ cups buttermilk

1 In a small bowl, combine cinnamon and sugar; stir until well mixed; set aside. In a medium bowl, whisk together flour, salt, baking powder, and baking soda. Cut in butter, using a pastry blender or two knives, until mixture is the size of peas. Add buttermilk; mix with a spoon just until dough comes together; it will be sticky.

2 Transfer to lightly floured work surface; bring dough together. Roll it into an 8-by-11-by-¾-inch rectangle; sprinkle ½ tablespoon cinnamon sugar over center section of rectangle. Use bench scraper or spatula to lift the ends, folding rectangle like a letter into thirds toward center. Before folding second end over, sprinkle another ½ tablespoon cinnamon sugar onto opposite flap. Fold second flap over. Give dough a quarter turn, and repeat rolling, sprinkling, and folding. Transfer dough to a parchment-lined baking sheet; wrap in plastic wrap. Transfer to refrigerator for 20 minutes.

3 Preheat oven to 500°F. Remove dough from refrigerator; return it to work surface. Roll out into a ½-inch-thick rectangle; repeat sprinkling and folding method as in step 2, except when rolling out second time, do not fold. Use a 2¼-inch round biscuit or cookie cutter to cut out biscuits; transfer to a baking sheet.

4 Sprinkle tops with remaining cinnamon sugar; bake for 4 minutes. Reduce the oven temperature to 375°F. Continue baking until the biscuits begin to brown all over, 20 to 25 minutes more. Remove from oven; cool on wire rack. Serve warm.

BRUSSELS SPROUTS

STEAMED BRUSSELS SPROUTS WITH LEMON-DILL BUTTER
SERVES 4

The butter can be made ahead of time and used on other vegetables, fish, or chicken.

8 tablespoons (1 stick) unsalted butter, room temperature

Zest and juice of 1 lemon, plus 1 lemon quartered

½ cup chopped fresh dill, plus more for garnish

1 garlic clove, finely chopped

2 teaspoons coarse salt

¼ teaspoon freshly ground pepper

1 pound brussels sprouts

1 Place butter in bowl of electric mixer fitted with paddle attachment or in a heavy bowl. Add lemon zest and juice, dill, garlic, salt, and pepper. Beat until well combined. Transfer herbed butter to a piece of parchment or waxed paper; roll into a cylinder, twisting both ends to secure. Place in refrigerator until ready to use.

2 Place a steamer basket in a saucepan filled with 1½ inches of water over medium-high heat. Trim the sprouts of their outer leaves; cut a small X in each base with a paring knife. When the water in the steamer is boiling, add the sprouts and the lemon quarters. Cook until the sprouts are tender and bright green, tossing occasionally, about 10 minutes.

3 Discard the lemon quarters, and transfer the sprouts to a serving bowl. Cut disks of herbed butter; toss with the sprouts. Serve sprinkled with fresh dill.

WILTED BRUSSELS SPROUTS SALAD WITH WARM APPLE-CIDER DRESSING
SERVES 6

1 pound brussels sprouts, trimmed

4 ounces (about 3 cups lightly packed) spinach leaves, washed, stems removed

1 small head radicchio

1 garlic clove, finely chopped

⅓ cup apple-cider vinegar

2 tablespoons honey mustard

1½ tablespoons sugar

1 teaspoon coarse salt

¼ teaspoon freshly ground pepper

½ cup extra-virgin olive oil

Goat cheese, for garnish

Toasted caraway seeds, for garnish

1 Thinly slice brussels sprouts crosswise into strips. Repeat with the spinach leaves and radicchio. Place the brussels sprouts, spinach, and radicchio in a large bowl; toss to combine. Set aside.

2 In a small saucepan, whisk the garlic, vinegar, honey mustard, sugar, salt, and pepper over medium heat. Slowly drizzle in the olive oil while whisking constantly. Bring to a simmer; cook until mixture thickens slightly, about 3 minutes. Pour over brussels sprouts mixture; toss to combine. Serve salad warm, garnished with goat cheese and caraway seeds.

FETTUCCINE WITH BRUSSELS SPROUTS LEAVES, BROWN BUTTER, AND TOASTED WALNUTS
SERVES 6

2 ounces walnuts

1 teaspoon coarse salt, plus more for cooking water and seasoning

16 ounces fettuccine

½ cup (1 stick) plus 3 tablespoons unsalted butter

1 medium red onion, sliced into thin wedges

2 garlic cloves, minced

1 pound brussels sprouts, leaves separated

¼ teaspoon freshly ground pepper, or more for seasoning

½ teaspoon fresh sage, finely chopped

¼ teaspoon fresh thyme, finely chopped

Freshly grated Parmesan cheese, for serving

1 Preheat the oven to 350°F. Spread the walnuts on a rimmed baking sheet, transfer to the oven; toast until fragrant, about 10 minutes. When cool enough to handle, chop coarsely; set aside.

2 Bring a large saucepan of water to a boil; salt the water. Add the fettuccine; cook until al dente, 8 to 10 minutes. Drain, transfer to a medium bowl, and toss with 1 tablespoon butter. Cover; keep warm while proceeding.

3 Place ½ cup butter in a small saucepan over medium-high heat. Cook until the butter begins to brown and is very fragrant, about 8 minutes. Strain, discarding solids, into a glass measuring cup or a small bowl. Set aside.

4 Heat remaining 2 tablespoons butter in a large skillet over medium heat. Add onion and garlic; cook until they start to soften, about 2 minutes. Add sprouts leaves, salt, pepper, and herbs; continue cooking until leaves are bright green and tender and onion is translucent, 3 to 5 minutes more. Add pasta to skillet; drizzle with brown butter. Toss to combine; cook until warmed through, seasoning with salt and pepper if desired. Transfer to a serving dish; garnish with walnuts and Parmesan cheese. Serve immediately.

SHRIMP COCKTAIL 101

SHRIMP COCKTAIL
SERVES 4 TO 5 AS AN HORS D'OEUVRE

Shrimp labeled "flash-frozen" are fine. If using fresh, buy them on the day you plan to use them. The flesh should be firm.

1 pound large shrimp (16 to 20 per pound)

8 cups water

½ lemon, plus wedges for serving

1 bay leaf

2 teaspoons coarse salt

Cocktail Sauce or Lemon Aïoli (page 252)

1 To shell shrimp, hold each shrimp leg side up, and peel the shell from the inside curve with your thumbs and forefingers, leaving the tail intact. Devein the shrimp: Gently run a paring knife along the center of the outside curve from head to tail, exposing the vein. Use the knife to remove the vein; discard.

2 Fill a pan with the water; add ½ lemon, the bay leaf, and salt. Cover; bring to a boil. Reduce the heat; simmer about 10 minutes. Return to a boil. Add the shrimp. Cook until bright pink and opaque, about 1 minute 45 seconds. Do not overcook.

3 Place a wire rack over a rimmed baking sheet. With a slotted spoon, transfer the shrimp to the rack; cover with ice to cool, about 5 minutes.

4 Keep cooked shrimp as cold as possible until serving. To store, fill a bowl three-quarters full with ice. Put shrimp in a resealable plastic bag. Place bag atop the ice; cover with more ice. Place bowl in refrigerator, replenishing ice as needed.

5 To serve, arrange the shrimp on a platter or along the rim of an ice-filled bowl, accompanied by lemon wedges and cocktail sauce or lemon aioli.

COCKTAIL SAUCE
MAKES 1 CUP

¾ cup prepared ketchup
2½ tablespoons prepared horseradish
2 tablespoons freshly squeezed lemon juice
½ teaspoon coarse salt
¼ teaspoon hot-pepper sauce

In a small bowl, combine the ketchup, horseradish, lemon juice, salt, and pepper sauce. Whisk to combine. Refrigerate in an airtight container for up to 3 days.

LEMON AIOLI
MAKES 1 CUP

1 large egg
1 teaspoon coarse salt, plus more for seasoning
½ cup canola oil
¼ cup extra-virgin olive oil
3 tablespoons freshly squeezed lemon juice
Zest of 1 lemon

Place egg and salt in bowl of a food processor; blend until foamy. With machine running, add canola oil, a few drops at a time and then in a slow, steady stream. Repeat with olive oil. Add lemon juice and zest; blend briefly. Adjust the seasoning with salt. Refrigerate in an airtight container for up to 2 days.

NOTE: Raw eggs should not be used in food prepared for pregnant women, babies, young children, the elderly, or anyone whose health is compromised.

THANKSGIVING OPEN HOUSE IN BROOKLYN

PUMPKIN DIP
MAKES ABOUT 4 CUPS

After the pumpkins are roasted, choose the most attractive one for the serving bowl. When scooping the flesh from this pumpkin, leave at least a half-inch thickness so the inside of the pumpkin doesn't collapse.

3 sugar pumpkins (about 2 pounds each)
5 tablespoons olive oil, plus more for pan
Coarse salt and freshly ground pepper
3 sprigs rosemary
3 garlic cloves, unpeeled
1 tablespoon grated Parmesan cheese
Crudités, bread, and crackers, for serving

1 Preheat oven to 425°F. Slice tops off pumpkins. Remove seeds. Drizzle cavity of each pumpkin with 1 tablespoon olive oil; season with salt and pepper. Place one sprig of rosemary and 1 garlic clove inside each pumpkin.

2 Oil an 11-by-13-inch pan. Place pumpkins in pan; transfer to oven until skin is easily pierced with a knife, 30 to 40 minutes. Remove pumpkins from the oven; allow to cool.

3 Carefully remove flesh from pumpkins, reserving shell from most attractive pumpkin for serving. Squeeze roasted garlic from the papery skins; place cloves in bowl of a food processor. Add pumpkin flesh; purée until smooth. If purée is watery or thin, place in a fine sieve lined with a damp layer of cheesecloth; allow liquid to drain for 20 to 30 minutes.

4 Add grated Parmesan and remaining 2 tablespoons olive oil to pumpkin mixture. Stir to combine. Adjust seasoning with salt and pepper if desired. Serve dip at room temperature in the pumpkin shell with crudités, bread, and crackers

VEGETARIAN PATE
MAKES 3 CUPS

5 large eggs
¼ pound string beans, ends trimmed, and cut into 1-inch pieces
1 tablespoon unsalted butter
1 red onion, cut into ¼-inch dice (1 cup)
¾ cup toasted walnuts
1 tablespoon soy sauce
2 tablespoons mayonnaise
1 tablespoon olive oil
2 tablespoons finely chopped chives
Coarse salt and freshly ground pepper
Bread or crackers, for serving

1 Fill a large bowl with ice and water; set aside. Place eggs in a medium saucepan with enough water to cover by 2 inches. Place over high heat; bring to a boil. Turn off heat; cover. Let stand for 12 minutes. Transfer eggs to the ice bath to stop the cooking. When eggs are cool, peel them under cold running water. Cut into quarters; set aside. Let the cooking water return to a boil. Blanch the beans for 2 to 3 minutes. Transfer to the ice bath to stop the cooking.

2 Melt butter in a medium sauté pan over medium heat. Add onion; cook until caramelized, 8 to 10 minutes. Remove from heat; cool to room temperature.

3 Combine eggs, beans, walnuts, soy sauce, mayonnaise, and olive oil in a food processor. Pulse until finely chopped but not puréed. Stir in sautéed onions and chives; season with salt and pepper. Serve at room temperature with bread or crackers.

FLAME-GRILLED EGGPLANT DIP
MAKES ABOUT 1½ CUPS

1 large eggplant
1 tomato, coarsely chopped
2 tablespoons red onion, finely chopped
1 tablespoon olive oil
1 teaspoon balsamic vinegar
2 tablespoons chopped fresh flat-leaf parsley
Coarse salt and freshly ground pepper
Crudités, bread, and crackers, for serving

1 Place eggplant over a gas burner set on high (or under the broiler). Cook, turning as needed, until blackened and soft. Set aside to cool. Remove and discard skin. Coarsely chop the eggplant; set in a colander to drain for 15 minutes.

2 Combine the eggplant, tomato, onion, oil, vinegar, and parsley in a serving bowl; season with salt and pepper. Serve at room temperature with crudités, bread, and crackers.

SPICE-CURED TURKEY

SERVES 12 TO 14 | **PHOTOGRAPH ON PAGE 267**

If you don't have a stockpot large enough to hold the turkey, use a new plastic tub.

FOR THE BRINE:

4 cups coarse salt

5 cups sugar

2 carrots, cut into 1-inch pieces

2 celery stalks, cut into 1-inch pieces

2 onions, cut into 1-inch pieces

2 leeks, well washed,
   cut into 1-inch pieces

3 bay leaves

1 head of garlic, cut in half crosswise

2 tablespoons whole black peppercorns

1 tablespoon ground cumin

2 teaspoons crushed red-pepper flakes

1 teaspoon cloves

2 teaspoons whole allspice

8 cups water

FOR THE TURKEY AND GRAVY:

1 eighteen- to twenty-pound
   organic turkey
   Apple-Chestnut Stuffing (page 255)
   Spice Butter, softened (recipe follows)

½ cup apple cider

3 tablespoons all-purpose flour

3 cups Homemade Chicken Stock (page 8)
   or low-sodium canned

1 To make the brine, in a large stockpot, combine salt, sugar, carrots, celery, onions, leeks, bay leaves, garlic, peppercorns, cumin, pepper flakes, cloves, and allspice. Add the water; bring to a boil. Remove from heat. Brine needs to cool completely before turkey is soaked in it: It can be made a day ahead or chilled over an ice bath.

2 Rinse turkey under cold water. Pat dry. Allow bird to come to room temperature. Place it in a large stockpot, breast side down. Add brine and enough water to cover. Cover stockpot; refrigerate overnight.

3 Preheat oven to 425°F. Remove turkey from brine; drain. Fill cavities with stuffing, being careful not to pack it too tightly. Secure skin over neck cavity with toothpicks or skewers; tie legs together with kitchen twine. Rub turkey generously with spice butter; place on a rack in a roasting pan.

4 Place the turkey in oven; roast 30 minutes. Baste, rotate the pan, and reduce heat to 350°F. Continue basting every 30 to 45 minutes, until the temperature taken in thickest part of thigh registers 180°F, 3½ to 4 hours. Once turkey is well browned, cover with foil—in sections, if necessary—to prevent overbrowning. Remove foil for last 30 to 60 minutes to crisp the skin. Allow turkey to rest at least 30 minutes before carving. While it's resting, remove the stuffing.

5 To make the gravy, pour liquid from the roasting pan into a gravy skimmer; set aside. Place pan on stove over medium-high heat, and deglaze it with the apple cider, using a wooden spoon to scrape up any browned bits stuck to the pan. Set aside.

6 In a small saucepan, combine 3 tablespoons of fat from reserved pan drippings with the flour; cook for 3 to 4 minutes, until browned. Add the reserved apple-cider mixture, the stock, and any separated juices from the pan drippings. Cook over medium heat until thickened. Serve.

SPICE BUTTER

MAKES 1 CUP

1 cup (2 sticks) unsalted butter,
   room temperature

2 teaspoons coarse salt

1 teaspoon freshly ground black pepper

1 teaspoon dried thyme

1 teaspoon ground cumin

1 teaspoon garlic powder

1 teaspoon crushed red-pepper flakes

¼ teaspoon ground allspice

¼ teaspoon ground cloves

¼ teaspoon ground nutmeg

Combine butter, salt, pepper, thyme, cumin, garlic powder, pepper flakes, allspice, cloves, and nutmeg in a bowl. Beat on medium speed with an electric mixer or by hand until thoroughly combined. Store in the refrigerator until ready to use, for up to 4 days.

CAULIFLOWER WITH HAZELNUT BROWN BUTTER

SERVES 12 TO 14 |
PHOTOGRAPH ON PAGE 267

1 cup hazelnuts (filberts)

3 small or 2 large heads cauliflower
   (about 3½ pounds)
   Coarse salt

10 tablespoons (1¼ sticks) unsalted butter

2 tablespoons freshly squeezed lemon juice

2 tablespoons finely chopped chives

1 Preheat oven to 350°F. Spread hazelnuts on a rimmed baking sheet; toast until fragrant, about 10 minutes. Transfer nuts to a kitchen towel; rub off the loosened papery skins. Coarsely chop nuts.

2 Trim the stems of each cauliflower so they sit flat, keeping the head intact if possible. Bring several inches of water to a boil in a large steamer or in a pot fitted with a rack; salt the water. Steam the cauliflower until just tender, about 10 minutes. Transfer to a serving platter.

3 Combine butter and hazelnuts in a small saucepan. Cook over medium heat until butter turns brown, 3 to 4 minutes. Remove from heat; add lemon juice and chives. Season with salt. Whisk to combine. Pour over cauliflower; serve.

BRAISED ONIONS

SERVES 12 TO 14 |
PHOTOGRAPH ON PAGE 265

3 pounds red and white onions
   (about 15 onions)

3 tablespoons unsalted butter

3 tablespoons sugar

1 teaspoon coarse salt

¼ teaspoon freshly ground pepper

1 Peel onions and trim roots, leaving enough to keep onion intact. Cut them lengthwise in halves or quarters, depending on their size.

2 Place onions in a large skillet with the butter, sugar, salt, pepper, and enough water to come halfway up the sides of the onions. Bring to a boil over medium-high heat. Reduce to medium-low; cook, covered, until onions are tender, about 20 minutes. Uncover, increase the heat to medium, and cook, stirring occasionally until caramelized, 30 to 40 minutes. Serve.

MASHED POTATOES AND CELERY ROOT

SERVES 12 TO 14
PHOTOGRAPH ON PAGE 267

If you prefer a completely smooth texture, pass the cooked potatoes and celery root through a food mill or ricer.

4 pounds Yukon gold potatoes
1 pound celery root
1 cup heavy cream
6 tablespoons unsalted butter
1 tablespoon coarse salt
¼ teaspoon freshly ground pepper

1   Peel potatoes; cut into 1-inch pieces. Peel celery root using a paring knife, following shape of the root; cut into ½-inch pieces. Place potatoes and celery root in a small stockpot with water to cover; bring to a boil over high heat. Reduce to a simmer; cook until tender, about 10 minutes. Drain, return to pot; place over low heat to dry out.
2   Combine cream, butter, salt, and pepper in a small saucepan; place over medium heat until butter is melted and mixture comes to a simmer. Pour over vegetables, and combine, using a potato masher, until fluffy and smooth.

VEGETARIAN MUSHROOM GRAVY

MAKES 3½ CUPS
PHOTOGRAPH ON PAGE 267

1 portobello mushroom
½ pound shiitake mushrooms
½ pound cremini mushrooms
4 cups organic mushroom or vegetable stock or Homemade Vegetable Stock (page 45)
4 tablespoons unsalted butter
2 shallots, finely chopped
1 tablespoon Marsala wine (optional)
3 tablespoons all-purpose flour
1 teaspoon fresh thyme leaves

1   Remove stems from mushrooms. Place the stems and the stock in a medium saucepan over medium-high heat; bring to a boil. Reduce the heat to low; simmer for 30 minutes. Strain; set aside.
2   Finely chop portobello cap, and thinly slice the shiitake and cremini. Place 3 tablespoons butter in a large sauté pan over medium heat; add shallots; cook until translucent, 3 to 5 minutes. Add chopped and sliced mushrooms; cook until mushrooms are soft and browned and all the liquid has evaporated. Add Marsala, if using, and cook, stirring to loosen any browned bits on the bottom of the pan. Remove from heat; set aside.
3   Place remaining tablespoon butter and flour in a medium saucepan over medium heat; cook until browned and combined, 2 to 3 minutes. Slowly whisk in enriched stock; bring to a boil, whisking until thickened. Add reserved mushroom mixture and thyme; stir to combine. Serve hot.

CHOPPED BEET SALAD WITH FETA AND PECANS

SERVES 12 TO 14
PHOTOGRAPH ON PAGE 267

½ cup pecans
4 bunches small beets (16 to 20 beets)
3 tablespoons cider vinegar
3 tablespoons olive oil
4 ounces feta cheese, crumbled
2 tablespoons chopped fresh flat-leaf parsley, plus sprigs for garnish
Coarse salt and freshly ground pepper

1   Preheat oven to 350°F. Spread pecans on a rimmed baking sheet; toast until fragrant, about 10 minutes. Transfer to a bowl to cool. Coarsely chop; set aside. Raise the oven to 450°F.
2   Trim the greens and long roots from the beets. Wrap beets in 2 to 3 foil packets, dividing beets according to size. Place in oven; roast until tender, 45 to 60 minutes, depending on size of beets. Using paper towels to protect your hands, wipe the skins from the beets. Cut into wedges; transfer to a serving bowl.
3   Drizzle the vinegar and olive oil over the beets; toss to coat when ready to serve (beets can be made ahead). Add the feta, parsley, and chopped pecans; season with salt and pepper. Toss to combine. Garnish with parsley sprigs.

HONEY-ROASTED SQUASH

SERVES 12 TO 14
PHOTOGRAPH ON PAGE 267

We looked for small squash and served them cut in half. You may quarter larger squash if necessary. Using various types of squash makes an attractive presentation.

8 squash, such as kabocha, acorn, delicata, and buttercup
4 tablespoons unsalted butter
3 tablespoons honey
1½ teaspoons fresh thyme leaves, plus 4 sprigs
Coarse salt and freshly ground pepper

1   Preheat oven to 450°F. Cut the squash in half; remove the seeds using an ice-cream scoop or large spoon. Arrange halves cut side up on a baking sheet.
2   Place butter, honey, and thyme in a small saucepan; place over medium heat until melted and combined. Using a pastry brush, coat squash with butter mixture. Sprinkle with salt and pepper; roast in oven for 30 to 35 minutes, until golden brown and tender. Serve.

CRANBERRY SAUCE WITH DRIED CHERRIES

MAKES 3 CUPS
PHOTOGRAPH ON PAGE 267

You can substitute dried cranberries or raisins for the dried cherries in this recipe.

3½ cups (one 12-ounce bag) cranberries
¾ cup dried cherries
½ cup finely chopped shallots
2 tablespoons red-wine vinegar
Zest and juice (about ½ cup) of 1 orange
2 teaspoons grated ginger, peeled
¾ cup packed light-brown sugar

Combine the cranberries, cherries, shallots, vinegar, zest and juice, ginger, and brown sugar in a medium saucepan; cook over medium heat until the cranberries pop. Reduce the heat to low, and cook, stirring occasionally, until cranberries release their juices, about 15 minutes. If sauce becomes too thick, add a little water until the desired consistency is reached. Transfer to a bowl to cool.

ESCAROLE WITH PERSIMMONS, POMEGRANATE SEEDS, AND LEMON-SHALLOT VINAIGRETTE

SERVES 12 TO 14

Fuyu persimmons, which also may be labeled "ready to eat," can be eaten while they are still firm, unlike Hachiya persimmons, which can be eaten only when very soft.

¾ cup freshly squeezed lemon juice (3 to 4 lemons)

¼ cup minced shallots

2 tablespoons grainy mustard

2 tablespoons chopped fresh marjoram

1 cup extra-virgin olive oil

1 teaspoon coarse salt

¼ teaspoon freshly ground pepper

2 heads escarole, washed and torn into bite-size pieces

5 Fuyu persimmons, very thinly sliced

Seeds of 1 pomegranate (optional)

1 Combine lemon juice, shallots, mustard, and marjoram in medium bowl; whisk to combine. Add oil, one drop at a time at first and then in slow, steady stream, whisking constantly, until incorporated. Season with salt and pepper.

2 Toss the escarole with just enough vinaigrette to coat. Arrange the persimmon slices over the greens; sprinkle with the pomegranate seeds, if using. Serve the remaining vinaigrette on the side.

APPLE-CHESTNUT STUFFING

SERVES 12 TO 14

PHOTOGRAPH ON PAGE 265

To save time on Thanksgiving Day, complete the first three steps and chop the onion and celery the day before. If using shelled chestnuts, chop, preheat the oven to 350°F, then proceed to step two.

2 cups chestnuts (12 ounces in the shells, 8 ounces shelled)

1 loaf rustic Italian or French bread (about 1 pound)

2 cups (12 ounces) prunes, coarsely chopped

1 cup apple cider

3 tablespoons unsalted butter, plus more for dish

1 large red onion, finely chopped

2 celery stalks, cut into ¼-inch dice

2 green apples, cored and cut into ¼-inch dice

2 large eggs, lightly beaten

½ cup heavy cream

3 tablespoons chopped fresh sage

Coarse salt and freshly ground pepper

1 Preheat oven to 350°F. Using a chestnut knife or small paring knife, make an incision about ⅛ inch deep through the shell and into flesh of each chestnut almost all the way around the circumference of the nut. Transfer to a chestnut pan or rimmed baking sheet. Roast in oven until chestnuts are tender, about 35 minutes. Turn oven off. Leaving sheet with chestnuts in oven, remove several at a time. Working quickly, place 1 chestnut in a towel; holding both, peel the chestnut while still hot. Repeat until all chestnuts are shelled. Remove and discard shells and inner skin; coarsely chop; set aside. Heat the oven to 350°F.

2 Remove crusts from bread; set aside. Cut bread into 1-inch cubes. Place cubes in a single layer on two baking sheets; toast in oven until dry, 5 to 7 minutes. Set aside to cool. Place the reserved crusts in the bowl of a food processor; pulse until coarse crumbs are formed.

3 Place the prunes and apple cider in a small saucepan; bring to a boil over medium-high heat. Reduce to a simmer; cook until all of the liquid has been absorbed, 20 to 25 minutes. Set aside.

4 Melt the butter in a large skillet over medium heat; add the chestnuts, onion, half the celery, and half the apples. Cook until the onion is translucent, about 7 minutes. Set aside to cool.

5 In a large bowl, combine the bread cubes and crumbs, prune mixture, chestnut mixture, remaining celery, apples, eggs, heavy cream, and sage. Stir to combine. Juices from the turkey brine will season stuffing cooked in the turkey.

6 The stuffing can be baked in the turkey until its temperature reaches 165°F. Season excess stuffing with salt and pepper, and bake in a buttered dish, covered, at 350°F for 30 minutes, and then uncovered for 10 minutes more.

HOMEMADE GINGER BEER

MAKES 16 CUPS

This drink is very spicy. Adjust the amount of lime juice and sugar to your taste.

2 pounds ginger, peeled, and cut into 1-inch pieces

1 gallon boiling water

1½ cups freshly squeezed lime juice (about 8 limes)

1½ cups superfine sugar

Place ginger in food processor; process until finely chopped. Transfer to a large pot or bowl; add boiling water. Allow to stand for 1 hour. Drain through a fine sieve lined with a double thickness of damp cheesecloth. Discard solids. Add the lime juice and sugar; stir to dissolve. Store, refrigerated, for up to 3 days.

SORREL PUNCH

MAKES 12 CUPS

Sorrel is also sold under the name dried hibiscus or Jamaica flowers.

12 cups water

2 ounces dried sorrel (hibiscus flowers)

2 inch piece ginger (2 ounces), peeled and thinly sliced

Juice and zest of 3 lemons

Juice and zest of 1 orange

8 allspice berries

4 cloves

2½ cups packed light-brown sugar

Bring the water to a boil in a large pot. Add the sorrel, ginger, lemon juice and zest, orange juice and zest, allspice, and cloves. Cover; let steep overnight. Strain; stir in the brown sugar until dissolved. Chill in the refrigerator. Serve over ice.

COCONUT PATTIES

MAKES 30 | **PHOTOGRAPH ON PAGE 270**

Coconut patties can be formed a day ahead and kept in the refrigerator, but they are best eaten the day they are baked.

- 1 coconut, or 4 cups unsweetened grated coconut
- 1 cup packed light-brown sugar
- ¼ teaspoon ground nutmeg
- 1 tablespoon water
- 1 tablespoon unsalted butter
  All-purpose flour, for work surface
  Flaky Pastry Dough (recipe follows)
- 1 large egg
- 1 tablespoon heavy cream

1 Preheat oven to 350°F. Use an ice pick or screwdriver to poke holes in the "eyes" of the coconut; drain the milk, and reserve for another use. Place the coconut in oven for 15 minutes; remove, wrap in a cloth towel, and hit with a hammer to crack it open. Separate the flesh from the hard outer shell; discard the shell. Use a vegetable peeler to remove the thin brown coating from the flesh. Grate the coconut on the largest holes of a box grater to yield 4 cups.

2 Combine grated coconut, brown sugar, nutmeg, and water in a medium saucepan; cook over medium-low heat, stirring until sugar has melted and coconut is thoroughly coated, 3 to 5 minutes. Transfer to a bowl; add butter, stirring until melted. Cool to room temperature.

3 Lightly dust a clean work surface with flour; divide the pastry dough into 2 pieces. Roll each piece to ⅛ inch thick. Use a 3½-inch round cookie cutter to cut out disks. Reroll the scraps; cut additional disks.

4 Make an egg wash by combining the egg and cream in a small bowl. Place 1 generous tablespoon of the coconut mixture on each pastry disk. Apply a light coating of egg wash to the edges using a pastry brush. Fold into half-moon shapes; press the edges together with the tines of a fork to seal.

5 Place patties on a baking sheet lined with a Silpat baking mat or parchment. Bake for 20 to 25 minutes, until golden brown. Transfer to a wire rack to cool.

FLAKY PASTRY DOUGH

MAKES ENOUGH FOR 30 PATTIES

- 1¾ cups all-purpose flour
- 1 cup (2 sticks) cold unsalted butter, cut into pieces
- 8 ounces cream cheese, cut into pieces
  Pinch of coarse salt
- 4 to 6 tablespoons ice water

Place flour, butter, cream cheese, and salt in a food processor, and pulse until thoroughly combined. Add ice water, 1 tablespoon at a time, until dough just comes together when pinched. Transfer to a piece of plastic wrap; flatten into a disk. Chill at least 1 hour before rolling.

PEAR-CRANBERRY UPSIDE-DOWN CAKE

MAKES 1 TEN-INCH CAKE |
PHOTOGRAPH ON PAGE 265

- 12 tablespoons (1½ sticks) unsalted butter
- 1¾ cups firmly packed light-brown sugar
- 3 firm but ripe pears, such as Anjou
  Juice of 1 lemon
- 1 cup cranberries
- 2½ cups all-purpose flour
- 2½ teaspoons baking powder
- ½ teaspoon table salt
- ½ teaspoon cinnamon
- ¼ teaspoon ginger
- 3 large eggs
- 1 cup milk, room temperature
  Spice Ice Cream (recipe follows)

1 Preheat oven to 350°F. Combine 6 tablespoons butter and ¾ cup brown sugar in a medium skillet; cook over medium-high heat, stirring constantly, until melted and thoroughly combined, about 6 minutes. Pour the mixture into a 10-by-2-inch round cake pan.

2 Peel pears, core, and slice into ½-inch-thick wedges. Coat with lemon juice; arrange on top of brown-sugar mixture in a spiral pattern around the edge of the pan. Fan out slices in center. Sprinkle ½ cup cranberries over pears.

3 Sift together flour, baking powder, salt, cinnamon, and ginger in a medium bowl; set aside. Place remaining 6 tablespoons butter and remaining cup brown sugar in the bowl of an electric mixer fitted with the paddle attachment; beat until

well combined. Add eggs one at a time, beating after each addition. Add milk alternately with flour mixture, beginning and ending with flour, beating until smooth. Stir in remaining ½ cup cranberries; pour over fruit in pan. Bake until a cake tester inserted into center of cake comes out clean, about 40 minutes.

4 Transfer to a wire rack to cool for 15 minutes. Run a knife around the edges of the pan, and invert onto a serving platter. Serve with spice ice cream.

SPICE ICE CREAM

MAKES ABOUT 1½ QUARTS

- 4 cinnamon sticks
- 1 whole star anise (optional)
- 2 cups milk
- 1 vanilla bean, split lengthwise
- 6 large egg yolks
- ¾ cup plus 2 tablespoons sugar
- 2 cups heavy cream, very cold

1 Place cinnamon sticks, star anise, if using, and milk in a saucepan over medium-high heat. Scrape vanilla seeds into pan; add pod. Bring mixture to a simmer, cover, and remove from heat. Allow to steep for 30 minutes; strain, discarding solids.

2 Combine the egg yolks and sugar in a bowl; whisk until pale yellow and thick, about 3 minutes.

3 Fill a large bowl with ice and water; set aside. Return milk to the stove, and bring just to a simmer. Slowly pour milk mixture into yolk mixture, whisking constantly. Return liquid to saucepan; cook over low heat, stirring constantly, until it is thick enough to coat the back of a spoon, about 5 minutes. The custard should retain a line drawn across the back of the spoon with your finger.

4 Remove pan from heat; immediately stir in the cold cream. Pass custard through a fine sieve into a bowl set in the ice bath. Stir occasionally until cool. Cover the bowl; place in the refrigerator until well chilled, preferably overnight.

5 Pour custard into an ice-cream maker; churn according to the manufacturer's instructions, until set but not hard.

6 Transfer the soft ice cream to an airtight container, and freeze at least 4 hours, or up to 1 week.

SWEET POTATO FLAN

MAKES 1 NINE-INCH FLAN
PHOTOGRAPH ON PAGE 270

*We made this in a four-cup savarin mold;
a nine-by-two-inch round cake pan or a
nine-inch glass pie plate can be used as well.*

2 sweet potatoes (1¼ pounds)
1¾ cups sugar
¼ cup water
¼ teaspoon ground allspice
½ teaspoon ground cinnamon
¾ teaspoon coarse salt
5 large whole eggs
2 large egg yolks
2 teaspoons pure vanilla extract
2 cups milk, scalded

1 Preheat oven to 450°F. Place the sweet
potatoes on a baking sheet, and roast in
oven until very soft, about 1 hour. Allow
to cool. Peel off and discard the skin.
Place the potatoes in the bowl of a food
processor; purée until completely smooth.
Measure out 1½ cups purée, reserving
excess for another use. This step may be
done a day in advance.
2 Reduce oven to 325°F. Combine 1 cup
sugar and the water in a small saucepan;
cook over medium heat. Cook, stirring
occasionally, until the sugar dissolves.
Brush down the sides of the pan with
a pastry brush dipped in water to prevent
crystallization. Increase the heat to medium-
high, and boil, without stirring, until the
syrup turns a deep amber, 5 to 6 minutes.
Pour the caramel into the savarin mold
or a 9-by-2-inch round cake pan. Holding
pan with pot holders, swirl to coat the
bottom and halfway up sides of the mold.
3 In a large bowl, combine the sweet-
potato purée, remaining ¾ cup sugar,
allspice, cinnamon, salt, whole eggs, and
egg yolks. Mix in the vanilla and scalded
milk, then pass the mixture through
a fine sieve. Pour into the caramel-lined
pan; cover with foil. Set in a roasting
pan; pour boiling water into the roasting
pan halfway up the sides of the flan dish.
4 Bake for 50 to 55 minutes, or until the
center of the flan is nearly set: A thin blad-
ed knife inserted in the center should come
out clean. Let cool to room temperature;
place in the refrigerator to chill overnight.
5 To unmold, run a sharp knife carefully
around the flan, and cover with a serving
plate; invert quickly. Remove the pan; serve.

CHESTNUTS

CHESTNUT MUSHROOM SOUP

SERVES 4 TO 6

*For a velvety-smooth texture, pass the soup
through a fine sieve after the mixture has
been processed and before adding the cream.*

1 pound fresh chestnuts
6 ounces cremini mushrooms, wiped clean
2 ounces shiitake mushrooms,
  wiped clean, stems removed
2 tablespoons unsalted butter
1 tablespoon extra-virgin olive oil
  Coarse salt and freshly ground pepper
1 small onion, chopped
1 garlic clove, halved
8 sprigs of fresh thyme,
  plus leaves for garnish
6 cups Homemade Chicken Stock (page 8)
  or low-sodium canned
2 cups water
½ cup heavy cream

1 Preheat oven to 350°F. Using a chestnut
knife or a small paring knife, make an
incision about ⅛ inch deep through shell
and into flesh of each chestnut almost all
the way around the circumference of the
nut. Transfer to a chestnut pan or rimmed
baking sheet. Roast in oven until chestnuts
are tender, about 35 minutes. Turn oven off.
Leaving sheet with chestnuts in the oven,
remove several at a time. Working quickly,
place 1 chestnut in a towel; holding both,
peel chestnut while still hot. Remove and
discard shells and inner skin; set aside.
Repeat until all chestnuts are shelled.
2 Roughly chop all but 2 cremini and
2 shiitake mushrooms. Heat 1 tablespoon
butter with oil in a small stockpot
over medium-high heat. Add chopped
mushrooms; season with salt and pepper.
Cook mushrooms, stirring occasionally,
until they start to brown, about 5 minutes.
Add onion, garlic, and thyme sprigs.
Reduce heat to medium-low; cook until
onions are translucent, about 8 minutes.
Add all but 4 chestnuts; cook until golden,
about 5 minutes. Add stock and water.
Raise the heat to high; bring to a boil.
Reduce the heat; simmer until chestnuts
are falling-apart tender, about 1 hour.
Remove and discard thyme sprigs; let
stand about 10 minutes.

3 Let the soup cool slightly. Pass it
through a sieve, and transfer the solids, reserving the liquid, to a food processor or
blender, filling it no more than half full.
Purée, in batches, until very smooth. Add
the reserved liquid; process for 1 minute.
Adjust seasoning with salt and pepper,
if desired. Transfer to the stockpot, stir in
cream, and place over low heat until hot.
4 Cut 4 reserved chestnuts and 4 reserved mushrooms into ¼-inch-thick
slices. Melt remaining tablespoon butter
in a small skillet over medium-high
heat. Add chestnuts and mushrooms;
cook until crisp and golden brown, 3
to 4 minutes. Divide soup among soup
bowls; garnish with sautéed chestnuts,
and mushrooms and the thyme leaves.

FRISEE, CHESTNUT, AND
PEAR SALAD

SERVES 6 TO 8

*If desired, the hazelnuts can be roasted
at the same time as the chestnuts. Since the
oven temperature is twenty-five degrees
lower, you will need to add five to seven
minutes to the roasting time of the hazelnuts.*

8 ounces fresh chestnuts
½ cup (2 ounces) hazelnuts
1 large head (about 12 ounces)
  frisée lettuce
1 tablespoon unsalted butter
1 pound Forelle or other small pears,
  such as Seckel, peeled, cored, and cut
  into ½-inch-thick wedges
1 tablespoon sugar
4 ounces pancetta or regular bacon
⅓ cup sherry-wine vinegar
¾ cup extra-virgin olive oil
  Coarse salt and freshly ground pepper

1 Preheat oven to 350°F. Using a chestnut knife or a small paring knife, make an incision about ⅛ inch deep through shell and into flesh of each chestnut almost all the way around the circumference of the nut. Transfer to a chestnut pan or rimmed baking sheet. Roast chestnuts in oven until tender, about 35 minutes. Turn oven off. Leaving sheet with chestnuts in oven, remove several at a time. Working quickly, place 1 chestnut in a towel and, holding both, peel chestnut while still hot. Remove and discard shells and inner skin; set nuts aside. Repeat until all chestnuts are shelled. Heat the oven temperature to 375°F.

2 Place hazelnuts on a rimmed baking sheet; toast in oven until golden, about 10 minutes. Remove from oven, place nuts in a clean towel, and vigorously rub between palms to remove skins. Roughly chop nuts; set aside.

3 Tear frisée into large pieces; transfer to a large bowl. Melt butter in a medium skillet over medium-high heat. Add pears and sugar; cook until caramelized, 6 to 8 minutes. Remove from pan; transfer to a dish.

4 Cut pancetta into ½-inch pieces. Place in skillet; cook until crisp, about 5 minutes. Remove from skillet; transfer to paper towels to drain. Set aside.

5 Return skillet with pancetta fat to heat; carefully add vinegar to pan. Raise heat to high; cook, stirring, until reduced by about one-quarter, about 2 minutes. Add olive oil; whisk to combine. Add chestnuts, adjust seasoning with salt and pepper, reduce heat to low, and simmer for 5 minutes. Add reserved hazelnuts, pears, and pancetta to frisée. Pour dressing and chestnuts over salad, toss to combine; serve.

LAMB AND CHESTNUT STEW

SERVES 6 | PHOTOGRAPH ON PAGE 268

Stews are best when cooked the day before they are served. Store in the refrigerator, covered, overnight.

14 ounces fresh chestnuts
2 pounds lamb stew meat, cut into 2-inch pieces
 Coarse salt and freshly ground pepper
 All-purpose flour, for dredging
3 tablespoons olive oil
6 ounces pearl onions
12 ounces small button mushrooms, wiped clean
1 cup red wine
3½ cups Homemade Beef Stock (page 11) or low-sodium canned
4 canned Italian plum tomatoes, drained and seeded
2 teaspoons chopped fresh sage
2 teaspoons chopped fresh rosemary
½ cup sun-dried cranberries
2 quarts water
2 cups quick-cooking polenta

1 Preheat oven to 350°F. Using a chestnut knife or a small paring knife, make an incision about ⅛ inch deep through shell and into flesh of each chestnut almost all the way around the circumference of the nut. Transfer to a chestnut pan or rimmed baking sheet. Roast in oven until chestnuts are tender, about 35 minutes. Turn oven off. Leaving sheet with chestnuts in oven, remove several at a time. Working quickly, place 1 chestnut in a towel and, holding both, peel chestnut while still hot. Remove and discard shells and inner skin; set aside. Repeat until all chestnuts are shelled.

2 Season lamb with salt and pepper. Dredge meat in flour; shake off excess. Set aside. Heat 2 tablespoons oil in a Dutch oven over medium-high heat. Add lamb pieces in a single layer without crowding; cook until browned all over, about 5 minutes. Transfer lamb to a dish. Repeat browning with remaining olive oil and meat.

3 Add the onions to the Dutch oven, cook until golden, about 4 minutes. Add mushrooms, season with salt and pepper, and cook until well browned, 5 to 6 minutes. Add red wine, scraping up any browned bits from pan. Cook until wine is reduced by half, about 5 minutes.

4 Add reserved lamb, beef stock, chestnuts, tomatoes, sage, and rosemary; bring to a boil. Reduce heat to medium-low, and simmer, uncovered, until meat is very tender, 1½ to 2 hours. Add cranberries; cook 2 minutes more. (Proceed with step 5, and serve immediately, or let cool, refrigerate overnight, and proceed with step 5 just before serving.)

5 Pour the water into a large saucepan; bring to a boil over high heat. Season generously with salt. Pour in polenta in a slow, steady stream while stirring constantly. Reduce heat to medium-low; cook, stirring with a wooden spoon, until polenta thickens, 3 to 5 minutes. Remove from heat; serve immediately with stew.

PERCIATELLI WITH ROASTED CHESTNUTS, BUTTERNUT SQUASH, AND GOAT CHEESE

SERVES 6 | PHOTOGRAPH ON PAGE 269

Perciatelli, a spaghetti-shaped pasta, can be found in specialty food stores. Bucatini, linguine, or spaghetti can also be used.

10 ounces fresh chestnuts
2 tablespoons unsalted butter
2 tablespoons extra-virgin olive oil
5 leeks, trimmed, white and light-green parts only, well washed, sliced ¼ inch thick
2 garlic cloves, thinly sliced
1 butternut squash (about 1 pound), peeled, seeded, and cut into ¾-inch dice
 Coarse salt and freshly ground pepper
¾ cup dry vermouth
1 cup Homemade Chicken Stock (page 8) or low-sodium canned
1 pound perciatelli
4 ounces fresh goat cheese, crumbled into small pieces
½ cup small fresh basil leaves, for garnish

1 Preheat oven to 350°F. Using a chestnut knife or a small paring knife, make an incision about ⅛ inch deep through shell and into flesh of each chestnut almost all the way around the circumference of the nut. Transfer to a chestnut pan or rimmed baking sheet. Roast in oven until chestnuts are tender, about 35 minutes. Turn oven off. Leaving sheet with chestnuts in oven,

remove several at a time. Working quickly, place 1 chestnut in a towel and, holding both, peel chestnut while still hot. Remove and discard shells and inner skin; set aside. Repeat until all chestnuts are shelled. Break chestnuts into halves or quarters; set aside.

2 In a large high-sided sauté pan, melt butter and olive oil over medium heat. Add leeks and garlic; cook, stirring occasionally, until softened, about 6 minutes. Add chestnuts and squash; season with salt and pepper. Cook until tender, 15 to 20 minutes. Add vermouth and stock, raise heat to medium-high, and cook until the liquid has been reduced by a little more than half, about 2 minutes.

3 Meanwhile, bring a large pot of water to a boil; salt water. Add pasta; cook until al dente, 8 to 10 minutes. Drain in a colander. Add pasta to sauté pan along with 2 ounces goat cheese; toss to combine. Transfer pasta mixture to a serving dish; serve garnished with remaining 2 ounces goat cheese and basil leaves.

CHESTNUT ESPRESSO CARAMEL-SWIRL ICE CREAM

MAKES ABOUT 1½ QUARTS

Let the ice cream stand at room temperature for ten to fifteen minutes before serving. Store extra caramel sauce in the refrigerator for up to one month.

12 ounces fresh chestnuts

3½ cups heavy cream

2 cups whole milk

1½ cups sugar

1 vanilla bean, split lengthwise

8 large egg yolks

¼ cup freshly brewed espresso or very strong coffee

2 tablespoons water

½ tablespoon unsalted butter

1 Preheat oven to 350°F. Using a chestnut knife or a small paring knife, make an incision about ⅛ inch deep through shell and into flesh of each chestnut almost all the way around the circumference of the nut. Transfer to a chestnut pan or rimmed baking sheet. Roast in oven until chestnuts are tender, about 35 minutes. Turn oven off. Leaving sheet with chestnuts in oven, remove several at a time. Working quickly, place 1 chestnut in a towel and, holding

both, peel chestnut while still hot. Remove and discard shells and inner skin; set aside. Repeat until all chestnuts are shelled.

2 Combine 2 cups cream, milk, ½ cup sugar, vanilla bean, and chestnuts in a medium saucepan. Place over medium-low heat; cook, stirring occasionally, until the chestnuts are falling-apart tender, 20 to 25 minutes.

3 Fill a large bowl with ice and water; set aside. In a large bowl, whisk together egg yolks and ½ cup sugar until mixture is pale yellow, about 2 minutes. Pour 1 cup chestnut mixture into egg yolks; whisk to combine well. Pour egg mixture back into pan; whisk to combine. Return saucepan to medium heat; stir constantly with a wooden spoon until mixture thickens and holds a line when a finger is drawn across the back of spoon, 3 to 5 minutes. Remove from heat; stir in 1 cup cream.

4 Transfer mixture to a food processor or blender, filling it no more than halfway. Purée, in batches, until smooth. Pass mixture through a fine sieve, pressing down on chestnuts to extract as much liquid as possible. Discard solids, pour mixture into a large bowl; set in ice bath, stirring occasionally, until cold.

5 Stir together espresso and remaining ½ cup cream; set aside. Combine remaining ½ cup sugar and water in a small saucepan; place over medium-high heat, brushing sides of pan with a pastry brush dipped in cold water to prevent crystals from forming. Cook until mixture turns dark golden, 13 to 15 minutes. To gauge color of caramel, dip a small piece of white paper into mixture. Carefully add espresso mixture; stand back. It will boil and sputter. Do not stir. When bubbling has subsided, about 1 minute, add butter. Stir well with a wooden spoon. Transfer pan to ice bath.

6 Freeze ice cream in an ice-cream maker, according to manufacturer's instructions. Quickly transfer half the ice cream to a 1½-quart container. Drizzle 4 or 5 tablespoons caramel over ice cream. Cover with remaining ice cream and drizzle with 4 or 5 tablespoons caramel. Drag a knife through caramel and ice cream creating swirl effect. Cover; place in freezer, about 6 hours or overnight.

CHESTNUT FLOUR CREPES

MAKES 22

Serve with chestnut ice cream. Store, refrigerated, in sealed plastic bags up to one week.

1½ cups chestnut flour

⅛ teaspoon table salt

1 cup milk

3 large eggs, lightly beaten

8 tablespoons (1 stick) unsalted butter, melted

2 tablespoons confectioners' sugar

Ice cream, for serving

1 Sift together the chestnut flour and salt into a medium bowl. Add the milk, whisking to form a smooth paste. Whisk in the eggs and 1 tablespoon butter until smooth.

2 Place a 7-inch nonstick skillet over medium-high heat; add a little melted butter. Pour 2 tablespoons batter into the center of the pan, and immediately swirl until the batter covers the bottom of the pan. Cook until the crêpe is almost dry on top and the bottom is golden, about 30 seconds. Flip; cook about 30 seconds more. Turn the crêpe out onto a clean surface. Repeat the cooking process until all the batter is used.

3 Brush the crêpes with the remaining melted butter; sprinkle with sugar. Fold into quarters, and serve with ice cream.

PAN-FRIED FENNEL

SERVES 4

For best results, use a heavy-bottomed sauté pan. Serve the fennel as an appetizer while preparing the meal.

2 medium fennel bulbs
1 cup all-purpose flour, for dredging
1½ cups fresh bread crumbs, for dredging
   Coarse salt and freshly ground pepper
3 large eggs
1½ cups vegetable oil, just enough to fill the pan about ¼ inch
2 lemons, cut into wedges

1 Remove tops and fronds from fennel bulbs. Slice bulbs in half widthwise. Cut each half into slices about ⅛ inch thick.
2 Pour flour into a medium bowl and the bread crumbs into another bowl. Add the salt and pepper. Crack eggs into a third bowl; whisk until frothy. Add the salt and pepper. Dredge the fennel lightly in the flour, then in the egg, and then in the bread crumbs, shaking off the excess after each step.
3 Heat oil in a large sauté pan over medium heat. Check to make sure the oil is hot enough by tossing a pinch of flour into the pan. If flour sizzles, oil is ready.
4 Fry fennel slices until golden brown on each side, about 30 seconds per side, working in batches so as not to crowd pan. Drain on paper towels; season with salt. Serve hot with lemon wedges.

SEA SCALLOPS WITH SHERRY AND SAFFRON COUSCOUS

SERVES 4

The scallops and couscous are prepared in the same sauté pan.

1 pound sea scallops, muscles removed and discarded
1½ teaspoons coarse salt, or more for seasoning
¼ teaspoon freshly ground pepper, or more for seasoning
2 to 3 tablespoons olive oil
¼ cup dry sherry
2½ cups Homemade Chicken Stock (page 8) or low-sodium canned
3 tablespoons unsalted butter, cut into small pieces
   Pinch of saffron
1 tablespoon fresh thyme
2 cups couscous

1 Season scallops on both sides with 1 teaspoon salt and the pepper. Heat 2 tablespoons oil in a sauté pan over medium-high heat. Add scallops, working in batches if necessary; cook until golden brown and caramelized, about 1 minute on each side. If cooking in batches, add 1 tablespoon oil to pan before second batch. Pour off any fat remaining in pan. Set scallops aside on a plate covered with foil.
2 Return pan to heat. Deglaze pan with the sherry, scraping browned bits from bottom of pan with a wooden spoon. Simmer until sherry is reduced by two-thirds. Add stock, butter, saffron, thyme, and remaining ½ teaspoon salt. Bring to a boil; add couscous. Cover pan; remove from heat. Let sit for 5 minutes. Uncover, fluff with a fork, and adjust the seasoning if necessary. Serve with scallops.

SAUSAGE-AND-PEPPER STEW

SERVES 4

¾ pound hot Italian sausage
1 medium yellow onion, cut into ¼-inch-thick half-moons
1 medium green bell pepper, seeds and ribs removed, cut into ½-inch-thick strips
1 medium red bell pepper, seeds and ribs removed, cut into ½-inch-thick strips
1½ teaspoons coarse salt, plus more for seasoning
¼ teaspoon freshly ground black pepper, plus more for seasoning
1 twenty-eight-ounce can whole tomatoes, seeded and chopped
¼ cup loosely packed fresh flat-leaf parsley, coarsely chopped

1 Remove casings from sausage; crumble into 1-inch pieces. Heat a large sauté pan over medium heat. Add the sausage; cook, stirring often, until browned and cooked through, about 8 minutes. Remove the sausage from the sauté pan with a slotted spoon; set aside.
2 Pour off all but 1 tablespoon of fat from the pan. Return to medium heat; add the onion. Sauté the onion until it is just beginning to brown and soften, about 5 minutes. Add the peppers; continue to cook for 10 minutes more.
3 Add salt and pepper. Add tomatoes; bring to a boil, and then lower to a simmer until vegetables are tender and the sauce has reduced and thickened slightly, about 12 minutes more.
4 Return sausage to pan; cook just enough to heat through. Stir in parsley; adjust seasoning with salt and pepper.

GRAPES WITH SOUR CREAM AND BROWN SUGAR

SERVES 4

We used red grapes, but green grapes can be substituted or used in addition. Make sure to use seedless grapes.

1 large bunch seedless red grapes
1 cup sour cream
2 tablespoons light-brown sugar

1 Wash the grapes; remove from stems. Transfer to the refrigerator to chill.

2 Whisk the sour cream in a small bowl. Place the grapes in serving dishes. Spoon the sour cream over the grapes, and sprinkle with the brown sugar.

FIT TO EAT: BETA-CAROTENE

BAKED SWEET POTATOES WITH CARAMELIZED ONIONS AND SHAVED PARMESAN

SERVES 6 | PHOTOGRAPH ON PAGE 266

6 medium sweet potatoes (8 ounces each)
1 tablespoon unsalted butter
4 large yellow onions, cut into ½-inch-thick half-moons
3 tablespoons sugar
1 teaspoon coarse salt
¼ teaspoon freshly ground pepper
2 tablespoons balsamic vinegar
1½ ounces freshly shaved Parmesan cheese (about ½ cup)

1 Preheat oven to 450°F. Place potatoes on a baking sheet; bake until tender, about 45 minutes. Meanwhile, melt butter in a large nonstick skillet over medium-low heat. Add onions; cook until soft, about 15 minutes. Sprinkle with sugar, salt, and pepper; toss to coat. Continue to cook, stirring occasionally, until onions are very soft and caramelized, about 1 hour more, adding water a tablespoon at a time if pan dries out. Stir in vinegar. Set aside; keep warm.

2 When potatoes are tender, split open, and top with caramelized onions and shaved Parmesan. Serve warm.

PER SERVING: 293 CALORIES, 5 G FAT, 13 MG CHOLESTEROL, 58 G CARBOHYDRATE, 124 MG SODIUM, 7 G PROTEIN, 3 G FIBER

SPINACH ROULADE

SERVES 6 | PHOTOGRAPH ON PAGE 266

6 tablespoons all-purpose flour, plus more for baking sheet
1½ cups skim milk
½ cup water
3 tablespoons unsalted butter
1½ teaspoons coarse salt
Pinch of cayenne pepper
2 large egg yolks
8 large egg whites
Pinch of cream of tartar
½ cup (1½ ounces) grated Parmesan cheese
2 pounds spinach, washed, large stems removed
1 onion, finely diced
16 ounces fat-free ricotta cheese
¼ teaspoon freshly ground black pepper
1 tablespoon heavy cream
Tomato-Pepper Sauce (recipe follows, optional)
Vegetable-oil cooking spray

1 Preheat oven to 400°F. Coat a 10-by-15-inch rimmed baking sheet with cooking spray, and line with parchment. Coat and flour parchment; shake off excess flour.

2 Heat milk in a saucepan until hot but not boiling; set aside. Place flour in an airtight container with water; shake until dissolved. Set aside. Heat 2 tablespoons butter in a medium saucepan over medium heat. Add flour mixture. Whisking constantly, cook until roux is lightly colored, 1 to 2 minutes. Whisk in hot milk. Cook, stirring constantly, until thick, about 3 minutes more. Remove from heat; season with 1 teaspoon salt and the cayenne. Lightly beat yolks in a bowl; gradually whisk some milk mixture into yolks to warm them. Whisk yolk mixture back into milk; set pan aside.

3 In a medium bowl, whisk egg whites until foamy. Add cream of tartar, and whisk until smooth, firm peaks form. Stir a quarter of whites and ¼ cup Parmesan into milk mixture; gently fold in remaining whites. Pour mixture onto prepared baking sheet; spread to fill all corners. Sprinkle with remaining ¼ cup Parmesan. Bake until top is browned and puffed, about 15 minutes. Remove from oven; let cool. Carefully invert onto a parchment-lined work surface; gently remove paper from bottom; set aside.

4 Bring a large saucepan of water to a boil. Fill a large bowl with ice and water; set aside. Add spinach to boiling water in bunches; cook until bright green and wilted, about 1 minute. Transfer to ice bath to stop the cooking. Transfer to a colander to drain; squeeze out excess water. Very finely chop spinach; set aside in a bowl.

5 Coat a baking sheet that is at least 15 inches long with cooking spray; set aside. Heat remaining tablespoon butter in a nonstick skillet over medium heat. Add onion; cook, stirring occasionally, until tender, about 10 minutes. Remove from heat; transfer to the bowl with the spinach. Add ricotta; season with remaining ½ teaspoon salt and black pepper. Stir until well combined. Spread filling over cooled soufflé base. Using parchment as a guide, roll soufflé tightly, starting with a long side; transfer carefully to baking sheet, seam side down. Brush with cream; bake until filling is heated through and soufflé is light golden, 25 to 30 minutes. Slice; serve hot or at room temperature with sauce, if using.

PER SERVING: 288 CALORIES, 11 G FAT, 110 MG CHOLESTEROL, 21 G CARBOHYDRATE, 615 MG SODIUM, 25 G PROTEIN, 4 G FIBER

TOMATO-PEPPER SAUCE

MAKES ABOUT 1 QUART

4 red bell peppers
1 tablespoon extra-virgin olive oil
1 onion, coarsely chopped
4 garlic cloves, minced
¼ teaspoon crushed red-pepper flakes
1 twenty-eight-ounce can crushed tomatoes
1 six-ounce can tomato sauce
1 14½-ounce can low-sodium chicken stock or Homemade Chicken Stock (page 8), skimmed of fat
3 sprigs oregano
Coarse salt, for seasoning
Pinch of freshly ground black pepper

1 Place bell peppers directly over a gas-stove burner on high heat. As each section turns puffy and black, turn with tongs to prevent overcooking. (Alternatively, place peppers on a baking sheet; broil in oven, turning as each side becomes charred.) Transfer to a large bowl; cover with plastic wrap. Let sweat until cool enough to handle,

about 15 minutes. Transfer to a work surface. Peel off and discard the blackened skin. Halve peppers; discard the seeds. Roughly chop the flesh, and set aside.
2 Heat the oil in a large saucepan over medium-low heat. Add the onion, garlic, and pepper flakes. Cook until the onion is tender, about 8 minutes. Add the tomatoes, tomato sauce, stock, oregano, and reserved peppers. Bring to a gentle simmer; cook until slightly thickened, 15 to 20 minutes. Season with salt and pepper; serve. The sauce can be made ahead and refrigerated for up to 2 days, or frozen for up to a month.

PER SERVING: 92 CALORIES, 3 G FAT, 0 MG CHOLESTEROL, 14 G CARBOHYDRATE, 703 MG SODIUM, 3 G PROTEIN, 4 G FIBER

WHOLE-WHEAT PENNE WITH BUTTERNUT SQUASH AND BEET GREENS

SERVES 6 | PHOTOGRAPH ON PAGE 266

Roast leftover beets to serve along with the pasta: Peel and cut into thin wedges, drizzle with a tablespoon of olive oil, season with salt and pepper, and roast in a 400°F oven until tender, about 30 minutes.

16 ounces whole-wheat penne, or other pasta
2 tablespoons unsalted butter
1 onion, cut into slivers
1 small butternut squash (1½ to 2 pounds), peeled, seeded, and cut into ½-inch dice
8 ounces shiitake mushrooms, wiped clean, stems removed, cut into ¼-inch-thick slices
¼ cup dry sherry
3 cups Homemade Chicken Stock (page 8) or low-sodium canned, skimmed of fat
3 ounces beet greens, from 1 bunch beets (or red or green Swiss chard), tough stems removed, cut into ½-inch strips
1 teaspoon coarse salt
¼ teaspoon freshly ground pepper
2 ounces low-fat goat cheese, crumbled

1 Bring a saucepan of water to a boil. Add the pasta; cook until al dente, according to the package directions. Drain; set aside, covered with plastic wrap.
2 Heat butter in a large skillet over medium-low heat. Add onion; cook until translucent, about 10 minutes. Add squash; cook until slightly softened, about 10 minutes. Add mushrooms; cook until tender, about 5 minutes. Add sherry; cook until the liquid evaporates. Add the stock; cook until the vegetables are tender and the stock is reduced by half, 15 to 20 minutes. Stir in greens, and cook until wilted, about 3 minutes. Add the pasta, salt, and pepper; toss to combine. Serve topped with cheese.

PER SERVING: 425 CALORIES, 8 G FAT, 14 MG CHOLESTEROL, 70 G CARBOHYDRATE, 523 MG SODIUM, 17 G PROTEIN, 12 G FIBER

CARROT SOUP

SERVES 6

1 tablespoon unsalted butter
1 onion, coarsely chopped
1 pound carrots, chopped
2 cups (16 ounces) freshly made or store-bought carrot juice
1 14½-ounce can low-sodium canned chicken stock, or Homemade Chicken Stock (page 8), skimmed of fat, or more for thinning
½ teaspoon ground cumin
1 tablespoon honey
2 teaspoons coarse salt
¼ teaspoon ground white pepper
2 tablespoons half-and-half (optional)
Chopped fresh chives, for garnish
Cayenne pepper, for garnish

1 Heat butter in a large saucepan over medium-low heat. Add onion; cook until translucent, about 5 minutes. Add carrots; cook until very tender, about 15 minutes. Do not brown. Add carrot juice, stock, cumin, honey, salt, and white pepper. Bring to a simmer; cook until vegetables are very soft, about 30 minutes.
2 Remove from the heat; cool slightly. Purée in batches in a blender or food processor, filling no more than halfway. Return soup to pan, and warm over low heat, thinning with stock or water if needed. Stir in the half-and-half, if using. Garnish with chives and cayenne, and serve.

PER SERVING: 116 CALORIES, 3 G FAT, 8 MG CHOLESTEROL, 21 G CARBOHYDRATE, 551 MG SODIUM, 2 G PROTEIN, 3 G FIBER

BRAISED ESCAROLE WITH CURRANTS

SERVES 6 | PHOTOGRAPH ON PAGE 266

1 tablespoon extra-virgin olive oil
½ teaspoon crushed red-pepper flakes
4 garlic cloves, thinly sliced
1 ounce (about ⅓ cup) slivered almonds
4 anchovy fillets, rinsed (optional)
¼ cup dry sherry
½ cup Homemade Chicken Stock (page 8) or low-sodium canned, skimmed of fat
1 tablespoon dark-brown sugar
2 bunches (about 2½ pounds) escarole, cleaned, drained, and torn into 2-inch pieces
¼ cup currants

1 Heat oil in a large, high-sided skillet over medium-low heat. Add pepper flakes; stir until fragrant, about 1 minute. Add garlic and almonds; cook until light golden, about 3 minutes. Add anchovies, if using; stir until mashed and well combined with the oil mixture. Add sherry; cook until most liquid has evaporated. Add stock and sugar; stir until sugar has dissolved.
2 Add escarole in batches, tossing and adding more as it wilts until all has been added to the pan. Cover; cook over low heat, stirring occasionally, until wilted.
3 Add currants; cook until escarole is tender, about 10 minutes more. Serve.

PER SERVING: 112 CALORIES, 5 G FAT, 0 MG CHOLESTEROL, 11 G CARBOHYDRATE, 175 MG SODIUM, 4 G PROTEIN, 6 G FIBER

APPLE PRALINE TART | **PAGE 249**

MAKING BISCUITS

1 To prepare biscuit dough, mix the dry ingredients with a whisk to distribute the leavening, salt, and sugar evenly throughout the flour.

2 Cut cold butter into the dry ingredients with a chilled pastry blender or two knives.

3 When the mixture resembles coarse crumbs, add the wet ingredients.

4 Knead the dough until it gathers together. Lay the dough on a lightly floured surface, and gently pat it out to a 1-inch thickness.

5 Cut the dough into rounds using a lightly floured 2½-inch round biscuit cutter or cookie cutter.

BACON-AND-ONION CORNMEAL DROP-BISCUIT | PAGE 250

HERBED BAKING-POWDER BISCUITS | PAGE 250

ANGEL BISCUITS | PAGE 249

LAYERED BISCUITS | PAGE 250

CHEDDAR BUTTERMILK BISCUIT | PAGE 249

WHOLE-WHEAT PENNE WITH BUTTERNUT
SQUASH AND BEET GREENS | **PAGE 262**

BAKED SWEET POTATOES WITH CARMELIZED
ONIONS AND SHAVED PARMESAN | **PAGE 261**

SPINACH ROULADE | **PAGE 261**

BRAISED ESCAROLE WITH CURRANTS | **PAGE 262**

PEELING CHESTNUTS

1 | Using a sharp knife, make an incision about ⅛ inch deep through each chestnut shell, just into the flesh of the nut, and work your way almost around its circumference.

2 | After slitting the shells, transfer the chestnuts to a chestnut roasting pan or a rimmed baking sheet, and roast them in a 350°F oven for about 35 minutes.

3 | While the chestnuts are hot, remove and discard each shell and papery skin.

LAMB AND CHESTNUT STEW | **PAGE 258**

PERCIATELLI WITH ROASTED CHESTNUTS, BUTTERNUT SQUASH, AND GOAT CHEESE | **PAGE 258**

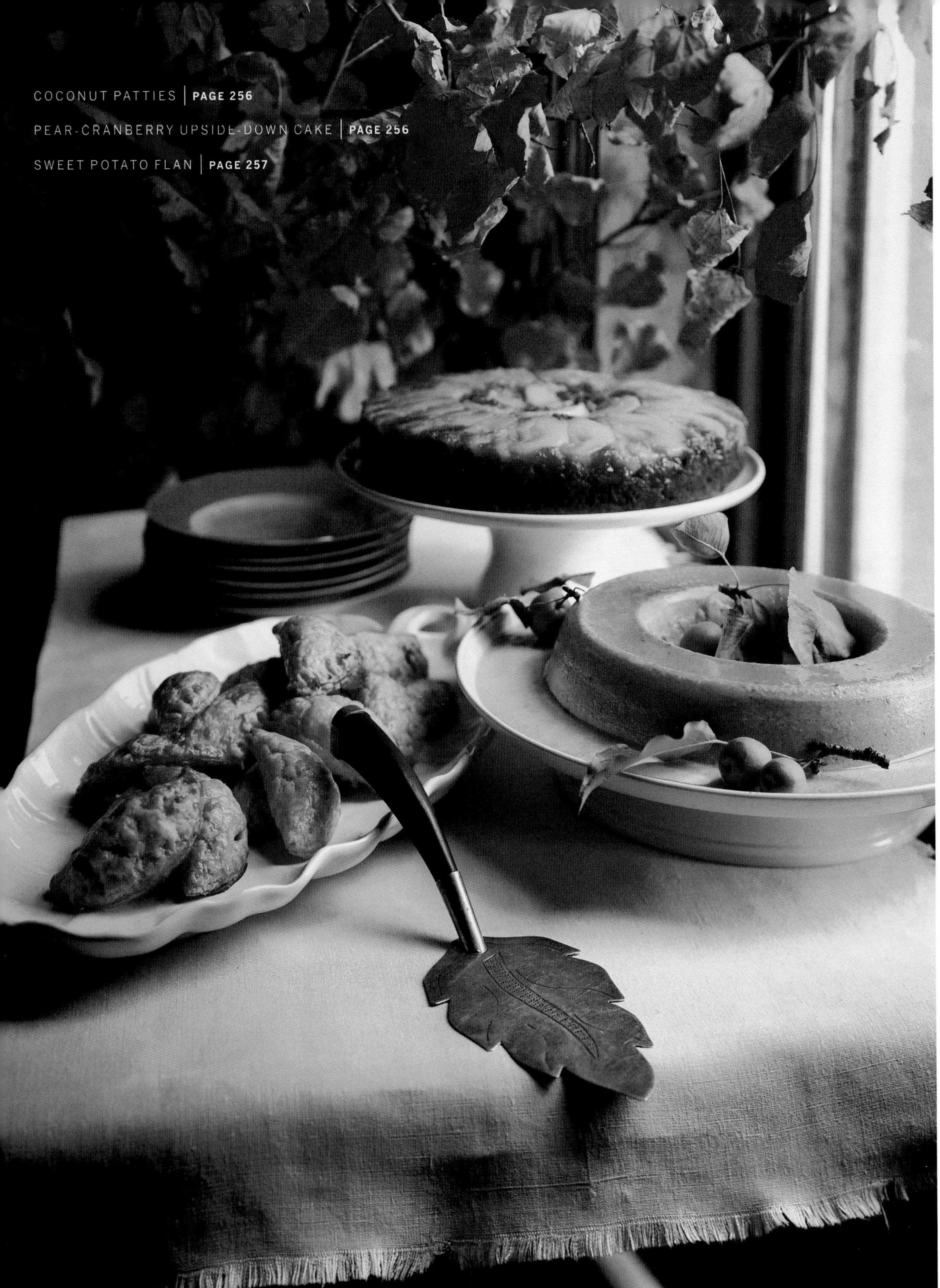

december

Zuccotto

Cranberry Caramel

Nut Brittle

Almond Croquant

Chocolate Macadamia-Nut Brittle

Toffee-Coated Popcorn Balls

Mixed-Nut Nougat

Chocolate-Pecan Butter Crunch

Chewy Nut Toffees

Gravlax

Gravlax with Curry Waffles

Gravlax with Boiled Potatoes and
Mustard Sauce

Cioppino

Roasted Poussins

White Beans with Gremolata

Roasted Baby Artichokes, Asparagus,
and Fennel with Olives

Citrus Tart

Mushroom Soup with Cracked Wheat

Roast Duck with Cherry Sauce

Carrot, Parsnip, and Pea Gratin

Lettuce, Red Cabbage, and Apple
Salad with Blue Cheese

Stollen Wreath

Oyster Stew

Pork Chops with Andouille-Pecan
Stuffing

Wilted Mustard Greens

Individual Maque Choux Puddings

Bread Pudding Soufflé with Whiskey
Sauce

Large-Quantity Guacamole

Spice-Rubbed Roasted Rack of
Venison

Four-Onion and Jalapeño Confit

Stewed Frijoles

Chile-Cheese Tamales

Sautéed Green Beans and Chayote
with Toasted Pine Nuts

Christmas Cornbread

Biscochitos

Mexican Hot Chocolate

Nutcracker Cookies

Marshmallow Mice

Seville Orange Chocolate Cake

Chocolate Mousse Cake

Chocolate Almonds

(continued on next page)

(continued from page 271)

Arabic Coffee

Turkish Delight

Coconut Sweetmeats

Baklava

Green Tea Sorbet

Chinese Hat Tuiles

White Russian Eggnog

Marzipan Cherries

Gingerbread Petits Fours

Sugar Plum Fairy

Chicory Salad with Lemon-Anchovy
    Vinaigrette

Chicken Livers with Shallots and
    Marsala

Creamy Polenta with Bacon and Sage

Roasted Pears with Pecorino Cheese

Scallops in White Wine

Warm Thai Squid and Shrimp Salad

Rolled Fillets of Sole

Mediterranean Vegetables

Steamed Chicken with Roasted
    Peppers and Prosciutto

Chestnut Chocolate Layer Cake

Chestnut Truffles

Chestnut Apple Strudel

Classic Light Rolls

Buttery Crescents

Twice Baked Potatoes

Mashed Potatoes 101

Glazed Ham 101

Roast Chicken 101

Perfect Roast Turkey 101

Classic Stuffing

Double Hot Chocolate Pudding

Date and Pine-Nut Tart

Three-Cheese Cake

DESSERT OF THE MONTH

ZUCCOTTO

SERVES 10 TO 12 | PHOTOGRAPH
ON PAGE 310

*If omitting the liqueur, substitute
a quarter cup water.*

4 ounces hazelnuts, plus more for garnish

½ cup sugar

¼ cup water

¼ cup Framboise or other
raspberry liqueur (optional)

Sponge Cake (recipe follows)

2 cups chilled heavy cream

¼ cup confectioners' sugar

4 ounces coarsely chopped chocolate-
covered toffee bars, such as Skor
or Heath, plus more for garnish

4 ounces (1 pint) raspberries,
plus more for garnish

Chocolate Ganache Icing I
(recipe follows)

Vanilla Bean Crème Anglaise
(recipe follows)

1 Preheat the oven to 350°F. Place the hazelnuts in a single layer on a rimmed baking sheet; toast until the skins begin to split, about 10 minutes. Rub the warm nuts vigorously with a clean kitchen towel to remove the skins. Return to the baking sheet; toast until fragrant and golden brown, about 1 minute more. Let cool; coarsely chop, and set aside.

2 Combine the sugar, water, and liqueur, if using, in a small saucepan. Bring to a boil, and stir until the sugar has dissolved. Remove from the heat, and set aside to cool completely. Line a domed metal or glass bowl that is about 9 inches in diameter and about 5 inches deep with plastic wrap.

3 Cut the rectangular sponge cake into thirds crosswise and lengthwise, making 9 rectangles. Reserve the round sponge cake layer to use on the top. Cut each rectangle diagonally in half, forming 18 triangles. Brush both sides of each triangle with some of the syrup. Line the inside of the mold with the triangle slices, pointed ends facing the bottom of the mold, to form a sunburst pattern. Fit the slices snugly so that the mold is completely lined. Use small pieces of syrup-

brushed cake to fill in any gaps. Trim the top to make it even. Transfer the lined mold to the refrigerator.

4 Place the cream and confectioners' sugar in the bowl of an electric mixer fitted with the whisk attachment. Beat on medium speed until stiff, about 3 minutes. Gently fold in the reserved hazelnuts, the toffee candy, and the raspberries. Remove the lined mold from the refrigerator, fill with the cream mixture, and cover the top with the cake round. This will become the bottom of the zuccotto when it is unmolded. Cover with plastic wrap, and refrigerate at least 12 hours or overnight.

5 Place a wire rack on top of the bowl, and invert the zuccotto onto the rack. Place on a rimmed baking sheet. Remove the bowl and plastic wrap. Using a ladle, pour the ganache over the top of the dome, letting the excess drip down the sides onto the rack. Make sure to coat the entire surface of the zuccotto. Cut into wedges. Ladle with the crème anglaise. Serve immediately, garnished with chopped toffee, nuts, and berries.

SPONGE CAKE

MAKES 1 ELEVEN-BY-SEVENTEEN-INCH
SHEET AND 1 NINE-INCH ROUND CAKE

Unsalted butter, room temperature,
for pans

¾ cup all-purpose flour, plus more for pans

¾ cup cornstarch

6 large eggs, separated

1½ teaspoons pure vanilla extract

¾ cup plus 6 tablespoons sugar

¼ teaspoon table salt

1 Preheat the oven to 350°F. Butter the bottom and sides of an 11-by-17-inch rimmed baking sheet and a 9-inch round cake pan. Line the bottom of each pan with parchment paper, and butter again. Flour the pans, and set aside. In a small bowl, sift together the flour and cornstarch; set aside.

2 In the bowl of an electric mixer fitted with the whisk attachment, beat the egg yolks, vanilla, and ¾ cup sugar on high speed until thick and pale, about 3 minutes. Transfer the egg-yolk mixture to a large bowl. Wash and dry the mixer bowl and the whisk attachment.

3 Combine the egg whites and salt in the mixer bowl, and beat on medium speed until soft peaks form, about 1½ minutes. With the mixer running, slowly add the remaining 6 tablespoons sugar. Continue beating until stiff and glossy, about 1 minute.

4 Fold the egg-white mixture into the egg-yolk mixture. In three additions, fold the reserved flour mixture into the egg mixture. Transfer two-thirds of the batter to the baking sheet, and smooth the top with an offset spatula. Transfer the remaining batter to the round cake pan, and smooth the top with the spatula. Bake the cakes until light golden brown and a cake tester inserted into the center comes out clean, about 20 minutes. Transfer the pans to wire racks to cool; turn out the cakes, remove the parchment paper, and wrap in plastic wrap until ready to use. The cakes can be made ahead, cooled completely, and frozen for up to 2 weeks. Thaw completely at room temperature before using.

CHOCOLATE GANACHE ICING I

MAKES ABOUT 1½ CUPS

This gets thicker as it sits. You want it pourable but thick enough to fully coat the cake.

9 ounces bittersweet or semisweet chocolate

1½ cups heavy cream

Finely chop the chocolate, and place in a medium bowl. Heat the cream in a small saucepan until bubbles begin to appear around the edges (scalding); pour over the chocolate. Let stand 5 minutes, then stir until smooth. Set aside at room temperature until cool but still pourable, stirring occasionally.

VANILLA BEAN CREME ANGLAISE

MAKES 2 CUPS

4 large egg yolks

¼ cup sugar

1 cup milk

¾ cup heavy cream

½ vanilla bean, split lengthwise

1 Fill a large bowl with ice and water; set aside. In a medium bowl, whisk together the egg yolks and sugar until light-

ened in color, about 2 minutes. Place the milk and heavy cream in a medium saucepan over medium heat; scrape the vanilla seeds into the pan, and add the pod. Bring to a simmer; reduce heat to low. Whisk about ⅓ cup of the milk mixture into the egg-yolk mixture to temper it. Return this mixture to the saucepan.

2 Cook the crème anglaise over medium heat, stirring constantly with a wooden spoon, until the mixture thickens to the consistency of heavy cream. Discard the vanilla pod, and strain the crème anglaise into a medium metal bowl. Place the bowl over the ice bath to chill until ready to serve. Can be stored in an airtight plastic container, refrigerated, for up to 4 days.

GOOD THINGS

CRANBERRY CARAMEL
MAKES 2 CUPS

2 cups sugar
½ cup water
1 cup cranberries
4 tablespoons unsalted butter

In a medium saucepan over medium-high heat, dissolve the sugar in the water. Bring to a boil. Using a pastry brush dipped in water, brush away any sugar crystals on the side of the pan to prevent crystallization. Cook the sugar until medium amber, and remove from the heat. Add the cranberries and 2 tablespoons butter, and stir until some of the cranberries begin to break up. Add the remaining 2 tablespoons butter, and stir to combine. Allow to cool slightly, and place in jars. Let cool completely; cover with lids. Caramel will keep in the refrigerator for up to 2 weeks. Reheat in the microwave or a small saucepan until it has a caramel consistency.

BRITTLES AND TOFFEES

NUT BRITTLE
MAKES 1 NINE-BY-THIRTEEN-INCH PAN | **PHOTOGRAPHS ON PAGES 308, 309**

Although peanut brittle may be the most common, you can also use other whole nuts, such as cashews, hazelnuts, almonds, or pecans, as well as pumpkin seeds. For a Caribbean twist, add 1 cup shredded coconut, and replace the peanuts with cashews.

Unsalted butter, room temperature, for baking sheet
1½ cups sugar
½ cup light corn syrup
¾ cup cold water
Pinch of table salt
2½ cups dry-roasted peanuts
1 teaspoon pure vanilla extract
1 teaspoon baking soda
Vegetable oil, for spatula

1 Brush a 9-by-13-inch rimmed baking sheet with butter; set aside. Combine the sugar, corn syrup, water, and salt in a medium saucepan. Bring to a boil over medium-high heat, stirring until the sugar has dissolved. Using a pastry brush dipped in water, brush away any sugar crystals on the side of the pan to prevent crystallization. Cook, swirling occasionally, until the mixture reaches the soft-ball stage on a candy thermometer (238°F).
2 Stir in the nuts. Continue to cook, stirring often so the nuts won't burn, until mixture is golden amber.
3 Remove the pan from the heat, and carefully stir in the vanilla and baking soda. The mixture will foam up in the pan.
4 Pour the mixture onto the prepared baking sheet, and quickly spread into a ½-inch-thick layer with an oiled metal spatula. Set the tray aside until completely cool. Break brittle into pieces, and store in an airtight container at room temperature for up to a month.

ALMOND CROQUANT
MAKES 1 NINE-BY-THIRTEEN-INCH PAN

This crunchy almond brittle is commonly enjoyed in the south of France as part of "Treize Desserts," a Christmas Eve tradition of serving thirteen sweets, representing Jesus Christ and the Twelve Apostles.

Unsalted butter, room temperature, for baking sheet
1½ cups sugar
½ cup corn syrup
2 cups finely chopped blanched almonds (about 9 ounces)
Vegetable oil, for spatula

1 Brush a 9-by-13-inch rimmed baking sheet with butter; set aside. Combine the sugar and corn syrup in a medium saucepan. Bring to a boil, stirring until the sugar has dissolved. Using a pastry brush dipped in water, brush away any sugar crystals on the side of the pan to prevent crystallization. Cook, swirling occasionally, until the mixture reaches the soft-ball stage on a candy thermometer (238°F).
2 Stir in the almonds, and continue to cook, stirring occasionally, until the mixture is light amber.
3 Pour the mixture onto the prepared baking sheet, and quickly spread into a ¼-inch-thick layer with an oiled metal spatula. Let sit about 2 minutes before cutting, if desired, with a sharp, oiled knife. (Alternatively, let cool completely before breaking into pieces.) Set the tray aside until completely cool. Store in an airtight container at room temperature for up to a month.

VARIATION: SESAME SEED CRUNCH

To make sesame-seed crunch, substitute 1½ cups toasted sesame seeds for the chopped almonds. Stir in 2 teaspoons of freshly squeezed lemon juice before pouring the mixture onto the prepared pan.

CHOCOLATE MACADAMIA-NUT BRITTLE

MAKES 1 NINE-BY-THIRTEEN-INCH PAN

3 tablespoons unsalted butter, room temperature, plus more for pan

1 cup coarsely chopped macadamia nuts (about 4½ ounces)

1½ cups sugar

½ cup light corn syrup

½ cup water

½ cup finely chopped semisweet chocolate (about 2¼ ounces)

Vegetable oil, for spatula

1   Brush a 9-by-13-inch rimmed baking sheet with butter. Sprinkle the chopped nuts over the baking sheet; set aside.

2   Combine the sugar, corn syrup, water, and butter in a medium saucepan. Cook over medium heat, stirring occasionally until the sugar has dissolved. Using a pastry brush dipped in water, brush away any sugar crystals on the side of the pan to prevent crystallization. Without stirring, continue to cook until the mixture reaches the hard-crack stage on a candy thermometer (300°F).

3   Remove the pan from the heat. Add the chocolate while stirring constantly.

4   Pour the mixture into the prepared rimmed baking sheet. Spread into a thin layer using an oiled metal spatula. Let cool completely. Break into pieces, and store in an airtight container at room temperature for up to a month.

TOFFEE-COATED POPCORN BALLS

MAKES 12 THREE-INCH BALLS

We formed this Cracker Jacks–like mixture into popcorn balls. For a quick holiday party snack, pour the hot mixture onto a buttered rimmed baking sheet, and let cool; break into pieces, and serve in a bowl. Follow the manufacturer's instructions for popping corn; avoid using microwave popcorn if possible.

½ pound (2 sticks) unsalted butter, room temperature, plus more for bowl and hands

12 cups plain unsalted popped popcorn

½ cup dry-roasted peanuts

⅓ cup water

1 cup sugar

1   Brush a large metal bowl with butter. Combine the popcorn and peanuts in the buttered bowl; set aside.

2   Place the butter and water in a large saucepan. Cook over medium-high heat until the butter is melted. Add the sugar, and stir constantly until dissolved and the mixture comes to a boil. Using a pastry brush dipped in water, brush away any sugar crystals on the side of the pan to prevent crystallization. Cook until the mixture is a dark amber.

3   Remove syrup from the heat, and pour over popcorn and peanuts. Toss until well coated; set aside to cool slightly.

4   Using buttered hands, quickly form the mixture into tight balls about 3 inches in diameter. Store in an airtight container at room temperature for up to a month.

MIXED-NUT NOUGAT

MAKES 1½ DOZEN PIECES OR
1 EIGHT-INCH SQUARE

Unsalted butter, room temperature, for pan

1 cup honey

3¼ cups (about 16 ounces) mixed nuts

1   Brush 18 miniature muffin tins (about 2 inches in diameter) with butter; set aside. (Alternatively, butter an 8-inch

BRITTLES AND TOFFEES

To make brittles and toffees, you'll need a candy thermometer and a thick-bottomed saucepan large enough to hold the sugar solution, which bubbles up and expands as it boils. Assemble all ingredients in advance; the caramelization process happens quickly and calls for a vigilant eye; watch closely for the moment the correct color and temperature are reached. A common pitfall is the recrystallization of sugar, called "sugaring," triggered by crystals on the side of the pan falling into the mixture. To help prevent this, use a pastry brush dipped in water to wash down the pan's sides once the sugar has dissolved completely in the solution. Using corn syrup further helps to deter recrystallization. Always have a bowl of ice water handy in case of accidental contact with the extremely hot and sticky mixture.

square baking pan, and line the bottom with a piece of parchment paper that extends up and over two sides. Butter the parchment, and set pan aside.)

2 Place the honey in a medium saucepan, and bring to a boil over medium-high heat. Continue to cook, stirring constantly, until it reaches the hard-ball stage on a candy thermometer (260°F). The mixture will thicken and change from golden to dark amber.

3 Stir in the nuts, and immediately spoon into the prepared tins or baking pan. Let cool completely before unmolding. Unmold, and cut nougat into pieces. Store in an airtight container at room temperature for up to a month.

CHOCOLATE-PECAN BUTTER CRUNCH

MAKES 2 TO 3 DOZEN
PIECES | PHOTOGRAPH ON PAGE 308

We coated our butter crunch with a layer of melted chocolate. You can leave it unadorned and simply cut it into squares or break it into pieces when cool.

½ pound (2 sticks) unsalted butter, room temperature, plus more for pan
⅓ cup water
1 cup sugar
2 cups chopped pecans, plus more halves (optional) for top
8 ounces semisweet chocolate (optional)
2 tablespoons light corn syrup (optional)

1 Butter a 9-inch square baking pan, and line the bottom with a piece of parchment paper that extends up and over two sides. Butter the parchment, and set the pan aside.

2 Place the butter and water in a large saucepan. Cook over medium-high heat until the butter is melted. Add the sugar, and stir constantly until dissolved and the mixture comes to a boil. Using a pastry brush dipped in water, brush away any sugar crystals on the side of the pan to prevent crystallization. Cook until the mixture is a dark amber. Remove from the heat, and stir in the pecans. Pour mixture into the prepared baking pan, and let stand at room temperature to cool completely.

3 Place the chocolate and corn syrup, if using, in a small heat-proof bowl set over a pan of barely simmering water. Stir occasionally until combined and completely melted. Let cool slightly, and spread over the top of the cooled toffee. Arrange the pecan halves, if using, over the top, and cool at room temperature until the chocolate has cooled completely and set, at least 2 hours or overnight. Carefully unmold by lifting out the parchment paper. Break or cut into pieces, and store in an airtight container at room temperature for up to a month.

CHEWY NUT TOFFEES

MAKES ABOUT 75 | PHOTOGRAPH ON PAGE 309

Toffees should be individually wrapped in cellophane or waxed paper so they keep their shape. This recipe is easily doubled if you want to make extra for gifts. For plain toffees, omit the nuts.

2 cups heavy cream
½ cup sweetened condensed milk
2 cups light corn syrup
½ cup water
2 cups sugar
½ teaspoon table salt
8 tablespoons (1 stick) unsalted butter, cut into 8 pieces
1 tablespoon bourbon or pure vanilla extract
1 cup chopped nuts, such as pecans or peanuts (optional)
Vegetable-oil cooking spray

1 Coat a 9-by-13-inch pan that is at least 1½ inches deep with cooking spray. Set aside. In a 2-quart saucepan, combine the cream and condensed milk; set aside.

2 In a heavy 3- to 4-quart saucepan, combine the corn syrup, water, sugar, and salt. Clip on a candy thermometer. Over high heat, cook, stirring with a wooden spoon, until the sugar is dissolved, about 5 minutes. Using a pastry brush dipped in water, brush away any sugar crystals on the sides of the pan to prevent crystallization.

3 Stop stirring, reduce heat to medium, and bring to a boil. Cook without stirring until the temperature reaches the hard-ball stage (260°F), about 20 minutes. Meanwhile, cook the cream mixture over low heat until it is just warm; do not boil. When the sugar mixture reaches 260°F, slowly stir in the butter and warmed cream mixture, keeping the mixture boiling at all times. Stirring constantly, cook over medium heat until the mixture reaches the firm-ball stage (248°F), about 15 minutes. Stir in the bourbon or vanilla and nuts, if using. Immediately pour mixture into prepared pan without scraping pot. Let stand uncovered at room temperature for 24 hours without moving pan.

4 To cut, coat a large cutting board generously with vegetable-oil spray. Unmold the caramel from the pan onto the sprayed surface. Cut the block into the desired-size pieces, and wrap each in cellophane or waxed paper. Store in an airtight container at room temperature for up to a month.

GRAVLAX 101

GRAVLAX

SERVES 4 TO 6

½ cup coarse salt
¼ cup sugar
1 tablespoon white peppercorns, crushed
1 tablespoon coriander seeds, crushed
2 1-pound center-cut salmon fillets, skin on
2 ounces fresh dill, coarsely chopped
¼ cup aquavit or vodka

1 Combine the salt, sugar, peppercorns, and coriander seeds in a small bowl. Set aside.

2 Place the salmon fillets on a parchment-lined work surface. Remove any remaining bones from the fillets. Gently rub the spice mixture onto the flesh side of each fillet. Spread the dill on top of the spices; pour the aquavit or vodka over the dill. Place one fillet on top of the other, and wrap tightly in plastic wrap.

3 Place the wrapped fillets in a glass or enamel pan. Place a heavy object, such as a can, in a smaller pan, and place on top of the fish. Transfer both pans to the refrigerator for 12 hours.

4 Remove the fish from the pan; pour off and discard the liquid that has accumulated in the pan. Turn the fish over, and replace the weighted pan on top of the fish. Refrigerate for 3 days more, turning the fish over every 12 hours.
5 After 3 days, remove the plastic wrap and discard. Scrape the dill and spices from the surface of both fillets.
6 To serve, slice each fillet on the diagonal, as thinly as possible. Wrap the remaining gravlax in plastic wrap and refrigerate. Store for up to 3 days.

GRAVLAX WITH CURRY WAFFLES

MAKES 30 | PHOTOGRAPH ON PAGE 304

The subtle curry flavor of the waffles complements the gravlax.

Curry Waffles (recipe follows)
1 pound Gravlax (page 276), thinly sliced
¼ cup crème fraîche
4 ounces salmon roe
Fresh chives, for garnish

Top each waffle with the sliced gravlax. Garnish with the crème fraîche, salmon roe, and chives.

CURRY WAFFLES

MAKES 30

1 cup all-purpose flour
1 teaspoon curry powder
½ teaspoon baking soda
½ teaspoon baking powder
½ teaspoon sugar
½ teaspoon coarse salt
2 large eggs, separated
1 cup nonfat buttermilk
4 tablespoons unsalted butter, melted

1 Preheat the oven to 200°F with a rack in the center. Line a rimmed baking sheet with parchment paper. Transfer to the oven.
2 Heat a waffle iron. In a large bowl, sift together the flour, curry powder, baking soda, baking powder, sugar, and salt.
3 In a medium bowl, whisk together the egg yolks, buttermilk, and butter. Pour into the dry ingredients; stir until just combined.
4 In a medium bowl, beat the egg whites until stiff but not dry. Fold into the batter.

5 Pour about 1 tablespoon batter onto each section of the waffle grid. Close the lid, and bake for about 3 minutes, until no steam emerges from the iron.
6 Transfer the cooked waffles to the prepared baking sheet in the oven until ready to use.

GRAVLAX WITH BOILED POTATOES AND MUSTARD SAUCE

SERVES 4 | PHOTOGRAPH ON PAGE 304

Gravlax and potatoes are a classic pairing. This dish makes a delightful light supper.

1¼ pounds small Yukon gold potatoes, scrubbed
2½ teaspoons coarse salt
1 small shallot, finely chopped
2 teaspoons champagne vinegar
¼ teaspoon freshly ground black pepper
2 tablespoons grainy Dijon mustard
½ cup extra-virgin olive oil
1 tablespoon caper berries, coarsely chopped, plus more for garnish
1 tablespoon fresh dill, chopped, plus more for garnish
10 ounces watercress, washed and trimmed
12 ounces Gravlax (page 276), thinly sliced
8 slices pumpernickel bread

1 Place potatoes in a medium saucepan; cover with cold water by 2 inches. Add 2 teaspoons salt. Bring to a simmer. Cook potatoes until tip of knife slips in and out easily, 12 to 14 minutes. Drain potatoes in a colander; set aside.
2 Combine shallot, vinegar, remaining ½ teaspoon salt, and pepper in a bowl. Allow to macerate for 10 minutes. Whisk in mustard. Slowly whisk in olive oil until emulsified. Stir in chopped caper berries and dill. Set aside.
3 Place watercress and potatoes in a large bowl, add 6 tablespoons mustard sauce, and toss well. Serve with gravlax, pumpernickel bread, and remaining mustard sauce. Garnish with caper berries and dill.

GRAVLAX

Dressed with salt and other seasonings, drizzled with high-test liquor, and chilled, salmon fillets slowly "cook," absorbing the preserving brine. During three days of curing, the assertive fishiness of the flesh mellows pleasantly. Crushed coriander seed, white pepper, and juniper berries will add faint, exotic piney notes to your gravlax; a layer of coarsely chopped dill between two fillets will infuse the fish with a grassy, minty essence. Vodka and aquavit are the most common liquors used to cure gravlax, though cognac and gin are appropriate as well. Any variety of salmon will do, as long as it is the freshest available. Ask the fishmonger to cut your fillets from the center of a side of salmon with the skin intact, because this helps to ensure freshness and secure the fish during slicing.

four American holiday menus

SAN FRANCISCO HOLIDAY MENU

CIOPPINO

SERVES 6

This is a refined version of a hearty classic. Serve as a first course, giving each person a variety of seafood.

¼ cup extra-virgin olive oil

1 medium onion, thinly sliced

4 garlic cloves, minced

1 dried bay leaf

2 tablespoons finely chopped fresh oregano

2 tablespoons finely chopped fresh flat-leaf parsley

½ teaspoon crushed red-pepper flakes

2 cups dry white wine

2 cups fish stock

½ cup clam juice

28 ounces crushed tomatoes, with juice

15 ounces plum tomatoes, drained and coarsely chopped

6 cherrystone clams, scrubbed

6 mussels, scrubbed, debearded

6 sea scallops, muscles removed

8 ounces cod or other white fish, cut into 1-inch pieces

8 ounces cleaned squid, bodies cut into rings

6 large shrimp, peeled, (tails intact), deveined

1 Heat the olive oil in a large pot over medium-high heat. Add the onion, garlic, and bay leaf. Cook until the onion is translucent, about 5 minutes. Add the oregano, parsley, and red-pepper flakes. Cook 1 minute. Add the wine, fish stock, clam juice, and tomatoes. Reduce the heat, and simmer gently 30 minutes. (Soup can be made through this point up to 2 days ahead and refrigerated. Reheat before adding seafood.)

2 Add the clams, and cook, covered, for 10 minutes. Add the mussels, and cook, covered, checking often and using tongs to transfer the clams and mussels as they open to a bowl. Discard any that do not open. Add the scallops, cod, squid, and shrimp to the pan; simmer gently until the seafood is cooked through, about 5 minutes. Gently stir in the cooked clams and mussels; ladle into bowls, and serve.

ROASTED POUSSINS

SERVES 6 | **PHOTOGRAPH ON PAGE 304**

Poussin is the French word for a very young, small chicken. Cornish hens can also be used.

½ cup extra-virgin olive oil

¼ cup balsamic vinegar

2 tablespoons Dijon mustard

3 garlic cloves, coarsely chopped

1 tablespoon chopped chives

1 tablespoon chopped fresh thyme

1 tablespoon chopped fresh oregano

1 teaspoon dry mustard

1 teaspoon coarse salt, plus more for sprinkling

¼ teaspoon freshly ground pepper, plus more for sprinkling

3 poussins (1 to 1½ pounds each) or Cornish hens

Vegetable-oil cooking spray

1 In a small bowl whisk together the olive oil, vinegar, and mustard until well combined. Whisk in the garlic, chives, thyme, oregano, dry mustard, salt, and pepper; set aside. Rinse the poussins well under cold water. Pat dry with paper towels.

2 Using kitchen shears, cut along either side of the backbone, and remove it. Turn the poussins over, and gently flatten with your hands. Place the marinade in a large, resealable plastic bag, and add the poussins. Seal and turn the bag over to coat the poussins well with the marinade. Refrigerate at least 2 hours or overnight.

3 Preheat the oven to 400°F. Position the rack in the middle of the oven. Place a flat roasting rack in a shallow roasting pan or rimmed baking sheet. Coat the rack with cooking spray; set aside.

4 Remove the poussins from the marinade, letting the excess drip off, and place on the rack, breast side up. Tuck the wing tips under the body. Sprinkle with salt and pepper, and roast until golden and cooked through, about 50 minutes. Cut each poussin in half through the breast, and serve.

WHITE BEANS WITH GREMOLATA

SERVES 6 | **PHOTOGRAPH ON PAGE 304**

Gremolata is a garnish made from chopped parsley, garlic, and lemon zest. It is traditionally served with rich osso buco, but here we have stirred it into beans for a refreshing accompaniment to roasted poussin.

1 pound dried cannellini beans

Finely grated zest of 6 lemons (about ¼ cup)

3 garlic cloves, minced

¼ cup finely chopped fresh flat-leaf parsley

2 medium shallots, finely chopped

¼ cup extra-virgin olive oil

2 teaspoons coarse salt

½ teaspoon freshly ground pepper

1 pint assorted cherry or grape tomatoes, quartered

1 Place the beans in a large pan, and cover with water by 2 inches; soak overnight. Drain the beans, and return to the pan. Cover with water by 2 inches, and bring to a boil. Reduce to a simmer, and cook until the beans are tender, adding water if necessary, about 1 hour. Drain and transfer to a bowl to cool.

2 Meanwhile, combine the lemon zest, garlic, parsley, and shallots in a bowl. Stir in the olive oil, salt, and pepper. Stir the gremolata mixture into the cooled beans, and let sit 1 hour to allow flavors to blend. Stir in the tomatoes, and serve at room temperature.

ROASTED BABY ARTICHOKES, ASPARAGUS, AND FENNEL WITH OLIVES

SERVES 6 | PHOTOGRAPH ON PAGE 304

1 bunch (12 ounces) asparagus
2 medium fennel bulbs
8 baby artichokes
1 lemon, cut in half
1½ cups large green olives, such as Cerignola
¼ cup extra-virgin olive oil
2 tablespoons freshly squeezed lemon juice
1 teaspoon coarse salt
¼ teaspoon freshly ground pepper

1 Preheat the oven to 375°F. Trim the ends of the asparagus, and cut the stalks into 3-inch lengths. Place in a large bowl, and set aside.
2 Trim the leaves from the fennel; cut the bulbs in half and then into thin wedges. Add to the bowl with the asparagus.
3 Remove and discard any tough outer leaves from the artichokes. Cut into quarters, and remove and discard the purple choke. Rub the artichokes all over with the cut lemon to prevent browning; add artichokes to the bowl with the the other vegetables. Add the olives, olive oil, lemon juice, salt, and pepper; toss to combine well.
4 Transfer to a large roasting pan or rimmed baking sheet. Roast until the vegetables are tender and just starting to brown, about 30 minutes. Serve hot or at room temperature.

CITRUS TART

MAKES 1 NINE-INCH TART

Look for orange marmalade that has long strips of zest.

All-purpose flour, for work surface
Pâte Sucrée (recipe follows)
Zest of 1 orange (about 1 tablespoon)
Zest of 2 lemons (about 1 tablespoon)
½ cup freshly squeezed orange juice
½ cup freshly squeezed lemon juice
¾ cup sugar
¼ cup plus 2 tablespoons crème fraîche or sour cream
6 large eggs
½ cup orange marmalade

1 Lightly flour a clean work surface. Roll out the pâte sucrée to ⅛-inch thickness. Place the dough in the bottom of a 9-inch tart pan with a removable bottom; transfer to the refrigerator for 30 minutes.
2 Preheat the oven to 375°F. Remove the tart pan from the refrigerator, and place on a baking sheet. Using a fork, prick the crust all over. Carefully line the pastry with parchment paper, pressing it into the corners and edges, and weigh down with uncooked beans, rice, or aluminum or ceramic weights. Bake about 20 minutes. Remove the foil and weights, and continue baking until the crust is light golden, about 10 minutes more. Transfer to a wire rack to cool for 15 minutes.
3 Whisk together the orange and lemon zest, orange juice and lemon juice, and sugar in a medium bowl. Whisk in the crème fraîche until well combined. Whisk in the eggs until well blended. Pour the mixture into the tart shell, carefully return tart to the oven, and bake until the filling is set, 25 to 30 minutes. Do not let it brown. Transfer to a wire rack, and let cool to room temperature.
4 Place the marmalade in a small saucepan, and stir over low heat until melted. Let cool a few minutes; spread over the cooled tart, forming an even layer. Serve at room temperature or chilled.

PATE SUCREE

MAKES ENOUGH FOR 1 NINE-INCH TART

1¼ cups all-purpose flour
1½ tablespoons sugar
8 tablespoons (1 stick) chilled unsalted butter, cut into pieces
1 large egg yolk, lightly beaten
2 tablespoons ice water

1 In the bowl of a food processor, pulse the flour and sugar to combine. Add chilled butter; pulse until the mixture resembles coarse meal, about 15 seconds.
2 In a bowl, lightly beat egg yolk with ice water. With machine running, add egg mixture in a slow, steady stream; process until dough just holds together. Transfer dough to a piece of plastic wrap. Press into a flattened disk; wrap in plastic. Chill at least 1 hour. Store up to 2 days refrigerated or 1 month frozen.

CHICAGO HOLIDAY MENU

MUSHROOM SOUP WITH CRACKED WHEAT

SERVES 6 TO 8 | PHOTOGRAPH ON PAGE 305

1 cup uncooked cracked wheat, such as wheat berries
3 tablespoons unsalted butter
1 onion, cut into ½-inch dice
2 carrots, cut into ½-inch dice
3 celery stalks, cut into ½-inch dice
2 pounds assorted mushrooms, such as cremini, button, or shiitake, stems trimmed, coarsely chopped
⅓ cup dry sherry
6 cups Homemade Beef Stock (page 11) or canned
2 sprigs thyme
2 sprigs rosemary
Coarse salt and freshly ground pepper

1 Bring a medium saucepan of water to a boil. Stir in the wheat; reduce the heat to a simmer, and cook, stirring occasionally, until just tender, 30 to 40 minutes. Drain and set aside.
2 Meanwhile, heat the butter in a large saucepan over medium-high heat. Add the onion, and cook about 4 minutes. Add the carrots and celery, and cook until softened. Add the mushrooms, and cook, stirring occasionally, until the mushrooms are tender, have released all their liquid, and most of the liquid has evaporated, about 15 minutes.
3 Add the sherry, and scrape the bottom of the pan with a wooden spoon to loosen any browned bits. Cook until most of the sherry has evaporated, about 2 minutes. Add the stock, thyme, and rosemary, and bring to a boil. Reduce to a gentle simmer, and cook 30 minutes to let flavors blend.
4 Stir in the cooked wheat, season with salt and pepper, and serve.

ROAST DUCK WITH CHERRY SAUCE

SERVES 6 | **PHOTOGRAPHS ON PAGES 304, 305**

1 duck (4 to 5 pounds), fresh or frozen, thawed, neck and gizzard reserved

1 lemon, cut into wedges

2 onions, 1 cut into 8 wedges, 1 cut into ¼-inch dice

4 tablespoons unsalted butter, room temperature

Coarse salt and freshly ground pepper

1 carrot, cut into ¼-inch dice

1 celery stalk, cut into ¼-inch dice

1 teaspoon freshly grated ginger

⅓ cup cider vinegar

3 tablespoons brandy

2 cups Homemade Beef Stock (page 11) or canned

2¼ cups water

10 ounces frozen cherries

2 tablespoons all-purpose flour

1 Preheat the oven to 450°F. Cut off the duck wing tips at the joint. Place the neck, gizzard, and wing tips in a medium saucepan; set aside. Trim the excess fat from the cavity of the duck. Rinse the duck well under cold water, and pat dry with paper towels. Fill the cavity with the lemon and onion wedges. Tie the legs together with kitchen string. Rub the skin with 2 tablespoons butter, and sprinkle with salt and pepper. Place in a roasting pan, and transfer to the oven. Roast the duck until deep brown and cooked through, about 1 hour. Cover with foil if it starts to brown too quickly.

2 While the duck is roasting, make the sauce: Add the diced onion, carrot, celery, ginger, cider vinegar, brandy, stock, and 2 cups water to saucepan with duck parts. Bring to a boil, reduce the heat, and simmer 1 hour. Remove duck pieces from the sauce and discard. Add the cherries; bring to a simmer. Place the flour in a tightly sealed jar or container with the remaining ¼ cup water; shake to dissolve. Stir into the simmering sauce, and cook until slightly reduced and thickened. Stir in the remaining 2 tablespoons butter; season with salt and pepper. Keep warm. Transfer the duck to a platter; let rest 10 minutes before carving. Serve with the sauce.

CARROT, PARSNIP, AND PEA GRATIN

SERVES 6 | **PHOTOGRAPHS ON PAGES 304, 305**

Butter, for baking dish

5 large carrots, cut diagonally into 1-inch pieces

5 large parsnips, cut diagonally into 1-inch pieces

10 ounces frozen peas, thawed

10 ounces frozen pearl onions, thawed

1 cup heavy cream

Coarse salt and freshly ground pepper

Preheat the oven to 375°F. Butter a 2-quart gratin or baking dish. Place the carrots, parsnips, peas, and onions in a medium bowl. Pour in the cream, and season well with salt and pepper. Toss until well combined. Pour into the prepared baking dish, and bake, stirring halfway through, until bubbly and golden brown, 40 to 50 minutes. Serve immediately.

LETTUCE, RED CABBAGE, AND APPLE SALAD WITH BLUE CHEESE

SERVES 6 | **PHOTOGRAPHS ON PAGES 304, 305**

1 red apple, cored and cut into ¼-inch-thick wedges

1 green apple, cored and cut into ¼-inch-thick wedges

Juice of 2 lemons (about 3 tablespoons)

½ head red cabbage, cored and shredded

1 head green lettuce, torn into bite-size pieces

Extra-virgin olive oil

Coarse salt and freshly ground pepper

4 ounces Maytag or other blue cheese, crumbled

Place the apples in a medium bowl, and toss well with the lemon juice; set aside. In another bowl, combine the cabbage and lettuce. Drizzle with olive oil, and season with salt and pepper; toss well to combine. Arrange the lettuce and cabbage on a platter, top with the apples, and serve, garnished with blue cheese.

STOLLEN WREATH

MAKES 1 LARGE WREATH OR 2 BRAIDS | **PHOTOGRAPH ON PAGE 305**

This yeasty fruit bread, originating in Dresden, Germany, is a Christmastime specialty served not only for dessert but for breakfast as well.

½ cup raisins

½ cup currants

1 cup mixed candied citrus peel, finely chopped

½ cup candied angelica, finely chopped

½ cup candied cherries, finely chopped

½ cup dark rum

¼ cup lukewarm water (110°F to 115°F)

2 packages active dry yeast (5 teaspoons)

½ cup plus a pinch of granulated sugar

1 cup blanched slivered almonds

5½ cups plus 2 tablespoons all-purpose flour

1 cup plus 2 tablespoons milk

½ teaspoon table salt

½ teaspoon pure almond extract

Finely grated zest of 1 lemon

2 large eggs, room temperature

12 tablespoons (1½ sticks) unsalted butter, cut into ¼-inch pieces, room temperature, plus 3 tablespoons melted

1 cup confectioners' sugar

1 Combine the raisins, currants, citrus peel, angelica, and cherries in a small bowl. Add the rum, tossing to coat fruits evenly. Soak at least 1 hour, stirring occasionally.

2 Pour the water into a small bowl, and sprinkle with the yeast and a pinch of sugar. Let stand 2 to 3 minutes, then stir to dissolve the yeast completely. Set aside until the mixture has almost doubled in bulk, about 5 minutes. Meanwhile, drain the fruit, reserving the rum; carefully pat the fruit dry with a paper towel. Place the fruit back in the bowl, add the almonds, and sprinkle with 2 tablespoons flour. Toss to coat evenly; set aside.

3 In a heavy saucepan, combine 1 cup milk, ½ cup granulated sugar, and salt. Heat until warm (110°F to 115°F), stirring until the sugar is dissolved. Transfer the liquid to the bowl of an electric mixer fitted with the paddle attachment, and add the reserved rum, the almond extract, and the lemon zest. Stir to combine. Stir in the yeast mixture and eggs. Gradually add 5 cups flour, 1 cup at a time, and beat until combined. Beat in the softened butter until well incorporated. Turn the dough out onto a surface that has been dusted with the remaining ½ cup flour. Knead the dough until all the flour is incorporated and the dough is smooth and elastic, about 5 minutes. Flour hands if dough gets sticky. Knead in one-third of the dried-fruit mixture until incorporated. Brush a large bowl with 1 teaspoon melted butter, and drop in the dough. Brush the top of the dough with 2 teaspoons melted butter, drape a kitchen towel over the bowl, and set in a warm, draft-free place to rise until doubled in bulk, about 2 hours.

4 Preheat the oven to 375°F. Line a large baking sheet with parchment paper; set aside. Punch the dough down, and roll into a long rectangle about 16 by 24 inches and ¼ inch thick. Sprinkle the remaining dried fruit over the pastry. Starting with a long side, roll up tightly, forming a long, thin cylinder. Carefully transfer the dough to the baking sheet, and join the ends together, pinching together with fingers if necessary to make it stick, forming a large circle.

5 Using sharp kitchen scissors or a knife, make cuts along the outside of the circle, in 2-inch intervals, cutting two-thirds of the way through the dough. Twist each segment outward, forming a wreath shape with all of the segments overlapping. Brush the dough with the remaining 2 tablespoons melted butter.

6 Cover the pastry with a clean kitchen towel, and set aside to rise for 30 minutes. The dough will rise only a little bit, not double. Bake until golden brown and crusty, about 45 minutes, rotating the dough halfway through baking. Place the baking sheet on a wire rack to cool before icing.

7 To make the icing, whisk together the confectioners' sugar and remaining 2 tablespoons milk until well combined. Drizzle over the cooled stollen.

NEW ORLEANS HOLIDAY MENU

OYSTER STEW
SERVES 6 TO 8

The simplest of soups, yet fancy enough for Christmas dinner, oyster stew is best made with freshly shucked oysters.

4 tablespoons unsalted butter
1 medium white onion, cut into ½-inch dice
2 celery stalks, sliced into ¼-inch pieces
4 cups milk
2 cups heavy cream
2 teaspoons coarse salt
½ teaspoon cayenne pepper
½ teaspoon ground white pepper
1 pint shucked oysters and their liquor (juice)
Paprika, for garnish
Hot sauce, for garnish (optional)
Oyster crackers, for garnish

Heat the butter in a large saucepan over medium-low heat. Add the onion and celery, and cook until softened, about 8 minutes. Do not brown. Add the milk, cream, salt, cayenne, white pepper, and liquor from oysters. Bring just to a boil, and cook, barely simmering, for 5 minutes to allow the flavors to blend. Add the oysters, and cook just until the edges of the oysters curl, 3 to 4 minutes. Serve immediately, garnished with a sprinkle of paprika, hot sauce, and oyster crackers, if using.

PORK CHOPS WITH ANDOUILLE-PECAN STUFFING
SERVES 6

Andouille is a spicy smoked pork sausage originally from France; it's a staple in Cajun cooking.

3 tablespoons extra-virgin olive oil
1 onion, finely chopped
3 garlic cloves, minced
1 celery stalk, finely chopped
1 carrot, finely chopped
4 ounces andouille or other spicy smoked sausage, finely chopped
3 ounces pecans, finely chopped
2 tablespoons bread crumbs
2 teaspoons chopped fresh thyme
2 tablespoons finely chopped fresh flat-leaf parsley
1½ teaspoons coarse salt
½ teaspoon freshly ground black pepper
Pinch of cayenne pepper
6 one-inch-thick pork rib chops

1 Heat 2 tablespoons olive oil in a large sauté pan over medium heat. Add the onion and garlic, and cook until they begin to soften, about 3 minutes. Add the celery and carrot, and cook until tender, about 3 minutes. Add the sausage, and cook until lightly browned, about 5 minutes. Transfer the mixture to a bowl, and stir in the pecans, bread crumbs, thyme, parsley, salt, black pepper, and cayenne; set aside to cool.

2 Preheat the oven to 350°F. With a sharp paring knife, make a horizontal incision along the side of each chop, and cut a deep, wide pocket in the chop. Fill the chops with the stuffing, and gently press the chops to pack and secure the stuffing.

3 Heat the remaining tablespoon olive oil in a large, heavy, ovenproof skillet (preferably cast iron) over medium-high heat until just starting to smoke. Sauté the pork chops, in batches if necessary, until browned, about 2 minutes per side. Transfer to a roasting pan large enough to hold all of the chops, and bake until cooked through, about 20 minutes.

WILTED MUSTARD GREENS

SERVES 6 TO 8

Mustard greens have a strong, peppery, almost bitter flavor. Kale, spinach, or Swiss chard can be substituted for a more mellow taste.

6 ounces (about 8 slices) thickly sliced bacon, coarsely chopped

2 shallots, finely chopped

3 garlic cloves, minced

4 pounds mustard greens, stems removed, cut into 1-inch pieces

2 cups Homemade Chicken Stock (page 8) or canned

2 tablespoons cider vinegar

Coarse salt and freshly ground pepper

Hot sauce (optional)

1   Heat a large soup pot (about 8-quart capacity) over medium heat. Add the bacon, and cook, stirring occasionally, until crisp. Transfer with a slotted spoon to paper towels to drain.

2   Add the shallots and garlic to the pan with the bacon fat. Sauté until tender, about 2 minutes.

3   Add the greens and stock, tossing well to coat. If all the greens don't fit in one batch, let them wilt in the pan until there is room to add more in batches. Cover, and cook until all the greens are wilted, about 10 minutes, tossing occasionally. Uncover, and cook until the greens are tender and most of the liquid has evaporated, about 10 minutes more.

4   Stir in the vinegar, season with salt and pepper, and serve warm garnished with the bacon and hot sauce, if using.

INDIVIDUAL MAQUE CHOUX PUDDINGS

SERVES 6

Maque choux is a traditional Cajun dish consisting of sautéed corn, onions, and peppers. We have turned the mixture into rich and dense savory puddings.

3 tablespoons unsalted butter, melted, plus more for ramekins

¼ cup bread crumbs

2 cups corn kernels (from about 4 ears), or thawed frozen

½ cup finely chopped red onion

½ cup finely chopped green bell pepper

1 small tomato, seeded and finely chopped

6 large eggs, lightly beaten

1 cup grated cheddar or Monterey Jack cheese

½ cup all-purpose flour

½ cup yellow cornmeal

¼ cup sugar

2½ teaspoons coarse salt

½ teaspoon freshly ground black pepper

¼ teaspoon cayenne pepper

½ cup heavy cream

1   Preheat the oven to 350°F. Butter six 8-ounce ceramic ramekins, and dust with bread crumbs; set aside.

2   In a large bowl, combine corn, onion, pepper, tomato, eggs, and grated cheese.

3   In another bowl, mix together the flour, cornmeal, sugar, salt, black pepper, and cayenne. Add to the egg mixture, and stir to combine. Stir in the heavy cream and melted butter.

4   Divide among the prepared dishes. Place the ramekins in a baking pan, and add water halfway up the sides of the ramekins. Bake until golden brown and a cake tester inserted in the center comes out clean, 40 to 50 minutes. Let cool slightly, and serve in ramekins or unmold.

BREAD PUDDING SOUFFLE WITH WHISKEY SAUCE

SERVES 6

This dessert takes the soufflé to another level by folding in cooked bread pudding that has been cut into cubes. New Orleans French bread is very light and tender. If you substitute a bread that is too dense, it will soak up all the custard and the recipe will not work.

Unsalted butter, for pan and ramekins

1½ cups sugar

1 teaspoon ground cinnamon

Pinch of freshly ground nutmeg

3 medium whole eggs

1 cup heavy cream

1 teaspoon pure vanilla extract

5 cups day-old French bread, or other light bread, cut into 1-inch cubes

⅓ cup raisins

9 medium egg whites, room temperature

¼ teaspoon cream of tartar

Whiskey sauce (optional, recipe follows)

1   Preheat the oven to 350°F. Butter an 8-inch square baking pan; set aside. Combine ¾ cup sugar, the cinnamon, and the nutmeg in a large bowl. Beat in the whole eggs until smooth; whisk in the heavy cream and vanilla. Add the bread cubes, and stir, allowing the bread to soak up the custard. Scatter the raisins in the pan, and top with the egg mixture. Bake until the pudding is golden and firm to the touch and a cake tester inserted in the center comes out clean, 25 to 30 minutes. It should be moist, not runny or dry. Let cool to room temperature.

2   Butter six 6-ounce ceramic ramekins; set aside. In the bowl of an electric mixer or in a large bowl, whisk the egg whites and cream of tartar until foamy. Gradually add the remaining ¾ cup sugar, and continue whisking until shiny and thick. Test with a clean spoon. If the whites stand up stiff, like shaving cream, when you pull out the spoon, the meringue is ready. Do not overwhip, or the whites will break down and the soufflé will not work.

3 In a large bowl, break half the bread pudding into pieces using your hands or a spoon. Gently fold in a quarter of the meringue, being careful not to lose the air in the whites. Divide this mixture among the ramekins. Place the remaining bread pudding in the bowl, break into pieces, and carefully fold in the rest of the meringue. Top off the soufflés with this lighter mixture, piling it high, about 1½ inches over the top edge of the ramekins. With a spoon, smooth and shape the tops into a dome over the ramekin rim. Bake immediately until golden brown, about 20 minutes. Serve immediately. Using a spoon at the table, poke a hole in the top of each soufflé, and spoon the room-temperature whiskey sauce into the soufflés.

ADAPTED FROM "COMMANDER'S KITCHEN," BY TI MARTIN AND JAMIE SHANNON, COPYRIGHT ©2000 BY COMMANDER'S PALACE, INC. USED BY PERMISSION OF BROADWAY BOOKS, A DIVISION OF RANDOM HOUSE, INC.

WHISKEY SAUCE

MAKES ABOUT 1½ CUPS

1½ cups heavy cream
2 teaspoons cornstarch
2 tablespoons cold water
⅓ cup sugar
⅓ cup bourbon

Place the cream in a small saucepan over medium heat and bring to a boil. Whisk together the cornstarch and water; add to the cream while whisking. Bring to a boil. Whisk, and let simmer for a few seconds, taking care not to burn the mixture on the bottom. Remove from the heat, and stir in the sugar and bourbon. Stir until the sugar dissolves. Let cool to room temperature.

SANTA FE HOLIDAY MENU

LARGE-QUANTITY GUACAMOLE

SERVES 6 TO 8 | **PHOTOGRAPH ON PAGE 306**

Guacamole is best eaten as quickly as possible after it is made; it will start to lose its color otherwise. Serve with corn chips or warmed flour tortillas.

6 large ripe Hass avocados
4 scallions, thinly sliced
3 tablespoons finely chopped fresh cilantro
2 tablespoons freshly squeezed lime juice
½ teaspoon ground cumin
Pinch of cayenne pepper
Coarse salt and freshly ground black pepper

1 Cut the avocados in half, and remove the pit by inserting the blade of a knife into the pit and twisting. Scoop out the flesh of the avocados into a medium bowl, and mash with a potato masher or large fork until semi-smooth, leaving some chunks of avocado for texture.
2 Stir in the scallions, cilantro, lime juice, cumin, and cayenne. Season with salt and black pepper, and serve immediately (or refrigerate, covering the top of the guacamole with plastic wrap, for up to a day).

SPICE-RUBBED ROASTED RACK OF VENISON

SERVES 8 | **PHOTOGRAPHS ON PAGES 306, 307**

2 tablespoons cumin seed
2 tablespoons coriander seed
1 tablespoon whole black peppercorns
1 tablespoon whole green peppercorns
1 tablespoon whole white peppercorns
4 shallots, minced
4 garlic cloves, minced
¼ cup coarse salt
4 tablespoons dark-brown sugar
1 rack of venison (about 8 chops or 2¾ pounds)
1 tablespoon vegetable oil

1 In the bowl of a food processor, pulse the cumin seed, coriander seed, and peppercorns until coarsely ground, about 1 minute. Add the shallots, garlic, salt, and sugar, and process to a thick paste; set aside in a bowl. Rinse the venison, and pat dry with paper towels. Rub a thin layer of the paste on all sides of the meat. Wrap with plastic, and refrigerate at least 4 hours or overnight.
2 Preheat the oven to 400°F. Rub off the excess spice paste from the venison. In an ovenproof skillet large enough to hold the venison, heat the vegetable oil over medium-high heat until just starting to smoke. Sear the meat until browned, about 2 minutes per side. Transfer the skillet to the oven, and cook until desired doneness is reached, 15 to 18 minutes for medium-rare. Remove the venison from the oven, and let rest 3 to 5 minutes before slicing.

FOUR-ONION AND JALAPEÑO CONFIT

MAKES ABOUT 3 CUPS | **PHOTOGRAPHS ON PAGES 306, 307**

This takes some time to prepare, but the flavorful result makes it worth the effort.

4 tablespoons unsalted butter
2 medium red onions, cut into ¼-inch slices
2 sweet yellow onions, cut into ¼-inch slices
4 large shallots, cut into ¼-inch rings
10 garlic cloves, halved lengthwise
1 bunch scallions, cut diagonally into 2-inch pieces
5 large jalapeño peppers, seeded and cut into ¼-inch-wide strips
¾ cup golden raisins
¼ cup packed light-brown sugar
½ cup cider vinegar
1½ cups water

1 Heat the butter in a large saucepan over medium heat. Add red and yellow onions, shallots, and garlic, and cook, stirring occasionally, until the vegetables begin to soften, about 8 minutes.
2 Add the scallions, peppers, raisins, brown sugar, cider vinegar, and water. Cook at a gentle simmer, covered, until vegetables are very tender, about 1 hour.
3 Uncover, and simmer until thickened and most of the liquid has evaporated, about 1½ hours. Serve warm, or keep refrigerated for up to a week.

STEWED FRIJOLES

SERVES 8 | PHOTOGRAPHS ON PAGES 306, 307

1 pound dried pinto beans

2 onions, 1 cut into ½-inch dice, 1 finely chopped

2 garlic cloves, minced

1 twelve-ounce ham hock

1 28-ounce can diced tomatoes, with juice

3 tablespoons extra-virgin olive oil

¼ cup finely chopped fresh cilantro

2 teaspoons coarse salt

½ teaspoon freshly ground pepper

1 Pick over the beans to remove any stones or broken beans. Place the beans in a large pot, and add cold water to cover by 2 inches. Cover, and soak overnight at room temperature.

2 Drain and rinse beans; return to pot, and add diced onion, garlic, ham hock, and tomatoes. Add water to cover by 1 inch. Bring to a boil; lower the heat, and simmer until the beans are very tender and most of the liquid has evaporated, 2½ to 3 hours. Remove ham hock; shred meat. Return meat to pot. Keep warm.

3 Heat olive oil in a medium skillet over medium heat. Sauté finely chopped onion until tender and just starting to brown. Stir in the cilantro, salt, and pepper, and cook, stirring, for 1 minute. Stir into the beans; serve immediately.

CHILE-CHEESE TAMALES

MAKES 16 | PHOTOGRAPHS ON PAGES 306, 307

Tamales can be made through step four up to a month in advance and frozen. You can steam them directly from the freezer, but the cooking time will be longer—follow the recipe directions to check for doneness.

4 ounces dried corn husks

3 cups corn kernels (2 fifteen-ounce cans), drained well

½ cup (4 ounces) fresh pork lard or solid vegetable shortening

2 cups masa harina, mixed with 1½ cups hot water and cooled to room temperature

2 tablespoons sugar

1½ teaspoons coarse salt

1½ teaspoons baking powder

2 poblano chiles, roasted, seeds and ribs removed, and cut into ¼-inch strips

2 cups (8 ounces) grated Monterey Jack cheese

1 Place the corn husks in a deep saucepan, and cover with water. Bring to a boil over high heat. Remove from the heat, and set a plate over the husks to keep them submerged. Soak 1 hour.

2 Meanwhile, prepare the batter. Place 2 cups corn kernels in the bowl of a food processor, and pulse to a medium-coarse purée. Add the lard or shortening, and pulse 5 or 6 times. Add the masa harina, sugar, salt, and baking powder; pulse until thoroughly combined. Process until the mixture is light, fluffy, and evenly combined, about 1 minute, stopping to scrape down the sides of the bowl once or twice.

3 Transfer the mixture to a medium bowl, and stir in the remaining cup corn kernels until combined. Chill the corn batter until ready to assemble.

4 Remove the husks from the water. Unroll one large piece; tear lengthwise along the grain to make ¼-inch-wide strips (you will need 2 per tamale). Remove another large piece; pat dry with a paper towel. Place on a work surface, pointed end facing away from you; scoop ¼ cup batter onto the middle, and spread into a 4-inch square, leaving a 1½-inch border all around. Place a few strips of poblano down the center, and sprinkle with 2 tablespoons grated cheese. Pick up the two long sides of the husk so the batter encases the poblano filling. Bring the two sides together to form a cylinder. Fold the flat end under; tie loosely with a husk strip. Tie the pointed end near the batter, and fray the exposed husk. Repeat with more husks and the remaining batter, poblanos, and cheese.

5 Fill a wok or large skillet with 2 inches of water. Line the bottom of a bamboo steamer basket with corn husks, and set the basket in place. Lay the assembled tamales in the steamer. Set the steamer over high heat. When the steam puffs out, reduce the heat to medium. Steam 1 hour 15 minutes, adding more water to the pan as necessary. To check for doneness, unwrap a tamale: If it's ready, the corn mixture will come free from the wrapper and feel soft. If the mixture sticks to the wrapper, rewrap, and steam and 15 to 20 minutes more. Remove from the heat; let stand 15 minutes for the tamales to firm up. Tamales will remain warm for about 1 hour.

SAUTEED GREEN BEANS AND CHAYOTE WITH TOASTED PINE NUTS

SERVES 8 | PHOTOGRAPH ON PAGE 306

Chayote, also referred to as mirliton in the South, is a green-skinned, gourdlike fruit about the shape of a large pear. It is widely available in most supermarkets throughout the winter months.

3 tablespoons extra-virgin olive oil

2 Chayote squash (about 12 ounces each), peeled and cut into ¼-inch matchsticks

1½ pounds green and yellow string beans, stem ends trimmed

3 tablespoons water

2 poblano chiles, roasted, seeds and ribs removed, and cut into ¼-inch-wide strips

Coarse salt and freshly ground pepper

Pine nuts, lightly toasted, for garnish

1 Heat 2 tablespoons olive oil in a large sauté pan over medium heat. Add the Chayote, and cook, tossing occasionally, until just tender, about 10 minutes. Transfer to a bowl, and keep warm.

2 Add the remaining tablespoon olive oil to the sauté pan; add the string beans. Toss to coat with oil. Add the water, cover, and cook, stirring occasionally, until bright and just tender, about 10 minutes. Add the cooked chayote and the poblanos to the pan, and stir until heated through.

3 Season with salt and pepper, and serve warm or at room temperature garnished with the toasted pine nuts.

CHRISTMAS CORNBREAD

SERVES 8 | PHOTOGRAPHS ON PAGES 306, 307

¼ cup plus 2 tablespoons vegetable shortening, plus more for pan

1¼ cups all-purpose flour

2¼ cups yellow cornmeal

2 teaspoons coarse salt

¾ teaspoon freshly ground black pepper

1½ teaspoons baking powder

¾ teaspoon baking soda

3 large eggs

2¼ cups nonfat buttermilk

1 cup corn kernels

2 jalapeño peppers, seeds removed, minced

1 small red bell pepper, seeds and ribs removed, cut into ¼-inch dice

1 cup grated cheddar cheese

1 Preheat the oven to 375°F. Coat a 9-by-13-inch baking pan with vegetable shortening. Whisk together the flour, cornmeal, salt, pepper, baking powder, and baking soda in a large bowl. Make a well in the flour mixture, and add the eggs to the center. Whisk the eggs into the dry mixture. Add the buttermilk, and combine. The mixture will be thick.

2 Stir in the corn, peppers, and cheese. Melt the vegetable shortening in a small pan over medium heat. Pour the hot shortening into the cornbread mixture. Stir well to combine. Spoon the batter into the prepared pan.

3 Bake until golden brown and cornbread is pulling away from the sides of the pan, 20 to 30 minutes; a cake tester inserted into the center should come out clean. Let stand until cool enough to touch; gently run a knife around the rim, cut into slices, and serve warm.

BISCOCHITOS

MAKES 4 DOZEN

These light and crumbly anise-flavored cookies are traditionally served throughout Mexico for weddings, christenings, or at Christmas.

1¾ cups sugar
1¼ cups lard or vegetable shortening
1 large egg
1 teaspoon pure vanilla extract
2 tablespoons Grand Marnier or triple sec
  Finely grated zest of 1 orange
3 cups all-purpose flour
½ teaspoon baking powder
¼ teaspoon table salt
2 teaspoons anise seeds
2 tablespoons water
½ teaspoon ground cinnamon
  All-purpose flour, for work surface

1 In the bowl of an electric mixer fitted with the paddle attachment, mix 1 cup sugar and lard or vegetable shortening on medium-high speed until light and fluffy, about 3 minutes. Add the egg; beat to combine. Add vanilla, Grand Marnier, and orange zest; beat to combine.

2 Sift together the flour, baking powder, and salt. Gradually beat the flour mixture into the sugar mixture on low speed. Beat in the anise seeds. On medium speed, gradually add about 2 tablespoons water or enough to form into a ball. Wrap the dough in plastic wrap, and refrigerate 30 minutes.

3 Preheat the oven to 350°F with a rack in the center. Combine the cinnamon and remaining ¾ cup sugar in a small bowl.

4 On a floured surface, roll the dough to ¼ inch thick. Cut moons, stars, or whatever shapes you like with a 2-inch cutter; lightly sift the cinnamon-sugar over each shape. Place on parchment-lined baking sheets. Bake, one sheet at a time, 12 to 14 minutes; the cookies should be set but not brown. Transfer the cookies and parchment to a wire rack to cool. Repeat with the remaining batches.

MEXICAN HOT CHOCOLATE

SERVES 6 TO 8

Mexican chocolate, flavored with cinnamon, almonds, and vanilla, is available in Mexican markets and some supermarkets.

1 quart milk
2 three-inch cinnamon sticks
10 ounces Ibarra or other Mexican chocolate, finely chopped
  Whipped cream, for serving
  Ground cinnamon, for serving

Place the milk and cinnamon sticks in a heavy medium saucepan. Bring just to a boil, reduce the heat, and add the chocolate. Let the mixture stand until the chocolate melts, about 3 minutes. Whisk until combined. Remove cinnamon sticks, and serve the hot chocolate immediately, topped with a dollop of whipped cream and a pinch of ground cinnamon.

NUTCRACKER SWEETS

NUTCRACKER COOKIES

MAKES 18

6 cups sifted all-purpose flour, plus more for work surface
1 teaspoon baking soda
½ teaspoon baking powder
1 cup (2 sticks) unsalted butter
1 cup packed dark-brown sugar
4 teaspoons ground ginger
4 teaspoons ground cinnamon
1½ teaspoons ground cloves
1½ teaspoons table salt
1 teaspoon finely ground pepper
2 large eggs
1 cup unsulfured molasses
  Gel-paste food coloring
2 recipes Double-Batch Royal Icing (page 317)
  Sanding Sugar
  Dragées

1 In a large bowl, sift together the flour, baking soda, and baking powder. Set aside.

2 In the bowl of an electric mixer fitted with the paddle attachment, cream the butter and brown sugar on medium speed until fluffy. Add the ginger, cinnamon, cloves, salt, and pepper, and beat to combine. Add the eggs and molasses, and beat to combine. Reduce the speed to low, and add the flour mixture; beat until incorporated. Divide the dough into three parts, and shape into flat disks. Wrap in plastic wrap, and chill at least 1 hour or overnight.

3 Preheat the oven to 350°F. On a floured work surface, roll out the dough to ⅛ inch thick. Cut out shapes using a nutcracker cutter, and transfer to baking sheets lined with Silpat baking mats or parchment paper. Refrigerate until firm, at least 15 minutes. Bake until crisp but not darkened, 8 to 10 minutes. Cool on wire racks. Using a toothpick, mix very small drops of the food coloring into the icing; stir by hand with a spatula until combined. Decorate with royal icing, sanding sugar, and dragées.

MARSHMALLOW MICE

MAKES ABOUT 18

You can pipe these mice two or three at a time, but they need to be decorated immediately for the decorations to really stick.

2 envelopes (5 teaspoons) unflavored gelatin
⅔ cup plus ½ cup cold water
2 cups granulated sugar
1¼ cups sanding sugar
    Cocoa powder or powdered food coloring
    Pink or red edible decorettes
    Blue and green dragées
    Sliced almonds
    Licorice shoelaces, cut into 4-inch lengths

1   In the bowl of an electric mixer, sprinkle the gelatin over ⅔ cup cold water. Allow to soften, about 5 minutes.
2   In a small saucepan, combine the remaining ½ cup water and the granulated sugar; stir over medium-high heat until dissolved. Stop stirring, and clip a candy thermometer onto the pan; wipe the sides of the pan with a pastry brush dipped in water to prevent crystallization. Boil the sugar until the temperature reaches the soft-ball stage (238°F). Remove the syrup from the heat; add to the softened gelatin. Beat on low with the whisk attachment to combine, about 1 minute. Increase the speed to medium-high, and beat until soft peaks form and the marshmallow mixture holds its shape, 8 to 10 minutes.
3   Transfer marshmallow mixture to an 18-inch pastry bag fitted with a large, plain round tip (Ateco #7). Mix sanding sugar with cocoa or powdered food coloring until the desired shade is achieved. Spread in an even layer on a rimmed baking sheet. Pipe a mound, 2 inches in diameter, directly onto the colored sugar, pulling the pastry bag to one side; the resulting peak will become nose of mouse. Spoon colored sugar over top and sides of the marshmallow until fully coated. Place a pink or red candy on the tip to create the nose. Place two dragées for eyes and two almond slices for ears. Insert licorice into the marshmallow, creating a tail.
4   Repeat step 3 until all the marshmallow is used. Keep stored in an airtight container lined with parchment paper for up to 2 weeks.

SEVILLE ORANGE CHOCOLATE CAKE

MAKES 1 NINE-INCH CAKE | **PHOTOGRAPH ON PAGE 303**

If you can't find Seville-orange marmalade, any orange marmalade may be substituted.

1   cup (2 sticks) unsalted butter, room temperature, plus more for pans
½   cup cocoa powder, plus more for pans and top of cake
1½ cups sifted all-purpose flour
1   teaspoon baking powder
¼   teaspoon baking soda
¼   teaspoon table salt
1½ cups sugar
2   large eggs
1   teaspoon pure vanilla extract
1   cup sour cream
1   cup Seville-orange marmalade
    Candied Kumquats (recipe follows), with poaching syrup
    Sugared Bay Leaves (recipe follows)

1   Preheat the oven to 350°F. Butter two 9-inch round pans; line with parchment. Brush the parchment with butter, and dust with cocoa. Sift together the flour, cocoa, baking powder, baking soda, and salt in a medium bowl; set aside.
2   Place the butter in the bowl of an electric mixer fitted with the paddle attachment. Beat on medium speed until creamy. Gradually add the sugar, and beat until fluffy. Add the eggs one at time, incorporating after each addition; add the vanilla.
3   Add the flour mixture and sour cream alternately, starting and ending with the flour mixture. Scrape down the sides of the bowl as needed. Divide the batter between the prepared pans; bake until a cake tester inserted in the center comes out clean, about 30 minutes.
4   Cool the cakes in pans on wire racks for 10 minutes. Unmold, and cool completely, right side up.
5   Heat the marmalade just until it reaches a spreadable consistency. Choose the more attractive cake layer, and set aside. Place the other layer on an 8-inch cake round, bottom side up. Using a pastry brush, coat the cake with the kumquat poaching syrup. Spread the marmalade over the cake, and allow to set, about 10 minutes. Brush the bottom of the

reserved layer with the kumquat poaching syrup, and place on top of the other layer, syrup side down. Dust the top with cocoa, and garnish with candied kumquats and sugared bay leaves.

CANDIED KUMQUATS

MAKES 1 PINT

The reserved poaching syrup is used for brushing the cake layers in the Seville Orange Chocolate Cake.

1   pint (12 ounces) kumquats
1½ cups sugar
1½ cups water

1   Rinse the kumquats, and place in a large saucepan with enough cold water to cover. Bring to a boil over medium-high heat. Drain immediately, and repeat the process two more times, always starting with cold water.
2   Place the kumquats, sugar, and water in a medium saucepan, and bring to a boil. Boil for 2 minutes until the sugar is completely dissolved. Immediately remove from the heat; allow kumquats to cool completely in syrup.
3   The candied kumquats can be used immediately or stored, refrigerated, in the syrup in an airtight plastic container for up to a month.

SUGARED BAY LEAVES

MAKES 30

1   large egg white
1   teaspoon water
30 fresh bay leaves
¼   cup superfine sugar

Place a wire rack on a baking sheet. Combine the egg white and water in a small bowl, and whisk to combine. Using a small brush, coat the bay leaves with the egg white, and spoon the sugar over it. Shake off the excess sugar, and place the leaf on the rack to dry. Repeat with the remaining leaves.

CHOCOLATE MOUSSE CAKE

MAKES ONE 10-BY-4½-BY-3-INCH LOAF;
SERVES 10 TO 12 | PHOTOGRAPH ON PAGE 303

Chocolate Génoise (recipe follows)
8 ounces bittersweet chocolate, finely
  chopped
3 large egg yolks
¼ cup sugar
2 tablespoons all-purpose flour
1 tablespoon cornstarch
1½ cups milk
1½ cups heavy cream
  Chocolate Ganache Icing II (recipe follows)
  Edible roses and rose petals (optional)
  Cinnamon Crème Anglaise (recipe follows)

1   Line a 10-by-4½-by-3-inch loaf pan
with plastic wrap, letting excess hang
over the sides of the pan. Line the pan
with the genoise: Cut two 9-by-3-inch
rectangles to fit the sides of the loaf and
one 9-by-4-inch rectangle to fit the
bottom. Cut a 10½-by-5-inch rectangle
to fit the top, and set aside. Cut four 2¼-
by-4½-inch pieces, and use two to fit each
end of the loaf.

2   Place the chocolate in a large heat-
proof bowl or the top of a double boiler
set over a pan of barely simmering
water; heat until melted. Set aside.

3   Combine the egg yolks and sugar in
a medium bowl, and whisk until pale yellow. Add the flour and cornstarch, and
whisk to combine. Place the milk in
a small saucepan, and bring to a boil.

4   Gradually pour the milk into the yolk
mixture, whisking constantly. Return
the mixture to the pan, and set over medium-low heat. Cook, whisking constantly,
just until the mixture comes to a boil.
Remove from the heat, and immediately
pass through a fine sieve into the melted
chocolate. Use a rubber spatula to combine,
and set aside to cool. When the chocolate
is almost cool, whip the cream to soft
peaks, and fold it into the chocolate.

5   Spoon the chocolate mousse into the
prepared loaf, and top with the reserved
genoise. Wrap the excess plastic over the
loaf, and place in the freezer overnight.

6   Unmold the cake onto a wire rack set
over a rimmed baking sheet. Pour the
chocolate ganache over the cake, coating
completely. Allow the ganache to set for
about 10 minutes. Scrape the excess
ganache from the baking sheet back into
the bowl. Pour a second coating of
ganache over the cake. If the ganache
gets too thick, it can be rewarmed slightly over a double boiler. Transfer the cake
to a serving platter, and refrigerate for 1
hour or until ready to serve.

7   Garnish with the edible roses and
rose petals, if using, just before serving.
Thinly slice the cake using a serrated
knife; serve with the crème anglaise.

CHOCOLATE GENOISE

MAKES 1 TWELVE-BY-SEVENTEEN-INCH
SHEET CAKE

  Unsalted butter, room temperature, for
  baking sheet
¼ cup plus 1 tablespoon all-purpose flour
¼ cup plus 1 tablespoon cocoa powder
6 large eggs, separated
¾ cup sugar

1   Preheat the oven to 400°F. Butter
a 12-by-17-inch rimmed baking sheet,
line with parchment paper, and butter the
paper. Combine 1 tablespoon flour and
1 tablespoon cocoa, and coat the pan, tapping out excess. Place the egg yolks in the
bowl of an electric mixer fitted with the
whisk attachment. Beat on high speed
until pale yellow, about 5 minutes. Transfer to a medium bowl, and set aside. Wash
and dry the mixer bowl and whisk.

2   Place the egg whites in the mixer
bowl, and whisk on medium speed until soft peaks form, about 3 minutes.
Increase the speed to medium-high, and
add the sugar gradually, until glossy stiff
peaks form. Transfer the egg-white
mixture to a large bowl.

3   Using a rubber spatula, fold the egg-
yolk mixture into the egg-white mixture.
Sift the remaining ¼ cup flour and ¼
cup cocoa powder over the top, and
gently fold in. Pour the batter into the
prepared baking sheet, and smooth the
top with an offset spatula.

4   Bake until the cake springs back
when touched, 10 to 12 minutes. Remove
the pan from the oven, and immediately turn out onto a wire rack covered
with parchment paper. Peel the parchment paper from the top of the cake, and
cool completely. Génoise should be used
the day it is made.

CHOCOLATE GANACHE ICING II

MAKES 2½ CUPS

12 ounces bittersweet chocolate
12 ounces heavy cream

  Finely chop the chocolate, and place in
a medium bowl. Heat the cream in
a small saucepan until bubbles begin to
appear around the edges (scalding);
pour over the chocolate. Let stand 5
minutes, then stir until smooth. Allow
to cool, stirring occasionally, until lukewarm. Use immediately.

CINNAMON CREME ANGLAISE

MAKES 2 CUPS

1 cup milk
¾ cup heavy cream
2 cinnamon sticks
4 large egg yolks
¼ cup sugar

1   Combine the milk, cream, and cinnamon sticks in a small saucepan, and bring
to a boil over medium-high heat. Remove
from the heat, and allow to steep for 30
minutes, until flavors are infused.

2   Fill a large bowl with ice and water;
set aside. In a medium bowl whisk together the egg yolks and sugar until lightened in color, about 2 minutes. Return
the milk mixture to medium heat, and
bring to a simmer; reduce the heat to low.
Whisk about ½ cup of the milk mixture
into the egg-yolk mixture, and return
it to the saucepan. Cook until the mixture thickens enough to coat the back
of a wooden spoon.

3   Strain the crème anglaise into a bowl
set in the ice bath, discarding the cinnamon sticks. Store in an airtight container
in the refrigerator for up to 3 days.

CHOCOLATE ALMONDS

MAKES 7 TO 8 CUPS | PHOTOGRAPH ON
PAGE 303

- 14 ounces unblanched whole almonds
- 1¼ cups sugar
- ¼ cup water
- 1 teaspoon ground cinnamon
- 1 pound best-quality semisweet chocolate, chopped
- ¾ cup Dutch-process cocoa powder

1 Preheat the oven to 350°F. Place the almonds in a single layer on a rimmed baking sheet, and toast until fragrant, about 10 minutes, shaking the pan halfway through. Line two rimmed baking sheets with parchment paper, and set aside.

2 In a medium saucepan, combine the toasted almonds, sugar, water, and cinnamon. Cook over medium-high heat, stirring constantly, until the sugar becomes golden, then starts to crystallize, and the almonds are completely coated, about 8 minutes. Pour the mixture into the prepared sheets. Chill in the freezer for 15 minutes.

3 Place the chocolate in a heat-proof bowl or the top of a double boiler set over a pan of simmering water. Stir until melted. Transfer half the chilled almonds to a large bowl, and pour half the melted chocolate over them. Stir until the nuts are thoroughly coated. Transfer the mixture to one of the prepared baking sheets, and separate the almonds with a fork. Place the pan in the refrigerator until the chocolate has set, about 5 minutes. Repeat with remaining almonds and chocolate.

4 Place the cocoa in a bowl, and add the almonds. Toss to coat, shaking off the excess cocoa powder. Store in an airtight container for up to a month.

ARABIC COFFEE

MAKES ABOUT 1½ CUPS

Traditional Arabic coffeepots are small with very long handles.

- 8 cardamom pods, smashed
- 2 cups cold water
- ½ cup coarsely pulverized dark-roast coffee beans

Combine the cardamom, water, and coffee beans in an Arabic coffeepot or a small saucepan. Bring to a boil over medium-high heat, reduce to low, and simmer, covered, for 15 to 20 minutes, until the grounds have settled and the coffee is very strong. Pour the coffee into small cups, taking care to keep the grounds in the bottom of the pot. Strain the coffee through a fine sieve if desired.

TURKISH DELIGHT

MAKES ABOUT 4 DOZEN PIECES

When pouring the syrup into the cornstarch mixture, be careful not to let the mixture coat the sides of the pan.

- 3 cups granulated sugar
- 3¼ cups water
  Juice of half a lemon
- 1 cup sifted cornstarch
- ¾ teaspoon cream of tartar
- 1½ tablespoons rose water or orange-flower water
  Gel-paste food coloring
- ½ cup sliced blanched almonds (optional)
- ¼ cup confectioners' sugar
  Vegetable oil, for pan

1 Combine the granulated sugar, 1 cup water, and lemon juice in a small saucepan, and stir to combine. Place over medium-high heat, and bring to a boil. If there are sugar crystals on the sides of the pan, brush down with a pastry brush dipped in water. Clip on a candy thermometer, and heat to 240°F. Remove from the heat, and set aside.

2 Combine ¾ cup cornstarch, the cream of tartar, and ¾ cup water in a medium saucepan, and whisk until smooth and fully combined. Bring the remaining 1½ cups water to a boil, and add to the cornstarch mixture, whisking constantly. Place over medium heat, and cook, whisking constantly, until the mixture becomes quite thick and just comes to a boil.

3 Pour the sugar syrup into the cornstarch mixture, whisking constantly, and reduce to a gentle simmer. Simmer for 1 hour 15 minutes, stirring frequently.

4 Stir in the rose or orange-flower water, food coloring, and nuts, if using. Pour into an oiled 8-inch-square pan, and let set overnight.

5 Combine the confectioners' sugar with the remaining ¼ cup cornstarch. Sprinkle some of the mixture in an even layer over a cutting board, and unmold the Turkish delight onto it. Sprinkle the top of the candy with more of the sugar mixture. Using a sharp knife, cut into 1-inch squares. Let sit overnight uncovered. Just before serving, dust with the remaining sugar mixture. Store in an airtight container for up to 2 weeks.

COCONUT SWEETMEATS

MAKES ABOUT 3½ DOZEN PIECES

This delicious coconut candy is from Iran.

  Unsalted butter, for baking sheet
- 2½ cups desiccated coconut
- 2 cups sugar
- ¼ teaspoon cream of tartar
- ½ cup water
- ½ teaspoon pure vanilla extract

1 Butter a 12-by-17-inch baking sheet, and set aside. Place ½ cup desiccated coconut in an 8-inch-square baking pan in an even layer.

2 Combine the sugar, cream of tartar, and water in a small saucepan, and stir to combine. Bring to a boil over medium-high heat, brushing down the sides of the pan with a pastry brush dipped in water to prevent crystallization. Clip on a candy thermometer, and cook, without stirring, until the temperature reaches 240°F.

3 Pour the sugar mixture onto the prepared baking sheet in a constant, steady stream, holding the pan close to the surface; do not allow any drips to fall onto the baking sheet. Allow the syrup to sit undisturbed until just warm to the touch on the surface (test often so the candy does not become too cool).

4 Using a wide offset spatula, lift the sides and fold over into the middle. Repeat this process, adding 1½ cups coconut and the vanilla extract, until the mixture becomes slightly stiff and opaque white, about 3 minutes.

5 Quickly press into the coconut-lined pan; flatten into an even layer. Cover with the remaining ½ cup coconut, and press to adhere. Let sit 5 hours or overnight.

6 Invert the pan to unmold. Carefully cut the coconut sweetmeat into eight 1-inch strips using a serrated knife. Cut each strip diagonally to make diamonds. Store in an airtight container for up to 2 weeks.

BAKLAVA

MAKES ABOUT 60 PIECES

1 cup finely ground almonds
1 cup finely chopped pistachios
2 cups sugar
1½ teaspoons ground cardamom
½ cup Clarified Butter (recipe follows)
12 sheets phyllo dough, cut in half crosswise
1 cup water
   Juice of half a lemon
1 tablespoon rose water

1 Preheat the oven to 350°F. Combine the almonds, pistachios, ⅔ cup sugar, and 1 teaspoon ground cardamom in a medium bowl; stir to combine.

2 Brush a 10-by-13-inch baking dish with clarified butter. Lay one half-sheet of phyllo in the prepared dish, and brush with clarified butter. Repeat with 5 more sheets, placing them on top of each other in the dish.

3 Sprinkle one-third of the nut mixture over the phyllo, and top with six more sheets of phyllo, brushing each with clarified butter before adding the next. Repeat two times, until all the nuts and phyllo are used.

4 Using a very sharp knife, cut into seven strips lengthwise. Cut across strips diagonally, 1¼ inches apart, to make diamonds. Pour the remaining clarified butter over the pastry. Bake until golden brown, 35 to 40 minutes.

5 Place the remaining 1⅓ cups sugar and the water in a medium saucepan, and bring to a boil, stirring until the sugar is dissolved. Add the remaining ½ teaspoon cardamom, and continue to boil for 10 minutes until the syrup has thickened slightly. Remove from the heat, and stir in the lemon juice and rose water. Pour over the baked pastry.

CLARIFIED BUTTER

MAKES 1¼ CUPS

1 pound butter

Cut the butter into tablespoon-size pieces. Place in a small saucepan over low heat. Cook until the solids sink to the bottom of the pan, skimming any foam off the top. Pour the clear yellow liquid into a glass jar, discarding the solids, and store in the refrigerator for up to a month.

GREEN TEA SORBET

MAKES ABOUT 1½ QUARTS

4½ cups water
1 teaspoon unflavored gelatin
2 cups sugar
¼ cup corn syrup
6 green tea bags
   Juice of 1 lemon
   Green food coloring
   Chinese Hat Tuiles (recipe follows)

1 Place the water and gelatin in a medium saucepan, and let dissolve for 5 minutes. Add the sugar and corn syrup, bring to a boil, and cook until the sugar is dissolved, about 2 minutes. Add the tea bags, and steep for 10 to 15 minutes to infuse the flavor.

2 Fill a large bowl with ice and water. Remove the tea bags, and transfer the mixture to a bowl set in the ice bath to cool. Add the lemon juice and food coloring, 1 drop at a time, until the desired shade is reached. The color will lighten slightly when the sorbet is frozen.

3 Freeze in an ice-cream maker according to the manufacturer's directions until set but not hard. Transfer to a chilled loaf pan, wrap with plastic, and place in the freezer until firm, 4 hours or overnight. Serve garnished with Chinese hat tuiles.

CHINESE HAT TUILES

MAKES ABOUT 4 DOZEN

These cookies are made of fortune-cookie batter and shaped to look like Chinese hats.

4 large egg whites
1 cup superfine sugar
1 cup all-purpose flour, sifted
   Pinch of table salt
5 tablespoons unsalted butter, melted and cooled
3 tablespoons heavy cream
1 teaspoon pure almond extract

1 Preheat the oven to 350°F. To make a tuile template, trace a 4-inch circle onto a piece of plastic, such as a coffee-can lid. Mark a notch from the center of the circle to two points on the circumference about an inch apart. Using a utility knife, cut out the wedge, leaving the notch intact. Discard the center.

2 In the bowl of an electric mixer, combine the egg whites and sugar, and beat on medium speed for about 30 seconds. Add the flour and salt, and beat until combined. Add the butter, heavy cream, and almond extract, and beat until combined, about 30 seconds.

3 Place the plastic template on a Silpat-lined baking sheet, and spoon about 2 teaspoons in the center. Using a small offset spatula, spread the batter until it fills the template in a thin and even coat. Lift the template, and repeat for a second cookie. Bake for about 6 minutes, until just barely beginning to brown. Remove from the oven, and lift immediately using an offset spatula. Overlap the ends to create the shape of a hat. Allow to cool completely on a wire rack. Repeat with the remaining batter.

WHITE RUSSIAN EGGNOG
MAKES 6 CUPS

This recipe may be doubled and made up to two days in advance. Add the alcohol and whipped cream just before serving.

3½ cups milk

5 large egg yolks

¾ cup sugar

2 cups heavy cream, cold

¾ cup vodka

½ cup coffee-flavored liqueur, such as Kahlúa

1 Fill a large bowl with ice and water. Place 2 cups milk in a small saucepan set over medium-high heat, and bring to a boil. Place the egg yolks and sugar in the bowl of an electric mixer fitted with the whisk attachment, and whip until pale and thick. Add the hot milk, whisking constantly, in a slow stream. Return the mixture to the pan, and cook, stirring constantly, over medium-low heat until thick enough to coat the back of a wooden spoon. Immediately add 1 cup cream and the remaining 1½ cups milk, and transfer the mixture to the ice bath.

2 When ready to serve, add the vodka and liqueur. Whip the remaining cup cream to soft peaks. Divide the eggnog among six cups, and garnish with whipped cream. Serve.

MARZIPAN CHERRIES
MAKES 14

1 seven-ounce tube marzipan
    Red, yellow, and green liquid food coloring

1 tablespoon vodka

14 slivered almonds

1 egg white

¼ cup superfine sugar

1 Divide the marzipan into three parts. Tint one dark red, one light red, and one yellow. Keep well wrapped until ready to form cherries.

2 Place the vodka in a small bowl, and tint it pale green. Add the slivered almonds, and let sit for 3 minutes. Remove from the liquid, and let drain on a paper towel.

3 Form the marzipan into 14 equal parts, each made by combining a small piece of each color. The colors can be blended and marbled by flattening and rerolling. Shape each to look like a cherry. Brush very lightly with egg white, and roll in the superfine sugar. Use a slivered almond to form the stem. Store in an airtight container for up to a week.

NOTE: Raw eggs should not be used in food prepared for pregnant women, babies, young children, the elderly, or anyone whose health is compromised.

GINGERBREAD PETITS FOURS
MAKES 2 DOZEN

Using a variety of colors for the fondant makes for a beautiful presentation, but you can make one single-colored batch as well.

1½ cups (3 sticks) unsalted butter, room temperature, plus more for pan

1½ cups all-purpose flour, plus more for pan

2 tablespoons ground ginger

2 teaspoons ground cinnamon

¼ teaspoon ground nutmeg

¼ teaspoon ground cloves

1½ cups sugar

3 tablespoons unsulfured molasses

6 large eggs, room temperature

1 teaspoon pure vanilla extract
    Ginger Simple Syrup (recipe follows)
    Swiss Meringue Buttercream (recipe follows)
    Poured Fondant (recipe follows)
    Gel-paste food coloring

1 Preheat the oven to 350°F. Butter a 10½-by-15½-inch rimmed baking sheet. Line with parchment; brush with butter, and dust with flour; set aside. Sift together the flour, ginger, cinnamon, nutmeg, and cloves into a medium bowl; set aside.

2 Combine the butter and sugar in the bowl of an electric mixer fitted with the paddle attachment, and beat on medium-high speed until light and fluffy. Add the molasses, and beat until combined.

3 Add the eggs one at a time, incorporating each and scraping down the sides of the bowl between each addition. Add the vanilla, reduce the speed to low, and

gradually add the flour mixture. Pour the batter into the prepared pan, and use an offset spatula to smooth into an even layer. Bake until a cake tester inserted into the center of the cake comes out clean, about 20 minutes.

4 Cool the cake in the pan on a wire rack for 10 minutes. Unmold, and allow to cool completely. Cut the cake in half crosswise, forming two 10½-by-7¾-inch rectangles. Using a pastry brush, coat one rectangle with the simple syrup. Spread 1 cup buttercream over the syrup. Using a 1½-inch round cookie cutter, cut a round out of the unfrosted rectangle. Leaving the cut round in cutter, cut a second round from frosted rectangle, forming a petit four. Transfer to a wire rack. Repeat until 2 dozen petits fours are cut.

5 Divide the poured fondant into three parts, and tint each a pastel shade. Working with one color at a time, warm over a pan of barely simmering water just until the fondant is pourable. You may have to return the fondant to the pot periodically to rewarm.

6 Place one petit four on a chocolate-dipping fork or a large dinner fork, and hold over the poured fondant. Use a small ladle to pour the fondant over the petits four until well coated. Allow to drip for a few seconds before transferring back to the wire rack. Repeat with the remaining petits fours and remaining colored fondant. Allow the fondant to set for at least 10 minutes before decorating. Decorate with the remaining buttercream as desired.

GINGER SIMPLE SYRUP
MAKES 1¼ CUPS

1 cup sugar

1 cup water

2 inch piece of ginger, thinly sliced

Combine the sugar and water in a small saucepan over medium-high heat. Bring to a boil. Add the ginger, reduce to a simmer, and cook for 5 minutes. Remove from the heat, and set aside to cool, about 1½ hours. Strain before using. Store in an airtight container in the refrigerator up to a month.

SWISS MERINGUE BUTTERCREAM

MAKES 1½ CUPS

If the buttercream appears curdled after adding the butter, don't worry; it will come together after beating with the paddle attachment.

10 tablespoons (1¼ sticks) unsalted butter, room temperature
½ cup sugar
2 large egg whites
½ teaspoon pure vanilla extract

1   Fill a medium saucepan one quarter full with water, and bring to a boil. Reduce to a simmer.
2   Beat butter in the bowl of an electric mixer fitted with paddle attachment until fluffy and pale. Transfer to a bowl.
3   Combine the sugar and egg whites in a heat-proof bowl or an electric mixer and place over the saucepan. Whisk constantly until the sugar is dissolved and the whites are warm to the touch, 3 to 4 minutes. Test by rubbing a bit between your fingers.
4   Beat the egg-white mixture on medium speed until fluffy and cooled, about 10 minutes. Increase the speed to high, and whisk until stiff peaks form. Reduce the speed to medium-low, and add the butter a few tablespoons at a time, beating well after each addition. Whisk in the vanilla.
5   Switch to the paddle attachment; beat on the lowest speed for 3 to 5 minutes. Leave at room temperature if using the same day, or store in an airtight container in the refrigerator for up to 3 days. Bring to room temperature; beat until smooth.

POURED FONDANT

MAKES ABOUT 2 CUPS

24 ounces powdered fondant
¼ cup hot water
Pinch of table salt
2 teaspoons corn syrup
2 tablespoons unsalted butter
1 teaspoon pure vanilla extract
Gel-paste food coloring
Ginger Simple Syrup, for thinning (page 290)

1   Bring 2 inches of water to a boil in a medium saucepan; reduce to a low simmer. Break up any lumps in the powdered fondant.
2   Place half the powdered fondant, the water, salt, corn syrup, and butter in a large heat-proof mixing bowl set over the pan. Using a spatula or wooden spoon, stir ingredients until smooth, about 3 minutes. Work quickly; the fondant will lose its sheen if heated for too long or at too high a temperature.
3   Add the remaining powdered fondant and vanilla, and stir until well combined and smooth. Using the end of a toothpick, add small drops of food coloring; stir until the color is evenly combined.
4   The fondant should be liquid enough to pour. If it is too thick, add simple syrup, 1 tablespoon at a time as needed to thin. As the fondant sits over the heat it will thicken; you may add more syrup as necessary.

SUGAR PLUM FAIRY

MAKES 12

You may use any flavor of jam in this recipe. Watch for our description of doneness when baking the meringue. The time can vary dramatically based on humidity.

Swiss Meringue (recipe follows)
6 ounces plum jam
1 pint raspberries
1 large egg white
½ cup superfine sugar
2 cups heavy cream
Spun Sugar (page 292)

1   Preheat the oven to 200°F. Line two baking sheets with parchment paper, and trace six circles measuring 3 inches in diameter on each. Turn the paper over so the ink is facing down.
2   Place the meringue in an 18-inch pastry bag fitted with a jumbo star tip (Ateco #824). Pipe the meringue into disks filling the circles, starting at the center and working outward in a spiral pattern. Pipe two more layers around the edge, forming a bowl.

3   Bake for 1 hour, until the meringue is set and no longer tacky. Reduce the heat to 175°F. Continue baking until the meringue is completely dry and crisp but not at all brown, 1 hour or more. Remove from the oven and store in an airtight container until ready to use, up to 2 days.
4   Place the jam in a small saucepan over low heat. Cook until the jam is liquid, about 5 minutes. Pass through a fine sieve. Discard the solids. Place the strained jam in an airtight container until ready to use.
5   Using a small brush, lightly coat the raspberries with the egg white. Sprinkle with the superfine sugar until well coated, shaking off excess.
6   Whip the cream to soft peaks, and add the strained plum jam. Fold in using a rubber spatula. Place the meringue bowls in jumbo paper cupcake liners set on plates. Spoon the cream into the meringues, and top with the sugared raspberries and spun sugar. Serve immediately.

NOTE: Raw eggs should not be used in food prepared for pregnant women, babies, young children, the elderly, or anyone whose health is compromised.

SWISS MERINGUE

MAKES ABOUT 6 CUPS

6 large egg whites
1½ cups sugar
Pinch cream of tartar
½ teaspoon pure vanilla extract

1   Fill a medium saucepan one quarter full with water, and bring to a boil. Reduce to a simmer.
2   Combine the egg whites, sugar, and cream of tartar in a heat-proof bowl or an electric mixer, and place over the saucepan. Whisk constantly until the sugar is dissolved and the whites are warm to the touch, 3 to 4 minutes. Test by rubbing a bit between your fingers.
3   Transfer liquid to the bowl of an electric mixer fitted with the whisk attachment, and whip on low speed, gradually increasing to high speed, until stiff, glossy peaks form, about 10 minutes. Add the vanilla, and mix until combined. Use immediately.

SPUN SUGAR

MAKES ENOUGH TO GARNISH 12 SUGAR
PLUM FAIRIES

*The best tool for making spun sugar is a
whisk with the ends cut off. Alternatively,
you may use two forks held back to back.
Make spun sugar the day it will be used.*

1¼ cups sugar

⅔ cup water

¼ cup corn syrup

Vegetable-oil cooking spray

1 Cover a 4-by-5-foot area of floor
with parchment or newspaper. Set a
pasta drying rack or a wooden clothes
drying rack on paper; coat well with
cooking spray.

2 Combine the sugar, water, and corn
syrup in a small saucepan, and stir to
combine. Place the pan over medium-
high heat, and bring to a boil. Use a pastry brush dipped in water to brush down
any sugar crystals on the sides of the pan.
Clip on a candy thermometer, and cook,
without stirring, until the temperature
reaches 290°F to 295°F (about 5°F lower
than the hard-crack stage).

3 Remove from the heat, and let sit for
about 5 minutes, until very fine threads
form when whisk or forks are lifted from
the sugar. Dip the whisk or forks into
the sugar, and swing over the rack, using
a quick motion, to create long threads.

4 When the rack is coated with a thin,
cobweblike layer of sugar, lift it in one
piece from the rack, and roll it gently into
a ball. Set on a parchment-lined baking
sheet. Repeat until 12 balls are formed.

CHICORY SALAD WITH LEMON-ANCHOVY VINAIGRETTE

SERVES 4

*Wash the radicchio and escarole—the
chicories—in advance, and keep them in
the refrigerator so the salad is cool and crisp
when served.*

1 lemon

½ teaspoon Dijon mustard

3 anchovy fillets, finely chopped

6 tablespoons extra-virgin olive oil

½ teaspoon coarse salt, plus more for
seasoning

¼ teaspoon freshly ground pepper, plus
more for seasoning

1 small head radicchio

1 small head escarole

1 Finely grate the zest from the lemon.
Squeeze the juice from the lemon, and
discard the seeds. Combine the lemon
zest, lemon juice, mustard, and anchovies in a small bowl. Whisk in the
olive oil, and season with the salt and
pepper.

2 Discard the outer leaves of the radicchio and escarole. Cut out the tough
cores, and tear the leaves into bite-size
pieces. Place in a mixing bowl. Season
with salt and pepper, and drizzle with
salad dressing. Lightly toss to coat. Serve
on salad plates.

CHICKEN LIVERS WITH SHALLOTS AND MARSALA

SERVES 4

1 pound fresh chicken livers, rinsed and
patted dry

1 teaspoon coarse salt, plus more for
seasoning

¼ teaspoon freshly ground pepper, plus
more for seasoning

½ cup all-purpose flour, for dredging

1 tablespoon extra-virgin olive oil, or
more if needed

3 to 4 tablespoons unsalted butter, or
more if needed

2 shallots, minced

½ teaspoon dried Italian herbs

½ cup Marsala wine

½ cup Homemade Chicken Stock (page 8)
or canned

1 Remove strings or sinew from livers.
Sprinkle with the salt and pepper. Dredge
lightly in flour, shaking off excess.

2 Heat the olive oil and 2 tablespoons
butter in a medium sauté pan over medium heat. Sauté the livers in two batches
(using more butter and oil if necessary
with the second batch) until nicely
browned and still pink in the center,
about 2 minutes on each side.

3 Remove the livers from the sauté
pan, and place on a plate, covered with
foil, to keep warm. Drain off all but 1
tablespoon fat from the pan and discard.
If there is not enough fat in the pan, add
more olive oil. Add the shallots and
dried herbs, and sauté until the shallots
are soft and slightly browned, about 2
minutes. Add the Marsala, and simmer
until reduced by half, about 2 minutes.
Add the stock, and simmer until reduced
by half, about 3 minutes.

4 Remove the pan from the heat, and
swirl in the remaining butter. Season with
salt and freshly ground pepper. Pour the
pan sauce over the livers before serving.

CREAMY POLENTA WITH BACON AND SAGE

SERVES 4

*Water or stock can be substituted for any or
all of the milk. The more milk you use, the
creamier the polenta will be.*

2 ounces thickly sliced bacon, cut into
½-inch pieces

1 teaspoon chopped fresh sage leaves, plus
more whole leaves for garnish

4 cups milk

¾ cup plus 2 tablespoons quick-cooking
polenta

3 tablespoons unsalted butter

½ teaspoon coarse salt, or more to taste

¼ teaspoon freshly ground pepper, or
more to taste

2 tablespoons extra-virgin olive oil

1 Place a medium saucepan over low
heat. Add the bacon, and cook until crisp
and golden, about 8 minutes. Remove
the bacon from the saucepan, and transfer to a paper-towel-lined plate. Set aside.

2 Add the chopped sage to the
saucepan, and cook in the bacon fat until
fragrant, about 30 seconds. Add the milk,
and bring to a boil.

3 Add the polenta in a steady stream, whisking constantly until it is smooth and creamy, about 6 minutes. Whisk in the butter, and season with salt and pepper. Transfer to a serving bowl, and crumble the reserved bacon on top. Heat the olive oil in a small sauté pan over medium heat. Add the whole sage leaves, and fry until crisp, about 30 seconds. Remove from the skillet, and scatter over the polenta.

ROASTED PEARS WITH PECORINO CHEESE

SERVES 4

Look for mild pecorinos from Tuscany, sometimes called cacicotta.

4 ripe Bosc or Anjou pears
2 tablespoons unsalted butter
6 tablespoons sugar
1 vanilla bean, split lengthwise
⅓ cup brandy
½ pound pecorino cheese

1 Preheat the oven to 350°F. Halve and peel the pears, and carefully remove the seeds and core.
2 Melt the butter in a large cast-iron skillet over medium heat. Arrange the pears, cut side down, in the skillet so they just touch one another. Sprinkle the sugar over the pears and butter. Cook, tilting the pan back and forth gently from time to time, until the sugar dissolves and melts into a golden caramel, about 4 minutes. Scrape the vanilla seeds into the pan, and add the pod. Reduce the heat, add the brandy, and cook a few minutes more. Be aware that the brandy may ignite, but the flames will die down quickly.
3 Carefully turn the pears over, and transfer to the oven. They should be deep golden brown. Roast until the pears are fork tender, about 10 minutes, depending on the ripeness and size of the pears. Serve with thick slices of pecorino and a bit of the caramel sauce.

FIT TO EAT: COOKING EN PAPILLOTE

SCALLOPS IN WHITE WINE

SERVES 4

Serve with your favorite wild-rice blend.

2 dozen sea scallops (about 1½ pounds), muscles removed
12 cherry tomatoes, cut in half
1 large red onion, cut in half, and cut into ¼-inch half moons
½ cup dry white wine
4 tablespoons unsalted butter
1 tablespoon chopped fresh thyme
1 teaspoon coarse salt
¼ teaspoon freshly ground pepper

1 Preheat the oven to 400°F. Fold four 18-inch lengths of parchment paper in half crosswise; cut each into a half-heart shape, and open. Place 6 scallops near the crease of each piece. Top each with a quarter of the tomatoes and onion. Drizzle 2 tablespoons wine over each pile. Dot each with 1 tablespoon butter. Season with thyme, salt, and pepper.
2 Fold the other half of the parchment over the ingredients. Make small overlapping folds to seal the edges, starting at the top of the heart. Two inches from the end, twist the parchment twice, gently but firmly, to seal. Repeat with the other pieces of parchment, making four packets.
3 Place the packets on a large rimmed baking sheet or in a heavy skillet (preferably cast iron), and bake 20 minutes or until fully puffed. Remove from the oven, and open the packets carefully. Transfer the scallops and vegetables to plates, and spoon some cooking liquid from the packet over them.

PER SERVING: 286 CALORIES, 11 G FAT, 81 MG CHOLESTEROL, 13 G CARBOHYDRATE, 754 MG SODIUM, 29 G PROTEIN, 2 G FIBER

PAPILLOTE PACKETS

While it sounds—and looks—fancy, preparing dishes en papillote, "in paper," is an easy way to make healthy meals without using much oil. To make a packet, fold an eighteen-inch piece of parchment paper in half crosswise. Starting from the folded edge, cut a half-heart shape (when open, parchment will be heart-shaped). Arrange the ingredients near the crease, then fold the other half of the parchment over the ingredients. Starting at the top of the heart, make small overlapping folds to seal edges. About two inches from the end, twist parchment twice, gently but firmly to seal. The paper puffs considerably while cooking, so the seams must be tightly sealed. Packets should not be prepared too far in advance, as the liquids can weaken the parchment paper.

WARM THAI SQUID AND SHRIMP SALAD

SERVES 4

Rice noodles turn this warm salad into a main-course meal.

1 red onion, thinly sliced

1 cucumber, peeled, seeded, thinly sliced

2 medium tomatoes, seeded, cut into ½-inch wedges

2 tablespoons chopped cilantro

1 fresh hot chile such as serrano or jalapeño, cut crosswise into thin rounds

8 ounces squid, cleaned and cut into ½-inch pieces

8 ounces medium shrimp, peeled and deveined

3 tablespoons dark sesame oil

3 tablespoons rice-wine vinegar

1 teaspoon coarse salt

¼ teaspoon freshly ground pepper

1 Preheat the oven to 400°F. Fold four 18-inch lengths of parchment paper in half, cut each into a half-heart shape, and open. In a medium bowl, combine the red onion, cucumber, tomatoes, cilantro, chile, squid, and shrimp. Divide the seafood mixture among the four parchment hearts, near each crease. Fold the other half of each piece of parchment over the ingredients. Make small overlapping folds to seal the edges, starting at the top of the heart. Two inches from the end, twist the parchment twice, gently but firmly, to seal.

2 Place the packets on a rimmed baking sheet or in a heavy skillet (preferably cast iron), and bake 15 minutes or until fully puffed. Remove from the oven, and let sit while preparing the dressing. Whisk together the sesame oil, rice-wine vinegar, salt, and pepper in a small bowl. Open the packets carefully, and transfer the mixture to a serving plate, discarding the cooking juice. Drizzle with the dressing, and serve hot or at room temperature.

PER SERVING: 185 CALORIES, 11 G FAT, 132 MG CHOLESTEROL, 11 G CARBOHYDRATE, 510 MG SODIUM, 10 G PROTEIN, 2 G FIBER

ROLLED FILLETS OF SOLE

SERVES 4

2 oranges

4 six-ounce fillets of sole, skin removed

1 bunch (about 6 ounces) arugula, stems trimmed

1½ teaspoons coarse salt

¼ teaspoon freshly ground pepper

2 tablespoons extra-virgin olive oil

2 tablespoons chopped fresh oregano

1 Grate the zest from the oranges, and set aside. Slice off the stem and flower ends of the oranges. Place the fruit on a work surface, cut side down; using a sharp knife, cut away the peel and white pith, in a single curved motion, from end to end. Working over a bowl to catch the juices, use a paring knife to slice carefully between the sections and membranes of each orange; remove the segments whole. Squeeze the membrane to release any remaining juice before discarding. Set aside the segments and juice.

2 Preheat the oven to 400°F. Fold four 18-inch lengths of parchment paper in half, cut each into a half-heart shape, and open. Lay the fillets on a work surface, skinned side up, and top each with a layer of arugula leaves. Season with half the salt and pepper, and roll up tightly. Place one fillet seam side down on each length of parchment paper near the crease. Combine the orange zest, juice, and segments, olive oil, oregano, and remaining salt and pepper. Spoon the dressing with segments over each fillet. Fold the other half of each piece of parchment over the ingredients. Make small overlapping folds to seal the edges, starting at the top of the heart. Two inches from the end, twist the parchment twice, gently but firmly, to seal.

3 Place the packets on a rimmed baking sheet or in a heavy skillet (preferably cast iron), and bake 25 to 30 minutes or until fully puffed. Remove from the oven, and open carefully. Transfer the fillets to a plate, and spoon the cooking liquid and orange segments over.

PER SERVING: 276 CALORIES, 11 G FAT, 54 MG CHOLESTEROL, 10 G CARBOHYDRATE, 832 MG SODIUM, 37 G PROTEIN, 1 G FIBER

MEDITERRANEAN VEGETABLES

SERVES 4

You can add or substitute your favorite vegetables. Carefully untwist the parchment to check doneness, as some vegetables may take longer to cook.

1 medium zucchini, cut in half lengthwise and cut across into ½-inch-thick half-moons

1 Japanese or 2 baby eggplants (about 6 ounces total), cut in half lengthwise and cut across into ½-inch-thick half-moons

2 medium tomatoes, seeded, cut into ½-inch-thick wedges

4 medium shallots, peeled, cut in half lengthwise

1 red, yellow, or green bell pepper, seeds and ribs removed, and cut into ½-inch strips

4 garlic cloves, thinly sliced

1 tablespoon chopped fresh thyme

1 tablespoon chopped fresh flat-leaf parsley

2 tablespoons extra-virgin olive oil

1½ teaspoons coarse salt

¼ teaspoon freshly ground pepper

1 Preheat the oven to 400°F. Fold four 18-inch lengths of parchment paper in half, cut each into a half-heart shape, and open. In a large bowl, combine the zucchini, eggplant, tomatoes, shallots, bell pepper, garlic, thyme, and parsley. Divide the vegetable mixture among the lengths of parchment, arranging near each crease. Drizzle the oil over the vegetables, and season with salt and pepper. Fold the other half of each piece of parchment over the ingredients. Make small overlapping folds to seal the edges, starting at the top of the heart. Two inches from the end, twist parchment twice, gently but firmly, to seal.

2 Place the packets on a rimmed baking sheet or in a heavy skillet (preferably cast iron), and bake 25 minutes or until fully puffed. Remove from the oven, and open the packets carefully. Transfer the vegetables to a serving plate, and spoon the cooking liquid over, if desired.

PER SERVING: 107 CALORIES, 7 G FAT, 0 MG CHOLESTEROL, 11 G CARBOHYDRATE, 726 MG SODIUM, 2 G PROTEIN, 1 G FIBER

STEAMED CHICKEN WITH ROASTED PEPPERS AND PROSCIUTTO

SERVES 4

Served with a green salad, this flavorful chicken dish makes a quick and easy supper. The chicken can be prepared a few hours ahead of time and kept in the refrigerator—don't place it in parchment until ready to cook, or the paper will get soggy.

2 red bell peppers
4 boneless, skinless chicken breast halves
1 teaspoon coarse salt
¼ teaspoon freshly ground black pepper
2 ounces thinly sliced prosciutto or other ham
4 ounces fresh mozzarella, thinly sliced
1 teaspoon unsalted butter, melted

1 Place the peppers directly over the burner of a gas stove over high heat or on a grill. Just as each section turns puffy and black, turn the pepper with tongs to prevent overcooking. (If you don't have a gas stove, place the peppers on a baking pan, and broil in the oven, turning as each side becomes charred.) Transfer the peppers to a large bowl, and cover immediately with plastic wrap. Let the peppers sweat until they are cool enough to handle, about 15 minutes. Transfer the peppers to a work surface. Peel off the blackened skin and discard. Cut each pepper in half, and discard the seeds. Set the four halves aside.

2 Meanwhile, preheat the oven to 400°F. Fold four 18-inch lengths of parchment paper in half, cut each into a half-heart shape, and open. Place each chicken breast between two layers of waxed paper, and pound with a meat pounder until ⅜ inch thick. Lay each breast, smooth side down, on a work surface, and season with half the salt and pepper. Top each with an equal amount of prosciutto. Place a roasted pepper half on top of the prosciutto, and top each with sliced mozzarella. Roll up each breast, and place, seam side down, on a piece of parchment near the crease. Brush with the melted butter, and season with the remaining salt and pepper. Fold the other half of each piece of parchment over the chicken. Make small overlapping folds to seal the edges, starting at the top of the heart. Two inches from the end, twist the parchment twice, gently but firmly, to seal.

3 Place the packets on a rimmed baking sheet or in a heavy skillet (preferably cast iron), and bake 30 minutes or until fully puffed. Remove from the oven, and open the packets carefully. Transfer the breasts to a plate, and spoon the cooking liquid over.

PER SERVING: 255 CALORIES, 10 G FAT, 91 MG CHOLESTEROL, 3 G CARBOHYDRATE, 1,082 MG SODIUM, 37 G PROTEIN, 1 G FIBER

HOLIDAY FAVORITES

CHESTNUT CHOCOLATE LAYER CAKE

MAKES 1 NINE-INCH LAYER CAKE

This cake is best when served the day it is made. You can bake it in the morning and finish it later in the day. It can stand in a cool place for about three hours before it is served. Marrons glacés, whole candied chestnuts, are available in specialty food stores.

Unsalted butter, for pans
14 ounces fresh chestnuts
1 cup sugar
4 large eggs, room temperature, separated
½ teaspoon cream of tartar
1 cup sifted cake flour (not self-rising)
⅔ cup sifted chestnut flour
2 teaspoons baking powder
½ teaspoon ground cinnamon
¼ teaspoon table salt
½ cup water
½ cup vegetable oil
1 teaspoon pure vanilla extract
6 ounces very finely ground semisweet chocolate
  Pastry Cream (page 296)
  Chocolate Ganache (page 296)
8 marrons glacés (optional)

1 Preheat oven to 350°F. Butter two 9-by-2-inch round baking pans; line bottoms with parchment. Butter parchment; set aside. Using a chestnut knife or a small paring knife, make an incision about ⅛ inch deep through shell and into flesh of each chestnut almost all the way around the circumference of the nut. Transfer to a chestnut pan or rimmed baking sheet. Roast in oven until chestnuts are tender, about 35 minutes. Turn oven off. Leaving sheet with chestnuts in oven, remove several at a time. Working quickly, place 1 chestnut in a towel and, holding both, peel chestnut while still hot. Remove and discard shells and inner skin; set nuts aside. Repeat until all chestnuts are shelled. Heat the oven to 325°F. Let chestnuts cool completely. Transfer chestnuts to a food processor. Add 2 tablespoons sugar; pulse until very finely ground; set aside.

2 Place egg whites and cream of tartar in bowl of an electric mixer fitted with the whisk attachment. Beat until foamy on medium-low speed, 5 to 6 minutes. With mixer running, slowly add ½ cup sugar. Raise speed to medium-high; beat until stiff peaks form, 6 to 7 minutes. Transfer whites to a large bowl.

3 Sift together the cake flour, chestnut flour, baking powder, cinnamon, salt, and remaining 6 tablespoons sugar into the bowl of an electric mixer fitted with the paddle attachment. Add egg yolks, water, oil, and vanilla, and beat on medium speed until smooth and well combined, about 1 minute.

4 Using a rubber spatula, carefully and gently fold flour mixture in 4 or 5 additions into egg-white mixture, until well combined. Gently fold in reserved ground chestnuts and chocolate. Divide batter between two prepared cake pans; bake on one shelf, rotating pans halfway through baking, until golden and a cake tester inserted into center of cakes comes out clean, about 65 minutes. Transfer to a wire rack until completely cool. Invert pans to remove cakes. Remove parchment.

5 Place one layer on a cake round or directly onto a cake stand or serving platter. Using an offset spatula, evenly

spread pastry cream on top to within ½ inch of edges. Place other layer on top.

6 Pour ganache on top; carefully spread to about ¼ inch from edges. Ganache will overflow slightly and gently brim edges. Arrange marrons glacés, if using, on top of cake at equal distances. Set cake aside in a cool place to allow ganache to firm up.

PASTRY CREAM

MAKES ENOUGH FOR 1 NINE-INCH LAYER CAKE

This recipe can be prepared up to two days ahead and stored, covered, in the refrigerator.

- 1½ cups milk
- 1½ tablespoons cornstarch
- 1½ tablespoons all-purpose flour
- ⅓ cup sugar
  Pinch of table salt
- 1 large whole egg
- 1 large egg yolk
- 1 tablespoon unsalted butter
- 1 teaspoon pure vanilla extract

1 In a medium saucepan, bring milk to a boil. Fill a large bowl with ice and water; set aside.

2 In a medium bowl, whisk together cornstarch, flour, sugar, salt, egg, and egg yolk until well combined. Pour one-quarter of boiling milk into egg mixture, whisking until combined. Whisk mixture back into pan; place over medium-low heat. Whisk until the mixture begins to bubble and has thickened, 4 to 5 minutes.

3 Remove from heat; whisk in butter and vanilla until butter is melted.

4 Transfer mixture to a medium bowl; place bowl in ice bath. Let stand until cold, stirring occasionally, about 10 minutes. Cover with plastic wrap; store in the refrigerator until ready to use.

CHOCOLATE GANACHE

MAKES ENOUGH FOR 1 NINE-INCH LAYER CAKE

- 5 ounces semisweet chocolate, finely chopped
- ⅔ cup heavy cream

Place chocolate in a small bowl. Bring cream to a boil in a small saucepan over medium-high heat. Pour boiling cream over chocolate. Cover with plastic wrap for several minutes. Remove wrap; stir until mixture is completely smooth and chocolate is melted. Set ganache aside in a cool place; let stand until thickened to consistency of thick cake batter, 10 to 15 minutes.

CHESTNUT TRUFFLES

MAKES ABOUT 2 DOZEN

- ½ cup heavy cream
- 8 ounces bittersweet chocolate, chopped
- 2 tablespoons dark corn syrup
- 12 chestnuts packed in syrup or in cognac, drained, patted dry, and coarsely chopped
- ¼ cup confectioners' sugar
- ¼ cup cocoa powder

1 Bring cream to a simmer in a small saucepan over medium heat. Remove pan from stove. Add chocolate and corn syrup, stirring until chocolate is melted. Fold in chestnuts. Transfer to a medium bowl; place in the refrigerator to chill until set, about 1 hour.

2 Using a dessert spoon, scoop out about 2 teaspoons of chocolate mixture, and, using fingers, form into a roughly shaped ball; place on a parchment-lined baking sheet. Repeat until all the mixture is used. Transfer to refrigerator until cold and firm, 15 to 30 minutes. The uncoated balls can be stored in an airtight container in the refrigerator, or a cool dry place, for up to 5 days.

3 Just before serving, roll half the balls in confectioners' sugar and half in cocoa, coating completely. Serve.

CHESTNUT APPLE STRUDEL

SERVES 10 TO 12

- 1 pound fresh chestnuts
- 4 cups water plus ¾ cup warm water
- 1 cup sugar, plus more for sprinkling
- 2 cups plus 2 tablespoons all-purpose flour, plus more for work surface
- ¾ teaspoon table salt
- 3 tablespoons vegetable oil
- 10 tablespoons (1¼ sticks) unsalted butter, plus more for pan
- 5 large apples (about 3 pounds), such as Empire, Gala, and Fuji, peeled, cored, and cut into ¾-inch cubes
- 1 slice white bread, crust removed
- ⅛ teaspoon freshly ground nutmeg
- 1 teaspoon ground cinnamon

1 Preheat oven to 350°F. Using a chestnut knife or a small paring knife, make an incision about ⅛ inch deep through shell and into flesh of each chestnut almost all the way around the circumference of the nut. Transfer to a chestnut pan or rimmed baking sheet. Roast in oven until chestnuts are tender, about 35 minutes. Turn oven off. Leaving pan with chestnuts in oven, remove several at a time. Working quickly, place 1 chestnut in a towel and, holding both, peel chestnut while still hot; remove and discard shells and inner skin. Transfer chestnuts to a medium saucepan. Heat oven to 375°F.

2 Add 4 cups water and ½ cup sugar to chestnuts; place over high heat, and bring to a boil. Reduce heat; simmer until most of the liquid has been absorbed and chestnuts are falling-apart tender, 40 to 45 minutes. Drain. Break chestnuts into small pieces; set aside to cool.

3 In an electric mixer fitted with the paddle attachment, combine flour and ½ teaspoon salt. Add oil and ¾ cup warm water; mix on medium-low speed until dough comes together, about 1 minute. Switch to dough hook; mix until smooth and shiny without sticking to fingers when squeezed, about 5 minutes. Turn dough out onto a clean surface; knead into a ball. Cover dough with a bowl; let stand at least 1 hour or up to 4 hours.

4 Melt 3 tablespoons butter in a large skillet over medium-high heat. Add half the apples and ¼ cup sugar; cook, stirring frequently, until just tender and golden on edges, 5 to 6 minutes. Transfer apples to a shallow bowl; set aside until cool. Repeat cooking procedure with remaining apples, 3 tablespoons butter, and remaining ¼ cup sugar.

5 Place bread in a food processor; pulse until texture resembles coarse meal. Add bread crumbs to reserved apples, along with reserved chestnuts, the nutmeg, the cinnamon, and remaining ¼ teaspoon salt. Toss to combine well; set aside.

6 Melt remaining 4 tablespoons butter. Brush a baking sheet with some melted butter; set excess aside. Place a clean sheet or a very large apron on a clean surface about 36 inches square; sprinkle with flour. Place dough in center; roll into a 12-inch square. Cover dough with a damp towel; let stand for 15 minutes. Remove towel; slide both hands, palms down, under dough. Lift dough; begin stretching until it becomes too big to stretch on top of hands. Carefully set dough back down on cloth, making sure to spread dough out without any wrinkles. Begin to pull dough out in all directions, maintaining square shape, until it is almost translucent and about 36 inches square.

7 Using a sharp knife or scissors, trim about ½ inch of the thicker edges off. The dough that remains should be only the very thinnest dough. Gently brush melted butter evenly all over dough; arrange apple-chestnut mixture on top, leaving a 1-inch border.

8 Lift front edges of cloth off table; flip dough and apple-chestnut mixture over onto itself, enclosing mixture. This first fold should be 3 to 4 inches wide. Continue folding dough in this manner, using cloth, until completely rolled up and with final edge on top. Carefully form dough into a C shape. Place prepared baking sheet right next to strudel; flip strudel over onto baking sheet so top becomes bottom. Brush with remaining melted butter; sprinkle generously with sugar. Bake, rotating pan halfway through, until top is golden brown and apples are tender, 45 to 50 minutes. Remove from oven, transfer baking sheet to a wire rack; let stand until strudel is warm or at room temperature.

CLASSIC LIGHT ROLLS

MAKES 2 DOZEN

For really fluffy yeast dinner rolls like these classic light rolls, don't gather and re-roll the scraps of dough, and be sure to give the dough generous rising time.

¼ cup warm water (110°F) plus 1 tablespoon water

½ cup plus a pinch of sugar

1 ¼-ounce package (2 teaspoons) active dry yeast

1¼ cups milk

¾ cup (1½ sticks) unsalted butter, melted and cooled, plus more for bowl

2½ teaspoons coarse salt

3 large eggs

4½ to 5 cups all-purpose flour, plus more for dusting

1 tablespoon poppy seeds

1 Line a baking sheet with parchment paper. In the bowl of an electric mixer, whisk together the warm water, a pinch of sugar, and the yeast. Set aside until the mixture is foamy, about 10 minutes.

2 Using the electric mixer fitted with the dough-hook attachment, mix together on low speed the milk, butter, the remaining ½ cup sugar, the salt, and 2 eggs. Gradually add enough flour to form a sticky but manageable dough. Transfer the dough to a lightly buttered bowl; cover tightly with buttered plastic wrap. Let the dough rise in a warm place until doubled in size, about 2½ hours.

3 Turn the dough out onto a lightly floured surface. With a floured rolling pin, roll the dough out to a ¾-inch thickness. Cut out 24 rounds, as close together as possible, using a 2¼-inch-round biscuit or cookie cutter. Place the rounds ¼ inch apart on the baking sheet. Cover with buttered plastic wrap. Let the rolls rise until light and the dough does not spring back when pressed with a finger, about 30 minutes.

4 Preheat the oven to 350°F. Whisk together the remaining egg and 1 tablespoon water. Brush the tops of the rounds with the egg wash. Sprinkle the rounds with the poppy seeds. Bake until the rolls are golden brown, 20 to 25 minutes. Transfer to a wire rack to cool for 5 minutes before serving. Serve warm.

BUTTERY CRESCENTS

MAKES ABOUT 3 DOZEN

Salted butter gives these rolls their light, flaky texture and just the right amount of seasoning.

1 cup (2 sticks) salted butter, cool but not cold

Classic Light Rolls dough (recipe above), made through step 2

All-purpose flour, for dusting

1 Line two baking sheets with parchment paper. Place the butter in the bowl of an electric mixer fitted with the paddle attachment. Beat on low speed until the butter is spreadable. Turn the dough out onto a floured work surface. With a floured rolling pin, roll the dough into a rough 10-by-25-inch rectangle. Spread the dough with the butter. Fold both 10-inch edges of the dough into the middle, then fold in half to form a rectangle that is about 10 by 6 inches. Wrap the dough in plastic wrap; place on a baking sheet. Transfer to the refrigerator to chill for 40 minutes.

2 On a lightly floured surface, roll the dough into a 10-by-25-inch rectangle. Fold into quarters as in step 1. Wrap in plastic wrap; return to the baking sheet. Chill 40 minutes more.

3 Roll the dough into a 15-by-25-inch rectangle. Using a pizza wheel or a sharp knife, trim the edges of the dough so they are straight. Discard the scraps. Cut the rectangle lengthwise into four equal strips. Cut each strip into elongated triangles, about 3 inches wide at the base. Starting at the base of the triangles, roll and shape into crescents. Transfer crescents to the prepared baking sheets, spacing them 1 inch apart. Cover with buttered plastic wrap. Let the dough rise in a cool place for 1 hour.

4 Preheat the oven to 350°F with two racks. Bake the crescents until golden and cooked through, about 20 minutes. Transfer to a wire rack to cool for 5 minutes before serving. Serve warm.

TWICE BAKED POTATOES
SERVES 6

6 Idaho potatoes, scrubbed
1 tablespoon olive oil
4 small garlic cloves, minced
8 medium shallots, minced
¼ cup plus 2 tablespoons nonfat ricotta cheese
¼ cup plus 2 tablespoons skim milk
1½ teaspoons coarse salt
¼ teaspoon freshly ground black pepper
4 medium tomatoes, seeded, cut into ¼-inch dice
1 tablespoon roughly chopped fresh marjoram, basil, or oregano

1   Preheat the oven to 400°F. Prick each potato several times with a fork or paring knife. Bake the potatoes on a baking sheet until tender, about 1 hour. Make about a 4-inch-long cut lengthwise along the top of each. Using a spoon or melon baller, remove the flesh of each potato; transfer the flesh to a medium bowl. Reserve the skins. Pass the potatoes through a ricer or a food mill fitted with a fine disc into a medium bowl.
2   Heat the oil in a nonstick skillet over medium-low heat. Add the garlic and shallots; cook, stirring frequently, about 6 minutes. Stir half the garlic and shallots into the riced potatoes. Set the remaining half aside in the skillet.
3   In the bowl of a food processor, purée the ricotta until smooth; mix into the riced potatoes along with the milk, 1 teaspoon salt, and ⅛ teaspoon pepper. Fill the potato skins with the cheese-and-potato mixture until brimming over the edges. Transfer to a baking sheet; place in the oven until the potatoes are heated through, about 15 minutes.
4   Return the remaining garlic and shallots to medium heat. Add the tomatoes and remaining ½ teaspoon salt and ⅛ teaspoon pepper; cook, tossing, until the tomatoes are warm, about 3 minutes. Stir in ½ tablespoon marjoram; cook 1 minute. Spoon 3 tablespoons tomato mixture over each potato; garnish with the remaining marjoram. Serve hot.

MASHED POTATOES 101
SERVES 4 TO 6

For stiffer mashed potatoes, use only three-quarters cup milk or cream; for richer mashed potatoes, add another two tablespoons butter.

2 pounds russet, Yukon gold, or long white potatoes
1 tablespoon coarse salt, plus more for seasoning
1 cup milk or cream
4 tablespoons unsalted butter
¼ teaspoon freshly ground pepper
¼ teaspoon ground nutmeg

1   Peel and cut the potatoes into 1½-inch-thick slices. Place in a medium saucepan, and cover with cold water by 2 inches; add 1 tablespoon of salt. Bring to a simmer. If using a potato ricer, fill another saucepan or the bottom of a double boiler with water; place over low heat. Cook the potatoes until the tip of a knife slips in and out easily. Drain the potatoes in a colander. Place the milk in a small saucepan set over medium-high heat.
2   If using a potato ricer, place a heatproof bowl or the top of a double boiler over the pan of simmering water. Press the hot, drained potatoes through the ricer into the bowl. (If using an electric mixer, proceed to step 4.)
3   Stir the potatoes with a wooden spoon until smooth, about 1 minute. Using a whisk, incorporate the butter. Drizzle in the hot milk, whisking continuously. Add the pepper, nutmeg, and salt to taste; whisk to combine. Serve immediately.
4   For the electric-mixer method, transfer the hot, drained potatoes to the bowl of an electric mixer fitted with the paddle attachment. Mix on medium-low speed until most lumps have disappeared, about 1 minute. Add the butter; mix until blended. On low speed, add the hot milk in a slow stream, then add the pepper, nutmeg, and salt to taste. Mix to combine. Do not overmix; do not increase speed. Serve immediately.

GLAZED HAM 101
SERVES 16

This is the traditional American ham, served across the country for holidays and gatherings. A ham this size can serve sixteen people for dinner and up to fifty for hors d'oeuvres. Using both light- and dark-brown sugar keeps the glaze from getting too dark while the ham cooks. Fresh bay leaves are soft and flexible and can be used as an attractive garnish.

¼ cup yellow mustard seeds
1 tablespoon whole fennel seeds
1 14- to 18-pound whole smoked ham, bone in and rind on
1 cup apple cider
2 teaspoons ground cinnamon
1 tablespoon ground ginger
¾ cup Dijon mustard
1 cup plus 2 tablespoons packed light-brown sugar
¾ cup packed dark-brown sugar
3 tablespoons light corn syrup
2 tablespoons unsulfured molasses
2 to 3 tablespoons whole cloves
4 fresh bay leaves (optional)

1   Heat a heavy skillet, such as cast iron, over medium-low heat. Add the mustard and fennel seeds, and shake the skillet gently to move the seeds around so they toast evenly and do not burn. Toast the seeds until they are aromatic and barely take on color. Let cool.
2   Rinse the ham with cool water, and dry with paper towels. Let the ham stand for 2 hours at room temperature. Preheat the oven to 350°F with a rack on the lowest level. Line a roasting pan with heavy-duty aluminum foil. Place a roasting rack in the pan. Transfer the ham, with the thicker rind on top, to the rack. Pour the apple cider over the ham. Cook for 2 hours, or until an instant-read thermometer inserted in the thickest part of the ham registers 140°F.

3 Place the toasted mustard and fennel seeds in a spice grinder or mortar and pestle, grind to a rough powder, and transfer to a medium bowl. Add the cinnamon, ginger, mustard, 2 tablespoons light-brown sugar, 2 tablespoons dark-brown sugar, the corn syrup, and the molasses. Combine well; set aside.

4 Remove the ham from the oven, and let cool for about 30 minutes. Using kitchen shears or a sharp knife, trim away the hard rind from the ham. Use a sharp knife to trim the fat to a layer of about ¼ inch all over the ham; it does not need to be perfectly even. The bottom of the ham will have less fat and more skin. Place ham bottom-side down. Score remaining fat on top of the ham into a pattern of 1- to 2-inch diamonds, cutting about ¼ to ½ inch through the fat and into the meat.

5 Insert a whole clove into the intersection of each diamond. Using a pastry brush or your fingers, rub the spice glaze all over the ham and deep into the cut diamonds. In a medium bowl, combine the remaining cup light-brown sugar and the remaining ½ cup plus 2 tablespoons dark-brown sugar. Using your fingers, gently pack the sugar mixture all over the scored fat. If using bay leaves, secure them with toothpick halves around the shank bone. Cover the toothpicks by inserting cloves on top of them. Return the ham to the oven, and cook for 20 minutes. The sugar will begin to crystallize, but there will be some hard spots of sugar; gently baste these areas with the remaining glaze. Cook 40 minutes more, basting with the remaining glaze after 20 minutes; do not baste with any pan juices (the melted fat from the ham will make the glazed ham less attractive). The ham should be dark brown and crusty; cook 15 minutes more if necessary. Remove and let cool slightly. Transfer to a serving platter, and let stand 30 minutes before carving.

ROAST CHICKEN 101

SERVES 4

A golden-brown chicken, its skin crisp and its meat juicy, makes a meal that is equally as appropriate for a casual gathering as for a small dinner party.

1 6-pound roasting chicken
2 tablespoons unsalted butter
Coarse salt and freshly ground pepper
2 medium onions, sliced crosswise ½ inch thick
1 lemon
3 large garlic cloves
4 sprigs thyme
1 cup Homemade Chicken Stock (page 8), or low-sodium canned, skimmed of fat, or wine, or water

1 Let the chicken and 1 tablespoon butter stand at room temperature for 30 minutes. Preheat the oven to 425°F. Remove and discard the plastic pop-up timer from the chicken if there is one. Remove the giblets and excess fat from the chicken cavity. Rinse the chicken inside and out under cold running water. Dry it thoroughly with paper towels. Tuck the wing tips under the body. Sprinkle the cavity liberally with salt and pepper, and set aside.

2 Place the onion slices in two rows down the center of a heavy-duty roasting pan, touching.

3 Press down on the lemon with your palm, and roll it back and forth several times (this softens the lemon and allows the juice to flow more freely). Pierce the entire surface of the lemon with a fork. Using the side of a large knife, gently press on the garlic cloves to open slightly. Place the garlic cloves, thyme sprigs, and lemon in the cavity. Place the chicken in the pan, on the onion slices. Cut about 18 inches of kitchen twine, bring the chicken legs forward, cross them, and tie together.

4 Spread the softened butter over the entire surface of the chicken, and sprinkle liberally with salt and pepper. Place in the oven, and roast until the skin is deep golden brown and crisp and the juices run clear when pierced, about 1½ hours. Insert an instant-read thermometer into the breast, then the thigh. The breast temperature should read 180°F and the thigh 190°F.

5 Remove the chicken from the oven, and transfer to a cutting board with a well. Let the chicken stand 10 to 15 minutes so the juices settle.

6 Meanwhile, pour the pan drippings into a shallow bowl or fat separator, and leave the onions in the pan. Leave any cooked-on browned bits on the bottom of the roasting pan, and remove and discard any blackened bits. Using a large spoon or a fat separator, skim off and discard as much fat as possible.

7 Pour the remaining drippings and the juices that have collected under the resting chicken back into the roasting pan. Place on the stove over medium-high heat to cook, about 1 minute. Add the chicken stock, raise the heat to high, and, using a wooden spoon, stir to loosen the browned bits from the bottom of the pan; combine with the stock until the liquid is reduced by half, about 6 minutes. Strain the gravy into a small bowl, pressing on the onions to extract any liquid. Discard the onions, and stir in the remaining tablespoon cold butter until melted and incorporated. Untie the legs, and remove and discard the garlic, thyme, and lemon. Carve, and serve the gravy on the side.

PERFECT ROAST TURKEY 101

SERVES 12 TO 14

If your roasting pan only fits sideways in the oven, turn the pan every hour so the turkey cooks and browns evenly. The cheesecloth is dipped in butter and wine to keep the breast meat moist and the skin from burning. Unlike frozen turkeys, fresh birds release a lot of juice as they cook. Watch your roasting pan for overflow, and scoop out liquid from the pan as the turkey cooks.

1 20- to 21-pound fresh whole turkey, neck and giblets (heart, gizzard, and liver) removed from cavity and reserved

1½ cups (3 sticks) unsalted butter, melted, plus 4 tablespoons room temperature

1 750-ml bottle dry white wine

2 teaspoons coarse salt, plus more for seasoning

2 teaspoons freshly ground pepper, plus more for seasoning

1 cup dry red or white wine, or water, for gravy (optional)

Homemade Turkey Stock (recipe follows)

1 Rinse the turkey inside and out with cool water, and dry with paper towels. Let stand for 1 to 2 hours at room temperature.

2 Preheat the oven to 450°F with a rack on lowest level. Combine the melted butter and wine in a bowl. Fold a large piece of cheesecloth into quarters, and cut into a 17-inch, 4-layer square. Immerse the cheesecloth in the butter and wine; let soak.

3 Place the turkey, breast-side up, on a roasting rack in a heavy metal roasting pan. If the turkey comes with a pop-up timer, remove it; an instant-read thermometer is a much more accurate indication of doneness. Fold the wing tips under the turkey. Sprinkle ½ teaspoon salt and ½ teaspoon pepper inside the turkey. If stuffing the turkey, do so now. Tie the legs together loosely with kitchen twine (a bow will be easy to untie later). Fold the neck flap under, and secure with toothpicks. Rub the turkey with the softened butter, and sprinkle with the remaining 1½ teaspoons salt and 1½ teaspoons pepper.

4 Lift the cheesecloth out of the liquid, and squeeze it slightly, leaving it very damp. Spread it evenly over the breast and about halfway down the sides of the turkey; it can cover some of the leg area. Place the turkey, legs first, in the oven. Cook for 30 minutes. Using a pastry brush, baste the cheesecloth and exposed parts of the turkey with the butter and wine. Reduce the oven temperature to 350°F, and continue to cook for 2½ hours more, basting every 30 minutes and watching the pan juices; if the pan gets too full, spoon out the juices, reserving them for gravy.

5 Carefully remove and discard the cheesecloth. Turn the roasting pan so the breast is facing the back of the oven. Baste the turkey with the pan juices. If there are not enough juices, continue to use the butter and wine. The skin gets fragile as it browns, so baste carefully. Cook 1 hour more, basting after 30 minutes.

6 Insert an instant-read thermometer into the thickest part of the thigh. Do not poke into a bone. The temperature should reach 180°F (the stuffing should be between 140°F and 160°F) and the turkey should be golden brown. The breast does not need to be checked for temperature. If the legs are not yet fully cooked, baste the turkey, return to the oven, and cook 20 to 30 minutes more.

7 When fully cooked, remove from the oven, and let rest for about 30 minutes. Transfer to a carving board. Make the gravy. Pour all the pan juices into a glass measuring cup. Let stand until the fat rises to the surface, about 10 minutes, then skim it off. Meanwhile, place the roasting pan over medium-high heat. Add 1 cup red or white wine to the pan. Using a wooden spoon, scrape the pan until the liquid boils and all the browned bits are loosened from the pan. Add the turkey stock to the pan. Stir well, and return to a boil. Cook until the liquid has reduced by half, about 10 minutes. Add the defatted pan juices, and cook over medium-high heat 10 minutes more. You will have about 2½ cups of gravy. Season to taste with salt and pepper, strain into a warm gravy boat, and serve with turkey.

HOMEMADE TURKEY STOCK

MAKES ABOUT 1 QUART

The giblets are the secret to a fine stock and gravy. Prepare it while the turkey roasts. To make it a day in advance, remove the neck and giblets from the turkey and return the bird to the refrigerator.

Giblets (heart, gizzard, and liver) and neck reserved from turkey

4 tablespoons unsalted butter

1 onion, cut into ¼-inch dice

1 celery stalk with leaves, strings removed, stalk cut into ¼-inch dice, leaves roughly chopped

1 small leek, white and pale-green parts, cut into ¼-inch dice, well washed

Coarse salt and freshly ground pepper

7 cups cold water

1 dried bay leaf

1 Trim the fat or membrane from the giblets. If the liver has the gall bladder attached, trim it off carefully, removing part of the liver if necessary. Do not pierce the sac; the liquid it contains is very bitter. Rinse the giblets and neck, and pat dry.

2 In a medium saucepan, melt 3 tablespoons butter over medium heat. Add the onion, celery and leaves, and leek. Cook, stirring occasionally, until the onion is translucent, about 8 minutes. Season with salt and pepper; cook 5 minutes more. Add the cold water, the bay leaf, gizzard, heart, and neck. Cover, and bring to a boil, then reduce to a simmer. Cook 45 minutes or until the gizzard is tender when pierced with the tip of a knife.

3 Meanwhile, chop the liver finely. Melt the remaining tablespoon butter in a skillet over medium-low heat. Add the liver; cook, stirring constantly, 4 to 6 minutes, until the liver no longer releases any blood. Set aside.

4 Simmer the stock until reduced to 2½ cups, about 45 minutes. Increase the heat, and cook 10 to 15 minutes more if necessary.

5 Strain the stock. Chop the gizzard and heart very fine; add to the strained stock along with the chopped liver. Pick the meat off the neck, and add to stock. Set aside until needed to make the gravy.

CLASSIC STUFFING

MAKES 12 CUPS

Stale bread gives this stuffing texture. If you like a very moist, soft stuffing, use a sturdy, chewy loaf.

12 tablespoons (1½ sticks) unsalted butter

4 onions (2 pounds), cut into ¼-inch dice

16 celery stalks, strings removed, cut into ¼-inch dice

10 large fresh sage leaves, chopped, or 2 teaspoons crushed dried sage

1½ quarts Homemade Chicken Stock (page 8), or low-sodium canned, skimmed of fat

2 loaves stale white bread (about 36 slices), crusts on, cut into 1-inch cubes

2 teaspoons coarse salt

1 tablespoon plus 1 teaspoon freshly ground pepper

3 cups coarsely chopped fresh flat-leaf parsley leaves (about 2 bunches)

2 cups pecans, toasted, chopped (optional)

2 cups dried cherries (optional)

1 Melt the butter in a large skillet. Add the onions and celery, and cook over medium heat until the onions are translucent, about 8 minutes. Add the sage, stir to combine, and cook 3 minutes. Add ½ cup stock, and stir well. Cook for about 5 minutes, until the liquid has reduced by half.

2 Transfer the onion mixture to a large mixing bowl. Add the bread, salt, pepper, parsley, pecans, cherries (if using), and the remaining 1 quart plus 1½ cups stock; mix to combine. Use to stuff the turkey immediately.

DOUBLE HOT CHOCOLATE PUDDING

SERVES 4 TO 6

The taste of the chocolate will come through very clearly in this pudding, so buy only the best. A pinch of cayenne gives it a slight bite. The pudding may be served lukewarm or chilled (with plastic wrap over the surface) for up to one day and served chilled.

¼ cup cornstarch

¼ cup plus 2 tablespoons sugar

3 tablespoons Dutch-process cocoa powder

¼ teaspoon ground cinnamon

1 tablespoon espresso powder (optional)

Pinch of coarse salt

Pinch of cayenne pepper (optional)

1¼ cups heavy cream

1¼ cups milk

7 ounces bittersweet chocolate, finely chopped

1½ tablespoons unsalted butter, cut into small pieces

1 In a medium saucepan, whisk together the cornstarch, sugar, cocoa, cinnamon, espresso powder (if using), salt, and cayenne (if using). In a measuring cup, combine the cream with the milk. Whisk 1 cup cream mixture into the dry ingredients until the cornstarch is dissolved. Whisk in the remaining cream mixture; place the saucepan over medium-high heat.

2 Cook, whisking constantly, until the mixture comes to a boil and thickens, about 5 minutes. Add the chocolate; cook, whisking, about 1 minute more. Remove from the heat; whisk in the butter until melted. Transfer to a bowl; place plastic wrap directly on the surface of the pudding to prevent a skin from forming. Let stand until lukewarm, about 45 minutes. Transfer the pudding to serving bowls or goblets.

DATE AND PINE-NUT TART

MAKES ONE 4¼-BY-13½-INCH TART; SERVES 1

You will need one four-and-a-quarter-by-thirteen-and-a-half-inch tart pan with a removable bottom.

1 cup pine nuts

½ cup all-purpose flour, plus more for work surface

½ recipe Pâte Brisée (page 10)

½ cup pitted dates, finely chopped

4 tablespoons unsalted butter, room temperature

½ cup sugar

2 large eggs, lightly beaten

½ cup honey

1 teaspoon pure vanilla extract

Grated zest of 1 lemon

½ teaspoon ground cinnamon

1 Preheat the oven to 350°F with a rack in the center. Place the pine nuts in a single layer on a rimmed baking sheet; toast until golden and aromatic, 8 to 12 minutes, shaking the pan halfway through toasting.

2 On a lightly floured surface, roll the pâte brisée into an 8-by-18-inch rectangle. With a dry pastry brush, brush off any excess flour; roll the dough around the rolling pin, and lift it over the tart pan. Line the pan with the dough; using your fingers, gently press the dough into the pan. Trim any excess dough flush with the edges of the pan. Transfer to the refrigerator to chill for 30 minutes.

3 In a small bowl, toss and separate the chopped dates with 2 tablespoons flour; set aside.

4 In the bowl of an electric mixer fitted with the paddle attachment, cream the butter and sugar. Add the eggs, honey, vanilla, and lemon zest. Stir in the remaining ¼ cup plus 2 tablespoons flour, the cinnamon, and the flour-dusted dates. Pour the batter into the chilled shell; sprinkle with the toasted pine nuts. Bake until the filling has browned and set, about 35 minutes. Transfer to a wire rack to cool. Serve.

THREE-CHEESE CAKE

MAKES ONE 8-INCH CAKE; SERVES 8

You will need one eight-inch springform pan.

¾ cup hazelnuts

8 navel oranges, peel and pith removed

6 tablespoons unsalted butter, plus more for pan

9 whole graham crackers

¾ cup plus 2 tablespoons sugar

5 ounces cream cheese, room temperature

6 ounces mild and creamy goat cheese, room temperature

1 teaspoon grated orange zest

1 tablespoon plus 1 teaspoon all-purpose flour

½ teaspoon coarse salt

1 tablespoon plus 1 teaspoon Frangelico (optional)

4 large eggs, separated

5 ounces mascarpone cheese

1 tablespoon plus 1 teaspoon freshly squeezed orange juice

1 tablespoon lavender-flavored or regular honey

½ teaspoon dried lavender (optional)

Lavender blossoms, for garnish (optional)

1 Preheat the oven to 350°F. Place the hazelnuts in a single layer on a rimmed baking sheet; toast until golden and aromatic, 8 to 12 minutes, shaking the pan halfway through toasting.

2 Working over a bowl to catch the juices, use a paring knife to carefully slice between the sections and membranes of each orange; remove the segments whole. Place each segment in the bowl as completed. Repeat the process with the other oranges; set aside.

3 Butter an 8-inch springform pan. In a small saucepan over low heat, melt the butter; set aside.

4 In the bowl of a food processor, pulse the graham crackers into fine crumbs, yielding about 1 cup crumbs. Place in a medium bowl; add ¼ cup sugar, and set aside. Place ½ cup toasted hazelnuts in the food processor; pulse until fine but not powdery. Add to the graham-cracker-crumb mixture. Using a fork, add the melted butter; stir to combine. Put the crumb mixture in the bottom of the pan, and press evenly around the bottom and halfway up the sides, about 1½ inches.

5 Bake the crust until golden brown, about 10 minutes. Transfer to a wire rack to cool.

6 Reduce the heat to 325°F. Place the cream cheese and goat cheese in the bowl of an electric mixer fitted with the paddle attachment, and beat on medium-high speed until light and fluffy, 2 to 3 minutes. Reduce the speed to low. Add ½ cup sugar, the orange zest, flour, salt, and Frangelico, if using; mix until combined. Add the egg yolks one at a time, mixing after each addition. Add the mascarpone cheese and the orange juice; mix just until the batter is combined and smooth. Transfer the batter to a large mixing bowl, and set aside. Clean the mixer bowl.

7 Place the egg whites in the clean mixer bowl. Using the whisk attachment, beat on medium speed until frothy. Increase the speed to medium-high, and gradually add the remaining 2 tablespoons sugar, 1 teaspoon at a time. Continue beating the whites until stiff but not dry.

8 Using a hand whisk, mix one-third of the whipped egg whites into the batter to lighten it. Using a rubber spatula, gently fold in the remaining whites. Pour the batter into the cooled crust.

9 Bake the cheesecake until the top is golden brown and the center has barely set, about 1 hour; the top should be cracked and will sink upon cooling, forming a "bowl." Transfer the cheesecake to a wire rack to cool completely. Cover with plastic wrap, and transfer to the refrigerator to chill several hours or overnight. To unmold, wrap a hot towel around the sides of the pan to help release the cake, and run a thin knife around the inside of the pan. Carefully remove the outside of the pan, and slide onto a serving plate.

10 Combine the orange segments, honey, and dried lavender, if using, in a medium bowl. Coarsely chop the remaining ¼ cup toasted hazelnuts, and add to the bowl. Spoon the topping into the bowl on top of the cheesecake. Garnish with the lavender blossoms, if using. Serve.

CHOCOLATE MOUSSE CAKE | PAGE 287
SEVILLE ORANGE CHOCOLATE CAKE | PAGE 286
CHOCOLATE ALMONDS | PAGE 288

GRAVLAX WITH BOILED POTATOES
AND MUSTARD SAUCE | **PAGE 277**

CHICAGO HOLIDAY DINNER | **PAGE 279**

SAN FRANCISCO HOLIDAY DINNER | **PAGE 278**

GRAVLAX WITH CURRY WAFFLES | **PAGE 277**

ROAST DUCK WITH CHERRY SAUCE | **PAGE 280**

MUSHROOM SOUP WITH CRACKED WHEAT | **PAGE 279**

CARROT, PARSNIP, AND PEA GRATIN | **PAGE 280**

LETTUCE, RED CABBAGE, AND APPLE SALAD
WITH BLUE CHEESE | **PAGE 280**

SANTA FE HOLIDAY DINNER | PAGE 283

MAKING NUT BRITTLE

1 To make nut brittle, allow the sugar mixture to reach the soft-ball stage. Stir in the nuts, and continue to cook, stirring often, until the mixture is a golden amber.

2 Carefully stir in vanilla extract and baking soda. The mixture will foam up in the pan.

3 Pour the mixture onto a baking sheet, and quickly spread into a ½-inch-thick layer with an oiled metal spatula.

CHOCOLATE-PECAN BUTTER CRUNCH | **PAGE 276**

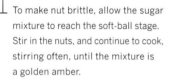

Once nut brittle is broken into pieces, it can be stored in an airtight container at room temperature for up to a month.

NUT BRITTLES | **PAGE 274**

CHEWY NUT TOFFEES | **PAGE 276**

ZUCCOTTO | **PAGE 273**

bonus recipes

Cookie Kisses

Olive Tartlets

Ginger Cookies

Coconut Soufflés

Mini Pavlova Cupcakes

Granola

Potato-Gruyère Biscuits

Pineapple-Papaya Bread

Cherry-Apricot Bread

Zucchini-Carrot Bread

Apricot Bellini

Citrus Cosmopolitan

Lollipop Garden Cake

Fish Cookies

Carrot Purée

Carrot and Potato Soup

Carrot Muffins

Carrot Croquettes

Carrot and Couscous Salad

Carrot Custard

Autumn Cookies

Potato-Leek Soup

Radishes with Chive Butter

Chocolat Blanc

Pissaladière

Madeleines

Petit-Pois Petits Fours

Cottage Cakes with Applesauce

Apple-Potato Pancake

Apple Oatmeal Bread

Apple Rice Pudding with
    Sautéed Apples

Cheddar Biscuit Pie

Baked Chicken Fingers

Spinach Dip

Fish Sticks

Parmesan Fish Crackers

Starfish Biscuit Sandwiches

Sparkling Limeade

COOKIE KISSES

MAKES 3 DOZEN

¼ cup blanched whole almonds

½ cup granulated sugar

1¾ cups all-purpose flour

½ teaspoon table salt

12 tablespoons (1½ sticks) unsalted butter, room temperature, plus 2 tablespoons, melted

1 large egg

2 tablespoons freshly squeezed lemon juice

½ teaspoon pure vanilla extract

1½ tablespoons strawberry jam

1½ cups confectioners' sugar

1 tablespoon heavy cream

1 Preheat the oven to 350°F. Line two baking sheets with parchment paper; set aside. Place the almonds and 2 tablespoons sugar in the bowl of a food processor, and process until very fine; set aside. Sift together the flour and salt into a small bowl; set aside. In the bowl of an electric mixer fitted with the paddle attachment, beat the 12 tablespoons butter and the remaining 6 tablespoons sugar until light and fluffy. Add the egg, lemon juice, and vanilla extract, and beat on medium speed until combined. Add the reserved almond and flour mixtures, and beat until combined.

2 Place the dough in a pastry bag fitted with a star tip with a ½-inch opening. Pipe out cookies, about 1 inch in diameter, onto the prepared baking sheets. With wet fingertips, shape the top of each cookie into a point to resemble chocolate kisses. Place in the oven, and bake, rotating the baking sheets halfway through cooking, until light golden brown, about 15 minutes. Remove the baking sheets from the oven, and transfer the cookies to wire racks to cool.

3 While the cookies are cooling, make the frosting. Place the strawberry jam in a small saucepan set over medium heat, and cook, stirring, until completely melted, about 2 minutes. Pour the liquid into a small bowl. Add the melted butter, confectioners' sugar, and heavy cream, and stir until combined and smooth. When the cookies are completely cool, spread ½ teaspoon frosting on the bottom of half the cookies. Top each with an unfrosted cookie to make a sandwich. Place the cookies on wire racks until the frosting has completely set. Unfrosted cookies will keep for up to 2 weeks in an airtight container.

OLIVE TARTLETS

MAKES 50 HORS D'OEUVRES

Any type of pitted olive may be used for these tartlets. A combination of ripe olives, such as Kalamata or Niçoise, and green Spanish olives is flavorful.

All-purpose flour, for work surface

1 17.3-ounce package store-bought puff pastry

10½ ounces goat cheese, room temperature

1 pound pitted olives, cut in half

Preheat the oven to 375°F. Line two baking sheets with parchment paper; set aside. On a clean, lightly floured work surface, roll the pastry ⅛ inch thick. Using a 2-inch round cookie cutter, cut out rounds, and place on the prepared baking sheets. Prick each round several times with a fork. Spread each with 1 teaspoon goat cheese, and top with 3 or 4 olive halves. Place tartlets in the oven, and bake until the pastry is puffed and golden, about 25 minutes. Serve hot.

GINGER COOKIES

MAKES 3 DOZEN

The dough for these cookies can be made several weeks in advance, wrapped in plastic, and frozen. Do this when the dough is in disks (step two), in rolled-out sheets (step three), or cut into cookies (end of step three).

3½ cups all-purpose flour, plus more for work surface

1⅓ cups unsalted butter, room temperature

1 cup sugar

1½ teaspoons baking powder

Pinch of table salt

¾ teaspoon ground ginger

5 large egg yolks

1 Preheat the oven to 375°F. In the bowl of an electric mixer fitted with the paddle attachment, mix the flour, butter, sugar, baking powder, salt, and ginger on low speed until the mixture is just combined but still crumbly, about 3 minutes.

2 Add the egg yolks, and mix 1 minute more. Divide the dough into thirds, shape each into a disk, wrap in plastic, and refrigerate until firm, at least 1 hour, or overnight.

3 On a clean, lightly floured work surface, roll the dough to ⅛ inch thick. Cut out cookies using a 3-inch oval cutter, and transfer to a baking sheet; refrigerate until firm. Continue the rolling process with the remaining dough, collecting scraps and rerolling as needed.

4 Bake until the edges are light golden, 10 to 12 minutes. Cool completely on a wire rack. Store in an airtight container for up to 3 days.

COCONUT SOUFFLES

MAKES 12 FOUR-OUNCE SOUFFLES

Leftover coconut can be toasted and added to cereals, salads, or snack mixes. You can substitute store-bought shredded sweetened coconut for the fresh.

1 fresh coconut

1½ tablespoons unsalted butter, plus more for jars

Granulated sugar, for jars

2 tablespoons all-purpose flour

1 cup canned unsweetened coconut milk (15% fat)

6 tablespoons confectioners' sugar, plus more for dusting

1 teaspoon pure vanilla extract

½ teaspoon pure coconut extract

1 teaspoon freshly squeezed lime juice

6 large egg whites

¼ teaspoon cream of tartar

1 Using a small screwdriver, pierce the "eyes" of the coconut, and drain the liquid. Place the coconut on a folded kitchen towel. While turning the coconut, gently tap with a hammer a few inches below the "eyes." Once the coconut splits, break it into pieces, and remove the white meat; cut away and discard the brown skin using a paring knife or a vegetable peeler. Thinly slice

the coconut meat on a mandoline or with a vegetable peeler. Measure out 1 cup of coconut, and set aside.

2   Preheat the oven to 350°F with a rack in the lower third. Butter the sides only of 12 four-ounce canning jars or ramekins, and coat with granulated sugar; tap out any excess sugar. Place the jars on a rimmed baking sheet, and set aside.

3   In a small saucepan, melt the butter over medium-low heat. Add the flour; whisk constantly for 3 minutes. Gradually whisk in the coconut milk. Bring the mixture to a boil, and continue to whisk until the mixture thickens, 2 to 3 minutes. Remove the saucepan from the heat, and whisk in 3 tablespoons confectioners' sugar, the vanilla and coconut extracts, and the lime juice. Transfer the mixture to a medium bowl; set aside.

4   In the bowl of an electric mixer fitted with the whisk attachment, beat the egg whites and cream of tartar on medium speed until soft peaks form, about 3 minutes. Gradually add the remaining 3 tablespoons confectioners' sugar. Increase the speed to high, and continue to beat until stiff peaks form, about 1 minute. Whisk the reserved coconut-milk mixture to loosen, and then whisk one third of the egg-white mixture into it to lighten. Gently fold in the remaining egg-white mixture. Pour the mixture into the prepared canning jars, filling to ¼ inch below the rims. Place several strips of coconut on the surface of each soufflé. Bake until puffed and golden brown, about 15 minutes. Remove from the oven; dust with confectioners' sugar, and serve immediately.

MINI PAVLOVA CUPCAKES

MAKES 4 DOZEN TWO-INCH CUPCAKES

4 large egg whites
1 teaspoon pure vanilla extract
½ teaspoon cream of tartar
1¼ cups superfine sugar
   Yogurt Cream (recipe follows)
   Mini Pavlovas (recipe follows)

1   Preheat the oven to 200°F. Line four miniature muffin tins with paper liners; set aside. In the bowl of an electric mixer fitted with the whisk attachment, whip the egg whites, vanilla, and cream of tartar on medium speed until soft peaks form. Gradually add 1 cup superfine sugar, 2 tablespoons at a time. Increase the speed to medium-high; whip until stiff peaks form. Using a rubber spatula, fold in the remaining ¼ cup sugar.

2   Transfer the meringue to a pastry bag fitted with a coupler but no tip. Pipe the meringue into the paper liners, filling just to the top. Bake about 1 hour, or until slightly puffed. The meringues should be crisp on the outside and have a soft center. Cool the pavlovas completely in the tins on wire racks. Remove from the tins, and store in an airtight container for up to 2 days.

3   To serve, use a pastry bag fitted with a #35 star tip to pipe a rosette of yogurt cream on top of each cupcake. Garnish each cupcake with mini pavlovas, and serve immediately.

YOGURT CREAM

MAKES 2 CUPS

We chose Greek-style yogurt for our topping because of its tangy flavor and firm consistency. Strained whole-milk yogurt can be substituted; place it in a cheesecloth-lined sieve, place over a bowl, and refrigerate overnight.

8 ounces cream cheese, room temperature
1 cup Greek-style whole-milk yogurt
2 tablespoons confectioners' sugar

In the bowl of an electric mixer fitted with the paddle attachment, beat the cream cheese on medium speed until smooth. Add the yogurt and confectioners' sugar, and beat to combine. Refrigerate in an airtight container for up to 3 days.

MINI PAVLOVAS

MAKES 4 DOZEN

Sugaring currants work best when you coat them with raw egg whites, which should not be consumed by pregnant women, babies, young children, the elderly, or anyone whose health is compromised. Powdered egg whites can be used instead.

1 large egg white
1 tablespoon water
1 pint golden currants
   Superfine sugar, for rolling

In a small bowl, whisk together the egg white and the water. Using a small paintbrush, apply a thin layer to each currant. Roll the currants in the sugar, place on a baking sheet, and set aside.

WEDDINGS: SPRING 2001

GRANOLA

MAKES 4 CUPS

Pumpkin seeds can replace the sunflower seeds, and pecans can replace the almonds.

2 cups rolled oats
¼ cup sunflower seeds
¼ cup wheat germ
1 ounce whole almonds (about ¼ cup)
2 tablespoons whole-wheat flour
3 tablespoons packed light-brown sugar
1¼ teaspoons ground cinnamon
¼ cup plus 1 tablespoon canola oil
6 tablespoons apricot nectar
2 tablespoons honey

Preheat the oven to 250°F. In a large bowl, mix the oats, sunflower seeds, wheat germ, almonds, flour, brown sugar, and cinnamon. Mix the oil, nectar, and honey in a liquid measuring cup. Pour over the oat mixture; toss to combine. Spread onto a baking sheet, and bake 2 hours, stirring every 45 minutes, until golden brown. When cool, store in an airtight container for up to 2 weeks.

POTATO-GRUYERE BISCUITS

MAKES 18 TWO-INCH BISCUITS

Swiss cheese may be substituted for Gruyère.

2 large potatoes, about 1 pound

2½ cups all-purpose flour, plus more for work surface

1½ teaspoons table salt

2½ teaspoons baking powder

1 teaspoon sugar

8 tablespoons (1 stick) unsalted butter, cold, plus 2 tablespoons melted

3 ounces freshly grated Gruyère cheese (about 1½ cups)

2 sprigs fresh thyme, leaves picked and stems discarded

1¼ cups milk

1 Preheat the oven to 400°F. Cut the potatoes in half lengthwise; reserve half of 1 potato. Place the remaining 1½ potatoes in the oven on the center rack. Bake until fork-tender, about 30 minutes. Remove, and set aside. Raise the oven temperature to 425°F. Once the potatoes are cool, use a paring knife to coax the skins from the flesh; discard the skins. Pass the potatoes through a potato ricer into a bowl to yield about 1 cup; set aside.

2 In a bowl, mix together the flour, salt, baking powder, and sugar. Using a pastry cutter, cut in the cold butter until it is the size of peas. Add the grated cheese and half the thyme leaves. In another bowl, mix the reserved riced potatoes and milk; add to the flour mixture. Mix just until moistened; turn onto a lightly floured work surface.

3 Flatten the dough into a ¾-inch-thick disk. With a 2-inch round cookie cutter, cut out 18 biscuits; place on an ungreased baking sheet. Cut the reserved raw potato half into 18 thin slices with the skin on. Lay 1 slice of potato on each biscuit, and brush with the melted butter; sprinkle with the remaining thyme leaves. Bake the biscuits until golden brown, about 20 minutes. Cool slightly on a wire rack, and serve warm.

PINEAPPLE-PAPAYA BREAD

MAKES TWO 2½-BY-5-INCH LOAVES, OR ONE 4½-BY-8½-INCH LOAF

Try this bread toasted and spread with a nut butter such as almond or macadamia.

1½ cups water

4 ounces dried papaya, cut into ½-inch pieces

4 ounces dried pineapple, cut into ½-inch pieces

4 tablespoons unsalted butter, melted and cooled to room temperature, plus more for pan

2 cups all-purpose flour, plus more for pan

2 teaspoons baking powder

¼ teaspoon baking soda

1 teaspoon table salt

¼ teaspoon ground allspice

1 cup sugar

1 large egg

½ teaspoon pure vanilla extract

1 Preheat the oven to 350°F. In a small saucepan, bring the water to a boil. Turn off the heat, add the papaya and pineapple to the water, and cover the pan. Let sit until the fruit is softened, about 10 minutes. Strain the liquid, reserving ½ cup; set the fruit and reserved liquid aside to cool.

2 Butter and flour two 2½-by-5-inch loaf pans or one 4½-by-8½-inch loaf pan; set aside. In a mixing bowl, combine the flour, baking powder, baking soda, salt, and allspice; set aside.

3 In the bowl of an electric mixer fitted with the paddle attachment, combine the melted butter, sugar, egg, vanilla, reserved fruit, and reserved soaking liquid on medium speed. Add the reserved flour mixture, and mix until smooth. Pour the batter into the prepared loaf pans; smooth the tops with a spatula. Bake until golden brown, about 40 minutes for small loaves or 50 minutes for a large loaf. Transfer to a wire rack to cool 5 minutes. Slide a knife around the sides of the loaves, then turn them out onto the rack; let cool. Bread will keep wrapped in plastic wrap for 2 days at room temperature or in the freezer for up to 2 weeks.

CHERRY-APRICOT BREAD

MAKES TWO 2½-BY-5-INCH LOAVES, OR ONE 4½-BY-8½-INCH LOAF

Dried pears and cranberries can be used in place of the apricots and cherries.

1½ cups water

4¼ ounces dried apricots, cut into ½-inch pieces

4¼ ounces dried cherries

4 tablespoons unsalted butter, melted and cooled, plus more for pan

2 cups all-purpose flour, plus more for pan

2 teaspoons baking powder

¼ teaspoon baking soda

1 teaspoon table salt

¼ teaspoon ground nutmeg

1 cup sugar

1 large egg

¼ teaspoon pure vanilla extract

1 Preheat the oven to 350°F. In a small saucepan, bring the water to a boil. Turn off the heat, add the apricots and cherries to the water, and cover the pan. Let sit until the fruit is softened, about 10 minutes. Strain the liquid, reserving ½ cup; set the fruit and reserved liquid aside to cool.

2 Butter and flour two 2½-by-5-inch loaf pans or one 4½-by-8½-inch loaf pan; set aside. In a bowl, combine the flour, baking powder, baking soda, salt, and nutmeg; set aside.

3 In the bowl of an electric mixer fitted with the paddle attachment, combine the melted butter, sugar, egg, vanilla, reserved dried fruit, and reserved soaking liquid on medium speed. Add the reserved flour mixture; mix until smooth. Pour the batter into the prepared loaf pans; smooth the tops with a spatula. Bake until golden brown, about 40 minutes for the small loaves or 50 minutes for a large loaf. Transfer to a wire rack to cool 5 minutes. Slide a knife around the sides of the loaves, then turn them out onto the rack; let cool. Bread will keep wrapped in plastic wrap for 2 days at room temperature or in the freezer for up to 2 weeks.

ZUCCHINI-CARROT BREAD

MAKES TWO 2½-BY-5-INCH LOAVES, OR
ONE 4½-BY-8½-INCH LOAF

*Serve with soft, spreadable cheeses such as
Brie, Camembert, and cream cheese.*

- 1 medium zucchini (about 8 ounces)
- 1 large carrot (about 8 ounces)
- 11 tablespoons unsalted butter,
   room temperature, plus more for pan
- 2 cups all-purpose flour,
   plus more for pan
- 2 teaspoons baking powder
- ¼ teaspoon baking soda
- ½ teaspoon table salt
- 1 cup sugar
- 2 large eggs
- ½ teaspoon pure vanilla extract
- 2½ ounces crystallized ginger
   (about ½ cup), finely chopped

1 Preheat the oven to 350°F. Using the
large holes of a box grater, grate the zucchini and carrot into a bowl; set aside.

2 Butter and flour two 2½-by-5-inch
loaf pans or one 4½-by-8½-inch loaf
pan; set aside. In a medium bowl, combine the flour, baking powder, baking
soda, and salt; set aside.

3 In the bowl of an electric mixer fitted
with the paddle attachment, beat the
butter and sugar on medium speed until
pale and fluffy, about 2 minutes. Add
the eggs one at a time, beating until each
is fully incorporated. Add the vanilla,
ginger, and reserved grated zucchini and
carrot. Add the reserved flour mixture;
mix on low speed until combined. Pour
the batter into the prepared loaf pans;
smooth the tops with a spatula. Bake until golden, about 45 minutes for small
loaves, or 1 hour for a large loaf. Transfer
the pans to a wire rack to cool 5 minutes. Slide a knife around the sides of the
loaves, then turn them out onto the
rack; let cool. Bread will keep wrapped
in plastic for 2 days at room temperature or in the freezer for 2 weeks.

WEDDINGS: SUMMER 2001

APRICOT BELLINI

MAKES 6 FIVE-OUNCE DRINKS

This is a fresh twist on the classic cocktail.

- 6 ounces apricot nectar, chilled
- 1 750-ml bottle sparkling wine, chilled

Fill six champagne flutes with 1 ounce
of apricot nectar. Top with 4 ounces
sparkling wine. Serve immediately.

CITRUS COSMOPOLITAN

MAKES 2 FIVE-OUNCE DRINKS

- 2 ounces orange-scented vodka
- 2 ounces Cointreau
- 2 ounces blood-orange juice
- 2 ounces orange juice
- 2 ounces red- or pink-grapefruit juice
  Zest of 1 blood orange

Place 2 martini glasses in the freezer for
at least 10 minutes. Fill a cocktail shaker
halfway with ice. Add the vodka, Cointreau, and juices. Cover; shake vigorously
for 30 seconds. Strain the liquid immediately into the chilled glasses, and garnish with strips of blood-orange zest.

BABY: WINTER 2001

LOLLIPOP GARDEN CAKE

MAKES 2 EIGHT-INCH LAYERS

*If you like, grate carrots for this carrot
cake on a box grater, and mix cake with a
mixer instead of in a food processor.*

-   Unsalted butter, for pans
- 1½ cups all-purpose flour, plus more for pans
- 4 medium carrots
- 1 cup golden raisins
- 1 cup walnut pieces
- ½ cup unsweetened applesauce
   Juice and zest of 1 lemon
- 1¼ cups sugar
- 1 teaspoon baking powder
- 1 teaspoon baking soda
- 1 teaspoon table salt
- 2 teaspoons ground cinnamon
- 1 teaspoon ground allspice
- ¾ cup vegetable oil
- 4 large eggs
   Large Quantity Cream Cheese Frosting
   (recipe follows)
   Green food coloring
   Lollipops

1 Preheat the oven to 350°F. Butter two
8-by-2-inch round cake pans. Line the
bottoms with parchment paper; butter,
and dust with flour. Grate the carrots
in the bowl of a food processor; measure
out 2 cups, and transfer to a medium
bowl. Add the raisins, walnuts, applesauce,
and lemon juice and zest.

2 Wipe out the food processor bowl;
fit with a blade. Add the flour, sugar, baking powder, baking soda, salt, cinnamon, and allspice; pulse to mix. With the
motor running, pour in the oil and
eggs; process until smooth, scraping down
the sides of the bowl. Add the reserved
carrot mixture; pulse. Pour into the prepared pans; bake about 40 minutes,
until a cake tester inserted into the middle comes out clean.

3 Cool in the pans on a wire rack for
20 minutes. Remove from the pans; cool
completely, right sides up.

4 Tint 2 cups frosting light green, and tint the remaining 5¾ cups dark green; chill at least 3 hours. Place the bottom layer on a cake round; use a small offset spatula to spread 1½ cups dark-green frosting over top. Add the second layer; spread 1½ cups dark-green frosting in a thin layer over the entire cake. Refrigerate 40 minutes until the frosting is firm.

5 Place the cake on a rotating cake stand; spread another layer of dark-green frosting over the cake. Fill a pastry bag, fitted with a #113 Wilton leaf tip, with light-green frosting. Place the tip at the base of the cake; pipe elongated varying sizes of leaves up the sides of the cake. Chill at least 1 hour before serving. Just before serving, insert lollipop sticks in the cake.

LARGE QUANTITY CREAM CHEESE FROSTING

MAKES 7¾ CUPS

24 ounces cream cheese, room temperature
1½ cups (3 sticks) unsalted butter, room temperature
6 cups confectioners' sugar, sifted

In the bowl of an electric mixer fitted with the paddle attachment, beat the cream cheese on medium speed until smooth and creamy, about 2 minutes. Add the butter ¼ cup at a time, and beat until smooth. Reduce the speed to low; add the confectioners' sugar 1 cup at a time, beating until fully incorporated. Chill before spreading.

FISH COOKIES

MAKES 35

2 cups all-purpose flour, plus more for work surface
½ teaspoon baking powder
¼ teaspoon table salt
8 tablespoons (1 stick) unsalted butter, room temperature
1 cup sugar
1 large egg
1 teaspoon pure vanilla extract
   Double Batch Royal Icing (recipe follows)
   Blue food coloring (optional)
¼ cup each white and blue sanding sugar

1 In a large bowl, sift together the flour, baking powder, and salt. Set aside.

2 In the bowl of an electric mixer fitted with the paddle attachment, cream the butter and sugar until fluffy. Beat in the egg and vanilla.

3 Add the flour mixture; mix on low speed to combine. Wrap in plastic, and chill 1 hour.

4 Preheat the oven to 325°F. On a lightly floured surface, roll the dough ⅛ inch thick. Cut into fish shapes, 1 to 3 inches long, using a paring knife or cookie cutter. Transfer to ungreased baking sheets; chill until firm, about 30 minutes. Bake 10 to 12 minutes, until the edges just begin to brown. Cool on wire racks. Once cool, decorate with royal icing, some tinted blue if desired; sprinkle with sanding sugar. Once dry, pipe on royal icing eyes.

DOUBLE-BATCH ROYAL ICING

MAKES ABOUT 2 CUPS

Meringue powder replaces raw egg whites, which should not be eaten by anyone who is pregnant.

¼ cup plus 1 tablespoon meringue powder
½ cup water, or more if needed
1 pound (about 4 cups) confectioners' sugar

In the bowl of an electric mixer fitted with the paddle attachment, beat the meringue powder and a scant ½ cup water on low. Add the confectioners' sugar, scrape down the sides of the bowl, and beat until soft peaks form and the icing holds a line when a spatula is pulled through it, 10 to 15 minutes. To thin the icing for filling, add a little more water. If making ahead, store in an airtight container.

CARROT PUREE

MAKES 1⅓ CUPS

Most pediatricians agree that six months is a good age at which to start your baby on some solid foods. This purée may be refrigerated for three days or frozen in small containers for up to two months. As your baby grows, use it as a building block in other recipes. Breast milk, formula, or the steaming water may be used to thin the purée.

6 carrots (about 1 pound)
   Breast milk or formula (optional)

1 Peel the carrots; chop into ½-inch lengths. Place a steamer basket in a medium saucepan filled with simmering water. Cook, covered, until soft, 20 to 25 minutes. Set the carrots and liquid aside to cool.

2 Transfer the carrots to the bowl of a food processor, and blend until smooth, adding breast milk, formula, or the steaming water 1 tablespoon at a time until desired consistency is reached.

CARROT AND POTATO SOUP

MAKES 4 SERVINGS (¼ CUP EACH)
FOR A BABY, PLUS 6 CUPS FOR THE
REST OF THE FAMILY

This soup may be refrigerated for three days or frozen for up to two months.

2 tablespoons unsalted butter
1 medium leek, white and light-green parts only, finely chopped and well washed (about 1 cup)
12 medium carrots (about 2 pounds), cut into ¼-inch pieces (about 4½ cups)
5 cups Homemade Chicken Stock (page 8), or organic low-sodium canned
2 Yukon gold potatoes, cut into ¼-inch pieces (about 3 cups)
¼ teaspoon ground ginger
   Coarse salt and freshly ground pepper
¼ cup sour cream (optional)
1 tablespoon finely chopped chives (optional)

1 Melt the butter in a large saucepan over medium-low heat. Add the leek, and cook until translucent, about 6 minutes. Add the carrots and chicken stock, and bring to a boil. Reduce to a simmer, and cook for 10 minutes. Add the potatoes, and cook until very tender, about 30 minutes.

2 Set aside ½ cup soup in a bowl for baby. Purée the remaining soup in batches in the bowl of a food processor or a blender until smooth. Stir ½ cup purée into the reserved soup for the baby. Season remaining puréed soup with ginger and salt and pepper to taste; garnish with sour cream and chives, if using.

CARROT MUFFINS

MAKES 2 DOZEN MINI MUFFINS

Babies can start enjoying these muffins at about eighteen months. Muffins will keep at room temperature for four days, or frozen, without the frosting, for up to three weeks.

Unsalted butter, for pans
¾ cup all-purpose flour, plus more for pans
2 medium carrots (about 5 ounces)
¼ cup unsweetened applesauce
Zest and juice of 1 lemon
½ cup sugar
½ teaspoon baking powder
½ teaspoon baking soda
¼ teaspoon table salt
1 teaspoon ground cinnamon
¼ cup plus 2 tablespoons vegetable oil
2 large eggs, lightly beaten
Cream Cheese Frosting (optional, recipe follows)
Orange and green food coloring (optional)

1 Preheat the oven to 350°F. Butter and flour two nonstick miniature muffin pans. Peel the carrots, and grate on the large holes of a box grater to yield 1 cup. Transfer the grated carrots to a medium bowl, and add the applesauce and lemon zest and juice.

2 In a medium bowl, stir together the flour, sugar, baking powder, baking soda, salt, and cinnamon. Add the oil and eggs; stir until smooth. Add the carrot mixture; stir to combine. Spoon the batter into the prepared muffin pans; bake until a cake tester inserted in middle comes out clean, about 20 minutes.

3 Cool the muffins in the pans on a wire rack for 5 minutes. Invert onto the rack to remove the muffins; let cool,

right side up. When completely cool, decorate with cream cheese frosting, if using. To make decorative carrots, tint two thirds of the frosting orange. Place in a 12-inch pastry bag fitted with a #5 Ateco plain round tip; pipe carrots onto the muffins. For carrot tops, tint the remaining frosting green; place in a pastry bag fitted with a #3 Ateco plain round tip; pipe carrot tops onto the muffins.

CREAM CHEESE FROSTING

MAKES ABOUT ½ CUP

4 ounces cream cheese, room temperature
3 tablespoons unsalted butter, softened
¼ cup confectioners' sugar

Place the cream cheese and butter in the bowl of an electric mixer fitted with the paddle attachment, and beat on medium-high speed until fully combined and fluffy, about 2 minutes. Reduce the speed to low, and add the confectioners' sugar. Beat until combined. If not using immediately, store in an airtight container in the refrigerator for up to 2 days.

CARROT CROQUETTES

MAKES ABOUT 3 DOZEN

Carrot-chickpea patties may be formed and refrigerated, without bread crumbs, for up to three days, or frozen for up to three weeks.

1 15-ounce can chickpeas, drained and rinsed
½ cup Carrot Purée (page 317)
1 tablespoon plus 1 teaspoon freshly squeezed lemon juice
2 carrots
½ teaspoon ground cumin (optional)
½ teaspoon coarse salt (optional)
1¼ cups dry bread crumbs
2 tablespoons olive oil
1 cup plain yogurt

1 In the bowl of a food processor, blend the chickpeas, purée, and 1 tablespoon lemon juice until smooth. Peel the carrots, and grate on the large holes of a box grater. Transfer the carrots to a bowl; add the chickpea mixture, the cumin if using, and ¼ teaspoon salt if using; stir to combine. Form heaping teaspoonfuls of the mixture into patties; dredge in the bread crumbs.

2 Heat 1 tablespoon oil in a large nonstick skillet over medium heat. Cook the croquettes in batches until golden brown, 4 minutes per side; add more oil as needed. Set aside on a paper-towel–lined plate.

3 In a small bowl, combine the yogurt, remaining teaspoon lemon juice, and remaining ¼ teaspoon salt, if using. Serve the croquettes with the sauce on the side.

CARROT AND COUSCOUS SALAD

MAKES 2¾ CUPS

This salad is perfect for one-year-olds; to make the couscous softer, increase the amount of chicken stock slightly. For older babies, this is a good dish to practice eating with a spoon. The finished salad will keep in the refrigerator for up to three days.

2 carrots
1 cup Homemade Chicken Stock (page 8), or organic low-sodium canned
½ cup couscous
1 tablespoon unsalted butter
⅛ teaspoon coarse salt (optional)

Peel the carrots, and grate them on the large holes of a box grater. Place the chicken stock in a medium saucepan, and bring to a boil. Add the carrots, couscous, butter, and salt if using; stir to combine. Cover and remove from the heat. Let stand 12 minutes. Toss with a fork to separate the grains; let cool before serving.

CARROT CUSTARD

MAKES 6

This custard contains egg yolks and cow's milk, so feed it only to children twelve months or older who aren't allergic to these foods.

3 carrots
2½ cups milk
5 large egg yolks
¼ teaspoon coarse salt

1 Preheat the oven to 300°F. Peel the carrots, and grate them on the large holes of a box grater. Bring the milk and carrots to a simmer in a medium saucepan. Cook until the carrots are very tender, about 10 minutes. Remove the saucepan from the heat, and set aside to cool, 10 to 15 minutes. Purée the milk and carrot mixture in the jar of a blender

until very smooth. Pass through a fine sieve, pressing with a rubber spatula; discard any solids.

2 Add the egg yolks and salt to the purée; whisk to combine. Divide the mixture among six ½-cup custard cups or ramekins; place them in a 9-by-13-inch baking pan. Skim any foam from the custards using a spoon. Cover each cup with a square of foil. Place the pan in the oven; pour boiling water into the pan, to halfway up the outsides of the cups. Bake until the custards are set in the center, about 30 minutes, rotating the pan once. Transfer the pan to a wire rack; let cool 30 minutes. Transfer the cups to the refrigerator; chill at least 45 minutes. The custards will keep for up to 2 days covered with plastic wrap.

BABY: FALL 2001

AUTUMN COOKIES
MAKES 4½ DOZEN

These cookies, full of healthful grains and fiber, are a perfect snack for a toddler or parent.

1 thirty-ounce can pumpkin purée
1 cup raisins
¼ cup boiling water
1 cup (2 sticks) unsalted butter, softened
¾ cup packed light-brown sugar
¼ cup molasses
2 large eggs
½ teaspoon table salt
2½ teaspoons ground cinnamon
1½ teaspoons ground ginger
¼ teaspoon freshly grated nutmeg
1½ cups all-purpose flour
1 teaspoon baking soda
½ cup toasted wheat germ
2½ cups rolled oats

1 Line a colander with a double layer of cheesecloth; set it over a bowl. Place the pumpkin purée in the colander; wrap the cheesecloth around the purée. Weigh down the purée with a small can of soup or something with a similar weight; let the purée drain for about 30 minutes.
2 Preheat the oven to 350°F. In the bowl of a food processor, purée the raisins with the boiling water until no large pieces

remain, about 1 minute. In the bowl of an electric mixer fitted with the paddle attachment, cream the butter and brown sugar on medium-high speed for 2 minutes. Add the molasses, and mix to combine, scraping down the sides of the bowl as needed. Add the eggs, and beat for 1 minute. Add the puréed raisin mixture and the drained pumpkin purée, and mix to combine.

3 In a medium bowl, combine the salt, cinnamon, ginger, nutmeg, flour, baking soda, wheat germ, and oats; stir to combine. Add the dry ingredients to the batter in the mixer bowl, and mix to combine.

4 Spoon the batter onto untreated baking sheets, making cookies about 1½ inches in diameter. Use the back of a spoon dipped in water to press the cookies down slightly. Bake the cookies until set and browning, 12 to 14 minutes. Transfer to wire racks to cool. Repeat with remaining batter. Store the baked cookies in an airtight container; they will stay soft for up to 1 week.

POTATO-LEEK SOUP
MAKES 6 CUPS

This soup can be made up to two days in advance.

1 small bay leaf
2 sprigs fresh flat-leaf parsley
10 whole black peppercorns
2 tablespoons unsalted butter
1 tablespoon olive oil
3 leeks, white and light-green parts only, cut into ½-inch pieces
2 shallots, finely chopped
1 pound potatoes, peeled, cut into ½-inch dice
1 quart Homemade Chicken Stock (page 8), or low-sodium canned
½ cup milk
¼ cup heavy cream
   Coarse salt and freshly ground white pepper
   Fresh chervil, for garnish

1 To make a bouquet garni, wrap the bay leaf, parsley, and peppercorns in a piece of cheesecloth. Tie with twine, and set aside.

2 Heat the butter and oil in a large saucepan. Add the leeks and shallots, and cook over medium-low heat until very soft, about 10 minutes, stirring occasionally. Do not brown. Add the potatoes, stock, and bouquet garni. Bring to a boil; reduce to a gentle simmer. Cook until the potatoes are very tender, about 40 minutes. Discard the bouquet garni.

3 Working in batches, pass the soup through a food mill fitted with a medium disk into a large saucepan. Warm over medium-low heat. Slowly stir in the milk and cream, and season with salt and pepper. Make sure the soup does not come to a boil. Spoon into small cups, and serve hot or cold, garnished with chervil leaves.

RADISHES WITH CHIVE BUTTER
MAKES 4 DOZEN

The flavored butter for these hors d'oeuvres can be made ahead and softened for piping before use.

8 tablespoons (1 stick) unsalted butter, softened
2 tablespoons finely chopped chives, plus more for garnish
2 bunches (about 1 pound) radishes, washed, trimmed, and halved lengthwise
   Coarse salt, for serving

Mix the butter and chives in a bowl. Transfer to a small pastry bag fitted with a #70 leaf tip. Pipe the butter onto the radish halves. Serve on a bed of coarse salt.

CHOCOLAT BLANC
MAKES 4 FIVE-OUNCE SERVINGS

2 cups milk
1 vanilla bean, split lengthwise
5 ounces good-quality white chocolate, coarsely chopped

1 Heat the milk and vanilla bean in a pan over medium heat until almost boiling. Remove from the heat. Remove the vanilla-bean halves; scrape the seeds into the milk. Stir, then let stand, covered, to infuse, 5 to 10 minutes.

2 Place pan over medium-low heat; add white chocolate. Whisk until completely melted. Serve immediately in mugs.

PISSALADIERE

MAKES 12 INDIVIDUAL TARTS

These savory tarts are a specialty of Nice, in southern France. Traditionally the pissaladière has a flaky crust, but this crisp crust gives it a lighter taste.

FOR THE DOUGH:

1¾ cups warm water (110°F)

2 tablespoons (2 packages) active dry yeast

3 tablespoons extra-virgin olive oil, plus more for baking sheets

4½ cups all-purpose flour, plus more for work surface

2 teaspoons coarse salt

FOR THE FILLING:

¼ cup extra-virgin olive oil, or more for drizzling

4 pounds onions, cut into ¼-inch dice

2 teaspoons sugar
Coarse salt and freshly ground pepper
All-purpose flour, for surface

4 Hard-Boiled Eggs (recipe follows), peeled and sliced ¼-inch thick

1 bulb fennel, trimmed, thinly sliced

3 ounces oil-cured black olives, pitted and halved lengthwise

3 ounces Gruyère cheese, grated
Fresh rosemary and thyme, for garnish

1 In a small bowl, combine the warm water and yeast. Let stand 10 minutes until foamy. Brush two baking sheets with olive oil.

2 Place the flour and salt in the bowl of a food processor. Add the yeast mixture and 3 tablespoons oil; process just until the dough comes together. Knead on a lightly floured work surface for 2 minutes. Divide the dough in half. Shape each half into a log; divide each log into 6 equal-size pieces, and flatten slightly with your palm to form disks. Transfer to the baking sheets. Cover with plastic, then with a hot, damp cloth. Let stand until doubled in size, about 1 hour.

3 Preheat the oven to 400°F. Heat a pizza stone for 30 minutes, or a large baking sheet for 15 minutes.

4 In a skillet over medium-low heat, heat 2 tablespoons oil. Add the onions, and cook until they begin to soften, stirring often, about 30 minutes. Add the sugar; raise the heat slightly. Cook until golden, stirring often, about 60 minutes more. Season with salt and pepper.

5 On a lightly floured work surface, gently roll or stretch each disk of dough into a ¼-inch-thick oval. Brush with the remaining 2 tablespoons oil, and top with the onion mixture, eggs, fennel, olives, and Gruyère. Sprinkle with salt and pepper. Transfer the tarts to the preheated pizza stone. Bake until the crust is golden, about 12 minutes. Garnish with the herbs, and drizzle with oil, if using. Cut into wedges, and serve.

HARD-BOILED EGGS

MAKES 12

These may be made up to one day ahead and kept refrigerated in an airtight container.

12 large eggs

Fill a large bowl with ice and water. Place the eggs in a saucepan large enough to accommodate them in a single layer. Fill the pan with cold water, covering the eggs by 1 inch. Place the pan over medium-high heat. Cover, and bring to a boil. Turn off the heat, and let stand, covered, for 12 minutes. Transfer the eggs to the ice bath. Let stand 2 minutes, then remove.

MADELEINES

MAKES 16

Madeleines are best the day they are made.

10 tablespoons (1¼ sticks) unsalted butter, melted, plus more for pan

½ cup all-purpose flour, plus more for pan

½ cup cake flour (not self-rising)
Pinch of table salt

2 large eggs

⅔ cup granulated sugar

1 teaspoon pure vanilla extract
Grated zest of 1 lemon
Confectioners' sugar, for dusting

1 Preheat the oven to 375°F. Butter and lightly flour a madeleine pan. In a medium bowl, whisk together the all-purpose flour, cake flour, and salt. In the bowl of an electric mixer fitted with the whisk attachment, beat the eggs and sugar. Add the vanilla and lemon zest, then the flour mixture; beat until just combined. On low speed, pour in the melted butter in a steady stream; mix until incorporated.

2 Spoon a rounded tablespoon of batter into each form. Bake 5 minutes. Reduce the oven to 350°F, and bake until golden, 8 to 10 minutes more. Let cool slightly; remove from the pan. Dust with confectioners' sugar, and serve.

PETIT-POIS PETITS FOURS

MAKES 16

Petit-pois is French for "polka dot." The petits fours can be made a day ahead. You will need a two-inch round cookie cutter.

Génoise (2 cakes; recipe follows)

1 cup orange marmalade, warmed, strained
Orange Glaze (recipe follows)
Double-Batch Royal Icing (page 317)
Lavender gel, paste, or liquid food coloring

1 Working with one cake at a time, invert the génoise onto a clean work surface. With a serrated knife, trim the cake level; cut in half horizontally. With a pastry brush, brush away any crumbs.

2 Spread ½ cup marmalade over the top of one layer. Using a 2-inch round cookie cutter, cut one round from the unglazed half, then move to the glazed half and cut again. The two pieces will stick, creating a petit-four cake. Remove the petit-four cake from the cutter, and set on a wire rack over a rimmed baking sheet. Cut out 7 more petit-four cakes; repeat the process with the second cake and remaining ½ cup marmalade.

3 Place a petit-four cake on a fork, and hold it over a pan of warm orange glaze. With a ladle, pour the glaze evenly over the cake, until all surfaces are covered. Slide the glazed cake onto a rack. Continue to coat the remaining cakes. Let the cakes set for 5 minutes.

4 Tint the royal icing by adding food coloring a bit at a time, stirring with a spatula. Fit a pastry bag with a #1 Ateco tip, and fill the bag with the royal icing. Pipe dots over each petit four. Serve.

GENOISE

MAKES 2 EIGHT-INCH CAKES

Make these cakes up to one week ahead and freeze.

6 tablespoons unsalted butter, melted, plus more for pans

2½ cups sifted cake flour (not self-rising), plus more for pans

1¼ cups sugar

¼ teaspoon table salt

4 large whole eggs

8 large egg yolks

2 teaspoons pure vanilla extract
Grated zest of 1 orange

1 Preheat the oven to 375°F. Place a rack in the lower third of the oven. Butter two 8-by-2-inch round cake pans. Line with parchment paper; butter and flour the paper. Sift together the flour, 2 tablespoons sugar, and the salt; set aside. Pour the melted butter into a large bowl, and set aside.

2 Combine the remaining 1 cup plus 2 tablespoons sugar, the whole eggs, and the yolks in the bowl of an electric mixer. Using the whisk attachment, mix on medium-high speed until pale in color and tripled in volume, about 5 minutes. Add the vanilla and orange zest.

3 Detach the bowl from the mixer. Add one-third of the flour mixture. With a spatula, gently fold in until just incorporated. Add the remaining flour mixture in two more additions. Add one-third of the batter to the butter; gently fold in until just combined. Fold in the remaining batter. Divide the batter between the prepared pans. Bake until just golden and the cake springs back when gently touched, 20 to 25 minutes. Remove the cakes from the oven. Let cool in pans, running a knife around the edges occasionally. Wrap in plastic, and refrigerate in the pans overnight.

ORANGE GLAZE

MAKES ABOUT 2 CUPS

2 tablespoons unsalted butter

5 cups confectioners' sugar, sifted

¼ cup milk, or more for thinning

¼ cup freshly squeezed orange juice, strained

Melt the butter in the top of a double-boiler or a heat-proof bowl set over a pan of simmering water. Add the confectioners' sugar, milk, and orange juice; stir until smooth and pourable. Thin with more milk a bit at a time, if needed. Keep warm; use immediately.

COTTAGE CAKES WITH APPLESAUCE

MAKES ABOUT 2 DOZEN SILVER-DOLLAR-SIZE CAKES

If using low-fat cottage cheese, drain it longer to remove the excess liquid.

¾ cup cottage cheese

¼ cup plus 2 tablespoons whole-wheat flour

¼ teaspoon baking powder

½ teaspoon ground cinnamon

¼ teaspoon coarse salt

2 large eggs, lightly beaten

2 tablespoons light-brown sugar

2 tablespoons unsalted butter, melted, plus more for griddle
Pink or Chunky Applesauce (recipes follow)

1 In a sieve placed over a small bowl, drain the cottage cheese in the refrigerator for at least 2 hours or overnight.

2 In a small bowl, whisk together the flour, baking powder, cinnamon, and salt. Set aside. In a medium bowl, combine the cottage cheese, eggs, brown sugar, and butter. Stir in the flour mixture until it is just combined.

3 Preheat the oven to 200°F. Place a baking sheet on the center rack of the oven. Heat a griddle or nonstick skillet over medium heat. Melt ¼ tablespoon butter on the griddle; wipe it across the surface with a paper towel. Working in batches, drop the batter, 1 tablespoon at a time, onto the hot griddle. Cook until lightly browned, about 2 minutes per side. Transfer the cottage cakes to the baking sheet in the oven until ready to serve. Cook the remaining batter, adding more butter as necessary. Serve the cakes with applesauce.

PINK APPLESAUCE

MAKES 1 QUART

Applesauce doesn't require sugar to make it delicious—just juicy, flavorful apples. Red-skinned apples make pink applesauce.

4 pounds organic or very well-washed red-skinned apples, cored (skins on)

⅓ cup water

Cut the apples into 1-inch pieces. Place in a large saucepan with the water, and simmer, covered, until tender, about 40 minutes. Working in batches, transfer the mixture to the jar of a blender, and blend; or pass it through the smallest disk of a food mill. For the silkiest purée, the mixture may then be passed through a fine sieve. For a coarser texture, pass the apple mixture through a larger disk of a food mill, or pulse in a food processor. The applesauce will keep refrigerated for up to 3 days or frozen in single-portion, airtight containers for up to 4 months.

CHUNKY APPLESAUCE

MAKES 1 QUART

Chunky applesauce is for older babies.

4 pounds organic or very well washed apples, peeled and cored

⅓ cup water

Cut the apples into 1-inch pieces. Place them in a large saucepan with the water, and simmer, covered, until tender, about 25 minutes. The applesauce will keep refrigerated for up to 3 days or frozen in single-portion, airtight containers for up to 4 months.

APPLE-POTATO PANCAKE

MAKES 1 LARGE PANCAKE

- 1 pound (2 large) baking potatoes, peeled
- 2 apples, peeled and cored
- 2 tablespoons vegetable oil
- 2 teaspoons coarse salt
- ¼ teaspoon freshly ground pepper

1 Preheat the oven to 350°F. Grate the potatoes and apples on the large holes of a box grater. Place the mixture in a clean kitchen towel, and squeeze tightly to remove the excess moisture.

2 Heat a 10-inch ovenproof nonstick skillet over medium heat; add 1 tablespoon vegetable oil. Add the grated potatoes and apples. Use a spatula to press the potatoes and apples into a flat, round shape. Reduce the heat to medium-low, and cook, shaking the pan periodically, until the pancake is browned, about 5 minutes. Place a large plate over the pan, and carefully invert the pan onto the plate to turn the pancake over. Add the remaining tablespoon of oil to the empty pan; slide the pancake back into the pan. Season with salt and pepper. Continue cooking until the other side is lightly browned and crisp, about 5 minutes more.

3 Transfer the pan to the oven, and cook until the potatoes are tender, about 20 minutes. Transfer to a cutting board, and cut into wedges. Serve hot.

APPLE OATMEAL BREAD

MAKES TWO 5¾-BY-3¼-BY-2¼-INCH LOAVES

- 1½ cups all-purpose flour
- 1 tablespoon baking powder
- 1 teaspoon coarse salt
- 1 teaspoon ground cinnamon
- 1 apple, peeled and cored
- 1 cup cooked oatmeal
- ½ cup milk
- ¼ cup Pink or Chunky Applesauce (page 321)
- 1 large egg, lightly beaten
- ¼ cup packed light-brown sugar
- 2 tablespoons rolled oats

Preheat the oven to 350°F. Place the flour, baking powder, salt, and cinnamon in a medium bowl. Whisk to combine. Grate the apple into a large bowl using the large holes of a box grater. Add the cooked oatmeal, milk, applesauce, egg, and brown sugar. Add the flour mixture; mix until just combined. Divide the batter between two 5¾-by-3¼-by-2¼-inch loaf pans. Sprinkle the oats over the loaves. Bake until the loaves are golden on top, about 1 hour.

APPLE RICE PUDDING WITH SAUTEED APPLES

MAKES 6 HALF-CUP SERVINGS

- 3 cups milk
- 1 cup heavy cream
- 1 vanilla bean, split lengthwise
- ⅛ teaspoon freshly grated nutmeg
- 3 tablespoons sugar
- ½ cup long-grain rice
- 2 apples
- 2 large egg yolks
- Sautéed Apples (optional; recipe follows)

1 In a medium saucepan, combine 1 cup milk, the heavy cream, vanilla bean, nutmeg, and sugar. Bring to a boil, remove from the heat, and let stand, covered, 30 minutes.

2 Remove the vanilla-bean halves from the milk mixture; scrape the seeds into the milk mixture. Stir in the rice. Cook, covered, over low heat, stirring occasionally, until the liquid is mostly absorbed, about 40 minutes.

3 Peel and core the apples; grate on the large holes of a box grater. In a small bowl, whisk together the egg yolks with the remaining 2 cups milk. Stir into the rice mixture with the grated apples, stirring well. Cook over medium heat, stirring constantly until thickened, 10 to 15 minutes. Do not boil. Remove the pudding from the heat. Transfer to a bowl, and let cool slightly. Transfer the pudding to individual dishes. Pudding may be eaten warm, at room temperature, or chilled. Top with sautéed apples, if using.

SAUTEED APPLES

MAKES 2 CUPS

Serve these meltingly soft apples with yogurt for a snack, or use them to top Apple Rice Pudding.

- 2 tablespoons unsalted butter
- 2 apples, peeled, cored, sliced ¼ inch thick
- 1 teaspoon sugar
- 1 teaspoon ground cinnamon

Melt the butter in a medium skillet over medium-high heat. Sprinkle the apple slices around the pan. Cook until the apples are beginning to brown and soften, about 5 minutes. Add the sugar and cinnamon. Cook, turning the apples as needed, until soft, about 5 minutes more.

CHEDDAR BISCUIT PIE

SERVES 4 TO 6

- 1 cup plus 1 tablespoon all-purpose flour
- 2 teaspoons baking powder
- 1 teaspoon coarse salt, plus more for seasoning
- ¼ cup pure vegetable shortening
- ½ cup sharp cheddar cheese, grated
- 7 tablespoons milk
- 1 pound fresh chicken sausage, casings removed and filling crumbled, or ground chicken
- 1 small onion, cut into ½-inch dice
- 1 carrot, cut into ½-inch dice
- 1 celery stalk, cut into ½-inch dice
- 1 apple, such as McIntosh, cored, cut into 1-inch dice (skin on)
- ½ teaspoon freshly ground pepper, plus more for seasoning
- ½ teaspoon dried thyme
- ¾ cup Homemade Chicken Stock (page 8), or low-sodium canned

1 Preheat the oven to 375°F. In a medium bowl, combine 1 cup flour, the baking powder, and ½ teaspoon salt. Using a pastry cutter or two knives, cut in the shortening until the dough resembles coarse meal. Stir in the grated cheese. Add the milk, and stir until just combined. Do not overwork the dough. Set the dough aside.

2 In an 8-inch ovenproof skillet, cook the chicken sausage over medium heat until cooked through, about 3 minutes. Remove the sausage with a slotted spoon; transfer to a medium bowl. Add the onion, carrot, and celery to the skillet. Cook for 3 minutes. Add the apple; cook until the vegetables and apple soften, about 6 minutes more. Add the remaining ½ teaspoon salt, pepper, and thyme. Add the remaining tablespoon flour; cook, stirring, 1 minute. Add the stock, scraping the bottom of the skillet to loosen any browned bits. Pour the mixture into the bowl with the sausage; stir. Season to taste with salt and pepper.

3 Return the mixture to the skillet or place in an ovenproof casserole. Drop spoonfuls of the reserved biscuit dough onto the sausage mixture. Bake until the crust is golden brown, 20 to 25 minutes.

KIDS: SUMMER/FALL 2001

BAKED CHICKEN FINGERS
MAKES 2 DOZEN

1 pound boneless, skinless chicken breasts
1 cup nonfat buttermilk,
   plus more if needed
⅔ cup cornmeal
½ teaspoon paprika
1 teaspoon coarse salt,
   plus more for seasoning
½ teaspoon freshly ground pepper
2 cups plain dry bread crumbs
3 large eggs
8 tablespoons (1 stick)
   unsalted butter, melted
   Vegetable-oil cooking spray
   Honey Mustard Sauce (recipe follows)

1 Preheat the oven to 450°F. Line a baking pan with a wire rack. Coat with vegetable-oil cooking spray; set aside. If needed, place the chicken breasts between plastic wrap and pound to ½-inch thickness. Cut the chicken breasts into ½-inch-wide strips. Place the strips in a medium bowl; add the buttermilk to cover, using more if necessary. Let sit 20 minutes.

2 In a medium bowl, combine the cornmeal, paprika, salt, and pepper; set aside. Place the bread crumbs in a separate medium bowl. Whisk eggs and a pinch of salt in a small bowl. One by one, remove the chicken strips from the buttermilk; dredge in the cornmeal mixture, then the egg mixture, then the bread crumbs; place on a wire rack.

3 Lightly brush both sides of the chicken strips with the melted butter. (At this point, the strips may be placed on a parchment-lined baking sheet in a single layer and frozen. Once frozen, the strips can be transferred to airtight bags or containers and stored in the freezer for up to 1 month.) Bake frozen fingers 12 to 14 minutes, unfrozen fingers 8 to 10 minutes, until crisp and golden brown; serve immediately with honey mustard sauce.

HONEY MUSTARD SAUCE
MAKES 1½ CUPS

½ cup Dijon mustard
2 tablespoons red-wine vinegar
¼ cup vegetable oil
¾ cup honey

In a medium bowl, whisk together the mustard and vinegar. Whisk in the oil; then whisk in the honey. This dipping sauce can be kept in an airtight container in the refrigerator for up to 1 week. Serve the sauce at room temperature.

SPINACH DIP
MAKES 2 CUPS

Serve this dip with toasted tortilla wedges or with vegetables.

1 garlic clove
4 scallions
1 tablespoon olive oil
10 ounces spinach leaves, cleaned and dried
8 ounces sour cream
   Juice of half a lemon
½ teaspoon coarse salt
¼ teaspoon freshly ground pepper

1 Finely slice the garlic and scallions. Reserve 1 tablespoon scallions for garnish. In a large skillet over medium-low heat, combine the oil, garlic, and all but the reserved scallions. Sauté until tender, about 2 minutes. Add the spinach; cover, reduce the heat to low, and cook until the spinach is just wilted, about 2 minutes. Remove the skillet from the heat, and let the mixture cool.

2 Transfer the cooked spinach to the bowl of a food processor, and process until smooth, about 20 seconds. Add the sour cream and lemon juice. Pulse to combine. Add the salt and pepper. Pulse to combine. The dip can be kept in an airtight container in the refrigerator for up to 1 week (refrigerate the sliced scallions for garnish as well). To serve, pour the dip into a bowl, and top with the reserved sliced scallions.

FISH STICKS
MAKES ABOUT 20

2 large eggs
¼ cup milk
1 cup dry bread crumbs
1 cup all-purpose flour
1 pound cod fillet,
   cut into ½-inch-thick sticks
   Coarse salt and freshly ground pepper
¼ cup plus 2 tablespoons olive oil
   Tartar Sauce (page 324)

1 In a shallow dish, beat the eggs and milk. Pour the bread crumbs and flour onto two separate plates. Sprinkle the fish sticks with salt and pepper. Dredge them in the flour, then the egg mixture, and then the bread crumbs, covering the fish completely with the bread crumbs, and pressing lightly to adhere. Place each fish stick on a wire rack once coated.

2 Heat 3 tablespoons oil in a large skillet over medium-high heat. Arrange half the fish sticks in a single layer without crowding; cook until golden brown, about 1 to 2 minutes on each side. Remove the fish sticks from the skillet, and transfer to a serving dish. Wipe out the pan, and repeat with the remaining oil and fish. Serve the fish sticks, hot or at room temperature, with tartar sauce.

TARTAR SAUCE

MAKES ABOUT 1 CUP

1   cup mayonnaise
2   teaspoons Dijon mustard
1   tablespoon minced shallots
¼   cup finely chopped dill pickle
1½ teaspoons freshly squeezed lemon juice
    Pinch of cayenne pepper

In a medium bowl, mix the mayonnaise, mustard, shallots, pickle, lemon juice, and cayenne until well combined. Store, covered, in the refrigerator until ready to serve, for up to 2 days. Stir again just before serving.

PARMESAN FISH CRACKERS

MAKES ABOUT 2½ DOZEN

This recipe can be made by hand using two knives or a wooden spoon. The Parmesan should be grated to almost powdery on the fine holes of a grater. You will need a two- to three-inch fish-shape cookie cutter to shape the crackers.

1½ cups all-purpose flour,
    plus more for work surface
8   tablespoons (1 stick) unsalted butter,
    cut into 5 pieces
½   teaspoon table salt
½   cup freshly grated Parmesan cheese
5   tablespoons plus 1 teaspoon cold water
1   large egg yolk

1   Preheat the oven to 425°F. Line two baking sheets with parchment paper. In the bowl of a food processor, combine the flour, butter, salt, and cheese. Pulse until the mixture resembles coarse meal. Add 5 tablespoons cold water; pulse until the dough just comes together. Shape the dough into a disk.
2   In a small bowl, whisk together the egg yolk and remaining teaspoon cold water; set aside. On a lightly floured surface, roll the dough ¼ inch thick. Cut out shapes using the fish-shape cookie cutter; transfer to the prepared baking sheets. Bring the scraps together, reroll the dough, and cut out more shapes. Brush each fish with the reserved egg wash. Bake until golden, about 10 minutes. Transfer to a wire rack, and let cool. Crackers may be kept at room temperature in an airtight container for up to 2 days.

STARFISH BISCUIT SANDWICHES

MAKES 16

You will need a three-and-a-half-inch star-shaped cookie cutter.

2½ cups all-purpose flour,
    plus more for work surface
¾   teaspoon table salt
1½ tablespoons baking powder
9   tablespoons cold unsalted butter,
    cut into small pieces
1   cup milk, plus more for brushing
    Cornmeal for sprinkling
1¼ pounds cheddar cheese, cut into
    ¼-inch-thick slices
3   tablespoons mayonnaise

1   Preheat the oven to 425°F. Line a baking sheet with parchment paper. In a large bowl, sift together the flour, salt, and baking powder. Using a pastry blender or two knives, cut the butter into the flour mixture until it resembles coarse meal.
2   Make a well in the center of the flour mixture; pour in the milk. Mix, using a fork, until the dough just comes together. Transfer the dough to a lightly floured work surface; press to form a 6- to 7-inch-diameter circle.
3   Roll out the dough ⅓ inch thick. Cut out with 3½-inch star-shape cookie cutter. Transfer to the prepared baking sheet. Lightly brush the tops with milk, and sprinkle with cornmeal. Bake until golden, 10 to 12 minutes. Remove from the oven, and transfer the biscuits to a wire rack to cool.
4   Cut the cheese into star shapes with the cookie cutter. Cut each biscuit in half crosswise. Spread one half with mayonnaise; top with a cheese star. Top with the other half, and serve.

SPARKLING LIMEADE

MAKES ABOUT 2½ QUARTS

1   cup sugar
1   cup water
¾   cup freshly squeezed lime juice
    (about 6 limes)
2   liters seltzer water

1   Combine the sugar and water in a small saucepan; place over medium heat. Cook, stirring occasionally, until the sugar has completely dissolved, about 5 minutes.
2   Remove from the heat, and let stand at room temperature until cool. Stir in the lime juice. Fill a large pitcher with ice, pour in the limeade, and add the seltzer. Stir well and serve.

sources

ALMONDS (WHOLE BLANCHED) *A.L. Bazzini Co.*

ANISE SEEDS *Penzeys Spices*

APRICOT HALVES (DRIED) *A.L. Bazzini Co.*

APRICOT NECTAR *EthnicGrocer.com*

ARBORIO RICE *Salumeria Italiana*

ARUGULA *The Herb Lady*

ASIAN PEARS *Frieda's Inc.*

BAKING PAN, 9-BY-13-BY-2-INCH
New York Cake & Baking Distributor

BAKING PAN, PROFESSIONAL *Bridge Kitchenware*

BAKING SHEETS *Martha by Mail*

BALL CANNING JARS, 4-OZ.
Broadway Panhandler

BAMBOO STEAMER *Broadway Panhandler*

BAMBOO STEAMER BASKET SET
Pacific Rim Gourmet

BAY LEAVES, FRESH *Balducci's*

BENCH SCRAPER *Kitchen Krafts*

BING CHERRIES, DRIED *A.L. Bazzini Co.*

BISCUIT CUTTERS *Martha by Mail*

BLACK MUSTARD SEEDS *Dean & DeLuca*

BOCCONCINI *Murray's Cheese Shop*

BOX GRATER *Kmart*

BREAD FLOUR, ORGANIC
King Arthur Flour Baker's Catalogue

BRIOCHE TINS *Bridge Kitchenware*

BUCHERON *Murray's Cheese Shop*

BUNDT PAN, 9-BY-4-INCH *A Cook's Wares*

BUNDT PAN, NONSTICK 10-INCH *Kmart*

CAKE FLOUR
King Arthur Flour Baker's Catalogue

CAKE PAN, NONSTICK 8-BY-8-BY-2-INCH
Kmart

CAKE PANS, ROUND
*New York Cake & Baking Distributor, Beryl's Cake
Decorating & Pastry Supplies*

CAKE RING, 8-BY-1¾-INCH
New York Cake & Baking Distributor

CAKE ROUNDS (CARDBOARD) *Beryl's Cake
Decorating & Pastry Supplies*

CAKE STAND (BEECHWOOD) *Martha by Mail*

CANARY MELON *Indian Rock Produce*

CANDY THERMOMETER (MARTHA STEWART
EVERYDAY) *Kmart*

CARDAMOM *Penzeys Spices*

CARDAMOM PODS *Kitchen Market*

CARROT JUICE, FRESH *Wild Oats Markets*

CELERY ROOT *Indian Rock Produce*

CHESTNUT FLOUR *Fante's Kitchen Wares Shop*

CHESTNUT KNIFE *Bridge Kitchenware*

CHESTNUT ROASTING PAN *Bridge Kitchenware*

CHESTNUTS, PACKED IN COGNAC
Earthy Delights

CHOCOLATE THERMOMETER, PROFESSIONAL
New York Cake & Baking Distributor

CHOCOLATES KIT (HANDMADE) *Martha by Mail*

CINNAMON STICKS (EXTRA LONG)
Martha by Mail

CITRUS PRESS, LIME AND LEMON
Martha by Mail

CLAMS (CHERRYSTONES, LITTLENECKS) *Citarella*

CLOVER SPROUTS *Indian Rock Produce*

COCONUT (DESICCATED)
New York Cake & Baking Distributor

COCONUT, UNSWEETENED GRATED
Lifethyme Natural Market

COCONUT EXTRACT *Adriana's Caravan*

COCONUT MILK *Pacific Rim Gourmet*

COLANDER, QUICK DRAINING *Martha by Mail*

COOLING RACK *Martha by Mail*

CORIANDER SEEDS *Penzeys Spices*

CORNHUSKS, DRIED *Kitchen Market*

CORNICHONS *Zingerman's Delicatessen*

CREME FRAICHE *Murray's Cheese Shop*

CRYSTALLIZED GINGER SLICES
EthnicGrocer.com

CUMIN SEEDS *Kitchen Market*

CUTTER SET, GIANT COPPER *Martha by Mail*

CUTTERS *Sweet Celebrations*

CUTTERS, 3-PIECE SET OF OCEAN ANIMALS
(CRAB, FLOUNDER, LOBSTER) *Sur La Table*

CUTTERS, 6-PIECE SET OF STARS
Beryl's Cake Decorating & Pastry Supplies

DAIKON RADISH *Indian Rock Produce*

DAIKON SPROUTS *Katagiri*

DECORETTES (EDIBLE)
New York Cake & Baking Distributor

DEMI-GLACE AND STOCK *Martha by Mail*

DOUGHNUT CUTTER, 3-INCH
thegadgetsource.com

DOUGHNUT CUTTER, 2¾-INCH STEEL
Pfeil & Holing

DOWEL (HARDWOOD) *New York Central Art Supply*

DRAGEES *New York Cake & Baking Distributor*

DRY MILK *King Arthur Flour Baker's Catalogue*

EGGPLANT, JAPANESE *Katagiri*

ELDERFLOWER CORDIAL *The Sweet Life*

ENOKI MUSHROOMS *Katagiri*

FAVA BEANS *Indian Rock Produce*

FENUGREEK SEED *Penzeys Spices*

FINGERLING POTATOES *Indian Rock Produce*

FISH SPATULA *Martha by Mail*

FISH STOCK (GLACE DE FRUIT DE MER GOLD)
Fancy Food Gourmet Club

FONDANT, POWDERED *Martha by Mail*

FOOD COLORING (GEL)
New York Cake & Baking Distributor

FOOD-PACKAGING PAPERS *Martha by Mail*

GARAM MASALA *Adriana's Caravan*

GOAT CHEESE, LOW-FAT *Murray's Cheese Shop*

GOURMET FRUIT SLICES *Martha by Mail*

GRAPE LEAVES *International Pantry*

GRAPESEED OIL *Dean & DeLuca*

GRAVY SKIMMER *thegadgetsource.com*

GREEN OLIVES, LARGE CRACKED WITH
THYME *Sultan's Delight*

GUMDROPS *The Sweet Life*

GUM PASTE PETAL CUTTERS
Beryl's Cake Decorating & Pastry Supplies

GUM PASTE PETAL CUTTERS (LARGE)
Creative Cutters

HIBISCUS FLOWERS, DRIED *Adriana's Caravan*

HORSERADISH, FRESH *Indian Rock Produce*

ICE CREAM MAKER (KRUPS) *Williams-Sonoma*

ICE CREAM SCOOP, PROFESSIONAL
Martha by Mail

JASMINE ESSENCE *Aphrodisia*

JASMINE RICE *Adriana's Caravan*

JASMINE TEA LEAVES *Adriana's Caravan*

JELLY ROLL PAN, 12-BY-17-INCH *Sur la Table*

JICAMA *Indian Rock Produce*

KALAMATA OLIVES, PITTED
La Cucina Rustica

KEY LIMES, FRESH *Indian Rock Produce*

KUGELHOPF MOLD *Bridge Kitchenware*

LAVENDER, DRIED *Adriana's Caravan*

LEMONGRASS
Indian Rock Produce, Kitchen Market

LICORICE SHOELACES *The Sweet Life*

LOAF PAN, 10-BY-4½-BY-3-INCH *A Cook's Wares*

LUSTER DUST *New York Cake & Baking Distributor*

LYLE'S GOLDEN SYRUP *Dean & DeLuca*

MADELEINE PAN *Martha by Mail*

MAJOR GREY'S MANGO CHUTNEY *Kalustyan's*

MANDOLINE *Martha by Mail*

MANDOLINE (MARTHA STEWART EVERYDAY) *Kmart*

MARRONS GLACES *Grace's Market Place*

MARSHMALLOW TREAT KIT *Martha by Mail*

MASA HARINA, DRIED *Kitchen Market*

MASCARPONE CHEESE *Murray's Cheese Shop*

MELON BALLER (MARTHA STEWART EVERYDAY)
Kmart

MELON BALLER, SINGLE AND DOUBLE
Bridge Kitchenware

MERINGUE POWDER *Martha by Mail*

METAL MOLDS, HALF-MOON
New York Cake & Baking Distributor

MEXICAN CHOCOLATE (IBARRA) *Kitchen Market*

MILLET *Dean & DeLuca*

MINI LOAF PANS, NONSTICK 5-BY-3-BY-2-
INCH; SET OF 4 *Cooking.com*

MISO PASTE *Katagiri*

MIXING BOWLS, STAINLESS-STEEL
Bridge Kitchenware

MUFFIN PANS, NONSTICK 12-CUP (MARTHA
STEWART EVERYDAY) *Kmart*

MUFFIN PANS (JUMBO) *Sweet Celebrations*

NUTCRACKER CUTTER *Martha by Mail*

OFFSET SPATULAS,
Bridge Kitchenware, Martha by Mail

ORANGE-FLOWER WATER
Adriana's Caravan

PANCETTA *Dean & DeLuca*

PAPAYA CHUNKS, DRIED *A.L. Bazzini Co.*

PARCHMENT PAPER
King Arthur Flour Baker's Catalogue

(continued on next page)

(continued from page 327)

PASTA DRYING RACK *Cooking.com*

PASTRY BAG *New York Cake & Baking Distributor*

PASTRY BLENDER *A Cook's Wares*

PASTRY FLOUR, UNBLEACHED
King Arthur Flour Baker's Catalogue

PEARL ONIONS (RED AND WHITE)
Indian Rock Produce

PEASHOOTS *Indian Rock Produce*

PECORINO TOSCANO *Murray's Cheese Shop*

PEPPERCORNS (BLACK, WHITE, AND GREEN)
Kitchen Market

PERSIMMONS *Melissa's World Variety Produce*

PICKLED GINGER (SLICED) *ThaiGrocer*

PIE PLATE (STONEWARE) *Martha by Mail*

PINEAPPLE RINGS, DRIED *A.L. Bazzini Co.*

PIPING TIPS *New York Cake & Baking Distributor*

PISTACHIOS *A.L. Bazzini Co., Martha by Mail*

PLUGRA BUTTER *Zingerman's Delicatessen*

PLUMS, DINOSAUR (AVAILABLE AUGUST AND
SEPTEMBER) *Indian Rock Produce*

POBLANO PEPPERS *Kitchen Market*

POTATO RICER *Cooking.com, Williams-Sonoma*

POUSSINS *D'Artagnan*

QUINOA *EthnicGrocer.com*

RADICCHIO *Indian Rock Produce*

RAMEKINS
Dean & DeLuca, A Cook's Wares, Cooking.com

REBLOCHON CHEESE *The Cheese Shop*

RED CURRANTS *Indian Rock Produce*

RING MOLD *Bridge Kitchenware*

ROASTED SEAWEED (SUSHI NORI)
Pacific Rim Gourmet

ROLLING PIN, OVERSIZE *Martha by Mail*

ROSES, EDIBLE (SMALL AND MEDIUM)
Sweet Celebrations

ROSE WATER *Adriana's Caravan*

SAFFRON *Vanns Spices, Adriana's Caravan*

SAFFRON THREADS *La Española Meats*

SAKE FOR COOKING (MORITA) *Katagiri*

SANDING SUGAR *Martha by Mail*

SANDING SUGAR, SUPERFINE
King Arthur Flour Baker's Catalogue

SAVARIN MOLD *Bridge Kitchenware*

SEMOLINA FLOUR
King Arthur Flour Baker's Catalogue

SERRANO HAM, 18-MONTH-OLD
La Española Meats

SHISO LEAVES *The Herb Lady, Katagiri*

SKILLET (FOUR-STAR HEAVY-GAUGE NONSTICK
ALUMINUM) *Kmart*

SILPAT BAKING MAT *Martha by Mail*

SOFT-SHELL CRABS *Citarella*

SOUFFLE DISH (PILLIVUYT) *Martha by Mail*

SOUFFLE DISHES, CERAMIC
New York Cake & Baking Distributor

SPARKLE DUST *New York Cake &
Baking Distributor*

SPATULAS, PROFESSIONAL *Martha by Mail*

SPRING ROLL WRAPPERS *Pacific Rim Gourmet*

SPRINGFORM PANS *Bridge Kitchenware*

SPRINKLES, PASTEL *Martha by Mail*

STAR ANISE, WHOLE *Penzeys Spices*

SWEDISH PEARL SUGAR
King Arthur Flour Baker's Catalogue

TART KIT *Martha by Mail*

TART PANS *Sweet Celebrations Inc., Broadway
Panhandler, New York Cake & Baking Distributor*

THAI CHILE PODS, DRIED *Kitchen Market*

THERMOMETER, DEEP-FRY
Bridge Kitchenware

TUBE PAN *Martha by Mail*

ULTIMATE STRAINER *Martha by Mail*

VALRHONA CHOCOLATES AND COCOA POWDER
*New York Cake & Baking Distributor,
Sweet Celebrations*

VANILLA BEANS *Martha by Mail*

VANILLA EXTRACT *Martha by Mail*

VENISON, (4-RIB RACK, 8-RIB RACK, FULLY
FRENCHED) *D'Artagnan*

VERMONT MAPLE SYRUP *Martha by Mail*

WALNUT HALVES AND PIECES *A.L. Bazzini Co.*

WALNUT OIL *Dean & DeLuca*

WARING BAR BLENDER *Martha by Mail*

WASABI, POWDERED *Katagiri*

WHISKS (STAINLESS-STEEL, STANDARD AND MINI)
Martha by Mail

WHITE GRAPEFRUIT SLICES *The Sweet Life*

WILD MUSHROOMS, DRIED
Urbani Truffles and Caviar

directory

A COOK'S WARES
211 37th Street
Beaver Falls, PA 15010
800-915-9788
www.cookswares.com

Bundt pans, loaf pans, pastry blenders, ramekins.

ADRIANA'S CARAVAN
Grand Central Food Market
78 Grand Central Terminal
New York, NY 10017
212-972-8804
800-316-0820
www.adrianascaravan.com

Catalog available. Spices and ethnic ingredients, including coconut extract, dried hibiscus flowers, dried lavender, garam masala, jasmine rice and tea leaves, orange-flower water, rose water, saffron.

A.L. BAZZINI CO.
339 Greenwich Street
New York, NY 10013
212-334-1280

Dried fruits and nuts.

APHRODISIA
264 Bleecker Street
New York, NY 10014
212-989-6440

Jasmine essence.

BALDUCCI'S
424 Sixth Avenue
New York, NY 10011
212-673-2600

BERYL'S CAKE DECORATING & PASTRY SUPPLIES
P.O. Box 1584
North Springfield, VA 22151
800-488-2749

Cake pans, gum paste petal cutters, star cookie cutters.

BRIDGE KITCHENWARE
214 East 52nd Street
New York, NY 10022
212-838-6746 or 212-838-1901
800-274-3435
www.bridgekitchenware.com

Catalog $3 (applied to first purchase). Brioche tins, chestnut knives, chestnut roasting pans, deep-frying/candy thermometers, kugelhopf molds, melon ballers, metal baking pans, mixing bowls, offset spatulas, Silpat baking mats, pastry bags, piping tips, ring molds.

BROADWAY PANHANDLER
477 Broome Street
New York, NY 10013
212-966-3434
www.broadwaypanhandler.com

Bamboo steamers, canning jars, tart pans.

THE CHEESE SHOP
2347 Black Rock Turnpike
Fairfield, CT 06432
203-372-2355

CITARELLA
2135 Broadway
New York, NY 10023
212-874-0383
www.citarella.com

Shucked oysters, cherrystone and littleneck clams, soft-shell crabs.

COOKING.COM
800-663-8810

Mini loaf pans, pasta drying racks, potato ricers.

CREATIVE CUTTERS
716-831-0562
888-805-3444
www.creativecutters.com

(continued on next page)

(continued from page 329)

D'ARTAGNAN
280 Wilson Avenue
Newark, NJ 07105
800-327-8246
www.dartagnan.com

Poussins, venison.

DEAN & DELUCA
560 Broadway
New York, NY 10012
800-999-0306
212-226-6800
www.deandeluca.com

Catalog available. Black mustard seeds, grapeseed oil, millet, pancetta, ramekins, walnut oil.

EARTHY DELIGHTS
1161 East Clark Road, Suite 260
DeWitt, MI 48820
800-367-4709
517-668-2402

Chestnuts, packed in cognac.

ETHNICGROCER.COM
800-803-1183

Apricot nectar, crystallized ginger slices, quinoa.

FANTE'S KITCHEN WARES SHOP
1006 South 9th Street
Philadelphia, PA 19147
800-443-2683
215-922-5723
www.fantes.com

Chestnut flour.

FRIEDA'S INC.
800-241-1771
www.friedas.com

Exotic and specialty produce.

THEGADGETSOURCE.COM
800-747-7224
www.thegadgetsource.com

Doughnut cutters, gravy skimmers.

GRACE'S MARKET PLACE
1237 Third Avenue
New York, NY 10021
212-737-0600
800-325-6126

THE HERB LADY
52792 42nd Avenue
Lawrence, MI 49064
616-674-3879

Arugula, shiso leaves.

INDIAN ROCK PRODUCE
530 California Road
Quakertown, PA 18951
215-536-9600
800-882-0512
www.indianrockproduce.com

Canary melon, clover sprouts, daikon radishes, fresh horseradish, jicama, Key limes, lemongrass, pearl onions, dinosaur plums.

INTERNATIONAL PANTRY
1618 West Lindsey
Norman, OK 73069
405-360-0765
www.intlpantry.com

KALUSTYAN'S
123 Lexington Avenue
New York, NY 10016
212-685-3451
www.kalustyans.com

KATAGIRI
224 and 226 East 59th Street
New York, NY 10022
212-755-3566
212-838-5453

Dumpling wrappers, enoki mushrooms, miso paste, sake (cooking), fresh shiso leaves, Japanese turning slicer, powdered wasabi.

KING ARTHUR FLOUR BAKER'S CATALOGUE
P.O. Box 876
Norwich, VT 05055
800-827-6836
www.kingarthurflour.com

Catalog available.

KITCHEN KRAFTS
P.O. Box 442
Waukon, IA 52172
800-776-0575
www.kitchenkrafts.com

KITCHEN MARKET
218 Eighth Avenue
New York, NY 10011
888-468-4433
212-243-4433
www.kitchenmarket.com
Catalog available.

KMART
800-866-0086
www.bluelight.com

LA CUCINA RUSTICA
P.O. Box 115
Wayne, IL 60184
800-796-0116
www.cybercucina.com

LA ESPAÑOLA MEATS
25020 Doble Avenue
Harbor City, CA 90710
310-539-0455
www.donajuana.com

Saffron threads, Serrano ham.

LIFETHYME NATURAL MARKET
410 Sixth Avenue
New York, NY 10011
212-420-9099

LOWELL FARMS
4 North Washington
El Campo, TX 77437
888-484-9213
www.lowellfarms.com

MARTHA BY MAIL
800-950-7130
www.marthastewart.com

Baking sheets, biscuit cutters, citrus presses, cake stands, colanders, cooling racks, Silpat baking mats, ice-cream scoops, food-packaging papers, fish spatulas, powdered fondant, madeleine pans, mandolines, marshmallow treat kit, meringue powder, sanding sugar, rolling pins, tube pans, vanilla beans, vanilla extract, Waring bar blender, whisks.

MELISSA'S WORLD VARIETY PRODUCE
800-588-0151
www.melissas.com

MURRAY'S CHEESE SHOP

257 Bleecker Street

New York, NY 10014

212-243-3289

888-692-4339

www.murrayscheese.com

Imported and domestic cheeses.

NEW YORK CAKE & BAKING DISTRIBUTOR

56 West 22nd Street

New York, NY 10010

212-675-2253

800-942-2539

www.nycakesupplies.com

Catalog $3. Baking and decorating supplies, including gel and paste food coloring, ice cream molds, fluted tart pans, luster dust, pastry bags, piping tips, sparkle dust, Valrhona chocolate.

NEW YORK CENTRAL ART SUPPLY

62 Third Avenue

New York, NY 10003

212-473-7705

PACIFIC RIM GOURMET

800-618-7575

www.pacificrim-gourmet.com

Bamboo steamer basket set, coconut milk, roasted seaweed (sushi nori), spring roll wrappers.

PENZEYS SPICES

800-741-7787

www.penzeys.com

Catalog available.

PFEIL & HOLING

58-18 Northern Boulevard

Woodside, NY 11377

800-247-7955

www.cakedeco.com

SALUMERIA ITALIANA

800-400-5916

www.SalumeriaItaliana.com

Arborio rice, amaretti cookies.

SULTAN'S DELIGHT

P.O. Box 090302

Brooklyn, NY 11209

718-745-2121

800-852-5046

www.sultansdelight.com

SUR LA TABLE

1765 6th Avenue South

Seattle, WA 98134

800-243-0852

www.surlatable.com

Catalog available.

SWEET CELEBRATIONS INC.

P.O. Box 39426

Edina, MN 55439

800-328-6722

www.sweetc.com

Cutters, jumbo muffin pans, edible roses, tart pans, Valrhona chocolate.

THE SWEET LIFE

63 Hester Street

New York, NY 10002

212-598-0092

Elderflower cordial, gumdrops, licorice shoelaces.

THAIGROCER

2961 North Sheridan Road

Chicago, IL 60657

866-842-4366

www.thaigrocer.com

URBANI TRUFFLES AND CAVIAR

29-24 40th Avenue

Long Island City, NY 11101

718-392-5050

800-281-2330

www.urbani.com

Catalog available. Fresh and dried mushrooms.

VANNS SPICES

6105 Oakleaf Avenue

Baltimore, MD 21215

800-583-1693

410-358-3007

www.vannsspices.com

WILD OATS MARKETS NATIONWIDE

3375 Mitchell Lane

Boulder, CO 80301

800-494-9453

www.wildoats.com

WILLIAMS-SONOMA

20 East 60th Street

New York, NY 10022

212-980-5155

800-541-2233

www.williams-sonoma.com

Catalog available.

ZINGERMAN'S DELICATESSEN

422 Detroit Street

Ann Arbor, MI 48104

888-636-8162

www.zingermans.com

Catalog available.

index

*Page numbers in **bold** italics indicate color photographs.*

photography

SANG AN *pages 52, 53, 71, 122 (top right), 146 (top left, top right), 183, 184 (bottom right), 194, 195, 198, 303*

CHRISTOPHER BAKER *pages 25, 98, 99, 101, 102, 148 (bottom left, bottom right), 149, 150, 304 (bottom left, top right), 305-07*

LUIS BRUNO *pages 191, 196 (top left, bottom left)*

BEATRIZ DA COSTA *page 26*

REED DAVIS *pages 24, 29*

FORMULA z/s *pages 47, 263, 310*

GENTL & HYERS *pages 74, 75, 148 (top left, top right), 184 (top right), 185, 186 (bottom left, bottom right), 190, 215-17*

LISA HUBBARD *pages 96, 119, 122 (all but top right), 264, 265, 268, 269, 308, 309*

RICHARD GERHARD JUNG *pages 97, 100, 120, 121, 123, 126, 184 (top left, bottom left), 220 (bottom left, top right), 221, 266*

ARTHUR MEEHAN *page 220 (top left, bottom right)*

WILLIAM MEPPEM *page 304 (top left, bottom right)*

JAMES MERRELL *pages 76, 77, 95*

AMY NEUNSINGER *pages 143-45, 192, 193, 196 (top right, bottom right), 197*

VICTORIA PEARSON *pages 27, 78*

MARIA ROBLEDO *pages 30, 48-51, 124 (bottom left, bottom right)*

DAVID SAWYER *pages 28, 146 (bottom left, bottom right)*

CHARLES SCHILLER *pages 186 (top left, top right), 222*

SIMON WATSON *page 188*

WENDELL T. WEBBER *pages 124 (top left, top right), 125*

ANNA WILLIAMS *pages 23, 54, 72, 73, 147, 187, 189, 218, 219, 267, 270*

COVER PHOTO
CHRISTOPHER BAKER (Martha), AMY NEUNSINGER (Cake)

BACK COVER
Top, from left: WILLIAM ABRANOWICZ, GENTL & HYERS, LISA HUBBARD, JAMES MERRELL *Middle, from left:* JOSÉ MANUEL PICAYO RIVERA, AMY NEUNSINGER, SANG AN, FORMULA z/s *Bottom, from left:* CHRISTOPHER BAKER, JOSÉ MANUEL PICAYO RIVERA, ANNA WILLIAMS, CHRISTOPHER BAKER